THE PSALMS

Other works by John Eaton

Obadiah, Nahum, Habakkuk, Zephaniah
Psalms: Introduction and Commentary
Kingship and the Psalms
Vision in Worship
Festal Drama in Deutero-Isaiah
The Psalms Come Alive: An Introduction to the Psalms through the Arts
Job
The Contemplative Face of Old Testament Wisdom
Interpreted By Love: Forty Expositions
Psalms of the Way and the Kingdom
The Circle of Creation: Animals in the Light of the Bible
Mysterious Messengers: A Course on Hebrew Prophecy from Amos Onwards

THE PSALMS

A Historical and Spiritual Commentary with an Introduction and New Translation

JOHN EATON

T&T CLARK INTERNATIONAL
A Continuum imprint
LONDON • NEW YORK

T & T CLARK
A Continuum imprint

The Tower Building, 11 York Road, London SE1 7NX
15 East 26th Street, New York, NY 10010, USA

First published 2003

British Library Cataloguing-in-Publication Data
A catalogue record for this book is available from the British Library.

ISBN 0–567–08979–7 (hardback)
0–567–08980–0 (paperback)

Typeset by YHT Ltd, London
Printed and bound in Great Britain by Cromwell Press, Trowbridge

Contents

Preface

The enjoyable path of Psalms study winds through several fields. Attention can turn first to the original meaning and use of the psalms. Then interest may be held by their subsequent use and interpretation, starting already with their collection and arrangement. And just as interesting, and often astonishing, is the discovery of what they can contribute to the life of faith and worship today.

I have shaped my treatment with these various fields in mind. In the Introduction I survey the historical areas and provide for convenient reference from the Commentary. For each psalm there is then a simple and regular pattern: I first give my own translation, then introductory remarks on the psalm's character, position and setting, then commentary on its sections, and so to a conclusion. In these conclusions I appreciate the psalm as a whole and in relation to spirituality today, especially in the Christian tradition; as a practical way of focusing this, I append a prayer I have drawn from my understanding of the psalm. Notes on textual details, poetic parallels and views of other scholars are gathered in an Appendix at the back of the book and are important for close study.

In my translation I have generally tried to meet the desire for inclusive language, but in some cases it seemed better to convey more exactly what is in the text. Already throughout Psalm 1 the dilemma arises (literally 'Happy is the man ...'). Some recent versions simply change to 'Happy those ...', but the reader will then not be able to appreciate the Jewish insight that sees here how the individual must be ready to stand against the crowd, or the Christian tradition that found here a prefigurement of Christ. Here and often, delicate judgements have to be made. Numbering of verses and even of psalms varies in old traditions; I have kept to the usual English numbers, as found for example in AV and NRSV.

Often my thoughts turn to the many, many good people to whom I am indebted, be it for their learning, their encouragement, their love. Here I mention only Henry Hart and Sir Henry Chadwick, formerly deans of Queens' College, Cambridge, my first tutors in theology. And in preparation of this book Margaret Lydamore has been immensely helpful and patient as copy-editor. Always ready with help and counsel has been my wife, Margaret. Let this work be for her – but also for every one who has a heart to love and use the Psalms.

John Eaton
July 2003

Abbreviations
and Guide to References

Abbreviations are given below for standard works of reference. Others works are cited by author and shortened forms of their titles. Publication details of these will be found in the Bibliography. Where an author's name only is given in the text, details of his or her work will also be found there. Where an author of several works is cited by name only, the reference is to the commentary.

ANEP	Pritchard, *The Ancient Near East in Pictures*
ANET	Pritchard, *Ancient Near Eastern Texts*
ANES	Pritchard, *The Ancient Near East, Supplementary Texts*
AV	Authorized (King James) Version of the Bible, 1611
BCP	The Book of Common Prayer (1662)
BDB	Brown, Driver, Briggs, *Hebrew Lexicon*, 1907
BHS	*Biblica Hebraica Stuttgartensia, Liber Psalmorum*, 1969 (the standard text of the Hebrew Bible)
BH3	*Biblica Hebraica*, third edition, *Liber Psalmorum*, ed. Buhl, 1937
BJRL	*Bulletin of the John Rylands Library*
ET	English translation
GK	Gesenius, Kautzsch, *Hebrew Grammar*, ET 1910
Int.	Introduction (of present work)
JSS	*Journal of Semitic Studies*
JTS	*Journal of Theological Studies*
LP	*The Liturgical Psalter*, London 1995
LXX	Greek 'Septuagint' version of the Bible
NL	Neale and Littledale, *Commentary on Psalms*
NRSV	New Revised Standard Version of the Bible (1989)
REB	Revised English Bible, 1989
RV	Revised Version of the Bible, 1884, 1898
TRP	Thomas, *The Text of the Revised Psalter*
TUAT	Kaiser, *Texte aus der Umwelt des Alten Testaments*
TWAT	Botterweck, *Theologisches Wörterbuch zum Alten Testament*
VT	*Vetus Testamentum*
ZAW	*Zeitschrift für die alttestamentliche Wissenschaft*

INTRODUCTION

I

The Importance of the Psalms

1a Words from worship

Each part of the Bible makes its own distinctive contribution to the enrichment of the spirit. The unique contribution of the Book of Psalms arises from the fact that here we have, for the most part, words addressed to God. Even where we find other kinds of speech, such as calls for praise or teachings addressed to the people, they are words spoken, we might say, in the presence of God. For the Psalms are words from worship, and mostly words of worship. Their extraordinary importance is that for thousands of years, and still in the modern world, they have been able to lead people into the heart of religion, the actual practice of communion with God. Before the Holy One, when their mouths and hearts might have been closed through inexperience or past alienation, the Psalms have enabled them to speak and to listen, to be at home in the practice of prayer and praise, to 'know the Lord'.

Each of the 150 psalms is a poem. This language of worship is all poetry, and generally intended to be sung or chanted with musical accompaniment. Yet it is not a stilted or artificial form of expression, but a natural outpouring of heart and soul – in need, in gratitude, in sorrow and in joy. The poetic art is here unobtrusive, but in its rhythms and patterns, its images and its purity of wording lies the proven power of the Psalms to enter and speak for the depths of human experience.

What has been true for modern users was no less true in their ancient context. It is here, in the Psalms, that the most significant moments of Hebrew religion are attested. The great traditional stories, the laws, the proverbs, the prophecies – all have much to tell those who study biblical religion in its ancient context. But for revealing the heart of that religion the Psalms must have pride of place. This has not always been recognized, and as a result many presentations of the ancient faith and sacred practice were impoverished. Perspectives which the Psalms offer on creation, the animal world, the nations, the holy centre of Zion, the king's vocation, the kingdom of God itself – these and other treasures of the Psalms were not properly taken into account.

1b Antiquity and integrity of the psalms

Sometimes this neglect has been due to misapprehension about the date and composition of the Psalms. Working from theories of how Israelite religion developed from a 'many-gods' to a 'one-god' outlook, some scholars have dated the Psalms very late in Old Testament history. They have explained the presence of obviously ancient passages as due to the method of the late authors who, supposedly, drew on pieces of old psalms and built them into their new compositions.

It is true that ancient authors sometimes incorporated older elements into their works; we shall see a likely case in Psalm 19. But this was something which could occur just as well in the early period. There was always something still earlier to draw on where appropriate. So the wisest procedure is first to receive the total impact of a psalm, to allow it to speak as a genuine unity, eloquent of one time and setting, before resorting to theories of editorial cuts, compilations or additions.

We then come to see the main period of composition as lying between 1000 and 400 BCE, with the early part of this period as having been especially fruitful. Favouring this conclusion are the obvious links with the dynasty of David and with the temple of Jerusalem in its first glory as royal and imperial holy centre. Furthermore, there are parallels in the prayers and hymns of neighbouring peoples from this period or before. And we may add that this period suits the poetic brilliance of so many psalms, for other biblical literature indicates in later times a decline in the poetic quality of religious utterance.

We have to think of the Psalms, then, as among the great foundational elements of Hebrew religion. In particular, our understanding of the prophetic books should reckon with this. From the Psalms we gain a vantage point to recognize when a great prophet is working with older ideas, especially the concepts, ceremonies and ideals of worship. In this perspective we may better understand his message.

2

The Authors

2a Relevance of headings

Many psalms have headings which at first sight seem to indicate their author, for example 'A psalm of David' (in 73 cases), 'A psalm of Solomon' (72; 127), 'A prayer of Moses' (90), 'A psalm of Asaph' (50; 73–83). However, caution is needed here. For one thing, textual evidence (for example from the ancient Greek translation) indicates variation in the occurrence of such headings, suggesting that some might be of late origin. For another, the meaning of the headings is often not certain. In 'Of David', for example, the preposition might have originally meant 'for' or 'pertaining to', while 'David' might have referred to the Davidic rulers in general.

Although many psalms are expressed as passionate statements of an individual, it is striking that there is scarcely anything that would identify any particular person. From various ancient sanctuaries across the Near East archaeologists have recovered prayers and thanksgivings and offerings which specify circumstances and record names, but there is nothing of this kind in the Psalms. We are led to think of the composing and the chanting of these pieces as the work of skilled circles in the service of the temple. Organized by the temple authorities under the hand of the king, they will have handed down their art and their compositions in largely hereditary guilds. Evidence of such guilds appears in the Books of Chronicles (especially 1 Chron. 15–16; 25) and in the headings 'Of the sons of Korah' (Pss. 42; 44–9; 84; 85; 87; 88), 'Of Asaph' (50; 73–83), 'Of Heman' (88), 'Of Ethan' (89) and perhaps 'Jeduthun' (39; 62; 77).

We may feel close to such a circle as we ponder 137. Here we are impressed by the cohesion which enabled the group of psalmists to survive exile 'by the waters of Babylon' and eventually make the difficult return. How faithfully they guarded 'the songs of Zion' and 'the song of the Lord'! Through all the terrible march into exile, which some would not survive, they did not part with their lyres; though their music should not be heard in the unclean land, they would not part with them. Half a century later, and back in Zion, they prized the fingers skilled in playing, and the tongue expert in singing praise; but even these they would destroy with a curse if they lost their all-surpassing love of God's holy place.

2b David

But how should we think of David's contribution to psalm composition? The ancient traditions had told of his gifts as composer, singer and lyrist. They told of his playing that healed Saul's spirit (1 Sam. 16.14f.). They told of his songs of lament that assuaged national tragedies (2 Sam.1.17f.; 3.33f.). He was remembered as one raised up by God, anointed, and filled with prophetic power to be the sweetest singer of Israel (2 Sam. 23.1f.). He was said to have devised and made instruments of music (2 Chron. 7.6; Neh. 12.36; Amos 6.5).

Later, when the kings were no more and a high priest ruled in the rebuilt temple, David was still seen as the one who had established the duties of the guilds of singers in Jerusalem's worship (1 Chron. 15.16f.; 16.4f.; 25.1f.). With cymbals, harps and lyres they played according to the cheironomer's gestures, the hand-signals inherited from the guild fathers, but ultimately from David (1 Chron. 25.6f.). In about 190 BCE the sage Jesus Ben Sira summarized David's role poetically, picturing him as personally singing praises to God throughout the events of his life, and also as appointing the music for festal and daily worship in the sacred courts:

> In all that he did he gave thanks.
> giving glory to the Holy One, the Most High.
> With all his heart he sang praise,
> expressing his love for his maker.
> He appointed singers to stand before the altar
> and sing sweet music to the lyre.
> He gave beauty to the festivals,
> and set their times through all the year,
> when they should praise the name of the Lord,
> the sanctuary resounding from break of day.   (Ecclus. 47.8–10)

Around New Testament times the idea that David was the main author of the Psalms was taken for granted. A Dead Sea scroll (11QPs*a*) from the first century CE includes a note detailing the numbers of his compositions made 'through prophecy given him from before the Most High'. It attributes to him 3600 'praises', 446 'songs' for daily and special worship, and four 'songs' to sing with harp or lyre over 'the stricken' (those afflicted by evil spirits) – in all, 4050 pieces. In the New Testament itself a number of quotations from the Psalms, taken to be prophetic of Christ, are attributed to David – he spoke 'by the Holy Spirit' or 'being a prophet'; God or the Holy Spirit spoke through him (Ps. 110 in Mark 12.36–7 and parallels; Pss. 69 and 109 in Acts 1.16f.; Pss. 16 and 110 in Acts 2.29f.; Ps. 32 in Rom. 4.6f.; and Ps. 95 in Heb. 4.7f.). A rabbinic opinion from the second century CE quaintly stated that David wrote the Psalms, helped by Adam, Melchizedek, Abraham, Moses, Heman, Jeduthun, Asaph and the three sons of Korah – that is, he incorporated some of their compositions. Early Christian writers continued to see the Psalms generally as the prophetic work of David.

Modern scholars have been inclined to turn their backs on the tradition of David's authorship. This was inevitable when the Psalms were dated after the end of the whole Davidic dynasty. But if it is right now to revise the dating and, as argued above, acknowledge the early monarchy as an important time in psalm composition, then the tradition of Davidic authorship may be viewed with respect. It may have valuable insights to give us.

Here we may take note of the thirteen cases where a psalm heading appears to have been expanded with an opinion of the circumstances which led to David's first uttering of the psalm (3, 7, 18, 34, 51, 52, 54, 56, 57, 59, 60, 63, 142). For the most part, these notices seem to be deductions which someone has made from statements in the psalm in question. The 'thirst' of 63.1, for example, has suggested David's time in the wilderness, while the 'prison', 'refuge' and 'traps' of 142 have suggested his time of hiding in a desert cave. But the instincts of these early exegetes are not insignificant, and when they link psalms to David's military campaigns (3, 18, 60) they may be working with a genuine recollection that some psalms originated as prayers of the kings in religious ceremonies on campaigns away from Jerusalem. While the kings will have had in their service sacred persons skilled in composing and offering for them prayers and praises, David himself, as tradition maintained, may have had here a special aptitude. Music and poetry, offered before the Lord, may have been among the gifts that won this skilful leader such fame and following. But though a number of psalms may date from his reign, it is hardly possible to demonstrate which could be his own compositions.

From all the traditions of David as composer and organizer of psalmody, three connections persistently recur and deserve respect. Firstly, there is the connection with the royal figure, the dynastic father; it may be, as we shall see, that in many psalms the person praying is indeed a king, representative of David's line, while there are other psalms which obviously concern the ideal of the royal calling. Secondly, there is the connection made with ceremonies of worship in the sanctuary; we shall find there the likely setting for many psalms, not least in the chief festival of the royal period.

And thirdly, there is the connection with prophecy; David and other psalmists were said to have 'prophesied' in their singing – they saw and set forth deep things of God by the power of the Spirit. This visionary quality of the Psalms is there for the modern reader to explore and go on discovering at ever deeper levels. But in particular we can see that the vivid experience of the God who makes all things new, an experience which lights up many psalms, easily takes on the aspect of prophecy of the world to come, the perfected kingdom of God. Thus the inherited idea of royal David, the Lord's Anointed, as supreme singer, musician and dancer becomes a precious symbol of the deepest significance of the Psalms. He is a witness to their messianic mystery.

2c Female psalmists

We should bear in mind the likelihood that there were female psalmists, just as there were female prophets. Egyptian and Assyrian pictorial records show how important were female instrumental players, dancers and singers in the worship of the surrounding peoples. As for Israelite society, it is clear that a high value was put on women singers. We hear of them as skilled mourners for the dead (2 Chron. 35.25) and as performers in the palace (2 Sam. 19.35). Some of them were included in the tribute sent to the Assyrian conqueror in 701 BCE to save Jerusalem. That they too, like their male counterparts, were organized in guilds seems to be implied by Ezra 2.65, which portrays an assembly of returning exiles as including 200 singers, male and female.

And so it seems likely that in religious ceremonies, at least in the royal period, skilled female singers made a contribution. They would be following in the tradition of Miriam, sister of Moses, a prophetess whose solo voice led the hymn and evoked response from women who danced and played hand-drums (Ex. 15.20–1). One of the mightiest hymns of old was composed and sung by a woman, the prophetess and ruler Deborah (Judg. 5.1, 7). There was also a powerful psalm ascribed to Hannah, mother of the prophet-leader Samuel; she is pictured as visiting the temple at Shiloh with her child to fulfil her vow, and the conclusion of her militant psalm anticipates the reign of a king, the Lord's Anointed (1 Sam. 2). Another notable psalm mirrors a festal procession in which young women with hand-drums complement the male singers and players of portable harps and lyres (68.25); these male and female companies may well be the ancestors of the singers in that assemblage of returning exiles. Like the male psalmists and priests, and like the singers and players in Egypt, such women will have served in a part-time manner, having turns of duty or roles on special occasions. The female contribution would impart brilliancy of tone to the singing, expressiveness to the dancing, and a complementary role in supplication and praise, sorrow and rejoicing, so that the whole soul of the people could be represented before the Creator.

It is interesting that though the authors of Sumerian hymns are not usually named, a cycle of 42 hymns praising the major temples and their gods is ascribed to the high priestess Enheduanna, daughter of King Sargon of Akkade, *c.* 2350 BCE (*TUAT* II, pp. 645, 686). Jacobsen (p. xi) describes her as 'a gifted poet'. In the Commentary, however, it will be practical to refer to the individual psalmist as a 'he', especially as by tradition, and with probability, it is often the king or someone from the male guilds who is speaking, and there are no indications to the contrary in particular psalms.

3

Psalm Music

3a The singing

Alas, the musical aspect of the original psalm-singing can only faintly be known to us today. The knowledge and styles handed down in the guilds of psalmists largely perished when the Romans put an end to the temple and its ministries in 70 CE. Nevertheless, enough clues remain to give us some idea of the character and significance of the music.

The singing itself was the heart of the music, while the instruments (appropriately known as 'instruments of song', *keley shir*, Amos 6.5; 1 Chron. 15.16) had deep significance as joined with the voices in a common endeavour. In most psalms the words appear to be those of a single voice, and it is likely that the role of the soloist was paramount. But there is also plenty of evidence that, as in Asian and African work-songs today, the singer interacted with a group. In addition to refrains and responses from the professional choir, there were the acclamations and affirmations voiced by the great assembly of pilgrims. In 8, for example, we may think of the graceful refrain that frames the soloist's meditation as sung by the choir, while in 118.1–4 the terse, rhythmic affirmation is evoked alternately from the priesthood and from the whole assembly. Such interplay was a significant feature of worship. Leader and community were encouraging each other, and the boundaries of the worshipping circle seemed to extend more and more until all living beings were called in (so 148 and 150). The essential structure of the Hebrew hymn in fact consisted of calls to praise supported by reasons for the praise, the soloist thus exhorting other worshippers to voice the traditional phrases acknowledging God's power and goodness.

The manner of singing was probably as emotional and passionate as that still to be heard in the liturgies and love-songs of the Mediterranean region. Between sorrowful lament and joyful praise, however, there would be a marked contrast. For the sorrowful song, displaying penitence and appealing for mercy, there was 'the voice of groaning' (title of 102). Here the vibrant murmuring could resemble the growling of bears or the moaning of doves (Isa. 59.11; Ps. 77.3). Terms for the singing of praise, by contrast, indicate joyful shouts with lively clapping and dancing. The Sumerians had even thought it best to allot the work of praise and lament to different orders of holy singers (the *gala* priests for lament, the *nar* priests for praise), and in

Jerusalem there would certainly be at least a keen sense of the difference of the two styles and their functions. All the more memorable, then, was an occasion when the order was for praise, with cymbals and trumpets and choral and congregational acclamations, but from some of the people there arose a spontaneous wailing, loud as the praises and mingling to produce a noise that carried far across the hills (Ezra 3.10f.).

Portrayals of singers among the neighbouring peoples suggest details of different singing styles. From a tomb in Saqqarah, Egypt, comes the stone relief of a blind harpist-singer kneeling at his harp. So carefully are the lines of his face represented that we can almost hear his nasal head-tone, expressing devoted rapture. Assyrian artists depict a group of Elamite singers and musicians, where one of the female singers taps her throat to produce a vigorous tremolo to heighten the songs of praise. In a joyful scene from Egypt four priests, shoulder to shoulder, lean forward and clap the rhythm as they sing out in concert with a priestly trumpeter who stands close and faces them.

3b The instruments

Such portrayals are especially helpful when we try to envisage the variety of instruments that were used in Israelite psalmody. It is clear from the accounts of David's procession with the ark (2 Sam. 6; 1 Chron. 13; 15), from Psalm 150 and from other references in psalms and stories, that the singing was accompanied by plucked strings, percussion and wind instruments no less than was the worship of neighbouring peoples. The form of the biblical instruments has mostly to be inferred from the abundant foreign sources – pictorial, textual, and sometimes actual remains.

First must be mentioned the lyre (*kinnor*). Made of wood, the instrument had a soundbox as its base. From here two side-arms rose to join a crossbar. Strings, which could number from four to eleven, were stretched from the crossbar to the soundbox. Several depictions of lyrists from the Palestinian region show how in processions the lyre was held with the strings horizontal and the base under the left arm. One hand could be used to dampen unwanted notes, while the other could play the strings with a plectrum or more softly with the fingers. The sound is described as 'sweet' or 'lovely' (*na'im*, 81.2), a vibrant 'murmur' (*higgayon*, 92.3).

To the lyres were often joined the deeper-sounding, more resonant harps (*nebel*). The portable, angular harps depicted by the Assyrians are probably our best guide. An arm joined the long soundbox at a right-angle or more acutely. The strings (between eight and twenty-two) ran diagonally and so with graded lengths from the arm to the box. One type was held with the strings vertical and box uppermost, while another was held with the box as the horizontal base. The player again might use a plectrum or only the fingers.

Some translators find a lute among the Israelite stringed instruments (so even NEB and NRSV for *nebel* in 150.3), but the evidence seems to be against this. The multi-stringed *nebel* ('ten-stringed harp', 33.2; 144.9) is obviously quite different from the lutes depicted by the Egyptians. These lutes had only two or sometimes three strings, which were of equal pitch. From a small oval soundbox ran a long narrow neck against which the strings were stopped with the fingers of the left hand, while those of the right hand, with or without a plectrum, were plucked near the box. One of the strings would be used for a drone note, while if there were two others they were played together for the melody as on a mandolin.

Instruments of the pipe family appear to be mentioned in 150.4 ('*ugab*, Targum *abbuba*), the heading of 5 (*nehilot*), and in scenes of prophets and pilgrims (*halil*, 1 Sam. 10.5; Isa. 30.29; cf. Mishna Arakhin 2.3). Types of flute, clarinet and oboe are well attested in the neighbouring countries; especially popular was the double oboe, where the mouthpieces of the two pipes each contained a double reed and were kept well inside the mouth and blown together. The pipes were of hollow cane and were held downwards, diverging a little from each other. The left pipe could be used to supply a droning note under the melody of the right pipe. It is likely that the Israelites used this popular instrument, along with the simpler vertical flute. The pipe family, like the clarinet today, could be eloquent as well of rejoicing (1 Kings 1.40) as of mourning (Jer. 48.36; Matt. 9.23).

A good deal of use was made of horns and trumpets. The horn (*shopar*) was that of a wild goat or ram. Its far-carrying blare made it especially suitable for solemn signals, such as those for the sighting of the moon for new year's day (Num. 29.1) or to mark the coming of God in worship (47.5; 81.3; cf. Ex. 19.13, 16, 19). The trumpet (*hasosera*) had a straight tube and flared end and was made of metal such as beaten silver (Num. 10.2). Although the Jewish trumpet depicted on the arch of Titus in Rome is noticeably long, a shorter type common in Egypt may have been normal. Brilliant in signals of acclamation, the metal trumpet could also be played with vigorous singing and dancing, as Egyptian portrayals show (cf. 98.4–6).

Of great importance were the instruments of percussion. The Babylonians had an especially sacred drum, large and goblet-shaped, resting on the temple floor. They also had a huge circular drum that required three men to carry and play it. In Assyrian processions we see players with a funnel-shaped drum fastened at their waist. Egyptian players sometimes have a barrel-drum hanging from their neck and across the stomach, a drum to be played at both ends. But the most widely used drum was related to our tambourine. Skin is stretched over a ring of wood or metal. The moving, dancing player holds it high with the left hand and taps it with the right. This is the instrument aptly named in biblical stories and psalms as *top*, plural *tuppim*. The combination of its rhythmic playing with dance or dancing procession is clearly shown (Ex. 15.20; 1 Sam. 10.5; 2 Sam. 6.5; Pss. 68.25; 149.3; 150.4).

There were several other percussion instruments to give effects of knocking, rustling, jingling and chiming – types of clackers, castanets, sistra and cymbals. Egyptian portrayals and references show their great importance and sacred associations, such as when sistra and pearl-strings were shaken to dispense blessings of life from heaven. Shakers, wooden bars and cymbals are mentioned in the ark-procession of 2 Samuel 6.5. Cymbals appear with special emphasis in Psalm 150. Two kinds may be intended, one (cymbals of *shemaʿ*) linked to proclamation of God's approach, the other (cymbals of *teruʿa*) to celebration of his victorious presence. Two kinds are in fact evidenced by archaeology, one where two bronze plates are clashed horizontally, the other where one bronze cone is struck downwards on another.

3c The character of the music

Some progress has been made by research into the actual music of the neighbouring peoples. There are clues in the details of surviving or carefully depicted instruments – fret marks on the lutes, the spacing of holes in pipes etc. Babylonian texts give information on the tuning of strings, and also on their re-tuning to pass through a series of modes. It seems that there were seven octave series similar to the modes of later Greek and Latin music. Those who today enjoy Gregorian plainsong would not have found the more ancient music too strange.

A tablet from the discoveries at Ugarit (on the North Syrian coast, a few centuries before David) gives a psalm to the goddess Nikal in the Hurrian language, and then a kind of musical notation where terms relating to intervals or chords alternate with numerals. Reconstructions of this music have been attempted and recorded. For the Hebrew psalms, surviving musical clues are more elusive. The accents written under or above most words in the mediaeval manuscripts of the Hebrew Bible have some significance for patterns of cantillation, which however vary considerably among Jewish communities. A French musicologist, Suzanne Haik Vantoura, believes that these signs represent ancient records of the hand-signals of the biblical cheironomers and specify notes on the scale and ornaments. She too has reconstructed and recorded the hypothetical music.

Enigmatic phrases in the psalm headings have been taken by some translators as musical indications. Names of tunes are thus discovered in 'The Hind of the Dawn' (22), 'Lilies' (45), 'The Dove on Far-off Terebinths' (RSV, 56), 'Do Not Destroy' (57 etc.). The common heading *lamenaṣṣeaḥ* (4–14 etc.) is often explained as 'for the choir-master / musical director'. 'Over the eighth' (6 and 12) has been related in some way to the scale's octave. All this interpretation, however, is very dubious and the references may sometimes be to rites or stages in liturgy. A manner of rendering suited to praise (literally 'for disposing to favour', cf. Targum here 'for praise') may be indicated by *lamenaṣṣeaḥ*, rather than any reference to a musical director. Concern for the appropriate liturgical style of the psalm rendering leads also to occasional specification of instruments – strings (4; 6 etc.) and perhaps flutes (5).

Another technical term that remains unclear is *sela*, which occurs within psalms and no less than 71 times. The Greek Version points to an interlude or pause, the Aramaic Targum to an affirmation, a kind of Amen. An interlude seems likely, and might have been the time for instrumental music or for a general obeisance with affirmations by the congregation.

3d The significance of the music

Such are the uncertainties that remain with us, particularly because so much of the closely guarded psalm-tradition was lost with its guardians in the tragedy of 70 CE. But fortunately it is a much clearer situation when we turn to the significance which was seen in the psalm music.

Psalmists sometimes deliver oracles (50.5f.; 81.6f. etc.), and the connection which was often made with prophecy (1 Chron. 25.1, 3; 2 Sam. 23.1–3 etc.) shows how the music was felt to be inspired. The psalm may pour from a heart seething with inspiration, a tongue driven by the Spirit (45.1). God puts the thankful song into the singer's mouth (40.3).

What was given was offered back again. Not for the pleasing of the congregation, but for the Lord, the music was offered and rendered with all possible skill and dedication. With all their heart the psalmists rejoiced in the Most High and to his name made music (9.1–2). With lyre and harp and a fresh song (33.2–3) they would make music for him. The psalmist's lifelong vocation was so to make music for the Lord, praying that the Lord would find it sweet (104.33–4). Best of all the offerings (69.30–1), it could dispose him to favour (19.14).

The time of offerings in the temple, accompanied by singing of psalms, was a time of communion, and the frequent reference to the name of God in psalm-praise is part of the experience of divine presence and revelation. 'Yah', the short form of the holy name 'Yahweh', resounded with emphasis in every 'Halelu-yah' ('Praise Yah'). The full depth of music's meaning is experience of the Lord himself: 'My glory and my music is Yah' (118.14).

Psalm music shares the universal dimension of the temple itself. As the space of the temple mysteriously merges with that of God's heavenly abode, so the music is one with the praises of the heavenly hosts and of all creatures when the world is made new – a truly visionary experience. On earth and in heaven there is acknowledgement of God's unique divinity – his holiness and glory (Isa. 6.1–4; Pss. 29.1–2, 9–10; 99.3, 5, 9). The playing, singing and dancing in the temple is joined with the music of all creation (98.5–9; 148; 150).

In lamentation the mournful chant was intended to move God's pity (Joel 2.17–18). The divine gift of music served to carry the appeal to heaven and the heart of God. Amidst life's perplexities, the lyre could bring relief and unlock the riddle (49.4).

Although our study of the Psalms has to become study of a text – words and sentences on silent pages – we do well not to forget the melody and movement, the music and dance that were essential aspects of psalmody. All together belonged to the divine gift which led the worshippers into communion with their Lord and fellowship with the cosmos.

4

The Poetry of the Psalms

4a Patterns of thought: parallelism

A good deal of European poetry sounds banal or even ridiculous when translated. Its carefully crafted wording, along with its metre and rhyme, cannot be carried across into another language, and so the beauty of the poem perishes. Hebrew poetry, however, has important qualities which can live on in translation. It is based on patterns of meaning rather than on the effects of particular words and their sounds, and these patterns – thoughts that weave, hover and dart – can be represented in other languages. The homely, unsophisticated wording – plain and unpretentious – and all the simple but strong imagery are also features which the translator can reproduce. And so we have this amazing fact: the poetry of the Psalms, torn from its beloved music and then in translation deprived of its own words with their own lilt and speech-melody, has yet lived on with great spiritual and aesthetic power among peoples and languages across the world.

The patterns of thought are easy to recognize in the layout of our modern Bibles. The main unit of the Hebrew poetry is usually called a 'line' or 'verse' (mostly identical with our numbered verses), and this usually falls into two parts (or 'members'), occasionally three. It is this prevailingly double structure which is so characteristic. The second part may indeed only repeat the sense of the first part ('synonymous parallelism' – strictly, where the correspondence is complete):

> The Lord will hear my pleading;
>> the Lord will accept my prayer.   (6.9)

There is nothing pedantic in the method, and in many of the repetitions not all the elements are matched:

> To the Lord belongs the earth and its fullness,
>> the world and all that dwell in it.
> For it was he who founded it on the seas,
>> and made it firm upon the floods.   (24.1–2)

> Show us your faithful love, O Lord,
>> and give us your salvation.   (85.7)

Sometimes the first part remains in suspense until the second part adds a vital element ('stair-like' or 'climactic parallelism'):

> For see, your enemies, Lord,
>> for see, your enemies shall perish...   (92.9)

> Give to the Lord, you powers above,
>> give to the Lord the glory and strength...   (29.1)

The double structure may comprise a comparison ('emblematic parallelism') or a contrast ('antithetic parallelism'):

> As arrows in the hand of a warrior,
>> so are the children born of youthful strength.   (127.4)

> The wicked one must borrow and cannot repay,
>> but the good person is ever giving to those in need.   (37.21)

Sometimes the flow of thought quickens, with the two parts of the verse having no repetition except in rhythm, constituting in fact a single statement ('formal' or 'synthetic parallelism'):

> And so they exchanged God's glory
>> for the likeness of a bull that feeds on grass.

> He made them also to be pitied
>> by all who had taken them captive.   (106.20, 46)

We have the impression that the Hebrew poets, having learnt the basic kinds of parallelism, had freedom to vary and develop them according to their inspiration. They might, for example, extend the echoing effects from parts of a verse to a series of verses (as in 124). Almost every psalm seems to have its own mix of varieties of parallelism, expressive of its own sorrow or joy, its own pathos or wonder or teaching.

4b Stanzas and metre

The same freedom can be observed in the use of stanzas and of metre. Much European poetry falls into stanzas (regular groups of lines), but little of the kind appears in the Psalms. If a psalm can be analysed into matching blocks of lines, the structure arises out of the needs of that particular psalm, in a way peculiar to itself, and not as an imposed system.

Metre, again, is a matter of much freedom. The most common rhythmic regularity is where a verse has parts that each consist of three words or three word-clusters, and so carry three stresses (a metre referred to as 3 + 3). English

needs more words than the Hebrew, but the three main beats of each part can
still be heard:

> The lions roar for their portion
>   and seek their food from God.
> The sun rises and they are gone,
>   to lie down to rest in their dens.   (104.21–2)

A favourite variation of the 3 + 3 rhythm is 3 + 2. The falling away of the
second part can have an effect of pathos:

> For you are God my refuge;
>   why have you rejected me?
>
> Why must I go about mournfully,
>   while the enemy oppresses me?   (43.2)

Urgent effects are felt in 2 + 2 rhythm:

> Rise, Lord;
>   save me, my God.   (3.7)
>
> I am weary with crying out
>   and my throat is burning,
> my eyes fail
>   with looking so long for my God.   (69.3)

4c Wording and images

The economy of the Hebrew wording is notable in the limited use of
adjectives, a marked contrast to English verse. Joseph Addison's hymn based
on Psalm 23, for example, has ten adjectives for a passage where the Hebrew
has none at all:

> When in the sultry glebe I faint
> or on the thirsty mountain pant,
> to fertile vales and dewy meads
> my weary wandering steps he leads,
> where peaceful rivers, soft and slow,
> amid the verdant landscapes flow.

In many cases the justifiable adjectives of our translations arise from a
favourite Hebrew construction which links up two or more nouns, sometimes leaving a rich ambiguity which the translator tends to flatten out. In 23,
for example, 'pastures of grass' is clear enough, but in 'waters of rest' is it the

water or the psalmist that is still? Are the 'roads of right' really 'right ways' or rather 'roads where right is shown' — the triumph-way of the vindicated Lord's Anointed? And mystery remains in 'the valley of the shadow of death' (NRSV 'the darkest valley').

Like all poetry, the psalms draw imagery from the natural world. Rainstorms, desert winds, earthquakes, snow and frost, night-time, morning light, burning sun and evening shadow — all speak of God. Mountains and crags, animals and wild flowers, long treks through the wilderness, the dramatic revival of parched watercourses, the wonder of trees — all contribute to the fullness of experience.

The world itself is seen imaginatively. The numerous depictions of the Beginning in the Bible (especially Gen. 1–2.4a; 2.4b–3; Job 38f.; Ps. 74.12–17; Prov. 8; John 1.1–5) vary remarkably because at bottom they are poetic interpretations of life's meaning, and each depiction has its own points to bring out. Psalm 74 has to express the Creator's power over chaos and so draws on an ancient poetry of the King-Creator who clove his adversary the chaos-sea and broke the heads of her dragon-allies. Elements from such ancient poetry occur in many psalms; the cosmic structure is the work of this royal victor — the heavenly ocean surmounted by his palace, the solid sky-vault that undergirds this ocean, the lower waters under the earth and at the mouth of Sheol (the caverns of death). For Psalm 8 creation, in all its vastness and detail, is the work of the Lord's fingers; this heightens the wonder that such a God yet loves and cares for our puny race.

It is in fact for the depiction of fellowship with the Lord that the imagery of the Psalms is most telling. In portraying the Lord whom we can approach, speak with, plead with, shelter in, the psalm-poetry has wisdom like a child's. Faced with the infinite and ineffable, it draws on the deepest simplicities of the heart. It calls on the Lord to wake up and act. It tells of his laugh, his smoking anger, his strides, his eyes and hands, his sheltering wings. It would spur him to act, move him to pity, appeal to his sense of honour, remind him of what he seems to have forgotten. To the psalmist the Lord is a light, a rock, a fortress, a spring. God holds him by the hand, or keeps him tenderly in his heart as one's eye may hold a tiny image of a person standing close (17.8). He knows how many are the suppliant's groans, and he keeps the tears in his bottle — so much he cares for every suffering (56.8). For this Lord the psalmist thirsts, and longs but to behold his beauty (27.4; 63.1–2). Utterly remote seems the sufferer from the light and life of God, as the prayer rises from the ends of the earth, from the subterranean death-land; but as the watchers of the night know that dawn will come, so the sufferer counts on the abundant and redemptive mercy of the Lord, and the watching and waiting are filled with hope (130).

4d Types and forms

An important angle of the study of psalm-poetry has been the recognition of types of psalm ('genres', 'forms', German *Gattungen*). Hermann Gunkel (1862–1932) was outstanding in his thorough study of the matter, and the types he identified remain the best starting point for continuing discussion. We have already noticed that there was a great difference of style between praise and lamenting prayer. Gunkel's analysis brings out and develops the distinction, but shows in more detail how the wording and build-up of thoughts took on their character from the function and 'setting in life' appropriate to the various types. These settings were generally to be found in the procedures of worship, but Gunkel also thought that, as the periods of history took their course, forms might come to be used away from their original settings and even mixed with other forms.

We may set out Gunkel's view of the types as follows:

1. Hymns, songs of praise to glorify God especially on the chief festal days (e.g. 33, 117, 145–50). Their thought-pattern is mostly made up of calls for praise and reasons for that praise. A variation or subclass are the Songs of Zion, which honour the holy city or sanctuary as God's abode (46, 48, 76, 87). Another subclass are the Songs for Yahweh's Throne-ascension, for the festal day which celebrated the Lord's ultimate triumph (47, 93, 96–9).

2. The People's Songs of Lament (/Complaint) for days of national penitence and fasting. They describe a calamity that has afflicted the people and aim to move God to intervene with mercy (44, 74, 79, 80, 83). The thought-pattern reflects this aim throughout, generally consisting of sharp pleas for God's attention and help, moving depictions of the calamity (the 'lament' proper), appeals to God's faithfulness and honour, and perhaps a final note of assurance that God has heard.

3. Royal Psalms, which may contain oracles and prayers in various patterns because from a variety of situations, but having in common an origin in outstanding royal ceremonies (coronations, commemorations, weddings, prayers before battle etc.; 2, 18, 20, 21, 45, 72, 101, 110, 132, and in part 89 and 144). These pieces from such special occasions have an outstandingly 'royal' character, but it is very doubtful that Gunkel was right to limit the king's psalms to this group.

4. The Individual's Songs of Lament (/Complaint), sung by an individual (not, Gunkel thought, the collective figure Israel) in personal need (3, 5, 6, 7, 13 etc.), a type originating in rites at the temple, but later arising more widely. This most numerous kind of psalm is generally formed with invocation of God's name 'Yahweh', cries for a hearing and for help, depictions of the suffering and the cruel enemies, appeals to God's promises, prayer for the doom of the enemies, and sometimes a concluding confidence that the prayer has been heard. All the elements in their different ways aim at moving the Lord to save. As an appendix Gunkel grouped here Psalms of Confidence, having something in common with the main type, but with confidence as the dominant mood (4, 16, 23 etc.).

5. The Individual's Songs of Thanks, where a saved person comes to the temple to fulfil the vow of sacrifice made during the affliction and bears witness to the Lord's faithfulness (30, 32, 116, 138 etc.).

Among types represented only sparsely, Gunkel noted Songs of Pilgrimage (84, 132), Israel's Songs of Thanks (67, 124), Sacred Legends (parts of 78, 105 and 106). From circles of the sages there came into psalmody, he thought, an influence that resulted in psalms of Wisdom Poetry, with style and concerns like those of Proverbs (Pss 1, 37, 73, 112 etc.). Combinations of elements in a form of dialogue or changing voices produced what he called Tora Liturgies (giving priestly teaching or 'tora'; 15, 24) and Prophetic Liturgies (with speech of God; 60, 75 etc.). For a really free mixture of various forms he used the name Mixed Poems (9–10, 119 etc.).

Gunkel's work of classification brought many benefits. In grouping like with like in a scientific manner he opened the way for others to follow new avenues of fruitful research. By identifying the component elements, the 'motifs' or traditional thoughts which are the building blocks for a particular type of psalm, he made it easier to follow the thought and purpose of the poet. But ironically, the attempt to classify and organize the material has also shown how much variation and fresh creation it contains. As we saw with metre, parallelism and stanzas, so here the traditional art is used with freedom and originality. This seems to correspond with the experience which the psalms express – an encounter with the Lord nurtured by tradition but ever born anew in the worshipper's own heart.

4e Alphabetic psalms

One other poetic device in the Psalms deserves mention, an acrostic or alphabetic scheme (found in 9–10, 25, 34, 37, 111, 112, 119, 145, and also in Prov. 31.10–31; Lam. 1; 2; 3; 4; Nahum 1.2–8 and three additional poems from the Qumran discoveries). The basic pattern, sometimes further developed, has each verse beginning with the next letter of the alphabet. In Babylon, where the writing was not alphabetic but syllabic, a kind of acrostic occurs with the first or last syllables of stanzas yielding a name or sentence when read downwards. The alphabetic method of composition was in use in Hebrew well before the Exile and was evidently found useful in providing a frame that gave order and a sense of wholeness. There may already have been a feeling for the wonder and mystery of the alphabet, the 22 signs that could express all sacred literature. Memory would be helped by the basic pattern, but not so much by the more elaborate examples (especially 119).

5

The Ancient Situations of Psalmody

5a Contexts in history

First we may consider historical contexts. Within the framework indicated above (1000–400 BCE, see 1b) it will be helpful to note certain periods and crucial events. The psalms contain, of course, references to earlier history, but these are retrospects, and they are not all that numerous – thus the patriarchs and the Exodus (e.g. 105; 106; 114) and the period of the Judges (*c.* 1230–1020, especially Ps. 78). Saul's kingship is almost ignored (78.67).

But it is especially from David's capture of Jerusalem in 1000 that our psalm tradition takes its rise. It had already been an important Canaanite city for some thousand years, with links especially with Egypt. David was able to bring some of its skills, including music and poetry, into his kingdom. Some of his psalmists may have come from the older population; thus Heman and Ethan (88 and 89) are called 'Ezrahites' ('natives'). Some psalm-themes have roots in the older city: Zion as abode of 'God Most High' (*el 'elyon*), city of 'right' (*sedeq*, cf. 'Melchizedek' and other royal names from the old city) and of 'peace' (*shalom*; 'Jerusalem' signifies 'Foundation of Peace'), the king as heir of Melchizedek (110). By this channel, too, may have come the Egyptian poetic influences evident in several psalms (104, 110 etc.).

David made Jerusalem the centre of an important empire and gave it religious pre-eminence for Israel by installing there the ark of the covenant, footstool of the invisibly enthroned Lord (2 Sam. 4–6). It will have rested in some kind of sanctuary called 'the house of the Lord' (2 Sam. 12.20). Here he could have established the services of priests and psalmists as tradition recounted. In this place and towards it, he could also pour out his own psalm-prayers and praises. With the peace and prosperity of his son Solomon's reign (970–31), it was possible to build the famous temple on the higher hill immediately north of the old city. In this feat, skills and materials from Canaanite Phoenicia played a big part. Psalm music will have been of a standard to match the architecture, and so the tradition which David had established entered a golden period.

When the empire split after the death of Solomon, Jerusalem was still able to continue for three and a half centuries as the seat of the Davidic dynasty and to uphold its claim to be Yahweh's throne-centre. The northern tribes had prestigious sanctuaries such as Bethel and Dan, and it is a question as to how much of their psalmody eventually found its way to Jerusalem, especially when the northern kingdom was crushed by the Assyrians (721). Whatever may have been adapted into the Jerusalem tradition, the claim was maintained that Yahweh's rule over the world and over his chosen people was mediated through the house of David and Zion / Jerusalem. And it will be the battles of David and his successors that are reflected in psalms that pray for help against terrible enemies (3, 44, 60, 140 etc.).

An era ended when the Babylonians destroyed the temple and put an end to the Davidic kingdom (587). But during the desolate half-century that followed, lamenting worship was still offered on the ruined site of the temple (74; 79), and in Babylonia the exiles met to commemorate Zion's tragedy, and the temple personnel were able to maintain their identity and sacred tradition (137). With the establishment of the Persian empire (539 BCE), the exiles could begin to return and the temple be rebuilt. It was dedicated in 515, and although not as fine as Solomon's temple, it was able to continue as the heart of Hebrew worship for nearly six centuries. Here psalmody had its place again. When the city walls were restored, psalmists led thanksgiving with cymbals, harps, lyres, trumpets, and all the musical instruments 'of David, the man of God' as the processions moved along the walls and ended 'in the house of God' (Neh. 12.27–43).

This era of reconstruction was also a time of building together the inherited resources of tora, story and poetry. Around the fourth century much of Hebrew scripture took its final form, and it is likely that near to that time (perhaps between 350 and 200 BCE, so Auwers, p. 170) smaller collections of psalms were gathered and arranged into the shape of the book we now have.

Another opinion, not so common today, has seen a much later period as originating many of the psalms. Greek empire replaced Persian from 333 BCE, but it was in 167–4 that the sharpest crisis arose for Judaism. The Hellenistic ruler Antiochus IV was in conflict with conservative Jews and for three years the temple was run in a way offensive to devotees of the Law, some of whom were martyred. The tensions of this crisis and the aftermath of sectarian strife till around 100 BCE seemed to some scholars to be reflected in psalms which show 'the faithful' in conflict with 'the wicked'. The royal psalms also were explained from the royal aspirations of Maccabean rulers. Such late dating now appears erroneous. That the Psalter was completed well before this period seems indicated by the Preface to Ecclesiasticus, which attests that Ben Sira (*c.* 190 BCE) studied scripture in the threefold division: Law, Prophets and (other) Writings. In the third part of this division the Hebrew Psalms come first. Ben Sira's praise of David (Ecclus. 47.8f.) is further indication of his familiarity with the Psalms.

It remains quite uncertain how to account for the deviant order of the psalms in some Qumran manuscripts – whether, for example, it arose from special liturgical requirements, or from the founders of the sect having originally broken away when the latter part of the collection was still fluid. (See Auwers, pp. 19–23.)

After a short period of independence under the priestly family of Hashmon (the Hasmoneans or 'Maccabees'), the country passed into Roman control (64 BCE). Rome sanctioned the reign of Herod (40–4 BCE), who undertook a massive reconstruction of the temple and its courts, extending the area with wonderful walls and substructures, as can still be made out today. In this great sanctuary, contemporary with Jesus and Paul, psalmody flourished with the daily rites of offerings and the vast gatherings of festal pilgrims, until war with Rome brought a catastrophic end. Temple and city were destroyed in 70 CE and Jews banned from the area. The guilds of psalmists, with their inherited knowledge and skill, were lost from view.

No doubt some psalm-songs had become known more widely through pilgrimages and in other pious circles. The hymn-singing of the disciples of Jesus (Mark 14.26) can be related to Jewish tradition that 113 and 114 were sung before the Passover meal, 115–18 after it. But synagogues were mainly places for the reading and study of scripture, for prayer and for administration, not for psalmody, and of all the instruments only the signalling ram's horn was permitted there. And yet, as part of Hebrew scripture, and no less in its widely used Greek translation, the written form of the Psalms was lovingly preserved, and so the way to a rebirth of psalm-singing was kept open.

5b Contexts in worship

Turning to contexts in worship, we find from Jewish tradition and from the character of many psalms that the pilgrimage festivals were of outstanding importance for psalmody. Daily offerings, sabbaths, new moons, fast days called in emergencies – all no doubt saw use of psalms or the like. But in the collection that has come down to us, much relates to the festivals.

Three main festal seasons are known (Ex. 23.14f.; 34.18f.). One fell in March-April and eventually came to combine two observances: the night of Passover and the week of Unleavened Bread. For many centuries the Passover remains in obscurity; celebration in the late monarchy (2 Kings 23.21–3) points to its development from a domestic observance to a national assembly commemorating the Exodus, prefixed to the feast of Unleavened Bread which marked the earliest harvest, that of the barley. The first produce of that harvest was offered to God so that the rest could be humbly taken for general use. The avoidance of leaven served to keep the new produce distinct from the old, and it came to be taken also as commemorating the haste of the meal in the Exodus.

Seven weeks later fell the feast of Weeks (Greek 'Pentecost') also called 'Harvest' as it celebrated the wheat harvest with presentation of the first crop. This seems to have been a one-day observance (Num. 28.26f.) until, perhaps in the third century BCE, it was developed into a week's celebration linked to the renewal of the covenant.

But the festival most prominent in the narratives from the time of the Judges until several centuries after the monarchy, and most reflected in the Psalms, is that of the autumn, September-October, called 'the *ḥag*' (the 'pilgrimage festival' *par excellence*) or 'the ḥag of the Lord' (cf. Arabic ḥaj). There will have been an extended holy season including items separated out in later times (and still today) as the Jewish New Year, Day of Atonement and week of Tabernacles / Booths (1, 10, 15–22 of the month Tishri). The vital importance of this time of year in ancient Palestine was that the new agricultural cycle was about to begin. Strongly felt was the need to renew the relationship with the Lord, master of all the forces of life, and to seek his gift of winter rains, which did not in fact arrive with unfailing regularity. Without them the cycle could not begin and starvation was inevitable. The ceremonies, prayers and psalms of this great festival amounted to a passionate evocation of the God of life.

The richness of meaning in the festival, however, was also connected with its sacramental character. The chief action in the ceremonies was felt to be God's. He came, he revealed his glory, he established afresh the living order, he gave blessings to his faithful worshippers. From many psalms we feel the drama of the moment of revelation:

> From Zion, perfection of beauty, God shines out;
> our God has come and will not keep silence.   (50.2)

Often the calls to praise are calls to acclaim this coming of God:

> Sing aloud to God our strength;
> with joyful praise greet the God of Jacob.
>
> Make melody and sound the drums,
> sweet lyres together with the harps.
>
> Blow the horns as for new moon,
> and as for full moon, on our festal day.   (81.1–3)

In this psalm, and similarly in 95, the acclaim at God's drawing near is naturally followed by his address to his people. Psalm 95 further helps us to see that this coming of God with glory and triumph into his sanctuary is part of the drama of his kingship. He is acclaimed as proved supreme, king above all gods, the Creator who must own and have power over all he has made (95.1–5). A number of psalms carry the proclamation 'The Lord is king!' or 'has become king!' (47, 93, 96, 97, 99), and despite much argument about the ideal translation of this announcement, it is obvious from the contexts that it is an exciting and dramatic moment. Chaos-foes and evil powers have been defeated, and the Lord has entered as victor, the most high God, the Creator-King.

The defeat of the adversaries (often envisaged as stormy waters) which has preceded this moment is alluded to in several of the triumphant psalms (29, 93 etc.). Ceremonies that signified the actual battle included especially processions (24, 68 etc.). In Babylonia and Assyria also, the subjection of the chaos-sea was signified by procession with the divine symbols to a ceremony at an outlying shrine, and in due course a triumphant return to the sanctuary with proclamation of the Creator's 'kingship', his supreme rule over all the living world.

As we begin to glimpse the setting of Jerusalem's triumphant psalmody, we see how the participation of all the pilgrims – with cries of praise and assent, with dancing and feasting – was part of their engagement in the festal drama. The full sequence included moments of penitence, purification, prayer and waiting. The joy was the final breaking through of the faith that through all suffering the good would triumph, and indeed does triumph. The meaning of the world, with all its myriad kinds and all its tragedies, came to glorious revelation in the climax of the festival, and through the acts of worship, including psalmody, the pilgrims took it into their hearts. They had come into the source of light and life and were made new.

It is probable that the autumn festival was also the setting for an important group of royal psalms. As the festival centred on the Lord's kingship, it was appropriate to consecrate there the office of the 'servant' of that kingship, the man 'chosen' and 'anointed' to effect on earth the heavenly King's will. It is known that in Egypt and Mesopotamia full inauguration and subsequent renewal of the royal office took place in chief festivals of 'new year' character where the heavenly kingship was celebrated; and in Jerusalem also, full years of a reign were counted from the (autumnal) new year. Psalms 2, 21, 72 and 110 can readily be seen in this setting. A number of others which in various ways envisage humiliation and deliverance (18, 89, 101, 118, 144) may reflect a dramatic character in the presentation and consecration of the royal office – scenes of desolation where faith, humility and righteousness were tested before glory was bestowed. More commonly these psalms are interpreted as referring to historical situations. One may note, however, that 2 already has a dramatic character connected with the royal installation. The elaborate royal dramas of Egypt may seem a long way theologically from the Davidic religion, but Egyptian influence is apparent in 2, 104 and 110. More comparable would be the Babylonian humiliation and reinstatement of the king before his god Marduk, in preparation for his leading duties in the new year festival. Divested of insignia, buffeted, dragged by the ears to bow low before the symbol of the god, he had to recite a protestation of right conduct before being re-invested and given favourable oracles. With this protestation several scholars have seen a parallel in 101. Another consideration is that liturgical scenes may well have been among the traditions that fed into the great prophetic vision of Isaiah 52–3, a drama of atonement won for the many by the suffering of a royal figure. All in all, the interpretation of these royal psalms in terms of liturgical drama is not in itself far-fetched.

Another situation of psalmody was the fulfilling of vows made in time of need. Especially at the pilgrimage feasts, individuals would present offerings with thankful testimony which could be expressed in song (30, 32, 116, 138; Job 33.27–8). National thanksgivings for deliverance also occur (67, 124). For national psalms of distress we see more clearly the setting at the temple, where the tragedy or danger would be lifted to God with fasting and lamenting intercession (44, 74, 79, 80, 83; Joel 2.15–17; 2 Chron. 20).

The situations of the numerous psalms expressing individual suffering and supplication have been much researched and disputed. Persistent character-istics running through these psalms have invited fairly comprehensive explanations. Twenty or more of these psalms have not infrequently been explained as pleas of persons on trial at the temple – such sacred ordeal trials being held when ordinary evidence was insufficient (1 Kings 8.31–2). Appropriate here, then, might seem the protestations of innocence, pleas for justice, denunciations of slanderous opponents (3, 4, 5, 7, 17, 26 etc.). But these and many other psalms have also been explained as prayers of fugitives come to the temple to request asylum or safe-conduct, and here the prayers for refuge and shelter in God would be especially significant. Asylum was indeed a function of the temple, but there is no evidence that psalms were sung either in asylum procedures or in 'ordeal' trials, or that psalms were adapted from inscriptions left in the temple by fugitives or plaintiffs. A few psalms more clearly seem to be prayers in sickness (38, 39, 41, 88), though little definite is known of this.

For many of these psalms of individual distress an approach closer to tradition has been advocated by some outstanding exegetes (Harris Birkeland, Sigmund Mowinckel, Aubrey Johnson, John Gray) and is favoured in this commentary. Here the supplicant is seen as David or (for the most part) one of his successors, or even an early post-exilic ruler. The king would be praying at the temple or (if on campaign) at a field altar, and he might be in danger from military enemies, from conspirators or rebels, or from sickness or national misfortunes which weaken his authority. The causes of distress would vary from time to time, but constantly in his prayers he would refer to the Lord's promises of faithful love for his servant, and his total reliance on these assurances in the face of hostile powers. Strong royal colouring in wording and thought in quite a number of these psalms would then be directly appropriate (not just adapted from royal prayers into common use), while the absence in many cases of decisive royal titles would be due to deliberate reticence. As in surrounding countries, the king in need would face his Lord in humility, with all the frailty of humanity, leaving the titles and insignia of high dignity for when he faced the people. It is notable that such royal interpretation of these psalms often reveals a powerful coherence in the psalm lost in other approaches (examples are 3, 4, 9–10, 17, 23, 40, 63). The frequent involvement of the whole people is also readily understandable in view of the king's responsibilities (e.g. 3.8; 28.8–9; 31.23–4; 51.18–19).

It was probably only in later times, about the third century BCE, that certain psalms began to be selected for fixed daily use in connection with the daily temple offerings. The Hebrew psalm headings note only one case, 92, for use on the Sabbath.

Unique is the note above 30, 'Song of the dedication of the house'. The psalm in itself seems to be a song of testimony sung at the temple when a healed person fulfilled a vow. The heading may have related to the dedication of the second temple in 515, but eventually the link was made with Hanukka ('Dedication'), the feast commemorating the Maccabean re-dedication of 165

BCE. This is a striking example of how an apparently individual psalm could come to speak for the whole community.

6

The Experience of the Holy

6a The unique God

Through all the kinds of psalms shines experience of God as unique, all-powerful being, above and distinct from all that exists, yet willing to be accessible. It is this almighty one, and no other, who makes, rules, purges and saves the world.

There is a remarkable lack of concern with other spiritual powers. Heaven indeed is imagined as peopled with many lesser beings, whose function is to serve God and carry out his orders. These beings are never addressed with prayer or praise, but only with the psalmist's terse calls for them to bow low before the Holy One and ascribe to him all glory. It is to God alone that prayer and worship of praise are addressed. Whether for the universal community, for the nation, or for the individual, relationship with the divine is focused on the Lord alone. To God alone is raised the supplication of the needy or the thanksgiving of the delivered. Deliverance may be effected through one of God's angels (*mal'ak*, 'one entrusted with a task', 34.7; 91.11), but these are treated just as bearers of the Lord's purpose and power.

Even for the spiritual forces of evil there is little attention. The Devil and his legions do not clearly feature in the religion of the Psalms, though there is sometimes reference to the harmful words and perhaps spells intended by enemies. Rather it is to the Lord's displeasure that sufferings are traced, and it is from his compassion that relief is hoped for. Not wholly past and done with is that old battle of creation, when, as envisaged by ancient poetic tradition, the Creator defeated the monster-like ocean of chaos and divided her body for the construction of the universe (74.12–17; 89.9–12). That chaos, the great negative force, can still threaten and seek revenge (8.2). But the Psalms are sure of the Lord's mastery, so much so that all hope is turned to him, all prayer is to him, all intercessory passion is working to call him from the semblance of absence, indifference or displeasure. And when he comes to save, the harming powers of chaos disperse like driven smoke, they melt like wax before fire (68.1–3).

6b The name 'Yahweh'

Of great significance in the Psalms, as in Hebrew scriptures generally, is that
God is known with a personal name. When we meet someone, we feel that
our acquaintance has taken a great step forward when we learn and use the
name of that person; the character becomes more distinct and definite, the
relationship has a foundation on which to develop. How much more when
the eternal and invisible one makes himself known through his holy name!
Here is distinctness from all other beings and powers, here is the basis for
'knowledge of God', a living relationship of grace and trust, guidance and
obedience, salvation and thanksgiving.

The famous story of Moses (Ex. 3.13–15) represents what was no doubt
fundamental also for the Psalms – that God himself has disclosed his name
'Yahweh' to his worshippers, thereby bestowing the means for him to be
invoked (*zikri*) through all generations. The story is probably also the best
guide to the meaning sensed in the name (playing on the verb 'to be', *hwh* /
hyh), appropriate for the One Who Is and Only Is, the unique, underived
reality, the absolute authority. The name 'Yahweh' occurs no less than 650
times in the Psalms, and its short form 'Yah' 43 times. It is usually found at the
beginning of psalms of distress (3, 5, 6, 7 etc.), as the essential grace-given
word that calls the Saviour into the encircling darkness. In psalms of praise
(not least in the name's short form in the phrase *halelu-yah*, 'alleluia') it marks
the Holy One who alone is to be worshipped. His exclusive role is marked
also in emphatic phrases such as 'Yahweh (and no other) reigns' (93.1),
'Yahweh is my shepherd' (23.1).

In later times there developed such awe for the name 'Yahweh', such
fear of using it unworthily, that open pronunciation of it was avoided. An
early example of this avoidance may be found in 42–83, where the more
general 'Elohim' ('God') is usually preferred – thought to be an editorial
revision carried through about the fourth century BCE before the blocks of
psalms had come together into their present combination. Subsequently it
became a standard practice (and to this very day) to pronounce 'Adonay' ('the
Lord') wherever *yhwh* (for 'Yahweh') was written. Already the Greek
translators (third and second centuries BCE) rendered the name throughout
with *kurios* ('Lord', sometimes with the article or possessive pronoun). This
was the practice inherited by our English Bibles, which generally have 'the
Lord', and in a few special cases offer 'Jehovah', a confused version of
'Yahweh'.

The Jerusalem Bible, emanating from the academic wisdom of the French
Dominicans, bravely returned to 'Yahweh' throughout. This procedure is
true to the original theology of God known by a name, but must struggle
against its strangeness in translation and against the gulf of millennia in the
tradition of usage. For Christians the wonder of God known in and through a
name has come to centre in the Lord Jesus Christ, to whom is given the name
above all names (Phil. 2.9); here they find the name, and indeed the person,
that brings the expression of the One Who Only Is.

Though the avoidance of pronouncing 'Yahweh' in later times was contrary to the very purpose of the revelation of the name, it was not altogether a surprising development in view of the theology of the name reflected in the Psalms. The name in effect is seen as little short of God himself made manifest. The name itself is praised as, like God, uniquely holy, powerful, faithful and saving. Revealed especially to his covenanted people (76.1), it is also the radiance of his glory which fills the world (8.1, 9). It is experienced as God's power and presence abiding in the sanctuary of Zion (74.7) and reaching from there in salvation (20.1–7).

6c Other divine names and titles

The richness of the experience of God, especially in the high moments of worship at his sanctuary, is expressed in a variety of phrases which include the name 'Yahweh' or alternative designations or titles of God. This variety witnesses also to the way in which the worship at Jerusalem had gathered up the manifold traditions and experiences of the Israelite tribes and of older sanctuaries and peoples of the land. It is an ecumenical tapestry, but woven with thorough discrimination.

The extended name 'Yahweh Sebaoth' (usually rendered 'Lord of Hosts') occurs forcefully in 24.10, where the context shows how this phrase evokes the all-conquering power of God. As is clear from the psalm, he is triumphant King not only in holy wars on earth (1 Sam. 17.45), but also in the cause of order and life on the cosmic stage (also 46.7, 11; 48.8; 84.1, 3, 12). The 'hosts' therefore extend beyond any earthly army to the vast hosts of the heavens. A fuller form, grammatically clearer but with the same meaning, is 'Yahweh God of Hosts' (89.8 etc.).

In addition to a few occurrences of 'Eloah' ('God'), there are in the Psalms over 360 occurrences of its plural 'Elohim' (if we include its construct and suffixed forms). Like our word 'God', it can be used as equivalent to a name, the plural form 'Elohim' appropriately expressing the majesty and fullness of the godhead. The occurrences of 'Elohim', rather than 'Yahweh', through most of 42–83 show how it could function as a name. But in addition, it lent itself to numerous important expressions of relationship. In close-knit phrases (Hebrew 'construct') it contributes to further designations or defining titles of Yahweh. Thus he is especially 'God of Israel' (41.13; 59.5; 68.8; 106.48) or 'God of Jacob' (20.1; 24.6?; 46.7, 11; 75.9; 76.6; 81.1, 4; 84.8), a title which brings to expression the long experience of the people's calling and the divine pledges. In one word (since Hebrew applies the possessive pronoun as a suffix) is expressed the immense reality of intimate bonding with the Lord: he is *elohay*, 'my God', or *eloheynu*, 'our God'. The two constructions (construct, and forms with suffixes) give manifold eloquent variations: 'God-of-my-salvation', 'God-of-my-right', 'God-of-my-love', 'God-of-my-refuge', 'God-of-my-praise'. Such expressions (including 'my God') are often used in prayers for help, appealing to the pledged goodwill of the Lord.

But in the best known example of 'my God', with pointed repetition and the clashing 'you have forsaken me' (22.1), the Hebrew uses another word, 'El'. This is the basic word for deity throughout the middle-eastern regions of the Semitic languages, signifying 'god' or, as a name, the chief god and the father of all, 'El'. The two usages are found in Hebrew, for example 'Elijah' ('Yahweh is my God') and 'Immanuel' ('El is with us'). In all, the Psalms apply 'El' to Yahweh some 75 times. Here again, then, is an ecumenical link, particularly as we find that the Hebrew deity 'El' has something, though by no means everything, in common with the 'El' of neighbouring Semites. The worship of 'El Elyon' ('El the Supreme' or 'God Most High') in pre-Israelite Jerusalem clearly bequeathed an important heritage to the worship represented by the Psalms. From Genesis 14.18–20, Psalm 110, and some other scraps of information, we can see that the pre-Israelite kings of Jerusalem were the sacred servants (high priests) of the deity who was reckoned above all others, the Creator, upholder of *sedeq* (right order, the essence of cosmic life), and especially manifest in Jerusalem. As king in Jerusalem, David (and then his dynasty) continued the line, 'the order of Melchizedek' (110.4), with 'El the Supreme' ('God Most High') being taken as an apt name of Yahweh (78.35, and with parallelism 57.2 and 107.11). If the older Israelite traditions sometimes give the impression that Yahwism was a tribal religion, fiercely concerned with the narrow interests of the one 'people of Yahweh', his covenanters, the El Elyon tradition gives more expression to experience of Yahweh as Creator and supreme ruler of the world and all creatures, concerned to make a universal kingdom of peace, through justice radiating from his presence in the city aptly named from pre-Israelite times 'Jerusalem' ('Foundation of Peace').

Parallel to the epithet 'Elyon', we find in 91.1 'Shadday' (cf. 68.14) and the combination 'El Shadday' is in fact applied to Yahweh in Genesis 17.1 etc. (there are 7 occurrences of the combination in the Old Testament, while 'Shadday' alone occurs 38 times, of which Job accounts for 31). One explanation of 'Shadday' has been sought in the Hebrew *shad* meaning 'breast', hence 'El Shadday', 'God with breasts', God with feminine aspect as nourisher, source of life – an explanation very appealing to those in quest of the apparently neglected feminine dimension. However, against the background of all the Semitic traditions of the chief God El, this seems an unlikely explanation, and mainstream opinion looks to an Akkadian word *shadu'*, 'mountain', hence 'El that dwells on the divine mountain'. This sense of the deity enthroned above all recurs often in the Psalms and is sometimes expressed also with the title *melek*, 'king', in various phrases – 'supreme king over all the world' (47.2), 'greatest king' (48.2), 'king of glory' (= to whom belongs all glory, 24.7f.), 'eternal king' (29.10). This title 'king', it is important to note, is particularly associated with the work of first creating and then reordering the world.

Associated with the expressions of Yahweh's supremacy, power and exalted kingship is the declaration that he is 'holy' (the sole true God, 22.3; 99.3, 5, 9; cf. Isa. 6.3) and is 'the Holy One of Israel' (the divine One in covenant with

Israel, the confederate tribes, 71.22; 78.41; 89.18). His authority as ruler and governor is especially expressed by the title *adon*, 'Lord' or 'Sovereign', and his rule of all the world and all its lesser authorities is here often explicit (8.1, 9; 97.5; 114.7; 135.5; 136.1–3). As many as 55 times we find in the Psalms the form *adonay*, where the addition of the ending *-ay* is best explained as emphatic, heightening the word's sense – 'Lord of all', 'almighty Lord', a title used for Yahweh from very early times. This was the word that eventually came to be pronounced in the reading of scripture generally where *yhwh* (for 'Yahweh') was written.

All in all, then, we have seen that on the one hand the Psalms express experience of God in his personal name ('Yahweh'), and on the other hand witness to the richness of the experience and to the uniqueness and universal authority of this Lord with a variety of other titles and epithets. In these names and titles is witness to the Creator and Master of all being, who yet will make himself known to a people or to an individual.

The manifold names and titles in the Psalms also show how in Zion's worship diverse older traditions have flowed together, sometimes indeed from springs outside the bounds of Israel. Much has come together in the service of 'Yahweh', and become a wonderful unity under the sovereignty of the ancient revelation of the One Who Only Is. If none of the titles, even 'El Shadday', defines God as feminine, it is still of great significance, against the middle-eastern religious background, that no female consort is envisaged. Metaphors of God as husband of Zion, the holy city, and as father of Davidic kings, are used in some psalms to express the loving bond, but there are no goddesses. It is striking that while the pre-Israelite El was characterized as father and father-creator (so at Ugarit), in the Psalms divine fatherhood is mentioned only in the simile of 103.13 and the metaphor of 68.6, along with the special bond with the Davidic king (89.26, cf. 2; 110). All in all, we discern in the God of the Psalms a revelation of the Holy One who transcends the sexual divide.

6d The fountain of life and the face of God

That this mysterious knowledge of God, a wonderful communion, was indeed experienced by the people of the Psalms appears from many striking statements. When much troubled and far from the holy place, the soul pants and thirsts for 'the living God', the very fountain of life; the need is compared to the plight of a deer that wanders through a drought-stricken land, straining her head upwards to catch the longed-for scent of water (42.1–2). And many were the pilgrims who could say 'Amen' to the psalm that told of the soul panting and fainting for the place where the Lord showed himself; heart and body cried out for 'the living God', and the holy abode would be reached with a satisfaction like that of the little bird making her nest near the altar (84.1–3). Not for a few heroic souls, but for all mankind the sheltering wings were there, and given there was the feast of goodness and quenching of the thirst for God; for there in the divine presence rose for all the fountain of life,

and the light of his face illumined the worshippers with the light of true life
(36.7–9). It is remarkable that in spite of the fear of death which the ancient
people sometimes connected with seeing God (Judg. 6.22f.; Isa. 6.5; cf. Ex.
33.18f.), the common phrase for attaining the goal of pilgrimage was 'to see
the face of God' (Ex. 23.15, 17; Ps. 42.2 etc.). The expression was indeed
bold, but with simplicity it caught the profound experience. Later, perhaps
from about 300 BCE, the vowels of the Hebrew here for 'see' were pronounced as for the passive 'be seen', and so from the resultant awkward phrase
arose the translation 'to be seen / to appear before the face of God'.

6e Turning aside to God

That some psalms have a special concentration on the wonder of experiencing
God is probably due to their purpose and setting in a kind of 'incubation'.
Particularly in the case of the king on the eve of a great crisis, the Lord's
invitation to draw near in the sanctuary, shelter under his wings, and be
renewed in spirit would be taken up. The supplicant would sometimes sleep
in the holy place in hope of a dream-vision and an encouraging word of God.
An example can be found in Psalm 63, apparently on the eve of battle. The
king, the anointed servant of the Lord, seeks him earnestly at the sanctuary,
thirsting for God in a parched land – a situation of danger and pain without
sign of divine salvation. He longs to see God's glory – his presence revealed in
the temple. Life itself is nothing compared with experience of his love.
Reciting God's holy name in formulas of praise throughout the night will
itself be contact with the wonderful presence, replenishing the soul as with
the finest nourishment. There, truly, will be joy in the shadow of God's
wings. The soul will cleave to him, held by his right hand. In similar fashion
the supplicant of 27, faced by terrible foes, recalls God's invitation, 'Seek my
face', and does indeed seek it; by comparison, nothing in the world matters
but to be near that presence in the sanctuary, to be granted to see the beauty
of the Lord, and to receive his guidance. Again we hear at the end of Psalm 17
of the enriching satisfaction, the utter fulfilment in seeing the face and form of
the Lord. Such a worshipper knew that there was no dissembling before the
Lord in such perfection of knowledge; this is his Creator who knows and has
always known him, who encompasses him and lays his hand upon him (139).

In these very psalms there is also more than an echo of the world of
conflict, voices of the ruthless and treacherous, the clash of armies. The one
seeking mystical contact, the vision and touch of the Holy One, is often one
responsible for affairs of state, the defence of the realm, the care of the
economy, the control of unruly forces. Thus the 'life' which wells up like a
fountain from the Lord's presence is thought of as a full-blooded life that
includes the work and cares of this world. The blessed hours of contemplation
are a time when strength is given to serve the Lord in his world.

If outstandingly contemplative psalms, such as those just cited, are prayers
of kings, the general ideal was nevertheless open to all pilgrims. All came 'to

see the face of the Lord' (Ex. 23.15f.; 34.20f. etc.) and be replenished by 'the living God' (Ps. 84.2, 7). The sheltering wings and the spring of life at Zion were for all mankind (*beney adam*). Immense as the mountains that reached into heaven and as the deeps of the world-ocean, the goodness of the sovereign Lord there gave salvation to all species, human and animal (36.5–9). The contemplative counsel to be still and know the Lord was given to the multitudes, perhaps indeed to all earth's warring peoples (46.10).

6f Zion and the house of the Lord

It is characteristic of the Psalms that such visionary knowledge of God is experienced at the temple. The Lord of all places and all times has his 'holy' place and time, his chosen instruments, peculiarly his, where he makes himself known (48, 76, 87, 132 etc.). His place and time are the focus of his universal light. They are an opening of heaven. So the Creator's throne in heaven is encountered also in the symbols of the 'house of the Lord' on the hill of Zion. There he can be said to dwell or rule from his throne. From Zion he sends help to one far off and in trouble (20.2; cf. 128.5). And there especially, at the climax of the annual festival, he reveals his glory in judgement and salvation, restoring and creating.

From David's time, the very beginning of Israel's worship at Jerusalem, this significance was seen in Zion. For in a number of details the tradition can be traced back into the pre-Israelite city (e.g. the paradise river, 46, and Zaphon, mountain of God, 48). David, and later Solomon, obviously adapted an older view of Jerusalem's hill as the mountain of the Most High and his heavenly council, the garden at the source of the world-river, a disclosure of heaven. By its very nature such thought had virtually no concern with other sanctuaries; already the basis was here for the doctrine (evident from Josiah's reforms of 621 onwards) of the sole legitimacy of Zion as Yahweh's temple.

The religious concentration on Zion was immensely important for the whole society:

> Jerusalem, you that are built
> as a city bound in fellowship!
> Here the tribes ascend, the tribes of the Lord,
> as is the law for Israel, to give thanks to the name of the Lord.
> And here stand thrones for justice,
> the thrones of the house of David.   (122.3–5)

The orderly assembly on Mount Zion for the great festival thus represented all the tribes (in former times often hostile to each other) 'united in fellowship', ruled by the Lord through the house of David, prospering as they prayed for and sought the good of the holy city (122.6–9). And in the encounter with the Most High, the sole God, the universal vision could transcend the national concerns. While it was for prophets to foresee the pilgrimage of all nations to Zion (Isa. 2; Micah 4), a number of psalms show how something of this light of universal peace broke through in the high moments of festal worship (47, 68, 87, 96–9, 148, 150).

6g The mystery of God's new reign

Such experience of the ideal divine kingdom is well expressed in the terse proclamation 'Yahweh is (now) king!' (93.1; 97.1; 99.1). The contexts of such proclamations are best suited by translations that suggest an event, not an unchanging state As was to be well understood by the seer of the book of Revelation (11.17; 19.6), there was a sense in which the eternal Lord could 'become king', taking open power for his new reign, applauded and worshipped by all heaven and earth (so also Zech. 14.9). For the seer, it was to happen soon in the great end-time. For the worshippers at Zion it was experience of the meaning of the heart of the festival, a disclosure in the presence of Yahweh Elyon. There was a powerful experience of present grace, evoking all the joy that resounds in the festal psalms. It remained for prophets at the festal gatherings to relate the conviction of the reign of God to the flow of world events.

Against the disappointments and tragedies of life, the dramatic character of the festivals opposed a message. God was not a static reality. The evils were not part of his eternal, unchanging reign. In the festival he was known as the one going out to conquer evil, the one returning in triumph, the one throwing down arrogant oppressors and lifting up the poor. Here in the drama a gospel was proclaimed, hope and faith evoked. And in the mysterious way of sacraments, with the gospel a reality was conveyed, a salvation given.

6h The Lord's royal Servant as channel of salvation

The dynamic nature of the ceremonies seems also to have embraced the vocation and destiny of the Davidic house. The royal psalms, as indicated above (see 5b), showed the will of God to send peace, life and salvation through his chosen minister, his 'servant', of David's line. In the ideal, this ruler was to mediate God's reign from Zion throughout the world. His bond with God was founded on the Lord's love, goodwill, grace and faithfulness, and on his own humility, obedience and trust. It resulted in the upholding of justice, especially in the care of otherwise defenceless people. Through this relationship of the 'Father' and 'Son' flowed power to defeat the armies of the wicked and to heal and bless nature and society, making abundance of 'right' and 'peace'. Dramatic presentation of this ideal within the broader festal themes of God's kingship meant that it contributed to the experience of all the worshippers. Tribulation and vindication, humiliation and crowning with glory – all the faithful seem to have been involved in the enactment. The Anointed One stood before the Lord on behalf of the people, their repre-

sentative. When his salvation was shown, the light of the Lord fell upon all
(118.27). When he was newly anointed on the holy hill, the concluding
benediction was for all who sheltered under the divine wings (2.6, 12). The
Lord was at once shepherd and refuge of his Anointed and of his people
(28.8). From beginning and end of the Davidic era we have other Old
Testament witnesses to the sense of salvation, the light and life, which the
people experienced through 'the Lord's Anointed' (2 Sam. 21.17; Lam. 4.20).

6i Bringing sufferings to God

The abiding appeal of the Psalms has no doubt been due in part to their
expression of sufferings. To the Holy One in Zion, kings and other worshippers told of troubles that were destroying their lives, bringing them near
to extinction. The exact nature of the distress is rarely apparent, all the
emphasis falling upon its terrible and deadly aspect and the urgency of the
situation. Sometimes the trouble seems to centre in illness, sometimes in the
assaults of enemies, sometimes in injustice, sometimes in the treachery of
friends. But it is the great images of fear and forsakenness, pain and exhaustion
which come to the fore and speak for so many through the ages.

Not into the void are the descriptions uttered, but directed to the Lord in
all his compassion and faithfulness: 'Out of the depths I cry to you, O Lord'
(130.1). Under the earth is imagined a subterranean ocean, and under that
again Sheol, the vast, dark, silent cavern for the dead. The mouth of Sheol is
therefore imagined as miry. The sufferer near to death is as one sinking in this
mud, with waters sweeping over his head. These are the 'depths' from which
the cry is made, from the very limits of human endurance, from the margin of
death:

> I sink in the mire of the great deep, and have no foothold;
> I have come into the depths of the waters,
>   and the flood overwhelms me.
> I am weary with crying out, and my throat is burning;
> my eyes fail with looking so long for my God.   (69.2f.)

In another image, the suffering is like a fire within. The loins are filled with
burning (38.7). The bones burn like a furnace and consume the days – the
days as times of life are destroyed by constant pain (102.3). Some sufferers
even feel they have sunk further than the mouth of Sheol, and have come into
the full darkness of the pit of death:

> My soul is full of torments,
>   and my life has come to the land of death.
> I am counted with those gone down into the pit;
>   I am like one whose strength has departed.

My couch is among the dead,
    with the slain that dwell in the tomb,
whom you remember no more,
    and they are cut off from the help of your hand.   (88.3–5)

All such experience of the extremities of suffering seems to be gathered up into the lamenting section of 22 – forsakenness, mockery, encirclement by the terrifying shapes of the demons of death, the pains of the onset of death in mouth, heart and bones. The sufferer says to the Lord: 'You have laid me in the dust (or 'mire') of death' (22.15). Some scholars suspect an error in the text and change it to 'they have laid me', but the fact is that it is usual in lamenting prayers for the suffering to be attributed to the Lord's will or action. A sick person says: 'Your arrows have sunk into me' (38.2). Another sufferer says:

You have set me in the lowest pit,
    in a place of darkness in the mighty deeps.
Your anger lies heavy upon me,
    and you have afflicted me with all your waves.
You have put my friends far from me,
    and made me to be abhorred by them.   (88.6–8)

Here in fact we have come to the most terrible but also the most significant part of the psalmists' suffering. The Lord himself, it seems, has turned against them, hidden his face from them, forsaken them, rejected them, and the arrows of suffering are his. Can the Lord who has pledged faithful love be acting so? But the significance is that no other person can decide the issue. To the Lord alone the sufferer turns and cries and looks still with hope: 'But you, Lord – how long?' (6.3).

6j Lament turning to praise

Most of the lamenting prayers in fact end with a note of confidence (e.g. 6, 13, 16, 27, 54, 56, 59, 69). Scholars still debate how to explain the change of mood. Can we assume in some cases that a priest or prophet has given assurance of a favourable hearing (cf. 20.6; 85.8)? Or is it rather a recognizable pattern of emotional recovery? Or again, should we think of the suppliant reinforcing his plea by an expression of faith? At all events, the texts can be read as witnesses to a moving experience of the Holy One. Suffering, injustice, betrayal are not considered outside his will and power. A good end is not yet known. But his faithfulness is sensed as a final reality, and through the wintry earth the green shoots of hope appear.

6k Prayer against enemies

The lamenting prayers often refer to enemies. They often appear as numerous, terrible, attacking without just cause. This is understandable if many of these psalms were prayers of a ruler. Invasions and rebellions were only too common. Assassination was a threat by day and night. The general nature of the allusions, however, has enabled other sufferers to enter readily into these prayers, holding before God the sense of manifold threats, a hostile world, and calling upon his powerful intervention.

In a few psalms the prayer against these threats takes on a character which jars against other Old and New Testament teachings of forgiving goodwill towards enemies (Gen. 45.5f.; 2 Kings 6.22; Prov. 25.21–2; Matt. 5.38–48 etc.). In this passionate prayer against enemies, old traditions of sacred cursing and ideas of collective guilt are drawn upon. Some commentators applaud the frank sincerity of these prayers, their appeal to divine rather than human vengeance, and their concern for justice on behalf of the oppressed. No doubt such features are instructive. But if the merciless passages are to be recited as still valid prayers, it can surely only be with some development of meaning. The early monks prayed them as a defence against demons. Today one might pray them as passionate entreaties for the end of the cruel as cruel (along with the 'offspring' of their ruthless minds), and for their rebirth in love.

It is notable that the accounts of the passion of Jesus quote bitterly lamenting psalms at least six times, as though to show how he too went down into that abyss of suffering, betrayal and cruelty. He knew that utter bitterness, but towards those responsible he showed a better way: 'Father, forgive them, for they know not what they do' (Luke 23.34). These psalms of terrible outpouring in the presence of God should not be ignored in modern devotion and worship, but their vehement meaning will best be transformed in the spirit of Christ's example. Certainly, there is ever an immense work of passionate intercession against evil to be done.

6l Counsel and encouragement

Experience of the Holy One gives rise to a desire to help others know that happiness. So there are some psalms where a sage-like figure seems to offer disciples or other seekers counsel – teachings and exhortations that help towards an ever closer relationship with the Lord. The sage would have us still trust in the Lord when times are evil: doing good, abiding in our given place, feeding on faithfulness, and so delighting in the Lord, who will not ignore the requests of our heart (37.3–4). Stillness towards the Lord and hope-filled patience are often recommended (37.7). The teachings of God must be treasured in the heart, and to their expression are devoted the mouth and tongue (37.30–1). The 'fear' of the Lord – awareness of his holy reality, practical acknowledgement of his lordship – is recommended as the foundation and crown of wisdom (111.10). The psalmist-teacher would draw all his circle into a life turned toward God, daily activity flowing from experience of the Holy One (112; 127).

6m Knowing God through his tora or word

In a few psalms communion with the Lord is linked with great emphasis to meditation in his tora (variously rendered 'law', 'teaching', 'direction', 'guidance'). Though the copying, reciting and memorizing of scrolls of scripture might well be involved, along with formulas of praise and invocations of the names of God, these psalms in fact never specify any book, writing or particular law. Nor is the divine teaching referred to in itself as an absolute ('the Law'), but rather with the suffixed or dependent forms which make the teaching subordinate to the Teacher – 'his-tora', 'your-word', 'tora-of-Yahweh' etc. From many verses and expressions it is plain that this way of tora-study and devotion is prized as a way of meeting and knowing the Lord, a way of living from the breath of his lips, in the light of his face. The longing, the fainting for God's ordinances (119.20, 40, 131), the watching for his word of promise (119.123) – all is a variation of the thirst for the living God expressed in other psalms. Constant occupation with the Lord's guiding words means to be nourished by his grace, as a tree rooted by constant channels of water is nourished and made lively and wholesome (1.2–3). Here was a revelation of God's life-giving light, which might however bring the disciple a sense of unworthiness. The course of meditation, therefore, ends with reliance on the redeeming goodness of the Saviour, the Lord sure as a rock, careful as a good shepherd for one that goes astray (19.12–14; 119. 173–6).

6n Discovering God in perplexity

Experience of God, according to a few psalms, is sometimes reached through deep perplexity. In such a time it seems that God has forgotten to be gracious (77.9). One singer, apparently representing the community, tells of a day of trouble with much seeking of the Lord in cries and appeals, hands still outstretched through the night, a soul that cannot be soothed: 'I think upon God and I groan; I ponder, and my spirit faints' (77.1–3). This psalmist takes the way of reciting God's ancient deeds of salvation, implying an earnest prayer that the mysterious Saviour, moving with unseen footprints, will come again to rescue his people (77.11–20).

In such perplexing times it was easy enough to lose one's footing on the mountainside of faith (73.2). The heart readily grew bitter; indignation gnawed at the inner parts (73.21). But in laying the perplexity and bitterness before the Lord and in drawing near to his presence in the temple, the psalmist finds relief in a sudden illumination. There dawns a fresh conviction of the worthlessness of the prosperity of the wicked and the inexpressible value of communion with the Lord (73.23–8).

6o The question of life after death

Here we come to the question of eternal life. In general, the psalmists share the strikingly unhopeful view of most of the Hebrew scriptures regarding existence after death. A mere vestige of the person persists, as it were in a place of deepest darkness and silence, remote from the life-giving, joyful work of God in his land of life. It seems that nowhere in the Psalms was there originally a doctrine of true 'after-life', resurrection or immortality. Glimpses of a more hopeful view can be found here and there (e.g. 16.10–11; 49.14–15), and influences in this respect from Egyptian wisdom teaching and from ideas widely associated with kings (cf. 21.4–7) would not be surprising. Psalm 73, however, witnesses to something still more precious – present experience of the Holy One which transcends the anxieties of time. Here is no theory of the learned, or a comforting flight into fantasy. Rather it is an experience of the Holy One, a knowledge of the ultimate, the discovery of a love which can have no end. To this experience all the sufferers represented by the Psalms have contributed, for it is a light that has broken through on a dark and difficult journey, where all the travellers have believed and testified that in the Lord alone was their hope.

6p Community and world before God

The mutual support of the fellowship of worshippers is indeed apparent at the end of 73: the psalmist rests in a great good – the opportunity to 'draw near to God' in the temple – and there he will recount to other worshippers all that God has done. And throughout the Psalms, the deep experiences from the hearts of individuals are woven into a greater pattern of a people's experience of the Holy One. God is known as 'the Holy One of Israel' (89.18), God who formed a bond with the ancestor Jacob / Israel and who has continued to work through the people that stemmed from him, through the confederation of tribes that bore his name. God is known as this Israel's God (68.8), Shepherd (80.1; 100.3) and Guardian (121.4). A 'memorial', or sacred recital, was maintained down the centuries, recalling the deliverance of the Exodus (81.6–7, 10; 105.26f.), God's choosing of this people (105.43; 135.4) and giving of the covenant with its grace and demands (50.5; 111.9).

This people came before God as their Lord who had both rescued them and made them the bearer of his special presence and work in the world (114.1–2). They themselves were his sanctuary, his temple of living stones, and the heart of his kingdom, his reign over all. As the people came together in the great assembly of worship, they were conscious of this divine centrality – the Lord manifest within this people, place and time, yet sending the rays of his divine rule to the ends of the world (59.13). 'In Judah', 'in Israel', 'in Salem', 'in Zion', he makes himself known, his power is exerted through the 'name' that is his self-giving, revelation, presence (76.1–3). Yet at the same time this is the God of all, uttering judgement from heaven to save all the poor of the earth (76.7–9).

As individuals experienced the Holy One as seemingly hostile, angry, distant or indifferent, so also the community had its fill of such bitter times. The communal laments are not nearly as numerous as those of the individual, but they cry to God from the extremes of suffering, from the ravages of famine or invasion, from ruins of the holy temple, from the havoc of human cruelty and corruption (e.g. 44, 74, 79, 80, 83). How hard it was to sustain the celebration of God's universal reign in justice and peace! But somehow the fellowship of pilgrims was able to hold on to the vision, to enter that timeless moment when all peoples and animals and cosmic identities dance and sing before the glorious Lord, led by the dancers and psalmists of the temple (150).

7

The Psalms Down the Ages

7a The headings

Superscriptions are found above 116 psalms. In spite of much obscurity, they can be seen as providing the earliest observations on particular psalms. Surveys of these headings in our commentaries usually find here five kinds of information (see e.g. Kirkpatrick, pp. xviii–xxxv; Anderson, pp. 43–51). Thus (1) there are headings (or parts of headings) that link a psalm with a named individual or group (e.g. David, Moses, the sons of Korah, cf. 2a, 2b above); (2) others indicate the type of composition (e.g. 'psalm', 'song', 'prayer; (3) some give the purpose or place in worship (e.g. 'for thanksgiving / for the thank-offering', 'for the memorial-offering', 'for the Sabbath'); (4) others again seem to give musical directions (e.g. 'with stringed instruments', 'for flutes'); (5) thirteen headings specify the situation in David's life (see above, Int.2b).

Such comments on the psalms must go back to at least the third century BCE, for they already lay before the Greek translators. Some may have been added in connection with the earlier processes of forming and gathering the smaller collections and then the assembling of the complete Psalter. But others may go back to the origin of the individual psalms, for information about the manner of rendering and the place in worship and tradition will have been useful from the outset. It is noteworthy that biblical psalms outside the Psalter sometimes have headings (e.g. Hab. 3.1, musical; Isa. 38.9, historical), while a sacred song found at Ugarit, centuries older than David, is furnished also with musical directions and other information.

Such headings, then, can reveal a little of how the psalms were used and regarded from their origin and down to centuries still before Christ. Puzzling as many of their terms are (especially the technical expressions relating to music and ritual), the headings combine to point to a psalm tradition that was at home in the temple's music and worship, and especially linked to the house of David and the guilds of sacred musicians. As noted above (see Int.2b), the thirteen cases of historical notes about David may be chiefly deductions from the psalms in question by very early researchers, but they may still preserve a recollection that some psalms arose in royal crises and military campaigns.

7b Division and order

Another kind of very early comment on the psalms, this time implicit, can be found in the way they have been arranged. Interpretations and understandings of individual psalms will have been involved wherever the grouping and ordering were carried out deliberately. And there are signs that such a work of conscious arrangement made a significant contribution, complementing other processes of tradition, and perhaps even having the last word.

In considering the arrangement of the psalms, one first notices the demarcation into five 'books'. This is indicated by formulae of blessing placed at the close of each book (41.13; 72.18–19; 89.52; 106.48; and perhaps Ps. 150 as a whole). With this fivefold division, we seem to have an interpretation of the Psalms as divine law or tora – teaching or guidance parallel to the tora of the five books of the Pentateuch, Genesis to Deuteronomy. A similar interpretation may have been held by those who placed Psalm 1, with its commendation of the Lord's tora, at the head of the entire collection.

Underlying the fivefold division, one notices from the nature of the psalms themselves three broad strata. In the first (1–41, Book One) almost all the psalms are headed 'of David' and there is no indication of the taking up of any smaller collections. In the second stratum (42–89, Books Two and Three), the headings show that several smaller collections have been used, especially psalms 'of the sons of Korah' (42–49; 84; 85; 87), psalms 'of Asaph' (50; 73–83), alongside psalms 'of David' (51–65; 68–70). There is even a note that 'the prayers of David the son of Jesse are ended' (72.20), apparently from a stage earlier than the present arrangement, which has still 15 psalms 'of David' to follow. Even more remarkable in this stratum is the fact that in 42–83 the normal usage of the names for God is reversed, so that here 'Elohim' (200 times) preponderates over 'Yahweh' (43 times). In the third stratum (90–150, Books Four and Five) most psalms are without names in their headings, and the obscure technical terms are also absent; and while *sela* ('pause', 71 times in the Psalter) occurs here only within 140 and 143, *halelu-ya* has all its 25 occurrences within this block. Broad differences in the character of the three strata are also noticeable. The first block has a great many psalms of apparently personal or individual character, often laments. The second has many psalms of clearly national character. The third has many psalms of rather general public praise.

Altogether, we have the impression of three great stages in the coming together of our Psalter, and behind these also much evidence of older collections that were gathered up. The process will in part have resulted from the flow of history, as one stratum was laid after another. But deliberate shaping and ordering also played a part. It is likely, for example, that Psalm 2 (without a heading) was placed at the front of psalms headed 'of David' (3–41) to make a decisive statement about the vocation of the king, perhaps with messianic intention. And as we have noted, Psalm 1 seems later to have been prefixed to the entire collection to bring out the aspect of tora. Deliberate also may be the concluding of the Psalter with a bright sequence of praise (145–150), giving the last word to positive hope, in agreement with the Hebrew title which the work came to have – 'the Book of Praises'.

One may find some deliberate ordering also in a number of cases where two successive psalms have resemblances of wording. Psalm 1 again provides a ready example, as it has at least four such links with 2 ('Happy' 1.1 and 2.12; 'law' 1.2 and 'statute' 2.7; 'mutter' 1.2 and 2.1; 'perish' and 'way' 1.6 and 2.12). Or again, the opening of 33 matches the end of 32, while 34 and 35 are the only psalms to mention 'the angel of the Lord'. The positioning of some strongly royal psalms, in addition to the case of 2, has been thought to be deliberate; falling at the 'seams' of the arrangement (especially 72 and 89), they encourage a messianic reading of the Psalter. While it is often difficult to be sure what is deliberate and what is more fortuitous, it seems fair to conclude that the arrangement of the Psalter does offer us glimpses of interpretation and application on the part of the arrangers.

7c Ancient translations

As all translators do, those who made the ancient versions of the Psalms interpreted their text and often let their own standpoint appear. The oldest and the most important of the versions known to us is the Greek, known as 'the Septuagint' (LXX). a name reflecting the legend of 'seventy' or seventy-two elders sent from Jerusalem to Alexandria to translate the whole Hebrew scripture. It was indeed probably done for the Greek-speaking community in Alexandria, with the Psalms completed by about 200 BCE. Many important versions, including the 'old Latin', were made in turn from LXX, so its influence was enormous. In general it is a good rendering and fairly close to our Hebrew text. The Hebrew headings are represented, but also extended to cover most of the psalms without headings in the Hebrew. There is a tendency to tone down the Hebrew's characteristically bold portrayals of God, moving, one might say, from the naive to the more sophisticated. Thus, for example, the 'gods' become 'angels' (8.5; 97.7) and God the 'rock' becomes the 'helper' (19.14). Following a Jewish oral custom, the Greek replaces the main name of God, 'Yahweh', with '(the) Lord', an important interpretation indeed. An inclination to take the psalms prophetically may be found in the Greek rendering of the common heading *lamenaṣṣeaḥ* (RV, 'For the Chief Musician', better, 'For favour') as 'For the end'.

Another valuable version is the Targum, a version which arose from the need to give oral translations and explanations (*targum*) to people more at home in Aramaic than Hebrew, a common situation in post-exilic Palestine (cf. Neh. 8.8). This version may date in the main from the turn of the era. It is notable for occasional freedoms and additional interpretations, a number of which relate the passages to 'King Messiah' (e.g. 21.1, 7; 45.2; 61.6, 8; 72.1; 80.15). The Syriac version (or 'Peshitta', 'the common version') dates from around 200 CE, having been made for the church in the region of Edessa. The language was a form of Aramaic, and its scriptures, liturgy and theological writings were of great importance as the churches of the East spread widely. The version shows influence from LXX and has similar theological tendencies.

The great scholar Jerome made outstanding contributions to the translation of the Psalms into Latin. First, about 383 CE, he revised the Old Latin Version that had been made from LXX; this revision is known as the Roman Psalter. About four years later he made a fresh revision, known as the Gallican Psalter and destined to have enduring use and influence. But soon afterwards he began the mighty work of translating the Old Testament, including the Psalms, from the Hebrew. When this version, the Vulgate ('common version'), became the approved Bible of the Latin church, however, the Gallican Psalter was now too familiar to be replaced and so became the Psalter of the Vulgate (and is referred to as such). The displaced translation of the Psalms from the Hebrew (referred to as 'Jerome') was fortunately preserved, but not in common use. It reflects for us a Hebrew text much earlier than our main surviving manuscripts, before the writing of vowel points and the other labours of the schools of Jewish mediaeval scholars (the Massoretes). Jerome inherited and has reflected for us the high scholarship of the Hellenistic world, and also the views of his Jewish teachers on questions of meaning.

These developments were significant for the translations into English in the sixteenth century. Coverdale states that his rendering was 'out of five sundry interpreters', and it no doubt owed much to continental scholars and Latin versions, especially the Vulgate. When the Book of Common Prayer became the enduring Anglican norm in 1662, Coverdale's Psalter was retained in it, against the claims of the King James or Authorized Version of 1611, which more accurately represented the (Massoretic) Hebrew. Thus it came about that for several centuries the great food of English spirituality was to be a version of the Psalms that had a lineage running from LXX through the Vulgate's Gallican Psalter, albeit affected by other influences. And still today, those who translate the Psalms into English for church use are inclined to hold on to as much of the Coverdale inheritance as possible.

Time and time again a Hebraist might demur a little at Coverdale's choice of words, or at least see a worthwhile alternative, and in these cases it will generally be found that Coverdale reflects words of the Vulgate Gallican Psalter, which in turn reflects words of LXX. For example, *tora* might well have been seen as 'revelation', 'teaching' or 'guidance', but we are solidly given 'law' (Latin *lex*, Greek *nomos*); *hesed* is the love or friendship that keeps faith, 'faithful love', but we are often given 'mercy' (*misericordia, eleos*); *hasid* denotes a (faithful) covenant-partner, but we are given 'godly' or 'holy one' (*sanctus, hosios*); *elohim* in certain contexts means 'gods', but we are given 'angels'. God is described in the Hebrew as 'shield' or 'rock', but we are given 'defender' and 'strength'. Those who 'shelter' in God are now those who 'put their trust' in him. New life, in the Hebrew, comes when God 'turns the turning' of the afflicted, working a mighty revolution or transformation; but for this Hebrew idiom we are given 'turns the captivity of . . .' (14.7/11; 85.1; 126.4/5). The Hebraist also notices in Coverdale words or sentences not represented in our Hebrew text, and these again can usually be traced through the Vulgate to LXX, for example 13.6: 'Yea, I will praise the name of the Lord most Highest' – none of which is in our Hebrew.

All this is but to illustrate what one finds fairly constantly throughout Coverdale's much-loved version. One deep in the Hebrew psalms might well feel that this English inheritance is too inadequate linguistically and textually to be still commended as a translation. But it is as well to remember that, apart from its beauty and spiritual power, it is a tradition of translation flowing from the earliest great work of transforming the Hebrew poetry into a European language, and linking us also with the way the Psalms were understood by the Christian church almost from the first and for many centuries. It will always deserve to be treasured.

7d The Dead Sea Scrolls

The Psalms are remarkably well represented among the writings that have so dramatically come to light in our time from the caves near Wadi Qumran, by the north-western shore of the Dead Sea. Some 39 manuscripts (but mostly only fragments) contain psalms and could date between the second century before and the first century in our era. They make a valuable, but hardly radical addition to our data for the text of the Psalms. The best preserved scroll (11QPsa), unrolled in 1961, is thought to be from the first century CE. Here 41 psalms are represented, all from the last third of our Psalter. Strikingly, they are in an order different from ours, and are occasionally interspersed with other texts, mostly of scriptural or apocalyptic character. From all the manuscripts, one might conclude that there were a number of copies of this arrangement in use, and that other such arrangements were also made; one might also conclude that the arrangement we are familiar with was also known in Qumran. Such conclusions, however, remain uncertain.

It is at all events clear that the Psalms were much used. Thinking very much of David as the author, the people of Qumran saw him as composing these and many other songs through the spirit of prophecy. Indeed, they appear to think of the Psalms, along with other prophetic scripture, as bearing upon these latter days in which they were now living. The placing of apocalyptic texts alongside psalms in several of the manuscripts is a sign of this, and in other kinds of Qumran writings we find several psalms (2, 37, 45, 128) interpreted as for the latter days.

In the collection of psalm-like pieces known as the Hodayot ('Thanksgivings') we find again the community's sense of identification with the troubles and deliverances depicted in the Psalms. The language of these pieces is full of words and figures from the Psalms, and several clear echoes happen to be from psalms seen in the New Testament as prophetic of Christ's sufferings. The singer tells of his bones pulled out of joint (Hodayot 7.4; Ps. 22.14; vv. 1, 7, 8, 18, 22 of this psalm are taken up in the New Testament); he complains of those who have eaten his bread and yet have lifted up their heel against him

(Hodayot 5.23–4; Ps. 41.9; John 12.18), and also of those who have given his thirsting people vinegar to drink (Hodayot 4.11; Ps. 69.21; Mark 15.36 etc.).

The Qumran writings reveal a kind of Judaism that sprang up in the Hellenistic period. The sect in question, which many scholars identify with the Essenes described by Josephus, Philo and the elder Pliny, seems to have centred in a priestly group that had broken away from the temple in Jerusalem, considering the High Priest and the ceremonies in breach of the Law of Moses. Led by their 'Teacher of Righteousness', they cultivated a strict monastic life in the remote quiet of a little plateau above the shore and beneath the cliffs. Buildings and installations were carefully designed, and here they could channel and store enough water from the ravine in winter to maintain life and provide for their frequent ablutions all the year round. Here they worshipped and studied according to their rule, until the war with Rome brought destruction even to this remote region. But they were able to hide away their precious writings in sealed jars in the caves, where the extraordinary Dead Sea climate preserved them to our own day.

And so it is that we have knowledge, still growing, of a community with zeal not only for the Law and the Prophets, but also for the Psalms. Their great use of the Psalms flowed from an interpretation of them as expressing their own struggles in what seemed to be the latter days. They felt themselves to be the pure and humble folk that the Psalms see oppressed by the wicked. And like many since, they found comfort in the ancient poetry of prayer and praise, as it gave them voice amidst the mighty conflict.

7e Midrash and synagogue

The general lines of Jewish interpretation that we have found, with varying emphases, in our preceding sections can be traced in the compilations formed by the Midrash on Psalms, the Mishnah and the Talmud. While these gather the traditions of several centuries and sometimes continue well into Christian times, their roots reach back to a period similar to that of the Dead Sea Scrolls. In the circles in question, the order of psalms seems always to have been that known to us, though there was sometimes variation in the dividing of one psalm from another, and hence in the resultant total of the psalms.

We find again the tendency to think of the whole Psalter as from David, in spite of occasional allowance for other contributors. He wrote prophetically, with the Shekinah, the divine Presence, resting on him (b. Pesachim 117a). And though the psalms might have reference to himself, they also concern all Israel and all times (Midrash T. on Ps. 18.1; cf. b. Pesachim 114a). The reference of the Psalms to the final days and the consummation is sometimes expressly asserted, as when the heading of 92, 'A song for the Sabbath', is explained as 'A song for the time that is to come, for the day that will be all Sabbath and rest in the life everlasting' (m. Tamid 7.4).

The Midrash (see the translation by Braude) has a wealth of interest. It sometimes has comments on every verse of a psalm, sometimes on a selection, and sometimes only on the first and last. The bulk of the material consists of miniature homilies, with views attributed to great rabbis of the past and many correlations with other passages of scripture. While plain meanings (*peshat*) are sometimes given, the preference is usually for the 'seeking' (*midrash*) of inner revelatory meanings. There was hardly a limit to the number of possible meanings; whatever someone was capable of receiving was revealed to him. Hidden meanings were often found in the admittedly mysterious psalm-titles, and, almost playfully, in acrostics, anagrams, numerical value of letters etc. David is seen as model of law-piety, and so the theme of the Tora is often discovered. Thus when 9.3 has 'I will rejoice in you', the Midrash finds as inner sense 'I will rejoice in the Tora', since the two Hebrew letters that spell 'in you' signify as numbers '22', suggesting the 22 letters of the Hebrew alphabet, and so the written Tora. The profundity of this apparently playful interpretation lies in the linking of absorption in the scripture with blissful experience of the self-revealing Lord. Again, the 'channels of water' in 1.3 are taken as images of the sacred learning that flowed from rabbis and their companies. One rabbi is said to have 'transplanted' (the word in 1.3) himself from one learned circle to another in order to fulfil the words of 119.99, taken to mean 'I have more understanding because of an abundance of teachers.' Along with such relating to law-piety, there is still messianic interpretation, especially in the strongly royal texts such as 2. Reference to Elijah is also found in conjunction with the Messiah (3.5/6).

While the earlier Jewish reverence for the Psalms was thus strongly maintained, their use in worship was somewhat restricted. The temple had been the place for music offered to God, with numerous instruments and psalms. The synagogues were places rather for reading and study of the Tora and for its practical administration in the local society. With the final destruction of the temple in 70 CE and the disappearance of the organizations of skilled musicians, the Psalms were now chiefly scripture to be studied and read or at most cantillated. The only musical instrument permitted at the synagogues was the ram's horn, and that only as an ordained method of giving sacred signals. We may suppose that some singing of psalms persisted in devotional meetings, rather as Philo describes among the community of the Therapeutae in the first century (*De Vita Contemplativa*, X.1) or as in the pilgrim-fellowship of the disciples of Jesus (Mark 14.26), but definite information on this is hard to find.

7f The New Testament

An essential feature of the early Christian faith was the belief that in the scriptures, in effect the Old Testament, the life, death and exaltation of Christ had been foretold, as was now revealed. Now of all this foreshadowing scripture, the most prominent was the Book of Psalms. Of all Old Testament books it is the most commonly cited in the New Testament. Over 90 passages are quoted, mostly from LXX, and some several times over (so the list in

Kirkpatrick, pp. 838–40, which includes some passages not introduced as quotations, but does not include the very numerous 'echoes').

Such prominence of the Psalms as prophetic scripture reminds us of the situation we have noted for the Dead Sea writings (see above, 7d). Indeed, the view of the Psalms as prophecy coming to fulfilment seems to have been widespread, for some New Testament citations of psalms are made in argument with other groups, which are here presumed to share common ground (Mark 12.36; Acts 2.25–35; 4.11; 13.33–6; the Epistle to the Hebrews cites ten psalms directly). But around the person and work of Jesus the Psalms as prophecies could come to clearer focus. David, again regarded as virtually the author of the Psalms, is described as a prophet through whom God by the Holy Spirit had given words concerning Jesus the Messiah (Acts 2.30–1; 4.25; cf. Matt. 22.43).

As the Gospels unfold their story of Jesus, references to the Psalms reveal the depth of meaning in the events by linking them to the ancient and ultimate purpose God. So the royal and messianic meaning of the baptism is signalled in the words that clearly echo 2.7: 'You are my son, the beloved' (Mark 1.11). The messianic struggle is evident in the tempter's words about the angels that God commissions to bear up his son (Matt. 4.6, citing Ps. 91.11–12). The Hosannas and blessing of 118.25–6 show the predestined solemnity of the entry into Jerusalem (Mark 11.9). At the cleansing of the temple, the divine purpose is signalled by reference to the consuming zeal of God's house from 69.9 (John 2.17). In the ministry of teaching, the question Jesus poses concerning 110.1 indicates the high mystery of the person of the Messiah, David's 'lord' (Mark 12.35–7); and likewise the destiny of rejection on the way to supremacy is conveyed in all its dread wonder by quotation of 118.22–3 (Mark 12.10–11). Divine purpose and ultimate significance are shown by use of psalms as prophecies throughout the narratives of the passion: the traitor at the table (John 13.18; Ps. 41.9); the mocking of the crucified Jesus (Matt. 27.43; Ps. 22.8); the sharing of his garments (Matt. 27.35; Ps. 22.18); vinegar for his thirst (John 19.28–30; Ps. 69.21); his cry of dereliction (Mark 15.34; Ps. 22.1); his committal of his spirit into God's hands (Luke 23.46; Ps. 31.5). And in the wonderful sequel, echoes of the Psalms continue to show the foreordained and mighty work of the Lord: fear and joy together at the tomb (Matt. 28.8; echoing Ps. 2.11); enthronement at God's right hand (Mark 16.19; Ps. 110.1).

Already in the first decades of the church the Psalms were sung, and new compositions overflowed from their inspiring words and patterns. We hear of such singing in the prison (Acts 16.25), and at meetings in Corinth where each person had a psalm or some other inspired contribution (1 Cor. 14.26). 'Be filled with the Spirit,' teaches the apostle; 'speak to one another in psalms, hymns and songs; sing and make music in your hearts to the Lord, and in the name of our Lord Jesus Christ give thanks every day for everything to our God and Father' (Eph. 5.19–20; cf. Col. 3.16 and James 5.13). The abundant flow of such psalm-like song is heard in the Magnificat, the Benedictus and the Nunc Dimittis (Luke 1.46f., 68f.; 2.29f.) and in the hymns of the

Apocalypse (Rev. 11.15–18; 15.3–4; 19.6). All in all, it is readily seen that the New Testament laid a massive foundation for the extraordinary love and use of the Psalms in the following centuries of the church's life. The poetry of the Psalms had been taken up into the greatest poem of all, and their music resounded constantly in the hearts of the early Christians.

7g Early Christian worship and exposition

Teachers of the second century (the 'Apostolic Fathers') turned readily to the Psalms to illustrate their admonitions to good conduct. The best example is the First Epistle of Clement, Bishop of Rome around 96 CE. In a dozen of his citations from the Psalms he takes the subject to be Christ. In 3.5, for example, 'I lay down and slept, I awoke for the Lord sustained me' refers to Christ's death and resurrection. An indication of use in worship from early times may be found in the tradition of the church in Antioch that the practice of singing the Psalms antiphonally was originated by their first bishop, Ignatius, around 100 CE, following a vision of singing angels (Socrates, *Church History*, vi.8). Tertullian's vivid depiction of the Christian fellowship around 197 (*Apologeticum*, 39) includes the singing of 'scriptural hymns', no doubt chiefly psalms, at the communion meals.

Great use of the Psalms in worship is also reflected in the burgeoning of homilies and expositions on them from the third century onwards. An early example is the great Origen who, in addition to treatment of the Psalms in his vast and unique textual work, the multi-columned *Hexapla*, gave many expositions on the Psalms in the form of glosses, homilies and commentaries, much of which has not survived. Following the tradition of Alexandria, he sought to penetrate beyond the plain outer sense to the spiritual or mystical meaning. We can see this in his treatment of 119, which features prominently in one of the later 'chains' compiled from a number of writers (see the volume edited by M. Harl). He found the image of the 'way' especially fruitful – the psalm sets out the way to God, the way prefigured by David and the other Old Testament saints, in the end the true way that is Christ. The alphabetic progression of the psalm represents steps on the way. The alphabet indicates the elementary beginning, while the eightfold patterns of the stanzas point to perfection in Christ. Beginning and end, action and contemplation, complement each other. Various expressions of God's manifestation are seen as virtually names of Christ – word, way, mouth, salvation, mercy, justice, face, hand, name. David's praying voice prefigures that of Christians who yearn for union with Christ, the fulfilment of God's tora. The theme of suffering in the psalm is connected with the ascetic and his struggle with Satan. So David prefigures the monks who recite the psalms in their battle with evil and receive from God the liberating room of salvation.

A different approach is found in the tradition of Antioch in Syria, where the preference was for the plain, non-allegorical meaning and the historical context. The strictest upholder of this approach was Theodore of Mopsuestia

(350–428). He begins with care to establish the correct text, then looks for the historical situation which the psalm requires – either in the life of David or in the history of Israel down to Maccabean times (which David is able to anticipate through the Holy Spirit). He relates only 2, 8, 45 and 110 to the Messiah (see Devreesse's book). His friend John Chrysostom (347–407) was a gifted preacher and has left 58 homilies on the Psalms, perhaps reworked with learned detail, and only a remnant of his output. He did not keep so strictly to the 'plain sense' tradition of Antioch and gave more room to messianic interpretation. It is Chrysostom who testifies so eloquently to the huge place occupied by the Psalms in Christian devotion. In all kinds of worship, he maintains, 'David is first, midst, and last', whether it be in church, at home, in the forum, in monasteries, or in the desert (NL, I, pp. 1–2 has the full passage). A similar testimony is given by Jerome, writing from Bethlehem (*Epistle* 46): the Psalms resound from work in the fields – ploughing, harvesting, vine-dressing, care of the sheep.

The attraction of the Alexandrian 'spiritual' interpretation grew ever stronger. The homilies of Basil of Caesarea on the Psalms show the influence of Origen. Basil takes 45 to be prophetically addressed to Christ, and the 'myrrh' alludes to his burial; the 'queen' is both the church and also the soul that will be espoused to Christ the Word. The church is summoned to contemplation in the words 'Hear, O daughter, and see'. Jerome tells us explicitly that he drew from Origen the substance of his *Commentarioli* (brief scholarly notes). The many homilies on the Psalms that have been attributed to Jerome now seem to be his translations from records of Origen's daily preaching in the church of Caesarea, interspersed with Jerome's comments (Rondeau, pp. 155–61).

Augustine of Hippo (354–430), a famed expositor of the Psalms, also constantly looked beneath the surface for relation to Christ. From his conversion onwards, the Psalms were a great resource for his devotion. Looking back to his preparation for baptism, he writes in his *Confessions* (60.4): 'How I addressed you (God) in these Psalms! How my love for you was kindled by them! How I burned to recite them, were it possible, throughout the world as an antidote to the pride of humanity!' In his *Expositions on the Psalms*, we see at once in Psalm 1 his Christ-centred reading: '*Blessed is the man* – this is to be understood of our Lord Jesus Christ, the Lord Man.' And that Christ delights and meditates 'in his law' indicates that he is not subject to it, but discerns it and does not depend on its letter. He bears fruit 'in his season' – when glorified by his resurrection and ascension into heaven. David is little considered in this exposition; Christ, the greater David, the Alpha and Omega, is found everywhere. Not that the interpretation is arbitrary; there is a regularity and system in its use of the symbolic, along with much spiritual penetration. Augustine's profound expositions ensured that this approach would characterize Western commentaries and the imbibing of psalmody in worship throughout the Middle Ages.

His work was the chief influence on a complete and well-organized commentary from the mid-sixth century, that of Cassiodorus (*c.* 485–580), who modestly states that he turned into shallow streams the ocean of Augustine's exposition (see the translation by Walsh of Cassiodorus, *Explanation of the Psalms*). Formerly a high Roman administrator, Cassiodorus was accomplished in the classical literary arts, and is careful to explain the rhetorical features of the Psalms. He develops the symbolic and spiritual approach even beyond Augustine, and while giving some introductory attention to the original historical context, concerns himself in the main with the prophetic reference to Christ and the church; as often prompted by the psalm-heading rendered 'To the end', he would have the mind set upon the Saviour, who is the End without end, the perfection of all blessings (see also 7h below). Himself the founder of a double monastery, Cassiodorus reveals the huge role of psalm-singing in the dedicated Christian life when he speaks in his preface of the psalms that make vigils pleasant in the silence of the night, beguile the first hour of the day, consecrate the third hour, make joyful the sixth hour with the breaking of bread, end fasting at the ninth, and bring the last hours of day to a close, taking darkness away from the mind.

7h The Middle Ages

Such use and understanding of the Psalms in the Christian life of the fifth and sixth centuries, East and West, set the pattern for the Middle Ages. So we find a continuance of the extraordinary prominence of the Psalms in individual prayer and corporate worship, and of the interpretation as centred in Christ. Recitation or chanting of the Psalter completed in a week was common, and some individuals undertook a daily completion. In the Gregorian scheme there were fixed psalms used daily at the offices of Lauds, Prime, Terce, Sext, Nones and Compline, while the remainder of the Psalter was covered weekly at Mattins and Vespers. It was often thought fit for ministers of the church to know the Psalms by heart; indeed the Council of Toledo (653, Canon 8) specified that no one henceforth should be promoted to any ecclesiastical dignity who did not perfectly know the whole Psalter.

A good impression of comment on the Psalms in the Middle Ages can be gained from the commentary of Neale and Littledale; a valuable survey of 28 works (mostly mediaeval) is given in Vol. I (pp. 76–87). There was evidently much carrying forward of older material. In the possession of most Western monasteries and other centres of learning would be the serviceable Latin commentary of Cassiodorus mentioned above, and it greatly served to shape the mediaeval interpretation. We can readily see here how the reciting of psalms was felt as a passing over holy ground, a continual touching on profound mysteries which were ready to show themselves to the attentive and devout imagination. In Psalm 23 (Latin 22) for example, Cassiodorus finds the faithful Christian who has been led from the desert of sin to the place of pasture, with the quickening waters of baptism and the table and cup of communion. Ten such gracious gifts are counted in this psalm, corresponding to the ten commandments. And the Latin number of the psalm, 22, corresponds to the 22 books of the Old Testament by the Jewish reckoning, and so denotes a wholeness of divine revelation. We should store up in our minds, says Cassiodorus, the song of this heavenly pipe, filled with its ten holy gifts – how sweet and wholesome to the soul is its melody!

For another example we can take the apparently plain statement of 33.6, 'By the word of the Lord the heavens were established, and all the power of them by the spirit / breath of his mouth'. Cassiodorus finds reference here to Christ the Word, by whom were established the apostles and saints, to fill the earth with their message of salvation and the power of their miracles. The mention of 'Word', 'Lord' and 'Spirit' in this verse alludes to the Son, the Father and the Holy Spirit, and the singular 'his (mouth)' corresponds to the unity of the Persons. Thus many a psalm, rich in itself, was read in a context which added new dimensions of meaning.

Nevertheless, stories of David, such as are sometimes alluded to in the psalm-headings, still held their fascination. Illuminators of psalters liked to depict such historical scenes in the ornate initial letters, showing that the experiences of David, and of Solomon also, were not forgotten in the use of the Psalms. Thus the Tickhill Psalter, written at Worksop about 1310, begins 27 ('The Lord – Dominus – is my light and my salvation') with the initial D of 'Dominus' containing four scenes of Saul's persecution of David, and two more are added below the verse. The Windmill Psalter (English, about 1270) begins with an elaborate design in which the second letter, the E of 'Beatus' ('Blessed is the man . . .') bears the scene of Solomon judging the case of the disputed child. With this historical allusion, the artist anticipates the modern classification of Psalm 1 as a Wisdom poem! In the Munich Psalter, perhaps from Oxford, about 1200, the initial B of the psalm is set in a frame which bears four scenes from the life of David, as well as portrayals of David with harp and (probably) Solomon. The leaves, blossoms and petals which generally adorn the initial letter of such psalters suit the theme of the flourishing tree in Psalm 1.

In another type of illustration, psalters might have at the front a whole cycle of miniatures showing the salvation won by Christ. An example of such aids to individual devotion is the Winchester Psalter, which begins with more than 80 scenes proceeding from the Fall to the Last Judgement. The life of David forms only a small part of the sequence, which above all features scenes from the Gospels and Christ in glory (see Haney). In the East we have the Simon Psalter, produced in Novgorod towards 1300. The text of the Psalms is here illustrated by 119 miniatures, and the first three are full-page illuminations. In one, David composes psalms and is accompanied by Solomon and musicians; in another, he writes down psalms. But the first page shows the risen Christ appearing in the garden to Martha and Mary. Christian interpretation is clear also in the Kiev Psalter, dated 1397; in the margin of 22, for example, three scenes from Christ's passion are each linked to appropriate verses by a thin red line: Christ surrounded by soldiers with heads like dogs' heads, soldiers nailing Christ to the cross, and soldiers sharing out the garments. (The Western illuminated initials can be seen in J. J. G. Alexander, and the Eastern miniatures in O. Popova.)

The methods of singing the Psalms will have varied according to the skill of the singers. The simplest method was to leave the main burden to one capable singer, to whom the group could give assent with periodic alleluias, amens, or even a whole verse as refrain. At a more skilled level the group might undertake the second part of each verse, responding to the soloist's first half. A well-trained choir, as in monasteries, would divide into two groups and sing the two parts of the verses antiphonally. The melodies seem sometimes to have descended from very early times. Their most esteemed form is usually known as 'Gregorian chant', which flourished as a remarkably uniform tradition in the West from about the eighth to the fifteenth centuries. For several centuries after this period it underwent various modifications, but more recently it has been restored to its former purity by the monks of Solesmes, so that it can be described by Mary Berry as 'spiritually, aesthetically, and practically the ideal kind of church music' (in J. G. Davies, p. 254).

The addition to each psalm of a concluding verse ascribing glory to the Father, Son, and Holy Spirit set the seal on the Christian interpretation. To apply the psalm more specifically to a particular day or season of the church's year, there was the use of antiphons. Here a line from the psalm, or some Christian phrase or sentence, was sung between each verse of the psalm, or as introduction and conclusion – an effective and beautiful way of bringing out the aspect suited to that moment of worship. Such establishing of a theme or aspect had ancient precedent. At Jewish Qumran in the first century, Ps. 145 was sung with a response of blessing after each verse: 'Blessed be the Lord, and blessed be his name for ever and ever.'

J. M. Neale (NL, I, pp. 34–69) gives an introduction to the vast subject of antiphons. The essence is explained thus:

> The same psalm was said at Christmas, and at Easter, said in Lent, said at Whitsuntide, said on the Festivals of Martyrs, said in the Office for the Dead; it could not, at all these seasons, be recited with the same feelings, in the same frame of mind. Its different emphases required to be brought out; the same sun-ray from the Holy Ghost rested, indeed, at all times on the same words, but the prism of the Church separated that colourless light into its component rays: into the violet of penitence, the crimson of martyrdom, the gold of the highest seasons of Christian gladness. Hence arose the wonderful system of antiphons, which, out of twenty different significations, definitely for the time being fixed one, which struck the right key-note, and enabled the worshipper to sing with the spirit and the understanding also.

Partly in reaction to the prevailing tendency of Christian interpretation, a succession of Jewish scholars commented on the Psalms with fresh concentration on the plainer meanings and matters of philology. Saadia (d. 942) translated the Hebrew Bible into Arabic and furnished it, including the

Psalms, with commentary. The scholarly tradition continues with Rashi (d. 1105), Ibn Ezra (d. 1167), and Qimhi (d. 1235). Of great value, their comments may yet be so terse and apt to assume knowledge of scriptural parallels and rabbinic tradition, that they may not be sufficiently appreciated. A good edition, however, will supply the missing links (thus for Rashi's commentary see Gruber). When one finds Rashi explaining the 'lilies' and the 'king' of 45 as tora-scholars, the 'arrows' as their disciples, and the 'Elohim-throne' as their judicial seat, one may think him fanciful, but it is all grounded in traditional correlations of scriptural and linguistic data.

7i The Reformation

The Renaissance saw the revival of the study of ancient languages and literatures, and biblical study began to swing again towards the foundations of language and history. In 1513 Luther began his academic lecturing at Wittenburg with exposition of the Psalms. The manuscripts of his notes for the lectures have survived, marginal glosses and wider 'scholia' for nearly two-thirds of the Psalter. Not surprisingly, he still takes account of the traditional four levels of interpretation (literal, allegorical, tropological or moral, and anagogical or mystical), but he is most concerned with the 'principal' sense, the relation to Christ.

He often spoke on the Psalms on various later occasions, and his collected expositions were published from notes made by his followers. Here we see a greater independence of thought and a great gift for uniting the ancient context and the life of his day. The message of the ancient faith, focused through Christ, was shown to bear powerfully upon all the troubles and dangers of Luther's time. Thus Psalm 2 leads from fear to hope: that God's king, Christ, is set in Zion brings home that the divine Son became man, one who can be touched and seen; and 'Zion' again is the people of Christ, holy because Christ dwells in them. In Psalm 23, the grass, water, path, rod, staff, table and balm of oil are all virtually names for the Word of God, 'for whenever God's Word is preached properly and purely, it creates as many good things and results as the prophet here gives it names'. Of great importance and influence was Luther's translation of the Bible into German; here in his Psalms was a spiritual treasure of eloquent force and homely warmth.

A decisive step towards the modern era of exposition comes with the commentary of Calvin (1564); it is as well organized as that of Cassiodorus, but decidedly turned away from allegorical interpretations. With scripture as the sole authority for the Reformers, it was necessary to have a firm foundation for interpretation, and hence the concentration on the literal sense and the author's intention in his own situation. Calvin does occasionally use the 'typical' method, where David is a 'type' prefiguring Christ, while Israel prefigures the church. Psalm 20, for example, is explained of David's prayer in some battle, but still a call can be heard in the psalm for much prayer on behalf of Christ's kingdom.

The moral and doctrinal use of the Psalms by Luther and Calvin was continued in numerous other commentaries from the circles of the Reformation and no less the Counter-Reformation. Learning increased, but often so did pedantry, and the poetic quality of the Psalms was somewhat buried. However, with the widespread translation of the Psalms into the common languages, there was new impetus for their role in popular piety. Hymns based on psalms, metrical paraphrases, and harmonized Gregorian chant (especially its offshoot, Anglican chant, that began to flourish in English cathedrals and collegiate churches) carried a knowledge of the Psalms into widening circles.

7j Eighteenth-century foundations of criticism

This was a period of reaction against the intense doctrinal conflicts of recent centuries. Dogmatism of Protestant and Catholic alike was abhorred by many leading spirits, who looked to reason and science, freedom, and progress through open-minded education. The most significant developments in the understanding of the Psalms were accordingly of a scientific nature – contributions to textual criticism, philology, and literary analysis. For establishing the Hebrew text, new tools were made from the massive labour of comparing hundreds of manuscripts. and clearly setting out their variations (Kennicott, 1780, and de Rossi, 1788). The elucidation of Hebrew from related languages was significantly developed. Much progress was made in the analysis of Hebrew poetry and hence the Psalms, especially the clarification of its parallel or repetitive structures (Lowth, 1753).

The life-giving breath of imaginative and sympathetic interpretation, however, was little in evidence until the work of J. G. von Herder (*On the Spirit of Hebrew Poetry*, 1782–3, ET 1833), in which many psalms were treated. Here was enthusiasm for the poetic spirit itself, and a readiness to share the feelings of the ancient poets through the heart's simplicity and love. The effect of Herder's work can be felt in some great commentators of later times, especially Gunkel; de Wette spoke of Herder as a seer who had appeared to him on barren slopes of criticism and rationalism, and directed him to green and living pastures.

The eighteenth century saw a great surge in the composition and singing of Christian 'hymns'. Especially gifted were Isaac Watts (1674–1748) and the prolific Charles Wesley (1707–88, credited with over 5500 hymns). Although the Psalms were drawn upon, most of this hymnody was so directly expressive of salvation through Christ that its ever-growing popularity was bound to weaken the appeal of psalm-singing for many worshippers.

7k The nineteenth century

The pace of discovery increased greatly through this century. Knowledge of the ancient context of the Bible came flooding in from expeditions to Egypt and the sites of Assyria and Babylonia. Theories of evolution challenged the old ways of regarding the Bible. Literary criticism, likewise, opened up to debate all the traditions of biblical authorship and literary unity. The textual and linguistic researches of the previous century were greatly developed. In Germany a series of learned commentators expounded the Psalms in the new perspectives of knowledge and criticism. The chief effect was to put in question the role of David. A view of the gradual development of Hebrew religion and literature became standard, and was such that the Psalms were usually given a rather late date, centuries after David. At the extreme, they were thought to be compositions of the last two or three centuries before Christ. Events of these late centuries were confidently traced in the Psalms, as in the sharp, concise explanations of B. Duhm (1899, 1922). Of course there were conservative scholars who maintained the old views as best they could amidst the new knowledge, for example E. W. Hengstenberg (1842–4). One of the most enduring contributions in fact came from such a writer, Franz Delitzsch (1859–60, 1894), who moved only slowly towards the newer perspectives, but wrote with such learning, cogency and theological instinct that his work will always be worth consulting. The passing of time has shown his wisdom in wrestling long with the received Hebrew text, rather than readily revising it as some did.

One of the most significant in the line of German commentators came at the beginning, and for most of the century was little regarded: W. M. L. de Wette (1811) took much from the spirit of Herder. Distrusting reliance on the search for the original historical circumstances, he preferred an aesthetic approach. He looked for the inner value of each poem, and so took much heed of imagery and literary form, anticipating H. Gunkel by nearly a century. In his second edition (1823) he was able to gain from use of the important new Hebrew dictionary by the great W. Gesenius.

In England the Oxford Movement influenced many churches towards the singing of the Psalms, as part of a revival in the depth and beauty of liturgy. One of the leaders, J. M. Neale, undertook indeed to bring to notice again the rich mystical interpretations of the primitive and mediaeval church, and began an extraordinary commentary made up from the ancient preachers and liturgies, which R. F. Littledale completed (1860–74). From the Nonconformist tradition came the prolific expositions of C. H. Spurgeon (1869–83), a testimony to the place of the Psalms in the hearts of many generations of evangelicals. But the last word on this period may be given to a work of 1902: the little, yet not so little, commentary of A. F. Kirkpatrick. He distils with sober judgement and remarkable detail much that was achieved in the century.

7l The twentieth century and beyond

The rather late dating of the Psalms just mentioned continued to have advocates, especially in some Catholic institutions on the continent (so P. Bonnard, A. Deissler, A. Robert, R. Tournay). Here most of the psalms are seen as having come from the hands of scribes or Levites in the late Persian and Greek periods, older materials having being re-worked and read in a new sense ('relectures').

Of great influence was the work of Gunkel, especially his thorough investigation of the 'forms' (*Gattungen*, genres) of the Psalms which has been outlined above (see 4d). He was much concerned also to compare the Psalms with all related materials from the ancient world. And above all, he approached the Psalms in the sympathetic spirit of Herder, aiming to hear from them and express again for today what the Hebrew poets had truly felt in their hearts.

His work gave basis and impetus to much that was soon to be done in the field, above all the work of the Norwegian Sigmund Mowinckel. In a long life of writing, Mowinckel made outstanding contributions in several areas of Old Testament research. His most significant contribution, it may be thought, was to show the dramatic, sacramental character of the autumn pilgrimage festival, and its fundamental importance in Israelite religion, and hence for the Psalms and Prophets. His views underlie the account of contexts in worship given above (see 5b). It was another Norwegian, Harris Birkeland, who led the way in explaining a great many psalms as arising from crises in the lives of the kings or the later governors. But this view had to compete with further attempts to link these 'personal crisis' psalms with ordinary individuals – for example, being tried by 'ordeal' at the sanctuary (H. Schmidt, W. Beyerlin) or seeking sanctuary there (L. Delekat, cf. 5b above), or even using the ministry of some more local 'ritual specialist' away from the temple (E. S. Gerstenberger).

The importance which Mowinckel found in the institutions of worship was not regarded sympathetically by some writers, anxious to distance scripture from what they took to be too close an association with foreign and magical ritual. Something of this antipathy can be found in the theologically strong commentary of H.-J. Kraus (1960, 1978), and also in the widely esteemed work of C. Westermann, who preferred the older view of psalms as evoked by historical events, and also worked at adjustments to Gunkel's system of classification. On the other hand, Mowinckel's view was the background of the penetrating and imaginative expositions of A. R. Johnson, who showed that a sympathetic investigation of the great rituals mirrored in the Psalms could yield rich theological results.

In the latter half of the century there was keen consideration of the Psalter as a whole and of the intention of the final compilers (see 7b above; Auwers). This in part reflected a certain frustration at the bewildering disagreements of scholars on the historical trail, and a desire to have a better basis for reading the texts as scripture. The quest, however, is still rather elusive, and the desire to go further back to the hearts of the first creators of the separate psalms will still burn brightly, if Herder, de Wette, Gunkel, Mowinckel and Johnson did not live in vain. M. Goulder, in an abundance of studies, has united interest in the liturgical and the historical origins of psalms, boldly proposing precise settings for the sequences as they stand, and always presenting his case with brilliance.

Study of the language of the Psalms received an important new resource with the discovery of much mythological poetry in a kind of early Canaanite, the tablets from Ras Shamra on the North Syrian coast, ancient Ugarit. The commentary of M. Dahood was like an enthusiastic experiment in exploring this material. He has many cogent suggestions, and sets out his evidence thoroughly, but he often may be thought to undervalue the traditional understanding of the text, and he piles up novelties that stretch credulity. But when all is said, his work remains a fine achievement and an enduring resource.

The singing of psalms in modern worship has been revived through new forms of the old responsorial method. The arrangements and settings of Joseph Gelineau, with translation approximating to the Hebrew rhythm, music in old modal and folk idioms, and key-verses as congregational response, have been widely used and have served as models for other arrangers and composers. But hymn-singing has generally remained more popular, and has itself been revitalized by much new composition of Christian 'choruses' and songs, often with rhythm and harmonies like those of modern popular songs. Many of these 'choruses' use words from scripture, not least the Psalms, in an excellently direct way and are found very helpful.

Nevertheless, the Psalms themselves can hardly be superseded in worship without serious loss. The hymns take up but a small part of their words and often debase it with the slickness or artificiality of their metre and rhyme. If scripture itself has a unique role in feeding the faith of the church and forming the life of converse with the Lord, then so does that part of it which has been to the fore from earliest times, the Psalter. Here in plain words and strong images scripture teaches, prophesies, and lifts the veil of the good world to come; it puts into the worshippers' mouths robust words of praise and thanksgiving, along with passionate entreaty from the lowest pit of suffering. The hymns we write ourselves are pleasant and easy to the feelings. Much in the Psalms may be difficult for the modern imagination, seeming primitive or harsh. But if the challenge of using them is met, they will be found to have a power and a fullness that modern compositions can hardly attain.

The challenge involves suitable translation, styles of singing and reciting, and the imagination (nourished by instruction) to relate the ancient ideas to the Christian realities. Given all that, the church may again find truth in St Basil's words (Letter 207): 'Why give such preference to the Psalms? Because hymns are human compositions, but the Psalms are the songs of the Spirit.'

COMMENTARY

PSALM 1: The Secret of Happiness

1   Happy the one who does not walk
        in the counsel of the wicked,
    or stand in the way of sinners,
        or sit in the circle of the scoffers,
2   but whose delight is in the teaching of the Lord,
    meditating in his teaching day and night.
3   Such a one shall be like a tree
        well planted by channels of water,
    giving its fruit at its proper time, its leaves never withering –
        yes, all this person does shall be fruitful.
4   Not so the wicked,
    for they are like chaff which the wind drives away.
5   Therefore the wicked shall not stand in the judgement,
    nor sinners in the assembly of the just.
6   For the Lord knows the way of the just,
    but the way of the wicked shall come to nothing.

Unlike most psalms, this simple but effective poem is not prayer, praise or oracle, but teaching. The style is like that of the wise, the sages who would hold up an ideal and warn against evil ways. The images of the well-watered tree and the two ways that part to opposite directions are characteristic of this tradition of Wisdom teaching, exemplified by the Book of Proverbs and much earlier Egyptian books. But in its focus on the Lord's tora ('teaching / law'), the psalm seems to reflect a development in which the old stream of Wisdom teaching has run together with another current of piety – devotion to tora, the scriptural commandments, teachings and revelations of the Lord. This is a development which can be traced in Deuteronomy (4.5–8 etc.) around the seventh century and in Ecclesiasticus (24.1–29) around 200 BCE. How the Wisdom tradition alone might have represented the message can be seen in the similar passage in Jeremiah (17.7–8), where tora is not mentioned.

There are several verbal coincidences with Psalm 2 (Int. 7b), and the two psalms in some manuscripts were joined as one (cf. Acts 13.33, which according to some witnesses cites Ps. 2 as the first psalm). It is possible that the teaching of Psalm 1 was originally directed to kings, who were meant to uphold and to study the tora of the Lord (Deut. 17.18–20), and in this case a linking to royal Psalm 2 would be fitting. The two psalms, however, are very different in form, and Psalm 1 may be a relatively late composition, which was given its place at the head of the whole collection of psalms to emphasize a theme dear to the hearts of the final collectors, the theme of God's tora. With their arrangement of the Psalter in five sections, they made a parallel with the five divisions of 'the law of Moses', and with Psalm 1 serving almost as an introduction, they presented the whole Psalter as further tora, divine revelation, and taught that meditation in the Psalms would be a way of blissful and fruitful communion with the divine Teacher.

1–3 Still today, happiness is most people's aim. Strikingly then, the first word of the Psalter, and probably quite deliberately, is 'Happiness'. The Hebrew, *asherey*, is a plural form, exclamatory and intensive: 'O the sheer happiness of the person who . . .' With this expression a way of living is going to be warmly commended with all the authority of generations of experience.

But now come surprises. The first is that the recommendation begins in the negative, indeed a threefold negative. What is this bad road which is marked with three 'no entry' signs for one seeking happiness? It is a way of conduct that is described as walking in the counsel of the wicked, standing in the way of sinners, and sitting in the sitting, the intimate circle, of scorners or scoffers. A progression seems to be intended: first an occasional compliance, then a lingering, and finally a settled identification. By the 'wicked', 'sinners', and 'scoffers' is meant those hardened in defiance of God and of all that is good; arrogant and unscrupulous, they would be god to themselves, attempting to procure their own gain, and callous towards the poor. The psalm is not referring to a situation like that in the Gospels, where Jesus reaches out to those, often poor, who have been labelled as 'sinners' by a fastidious and sometimes hypocritical religious élite. The reference is rather to participation in cruel designs and practices, perhaps especially the corruption of power. The way to happiness begins with a decided turning from these.

The second surprise is that the positive recommendation for 'sheer happiness' amounts to only one thing, and that something few today would have thought of – meditation in the Lord's tora. This expression must be distinguished from an absolute, 'the Law', which never occurs in the Psalms. What is meant is the teaching of the Lord in person, imparting his word and his will, his guidance and his grace, and, at the deepest level, his very self. A written form, a scroll, is probably involved, and the content originally would be scripture such as was current at the time of the psalm's origin; eventually, as suggested above, reference might be intended to the Psalter itself. The 'meditating' (*haga*) suggests the murmur of recitation; the scroll is read, or passages are recited from memory, all in a kind of intoned way, and mingled with formulas of praise and prayer, sounding especially the names of the Lord. It is because this 'meditation' is a communion with the Lord that, ideally, it would be continued day and night. And for the same reason, it is not an irksome labour, but the highest delight.

And again for the same reason, it is indeed fruitful. With this thought the devout poet introduces his great central image, a comparison which gives his teaching beauty and power. We are shown a tree. It has been planted deep and firm beside running water – probably channels leading water around it from a fountain, a wise provision against the regular long, hot droughts. The word used here for the planting (*shatul*) denotes 'transplanting' and, according to rabbinic tradition, means a firm planting to withstand tempest. In this situation, its roots firm and well nourished, the tree grows healthy and wholesome leaves, and gives its fruit in due season. Blessed itself, it gives blessing again in shelter, healing and life. So too the one whose roots draw deep from the channels of the Lord's life-giving grace – one whose mind and heart are constantly exercised in scripture and the related means by which the Lord reveals himself, guides and gives communion. All that this person does, or 'produces' (*ya'aseh*), succeeds and prospers, or rather 'is fruitful'; the fruit of such a life is good, serving God's will, benefiting many. It is not always seen, but at the time of God's appointing does not fail.

4–5   The thought of the 'wicked' returns from v. 1. The contrasting image for them is the 'chaff', harvest waste, light as dust, blown who knows where. On the hills of Palestine, the evening breeze arises as the earth cools quicker than the sea (cf. Gen. 3.8). As the farmer tossed up his threshed mixture into the breeze, the heavy, good grain fell into a golden heap, while the chaff was whirled away towards the desert. So the wicked life has no weight of worth, no root against the tempest, no abiding in God's world. It cannot 'rise up' or 'stand' (*qum*) when tried in God's 'judgement'. The reference here may be to the judgement which is ever close at hand, ever manifesting itself in the trials of life. Or the thought may be of the final judgement, when God makes an end of this world (cf. Zeph.1; Mal. 4). Whatever the form of judgement envisaged by the poet, he seems to have thought of it as a test for entering into the assembly of the just, the community accepted by the Lord, in harmony with him (*saddiqim*).

6   The teaching of the psalm is summarized with a concluding image, the two ways. One way, that of the just, the Lord 'knows' – he watches over it with love and care; we might say he is beside the traveller in every need, guiding and protecting. The other way, that of the wicked, has no true direction, running out into a trackless waste, lost to all that is good.

The psalm's view of the way that brings happiness and prosperity may seem unrealistic. It is the wicked who often gain wealth, power and success, as other psalms lament. It is possible that with the 'judgement' and the 'assembly of the just' (v. 5) thought turned to the end of this age, and a new world where the injustices would be put right. But we may rather have the pro-found and hard-earned thought that, despite appearances, the good way of life in itself finds true happiness and is ever fruitful, while the bad way in itself swerves into misery and a meaningless waste. Judgement, on this latter view, is inherent in life's living, active here and now, and it is here and now that the just have the companionship of the Lord on their way, and indeed bear good fruit, often in a mystery. This 'way' means rejecting temptations to corruption and centring all one's thought and delight in 'the Lord's teaching'. A modern application might think of the individual refusing to be carried along by the pervasive influences to greed and baseness that come from every angle; devoted rather to practices of constant prayer and turning to the word of God;

nourished in the deepest being by the currents of communion that alone give life and joy.

'I Am That I Am, and my counsel is not with the wicked, but in the law of the Lord is my delight, alleluia.' Such was the ancient Christian antiphon, the theme-setting refrain interwoven with this psalm at Easter. In the great poem formed by the year of worship, the figure of the risen Lord was thus put first, as the one who had not made compromise with evil, but was wholly given to the Father's will, and whose cross bore healing leaves and saving fruit for all the world. Under this bright figure, so the church intended, the weak and wayward would gather and come to be made like him, to find all their pleasure in the Lord's word, and all along their way grow in knowledge of him.

Grant, Lord, that through study of your word and nourishment by your grace, we may know the happiness of walking the good way where you are ever at our side.

PSALM 2: A Message to Rulers

1   Why are the nations in tumult,
    and the peoples muttering folly,
2   the kings of the earth rising up,
        and the rulers conspiring together,
    against the Lord and his Anointed?
3   Let us break their bonds, they say,
    and throw off their cords from us.
4   He who thrones in heaven laughs,
    the Lord of all derides them.
5   Then he speaks to them in his wrath,
    dismaying them in his anger:
6   Enough that I have anointed my king,
    on Zion my holy mountain!
7   I will quote from the Lord's decree:
    he says to me, You are my son;
        this day have I begotten you.
8   Ask of me, and I will give you the nations as your inheritance,
    and the ends of the earth as your possession.
9   You shall break them with a rod of iron,
    and shatter them like a potter's vessel.

10 So now be wise, O kings,
    be prudent, you rulers of the earth.
11 Serve the Lord with fear,

and rejoice before him with trembling.
12   Pay homage sincerely, lest he be angry,
     and you perish from the way.
     For his anger can blaze in an instant,
     but happy are all who shelter in him.

With modern knowledge of the ancient Near East, this highly dramatic psalm has been recognized as originally from enthronement ceremonies of the Davidic kings in Jerusalem. The freshly installed king is the speaker in vv. 7f., and likely enough throughout the psalm. With the anointing and installation on the holy hill of Zion, God has declared him to be his 'Son', the one who is to carry out the wishes of the true king, God himself. It is thought of as a single kingdom or kingship – God's rule mediated through his Chosen One. After the ceremonies of anointing, enthronement, and the presentation of an oracular scroll as the deeds of office (the 'decree' of v. 7), the Davidic ruler issues a warning to earth's princes not to rebel against this divine sovereignty. The very high claim of the Davidic ruler to represent a universal kingdom seems historically to be an echo of the style of great empires, such as that of Egypt or Assyria. But it was joined to the visionary ideas concerning the Lord as the Most High God and Creator-King, and so nourished the religious faith that we later see blossoming in the hope of the Messiah (Hebrew for 'Anointed', Greek 'Christ'), who would represent the final kingdom of God.

There are indications in the Old Testament that the full installation of a Davidic king would take place in the autumn festival, and there his role would appropriately be set forth in the framework of the festival's main theme – God as universal King and Creator, manifest at this time of new beginning (Int. 5b; my *Kingship*, p. 112f.). On the analogy of the great empires, it is likely that commemorations, renewals and jubilees of the Davidic king's enthronement would also take place in this festival in other years. Whether the dramatic moment brought to life by our psalm was part of an extended drama (including divine election of the king, his empowerment, contest with hostile forces, salvation and exaltation) can hardly now be proved, but has seemed likely to a number of specialists in the field. In such a sacramental drama, the psalm would have belonged to the moment when the kings of the earth were imagined as rising in rebellion against the Lord and conspiring to assault Zion. But even if there were no such extended drama, the psalm brought to the ceremonies remarkable prophetic vision and power, conveying a promise of God's salvation from the attacks of potential enemies. (For the joining of Ps. 2 to Ps. 1 in some manuscripts, see above on Ps. 1.)

1–3   A scornful question brings before us the folly of the world's rulers and their peoples. Instead of living quietly in the peace of God's kingdom, they are seething and rumbling with plans for rebellion. Kings and princes posture and plot together against 'the Lord and his Anointed', against the divine kingdom which David and his heirs are anointed to represent. They think the moment propitious for breaking off the restraints which hold them in submission to God's just reign.

4–6 Terrible as the prospect of such universal uprising might seem, it is utterly deflated by a glimpse of the glory of God. The psalm simply reports that he who reigns ('sits') in heaven laughs at them, deriding their pretensions, and then utters his word of wrath, the sentence that will rout their forces. And all that it is, this conquering word, is a simple statement that God has anointed and installed his king on Zion (the hill of Jerusalem where the divine presence and reign are symbolically centred). What economy in this portrayal, and with what concentrated force the importance of the office of the Lord's Anointed is presented!

7–9 As part of his installation, the king has been given a document containing oracles of God; these appoint and acknowledge him, bestow blessings and probably make requirements. This document, called here the 'decree of the Lord', is probably the 'testimony' given with the crown in the story of 2 Kings 11.12; a comparable document featured in Egyptian enthronements. From this 'decree' the king now quotes, as part of his warning to the rebellious rulers. The citation first gives the essential, showing that the Lord has made him his 'Son', that is, the one who, in the Lord's favour, will share the divine rule, serving to execute God's reign on earth. Such sonship has taken effect 'this day', the day of the installation, and so is here expressed as like an adoption. It is a high office indeed, for here is one anointed by the Lord with the oil of divine holiness, and placed upon the throne of the Lord's own reign. He has only to ask (for he is granted a special grace of prayer) and God will give him the world and its peoples, through a fearsome power to shatter the force of his enemies. The victorious 'rod of iron' is symbolized by his sceptre, and there may be an allusion to a symbolic breaking of 'potter's vessels' that represented evil forces (a rite of this kind is known from Egypt; see Noth, 'Thebes'; cf. Jer. 19.10–11).

10–12 Dramatically the king admonishes earth's rulers. Into the midst of their rebellious preparations he directs his urgent warning. They should wisely hear his reproof and serve the Lord ('Yahweh') with reverence and awe. There is some question about the text and translation of the last phrase of v. 11 and the first of v. 12, though the general sense of these verses is clear. RV 'and rejoice with trembling' follows the usual meaning of the Hebrew words, and we may understand 'rejoice' in a context of worship (parallel to 'serve') and with the helpful addition of 'before him' as in LXX. RV 'Kiss the Son' would denote a gesture of submission to the Lord's Anointed, but St Jerome's translation 'Adore purely' is more likely. The dire warning finally gives way to a positive note. For 'all' who shelter in the Lord, putting their trust in him, there is great happiness (*asherey*, cf. above on 1.1) – a concluding invitation and promise from the Lord's 'Son' to all throughout the world.

The psalm presents a visionary scene and quotes an oracular promise of God. This is typical of the psalms that stem from the great festal ceremonies in Jerusalem, worship that set forth ideals and was full of expressions of the divine purpose. The original function of the psalm was to serve in the establishment of David's dynasty as instrument in God's government of his creation. It interpreted the ceremonies of anointing and coronation as action of the Lord who declared the ruler to be his 'Son', the beloved partner of his own reign, and bestowed on him power to overcome evil; and the psalm called the world to turn from rebellion and embrace the good reign of God. This all amounts to a poetic vision, which knows the ideal unity of the world, and the misery that results from the uprising of selfish ambition and greed against the divine order – knows all this, yet is sure that the Creator's good kingdom will prevail, and do so through his purpose in David and Zion.

When the house of David suffered a cruel fate and from 587 BCE reigned no more, the psalm was seen as prophecy yet to be vindicated. For the New Testament it told of the cruel hostility that crucified Christ, the Lord's Anointed (Acts 4.25f.), but also of the resurrection which revealed him as Son of God (Acts 13.33; Rom. 1.4; cf. Heb. 1.5; 5.5), and of the certainty of his ultimate victory over evil (Rev. 6.15f.; 12.5; 19.15; cf. 2.26–7). The church continued to find in the psalm the message of that certainty, strengthening the faith of all who love what is good; and calling to the destroyers and corrupters to return, before they are shattered in a sudden and certain doom. And through all the cataclysms the psalm's last word still sounds: O the happiness of all who shelter in him!

Lord, speak your mighty word upon the nations, that they may turn back from the ways of destruction, and find happiness in reverence for your good laws.

PSALM 3: When Foes Increase

Psalm.   Of David.   When he fled from before Absalom his son.

1   Lord, how my foes increase;
     so many are rising against me!
2   Many are those who say of my soul,
     He will have no salvation from God.   *[Pause]*
3   But you, Lord, are a shield about me,
     my glory, and the one who lifts up my head.
4   When I cry with my voice to the Lord,
     he hears me from his holy mountain.   *[Pause]*
5   I lie down and sleep;
     I wake again, because the Lord sustains me.

6   I will not be afraid of a host of ten thousands,
     which is arrayed against me.
7   Rise, Lord, save me, my God;
     smite the jaws of all my enemies,
        and break the fangs of the cruel.
8   Salvation is the Lord's!
     Your blessing be on your people!   *[Pause]*

We come to a series of psalms (3–41) which, with the exception of 10 and 33, are headed 'Of David'. They appear to have formed an independent collection prior to the completion of the Psalter and having a special association with 'David', the famous king or at least his dynasty. Although modern scholars (perhaps inclined to later dating) have often discounted this association, it is likely that there is some substance in it. Psalm 3 is first headed *mizmor*, 'Psalm' (a sacred chant with accompaniment usually of lyre or harp), then 'Of David' (Int. 7a); and then is added a further note on the circumstances said to have given rise to the psalm. This is one of the thirteen cases of such additional explanations from David's career, which could be later theorizing from the text (Int. 2b). But whether or not real knowledge linked this psalm with Absalom's rebellion (2 Sam. 15–19), the piece does fit with a situation of royal warfare, and bases its plea upon the pledges of God to his Anointed. The liturgical notice rendered 'Pause' (*sela*, apparently an interval, perhaps for obeisance or for an instrumental passage, Int. 3c) divides the psalm into three sections, vv. 1–2, 3–4, 5–8, but logically we might divide: lament (portraying the evil situation, vv. 1–2), grounds for trust (with implied appeal, vv. 3–4, 5–6), and direct petition (vv. 7, 8).

1–2 The 'lamenting' prayer-songs, which are the most numerous kind of psalm, keep closely to one aim, however varied their contents seem – the aim of moving God to come to the supplicant's aid. One of the main elements in such pleading prayer is a description of the suffering, not usually very specific, but enough to show how sharp the anguish, how urgent the situation. The first word is very often the name of God, 'Yahweh' (traditionally rendered 'Lord'; Int. 6b); and so it is here. In the use of this one word so much is compressed, especially allusion to the personal relationship with the Lord, and the confession that he alone can save. The situation now laid before the Lord is of a growing multitude of enemies. It seems to be the situation of a king whose weak position leads more and more subjects and allies to defect, so as to be on the winning side. The damaging idea is spread that God has withdrawn his support, so that it is indeed a hopeless cause.

3–4 In earnest appeal to the Lord, the supplicant sings of the protection and glory with which God raised him to eminence, and of the special grace of powerful prayer given to him (cf. 2.8; 4.3; 20.1–6; 21.2; 57.2–3; 89.26; 91.15; 1 Kings 3.5). Now, if ever, is the time for this promise to be proved. May the

Lord answer and send help from the holy mountain of Zion, symbol of the heavenly throne (cf. 20.2).

5–6 The king declares his confidence in the Lord's support, and so strengthens his appeal as one depending on God alone. The hours of sleep were a vulnerable time for a leader, but he has committed himself into the Lord's protection. It is possible that this thought arose as the psalm was sung with an early morning offering at a field altar. Military terms are used of the enemy: they are an 'army' (*'am*), 'deployed' (*shatu*), in hosts of 'ten thousands'. But though the hostile hordes seem all around him, he renounces fear through his trust in the Lord.

7–8 Now comes his direct petition, calling on the Lord to spring into action on his behalf and so to save him. Picturing the foes as demonic beasts with ravening jaws and fangs, he calls on God to smite their jaws and break their teeth (the Hebrew perfect tenses for 'smite' and 'break' are best taken, with Dahood and others, as expressing request, 'precative' rather than 'prophetic' perfects). The conclusion rings out confidently with the exclamation that salvation and victory belong to the Lord, and his blessing is called down on his own 'army / people' (*'am*).

The sense of friends falling away and enemies increasing is indeed a dreadful experience. How fickle and false the many appear as they shift loyalties to suit their own safety! David and many another leader have known it, and the church has traced here a prefigurement of the hostility and desertion experienced by Jesus. Through him his followers are to know the Lord as their shield, their glory and the lifter up of their head, and to see the angels of salvation sent out in answer to their prayer; through him also they lie down and sleep, even to the last sleep, and awake to the morning of salvation. Passing through the psalms, here one meets for the first time the mysterious *sela* (see above), and three times at that. It will occur very often, and while its full significance is not known, it certainly carries an advice to pause, whether to kneel in supplication or adoration, or to listen and let the music speak, or just to pause before the glory and mercy of the Lord. To pause is always good, and other psalms will develop the counsel of stillness before the Lord (46, 62, 131).

Almighty God and Father, when our enemies seem many and on all sides, help us to trust in your promises, to know that your love and power are a shield about us, and that nothing can part us from the salvation which you have given us in your Son Jesus.

PSALM 4: Commune with your Heart

For favour.   With stringed instruments.   Psalm.   Of David.

1   Answer me as I call, O God my Saviour;
    in my distress give me room,
        be gracious to me and hear my prayer.
2   How long, fine people, shall my glory be scorned,
    while you love what is worthless,
        and set your heart on a lie?   *[Pause]*
3   Yet know that the Lord wonderfully answers
        the one who is close to him;
    the Lord will hear when I call to him.
4   Tremble then, and sin no longer;
    commune with your heart upon your couch
        and be still.   *[Pause]*
5   Offer the sacrifices that make for peace,
    and put your trust in the Lord.
6   Many are saying, O that we might see good!
    The light of your face has fled from us, O Lord.
7   You will put joy in my heart again,
    more than when their corn and wine abound.
8   In peace I will lie down and sleep,
    for only you, Lord, make me dwell in safety.

We notice several links with the preceding psalm: the 'many who say', and the themes of effective prayer, safe sleeping, glory and abuse. If we can hardly conclude (with Delitzsch and Kirkpatrick) that these psalms are from the same situation, they appear to come from the same circle and period. Notable is the long address to an opposition that is both scorning the psalmist and turning from the Lord. This address has an authoritative tone culminating in a series of seven imperatives, and warns of the power of prayer bestowed on the psalmist as God's *ḥasid*, his covenant partner. The signs are, then, that the psalmist is the Lord's Anointed, sharing the divine sovereignty (we may compare royal Psalm 2 for the joint reign, the grace of prayer, and the weighty address to the opposition). His plight is not so evidently military as in Psalm 3; in the foreground seems rather to be disaffection connected with drought or dearth. The psalm is furnished with four items of heading and two occurrences of the liturgical notice 'Pause' (see above on Ps. 3). 'For favour' (*lamenaṣṣeah*) gives the liturgical aim, to 'make bright' the face of God (so Mowinckel, *Psalms* II, p. 212; others take this term to mean 'for the director', Int. 3c). The 'stringed instruments' would be lyres and harps (Int. 3b).

1 The singer cries out to God for a hearing, praying that in his pity he would give him room or liberty from forces that press in on him. (For 'Give me room' the Hebrew tense is taken as 'precative'; otherwise, 'You gave me room', a rather abrupt reference to past salvation.) He invokes the Lord as 'God of my right (*sedeq*)'; the idiom may mean 'God who secures my salvation'.

2–5 This relatively large central section, a little over half the psalm, is addressed to 'sons of a man (*ish*)', an idiom for people in general or perhaps people of substance (cf. *ish* in 49.2; Isa. 2.9). It is a striking feature in a small psalm of urgent prayer. As in the speech of 2.10–12, there is an authoritative tone and a linking of the speaker's cause with that of the Lord; but 2 was not a prayer, and its dramatic character suited the royal ceremonies. In the present case we may understand the composition by reference to the prophetic aspect of psalmody. It is as though the supplicant, through converse with God, gains strength to address words of inspired power to the hostile people, a power which is conveyed across the wide world. At the same time, the scene of trust in the face of hostility is being indirectly portrayed before the Lord. In his address the singer admonishes those who bring his 'glory' into disrepute and who pursue some false course that is a turning against himself and against the Lord (cf. 2.1 'against the Lord and his Anointed'), and he goes on to warn of his gift of powerful prayer (cf. 2.8; 3.4) – the Lord 'wonderfully acts' for the one specially bound to him, his faithful partner (*hasid*). They should tremble and repent, stilling rebellious thoughts (cf. 46.10). They should renew their bond with God, trusting him and offering 'the sacrifices of right (*sedeq*)', sacrifices for making things right, for seeking peace.

6–8 Here we discern the likely cause of the disaffection. The lack of 'good', the departure of the 'light' of God's favour, and the reference to 'corn and wine' (LXX has also 'and oil') suggest that harvests have failed, perhaps for several years, a devastating situation. Such a crisis could induce a turning to the fertility deities of Canaan, and also anger against the king, for it was thought that a good king in favour with heaven should ensure fertility (72.3, 6, 16). But our psalmist concludes with words of trust in the Lord, indirectly strengthening his opening plea for help. The 'joy' (*simha*) is the festal merriment so markedly absent at present, yet confidently hoped for (here we take the perfect tense as expressing confidence, 'you will put joy', rather than 'you have put joy'); we could translate 'from the time that their corn and wine increase', but that would be somewhat banal; the thought is deeper – God will give the joy in his own way and time. And the psalmist will not fear the vulnerability of sleeping amidst such hostility, having God's protection (cf. above on 3.5).

Well known from its daily use in the office of Compline, this psalm is also much loved for its depth of meaning. It speaks for an individual who, for the sake of the Lord, is beset by much hostility and scorn. It is a time when prosperity has fled away, and people of power have turned their backs on

God's values, and love rather goals that are in reality worthless. On every hand, also, there are many who despair of ever seeing good again. The faithful person turns to prayer and also witnesses to the good way, where there is awe of God, turning from sin, stillness and meditation, worship that finds and holds to God, and above all, trust in him. In such trust the psalmist concludes, confident that the Lord in his own time will fill the heart again with rejoicing, and make his peace known in every danger. In the royal figure that can readily be discerned in our psalmist, the church has seen a prefigurement of Christ, with his powerful prayer to the Father, his glory despised, his teaching of humility and faith, his surpassing joy, his trustful sleep of death that won peace for the many. So the follower of Jesus feels close to him in this psalm, and asks to be led into that same joy of trust, which overcomes even in the last night.

Lord, by your grace may we learn to be in awe and sin no longer, to commune with our heart and be still before you, that when many lose heart, we may abide in confidence that you will wonderfully answer all our needs.

PSALM 5: Lead me, Lord

For favour.   With the flutes.   Psalm.   Of David.

1   Listen to my words, O Lord;
     take heed of my lamentation.
2   Attend to the voice of my crying, my King and my God,
     for to you alone I pray.
3   Lord, in the morning you will hear my voice;
     early in the morning I will make ready for you,
          and will look up.
4   For you are not a god pleased with wickedness;
     evil shall not dwell with you.
5   The arrogant shall not stand before your eyes;
     you abhor all evildoers.
6   You put an end to those who speak falsehood;
     a murderous and deceitful man the Lord condemns.
7   As for me, in the abundance of your faithful love
          I will come into your house;
     I will bow down towards your holy temple in awe of you.
8   Lead me, Lord, in your goodness,
          against those who lie in wait for me;
     make your way plain before my face.
9   For there is no truth in their mouth,
          but in their heart is a gaping pit;

> their throat is an open tomb,
>   while they flatter with their tongue.
> 10 Condemn them, O God, let them fall by their own counsels;
>   for their many sins drive them out,
>   for they have rebelled against you.
> 11 But let all who shelter in you rejoice and ever sing for joy,
>   that you are a wall about them,
>   and let those who love your name exult in you.
> 12 For you, Lord, will bless your faithful one;
>   you will surround him with your favour as with a shield.

This lamenting supplication was made in connection with ceremony at the sanctuary at break of day. Mention of the Lord's house and temple may refer to Solomon's fine courts and building, but could otherwise refer to the earlier sanctuary of David's time (cf. 2 Sam. 12.30). Though some think of the psalmist as a private citizen, seeking asylum or justice by oracular decision, there are indications that he is a king troubled by rivals or plotters (my *Kingship*, p. 65). The reference to flute-playing in the heading may be to a traditional kind of lamenting accompaniment (for the rest of the heading see above on 3 and 4).

1–3 The appeal for a hearing is made with urgent repetition, as for an acute need. The 'lamentation' involves groaning or sighing (cf. Rom. 8.26). In addressing the Lord as 'my King and my God', the supplicant is using a phrase found in national prayers (44.4; 68.24; 74.12; 84.3); it pictures God as the Creator who vanquishes chaos-foes, and yet is in close bond with the singer and those he represents. The worshipper 'makes ready' in the sense of putting in order either his thoughts and prayers, or the offerings that would accompany the seeking of guidance. He 'looks up' or 'keeps watch' for an indication of God's will.

4–7 The opening appeal is now developed by an expression of faith in the Lord's justice. The description of the heavenly King's righteousness is reminiscent of the code laid upon the Davidic king (101); he reigns through servants that are humble and truthful. The supplicant implies that his present troublers would not pass this test. For himself, however, he claims that he can enter the sanctuary as one governed by the fear of the Lord and conscious of God's faithful love (*ḥesed*), the good-will promised and covenanted to him by God. Enabled by this love, he can enter the Lord's courts and make obeisance towards the inmost holy place, the shrine so rarely entered.

8–10 The theme of confidence in God's goodness opens out into prayer for protection from the enemies and for their just condemnation. As good shepherd and as conqueror of evil, the Lord is implored to lead the way, driving out the lurking foes, clearing away the dangerous obstacles. Prayer for the defeat and fall of the foes is built up with portrayal of them as deceivers, smooth in talk, deadly in heart, rebels indeed against God, deserving to be caught in the plots they devise against others.

11–12 In contrast with the end desired for these foes, the concluding prayer is for the joyful experience of God's defence and blessing – not narrowly envisaged, as though only for the psalmist and his supporters, but requested for all who shelter in the Lord, all who love his name. The word for the 'faithful' or 'righteous' one (*saddiq*) may allude especially to the psalmist's calling, the king who is God's Chosen One, marked by his 'favour' (*rason*) and protection.

In this psalm we have had glimpses of ceremony: the approach at break of day, a 'making ready', the entering into the temple courts, the prostration before the holiest place. It may be that the prayer is preparatory to such ceremony, and so the repeated plea for a favourable hearing arises while it is still dark, when the foes, as servants of the sinister powers, are all the stronger. From the night, then, the psalmist looks towards the morning, and prepares in hope for the Lord's response in his goodness and blessing. His trust is in God's faithful love, but with awe of his majesty. Through the valley of shadow and danger he would follow his good shepherd, trusting him to make the way plain. Only this Lord can drive out the evil ones, so subtle in their tongues and voracious in their hearts, and so he prays strongly to this effect. His prayer has been sustained in the church down the ages; not vindictively, but seeking from God that the destroyers should come to the end of that sinister existence, to live anew among those who shelter in God and exult in love of his name.

Lead me, Lord, in your goodness, and make your way plain before my face, that I may pass through every danger and perplexity, and come with awe and thanksgiving into your holy temple.

PSALM 6: Prayer with Tears

For favour. With stringed instruments. Upon the eighth. Psalm. Of David.

1 Lord, do not in your anger rebuke me,
   or correct me in your wrath.
2 Have pity on me, Lord, for I am weak;
   Lord, heal me, for my bones are troubled.
3 My soul also is sorely troubled;
   but you, Lord – O how long ?
4 Return, Lord, rescue my soul;
   save me, for the sake of your faithful love.

5   For there is no remembrance of your name
         in the land of death,
     and in the great darkness who will give thanks to you?
6   I am weary from my groaning;
     every night I wash my bed
         and water my couch with my tears.
7   My eye is wasted with grief,
     grown old because of all my foes.
8   Get away from me, all you that work evil,
     for the Lord will hear the voice of my weeping.
9   The Lord will hear my pleading;
     the Lord will accept my prayer.
10   All my enemies shall be put to shame and confusion;
     they shall suddenly turn back in shame.

This is the prayer of one brought very low by suffering, apparently illness. After depicting to the Lord the extremity of the suffering and asking for mercy and healing, the supplicant finds confidence to bid his troublers to depart, and he envisages their defeat. In the view of some scholars, prayer at the temple has elicited a sign or word from priest or prophet, signifying God's response; so, resuming at v. 8, the supplicant can say 'the Lord has heard'. Another explanation is that at this point the one who has poured out such entreaty suddenly receives an inward conviction of acceptance. Neither view, however, is quite satisfactory, and it may be better to translate not 'he has heard' but (as above) 'he will hear' (Hebrew perfect tense to express confidence). The point of the passage (vv. 8–10) will then be to reinforce the supplication by an expression of faith. The hostile forces may be imagined as a combination of demonic and human adversaries, finding opportunity to attack when the psalmist in some way offended the Lord, but now to be routed as the Lord turns again in grace. In the heading we meet the unexplained technical term 'upon / over the eighth' (found also in 12 and 1 Chron. 15.21). Some connect it with the musical 'octave' or an eighth mode, while Mowinckel suggests an eighth and decisive moment of ceremony (*Psalms* II, pp. 215f.). For the rest of the heading see above on 3 and 4.

1–3   The prayer from deepest affliction begins with the holy name, which will continue to be prominent; in 'Yahweh' alone is power to save, this Lord who has given his name that he may be called upon (cf. above on 3.1; Int. 6b). The supplicant appears to accept that he has merited rebuke and correction, but he prays for alleviation. In pleading for grace and compassion, and so healing, he depicts his condition as like a withered and drooping plant; his frame and the very life within him are shaken and bewildered. Words fall away (v. 3b) as he puts the whole situation into the hands of God with longing for speedy relief.

4–5 The prayer for the Lord to 'return' is especially that he should be known again in his saving, faithful love. In childlike fashion, the psalmist urges, as it were to the Lord's own advantage, that his death would only cut him off from any opportunity to give praise (for the land of death, 'Sheol', imagined as the subterranean abode of the shades, silent, remote from divine grace, see Int. 60). This plea, however, also adds to the pathos of the prayer, which becomes a cry from the weakness of all earthly life, so brief and fragile, a little space of light in an encompassing darkness.

6–7 The psalmist puts to the Lord further depiction of his suffering in nights of copious weeping, with eyes worn out, prematurely aged. It is a suffering caused by adversaries – malevolent forces, perhaps in part spiritual, in part human troublers, who bring on him sickness in the opportunity afforded by the Lord's displeasure.

8–10 As often in the lamenting psalms, the conclusion is on a note of hope and confidence. The psalmists endeavour to strengthen their prayer by expressing a faith which the Lord would not lightly disappoint. The passage may not begin with such an abrupt change as the usual translations show ('the Lord has answered' – see above). But it is a brave statement of hope and trust, beginning with the defiant address to the tormenters, 'Get away from me, you who work harm!' (words echoed in Matt. 7.23; Luke 12.27). When the Lord wills, how swiftly the horde of assailants will melt away!

The prayer of this sufferer draws upon the typical experience of all who know deep pain and misery. It has therefore continued to be much used, especially since it is one of the seven 'Penitential Psalms' chosen (with 32, 38, 51, 102, 130, 143) by the church for additional uses (e.g. on Ash Wednesday). The beginning of v. 3 is echoed in the words of Jesus (John 12.27), and the psalm has continued to be associated with Christ's weeping, pleading, loss of strength and beauty, and at last victory over the evil one. Thus, while it is used to express human need in great sufferings, whether individual or communal, it is with faith that he who came down into our lowest weakness will raise us in his victory.

Faithful Lord, have pity on those who are sorely troubled and wasted with grief; hear the voice of their weeping, and drive away all that troubles them, so that they may bear witness to your salvation in the land of your light.

PSALM 7: Rise up, Lord

Lament.   Of David.   Which he sang to the Lord on account of Cush the
Benjaminite.

1   Lord, my God, I take shelter in you;
     save me from all who pursue me, and deliver me,
2   or they will tear my soul like a lion,
     rending me, with none to deliver.
3   Lord, my God, if I have done this,
     if there is guilt upon my hands,
4   if I have done harm to one at peace with me,
     or plundered my foe without a cause,
5   then let the enemy pursue and overtake my soul,
     tread my life to the ground,
       and lay my glory in the dust.   *[Pause]*
6   Rise up, Lord, in your wrath,
       be exalted against the raging of my foes,
     and stir up for me the judgement you have commanded.
7   Let the assembly of the nations gather about you,
     and over it take your seat on high.
8   Lord, Judge of the peoples,
       give judgement for the rightness of my cause,
     and according to the innocence that is in me.
9   May the evil of the wicked come to an end,
       but establish the one who is just,
     for you try hearts and inner thoughts, O God of justice.
10 For my shield I trust in God,
     who saves those who are true of heart.
11 God is a judge who does right,
     and a God who condemns evil every day.
12 For the unrepentant he sharpens his sword,
     he bends his bow and makes it ready;
13 yes, for such he has prepared the weapons of death,
     he makes his arrows shafts of flame.
14 See the one who travails with evil!
     He grows great with mischief, then gives birth to falsehood.
15 He digs a pit and makes it deep,
     and falls into the trap of his own making.
16 His mischief will return upon his own head,
     and his violence will fall on his own skull.
17 I will give thanks to the Lord for all his justice,
     and will make music to the Lord Most High.

The heading 'Lament' (*shiggayon*) is found elsewhere only once (Hab. 3.1), where it heads a psalm that prays for king and people and sees God rout his foes. Our psalm also appeals to the just ruler of the nations, warrior against the wicked, and attains a confidence where the enemy is graphically seen to suffer the fate he prepared for others. If the connection with David's life given in the heading should be treated with reserve (Int. 2b), yet there are signs that this is an ancient prayer of a king who faces a national foe (vv. 4–8). The reference in the heading to the otherwise unknown 'Cush' may reflect an episode not preserved in our histories; the Targum rather unsuitably identified him with King Saul, son of Kish, and others have suggested the rebel Shimei (cf. 7.16 with 1 Kings 2.8f.).

1–2   The prayer of distress begins with the holy name (cf. above on 6.1), but to this is added 'my God', one word in the Hebrew, expressing mutual commitment (Int. 6c). This doubly strong invocation is repeated in v. 3. The supplicant seeks to shelter in the Lord from fierce 'pursuers', but in v. 2 the literal Hebrew may indicate a single figure, the chief adversary, ready to attack and rend like a hunting lion. (Some prefer to give *nephesh* here its possible physical sense: tear my 'throat' rather than 'soul'.) Right at the outset of the psalm, marking the urgency of the situation, the direct prayers ring out: 'Save me, deliver me.'

3–5   The passion of this lamenting psalm is manifest now in an oath of innocence in the drastic self-cursing form: 'If I am guilty, may I be trodden into the dust of death.' In such a form, more extended, did Job fight against all odds for his innocence (Job 31.5f.). Appealing to the just God, the psalmist too will stake all on his conviction that he has not wronged his adversary. With the terrible self-curse, he avows that he has not rewarded with evil one with whom he was at peace (perhaps in formal covenant), nor wantonly plundered his adversary. So he rebuts the pretext with which the war against him is being justified.

6–9   With bold phrases traditional in the great national intercessions, the psalmist invokes the Lord: 'Rise up, raise yourself.' So he invokes God to come in the power of his fury against the raging of the evil enemy: 'Rouse up (*'ur* taken as transitive) for me the judgement you have commanded', that is, 'Put into effect the justice which you have pledged to me.' The thought would suit the covenantal assurances given to David and his heirs. A striking scene is now envisaged – the nations gathering in a vast circle, and in the midst the Lord taking his exalted throne (this is all the clearer if in v. 7b we alter, as above, the vowel of *shuba*, 'return', to *sheba*, 'be seated'). Appealing for justice in such a setting, the psalmist appears clearly as head of his people, acting on a national scale; the Lord 'judges' the peoples, or is their 'judge' (*yadin* taken as a noun, with form like *yarib*, GK 85d). In a world full of false propaganda, only God who tests 'hearts and kidneys' (regarded as the seat of thoughts and purposes) can vindicate the true of heart.

10–16 The psalmist now supports his plea by declaring confidence in God's just rule. He depicts God as holding judgement every day, saving the just and condemning the oppressors. He prepares his weapons against those who will not turn from their evil. (Verses 12–13 can otherwise be taken throughout to depict the aggressor: 'Ever and again he sharpens his sword . . . but for himself he has prepared the weapons of death . . .') The doom of the wicked is vividly portrayed, rather as prophets used strong images to carry the power of God's judgement. The wicked swell with their pride and violent schemes, but from this pregnancy they give birth to 'falsehood', which brings ruin and failure for themselves. The deviser of evil finds it rebounding; the cruelty returns and lands on his own skull.

17 The conclusion adds to the plea with further expression of confidence, now in the form of a promise to give thanks when deliverance comes; testimony to salvation will be made through the playing and singing of a thankful psalm.

This is prayer in a fighting spirit. With its self-curse, it calls upon God in the most drastic fashion. But it is probably the prayer of one responsible for a people, and carrying duty and promise from the Lord. Here is a way of prayer which knows God as the only shelter and shield, the sure upholder of what is good and true, but knows also that there is a battle to be fought in prayer, a battle on which life itself must be bravely staked. The church found allusion to Christ's innocence and intercession, and also (v. 6) to his resurrection; against the roaring lion of evil the needy ones must set the victory of the righteous Lion of Judah.

O God of Justice, rise up to save all the abused of the earth, for only by your might can the forces of evil be driven back, and we call upon your holy name through the merits of your Son Jesus.

PSALM 8: Crowned to Love

For favour.   Over the Gittith.   Psalm.   Of David.

1   O Lord, our Lord, how glorious is your name in all the earth,
    while your splendour is chanted over the heavens!
2   Out of the mouth of babes at the breast
        you have founded a stronghold,
    to counter your foes,
        and still the enemy and the avenger.
3   When I see your heavens, the works of your fingers,

the moon and the stars which you have created,

4   what is man that you remember him,
      and the son of man that you care for him?

5   For you have given him little less than the angels,
      and crowned him with glory and honour.

6   You gave him rule over the works of your hands;
      you put everything under his feet,

7   flocks and herds of every kind,
      even the animals of the wild,

8   birds of the heavens and fish of the sea,
      and all that moves along the paths of the seas.

9   O Lord, our Lord,
      how glorious is your name in all the earth!

Although this wonderful psalm can be fairly described as a hymn or song of praise, its form is unusual. It does not contain the usual calls to praise and is throughout addressed to God. The opening line is repeated at the end, and in a choral form (note 'our'), whereas the inner section is markedly borne by a single singer (v. 3 'I'). The theme centres in the sovereignty of the Creator, manifest in royal glory, vanquisher of chaos, maker of the mighty elements, yet, amazingly, willing to make man the earthly agent of his sovereignty, treating him with love and honour. The thought is all enfolded in the wondering adoration of God, the only true sovereign and master.

All this points to a connection with the chief festival of early times, the autumnal new year celebration of Yahweh as king and master of nature (Int. 5b). The obscure heading 'Over the *gittith*' is found also with 81 and 84, which also appear to belong to this festal season; some have looked for a link with the Philistine town of Gath (giving a feminine adjective, 'Gittite', hence perhaps an instrument from Gath – so the Targum – or a melody), while others think of *gath* 'wine-press' and so the autumnal celebration of the grape harvest (so apparently LXX). Mowinckel (*Psalms* II, p. 215) suggested a connection with the festal procession of the ark, since tradition told of a Gittite home as starting point (2 Sam. 6.10f.). Although there is some similarity between our psalm and the tradition of Creation found in Genesis 1, where also the human race is appointed God's viceroy, the psalm has distinctive character (e.g. in mentioning the 'fingers' of the Creator and seeing chaos as personified vengeful enemy). The poet of the Book of Job seems to have been familiar with the psalm, giving it a bitter application in Job 7.17–18.

1–2   The address is to 'Yahweh, our Lord / Master (*adon*)'. The chorus utters exclamation at the majestic shining of this 'name' over all the earth, the name that is the showing of God's holy being (Int. 6b). It is likely that the psalm is sung at a high moment of such revelation, the moment in the drama of worship when the faithful are conscious of the Creator manifest in victory, and of the world made new (Int. 5b). A parallel statement is then made about corresponding worship over or across the heavens; at this climactic moment the heavenly beings also worship and sing responsively of God's glory (cf. 29.9; Isa. 6.3). Profound wonder develops in v. 2 that out of the praising mouths of mere 'babes and sucklings' the Lord has founded a fortress against the vengeful chaos, which would return if it could. The context suggests that these 'babes' are the weak and humble worshippers, whose inadequate singing of God's glory is yet used by him to still the avenger. So long as they sing, the chaos is silenced, the meaninglessness repulsed.

3–8 The arresting thought of such humility in God is continued through meditation on the night sky, so brilliant over Jerusalem. The Lord, whose fingers made these bright hosts, yet stoops to attend lovingly to the needs of our tiny race. Moreover, he has given (traditionally 'made') man little less than the angels (*elohim*, strictly 'gods, heavenly beings'; the sense 'God' seems unlikely in an address to God), and has crowned him with royal honour, putting all the other creatures of the earth 'under his feet' – under his dominion. The strong expression 'under his feet' is an echo of the traditional near-eastern formulas of kingship, where kings would be commissioned by heaven to rule justly and compassionately, but have conquering power against evil. The kingship which the Lord has bestowed on man is intended as the mediation of God's own rule. There is to be but one kingdom, the just and saving reign of the Creator, and puny man, amazingly, is appointed as the royal steward, the one who is to represent and carry out the wishes of the Lord.

9 The conclusion resumes the opening words. Such use of a refrain here is not just for artistic effect, but brings home the absolutely essential point: through all the earth it is the Lord's name that is glorious; the kingdom, the power and the glory are his and his alone. Woe to man if he should imagine the glory is his own and come to abuse the creatures entrusted to his care!

To achieve inclusive language, many recent versions render a little freely but not unfairly in the famous verses 4f.; thus NRSV 'what are human beings that you are mindful of them, mortals that you care for them? Yet you have made them a little lower than God and crowned them with glory and honour ...' My translation has kept the older, more literal style, and so a clearer connection with the tradition of the Beginning as seen in the New Testament. The psalm does indeed breathe a paradisal air; no mention is made of the failure of man, his treachery and cruelty, the sufferings of the creatures, the obscuring of God's glory throughout the earth. The moment of worship which it seems to reflect was touched with a vision; perfection both primal and ultimate is glimpsed by the eye of faith. The crowned figure in this vision is representative and head of our race, the ideal that the New Testament declared manifest in Christ (Heb. 2.6–8; 1 Cor. 15.20–8; Eph. 1.22). With the light of the resurrection and new creation, the vision is given again. Amidst all the failure of human responsibility come glimpses of what can and will be. Crowned with honour, close to the angels, the race made new will love those under their rule as they themselves are loved by God.

O God, glorious in heaven and earth, in your grace you make the praises of the humble a stronghold against evil, and have appointed the human race to be your royal minister on earth; grant that we may rule your creatures with love, until with them we are made perfect in joyful subjection to your Son, our Lord Jesus Christ.

PSALMS 9 and 10: Holding on to the Music

For favour.   Ceremonies at Full Moon.   Psalm.   Of David.

9.1 I will give thanks, Lord, with all my heart;
    I will tell of all your marvellous works.
2   I will be glad and rejoice in you;
    I will make music to your name, Most High.
3   When my enemies turned back,
    they stumbled and perished before you.
4   For you upheld my right and my cause;
    you took the throne and acted justly.
5   You rebuked the nations and brought the wicked to ruin;
    you put out their name for ever and ever.
6   The enemy was utterly laid waste,
    you pulled down cities, and even their memory perished.
7   But the Lord shall be enthroned for ever;
    he has made fast his seat for judgement.
8   And he shall rule the world aright;
    he shall govern the peoples justly.
9   The Lord will be a high tower for the oppressed,
    a high tower in times of need.
10   And those who know your name will trust in you,
    for you, Lord, have not forsaken those who seek you.
11   Make music to the Lord enthroned in Zion;
    tell among the peoples the things that he has done,
12   that the avenger of bloodshed remembered them;
    he did not forget the crying of the poor.

13   Have pity on me, Lord;
    see what I suffer from those set against me,
    you that lift me up from the gates of death,
14   that I may tell all your praises in the gates of fair Zion,
    and rejoice in your salvation.

15 The nations shall sink in the pit of their own making;
in the net which they spread, their own foot shall be caught.
16 When the Lord makes himself known in doing judgement,
the wicked shall be snared
in the work of their own hands. *[Music. Pause]*
17 The wicked shall return to the land of darkness,
all the nations that forget God.
18 For the needy shall not be utterly forgotten,
nor the hope of the poor be lost for ever.
19 Rise up, Lord, do not let man prevail;
let the nations be judged before your face.
20 Put fear upon them, Lord;
may the nations know they are but dust. *[Pause]*

10.1 Why, Lord, do you stand far off,
and hide yourself in times of need?
2 In arrogance the wicked blaze against the poor;
may they be caught in the schemes they have devised.
3 For the wicked man boasts of the craving of his soul;
in his greed he curses and despises the Lord.
4 With haughty brow he says, God will not inquire;
in all his schemes there is no God.
5 His ways are ever brazen,
your judgements far above his sight;
he scoffs at all his foes.
6 He says in his heart, I shall not be moved;
I shall never come to harm.
7 His mouth is full of cursing, lies and oppression;
under his tongue lie trouble and evil.
8 He lurks in the cover of villages,
in dark places he murders the innocent;
his eyes spy out the helpless.
9 He waits in hiding like a lion in his covert,
he lies in wait to seize the poor;
he will seize the poor indeed,
when he catches them in his net.
10 He crouches and lies low,
and the helpless fall by his might.
11 He says in his heart, God has forgotten;
he hides his face, he will never see it.
12 Rise, Lord God, lift up your hand;
do not forget the poor.
13 Why should the wicked one be scornful of God,
and say in his heart, You will not avenge it?
14 Surely you must see the trouble and misery;
you regard it and will take it into your hands.

> The helpless throws himself upon you,
> for you are the helper of the fatherless.
> 15 Break the arm of the wicked and evil one;
> search out his wickedness till you find no more.
> 16 The Lord shall be king for ever and ever;
> the nations shall vanish from his land.
> 17 The desire of the humble, Lord, you will hear;
> you will listen to the fullness of their heart,
> 18 to do right for the fatherless and needy,
> so that mere man may cause terror no more.

The unity of 9 and 10 can be argued on several grounds. They are joined in LXX and a few Hebrew manuscripts; 9, uncommonly, ends with a 'Pause', and 10, surprisingly in this group, lacks a title; they are acrostic psalms (Int. 4c), with 9 following the first half of the alphabet and 10 (falteringly) the second; there are similarities of style, such as the peculiar phrase rendered 'in times of need' in 9.9 and 10.1. Nevertheless, there is a distinction of content, with praise preponderating in 9, lament in 10. What we have, then, is an extended composition in two main parts, a ceremony of prayer in two phases, balanced across the two halves of the alphabet. The rather surprising pattern of praise-followed-by-lament is in fact not unusual (cf. 27, 40, 89).

The alphabetic scheme is in parts poorly preserved (especially in 10.3–11) and the text likewise difficult in some details. The piece, with resemblance to Habakkuk, may be quite ancient, from the seventh century or earlier. It points up the contradiction between the praise of God's good rule (with justice for the poor) and current affliction. Enemy nations are often mentioned; they invade the land (cf. 10.16) and murder and oppress. Their activity is generally depicted in the figure of a wicked man who preys on helpless folk, a picture to challenge God's justice. The suffering caused by the nations weighs on the psalmist personally (9.1–5, 13–14) and he must surely be the nation's leader in these prayers. Like the king in 18, he addresses the Lord as his saviour from the gates of death (9.13). Little can be deduced from the peculiar second phrase in the title, which LXX rendered 'Concerning the secrets of the Son' and the Targum related to the death of Goliath. Some think of the name of a melody ('The Dying of the Son'), while Mowinckel (*Psalms* II pp. 216f.) wonders about 'secrets' (*'alamot*) in a ritual sense, with *lbn* as possibly 'full moon' (*lebana*).

9.1–12 The singer has a representative character, for it soon becomes clear that 'my enemies', 'my right' and 'my cause' (vv. 3–4) relate to conflict with the nations (vv. 5–6). It is probable that he is a king, and it is notable that his opening words resemble the conclusion of 7. It was a royal duty to witness to the Lord's faithfulness and justice (cf. 89.1–18; Isa. 55.3–4; my *Kingship*, pp. 182f.), and it seems that in time of great need the king might first show himself as such a witness before bringing forward his petition. The hope was that the Lord would respond for the sake of the faithfulness so freshly praised.

So the psalmist sings in testimony to past wonders of salvation, when nations unjustly making war were repulsed and their cities ruined. The just kingship of the Lord was manifested, and the hope of his protection of the poor established for all time to come. Already we see what will be prominent in 10, that the king and his people present themselves to God as needy, poor, oppressed people. They will mount their appeal from lowliness and affliction.

9.13–14 It suddenly emerges that all the resounding praise and testimony is from one brought low by his 'haters', those implacably set against him. He pleads for the Lord to see his suffering with pitying eye, the Lord who lifts him from the gates of death. Here he may echo a scene from the ceremonies installing the king, a scene showing his symbolic rescue from the clutches of death (Int. 5b). At all events, the phrase appeals to the Lord's committed love and his power to save. 'Fair Zion' is more literally 'Daughter Zion' (not 'Daughter of Zion', cf. GK 128k); the holy city is affectionately personified and seen as the supreme place of communion with the Lord.

9.15–18 If translated in the past tense, vv. 15–16 are a resumption of the opening testimony. All the sharper, then, would be the contrast between current suffering and the stoically maintained praise of God's just and saving rule. It may be better, however, to render as above in the future tense (a Hebrew 'perfect of confidence'), agreeing with vv. 17–18. The effect of such an expression of hope and faith would be to strengthen the appeal. The thought of cruel deeds rebounding on the perpetrating nations is another resemblance to 7 (vv. 11–16). The 'land of darkness' (lit. 'Sheol') signifies death and its realm, seen as manifest in destructive deeds. Preceding the 'Pause' is another term, *higgayon* (found within the text of 19.14 and 92.3); it may refer to music, perhaps combined with formulas of praise.

9.19–20 The first half of the great whole concludes with bold invocation of the Lord to 'rise up' (another link with 7, v. 6). This clearly shows the beseeching aim of all the preceding verses, however much they have told of God's just and saving deeds. It is also again made clear that the singer carries the burden of his own suffering nation as he faces powerful and aggressive peoples. May God bring home to the arrogant nations that they are not God but 'man' – creatures answerable to the just sovereign of all.

10.1–11 The second part of the composition begins with the traditional thrust of lamenting prayer: 'Why, Lord, stand far off?' (cf. 22.1, 11, 19). While the Lord appears to hide himself, the weak are cruelly preyed upon; and the impassioned prayer conveys to God such a description of injustice as should rouse the guardian of royal justice. Most of this description pictures a wicked individual, hardened against God's requirements, and like a murderous robber who watches for vulnerable passers-by. While foreign oppression did lead to much abuse within society, it is likely that the picture is a kind of symbol for national and military attacks (as also in Habakkuk), a pointed appeal to God's obligation as royal defender of widows, orphans and other vulnerable people.

10.12–15   The lamenting depiction has led to a fresh outburst of direct petition. The Lord is called upon to arise, lift his hand in action, even to 'break the arm' of the one who strikes the helpless. Surely God must see the need, surely he knows that on him alone, defender of the fatherless, the oppressed have thrown themselves.

10.16–18   The conclusion adds to the appeal with further statements of trust. There is confidence that the kingly rule of God, just and radiant, will be openly established, with oppressors vanishing from the land. So the Lord will have responded to the sufferings that fill the heart of his people, and human tyrants will no longer be allowed to terrorize them.

It is hard to maintain belief in God's just and compassionate rule of the world when one sees on every hand abuse and slaughter of the innocent. Facing such appalling situations in our own day, we can reflect that it is no new anguish of belief, but one often borne by the people of the Psalms. In such a terrible situation the singer of 9 and 10 held on to the music; he sang traditional praise of God's just rule along with depiction of present atrocities and with invocations to action, all in one tightly knit composition. In this way he sharpened his lament, and gave strength of hope and faith to his petitions. One may wonder if the psalm-collectors saw a relation to the 'stronghold' founded out of the praises of 'babes at the breast' in 8. As long as the poor worshippers sing, 8 seems to say, the enemy and avenger is stilled; and here in 9 and 10 is the representative of the poor, assailed by that enemy, and yet beginning his intercession making music and singing thankful praise with all his heart. At all events, he shows a way of outspoken and passionate prayer against the cruel and on behalf of the helpless, a way that holds the evil up before God, and somehow holds on also to the all-encircling faith in the just Creator-King, the high tower for the poor, the one who raises his beloved from the gates of death. In Christian usage these psalms have brought to mind the strong prayers of Christ and his church for the poor and vulnerable, enfolding their sufferings in faith in the divine victory over cruelty and chaos. However great the troubles, the music of hope will ever sound before the Lord of the resurrection.

O God Most High, we praise and thank you for your marvellous works and for the sure hope of the triumph of your kingdom; and we commend to your pity those who are crushed in this present world, that you will save them from the cruel and lift them up with your Son Jesus from the gates of death.

PSALM 11: Resolving Not to Run Away

For favour.   Psalm.   Of David.

1   In the Lord I shelter, so how can you say to my soul,
    Flee to the mountains like a bird;
2   for look how the wicked bend their bow;
    they set their arrows on the string,
       to shoot from darkness at the true of heart;
3   if the foundations are ruined,
    what can the faithful do?
4   But the Lord is in his holy temple,
       the Lord has his throne in heaven;
    his eyes see, his very eyelids try the children of earth.
5   The Lord tries the good and the bad,
    and his soul abhors the lover of violence.
6   On the wicked he will rain coals of fire and brimstone,
    and a scorching wind shall be the portion for their cup.
7   For the Lord is just and loves just deeds;
    the true of heart shall see his face.

This is rather dramatically formed as a dialogue with those who counsel flight, and there is no address to God. However, we must feel that a rejoinder to these fearful counsellors was not the psalmist's real concern; that would hardly call for a psalm. More probably, he is concerned to put before the Lord the dangerous situation, and to press further for help by declaring his confidence in God's just rule. There were various ways of intercession; it was considered an inspired calling which needed gifts of boldness and of skill. It is the skill which we notice here; much is conveyed in a few verses, and all in imaginative and dramatic form. Although at first sight there is not much to clarify the singer's situation, comparison with preceding and with other psalms takes us some way. Images and phrases indicate that it comes from the same circle as many others in this 'Of David' group (cf. 3.2; 5.4–5; 7.1, 9, 10, 12; 10.14; 14.2; 17.2, also Ps. 4 for a rejoinder to the weak in faith). The events are drawn on a large scale – the foundations of world or national order in turmoil, judgement to come as fire and brimstone from heaven. So the psalmist may be a king who represents his people, and possibly is drawing near to the Lord at the sanctuary in hope of a strengthening vision before conflict (v. 7).

1–3   The imaginative scene of faint-hearted counsel and stalwart rejoinder provides indirectly the portrayal of peril and faith normal in lamenting prayers. No doubt actual experience is reflected. Counsellors have judged the situation hopeless, and flight to the rugged crags and caves of the Judean desert the only resort. As in Psalms 9–10, the enemies are depicted in the figure of villains who strike from the shadows at the innocent. The great scale of the assaults, however, is suggested in the phrase 'the foundations are destroyed' (cf. the world anarchy in 82.5). The term for the faithful or just person (*ṣaddiq*, v. 3b) sometimes, and perhaps here, alludes to the rightful king (cf. 5.12). The image of a bird for the soul was common (e.g. 1 Sam. 26.20 in LXX); Assyrian annals describe how a Babylonian king fled like a bird, and how King Hezekiah was shut up like a bird in the siege of Jerusalem.

4–7 The psalmist answers the counsel to flee with testimony to the Lord's just rule, which defends the humble and faithful against the cruel and violent. The 'throne' in the heavenly 'temple' or 'palace' (*hekal*) signifies the active reign that encompasses the world and (lit.) all the 'children of man', and responds to full knowledge of all that they do, testing and trying hearts like a refiner of metal. The awful power of volcanic flame and sulphur and scorching wind points to a might of judgement which must at last overwhelm wickedness. The final thoughts turn to the Lord's just nature as world sovereign and his love of doing saving acts; he will grant the one that is true-hearted to see his face (cf. 17.15; Matt. 5.8; Rev. 22.4). In that gift of vision is given also true life and salvation (Int. 6d). If this is granted to the psalmist, he will have strength to face the cruel darts and destroyers.

This small but striking psalm leads worshippers to pray with imagination. In the dramatic scene enacted before God, they may well think of the courage of Jesus, who strengthened his fearful disciples and went consciously into the dangers of Jerusalem. Often indeed the good foundations are overthrown, and hidden archers pierce the true of heart. But the psalm maintains faith that those who see the face of the Lord will be given courage to believe that his power and goodness will prevail.

Help us, Lord, to shelter in you and not flee away, to trust in your rule and not despair, and being found true of heart, to see the beauty of your face.

PSALM 12: The Silver-Pure Word of Salvation

For favour. Upon the eighth. Psalm. Of David.

1   Save, Lord, for there is not a faithful person left;
    the trustworthy have vanished from among earth's peoples.
2   They speak falsely to their neighbour;
    with flattering lips they speak, and a double heart.
3   May the Lord cut off all flattering lips,
    and the tongue that speaks great boasts.

4   For they say, With our tongue we will prevail;
     our lips fight for us – who will be our master?

5   For the plundering of the poor, for the groaning of the needy,
          now I will rise up, says the Lord;
     I will place the hunted one in safety.

6   The words of the Lord are words so pure –
          silver refined in a furnace,
     seven times purified to the ground.
7   You, Lord, will keep us,
     you will ever guard us from this generation.
8   On every side the wicked strut,
     as vileness is exalted among earth's peoples.

This is one of the few psalms of lament where the appeal is followed by an answering oracle (v. 5); this oracle in turn elicits an appreciative but still appealing response. So we have a complete liturgy of intercession in miniature. Some acute need is linked to the deceitful, untrustworthy ways of humankind (vv. 1, 8, lit. 'children of man'). It involves the plundering of society's poor, but, as in 7, 9–10 and 11, this may in part be a figure for conspiracy and aggression by foreign powers, and hence the lament about a universal falsehood. (For the heading 'Upon the eighth' see above on 6, also a lament.)

1–4 LXX begins: 'Save me, Lord', but the Hebrew has just 'Save, Lord', and the only indication of the psalmist's person is the 'us' probably to be read in v. 7. So he voices the need of the community, and expresses it at length under one selected aspect – the untrustworthiness that prevails on earth. The damaging deceit operates especially through speech which is outwardly 'smooth', but in fact comes from a 'double heart', like the weights of a fraudulent merchant, who deftly deceives with two sets in his bag, one for selling, one for buying (Deut. 25.13). The deceitful words are like a weapon of war; the literal 'Our lips are with us' means 'they fight for us', we trust in them for victory. With prophetic force, the psalmist invokes judgement on this brazen challenge to God's authority.

5 Complaining prayer generally sought an answering word, an oracle from the Lord, but it is quite rare for such an answer to be recorded (other examples are 60.6–8; 85.8; 108.7; see further my *Vision*, pp. 54–88). There was something of the prophetic office involved in the great moments of intercession, a calling and equipment to come near and wrestle; and of a piece with this was the transition to the task of bringing back a word of God. In some way it could happen that such a moment of inspiration became part of a psalm for continuing use. The original prayer and the answering promise of God represented a movement between earth and heaven which had enduring validity. The oracle promises immediate action by God, and it is interesting to see that again the community's need is expressed in one aspect, and one not really mentioned in the prayer. The need is now charactized by the 'plundering of the poor', 'the groaning of the needy', and a merciless pursuit ('the hunted one' – lit. 'one for whom they pant').

6–8 Praise of the Lord's words shows the difference from the deceiving speech prevalent on earth. They are pure as silver refined and flowing down through a duct, over and over again. The praise adds to the intercession – surely the Lord will be true to his word of salvation. The thought becomes explicit in v. 7, where there is some doubt about the object – 'them', 'him', or more likely 'us' (so a few manuscripts and LXX). And the note of supplication sounds still in v. 8, as the evil situation is depicted and raised to God. The description is still general, but vivid; all around the wicked parade, and what should be most despicable is most highly prized.

The situation lamented in this psalm may be difficult for the historian to determine, but it is presented in a way instantly recognizable to the sensitive soul in most periods. Faithfulness and truth are discounted, indeed they seem to have vanished. Words are used smoothly to deceive. The underlying spirit is of arrogance and self-worship. Vileness is glorified. Villains openly strut on every hand. And the result – most painful to the heart of God – is seen in cruelty to the weak. The cry of the hunted one pierces the heavens. To be saved from such a generation, the psalmist holds on to the precious word of God which does not flatter to deceive. Not in the 'children of man', he testifies, but here alone is hope, which in the end will not be disappointed.

Save, Lord, for your little ones are exploited and vileness is exalted; and help us to receive your words and hold them fast in a pure heart, that we may be defended from the guileful speech of the deceiver.

PSALM 13: When Suffering Seems Endless

For favour.   Psalm.   Of David.

1   How long, Lord, will you utterly forget me,
    how long will you hide your face from me?
2   How long shall I have anguish in my soul
        and sorrow in my heart all day,
    how long shall my enemy be exalted over me?
3   Look down and answer me, Lord my God;
    give light to my eyes, or I shall sleep in death,

4   and my enemy shall say, I have prevailed against him,
     and my foes rejoice that I am overthrown.

5   But I trust in your faithful love;
     may my heart rejoice in your salvation.

6   And I will sing of the Lord,
     that he has dealt so lovingly with me.

This may be a prayer for deliverance from grave sickness. Its style of lamentation is very ancient, the use of a repeated 'how long' being found earlier in Mesopotamia. The three references to enemies may reflect an idea that some have 'wished' the evil on the sufferer, and may be an indication of his responsible position, ever beset by foes.

1–4   The supplication begins with stress on the duration of the unrelieved suffering. With the four repetitions of 'How long' are other strong expressions of distress. The sufferer feels forgotten by God – 'utterly' (rather than RV 'for ever'); or the Lord has hidden his face, as though refusing the life-giving communion. The soul is full of 'anguish' (rather than RV 'counsel', *TRP*); the enemy rise in exultation. In v. 3 comes direct petition for the light of life. The eyes were often felt to be a measure of vitality, wasting or darkening in sorrow (cf. 6.7), brightening when God gives new life (cf. 19.8).

5–6   As often, a prayer that first pressed upon God by portraying the anguish passes on to a statement of trust, and also a promise to testify when salvation is given; the hopeful words are intended to reinforce the prayer, for how could the trust and the readiness to give thanks be ignored? So it is hardly correct to speak here of a change of mood, a resurgence of faith (cf. Spurgeon: 'What a change is here! The rain is over and gone ... The mercy-seat has so refreshed the poor weeper, that he clears his throat for a song.') Rather, the little psalm is a close-knit unity, that holds up to the Lord both the sense of unending pain and the unquenched hope in him alone. Appeal is made equally through the pain and the trust and the seed of thankful witness that waits to break into life.

Through long, long agony the psalmist holds on to the 'faithful love' (*ḥesed*) of the Lord, that love which lasts longer than any suffering. His psalm has continued to inspire sufferers with faith that through this *ḥesed*, this revelation of God's heart, and in his way and time, salvation will be given, calling forth the song of responding love.

Look with pity, Lord, on your servants who see no end to their sufferings; give light to their weary eyes, and help them to trust in your faithful love, until the song of thanksgiving can be sung and their hearts rejoice in your salvation.

PSALM 14: Longing for the Great Turning

For favour.   Psalm.   Of David.

1   The fools say in their heart, There is no God;
    they are corrupt and vile in all they do,
        there is no one that does good.
2   The Lord has looked down from heaven upon earth's peoples,
    to see if there is anyone acting wisely and seeking God.
3   But all have turned aside, all alike corrupted;
    there is no one that does good, not even one.

4   Are all the evildoers without understanding,
        that they eat up my people as though they ate bread,
    and do not call on the Lord?
5   But there shall they fear with great fear,
    for God is in the circle of the just.
6   Though you would confound the counsel of one who is poor,
    yet the Lord shall be his refuge.

7   O that the salvation of Israel were given from Zion!
    When the Lord turns the life of his people,
        Jacob shall rejoice and Israel be merry.

Another version is preserved as Psalm 53, the chief differences being in 14.5–6 as against 53.5. Both versions contain the final verse, which seems to clarify the subject of the psalm as national affliction. In Paul's quotation of the opening lines in Romans 3.10f., there is an addition of several lines; this is a chain of similar sentiments from Pss 5.9; 140.3; 10.9; Isa. 59.7, 8; Ps. 36.1. This supplementary passage found its way from Romans or from Paul's source back into Psalm 14 not only in Greek but also in two Hebrew manuscripts; so it passed into other versions, and was long familiar through the Book of Common Prayer. As in several preceding psalms (10, 12 etc.), the suffering is introduced from a particular angle, which obscures it somewhat for the historian. The general corruption of mankind is lamented – behaviour as if there were no God to take account of. The focus becomes clearer as God speaks of the oppression of 'my people'. Then there is mention of 'the circle of the just' and one that is 'poor, afflicted'. And finally, hope centres on renewal for 'Israel, Jacob' to be sent out from Zion. It seems, then, that the nation suffers from an oppression, conditions which eat into its moral fabric. The psalm well illustrates the closeness of psalmody to prophecy (Int. 2b), and our psalmist is able to tell of the Lord's looking down from heaven, with resultant thoughts and words. (Similar ideas may be noted in Isa. 59.3f.; Jer. 5.1f.; Hos. 4.2.)

1–3 Instead of direct lament, seeking to move God, we have an opening passage where psalmist and God concur about the corrupt behaviour evident throughout the earth. It is a prophetic insight, where the singer is caught up into God's own pain. He can even report how the Lord has searched for goodness throughout (lit.) 'the children of man', all peoples on earth, only to find that all have swerved aside from a life based on awe and love of God. The 'fool' is everywhere – prominent persons, of hard and ruthless disposition, who act continually as though they were their own sufficient god; that they 'say in their heart ...' means that in practice this is how they behave, irrespective of what they profess. (The Hebrew begins as singular 'fool', v. 1a, but becomes plural in v. 1b.)

4–6 The singer seems to voice the Lord's own words in a question that expresses amazement at the moral ignorance of the 'evildoers'. Here the focus has sharpened; rather than the fault of all humanity, it is the cruelty of certain oppressors which seizes attention. The victims are seen as 'my people' (the speaker here probably being the Lord), and also as 'the circle of the just' (RV, 'the generation of the righteous'), and 'the poor / afflicted one'. The psalmist, in prophetic style, can declare God's warning to the cruel, and his sure defence of the afflicted. In the midst of those who know his will, the Lord himself is present; the attackers will find more than they reckon on.

7 The conclusion is a response to the foregoing prophetic word (cf. 12.6–8). The yearning of the Lord's people is voiced: may salvation be given from the Lord's throne (mysteriously present in Zion, Int. 6f). And a vow is indicated; thankful worship will resound when the Lord 'turns the great turning' of his people. This last idiom is best grasped through the wonderful image linked to it in 126.4: as he brings the dry wadis of the southern wilderness to new life through the winter rains, their banks becoming lush with green and flowers, so he will restore the life of his people from the clutch of death to the fresh beauty of his kingdom.

The singer's thought has led through three fields of vision. First, there was the exposure of the human heart, the nature that is found throughout earth's peoples; failure in practice to heed God meant that all that was done became corrupted. Secondly, distinctions began to emerge; by some miracle, there was yet a people God would call 'mine', a circle or company that was 'just', looking to him, knowing his will; a people inevitably suffering from the ruthless. Thirdly, seen only in hope and faith, was a great vision of transformation, a world made new, when the Lord would send out salvation for his people and turn their deserts to life, beauty and joyful praise. For all their contrasts, these perceptions have been sustained down the ages. Entering into this psalm, the circle that looks to God knows that its loyalty is often precarious, raised by a miracle from the corruption of all the earth. In spite of their failures and sufferings, they believe that their Lord is in their midst, and, because of what he is, their hope stands fast, trusting that he will indeed bring about that great turning, and make all things well.

O Jesus, Word of the Father, and Saviour in the midst of the humble, we pray that all may know you, as your salvation goes out to turn earth's corruption to the beauty of life in your presence.

PSALM 15: At the Threshold

Psalm.   Of David.

1   Lord, who will be welcome in your tent,
     who may stay on your holy mountain?
2   One who walks whole,
     and ever does what is just;
     who speaks truth even in his heart,
3   and bears about no slander on his tongue;
     who does his fellow no harm,
     and raises no abuse against his neighbour;
4   who is lowly in his own eyes and humble,
     but honours those who fear the Lord;
     though his pledge prove to his disadvantage,
     he will not go back on his word;
5   he does not lend his money to make ruthless gain,
     and he takes no reward against the innocent.
     Whoever keeps to these words
     shall never be overthrown.

This has the pattern of a question to God relating to his sanctuary, followed by his answer, mediated by priest or prophet. Such an answer was called *tora* – authoritative teaching or ruling (cf. Mal. 2.5–7 and examples in Zech. 7.1f., 2 Sam. 21.1, Micah 6.6–8). The form and the topic are similar in 24.3–5 and Isaiah 33.14–16, and can also be compared with inscriptions of other peoples on the gates of places of worship, warning those who would enter of certain requirements of conduct. It is possible that Psalm 15, like 24, functioned in some processional entry of pilgrims to the holy place, though some scholars argue for a more general instruction. A few have connected it with royal ceremony, but the teaching seems of broader application than that applied to the king elsewhere, for example in 101.

The poetic structure, as against the traditional verse numbers, appears to set out the requirements in six couplets (as above). This would yield a list of twelve requirements, except that those falling under v. 4 may be counted as only two requirements, expressed with a whole couplet each. The number of requirements would then total ten, like the Ten Commandments (recited on ten fingers?). Some scholars (e.g. Craigie) indeed count five that are positive and five negative, but for this v. 4b would have to be translated as positive, which is dubious. We may rather think, as for 101, that the poet has been content to follow the general form of a ten- or twelve-point instruction without being too precise.

1   To the Lord himself the question is put: who may come into the holy place and abide so close to the holy presence? The thought would be focused on the entrance of pilgrims to the great central sanctuary and the 'sojourn' in and about Zion during the festal days. To come and receive blessing entailed preparation in confession and purification, and earnest thought about what the Lord required of his worshippers.

2   The answer is given – it is understood – in the name of the Lord. It begins to portray an individual who would be his welcome guest, someone who 'walks whole', living from day to day wholeheartedly for the Lord (cf. Prov. 28.18; Deut. 18.13; Matt. 5.48); and not just talking of what is good, but doing it. Sincerity and consistency mark this person, and truth is spoken not just with the lips, but in the heart.

3   This person does nothing hateful or injurious against a neighbour, not spreading slander or shouting abuse in taunts or rage.

4   My translation follows the tradition of the Targum, likewise BCP: 'he that setteth not by himself, but is lowly in his own eyes.' This understanding is stoutly defended by Delitzsch, who compares 1 Sam. 15.17 and 2 Sam. 6.22. But others translate: 'in whose eyes a base person is despised,' giving a more obvious contrast with the following line. The next couplet refers to a promise or sworn oath which the giver in time finds inconvenient or hurtful to himself; one who is pleasing to God will keep it nevertheless. (A simpler situation is given in LXX: 'He swears to his neighbour and does not change.')

5   Literally: 'He does not lend his money on interest', but such loans are seen in the context of extending help to fellow-citizens fallen into poverty and starvation, a common plight in a country of subsistence farming and uncertain rains. To make a profit out of this misery was prohibited by a sacred law against the charging of interest (Deut. 23.19–20), especially since the practice was sometimes deliberately used to bring about permanent disappropriation and enslavement. Finally, reference is made to the bribing of judges or witnesses to secure condemnation of the innocent, a practice often rife, though condemned by laws and prophets (Ex. 23.7, 8; Deut. 16.19). The concluding sentence draws it all together. A person keeping the foregoing requirements will never be 'moved' or 'thrown down'. In the first place, this promises a safe and secure resting in the Lord's dwelling; and beyond that, his sure support through all the circumstances of life.

The psalm brings home a striking selection of sacred teachings. On the threshold of the holy dwelling, the pilgrim is to ponder especially what the Lord requires in personal relations, for the health of individuals, families, and society. Here are laws of the heart, making for sincerity, humility, reliability, compassion and fairness. It is assumed that the pilgrim comes to a God who has first been known as gracious Saviour, but there is a pattern that this God commands for continuing fellowship, a pattern which must ever be taught afresh, so prone are his worshippers to neglect it. Positive and negative mingle in these requirements, each with its own usefulness. The positive holds up an inspiring ideal, the negative is challengingly specific.

Cassiodorus (cf. Int. 7g, h) describes the psalm as a divine decalogue, a spiritual psaltery of ten chords which only Christ could fulfil, and adds, 'Let us pray to him that we, who cannot of ourselves perform such acts, may do them by being enriched with his gift.' In the music of this 'psaltery' it would seem that the first clause gives the key-note, the ground-tone – the daily life that is 'whole', whole-hearted for the Lord, wholly given to him.

Lord, as ever and again we would cross the threshold to come and rest before your face, grant that we may take to heart your will for us to love our neighbour as ourselves.

PSALM 16: To Know the Path of Life

Atonement.   Of David.

1   Keep me, O God,
     for I take shelter in you.
2   I say: Lord, you are my Lord;
     I have no good apart from you.
3   As for spirits below and lords that others delight in,
4   many shall be the troubles of those who turn back after them.
     Their drink-offerings of blood I will not offer,
     nor will I take their names upon my lips.
5   The Lord is my portion and my cup;
     it is you that hold my lot.
6   My share has fallen in pleasant land;
     my heritage shines fair upon me.
7   I will bless the Lord that he counsels me,
     and in the depth of the night instructs my heart.
8   I will set the Lord always before me;

> with him at my right hand, I shall not be overthrown.
> 9   Therefore my heart shall rejoice, and my glory be glad,
>   and my flesh shall abide in safety.
> 10 For you will not abandon my soul to the land of death;
>   you will not hand over your faithful one to see the abyss.
> 11 You will cause me to know the path of life,
>   fullness of joys before your face,
>   and pleasures in your right hand for ever.

This prayer for the Lord's protection is supported by eloquent statements of loyalty and close fellowship with God. This relationship and also the hope of deliverance from death are expressed in such heightened terms, that we may well think the one praying is a king, Yahweh's elect and beloved. The heading *miktam* may mean 'Atonement' and refer to ceremonies on a national day of penitence and intercession in time of peril (Mowinckel, *Psalms* II, p. 209). Following LXX, however, some think of an 'inscription', supposing the psalm to have been carved on stone (so Dahood and Seybold; the same heading is found over 56–60).

1–4   Direct prayer in this psalm is brief and comes at the very outset (v. 1). It is followed by an avowal of exclusive loyalty; the psalmist calls Yahweh alone his master (*adon*), and will have no other god. Further, he specifically renounces any worship of chthonic deities (literally 'holy ones of the earth / underworld'), cults which some reverted to in dangerous times. On worshippers of such, he declares, fall many 'troubles', a word in Hebrew close to that for 'idols'; and he vows never to pour out libations in such cults or invoke the names of these spirits.

5–6   The psalmist's close bond with the Lord is now described in striking images. The first resembles something that was said of the priesthood (Num. 18.20; Deut. 10.9; Josh. 13.14): others had territories as their portion to live off, but the priests, as it were, had the Lord, in that they lived from a share of the offerings. The psalmist is here affirming that he lives only from the grace of the Lord, and only from him comes the cup of salvation (cf. 116.13). The following images also relate to the sharing out of land. By the casting of lots, borders could be determined and marked with lines or ropes; the psalmist means that his destiny and all that makes up his life is in the power of the Lord to give and shape. And he adds that his share is indeed beautiful – the gift that is the Lord himself.

7–9   The singer is thankful for the Lord's counsel and instruction, and mentions receiving it in the night-watches ('heart' here is lit. 'kidneys', regarded as a seat of wisdom and feeling). 'Counsel' was thought vital for a king, and there may also be an allusion to royal 'incubation', sleep at the sanctuary in hope of a guiding dream-revelation; perhaps indeed the psalm was in preparation for such a visitation (Int. 6e). Looking always to the Lord, knowing him always close, the singer has confidence that he will not be cast down. In joy and tranquillity his whole being will find peace – his 'heart', 'flesh', and 'glory' (some alter the Hebrew vowel to make this last term 'liver', but the reference could be to a royal glory, the king's soul).

10–11   The expression of trust and confidence, adding force to the opening prayer, now reaches a wonderful climax. God will not abandon to death his *ḥasid*, his covenant-partner, bonded to him in faithful love. A common interpretation is that the reference here is to deliverance from a current danger; he is not to die on this occasion. This would suit the usual trend of Old Testament thought (Int. 60), but it is possible that, beyond this, the passage is coloured by ancient ideas of the continuing life of kings – one made so close by God, called his 'Son', filled with abundant life, would in some way ever remain with God, and this royal destiny would work for the benefit of all his people. Such thought is not spelt out, but seems to shine through several passages (e.g. 21.2–7; 45.2, 6; 61.6–8; 72.5; 110.4; my *Kingship*, pp. 160–8). The train of thought in our psalm would be that deliverance in a present crisis (v. 1) would confirm the king's position in the Lord's choice and favour, and so maintain his hope of everlasting communion. Such an interpretation fits with the fact that in New Testament times the psalm was understood to refer to the new 'David', the royal Messiah and is applied by the apostles to the risen life of Christ (Acts 2.24f.; 13.34f.). The conclusion (v. 11) describes fulfilment of the joy in God expressed in vv. 2, 5–6. So present knowledge of the Lord as the surpassing good will blossom to perfection on the eternal path in the nearer light of his face.

The psalmist, praying first for God's protection, passes on to affirm his devotion. The Lord alone is his master and God. Recourse to other powers is abhorred. The Lord alone is the very ground of his life, source of sustenance, delight, counsel and instruction. On the Lord he sets his gaze, and trusts that he will not forsake him. In present danger and even, it seems, at the end of earthly life, he trusts that the Lord will bring him through to the path of life, away from the abyss of death, into the fullness of unending joy before God's face. The emphasis of the song is upon total devotion to the Lord. Wanting the Lord alone, the singer gains in and from the Lord all that is good. Having this God only, he has all, and for ever. Following Acts 2 and 13, the church has seen this psalm as especially prophetic of Christ's resurrection. 'Who is the Path of Life but the Lord himself?' asks Augustine, and proceeds to make relation also to the ascension and to the believer's destiny through Christ.

Lord Jesus, our portion and our cup, our heritage that shines fair upon us, keep us and counsel us; and by the power of your resurrection cause us to know the path of everlasting life and joy before your face.

PSALM 17: The Face and Form of God

Prayer.   Of David.

1   Hear a just cause, Lord, attend to my cry;
    listen to my prayer from lips without deceit.
2   May judgement for me go out from your presence,
    may your eyes look on what is right.
3   You shall try my heart, when you visit me in the night;
    test me, and you shall find in me no evil purpose.
4   My mouth has not transgressed for rewards of man;
    I have kept to the word of your lips.
5   My steps have held to the way of your commandment;
    my feet have not stumbled from your paths.
6   As I call to you, O God, surely you will answer me;
    turn your ear to me and hear my words.
7   Show the marvels of your faithful love,
    O saviour of those who take refuge
        from rebels against your hand.
8   Keep me as the little one mirrored in your eye;
    hide me in the shadow of your wings,
9   from the wicked that ravage me,
    from my enemies that greedily surround me.
10 They have closed their heart to all feeling;
    they speak in arrogance with their mouth.
11 Now they hem in our steps all around;
    they set their eyes to spread into the land.
12 They are like a lion thirsting for the prey,
    a hunting lion crouching in a covert.
13 Rise up, Lord, confront him, and subdue him,
    by your sword deliver my soul from the evil one.
14 They shall be slain by your hand, Lord, slain;
    their portion shall be to go suddenly from this world.
    But your treasured ones you will replenish,
    and they shall be satisfied with children,
        and have increase to leave to their young.
15 I, found true, will see your face;
    awaking, I shall be replenished by the vision of you.

This resembles 16 in several details (cf. Kirkpatrick), and probably comes from
the same circle and from a similar situation. The psalmist prays urgently for
deliverance on the grounds that his cause is just, the enemy ruthless and
rebellious against God. While his cause seems to be that of his people also
(plurals in vv. 7, 11), he claims an intimate relation with God (vv. 8, 15). We

may well think, therefore, of a king who is praying in some national emergency. The enemies seek to plunder and encircle, and have 'set their eyes to spread into the land' (vv. 9–11). So this 'royal prayer' (as we may render the title) takes up the Lord's promises and invitations to his Anointed, and probably is made in connection with vigil and sleep in the sanctuary, in hope of the Lord's drawing near to give his embrace of support and word of blessing and victory (v. 15, Int. 6e).

1–2 With his 'cry' and 'prayer', the supplicant calls for the Lord's favourable attention and decision, in confidence that the cause is 'just' and 'right' and uttered by truthful lips.

3–5 In furtherance of this claim, the psalmist looks to God's testing of his heart (the Hebrew perfect tenses for this 'trying' and 'testing' are best taken as future or precative, cf. Dahood). He expects this testing 'in the night', probably referring to the forthcoming night to be spent in the sanctuary; the hoped-for blessing must be preceded by God's trial of his sincerity. And he solemnly affirms that he has kept to the paths of the Lord's requirements.

6–9 In his central petition, the psalmist now asks for the wonders of God's *ḥesed*, the saving acts that spring from his committed love. King and people would shelter in this saviour, away from those that rise up against the divine rule, arrogant and wreaking havoc. For king or for beloved people of God the tender image is appropriate: they would be cherished as 'the little one, daughter of an eye', the tiny figure reflected in the pupil when someone is very close, virtually as a lover who looks into the beloved's eyes, or as the babe at the breast who looks into the eye of the mother. And another remarkable image follows: the psalmist would shelter in God as the fledgling nestles under its mother's wing.

10–12 Further description of the enemies adds to the urgency of the appeal. Pillaging, encircling (v. 9), they have closed off their organs of reason and feeling, and speak only in self-vaunting arrogance. Having encompassed the borders, they prepare to 'spread into the land' (the same phrase as in Num. 21.22; so Birkeland, p. 255). They keep watch on their prey like a young lion ready to spring from hiding.

13–14 A bold prayer now invokes the Lord to action, to rise up and come with divine sword against the evil one (cf. 3.7; 7.6; 9.19; 10.12). The translation of v. 14 is so uncertain that it is almost best left out of account. Some take it as calling for judgement on the whole brood of the wicked (so NRSV); others as depicting the enemies as made wealthy by God (AV, RV). My translation finds a contrast – a hope that the aggressors be suddenly swept away, while the Lord's treasured ones be granted well-being and continuance.

15   The psalmist concludes in hope of being granted vision of the face and form of God. In the depth of the night, the Lord, he prays, will draw near and by his revelation fill him with the blessing and strength to go out to the hard task ahead. On awaking after such a visitation, he will indeed be (lit.) 'satisfied', deeply replenished.

It is remarkable how the most intimate and tender expression of devotion, the most intense and beautiful spiritual moment, is linked here to the harsh affairs of the world. Faced with terrible foes that surround and pillage his land and prepare to overrun it, the psalmist, who is surely the king, is above all concerned to draw near to God; to know such nearness, to see the beauty of God's self-revelation, this is to triumph over the world's wickedness, but not to run away from it. He speaks of a profound 'satisfaction', and would no doubt agree with Augustine's comment here that 'without God, all is emptiness'. And for this satisfaction he looks to the God who comes in the night. In time of fear and loss, God comes through the darkness, and by the beauty of his presence drives away fear and bestows the fullness of his grace.

With various terms – 'glory', 'name', 'face', 'form' – the Old Testament speaks of the revealed presence of God, the mysterious, the utterly beyond, who yet wills to makes himself known and near in blessing. With these terms the New Testament finds a way of understanding his coming and self-revelation in Christ, 'the effulgence of his glory, the impress of his substance' (Heb. 1.3), 'Christ who is the image of God' (2 Cor. 4.4). While the psalm stresses the need for truth of heart in the near approach to God, Christian thought turns to Christ as the pure one through whom disciples too can enter the most holy presence. In the name of Jesus they can shelter under the protecting wings, look into the eye of the beloved, be satisfied with the face and form of God. Into the last night also, the night of death, they can go in sure hope of that encounter and a glorious awakening.

Eternal Father, receive us through the purity of your Son Jesus; and keep us then as the little one mirrored in your eye, hide us under the shadow of your wings, and grant that, through vision of you in all our darkness, we may be satisfied with your ever-lasting peace.

PSALM 18: Prefiguring the Victory over Death

For favour. Of the Servant of the Lord. Of David. Who spoke to the Lord the words of this song on the day when the Lord delivered him from the hand of all his enemies and from the hand of Saul. And he said:

1   I love you, Lord, my strength.
2   The Lord is my crag, my fortress, and my deliverer,
      my God, my rock where I take shelter,
      my shield, the horn of my salvation and my stronghold.
3   With anguished prayer I cried to the Lord,
      and I was saved from all my enemies.
4   The cords of death entwined me;
      the torrents of destruction overwhelmed me.
5   The cords of darkness closed around me;
      the snares of death took hold of me.
6   In my distress I called to the Lord,
      and I cried to my God for help.
      From his temple he heard my voice,
      and my cry came before him into his ears.
7   Then the earth trembled and shook;
      the foundations of the mountains quivered,
         and shook because he was angry.
8   Smoke rose from his nostrils,
         and devouring fire from his mouth;
      hot coals blazed out from him.
9   Then he parted the heavens and came down,
      and thick darkness was under his feet.
10   He mounted a kerub and flew;
      he came swooping on the wings of the wind.
11   He made darkness his covering round about him,
      dark waters and heavy clouds his pavilion.
12   From the brightness of his presence, his clouds blazed out
      with hailstones and coals of fire.
13   And the Lord thundered out of heaven;
      God the Most High sounded his voice.
14   He sent out his arrows and scattered them;
      he shot his lightnings and put them to flight.
15   The springs of the ocean were seen,
      and the foundations of the earth uncovered,
      at your rebuke, O Lord,
      at the blast of the breath of your displeasure.
16   He reached from on high and took me;
      he drew me out of the mighty waters.

17 He delivered me from my cruel enemy,
    and from my foes that were too strong for me.
18 They came upon me in the day of my trouble,
    but the Lord was my upholder.
19 And he brought me into a place of freedom;
    he rescued me, because he delighted in me.
20 The Lord rewarded me for my just dealing;
    according to the cleanness of my hands he recompensed me.
21 For I had kept the ways of the Lord,
    and had not wickedly gone away from my God.
22 For all his judgements were before me,
    and I did not put away his statutes from me.
23 And I was wholehearted with him,
    and from my failings I guarded myself.
24 So the Lord rewarded me for my fair dealing,
    for the cleanness of my hands before his eyes.
25 With one who is faithful you show yourself faithful;
    with one who is true you show yourself true.
26 With one who is pure you show yourself pure;
    with one who is devious you show yourself perverse.
27 For you will save a humble people,
    but haughty eyes you will bring low.
28 You will light my candle;
    the Lord my God will make my darkness to be light.
29 For by you I shall run at a host of foes;
    with the help of my God I shall leap over the wall.
30 As for God, his way is true;
      the word of the Lord is tried in the fire;
    he is a shield to all who shelter in him.
31 For who is God but the Lord,
    and who is the rock except our God?
32 It is God who girds me with strength,
    and appoints for me a way that is true.
33 He makes my feet like the feet of a deer,
    and makes me firm upon the heights.
34 He trains my hands for battle,
    and my arms shall bend even a bow of bronze.
35 And you have given me the shield of your salvation;
    your right hand upholds me,
      and your grace has made me great.
36 You enlarge my strides beneath me,
    yet my ankles do not falter.
37 I shall pursue my enemies and overtake them,
    and shall not turn back till they are at an end.
38 I shall smite them so that they cannot rise;
    they shall fall beneath my feet.

39   You have girded me with strength for the battle;
     you will subdue my foes beneath me.
40   You will make my enemies turn their backs upon me,
     and I shall make an end of those that are set against me.
41   They shall cry out but find no helper,
     cry even to the Lord, but he will not answer them.
42   And I will make them as dust on the wind;
     I will clear them out as mire from the streets.
43   You will deliver me from the strife of peoples;
     you will make me the head of the nations.
     People I have not known shall serve me,
44   and as soon as they hear me they will obey me;
     the strangers will humble themselves before me.
45   The alien hosts will lose their strength,
     and come trembling out of their strongholds.
46   The Lord lives, and blessed be my rock,
     and praised be the God my salvation,
47   the God who gives me victory,
     and subdues the peoples under me.
48   You that save me from my enemies,
        you will exalt me above those that rise against me;
     you will deliver me from the violent man.
49   Therefore I will give you thanks, Lord, among the nations,
     and make music to your name,
50   the One who gives salvation to his king,
     and shows faithful love to his Anointed,
        to David and his seed for ever.

Another form of this great psalm appears in 2 Samuel 22, and much of our long heading seems to have been borrowed from there. Its earlier form will have ended at 'Of David' and thus have been identical with the heading of 36. Our psalm's language and martial vigour could well suit the period of David's reign or soon after. A king gives thanks most warmly and poetically for salvation and exaltation. Some translators maintain the reference to past deliverance throughout, but it is also possible, and perhaps preferable, to move to a future prospect from v. 28 and especially in vv. 37–45, as in my translation. In any case, the psalm does not really fit the account given in the long heading. It does not describe the hostility of Saul or the many and varied military campaigns of David's reign. Some therefore explain it as a thanksgiving after one particular victory; but there is nothing to identify the occasion, and tradition about the psalm did not recall it. It may be, therefore, that the great event of 'salvation' was not military but liturgical. Ceremonies installing kings or renewing their reigns were full of poetry and imagination, verging on drama. The rites had a sacramental character, divine action endowing the king with salvation and inculcating the ideal of just rule in obedience to God. In such a context our psalm would have unfolded the meaning of some great rite (perhaps baptismal, in the caverns of the spring Gihon) – how the Creator had raised his chosen servant and 'Son' from the waters of death, and girded him with strength to rule the peoples; but all on the basis and condition of purity, truth, justice and humility.

1–3 The king begins his testimony and thanksgiving with a warm declaration of love (cf. 116.1). With a series of images, he characterizes the Lord as his faithful and mighty saviour. The 'horn' is an image from a great animal such as the wild ox (Deut. 33.17) and represents the saviour's power to drive away the foes. Verse 3 appears to begin 'Praiseworthy', or with change of vowels 'Praising' (so LXX); but if we derive from another root (Hiphil of *yll: mehelil*) we have the more suitable sense 'wailing / lamenting'.

4–6 The king describes how he called to the Lord when in the grip of death, and the Lord in his heavenly abode heard his voice. This 'death', however, is seen poetically as a personification of all that is opposite to life, and is called 'death', 'Belial' (perhaps 'the swallower') and 'Sheol' (imagined as the subterranean land of darkness and the dead). The king tells how, like a deadly hunter, this terrible power set upon him with traps and cords to draw him into its abyss.

7–15 Terrible as was this enemy 'death', more terrible by far to all the forces of darkness was the Saviour. The poetry strives to convey the fearsome will and power of God to rescue his Chosen One. The imagery draws on the mighty irruptions of nature – storms of hail, thunder and lightning, earth-quakes, volcanic terrors. The 'kerub' is a personification of the storm-wind – a winged heavenly steed, part lion, part human in form. Riding this creature through the skies, the Lord came thundering and flaming through the sky-vault and down upon the foe. The whole world was shaken, and the ocean driven apart by the blast of his thunderous battle-roar.

16–19 For the ancient poets, the 'mighty waters' were closely associated with death and Sheol. They were part of the chaos that the Creator had to conquer in order to bring them into the living order. Seen here in their former character, they represent the king's 'cruel enemy', the foes too strong for him, eager to swallow him up. From their surging waves, in the very jaws of the underworld, the Lord drew him up and set him in 'a wide place', a place of freedom. Such was the salvation of the one in whom the Lord 'delighted', his chosen and beloved Son and servant, his anointed king (cf. 2 Sam. 15.26; 1 Kings 10.9; Isa. 42.1; Pss. 22.8; 41.11; Mark 1.11).

20–29 The psalm now teaches God's requirement of justice and humility in king and people. The matter is seen in a context and from an angle different from those of St Paul's statement, 'While we were yet sinners, Christ died for us' (Rom. 5.8). The psalm aims to bring home with the utmost emphasis to kings and to the powerful people around them that God's support is for those who are just and true and humble before him. This is all the clearer if the text expounded part of the royal rites. It is not as though an individual here professed his virtue, but rather we have a liturgical model of what God requires in the rulers who serve him – care of the poor, hatred of corruption, a walking in God's way, close and responsive to him. In vv. 25–7 the model is developed to cover the whole people, no doubt with people of wealth and power especially in mind. They too, like the king, are not to expect to retain God's favour and support if they go against all that he loves. The evil they do will return upon them. In vv. 28–9 the king pictures the effect of his deliverance, and one can easily interpret his hopes as based on the meaning of a foregoing sacrament; God has in symbol 'saved' him and confirmed his choice of him, and so the king looks forward to having the divine help in struggles that lie ahead. In times of darkness God will light his 'candle' (the picture will be of a lamp made of a wick set in a saucer of oil). It is a picture of one who has to go through much darkness, but whose little light is sufficient because it is lit by the Lord. Through God this warrior will not fear to run at a whole troop of foes, and a mighty city wall will be no obstacle to him.

30–45 Before the king unfolds further what the Lord's salvation will mean to him, he takes up again the wider application. To all who shelter in the Lord there is a sure promise; and his way is always true ('perfect'), his word pure as precious metal from the furnace (cf. 12.6), utterly reliable. Of all the powers that may be named as gods, only Yahweh ('the Lord') is truly God. 'Rock' is a title frequently used for the Lord (Deut. 32.4, 15, 18, 30, 31; 1 Sam. 2.2; Ps. 19.14), indicating his might and his unchanging readiness to protect. Fleeing to this rock for shelter is an image for trusting in the Lord alone. From this refuge the king will be able to go out and face the most terrible foes, given by God all that he needs for victory. In v. 35 'your grace' is more literally 'your humility', but some scholars prefer to adjust the vowels to give the sense 'your affliction / correction', or 'your response'. The language of conquest becomes fearful, especially in v. 42; as in royal 2.9 and 110.6, the text is worded to express the utmost certainty of the defeat of the forces that withstand God's kingdom. The sacraments bestowing ultimate victory on the Lord's Anointed meant to bestow it with no uncertain power. The language, like a prophet's symbolic action, already strikes the blow against evil.

46–50 'The Lord lives!' is a cry resembling that used in more ancient times to celebrate the triumph of the god of life and growth over the powers of death. In its present context it echoes the theme of vv. 4–19, the Lord's victory over death when he saved his Anointed; but it may still be a clue to a link with the ceremonies of the autumn festival, when proclamation was made of the Lord's reign and the victory of life. The king gives thanks and testimony 'among the nations', exalting the name of the Lord in the melody of psalms. Thus the king's salvation has a universal context. It is a central moment in God's work with his world (cf. the citation in Rom. 15.9). From so rich an experience of God's faithful love, the widest testimony must be made, that all may come to believe, obey, and worship the Lord alone.

The psalm is a testimony to the God who gives salvation to his king, showing faithful love to his Anointed, keeping his promise to the house of David for ever. This 'king', belonging to the Lord, is presented as an ideal figure, whole and true of heart, living in God's ways. History was to tell of the terrible end that befell the dynasty in Jerusalem, and blame was laid on the later kings of the line. The religious tradition, however, continued to believe that God's faithfulness, his *ḥesed*, would not fail, and would be fulfilled in one of David's seed who was yet to come. The psalm itself gives a fine foundation for such messianic interpretation in the way it depicts the relation of the Lord to his Anointed, the mission of this Anointed, and the nature of the suffering and salvation. Particulars of history, of local wars and enemies, fade away. Here is the Lord's Son and servant, appointed to rule for God in God's kingdom, plucked from the terrible waters of death, as God shakes the cosmos and blasts and scatters the forces of chaos. So, as it were in a vision, the Lord's Anointed is raised to supremacy and the sureness of his victorious reign with God is powerfully emphasized.

Christian interpreters have made connections with the baptism, passion, and exaltation of Christ and the victory over the satanic hosts. The assurance of the victory over evil, through the faithfulness of the Lord, is prized as the psalm's great message. But many details, too, found application. How should those who have been blessed by the 'humility' of God not also walk humbly themselves (vv. 27, 35)? How should those rescued from the torrents of Belial and the cords of death not also in their turn give thanks and sing of the wonder of the Lord to all people? And though they are presently surrounded by much darkness, they hold a candle, a little lamp, lit by the Lord himself, which is enough to make a path of brightness through the darkness (v. 28). How should they also not love their saviour, glad indeed to find all their strength in him (v. 1)? It is with this thought that a Gregorian antiphon set the theme for the psalm's recital: 'I will love you, Lord, my strength.'

O God, who drew your faithful Son from the waters of death, give us through him the desire of loving you; and send forth your arrows to disperse our enemies, that their hearts may be turned, and we with them may ever make melody to your name.

PSALM 19: The Heavens and the Heart

For favour.   Psalm.   Of David.

1   The heavens are telling the glory of God,
    and the sky-vault recounts the work of his hands.
2   One day pours out the story to the next,
    one night to another unfolds the knowledge.
3   They use no earthly speech or words;
    their voice cannot be heard.
4   Yet their music goes out through all the earth,
    and their words to the end of the world.
5   He has put a tent among them for the sun,
    which comes out like a bridegroom from his bower,
        and rejoices as a champion to run the track.
6   At one end of the heavens is its rising,
        and its circuit passes over their farthest bound;
    and nothing is hidden from its heat.
7   The Lord's teaching is perfect, reviving the soul;
    the Lord's testimony is trustworthy, making the simple wise.
8   The Lord's precepts are right, and gladden the heart;
    the Lord's command is radiant, giving light to the eyes.
9   The fear of the Lord is pure, and continues for ever;
    the Lord's commandments are true and altogether right,
10 more desirable than gold, even much fine gold,
    and sweeter than honey, flowing from the comb.
11 Your servant also has light from them;
    in keeping them there is great reward.
12 Who can discern their unwitting errors?
    O cleanse me from my hidden faults.
13 Hold back your servant also from deliberate sins,
        may they not rule over me;
    then I shall be whole, and innocent of great offence.
14 May the words of my mouth find favour,
        and the music of my heart rise before you,
    Lord, my rock and my redeemer.

Metre, style and topic change abruptly at v. 7, and some scholars have preferred to speak of two psalms, 19A (vv. 1–6) and 19B (vv. 7–14), which deal
respectively with wonders of the heavens and with the perfection of the law
of the Lord. However, the two parts are united in all ancient tradition and
would seem incomplete on their own. There are several indications of unity,
especially the use in the second part of sun-imagery to glorify God's teaching,
and so linking with the portrayal of the sun in vv. 4b–6. Read as a whole, the

psalm in fact has an inexhaustible richness of theme, making it one of the greatest treasures of religious devotion. We may best think of a psalmist who was deeply familiar with ancient hymnody on the lines of vv. 1–6, and who was also familiar with a style of appreciating the Lord's teaching with use of several parallel terms for it ('precepts', 'commandments' etc.). Meditating with his harp or lyre in the open court of the temple as night gave way to day (cf. 8.3; 57.8; 108.2; 130.6), he draws on familiar words from deep within to express his experience of God in the wonders of the heavens and the salvation that comes with his word. Like an emblem of the Lord's revelation in his teaching, the sun has arisen; the priests around him are busy with the morning offerings, and he too offers up 'for favour' the music of his meditation (v. 14). The date of the completed psalm is judged from the nature of the special praise of the Lord's teaching (vv. 7–10). This anticipates the more developed treatment of 119, and has some affinity (in spirit and in the use of synonyms) with Deuteronomy and its kindred works. A late post-exilic dating seems unjustified, and it may be best (especially in view of the psalm's position between royal psalms, and cf. 18.30) to think of the middle or late monarchy.

1–4a In profound meditation, the psalmist has become aware of what the ear of itself cannot hear – the singing of the heavens, the sky-vault, and all their lights. They have their being and their orderly and beautiful functions as they in their own way adore their Creator, and hand on within their own kind a testimony to his mighty work, a testimony of praise and thanksgiving passed down from the elements that first witnessed the working of his hands. Down the succession in the species, from day to day, from night to night, the testimony is borne, an inspired singing which bubbles and overflows as, by divine force, the mystery is shown. Their music fills the world, indeed the cosmos, but we do not hear its melody or understand its story. Only an enraptured soul, like that of the psalmist, may become aware that it goes out through all existence, sustaining the gaze of all the elements towards their Creator.

4b–6 The present Hebrew seems to mean that the tent which God has set up for the sun (to rest in at night) is in the remote heavens, where nights and days too have their home (cf. Job 38.19–20). But the context makes a small emendation very plausible (changing *bhm* 'in them' to *bym* 'in the sea'); the thought would be of the sun, having set and passed through the underworld, resting in a pavilion in the ocean before emerging on the eastern horizon. The comparisons with a bridegroom and an athlete almost merge. Still today in some Arab lands the newly-wed comes out of the nuptial chamber, where the marriage has been consummated, to great acclaim and a celebratory procession. Our poet sees the rising sun also come forth with joy and ardour, to pass on his way like a champion runner, happy in the strength God has given him. Such an extended, poetical and enthusiastic depiction of the sun is unusual in Hebrew literature. We may contrast the avoidance of the very word 'sun' in Genesis 1.16, and the terse reference in Psalm 104.19. The passage thus takes on a special significance for the thought of the psalm as a whole. The first thought must be how this wonderful sun is in itself a tribute to the Creator, who made it and provided for its marvellous function. But thought is also prepared for the sun-like qualities of the Lord's law and teaching – whole and unblemished, life-reviving, gladdening, constant and enduring, guardian of justice, illuminating and so making wise (cf. the sun-imagery for God's revelation in Deut. 33.2f.; Isa. 51.4; 60.1–3; Zeph. 3.5; Mal. 4.2).

7–10 In vv. 7–9 there are six lines built on the same pattern and metre, praising the Lord's teaching or law, which is named in six synonyms. Some written and early form of the 'law through Moses' may well have been in mind as focus of life lived in the way of the Lord, but it is not specified as such. The psalmist was content to present it as Yahweh's teaching and commandment, sent out, as it were in great rays, to give life, light and joy. With each synonym the name 'Yahweh' is emphatically spelt out as the governing word of the construction ('tora-of-Yahweh' etc.), and these six repetitions are the more striking as God has previously been named only once, and that as 'El' (v. 1, cf. Int. 6b, c). We have the impression of the Lord in action, the Lord making a claim upon his creatures, the Lord giving authoritative guidance, but all for their good and for their happiness; it is all very far from 'the Law' as an absolute, which many commentators loosely speak of here and in 119.

The six synonyms are *tora* (law, teaching, guidance), *'edut* (testimony, solemn assurance), *piqqudim* (precepts, ordinances), *mișwa* (command), *yir'a* (fear – the pious way taught by the Lord; but the original reading may perhaps have been *imrat*, word, promise, cf. 119.38), *mishpatim* (rules, commandments). The utterance they denote is praised as 'whole, perfect' and 'bringing back the soul' (restoring and refreshing life); 'trustworthy' and 'making even the simple wise'; 'straight, plain, true' and 'making the heart glad'; 'radiant' and 'brightening the eyes'; 'pure, clear' and 'lasting for ever'; 'truth, reliability' and 'altogether right'. The total picture is of the Lord's word, ruling and teaching with authority, but faithfully bestowing the blessings of light, life, wisdom and joy. And v. 10 gathers up the mood of appreciation and love by comparison with gold and honey: the utterance of the Lord to his world and his people is utterly precious and desirable, sweet and beautiful. In all this praise one can feel the effect of the preceding portrayal of the sun. Here indeed is the sun of the soul, the true light of all existence – radiant and unblemished, pure and clear, golden and sweet (cf. Eccles. 11.7), enduring (cf. 72.5,17; 89.37; 148.6), reviving, enlightening, gladdening.

11–14 The meditation has led the psalmist ever closer to the God who knows and meets every one of his creatures – from the Creator of the cosmic order, to the Lord who rules and blesses through his word, and now to the bond with this one worshipper, 'your servant'. First, the psalmist testifies from his own experience that the Lord's commandments have given him light (*nizhar* here 'illumined' rather than RV 'warned') and much reward. But close to his Lord, he feels his unworthiness. May God cleanse him from sin which has crept into him unawares, and may he restrain him from deliberate offences, so easily committed in the heat of the moment (*zedim* lit. 'seething ones', less likely here 'arrogant people'). His longing is to be, by God's grace, 'whole' in obedience and in love of his Lord. So he has passed from contemplation of night sky, dawning, rising sun, the light of the Lord's word, to prayerful encounter with the Lord himself. He has embodied his meditation in string music and song, and offers it up to find 'favour', acceptance, just as the priests are sending up their morning offerings also 'for favour'. So his music rises, with the song of his lips and the inner melody of the heart (*higgayon* denotes reverberating music rather than RV's 'meditation', cf. 9.16; 92.3). The concluding thought is in the deepest reaches of contemplation: the immediate knowledge of the Lord as 'my rock and my redeemer', the one who saves from perils and from sin, and through his faithful care gives true life in all its goodness.

The marvel of this psalm lies somewhere in its connection of the vast natural phenomena with the individual's moral way. There is perception of a Creator whom the bodies and lights and darks of the heavens revere; what a revelation, what a rapture to know of their melodious outpouring of testimony! There is appreciation of the beneficial and beautiful word of the Lord, that orders and restores the life of his servants. And there is a prayerful communion with him, the individual's rock and redeemer. Through all these runs the thread of contemplation, a thread indeed to guide one with meaning and fulfilment through the vast and complex world. And to the one who gives all, something of beauty in music and poetry, something pleasing to him, is offered up again. The psalmist indeed has found the place of sweet light and gladness.

Interpreters in the church for many centuries found here figures of the apostles who preached through all the earth (vv. 1–4a, cited on these lines in Rom. 10.18), then of the incarnation (vv. 4b–6), then of the commandments of Christ (v. 7f.). Christians today still honour their Lord in the psalm with contemplation of him as the Word by whom all was created, and who was further revealed in the Gospel as the Word who saves and directs, cleanses and revives, giving gladness and light. And still the psalm may lead them into the rapture of knowing the cosmic fellowship of praise, where humans are but one kind in the vast array that revere the Creator, and where, like St Francis, they may extend their love to their Brother Sun and their Sister Moon, and even welcome their Sister Death.

Word of the Father, adored by the skies, their lights and their darks, grant us so to embrace your law, that we may be cleansed from all our sins and filled with your light; and so may we ever praise you as our sure rock and faithful redeemer.

PSALM 20: The Name that Saves

For favour. Psalm. Of David.

1   The Lord answer you on the day of distress;
    the name of the God of Jacob set you up on high.
2   May he send you help from the holy place,
    and out of Zion may he uphold you.
3   May he remember all your offerings,
    and receive your sacrifice with favour. *[Pause]*
4   May he grant you the purpose of your heart,
    fulfilling all your counsel.
5   May we rejoice in your salvation,
        and in the name of our God set up our banners;
    the Lord fulfil all your petitions.
6   Now I know that the Lord will save his Anointed;
    he shall answer him from his holy heavens,
        with the saving strength of his right hand.
7   Some look to their chariots and some to their horses,
    but we will call upon the name of the Lord our God.
8   They shall stumble and fall,
    but we will rise and stand secure.
9   Lord, save the king.
    May he answer us on the day when we call.

With a prospect of battle ahead, the psalmist, with prophetic power, addresses the king with a blessing or indirect prayer, that he may have the mighty help of God. It may well be that the occasion is a 'day of distress' as mentioned in v. 1; the king has offered up prayer and sacrifice (vv. 5, 3) and commended his plan to the Lord (v. 4), and the prophetic psalmist receives a word or sign of acceptance from the Lord (v. 6), evoking statements of faith. Comparison for all this procedure can be made with the story of 2 Chron. 20, where the king faces invasion, offers prayer and sacrifice, and receives an affirming oracle from one of the psalm-guild of Asaph; king and people bow before the Lord, while a psalm-choir raises loud praise, and next day they go out to battle. Some scholars, however, note the measured, calm style and the absence of lament, and relate it, like the following psalm, to the inauguration or renewal of a reign, where the king would be empowered for conflict in general (cf. above on 2; 110).

1–5   On behalf of the people ('we' in v. 5), the singer addresses the king. His words are like a blessing, gathering strength from God to bestow good upon the king, that his prayer in time of need be answered and his offerings accepted with favour, and his plans and stratagems be brought to success. We note here the centring of all the people's needs and hopes in their king, and the reliance on what the Lord will do. The salvation, which is in the hand of the Lord alone, is seen as mediated through the divine presence in Zion and through God's name – two concepts which sometimes merge. In his name the Lord makes himself known and present, and is ready to answer the prayer which calls upon this name (Int. 6b).

6   The sudden prominence of the 'I' may be due to the psalmist emphasizing his inspiration to hear a word or read a sign from the Lord (cf. 81.5; 85.8), though some have thought of a response from the king himself. A conviction is expressed that the Lord will answer and save 'from his holy heavens', from his heavenly abode with which the Zion sanctuary is mysteriously identical (cf. 11.4; 18.6; Int. 6f).

7–9   In v. 7 the only verb in the Hebrew comes at the end: 'we invoke' (but LXX and Syriac have 'we shall be strong', reading *nagbir*). The sense of the Hebrew is then that while some 'invoke' (call to their aid) their great armaments, the Lord's people rely only on invoking his name (cf. 33.16f.; 75.6–7; Isa. 31.1–3). The final verse renews the opening blessing-wish, looking for salvation focused in the person of the king (the translation of RV follows traditional punctuation: 'Save, Lord; let the King answer us when we call'). Some emend in v. 9b to 'and answer us.' (so LXX); however, the slightly more awkward Hebrew ('let him answer us') gives a conclusion to match the psalm's opening words.

The psalm is testimony to the faith that it is the work of God, not earthly wealth and power, which is decisive in human affairs. This faith has here specific, concrete supports, definite manifestations of God's grace: the sanctuary, the name of God, his choice of his Anointed. In the person of this Anointed the people are content to be gathered up, letting his offerings and prayers plead for them. There is nothing 'automatic' about the salvation they look for. All rests with the will of the Lord; on this his people wait, and sometimes – but not always – receive for their comfort a clear word of response.

The church readily found the psalm prophetic of Christian experience. Spurgeon represented the ancient tradition when he said: 'All loyal subjects pray for their king, and most certainly citizens of Zion have good cause to pray for the Prince of Peace ... All the Saviour's days were days of trouble, and he also made them days of prayer; the church joins her intercession with her Lord, and pleads that he may be heard in his cries and tears.'

Answer us, O God, in the day of our troubles; send us help from the sanctuary and accept our sufferings as a sacrifice to you, that you may breathe into our hearts your counsels, and save us by the mighty name of your Son, our Lord Jesus Christ.

PSALM 21: Blessings for Ever

For favour.   Psalm.   Of David.

1   Lord, in your strength the king is glad,
    and in your salvation how greatly he rejoices!
2   You have granted him the desire of his heart,
    and have not withheld the request of his lips.   *[Pause]*
3   For you came to meet him with blessings of good;
    you placed a crown of pure gold upon his head.
4   When he asked you for life, you gave it him,
    length of days, everlasting and for ever.
5   Great is his glory in your salvation;
    splendour and majesty you have laid upon him.
6   Truly, you have appointed him blessings for ever;
    you have gladdened him with joy before your face.
7   For the king trusts in the Lord,
    and through the love of the Most High,
        he will not be overthrown.

8   Your hand shall find all your enemies;
    your right hand shall find your foes.
9   You will make them as a fiery oven in the time of your anger;
    the Lord will confound them in his wrath,
        and the fire devour them.
10 You willl destroy their fruit from the land,
    and their seed from the peoples of earth.
11 For though they intend mischief against you and purpose evil,
    yet they will not prevail.
12 For you will put them to flight,
    when you aim at them with your bow-string.

13 Be exalted, Lord, in your strength;
    so shall we make music and sing of your power.

This psalm appears to have belonged to the great royal rites in the autumn festival – enthronement or renewal of reign (see above on Ps. 2). The first half brings an address to the Lord, acknowledging what he has done for the king in this sacramental rite; the Lord himself has set the crown on his head, answered his prayer for abundant life, and endowed him with majesty and salvation. This section is rounded off by v. 7. Verses 8–12 consist of an address to the king, like a power-filled word of prophetic blessing, and the whole is rounded off with a choral address to the Lord, v. 13. Some have taken the psalm to be a kind of thanksgiving after a victorious battle that had been anticipated in 20; this seems less appropriate.

1–6 This address to the Lord can be taken to acknowledge what he has done for his king in a preceding sacrament. It is not really expressed in the customary way of a thanksgiving; it serves rather to expound for the king and all in attendance what God has done in the ceremony and what the effects will be. By his power and salvation, God has brought joy to his Anointed. He has answered his prayers (as specially promised, 2.8; 3.4; 4.3; 89.26), granting him long life. Here was grace for the individual king, and for the continuance of the dynasty. But with the expansive promise of life 'for everlasting and for ever', there may have also been a thought of communion with God beyond this life, an ancient hope of kings (cf. above on 16.10–11). The crowning, like the anointing, was said to be the very action of God, and with it he bestowed 'blessings of good', all that made for healthy life for the king, his land and people. The greatest blessing, life in its deepest meaning, was to live before God's face, in his presence, in harmony with his will.

7 Here the speech refers to the Lord in the third person, as though to round off the foregoing direct address. Tremendous weight must fall on the one item mentioned as required in the king – that he trusts in the Lord. From the Lord's minister is required continual trust, and from the Lord himself flows the rich counterpart, the *ḥesed* of the Most High, of all loves the most faithful and invincible.

8–12 The singer now (as seems most probable) addresses the king in the manner of prophetic blessing (cf. 20.1–4), depicting that power of victory which will flow from all that the Lord has now done. The fierce vigour of the language, as usual in such rites, is meant to convey the certainty that evil powers, enemies of God himself, will be overcome (cf. above on 18.42). To 'find' the foes probably means to strike with unerring aim.

13 The choral conclusion looks to the outworking of the sacramental grace in the conflicts which king and people will inevitably have to face. The prayer (cf. above on 7.6) calls on the Lord to appear in his power (*'oz* as in v. 1), and the promise is made to give thanks and testimony then with instruments and voices in the praise of psalmody.

This relatively simple and clear psalm gives a vivid insight into the ideals linked to Israel's kings. Fundamental is the requirement of trust in the Lord, a trust which answers the invincible divine love. In this close relationship with the Lord, the king is encouraged to pray, to ask at every turn for God's help. As he asks, God is already, as it were, on the way to meet him, bearing the goodly blessings. Prominent among the king's requests is that for 'life', and the ancient people's hope was for their king's long life indeed, but also for it to have an abundant quality which would quicken all the springs of life to run through society and nature. Yes, for ever and evermore he shall have such life – so the psalmist reports God's answer, a prospect which seems to swim away from earthly calculation into an ideal world, or, we might say, a glimpse into the purpose hidden in God's heart. Strongly then is stated the king's promised defeat of evil forces. and the Lord beside him means nothing less than to destroy them for ever. Many would be the down-to-earth occasions when all this faith and hope was sorely tested, and the cry would go up for the Lord to arise and be exalted in his strength. For Christian interpreters this ideal of the Lord's Anointed was eloquent of Jesus the Messiah. Following the great work of the divine 'strength' and 'salvation' in the resurrection, Christ has ascended to receive the crown, and with mighty prayers brings blessing to his people. Especially he has obtained 'life', an eternal life, into which may enter all who come to trust in him: 'Because I live, you shall live also' (John 14.19).

Almighty God, who raised up your Son and crowned him with glory, rise up against all who still despoil your world, and hasten the victory of your kingdom, that we may live and sing your praise for ever.

PSALM 22: Far from my Crying

For favour.　Over the help of the dawn.　Psalm.　Of David.

1　My God, my God, why have you forsaken me,
　　　and are so far from my salvation,
　　　　and from the words of my crying?
2　My God, I call out by day, and you do not answer;
　　　by night, and still I find no rest.
3　And you sit enthroned as the Holy One,
　　　you that are the glory of Israel.
4　In you our fathers trusted,
　　　they trusted, and you delivered them.
5　To you they cried, and were rescued;
　　　in you they trusted, and were not put to shame.
6　But I am a worm, not a man,
　　　the scorn of all, despised by people.
7　All that see me mock me;
　　　they curl their lips and wag their heads.
8　He relied on the Lord, they say, that he would deliver him;
　　　let him save him, since he delights in him!
9　But you were the one who drew me from the womb,
　　　and laid me on my mother's breast.
10　On you I was cast at birth;

    from my mother's womb you have been my God.

11   Do not stay far from me, for trouble is near,
    and there is none to help.

12   Great bulls have come about me;
    the mighty ones of Bashan have surrounded me.

13   They gape upon me with their mouths,
    like a lion that rends and roars.

14   I am poured out like water, and all my bones are come apart;
    my heart has become like wax, melting through my body.

15   My strength is dried up like a potsherd,
      and my tongue cleaves to my jaws;
    and you have laid me on the dust of death.

16   The dogs are all about me,
      the deadly pack have surrounded me;
    they pierce my hands and my feet.

17   I can count all my bones,
    and they stare back and gaze upon me.

18   My garments they divide among them,
    and cast lots for my clothing.

19   But you, Lord, do not stay far away;
    O my help, come quickly to my aid.

20   Deliver my soul from the sword,
    my poor life from the grip of the dog.

21   Save me from the lion's mouth,
    and from the horns of the wild oxen –
      you will surely answer me.

22   I will tell of your name to those who worship with me;
    in the festal assembly I will praise you.

23   You that fear the Lord, praise him,
      all you seed of Jacob, glorify him;
    stand in awe of him, all you seed of Israel.

24   For he has not despised or abhorred the sufferer's pain;
    and did not hide his face from him,
      but heard when he cried to him.

25   From you comes my praise in the great assembly;
    my vows I fulfil in the presence of those who fear him.

26   The poor shall eat and be satisfied;
    those who seek the Lord shall praise him –
      may your heart live for evermore.

27   Let all the ends of the earth remember and return to the Lord,
    and all the families of the nations worship before you.

28   For the kingdom is the Lord's,
    and he is the ruler over the nations.

29   All the living shall eat together and worship,
      and all gone down to death's dust shall bow before him,

> for he has made my soul live again to him.
>
> 30 My seed shall serve him;
> witness shall be borne to the Lord for ever.
>
> 31 They shall come and declare his saving work,
> telling a people yet to be born all that he has done.

The psalm falls into two parts: lament in vv. 1–21, and praise in vv. 22–31. The last Hebrew word of the first part seems to prepare for the following praise – a confident 'you-have-answered-me' or 'you-will-answer-me', though some prefer an emendation here. In any case, the two parts form an amazing contrast. The sufferer's lament rises from a desolation that becomes so extreme that it is virtually from the sphere of death, pictured in abysmal horrors. His subsequent thanksgiving presses to the other extreme; before the full festal assembly of Israel he tells of a salvation which will resound to the ends of the earth and even into the silence of the underworld, evoking universal worship of the Lord and acknowledgement of his kingdom.

Adhering to the lines of interpretation developed by Gunkel, whereby most of the lamenting psalms were connected with the distress of a private individual, many scholars have attempted to read this psalm as an expression of someone's illness (or other misfortune) and recovery. This has proved scarcely feasible, and while some (e.g. Kraus, Craigie) shifted to the idea of a formula, a statement of fundamental suffering and relief which could be recited for any afflicted pilgrim, others marked off parts of the psalm as much later additions, when an individual's prayer was developed into a general hope for the end of the age. Girard, however, is emphatic that his structural analysis absolutely rules out such a theory of later expansions and demonstrates the original unity and homogeneity of the entire psalm.

A juster view of the psalm was taken in an earlier period of scholarship, when Kirkpatrick, for example, wrote that the psalmist was a representative character, 'to some extent, secondarily at any rate, the mouthpiece of the nation'; while, earlier, Delitzsch had said that no one in the pre-Christian period could link such universal effects with his deliverance except 'the theocratic king', the Lord's Anointed. The scale of the psalm in fact suits best a royal speaker, as in several adjacent psalms. The Davidic kings witnessed to the world in their psalms (2, 18 etc.); their situation was linked with God's own kingship (2 etc.).

But also in the lamenting section of our psalm we easily discern the royal figure, though (like the Man of Sorrows in Isa. 53) deprived for a while of his outward glory. A special bond with the Lord is indicated at the outset in the threefold 'my God' (also v. 10) and more vividly in the appeal to God as the one who, as father, had drawn him from the womb and committed him to his mother's breast. The mocking of enemies has its point in the psalmist's having been supposed to be the chosen of the Lord, the one in whom he 'delighted' (v. 8, cf. above on 18.19). His abasement has an archetypal character, an exposure to the terrible shapes of death – the scale here could be compared with that of royal 18, and again of Isaiah 53. To such a depth of horror, the unbounded exaltation of vv. 22–31, with effulgence of God's kingdom, seems the fitting counterpart.

If, then, the speaker is best regarded as the Lord's Anointed, from what situation does he lament and give thanks? The mediaeval Jewish scholar Rashi says that David composed the prayer with reference to the Exile, foreseeing what would befall the congregation of Israel. Mowinckel favoured the view that the occasion was an extreme crisis such as that suffered by King Hezekiah in the Assyrian invasion of 701. But there are really no indications of such a situation, and it has still to be explained how the exaltation could follow the abasement as part of one composition, for just as the lament rises from one actually in the grip of death, so the thanksgivng rises from one actually delivered, not just foreseeing deliverance.

In view of all this, consideration may fairly be given to the possibility that we have here a kind of liturgical drama in two scenes, a profound and prophetic mystery of salvation from death comparable with liturgy that may lie behind 18, 118, Isa. 53, Zech. 9.9f. Such an enactment at the year's turning-point would focus in the person of the king all the sorrows of mortality and all the hopes of life in God. In comparison with prayer from a historical incident, it was not artificial. Like all great art – poetry, drama, music – it caught the truth of existence, and like all great sacraments of worship, it was open to the divine grace. In such liturgy the psalmists, headed by God's royal 'Son', were prophets indeed, seeing into the depths and heights, and mediating the power from beyond (cf. *Kingship*, pp. 18f., 34f.). The peculiar heading may indicate a rite that began in darkness and culminated with joy at break of day. While LXX found here the word *eyalut*, 'help', as in v. 19, the Hebrew vowels give 'hind' (an animal that may have been used in the morning sacrifice in early times; cf. Gen. 27; Isa. 40.16; Ps. 50.10–12; ct. Deut. 12.15).

1–2 The opening cry to God is unique in beginning with the repeated 'My God', *eli, eli . . . elohay*; the expression makes a jarring contrast with the description of forsakenness (Int. 6c) – you that have been so close, so strong in commitment and promise of faithfulness, can you so abandon me? Long crying to the Lord, by day and by night, has brought no response and no relief (for 'far from my salvation' a change of vowels is sometimes favoured, giving 'far from my cry for help', *shaw 'ati*).

3–5 The appeal is now supported by reference to the case of the ancestors. Sacred tradition told how they cried to God in need and were saved; their trust was not disappointed. The argument seems to reflect a representative and national dimension in the sufferer's person. In v. 3 the traditional phrasing gives a translation like that of RV margin 'But thou art holy, O thou that art enthroned on the praises of Israel'; but metre and simpler sense favour division and translation as above.

6–11 Another sharp contrast is presented, as the opening word ('And–I') corresponds to v. 3 ('And–you'). The heavenly king has been pictured on his throne in divine glory; from the psalmist all glory has been taken; he is accounted a worm, not a man, an object of derision (cf. Isa. 41.14 of Israel; 52.2–3 of the royal servant). The taunting plays on his former status, as the one so close in bond with the Lord, the one in whom the Lord 'delighted', his Chosen One (cf. above on 18.19). But the psalmist will not let go the truth which they mock. He tells of the Lord's care at his birth, picturing him as the father who acts as midwife and so calls him his own child in the most complete manner (cf. Gen. 50.23); yes, he is this 'Son' who now calls out to the Father (cf. 2.7; 89.26), mock as they may.

12–18 He now adds to his pleading a portrayal of his plight. The symbolic poetry describes no less than a sinking into death. There are fearsome animal shapes – massive bulls, a ravening lion, a pack of savage dogs – all shapes of the destructive demons of the underworld, leering and attacking from every side. Death strikes into the sufferer's body. The life-force is all poured out. The bones fall apart. The heart itself melts away. As the sap of life is fled, dryness prevails. The sufferer lies 'on the dust of death'.

19–21 The dire situation has been portrayed and thereby commended to the divine compassion. The appeal comes to a final climax with a series of direct and urgent petitions for the apparently remote Lord to come quickly and save. The demons of death are pictured with swords or again in animal shapes – dogs, lions, and gigantic yore-oxen.

22–26 The scene has changed. The psalmist, saved and joyful, is bent on giving thanks and testimony. He is not vowing praise, or anticipating the joyful situation. He sings as already in the midst of the great festal assembly, telling of his answered prayer, and calling on all to join in the praise of the Lord. He bears witness to 'the name of the Lord', the Lord as a very present and unique help, and the message is first (lit.) 'to my brothers' – all in the fellowship of the festival (cf. 131.1; also David's use of 'brothers' to his men and to the people of Judah, 1 Sam. 30.23; 2 Sam. 19.12). The whole people, 'all the seed of Israel / Jacob', is to give praise to the Lord because he has not hidden his face or turned away in disgust from this sufferer (cf. Isa. 53.3), but answered his prayer; it is an event central to the nation. In v. 25a the psalmist may mean that his new splendour (his 'praise' or 'glory') is the result of God's act; or he may mean that he has 'praise' to sing because of this act. He makes the thank-offerings which he vowed when afflicted (cf. 116.17–19; Lev. 7.15f.). The other worshippers share in the sacrificial meal; the 'poor' or 'humble' are thus satisfied, and he pronounces over them the blessing-wish 'May your heart live for ever.' God has now given salvation and abundance of life, and in this meal in the presence of God all hearts are quickened anew (cf. the scene in 2 Sam. 6.17–19).

27–28 But if the immediate fellowship of the festival consists chiefly of 'the seed of Israel', a people near the Lord (148.14), this is only the first-fruits of a universal kingdom. The Lord, the Creator, is the sovereign of all that exists. So the psalmist calls for all the ends of the world to remember and return and worship. The salvation from death that he has so wonderfully experienced sends an impulse through all creation. He proclaims the kingship, manifest in this salvation, as belonging to the Lord and to no other power, a kingship that embraces all peoples, bringing them light and justice.

29–31 The 'saving act' (v. 31a, *sedaqa*), the work of the just and faithful Lord that has brought the psalmist back from death, will be preached and celebrated yet wider than earth's bounds. It will be passed on through generations yet unborn, witness being borne by descendants who in their turn will also make solemn entry – a reference, it seems, to Davidic heirs and their role as witnesses in the festal assembly (cf. above on 18.49–50). The light of this salvation will even strike into the underworld, and cause the shades to bow to the Lord. Because he has made the psalmist's soul live again to him, even the dead will share the reverence of all those still flourishing in life on earth, who eat of the thanksgiving sacrifices and worship the Lord.

The psalm expresses a terrible suffering which has its sharpest point in the sense of being forsaken – and forsaken by the God who made promises and declared special love, and was trusted. How far away this God seems, far from the agony, far from the cry for help! No answer is heard from him. Society too has little time for this unfortunate, who is aware only of its scorn and even mockery and gloating. The shapes of death gather all around. They attack ferociously, and the final shadow spreads over the sufferer; the living strength ebbs away, and the sense of dissolution and dust prevails. Yet all that is thus expressed is expressed still to the Lord; all is prayer. And the end is a repeated calling for him to come quickly; and in the very last Hebrew word there has entered a tone of hope – 'you will answer me.'

The second scene of the psalm is there without explanation. All that is known is that the Lord kept faith. He answered the prayer of the sufferer. He did not hide his face. How salvation came from death's grip remained a mystery. But to the faithfulness of the Lord the psalmist could witness with joy, before all the world and to ages yet to come. Who could praise enough this faithful saviour? Let the witness be made in the fellowship of worshippers, in the meal of communion, and to the ends of the world, and for ever.

For the New Testament, the psalm appeared as prophetic of the way Jesus took – especially of the mockery of the sufferer purporting to be Son and King (Matt. 27.39–44; Mark 15.29–32; Luke 23.35–9), the soldiers' sharing out his garments (Matt. 27.35; Luke 23.34; John 19.23–4), the use of v. 1 in the Aramaic language of Jesus (Matt. 27.46; Mark 15.34), and the testimony to his brothers of the one raised from death (Heb. 2.12). Though the circumstances that gave rise to this psalm remain uncertain, Christians have felt that the author was led to a mystery of ultimate sorrow and salvation which corresponded with the passion and resurrection. Through the words of this great psalm, worshippers have voiced the tragedy of forsakenness and death, and seen the light beyond. Linked to the work of Christ, the psalm brings the light into the sufferer's abyss, and encourages the redeemed to rejoice in the meal of thanksgiving, and testify to the saving act that will shine upon the living and the dead, to the bounds of existence and for ever.

O Christ, who well knew the hour of forsakenness and the sharpness of death, do not stay far from us in our sorrows; come quickly to our help, that we may arise to offer ourselves as a living sacrifice of thanksgiving, and to tell of your goodness to all the world.

PSALM 23: Coming Home

Psalm.   Of David.

1   With the Lord as my shepherd,
    I shall not be in want.
2   In green pastures he will let me lie;
    by still waters he will lead me.
3   He will restore my soul;
    he will guide me in ways of salvation for his name's sake.
4   Even though I walk in the valley of the shadow of death,
        I will fear no evil;
    for you will be with me;
        your rod and your crook will comfort me.
5   You have prepared a table before me,
        a sign to my foes;
    you have anointed my head with oil;
        my cup runs over.
6   Truly, goodness and love will follow me
        all the days of my life,
    and I shall come home to the house of the Lord for ever.

Through the images of the good shepherd (vv. 1–4) and bountiful host (vv. 5–6) the psalmist testifies to the Lord as his King – caring, providing, mightily protecting. The shepherd was a much-used image for the duties of kingship in the ancient Near East and in Israel, symbolized in sceptre ('rod') and crook. Elsewhere in the Old Testament God is described as shepherd only of the nation, except for one reference to his shepherding of the nation's ancestor (Gen. 48.15; for shepherd of the nation see Pss 74.1; 77.20; 78.52; 79.13; 80.1; Isa.40.11f. the Targum accordingly explains Ps. 23 of God's shepherding the nation in the wilderness). So there is something remarkable here in the extended application of the theme in such a personal way; even in the closing verses also we are aware of just the two figures, the Lord and his treasured one, with a background of hostility or danger.

If the psalm is the song of a king (David or a successor), all this can be well understood. As representative of his people, and as sharing the royal task with the true King, God, he could dwell on the thought of his relation to this supreme sovereign and shepherd. To him he owes his anointing and the covenant of protection against foes (v. 5); from God are sent the angels of covenant-grace to attend him closely on dangerous missions (v. 6a); and to God he returns to dwell on the sacred hill of Zion (where temple and palace adjoined, v. 6b; cf. above on Ps. 5 for God's 'house' before Solomon).

The form of the psalm is unique in consisting only of testimony and trust – testimony about the Lord, and trusting words to him. There is no prayer, no lament, no general praise. Parallels for the themes can be found in 61 and 27.1–6, where there is more obvious reference to the king's foes. The unusually restricted form-pattern may suggest that the psalm was part of a sequence in worship, and, as Delitzsch long ago observed, there are in fact important points of connection with the great preceding psalm. After the exciting public testimony and praise of Psalm 22B, we have here a more intimate reflection on the grace of the heavenly ruler to his Anointed – the restoration of soul, the protection from death, the gifts of abundant and unending life, the meal in God's presence.

1–4 The singer expresses his confidence in the loving care of the Lord. The shepherd's task in the mountainous wilderness of Palestine is one calling for the greatest devotion, skill and courage. Want, hardship, injury and death are never far from the sheep and goats and their young. But the good shepherd knows how to find the pastures of fresh grass where the animals can graze and lie down, and the still pools formed with rocks in the waters of mountain springs, where the thirst, so sharp from the heat, can be safely quenched. So the exhausted life is brought back and strength renewed to follow the wise shepherd on the good ways that he knows how to find. And even in dark ravines, he dispels fear, as he keeps on the watch with his club against foes and his crook to guide and support the little ones.

Thus far the images arise from the shepherd's work, and yet they are rich in spiritual meaning, especially as testimony to the faithful love of the divine King. Pastures and pools speak of the true life that he gives and replenishes. The restoring of soul speaks of his delivering from death, and the good ways are properly 'roads of right / salvation', suggesting the joyous route of the rescued one, leading through the 'gates of righteousness' into Zion. The 'valley of the shadow of death' speaks of that land of darkness where the grim shepherd death (49.14) claims dominion, but where the sceptre and crook of the Lord, the signs and instruments of his almighty kingship, are ready to defend and save.

5–6   The Lord is now pictured as host to the psalmist, with only the two figures at the table. The Lord has 'arranged' or 'put in order' the table – spread it with good fare; he has anointed the psalmist's head with oil, a custom for a festive meal; and he has amply filled his cup. The scene suggests the communion meal of worship, where offerings were made and from them a meal shared as it were with the deity (cf. 22.25f.). But there is also here the theme of the royal covenant. The generous gestures of the Lord to this single guest are done in the sight of and over against his adversaries; they are demonstrative, warning foes that the Covenant-Lord will protect this his Chosen One. (Gunkel and Kraus rightly compare an Amarna text which speaks of Pharaoh's gifts to vassal princes in Canaan to be made 'while our enemies look on'.) Immediately after this allusion, v. 5b is readily seen to evoke the royal anointing, although the verb here is not the usual term for this (we have *d-sh-n*, not *m-sh-ḥ*; the mediaeval Jewish authority Rashi takes v. 5a as a metaphor for the kingship, and paraphrases v. 5b 'By your decree I have already been anointed king'). 'Goodness' and 'Love' are pictured as angelic helpers, representing the generous and faithful love that the Lord has for his Chosen One. These angels are appointed to 'pursue' or attend the psalmist most closely and unceasingly in all his dangerous missions and expeditions. And from these dangers he returns at last to dwell for ever with the Lord. The picture will be based on the fact that the royal residence was beside the Lord's sanctuary, but there seems also to be allusion to the royal hope of everlasting communion with the Lord (cf. above on 16.10–11).

Many read this psalm with delight in its imagery for divine care and grace, and they readily identify with the psalmist's relationship to the Lord. Especially telling is the assurance of his companionship in the valley of death's shadow, and the confidence of dwelling in his eternal house. But in the considerations put forward above, something deeper has emerged. If the psalm is the testimony of the Lord's Anointed, the tender and faithful relationship with the heavenly king is bound up with his royal calling. That calling is for the benefit of all, and so that relationship becomes a fountain of grace and blessing for all. Their life is hidden in his, as he moves in the intimate presence of God. In the Christian context, therefore, the psalm has fullest depth when related to Christ and his Father. It evokes the passion and new life of Jesus, and the gifts of the Lord's table. Unworthy, unclean as they are, the pilgrims come to know through Christ the true wonders of the pastures of young growth, the still waters, the grace of communion, the angels of love, the comforter in the valley of the shadow of death, and the great homecoming. Nor is the relation to the preceding psalm without deep significance. To enter fully into the peace of 23, the pilgrim must first make the daunting journey through 22, through that place where the lonely representative suffers to the uttermost, holds true, and obtains victory; having stood with him in that awesome place, the pilgrim will know the joy of the homecoming.

O God, our sovereign and shepherd, who brought again your Son Jesus from the valley of death, comfort us with your protecting presence and your angels of goodness and love, that we also may come home and dwell with him in your house for ever.

PSALM 24: At the Everlasting Doors

Of David.   Psalm.

1   To the Lord belongs the earth and its fullness,
     the world and all its teeming life.
2   For it was he who founded it on the seas,
     and made it firm upon the floods.
3   Who shall ascend the hill of the Lord,
     and who shall stand in his holy place?
4   The clean of hands and the pure in heart,
     who have not lifted up their soul to false things,
         or sworn only to deceive.
5   These shall carry home blessing from the Lord,
     and goodness from God their Saviour.
6   May such be those now seeking him,
     seeking the face of the God of Jacob.   *[Pause]*
7   Lift up your heads, O gates,
         and be lifted up, you everlasting doors,
     and the King of Glory shall come in.
8   Who is the King of Glory?
     the Lord, strong and mighty, the Lord who is mighty in battle.
9   Lift up your heads, O gates,
         and be lifted up, you everlasting doors,
     and the King of Glory shall come in.
10   But who is the King of Glory?
     The Lord of Hosts, he is the King of Glory.   *[Pause]*

The psalm evidently accompanied a procession that ascended the sacred hill and entered the gates of the Lord's house. Moreover, it all signified the procession and entry of God himself, and so probably involved the transporting of the ark, symbol of the divine presence and glory (cf. 47; 68; 132). From the opening and closing themes it may be deduced that this grand procession was part of the ceremonies of the chief festival, at the turn of the year in the autumn (Int. 5b). With conquering power over the primaeval waters, the Creator has secured the living world. The original event has, as it were, been relived in the drama of the festival, which also emphasized that this King of all was none other than Yahweh, God of Jacob / Israel, requiring faithfulness and truth from his worshippers. The greater part of the psalm, vv.

3–10, is made up of questions and responses, a lively liturgical dialogue. Such psalms were thus not mere songs incidental to the ceremonies, but texts which carried the worship forward and unfolded the meaning of the rites.

1–2   Not some broad philosophical reflection, but rather a cry of triumph opens this exciting psalm, as indeed befits the moment of the return of the victorious Lord to his eternal gates (vv. 7, 9), the heavenly event mirrored in Zion's festal procession. Like the militant cry that ends Psalm 3 (literally 'To the Lord the salvation!'), the cry now is 'To the Lord the earth and her fullness!' The living, teeming world belongs to him, and to no other power, because he has conquered chaos, stilled the raging ocean, and built the earth over the subdued waters on the pillars of the great mountains. He enters now as victor, the king who will faithfully sustain the good order of life in all the cosmos. Such is the pattern of thought that lies in the opening song of jubilation and the later verses that speak of the God supreme in battle and in glory. But more than this, the ceremony was a sacrament in which the work of the Creator was present as at the beginning, and the worshippers rejoiced in the new springs of life.

3–6   As the procession up the sacred way approaches the sanctuary gates, the awe of the holy realm prompts the ancient question (cf. 15): who is fit to endure it? Who may dare to enter as the Lord's guest? The authoritative answer is here put briefly. In action and in motives let the worshipper be 'clean' and 'pure', and let not the soul be lifted up to what is false, or solemn assurances given to deceive. The Lord will not abide the defilement of cruel and treacherous deeds, nor the worship of false gods and the cynical breaking of promises. The worshipper true to these requirements will 'carry' blessing and goodness ('right' in its sense of divine gift and salvation, cf. 23.3) from the Saviour, returning home laden with such gracious gifts. Verse 6 seems to be a rejoinder to the foregoing answer: may this processional company or throng (*dor*) of worshippers (called 'seekers of God's face') find such acceptance with the Lord.

7–10   The preceding question, answer and rejoinder have seemed like dialogue between the procession and guardians of the gates. And now again, even more dramatically, such an interchange rings out, as the gates are called upon to open, and responding inquiry is made and answered as to who is seeking entry. Why the gates are to raise their heads is not quite clear to us. A portcullis structure is not evidenced. Some explain from the thought of the towering divine presence which is to pass through; others think of the gates personified as sleepy guardians who must bestir and arise; others again suggest that 'Lift up your heads' just means 'Rejoice' (cf. Dahood and Craigie with Ugaritic references). It is at all events a vivid conception. Like all features of the temple, the sanctuary gates are symbolic of heavenly reality; they are 'gates of eternity (*'olam*)', corresponding to the entrance of the victorious Creator's residence above the heavenly ocean (cf. below on 93.5; 104.3).

The titles and epithets cited, as it were, to identify the one that would enter, are sung out in climactic fashion. As 'King of Glory' he is the supreme power of all the cosmos (cf. 29.9; Isa. 6.3. and for the ark as manifestation of this divine glory 1 Sam. 4.21f.). As 'Yahweh, Champion in War' he is, further, the Lord who saved and now works through the people 'near to him', Jacob / Israel (cf. v. 6 and above on 22.23). As 'Yahweh of Hosts' he is at the head of the hosts of heaven, or, on another explanation, he is 'Yahweh Omnipotent' (*sebaot* taken as an abstract noun in apposition). With this final citation of the dread name, the barriers must give way, and the triumphal ascension is accomplished.

One can see here how reading the Psalms only as 'instruction' must fall short. One who sings, hears or reads this poem with sympathy is caught up in a most powerful action. An ancient ceremony of worship lives again, and carries us into the very springs of existence. The Creator becomes present, and his work is known in the marvel of its first perfection. The music of triumph celebrates the conquest of evil. And within the cosmic order appears the aspect of revelation and covenant – God's work through chosen ones, and his insistence on the wholehearted love of truth and goodness. The psalm would gather all so minded, the seekers of God's face, into the throng that passes through the eternal gates.

The church has sung the psalm especially at Ascensiontide, and seen in Christ the manifestation of the King of Glory. Important here is the thought that he alone is worthy to enter, but by his suffering and salvation he makes possible the entry also of sinners who join themselves to him in penitence and faith. And beyond even this rises the faith that, through him, all shall be well, as God saw all was good in the beginning. For to him belongs all the teeming life of the world; he is the good sovereign and shepherd of every creature. He will not forsake them, but in the end will win back every one. The glory of his kingship will be known in his victorious power, justice, and compassionate redemption.

O God, in whose hand is all the plenitude of the earth, restore in us true innocency of life, that, following your Son, we may ascend your holy mountain and rejoice in the completion of your good kingdom.

PSALM 25: The Friendship of the Lord

Of David.

1   To you, Lord, I lift my soul;
2   my God, I trust in you.
     May I not be put to shame;
         may my enemies not triumph over me.
3   May none who wait for you be ashamed;
     rather let the treacherous be frustrated and put to shame.
4   Lord, make me to know your ways,
     and ever teach me your paths.
5   Cause me to walk in your truth and teach me,
     for you are the God of my salvation;
         all the day long I look for you.
6   Remember, Lord, your tender mercies,
     and your faithful kindnesses, which have been from of old.
7   But do not recall the errors of my youth and my sins;
     think of me according to your faithful love,
         for the sake of your goodness, O Lord.
8   The Lord is generous and true;
     therefore he teaches sinners in the way.
9   He will guide the humble in judgement,
     and will teach the lowly his way.
10   All the paths of the Lord are faithful love and truth,
     to those who keep his covenant and his testimonies.
11   For the sake of your name, O Lord,
     forgive my sin that is so great.
12   Who is he that fears the Lord?
     Him will he teach in the way that he should choose.
13   His soul will abide in goodness,
     and his seed will inherit the earth.
14   The friendship of the Lord is for those who fear him,
     and he will make known to them his covenant.
15   My eyes are continually towards the Lord,
     for it is he that shall deliver my feet from the net.
16   Turn to me and be gracious to me,
     for I am alone and very troubled.
17   Relieve the distresses of my heart,
     and bring me out of my sufferings.
18   Look upon my affliction and trouble,
     and put away all my offences.
19   See my enemies, how many they are;
     and they hate me with a cruel hatred.

20   Keep my soul and deliver me;
     may I not be put to shame, for I shelter in you.
21   May integrity and truth protect me,
     for my hope, Lord, is in you.
22   Redeem Israel, O God,
     from out of all his troubles.

This is the second of the four alphabetic compositions which occur in Book One (Int. 4e). Each verse begins with the next letter of the alphabet, although this has become obscured in vv. 2, 5c, 18 (and it may be that, as in Ps. 34, the letter *waw* was deliberately omitted from the sequence). When the alphabet has been traversed, an additional verse beginning with 'P' provides a general concluding prayer. Psalm 34 likewise concludes with an additional 'P' verse; perhaps the intention was to spell out the root 'Learn' (*'-l-p*), made from the first letters of the two halves plus the additional 'P', echoing also the first letter, *'alep*. The thoughts in such alphabetic psalms at first sight appear somewhat fragmented, but in the present case we are never far from 'lament', prayer from affliction; and there are three recurring themes: desire for deliverance from suffering, for forgiveness of sin, and for the Lord's instruction and guidance. There is little indication of the original circumstances. The use of an acrostic and resemblances to Wisdom literature do not prove a post–exilic date, and it is possible that the psalmist was a royal figure who could speak for Israel (v. 22) through his apparently individual prayer.

1–7   The opening verse strikes the characteristic note of this psalm, the singer being conscious of direct relation to the Lord, lifting his soul in worship and in longing for help in present sufferings. To restore the verse that should begin in Hebrew with 'B' (v. 2), some conjecture changes thus: 'For you, Lord, I wait; I lift my soul to my God. I trust in you ...' (so *BHS*). The prominence of treacherous and violent enemies in the psalm perhaps points to the psalmist being a king. Verse 3 is literally 'Let not all who wait ...' and seems to anticipate v. 22 in revealing the representative dimension in the prayers. In vv. 4–5 the psalmist repeatedly asks the Lord to teach him, that he may live daily in the ways of the Lord, knowing well the ways and treading in the path of God's faithfulness ('truth'); not commandments and principles in themselves are to be treasured, but the One who teaches and guides – 'all the day long I look for you (/long for you / hope in you'). Recognizing his need of forgiveness, the psalmist appeals to the compassionate aspect of God's abiding love.

8–14   The style here is chiefly that of testimony in praise of God, encouraging to a gathering of worshippers. Several plural expressions seem to draw in such a group: '(penitent) sinners', 'the humble', 'those who keep his covenant', 'those who fear him'. The message centres on the faithfulness, grace and love of God, which are so wonderfully discovered by those who are humble towards him, willing to be taught, eager for his way. Strikingly, it is said that fear of him finds his friendship; the sense is that those who know him as God, the chief factor in every circumstance of their lives, find that he draws close in counsel and companionship (the word rendered 'friendship', *sod*, denotes the circle of trusted intimates who counsel and encourage each other). But significantly, at the centre of this passage, in v. 11, the singer repeats his prayer for forgiveness, confessing to great sin; such penitence, he seems to say, is fundamental to the blessedness of intimacy with the Lord.

15–21 The tone of lament – prayer from suffering – is here more plaintive and urgent. The psalmist's troubles are like a net trapping his feet; he is 'alone', that is, without any who can help, save the Lord. The enemies are many and cruelly violent, unrelentingly hostile. He asks the Lord to turn his face to him, as he looks in yearning hope ever towards the Lord. In v. 21 'integrity / perfectness' and 'justice / right' are best understood (in view of v. 21b) as qualities of God that come in the form of angels to protect the trusting one, rather than as human moral qualities.

22 This last verse, as mentioned above, lies outside the alphabetic scheme, but seems to play further on the pattern of letters, which was no doubt seen as touched by the wonder of divine revelation. Some have thought of the verse as added to adapt an individual prayer to congregational use. But we may rather think that it is part of the original design, and resoundingly makes explicit that suffering and hope of a whole people which were already borne throughout in the person of the psalmist.

The alphabetic type of psalm (most fully developed in 119) has an eloquence of its own. It has a pithy character, as brief prayers and testimonies are shot off like arrows of the spirit. Under the variety of the verses lie fundamental themes. Our psalm has expressed a concentration of yearning hope for God's salvation, that he would deliver from sin and from violent foes. Also, there is openness for his teaching, valued above all for the relationship with him; his ways are the true ways of life; and in a practical consciousness of the divine majesty, the disciple comes to be rewarded with God's 'friendship' – his company and counsel. The element of testimony and the concluding verse especially show how the individual prayer bears in itself a loving hope and intercession for all God's suffering ones.

Father, forgive our sin, which is so great; and cause us to know your ways and to walk in your truth, that we may be saved from cruel enemies, and daily rejoice in the goodness of your friendship.

PSALM 26: Washing the Hands in Innocence

Of David.

1   Judge me, Lord, for I have walked in sincerity;
     I have trusted in the Lord, and have not wavered.
2   Prove me, Lord, and test me;
     try my heart and inward thoughts.
3   For your faithful love has been before my eyes,
     and I have walked ever in your truth.
4   I have not joined with those that are false,
     nor consorted with deceivers.
5   I have abhorred the gathering of evildoers,
     and had no place in the circle of the wicked.
6   I have washed my hands in innocence,
     that I might go around your altar, Lord,
7   to sing aloud with the voice of thanksgiving,
     and to tell of all your wonders.
8   Lord, I have loved the dwelling of your house,
     the place where your glory abides.
9   Do not gather away my soul with the sinners,
     my life with the murderous ones,
10   in whose hands is evil purpose,
     and their right hand is filled with bribes.
11   For I have walked in sincerity;
     redeem me, Lord, and be gracious to me.
12   My foot will stand on fair ground;
     in the great assembly I will bless the Lord.

The singer avows that he has not departed from the requirements of the Lord, and is ready to be examined and judged by him. Beyond this, he seeks grace and redemption, and looks forward to being able to give thanks for such deliverance. One may conclude that, as in the psalms where there is indication of 'incubation' (Int. 6e), the psalmist is facing a severe crisis, and draws close to God earnestly and solemnly beseeching his aid. In such a case, he has to be ready to bare his soul to the divine testing. If God judges him loyal and innocent of evildoing, the help will be granted. The way the requirements of the Lord are reflected resembles the teachings of royal 18.20f. and 101, and we may think of a king in crisis as in the partly similar 17 and 28.

1–2   The psalmist asks the Lord to judge, prove, test and try him, looking deep within him (lit. 'my kidneys and my heart'). He claims to have lived daily with a heart whole towards the Lord (lit. 'in my wholeness'), trusting him alone. Such trust cannot but govern conduct; as Spurgeon says, 'Faith is the root and sap of integrity.'

3–5 There is at first sight an ambiguity here in the reference to faithful love and truth. These are indeed reciprocal virtues in the covenant-bond with the Lord; he is committed and steadfast in his goodwill to his servant, who likewise undertakes a matching loyalty. But (as also in the similar case of 101.1) the context shows the main thought here to be of the fidelity required of the Lord's covenant-partner. This commitment that God requires, answering his own, has been ever before the psalmist's eyes, and has governed his daily conduct. He has not allied himself to idol-worshippers or sorcerers (so probably the reference of v. 4), or to those given to cruel and corrupt actions (v. 5).

6–7 That hands are washed 'in innocence' signifies sometimes a demonstrative avowal of innocence in a particular case (Deut. 21.6; Matt. 27.24); or again the phrase may just refer to a pure life (Ps. 73.13). The latter sense seems satisfactory here; the psalmist rounds off his avowal of loyalty to the Lord with this image and looks forward (with a kind of implicit vow) to passing around the altar in the open court, singing a testimony when he receives the salvation he seeks.

8–11 Concluding prayer is preceded by another consideration to move the Lord – the psalmist claims to have 'loved' the holy place, where the divine presence or 'Glory' dwells. This can be well understood as a reference to the practical care of the sanctuary, such as was particularly the responsibility of the king (as in the work of David and Solomon, also Josiah in 2 Kings 22.3f.). The prayer then resumes the thought of the opening verses: may he not have the fate earned by the murderous and corrupt. 'Redeem me, Lord' is a prayer to be delivered from any heavy oppression.

12 This is probably an anticipation of deliverance: 'My foot will stand' (the Hebrew perfect tense for confidence); it will stand 'in levelness' – a double sense: 'fairness, justice', and 'on level ground' (safe and pleasant). His hope is high in the saving justice of the Lord, and he promises to acknowledge it with testimony and thanksgiving in the great festal assembly.

The psalm brings to the fore the mutual nature of the covenant-bond. There is indeed from God's side faithful love and compassion, but for a true relationship these must be answered with loyalty and trust, from which is born a purity of heart and an abhorrence of evildoing. From such a relationship the prayer for rescue in sudden troubles rises with strength, and the way is open for the wonders of the Lord's salvation. The church teaches that there is by grace a washing from sin, a new birth, a growing into Christ's innocence and wholeness towards the Father; but also that the disciples must be responsive in trust and purity on the daily path. Washing their hands in innocence before they go to his altar, they both ask to be cleansed by his grace, and also recognize their own responsibility to live in the path of purity, whole-heartedly for him.

Help us, Lord, in the way of trust and wholeness towards you; that we, being washed in the innocence of your Son, may love the place of your glory, and ever abhor all that is evil.

PSALM 27: One Thing I Ask

Of David.

1   The Lord is my light and my salvation – whom shall I fear?
    The Lord is the stronghold of my life –
        of whom shall I be afraid?
2   When deadly ones draw near to me to eat up my flesh,
    my adversaries and my foes – see, they shall stumble and fall.
3   Though a host encamp against me, my heart shall not fear;
    though the line of battle rise upon me, yet shall I trust.
4   One thing I have asked of the Lord, and that alone I seek,
    that I may dwell in the house of the Lord
        all the days of my life,
    to look on the beauty of the Lord,
    and seek guidance in his temple.
5   For he will hide me in his shelter in the day of trouble;
    he will conceal me in the covering of his tent,
        and lift me high upon the rock.
6   And then shall my head be high,
    above my enemies round about me.
    And in his tent I shall offer sacrifices in joyful thanksgiving;
    I shall sing and make music to the Lord.
7   Lord, hear my voice;
    as I call, be gracious and answer me.
8   My heart recalls your word: Seek my face;
    your face, Lord, I do seek.
9   Do not hide your face from me,
    or turn away your servant in displeasure.
    You have been my helper;
    do not leave me or forsake me, O God of my salvation.
10 Though my father and mother forsake me,
    the Lord will take me up.

11 Teach me, Lord, your way,
    and lead me on a good path
        against those who lie in wait for me.
12 Do not give me up to the desire of my adversaries,
    for false witnesses have risen against me,
        and those who breathe out violence.
13 But I believe that I shall see
    the goodness of the Lord in the land of the living.
14 Wait for the Lord, be strong, and let your heart take courage;
    yes, wait in hope for the Lord.

A remarkable feature of the prayers of the kings is the combination of harsh military situations with thoughts of tender intimacy in the relationship with the Lord (3; 61; 63; 91). It is in the time of peril, over against terrible enemies, that the Lord's 'Son' makes appeal to the loving bond in which alone the royal calling can exist. This psalm is surely another example. The first section (vv. 1–6) prepares the way for the following supplication by making testimony, apparently to a gathering of worshippers, about the confidence that the royal psalmist has in the Lord's salvation. He testifies further of his single-minded desire ever to be close to the Lord and follow his will. And looking forward in faith, he promises to bring thank-offerings in acknowledgement of victory. Altogether, we may say he makes it difficult for the Lord to reject him! Then comes the supplication (vv. 9–13), into which are woven more reinforcing considerations. The concluding verse may be a choral rejoinder on behalf of the other worshippers, encouraging the psalmist to hope in the Lord; the singular of the verb 'wait' favours this, rather than the verse being an address to the other worshippers. Some think of it as an oracle responding to the psalmist's prayer. The pattern of praise-followed-by-lament thus has its own logic and is attested in several psalms (9–10, 40, 89). The once common view that we have here two psalms was based on a narrow understanding of forms. There are in fact many echoes of vocabulary and motifs between the two sections, and the whole is described by Girard, after structural analysis, as 'a marvel of literary architecture'.

1–3 The singer begins his avowal of trust and devotion, all in preparation for the supplication that will follow. Throughout vv. 1–6 he refers to God in the third person and seems to address his words to supporting worshippers. He uses epithets for the Lord as his saviour in the way prominent in royal psalms (e.g. 18.1–2); with 'my light' we can compare 'thy light' (addressed to Zion) in Isaiah 60.1f. (cf. also Isa.10.17); the saviour comes to his beloved like the rising sun to scatter the perils of night. The 'deadly ones' (lit. 'harmers / evildoers')seem to be sinister beast-like shapes (cf. 22.12–13, 20–1) eager to devour him (RSV 'uttering slanders' relies on an Aramaic idiom, cf. Dan. 3.8; 6.24). Enemies are also envisaged as a great army. Not in human strength, but by trust in the Lord, the singer would banish fear.

4–6   To the consideration of his trust, the psalmist adds that of his single-minded devotion; his desire is only to dwell in the house of the Lord, and there see the beauty of his revelation and divine his will. This indication of his love seems also to carry the thought of his hope to return in peace and safety after confronting present dangers. The 'dwelling' or 'sitting' in the house of the Lord resembles the thought of 23.6 and may relate to the royal residence that was joined to the sanctuary; the high moments in the royal worship would be the experience of the revealed 'face' of God (see above on 17.15) and the ascertaining of divine guidance (cf. 5.3; 2 Kings 16.15) in the difficult decisions of state in war and peace. And the section concludes with a statement of trust in the Lord's protection in time of affliction. The Lord's 'tent' and 'rock' refer again to the Zion sanctuary, where he will keep his beloved safe under his shadow (cf. 61.2–4; 91.1–4). The psalmist's head will be raised high in victory (cf. 3.3; 18.48; 110.7). He promises then to bring the sacrifices of thanksgiving for victory (sacrifices of *teru'a* – with trumpet blasts and martial acclamations of God), singing in psalms the story of salvation.

7–12   After the preparation, the lamenting prayer. The peril seems to have deepened over some time, as though the Lord were 'hiding his face' (v. 9, cf. 22.24), and an apprehension of being forsaken has crept in (vv. 9, 12; cf. 22.1). Verse 8a may be interpreted as a recollection of the Lord's invitations to his worshippers, 'Seek (ye) my face' (the phrase is used of worship in 24.6; 105.4). Now indeed the psalmist earnestly seeks the face and favourable acceptance of God (v. 8b), and prays they may not be denied him (v. 9). Verse 10 uses a theme found also in neighbouring countries – the ruler as adopted by the deity, who is more than mother and father to him; thus Gudea of Lagash says to his goddess: 'I have no mother – you are my mother; I have no father – you are my father' (my *Kingship*, p. 203, n. 13). So our psalmist takes up the sonship bestowed on him (2.7; 89.26) and builds it into his supplication (cf. 22.9–10). He pleads for guidance on a 'path of equity', which means also a level path (cf. 26.12) safe from ambush. The reference to 'false witnesses' in v. 12 is taken by some to support the linking of the psalm to sacred trials, but it might refer to false reports about the king to other rulers, or more generally to the pouring out of harmful words and false propaganda against him as war is prepared; the 'breathing out' of violence is literally a 'puffing out' and suggests the use of harmful spells (cf. Num. 22.2–6).

13–14   The supplication is finally reinforced with a statement of confidence that the Lord will not fail him (v. 13). The 'goodness' of the Lord may have a sense similar to the 'beauty' of v. 4. The thought would be of returning alive from danger to dwell again in Zion. Verse 14 is perhaps best understood as a choral conclusion. The psalmist is bidden to continue in hope of the Lord's help, and so to be brave in the forthcoming conflict (cf. Deut. 31.7, 23; Josh. 1.6f.).

The pattern of this psalm may give the impression of a person in two minds. Such profession of trust, such apprehension of being abandoned! Is it possible so to believe while doubting, to be both brave and fearful? It seems to have been so for our psalmist; and a tradition of combining in one song praise and lament, confidence and supplication, gave him a way of honest communion with his God. Most urgently he prayed in the face of great dangers, prayed with passion and pathos; but all about his prayer, and in the midst of it, burned beacons of faith, and at the end he is confident of seeing the goodness of the Lord, though there remains a waiting; for the waiting will be 'for the Lord', a steadfast looking to him in hope and trust. The psalm focuses all that can be desired into one all-sufficient desire: to dwell with the Lord, in that nearness seeing the beauty of his face and receiving his word. This would be in response to the Lord's own invitation to his worshippers, 'Seek my face'. Here is religion in a form not always practised: to seek the beauty of the Lord, the face with which he reveals to a worshipper his particular love and acceptance. And the one who is granted to see this beauty responds with the poetry and music of a song of testimony, the melody of a devoted heart.

Almighty Father, who showed us your face in Jesus, and gave him to be our light and salvation, save us from our adversaries, and set us high upon the rock, that we may dwell in your house, and evermore behold your beauty.

PSALM 28: The Shepherd Who Carries the Lambs

Of David.

1   To you, Lord, I call, O my rock, do not be deaf to me;
    if you are silent to me,
        I shall be as those gone down into the abyss.
2   Hear the voice of my supplication, as I cry out to you,
    as I lift up my hands to your holy dwelling.
3   Do not drag me away with the wicked,
        the workers of mischief,
    who speak peace with their neighbours,
        but in their heart mean harm.
4   Give them according to their doing and the evil of their deeds;
    give them according to the work of their hands,
        and render to them their due reward.
5   As they do not heed the acts of the Lord
        and the work of his hands,
    he will pull them down, and not rebuild them.
6   Blessed be the Lord,
    for he will surely hear the voice of my supplication.
7   The Lord is my glory and my shield, my heart trusts in him;

and when I am saved my heart shall exult,
   and I will thank him with my song.
8 The glory is the Lord's,
   and he is the stronghold of salvation for his Anointed.
9 O save your people, and bless your heritage;
   be their Shepherd, and carry them for ever.

Lifting his hands towards the inmost and holiest room of the sanctuary, the singer voices an urgent supplication. He is threatened by death, perhaps through sickness, and troubled by enemies who speak peace but intend harm. As he ends with some confidence of being heard, his words seem to show that the supplication is that of the Lord's Anointed, and in the interest also of the Lord's people (vv. 8–9).

1–2   The supplicant seems to be standing in the open court or in the nave of the temple, and with raised, imploring hands (cf. 1 Tim. 2.8 and comparative material in Gunkel) he directs his entreaty to the inmost shrine, the *debir*, where in darkness stood the ark and other symbols of the divine presence (cf. 5.7; 1 Kings 6.19f.). He is in some mortal peril, fearing that he is near to being counted with the dead in the abyss of Sheol. The epithet 'my rock' joins with 'my strength and my shield' (v. 7) and 'stronghold of salvation for his Anointed' (v. 8) as typical of the king's prayers (18.1–2).

3–5   His prayer now turns sharply against the sinister 'workers of mischief', such as secretly harm him and all the society. With their outward show of peace, they are hard to identify and deal with by means other than the king's weapon of prayer, which indeed mounts to a kind of prophetic force (v. 5b – hardly an answering oracle as Craigie thinks; for the phrase cf. Jer. 24.6).

6–8   There is now a note of confidence in the prayer being favourably received, and many suppose that an oracle of acceptance has been spoken by a minister, or at any rate that such a procedure lies behind this pattern of a switch to confidence. Verse 6a can indeed be rendered '. . . for he has heard'; but it may be simpler and more in tune with the sequel to render '. . . for he will surely hear' (cf. 22.21). The point would be to add the expression of confidence as reinforcing the supplication; petition is still the main concern at the end of the psalm. The psalmist gives thanks warmly at the prospect of his deliverance and vows to sing praise (the style here resembles that of royal 18.1–2, 46, 49; 144.1–2). In v. 8b the reference to 'his Anointed One' is most simply taken as the psalmist's designation of himself (cf. 61.6f.; 63.11) as king anointed by the Lord. In v. 8a the 'power / glory' is ascribed as solely the Lord's (*lamo* as 'to him'), though a few manuscripts, with LXX and Syriac, have 'The Lord is the strength of his people' (*le'ammo*).

9   The concluding petition brings to the fore the involvement of the whole people in the fate of the psalmist. He prays that the Lord, the true king and shepherd (cf. above on 23), will care for this his flock and ever carry them through danger (cf. Isa. 40.11) – a prayer that was to be taken up in the church's Te Deum and daily responses.

In the lifting up of the psalmist's hands is seen the urgency of his supplication, and its direction right to the presence of the Lord. The prayer is for life and salvation beyond the harm purposed by secret workers of mischief. The elements of trust and hope, which usually bear up and support the entreaties of the psalms, suddenly break through; but as the Lord's Anointed praises God as his own 'stronghold of salvation', he holds up all God's people in prayer to the shepherd who will carry them in his bosom. Bede sums up a long tradition when he hears in this psalm the Lord Christ praying, giving thanks, and finally asking that, as he himself is lifted up in his resurrection, so may be all who believe in his name. The disguised evils that would pull down the good fabric of creation and society ever menace, and prayer still rises against them. Those who undertake the heavy task at God's bidding know that their voice is joined to that of the beloved Son, and their hands lifted with his towards the Father's throne. Daily the prayer continues: 'O save your people, and bless your heritage; shepherd them and carry the lambs for ever.'

Almighty God, we lift our hands to you, our rock and our shepherd; may the works of destruction themselves be destroyed, that we may all speak peace sincerely, and live with your blessing on our lips and in our hearts.

PSALM 29: The Word in the Thunder

Psalm. Of David.

1 Give to the Lord, you powers above,
   give to the Lord the glory and strength;
2 give to the Lord the glory of his name;
   bow low to the Lord in the beauty of his holiness.
3 The voice of the Lord against the waters!
     The God of glory thundered,
   the Lord, against the mighty waters!
4 The voice of the Lord with might,
   the voice of the Lord with majesty!
5 The voice of the Lord breaking cedar-trees –
   so the Lord broke the cedars of Lebanon.
6 He made Mount Lebanon skip like a calf,
   and Sirion like a young wild-ox.
7 The voice of the Lord cleaving flames of fire!

8 The voice of the Lord made the wilderness whirl;
      the Lord set whirling the wilderness of Kadesh.
9 The voice of the Lord bowed the oak-trees,
      and stripped the forests bare.
      Now in his temple all cry, Glory!
10 The Lord has taken his seat above the ocean of heaven,
      enthroned as King for ever.
11 The Lord will give strength to his people;
      the Lord will bless his people with peace.

In the usual style of a 'hymn' (Int. 4d), this magnificent psalm opens with a call to worship (vv. 1–2), followed by reasons (vv. 3–9b) and a conclusion (vv. 9c–11). In other respects, however, it is quite distinctive (the nearest comparison is 93). Its poetry is in an ancient style, with ample use of climactic parallelism (Int. 4a). Its theme also is remarkable, the eleven verses containing seven references to Yahweh's (thunder-) voice and, in all, eighteen occurrences of the name 'Yahweh'. Clearly, it is a powerful declaration in a special setting.

A heading in LXX gives the first clue to this setting: 'for the finale of Tabernacle(s)', and indeed the psalm's content agrees in pointing to a climax in the ceremonies of the autumn festival at the turning of the agricultural year (cf. Int. 5b). Psalm 24 has already given us a glimpse of the excitement as the Lord's procession arrived back at the temple gates, after a symbolic re-enactment of the subduing of the primaeval waters. Now 29 takes us on to the climax: the ark returns to the *debir*, the inmost sanctuary, and proclamation is made that the Lord has taken his throne in heaven (cf. v. 10; 93.1). He, and he alone, is supreme over all the cosmos. Our psalm shows the response of worship in heaven and earth, and recounts his great work of creative power, and looks to the life that will flow from it (v. 11). It is significant that still in post-exilic times a prophet could look forward to the manifestation of Yahweh as King, and declare that those who were missing from the gathering of all nations for the autumn festival in Jerusalem, with its worship of Yahweh as King, would lack rain (Zech. 14.9, 16–17).

1–2 The opening call to praise illustrates the universal dimension of worship in the temple, where all heaven and earth meet. The singer directs his call to 'the sons of the gods', the company of the divine attendants and ministers in heaven. They are to ascribe the power and the glory to Yahweh and (so v. 2b) prostrate themselves before the manifestation of (his) holiness, his divine majesty. They are picked out in the call to praise to emphasize the significance of the moment – that Yahweh is revealed as the utterly supreme, the cosmic victor, power above all powers, God above all gods.

3–9b This central section now glorifies the Lord by giving the grounds for the praise, his mighty deeds preceding this scene of acknowledged triumph. The first and fundamental act was his subduing of the chaos-waters; the

ancient poetic style represented this as the cleaving of the chaos-monster
(74.12f.) or the routing of the waters with a thunder-roar (*ge'ara*, 18.15;
104.7). Our poet follows this latter tradition; the Lord's thunder-voice (*qol*)
went out against (RV 'over') the waters, his might and majesty confronted
and prevailed over the 'mighy waters' that had pretensions to sovereignty
(93.3). From v. 5 the narrative reflects experience of the winter storms in the
north of the Davidic kingdom, around the great mountain ranges of the
Lebanon and Anti-Lebanon (Sirion, Hermon). From time immemorial in the
cultures of Western Asia, the breaking of the long summer drought by the
winter rains had been seen as a drama of the gods, a battle that resulted in the
earth's new life. For the Israelite faith of our poet, it is Yahweh whose power
subjugates the cosmic ocean and so gives rain and life. In evoking the first
work of creation, our poet passes easily to the portrayal of the annual winter
storms, taking them as the Creator's own renewal of his original 'victory'. So
we hear of the irresistible power of his voice in the storm that breaks giant
trees, shakes the huge mountains, sends flying the dust of the wilderness, and
divides the tongues of lightning. The 'wilderness of Kadesh' is probably in
Syria (the phrase occurs in a Ugaritic text, see Dahood) rather than around the
Kadesh oasis of the southern wilderness (Num. 20.16). In v. 9, RV 'The voice
of the Lord maketh the hinds to calve' represents traditional Hebrew vowels,
but it is more likely that the 'writhing' is of 'oaks' (*eylot*) rather than of 'hinds'
(*ayyalot*).

9c–11 After the retrospect, which has given a vivid impression of Yahweh's
assertion of power in his preparation of life, the psalmist returns to the present
scene of homage. Verse 9c resumes from the opening the theme of 'glory': all
in God's temple – primarily his heavenly abode (11.4; 104.3), with which
those in the earthly temple feel united – sing acknowledgement that the glory,
the divine supremacy, is his alone. They are responding to the climactic event
of v. 10, when the Lord took his throne over the *mabbul*, the cosmic ocean
pictured especially as the waters gathered above the firmament or sky-vault.
The throning of Yahweh above the heavenly ocean signifies that he is the
Lord of life; he has subdued and made serviceable the otherwise unruly
cosmic waters, and from them he ensures the rains and fountains on which
earthly life depends. (*Mabbul* is taken by some as a reference to Noah's Flood,
but the term came to be used in that story because the flood-waters were seen
as an irruption of the cosmic waters, *TWAT* IV, cols 633–8.) In v. 11 some
translate as a prayer-wish; so NRSV: 'May the Lord give strength . . . May the
Lord bless.' The order of the Hebrew, however, with 'Yahweh' in emphatic
position, favours the declarative 'The Lord will . . . 'The verse is essential to
the meaning of the psalm. By his kingship, that rules the great forces to
nourish life, Yahweh will give vital strength and abundant, healthy growth
and provision (*shalom*, 'peace', harmony in nature and society) to his worshippers. The word 'strength' (*'oz*) resumes the opening call, and with the last
words of 'blessing' and *shalom*, the psalm concludes on the good meaning of
all the terrible might and majesty that it has evoked.

What terror and consternation, to be out on the mountainsides in the fury of a winter storm, with the lightning ripping through the skies and the mighty crack of thunder, the tops of great trees splintered off, the forests whirling, the very mountains vibrating, and out to sea a battle seeming to rage between the rearing waves and the missiles from on high! From age-old experience of such awesome tempests the psalm-poetry draws, and makes its tribute to the seven-fold 'thunder-voice of Yahweh'. But this is not a poem on natural phe-nomena. In the convulsions of nature a meaning is seen and now declared: the Lord – who has a bond with his worshippers and gives them blessings of life and well-being – he, and he alone, is sovereign of the great forces of the cosmos; through all their awesome operations he is at work, preparing his blessings. Even in the shatterings and flames, he is creating life and shaping salvation. In the high moment of worship there has come a glimpse of the eternal moment, the moment which is also the final fulfilment, when all creation acknowledges the royal glory of the Lord and kneels before the revealed beauty of his holiness, rejoicing in his victory, his blessing and his peace.

The Lord's 'thunder-voice' is thus an aspect of his creative Word; within the shattering power is this good Word, the divine purpose and power that makes and shapes the world, the Word known at last, says the New Testa-ment, as grace and truth in the person of Jesus (John 1.1–18; cf. Wisd. 18.14f.). The psalm thus leads to meditation on the power of the Word incarnate, and on the fullness of glory that is his in the unity of the Father, Son and sevenfold Spirit.

Eternal God, who make and direct all things by your mighty Word, in all the storms of life give us your peace; until we come to sing of your glory, when you bring all things to perfection and appear for ever in the beauty of your holiness.

PSALM 30: Cause for Dancing

Psalm. Song for the Dedication of the House. Of David.

1 I will exalt you, Lord, for you have drawn me up,
and not let my foes rejoice over me.
2 O Lord my God,
I cried aloud to you, and you have healed me.
3 Lord, you have brought my soul up from the darkness;
you have restored my life from those gone down to the abyss.
4 Make music to the Lord, you his faithful,
and give thanks to his holy name.
5 For a moment is spent in his anger, but life in his favour;

> in the evening tears may visit, but joy comes in the morning.
>
> 6   But when I was at ease I said,
> I shall never be overthrown.
>
> 7   Lord, in your favour you had made my hill so strong.
> You hid your face from me, and I was troubled.
>
> 8   To you, Lord, I called out;
> to the Lord I made my supplication:
>
> 9   What gain is there in my blood, if I go down into the abyss?
> Can dust thank you? Will it tell of your faithfulness?
>
> 10 Hear, Lord, and be gracious to me;
> come, Lord, as my strong helper.
>
> 11 You turned my sorrowing into dancing;
> you took off my sackcloth, and girded me with joy,
>
> 12 that in glory I should make music to you, and not be silent;
> O Lord my God, I will give thanks to you for ever.

The psalm in itself appears to be the testifying praise made at the temple by one recovered from grave illness. The situation might thus be like that described in Job 33.24–8, and illustrated by the similar psalm of King Hezekiah after his recovery (Isa. 38.9–20). Although there is no mention of thank-offerings (ct. 116.17–19), the setting in a gathering for worship seems indicated in v. 4. Granted this was probably the original purpose of the psalm, later usage represents interesting applications to other situations. The Mishna (Bikkurim 3.4) tells of its use at the presentation of the first-fruits (the ceremony of Deut. 26.1–11). The later Jewish tractate Soferim (18.3) tells of use in the festival of Hanukka, which commemorates the dedication of the restored temple after the desecration in 164 BCE (1 Mac. 4.52–9). This latter use connects with the distinctive heading of the psalm, and could have been suggested by it. But the heading might have originated in earlier usage, perhaps for the dedication of the second temple in 515 (Ezra 6.16); or it might even have referred to the dedication of a palace (e.g. David's, 2 Sam. 5.11; LXX translates 'Song at the dedication of the house of David'). At all events, the later uses show how the poetry of the Psalms sounded with many resonances.

1–3 The singer addresses the Lord in thankful praise, recalling that he answered his cry by healing him, drawing him up, as it were, from Sheol (land of the dead, imagined as a vast pit beneath the subterranean waters). The reference at once to enemies is perhaps a feature from royal psalmody, the king always having to reckon with adversaries that would exploit every weakness and rejoice in his overthrow.

4–5 The setting in a gathering for worship becomes clearer as the singer calls for praising, thankful psalmody from the Lord's 'faithful ones' (*hasidim*), people of his covenant. The salvation of this one person is cause for joy to all his community. The 'name' here is literally 'remembrance / citation', meaning the name of God as invoked or chanted in praise; gratitude is felt for the very means by which the saviour makes himself near and available to those in need. In the time of salvation it seems that the suffering was but a moment, or like a night that was dispersed by the coming of glorious day. (For 'moment' some prefer to hazard the translation 'disturbance, trouble': 'in his anger, trouble; in his favour, life'.)

6–12 The singer now gives his story. He had grown complacent, and incurred the Lord's displeasure; his world was overturned. Verse 7a is perhaps best taken as his present comment, not a continuation of his former thought in 6b; the image may reflect the situation of a king established on the fortified hill. He recalls his supplication – how he had put it to the Lord that he would gain nothing from consigning him to Sheol, where all is silence; but if he saved him, what glad testimony he would receive! In such frank and childlike manner the psalmist had pleaded for his Lord to come as his 'helper', or rather 'saviour'. And so, through God's compassion, it had come about, and the psalmist was healed and put away the sackcloth of penitence; wearing the joyful garb of worship, he comes with dancing step to the altar to offer his song of praise. In v. 12 we may read '*my* glory' with LXX, to give a literal 'that my glory should make music to you and not be silent', a reference to his soul in restored royal glory (cf. 16.9; 57.8; 108.1; but some change the vowels to give 'my liver' and then render 'my heart').

Taken as the thankful praise of a person restored from being near death, the psalm well illustrates the practice of telling the story in the community, a testimony to the grace and power of the Lord towards those who, trusting in him alone, cry out to him. The glad worship is filled with poetry, music and dancing; the worshipper's soul is bright with the glory of one who has experienced the saviour, having confessed and put away the sin of complacency. Not for a day or a season would this worshipper praise God for his healing, but for ever. But threads of meaning were found here for the experience of a whole community. And later the church related the psalm to her times of penitence and re-dedication, times when the grace of God drew her up from the abyss of death, healed her, clothed her with gladness and led her to a time of dancing, celebrating afresh the resurrection from which her life first sprang. So for the church, as well as for the individual, the psalm prompts the glad testimony of the dance, and the music of love that honours his holy name.

Lord, deliver us in times of ease from the false security that hardens our hearts towards you; and when troubles abound, help us to cry to you with simple faith, and so be granted the morning of healing, and the new life of thankfulness without end.

PSALM 31: Into Your Hand

For favour.   Psalm.   Of David.

1   In you, Lord, I would shelter, let me never be put to shame;
    in your goodness deliver me.
2   Turn your ear to me, quickly rescue me;
    be to me a rock of defence, a strong castle for my salvation.
3   For you alone are my crag and my defence,
    and for your name's sake you will guide me
        and lead me to safety.
4   You will bring me out of the net they have laid for me,
    for you alone are my stronghold.
5   Into your hand I commit my spirit;
    you will redeem me, Lord and faithful God.
6   I have abhorred those that cherish worthless idols,
    and for my part I have trusted in the Lord.
7   I will rejoice and be glad in your love,
    when you look on my distress,
        and take heed of the troubles of my heart,
8   and have not shut me in the hand of the enemy,
    but on a wide place set my feet.
9   Be gracious to me, Lord, for I am distressed;
    my eye is wasted with grief, my body and soul alike.
10 For my days are consumed with sorrow,
        and my years with sighing;
    my strength fails through my suffering,
        and my bones, they waste away.
11 I have become the scorn of all my foes,
        a burden to my neighbours,
    a horror to my acquaintance,
        and those who see me outside flee from me.
12 I am forgotten like a dead man passed from mind,
    discarded like a broken pot.
13 I hear the whispering of many, a terror all around,
    as they confer against me, and plot to take away my life.
14 But I trust in you alone, O Lord;
    I have said, You are my God.
15 My times are in your hand;
    O deliver me from the hand of my enemies and pursuers.
16 Make your face to shine upon your servant;
    save me in your faithful love.
17 Lord, let me not be put to shame,
    for I have called upon you.

18 Let those false lips be closed,
    that with arrogance, disdain and contempt
        speak against one who is true.
19 How great is your goodness, Lord,
        which you have stored up for those who fear you,
    and openly accomplish for those who shelter in you!
20 In the covering of your presence
        you will hide them from the plots of men;
    in your shelter you will guard them from the strife of tongues.
21 Blessed be the Lord,
    who in a besieged city wonderfully shows his love for me.
22 As for me, I said in my haste,
        I am cut off from before your eyes.
    But you hear the voice of my supplication,
        when I cry to you for help.
23 Love the Lord, all you his faithful;
    the Lord keeps the steadfast, but fully rewards the proud.
24 Be strong and let your heart take courage,
    all you that wait for the Lord.

This is a prayer from a situation of great distress. But with depictions of suffering and humiliation go also expressions of trust and anticipations of thanksgiving; vv. 21–4, especially, express such a grateful confidence that many suppose a sign or oracle of favour has intervened (cf. Int. 6j). The situation is presented with such abundance of traditional motifs of suffering that it is hardly clear to us. That the psalmist is a king may be indicated by the close relationship with the Lord – his rock of refuge, his castle, crag and stronghold, emphatically 'my God' (cf. 18.1–2; 22.1,10; 89.26 etc.); he is the Lord's 'servant', before his face (v. 16), looking for the angel-graces of God's fidelity, truth, righteousness, goodness; beset by hosts of enemies that take counsel against him and (perhaps lit.) besiege his city (v. 21), encircling him with terror. And as a representative figure, he involves all the faithful, God's covenanters (v. 23), and in military style calls them to courage (v. 24). Against this may seem the traits of an outcast of society (vv. 11–13) and of physical distress (vv. 9–10). But these can be taken as traits of archetypal misery which were often included in royal or representative supplications. The image of the broken and discarded pot (v. 12) is applied to a king in Jer. 22.28.

1–4 With phrases that often seem connected with warfare, the psalmist weaves together his appeal for a hearing and for deliverance with his avowals of trust in the Lord as his only true defender, the 'strong castle' of his salvation. In v. 1b the 'goodness' or 'rightness' of the Lord means his faithfulness towards his servants, his readiness to save. Here, and with three expressions in v. 3b, we are reminded of 23: the Lord's name is upheld when he publicly saves his Chosen One, to whom he is also the good shepherd, leading to safe waters.

5–8   His supplication is now supported by especially strong statements of his trusting relationship to the Lord. His 'spirit', the mysterious essence of his life, he places in God's care, gives it into the charge of his 'hand'. He himself has not the strength to guard it, so he gives it over to the protection, rule and ownership of the one who can. Verse 5b is either an expression of confidence that in the present peril the faithful Lord will save him; or, with the familiar rendering 'You have redeemed me', he acknowledges past salvation, through which his spirit now belongs to the Lord. He then makes a solemn rejection of the worship of other gods, and affirms again his bond with the Lord. In vv. 7–8 he promises testimony and praise when saved (though some translate '. . . for you have seen my distress and taken heed' – a confidence like that of vv. 21f.). The idea of being shut in the hand of the enemy makes a dark counterpart to v. 5a.

9–18   The psalmist now increases the urgency of his appeal by depicting his suffering. The anguish affects his eyes, his soul (or we may translate *nephesh* here as 'throat') and body (lit. 'belly'), his strength and bones. In v. 10b 'because of my suffering' seems the more probable reading with support from Greek versions, instead of the very similar word in the Hebrew, 'because of my wrong-doing'. He portrays himself as an unfortunate whom enemies deride and acquaintances shrink from (as they fear the contagion of ill-fortune), one who feels that all around are whisperers plotting to destroy him. This is the ultimate misery in a tightly knit society – to be no longer accepted, a liability, best soon disposed of. To this depiction of utter humiliation, the psalmist adds fresh declarations of trust. Again we have the antithesis 'in your hand . . . from the hand of my enemies'; his faith is that the Lord's will for him must be decisive. He longs to have again the light of God's face and the joy of his faithful love. The final argument in his plea is that his enemies are cruel, false and arrogant.

19–24   The conclusion can be seen as the ultimate word of persuasion in a prayer – thanksgiving in anticipation. Indeed, the experience of acceptance seems here so definite and present that many interpreters assume that a sign or oracle of favour has been given (2 Chron. 20.14f.). At all events, the psalmist is now seen praising the rich goodness of the Lord and his wonderful, faithful love. He rejoices that his prayer has been heard, and he calls on all the covenanted people to 'love' their Lord, to follow him with single-minded trust and obedience. The closing words seem to envisage a community that still must await the realization of deliverance; a conflict lies ahead, but the soldiers of the Lord will be brave through trust in him (cf. 27.14).

The psalm holds together three conditions that may be known by the Lord's servants. The first of these is suffering, and it is indeed a very acute distress which is here held up to the divine pity; the very gift of life is consumed away, as bodily strength fails, and a sense of isolation and a fear of ill-wishers oppress the spirit. But, mysteriously, there steals upon the sufferer an awareness of the great goodness of the Lord, miracles of faithful love which come like rescuing angels into the city under siege. The besieged ones then know that they are kept under God's wings, protected in his shelter from all the plots of men and strife of tongues. Between these two contrasting situations comes, almost as a bridge, the other great element that makes up this psalm – trust in the Lord. Rejecting false idols, the psalmist sees the Lord alone as his rock of defence, his faithful shepherd, his God. Into the Lord's hand he commits his spirit; in his hand are his times, his daily experiences. He is saved from the hand of the foes and pursuers, and from the hand of the last enemy, for the hands of God are all-powerful, and sure in their accomplishing of his never-failing love.

The words in which the trust of the psalmist is most evident are recorded in Luke's Gospel (23.46; cf. Acts 7.59) as the last utterance of Jesus on the cross: 'And when Jesus had cried with a loud voice, he said, Father, into your hand I commit my spirit. And having said this, he breathed his last.' The church continued to find the psalm prophetic of his steadfast trust in suffering and of his triumph. St Athanasius (see NL), seizing on the representative aspect, believed that with these dying words Christ entrusted the souls of all good people to that loving care, for it was Christ's desire that his people should have no less secure place of refuge at the hour of their death than he had at his. Nevertheless, there is in these great words a thought and an act for every day of life. In the strength of Christ, his people continually give back their life to the God who first gave it; here is a daily dying to self which death only completes.

We bless you, Father, that even now, in the days of our tribulation, beset as in a besieged city, we are shown the light of your face; and we pray that we may daily be led by your Son Jesus to lay our times and our spirit into your hands.

PSALM 32: A Song of Forgiveness

Of David. Poem.

1   Happy the one whose sin is forgiven,
     and whose transgression is covered.
2   Happy the person to whom the Lord imputes no wrong,
     and in whose spirit is no deceit.
3   While I would not admit my fault,
     my bones were consumed through my groaning all day long.
4   For day and night your hand was heavy upon me;
     the springs of life within me turned to summer drought.
5   Then I acknowledged to you my transgression,

and no longer covered my wrongdoing.
  I said, I will confess my sin to the Lord,
    and you put away the guilt of my transgression.
6   Therefore let every faithful soul pray to you
      while you may be found;
    even when the great waters surge,
      they will not sweep over them.
7   You are a shelter for me, to guard me from trouble;
    you will surround me with songs of deliverance.

8   I will instruct you and guide you in the way you should go;
    I will counsel you, with my eye watching over you.
9   Do not be like a horse or mule not yet trained;
    with bit and bridle their course must be checked,
      or they will not come with you.
10 Many pains are prepared for a wicked person,
    but the one who trusts in the Lord
      will be circled by faithful love.
11 Rejoice in the Lord, you faithful, and be glad;
    sing out, all that are true of heart.

This is the first of thirteen psalms headed *maskil* ('poem'?), the others being 42, 44, 45, 52–5, 74, 78, 88, 89, 142. The technical reference of this term must be regarded as quite uncertain, although the underlying Hebrew verb is well known and has prompted the translations 'instruction' (cf. the verb in 32.8) and 'skilful psalm' (cf. *maskil* in 47.7). The psalm is also the second of the church's Penitential Psalms (see above on 6); appropriately so because of its theme of confession and forgiveness, although its tone is essentially joyful. In spite of some unusual features, it can best be regarded as thanksgiving and testimony in a gathering for worship. The psalmist tells his story as one who experienced deliverance from trouble, when at last he confessed his sin to the Lord. The beginning (vv. 1–2) and ending (vv. 10–11) direct the lesson of this experience to the gathering, while the heart of the psalm takes the form of address to God (vv. 3–7) and God's reply (vv. 8–9, taken however by some as the psalmist's instruction to his disciples). Rashi believed that the *maskil* psalms were cases where David had uttered the basic idea and another had elaborated it.

1–2 The theme of happiness is introduced strongly with four clauses governed by 'O the sheer happiness of ...' (*asherey*, see above on 1.1). A supremely happy person is envisaged as one whose sin has been 'borne away' or 'covered' – forgiven by God and no longer pretending there was no sin to confess.

3–7 Speaking to the Lord, but for the benefit of the circle of worshippers, the psalmist recounts his own experience. While he was unwilling to confess his sin, he was in physical distress; his bones were troubled, the sap of life dried up within him. But when he acknowledged to the Lord his wrongdoing, the burden of it was lifted from him; the Lord forgave him. The personal story carries a message for every *ḥasid*, committed to God but yet frail and liable to err. Through timely prayer they will find the help of God in the midst of peril. When the waters of chaos come rushing like the furious winter-floods down the gullies, the person so reconciled to God need not fear. In v. 7 the psalmist tells the Lord of his trust, and seems to ask with this that the Lord's protection and deliverance may be ever known in days to come.

8–9 This promise of guidance is addressed first to a singular, and is best taken as words of the Lord in response to v. 7. He promises to guide and enable the psalmist to take a good way through the problems of life, ever counselling him and watching over him with loving care (cf. the eye of the Lord in 33.18; 34.15; Jer. 24.6). The image of 'horse or mule' adds the thought that on this good way the disciple should walk with the Lord in trust and close accord, not like a horse or mule yet untrained, struggling against bit and bridle (Dahood: 'muzzle and straps'), trying to flee its master.

10–11 The conclusion gives first, as a kind of appreciation of the foregoing word of the Lord (cf. 12.6), a confirming testimony: while the life of wickedness brings its own torments, the life of trust in God is surrounded by his *ḥesed*, his unfailing care. So the final verse summons the circle of worshippers to joyful praise; these 'faithful / right' and 'true of heart' are thought of, as the psalm has shown, as those in sincere relation to the Lord, open to him in confession and forgiveness, content to take the way of his guidance, the way of closeness to him.

In giving the view that this much-loved psalm has been overrated, some critics (e.g. Duhm and Gunkel) have linked the author with the kind of doctrine attacked by the Book of Job, the doctrine that the sufferer must have some sin to confess, and if he refuses, will only get worse. But the author of Job is dealing with doctrinaires who abuse a religious insight. The psalm in itself puts forward advice based on experience, which finds an echo in many a heart (e.g. St Augustine, who in his last illness had the psalm written on the wall before him). It testifies to a surpassing happiness given by way of confession and forgiveness, and sustained in a walk with the Lord. Here indeed is a positive note for the Penitential Psalms; for confession is seen as the gate to a life of happiness, surrounded and upheld by the God's faithful love. But there is another key-word in the psalm – 'trust'; and here is a link to the Christian experience of forgiveness. By trusting in what the Lord has done to overcome the barrier of sin, by trusting in the Lord as the individual's guide and faithful companion, the pilgrim finds that sheer happiness of which the psalmist sings.

Lord Jesus, from whose cross run the springs of life, grant us by faith and sincere confession to be delivered from the drought of a guilt-laden spirit, and so to know the happiness of your guidance and fellowship along our way.

PSALM 33:   Music Full of Meaning

1   Rejoice in the Lord, you faithful;
    beautiful is praise from the true of heart.
2   Give praise to the Lord with the lyre;
    with the ten-stringed harp make music for him.
3   Sing to him a new song;
    raise the music of strings with shouts of joy.
4   For the word of the Lord is true,
    and all his work is in faithfulness.
5   He loves right and justice;
    the earth is full of the faithful love of the Lord.
6   By the word of the Lord the heavens were made,
    and all their hosts by the breath of his mouth.
7   He gathered up the waters of the sea as in bottles,
    and laid up the deep in stores.
8   Let all the earth fear the Lord;
    let all that dwell in the world stand in awe of him.
9   For he but spoke, and it was so;
    he commanded, and it was established.
10 The Lord made null the counsel of the nations;
    he brought to nothing the plans of the peoples.
11 The counsel of the Lord shall stand for ever,
    the plans of his heart to all generations.
12 Happy the nation whose God is the Lord,
    the people he has chosen for his possession.
13 The Lord looks down from heaven;
    he sees all the people of earth.
14 From the place of his throne he peers down
    upon all that dwell in the world,
15 he who has formed the hearts of each one,
    and understands all their deeds.
16 A king is not saved by the greatness of an army;
    a warrior is not delivered by greatness of strength.
17 A war-horse is a vain hope for safety;
    by the greatness of his strength he cannot deliver.
18 But the eye of the Lord is on those who fear him,
    on those who wait for his faithful love,

19 to deliver their soul from death,
    and to keep them alive in famine.
20 Our soul has waited for the Lord,
    for he is our help and shield.
21 Our heart will rejoice in him,
    for we have trusted in his holy name.
22 Lord, may your faithful love be upon us,
    as we ever wait for you.

Here we have the basic pattern of the 'hymns' or songs of praise: first the call to praise (vv. 1–3), then grounds for the praise (vv. 4–19), then the conclusion (vv. 20–2). As usual in the hymns, the address is to the worshippers rather than to the Lord, but at the end a short prayer is addressed to him (v. 22). Although the psalm is not an acrostic (Int. 4e), the total of its verses matches that of the letters of the Hebrew alphabet, perhaps for a sense of completeness (so also Ps. 38 and Lam. 5; also, by the sum of the half-verses, Ps. 146). It is the only psalm in the series 3–41 to lack a heading, apart from 10 which is really a continuation of 9. It is a fact that the end of 32 and the beginning of 33 are similar, and the two psalms are joined as one in a few manuscripts. But otherwise they are quite different and our main tradition is surely right to separate them. (The title 'Of David' found in Greek manuscripts with 33 is not textually secure.) The ample reference to music (with a 'new' song) and to the worshipping people (v. 1, cf. v. 12) and the themes of the Lord's rule of nature and nations point to a setting in the chief festival, in the high moment of Yahweh's presence in full majesty. One may think of the times of the kings (cf. v. 16); the ideas are similar to those prominent in Isaiah.

1–3 The call to praise brings before us a lively scene. The congregation (who must be 'right' and 'true' for the Lord, sincere and humble, if their worship is to be acceptable) join in 'ringing cries', acclamations of praise in response to the psalmody of cantor and instrumentalists. The instruments mentioned, perhaps only a selection of those deployed (cf. 150), are the *kinnor*, the lyre, and the *nebel*, the harp, here specified as of ten strings (Int. 3b). The call for a 'new' song (so also 40.3; 96.1; 98.1; 144.9; 149.1; Isa. 42.10; Rev. 5.9) fits the experience in the festival that the Lord who makes all things new is manifest; the moment of creation shines afresh in a vision of all things made well. As always in the Psalms, the music is for the Lord, and in no sense for the satisfaction of the worshippers; the beauty, the skill and the willing spirit of it all are for him, who is at this moment and in this place revealed in holy splendour.

4–9 Now come the reasons supporting the call for praise (as usual introduced by *ki*, 'For'). This element of the hymns was valuable as teaching, but it also had a kind of sacramental force, supporting the drama of worship by filling out the experience of God's presence, conveying to mind and heart something of the nature of his holy being. The first theme here centres on the

Creator's word. There is the wonder of his power that all sprang into existence, including the starry hosts, at the word of his mouth, the going forth of the breath of his lips. Not just a physical marvel was this, for all its vast scale and complexity; but all was made 'in faithfulness'. The word of the Lord is just, right and trustworthy; and the earth he created is filled with his *ḥesed*, his steadfast love, goodness and compassion. To set upon it, as man has often done, without respect for this divine faithfulness, justice and love would indeed be ignorant and arrogant folly. In v. 7a the traditional Hebrew vowels, giving 'as a heap', seem to associate the collecting of the waters with the miracle of the Exodus (78.13; Ex. 15.8), but the context favours the reading of LXX (*ne'od* rather than *ned*), giving 'as in a bottle'; the poetic idea is like that of Job 38.22, 37; the stored-up water-skins are brought out and tilted to give rain. In v. 8 the call to revere the Creator is probably meant to include all creatures.

10–19 After the 'Lord of creation', the 'Lord of history'; the grounds for praise now centre on his work among the nations. When they rise up in arrogance against his good rule, he brings their stratagems to nothing, while his own plans and purposes ever continue their course. Happy, in contrast, the people he has chosen, and who know and follow him. This thought, as the context shows, is filled with latent meaning. In the purpose of God, this people are the first-fruits of all earth's inhabiters, sending far and wide the call to worship and to know the Lord as God, and so to share the true happiness. For he is concerned with all – with each one, individually made by him (*yaḥad*, so Delitzsch); he watches over each one and understands their deepest thoughts. Not in the force of armies and armaments lies salvation, but in the help of the Lord; his caring eye (cf. 32.8) is on all who honour him as God, the true power. This honouring is done in worship, but also in that 'waiting' which gathers soul and body in acknowledgement that his will and his work are decisive and faithful; a waiting that is therefore a kind of stillness, hope, and trust. Mentioned along with the frequent suffering of military aggression is the other common scourge in a land of subsistence farming and uncertain rains – famine.

20–22 The conclusion comes as a choral rejoinder to the cantor. The worshippers affirm that they have such trust in the Lord and in his 'holy name' (cf. above on 30.4; Int. 6b). And they end with a prayer, which brings out again the intercourse of the faithful love of God and the quiet trust of his people.

Sounding out with musical instruments and with clear and colourful poetry, our psalm is ever and again a 'new song' to all whom it leads into the presence of the Creator. Through this music, so full of meaning, they know him anew, and see the world made new. The vast creation is found to be full of the divine faithfulness and truth, its very existence given by the Word that expresses his purpose; and all is seen to be under his caring eye, as he brings to nothing the pretensions of aggressors and cherishes those who wait upon him. Here indeed is an experience of new birth, to which this psalm would joyfully lead. The Word of creation is indeed ever the Word of new creation, and for this his creatures wait and at last have cause to rejoice.

Eternal Father, Creator of all things by your Word, cause us by that same Word to be made new, that we may sing to you the new song in faithfulness and love.

PSALM 34: Taste and See

Of David.   When he feigned madness before Abimelek, so that he drove him away, and he departed.

1   I will bless the Lord at all times;
     his praise shall ever be in my mouth.
2   My soul shall glory in the Lord;
     the humble will hear it and be glad.
3   Tell out the greatness of the Lord with me,
     and let us exalt his name together.
4   I sought the Lord and he heard me,
     and delivered me from all my fears.
5   Those who look to him become radiant,
     their faces no longer downcast.
6   Here was a sufferer who called, and the Lord heard his cry,
     and saved him from all his troubles.
7   The angel of the Lord encamps around those who fear him,
     that he may deliver them.
8   O taste and see that the Lord is good;
     happy the person who shelters in him.
9   Fear the Lord, you his holy ones,
     for those who fear him shall lack nothing.
10 When even lions lack and hunger,
     those who seek the Lord shall not lack anything good.
11 Come, children, listen to me;
     I will teach you the fear of the Lord.
12 Who among you is eager for life,
     longing for days to enjoy what is good?
13 Then keep your tongue from evil,
     and your lips from speaking deceit.
14 Turn away from evil, and do good;
     seek after peace and pursue it.
15 The eyes of the Lord are towards the faithful,
     and his ears are open to their cry.

16 The face of the Lord is against those that do evil,
    to cut off their memory from the earth.
17 When the faithful cry out, the Lord will hear,
    and deliver them out of all their troubles.
18 The Lord is near to the broken-hearted,
    and he saves those that are crushed in spirit.
19 Though the sufferings of the faithful one be many,
    the Lord will deliver him out of them all.
20 He keeps all his bones,
    so that not one of them is broken.
21 Evil will slay the wicked person,
    and those who hate the just shall be condemned.
22 The Lord redeems the soul of his servants,
    and none that shelter in him shall be condemned.

This is one of the thirteen psalms where the heading 'Of David' has been expanded to give the circumstance in David's life (Int. 2b). The expansion here is perhaps a later theorizing based on the occurrence of two verbal roots which come also in the story of David (*hll* and *t'm*, vv. 2, 8; cf. 1 Sam. 21.13). In that incident the name of the king, according to 1 Samuel, was 'Achish', but 'Abimelek' was perhaps his Semitic name or a dynastic title (cf. Gen. 20; 21; 26). This is one of the alphabetic psalms (Int. 4e). There is no verse beginning with W (awkward as an initial letter), but the total is made up by concluding with an additional P verse (v. 22, cf. above on Ps. 25). Some think that, in the original, v. 17 followed v. 15, and that it was later switched with v. 16 to conform to what had become the normal order of the alphabet, thereby causing a slight difficulty of sequence, which ancient and modern translators overcome with a little freedom. The alphabetic form is handled skilfully, and is used to express the usual thoughts of a thanksgiving, a testimony of personal salvation. However, the application of the personal experience as carrying a lesson for others is extensively developed, and in the Wisdom style akin to Proverbs. Too much should not be concluded from the use of this style; the Wisdom schools will have been close at hand in Jerusalem from the early monarchy, and their style easily passed into psalmody and prophecy. The psalm is aptly positioned; cf. v. 15 with 33.18, and v. 7 with 35.5–6.

1–3 In the common style of a thankful hymn, the psalmist declares that he will praise the Lord not only now, but continually. His soul will fully enter into the witness to God's grace and power (v. 2a), and the circle of worshippers now gathered about him will hear and rejoice (v. 2b). He invites them to join in the praise, exalting the 'name' in which the Lord is open to prayer and present in salvation (cf. on 33.21).

4–10 Still in the style of a thanksgiving, the psalmist bears witness before the gathering that the Lord answered his cry in need and delivered him from the troubles (v. 4, and probably v. 6). But the teaching aspect is now greatly developed, as the lesson of the experience is drawn out. From misery the sufferer may look up to the Lord, see the light of his face, and so receive and reflect the light of salvation (cf. 2 Cor. 3.18), a radiance of joy (v. 5, where some translators adopt another reading 'Look to him and be radiant', and emend after LXX to 'your faces'). As in Proverbs, there is emphasis on the value of 'fearing' the Lord, truly taking account of him as God in all one's acts and thoughts (vv. 7, 9, 11); round about such humble folk is a ring of divine care, an encampment of angelic powers (v. 7, cf. Ex. 14.19; Josh. 5.14; 2 Kings 6.16–17).

Boldly, the psalmist exhorts his hearers to 'taste' for themselves the goodness (or 'sweetness', Vulgate and Dahood) of the Lord – make but trial and experience will decide. In v. 9 'his holy ones' (only here of human beings) means the people of the Lord as bearing his presence, and endeavouring to be in harmony with him (114.2; Ex. 19.6; Lev. 11.44–5). The thought of v. 10 will be that in the extreme case when young hunting lions are in want, people who seek the Lord will yet lack nothing good (NEB follows a sense in later Hebrew and in Arabic to get 'Unbelievers suffer want').

11–14 The style of Wisdom teaching is now very marked. The disciples or pupils are addressed as 'sons'. They are to heed the fundamental teaching, to 'fear' the Lord, recognizing his reality in every circumstance. Question and answer were ever the favourite method in oral teaching. The psalmist's question is well directed to those full of the questing of youth – how to find and enjoy what is good. Though the values are put broadly (avoidance of evil and deceit, striving for good), there is practical focus: control the tongue and lips, turn away from an evil path; do, seek, pursue the good. 'Peace' here (*shalom*) will mean harmony with the Creator, as the foundation of health and of good relations with others (cf. Rom. 14.19; Heb. 12.14; 1 Peter 3.8–12).

15–22 The psalm eloquently develops the teaching considered so vital and urgent for the young to absorb – the surpassing benefit of taking the right way, the fatal calamity of embracing evil. For the 'faithful' (or 'righteous') – true-hearted, sensitive to God – his eye is watchful in care, his ears open to their cry. Their sufferings are many and great; they may be broken-hearted, crushed in spirit. But the Lord is near them; the saviour will give them new life. The 'bones' have been kept intact: taken figuratively, this will mean that, for all the suffering, the essential person was kept safe for the saviour to restore. But the person devoted to wickedness and cruel to the faithful dies by that same wickedness (v. 21).

This psalm has been especially prominent in Christian tradition, beginning with the citation of seven of its verses in the New Testament (John 19.36; 1 Peter 2.3; 3.10–12; cf. Rom. 14.19 and Heb. 12.14); often recited during communion, it has been applied both to Christ and, in the Christian life, to suffering and the pursuit of peace. At the end of his life, St Columba of Iona was transcribing the Psalter and finally laid down his pen after completing v. 10 (see Kirkpatrick). But how difficult it can be to commend to others the faithfulness of the Lord in hearing prayer, delivering from all troubles, ringing those who fear him with the defence of angelic powers! The friends of Job were eloquent in such counsels (Job 4; 8; 11; 15; 22) but were in the end to be condemned (Job 42.7). Somehow the truthful recognition of earth's injustices and apparently blind calamities has to be balanced with the testimony to the experience of divine mercy and love. The church begins from the crucifixion (cf. John 19.36), the atrocity which no ring of angels prevented; and she comes to celebrate it as the burning heart of all faithfulness, the salvation that shone out in the resurrection. Whatever earthly cruelties befall the faithful, they look to this holy fire and are made radiant, their faces no longer downcast. In the sacrament they taste and see that goodness of the Lord which surely saves the broken of heart who shelter in him.

Lord, whose angels encamp around those who fear you, hear our cry when we are broken-hearted, that we may taste of your goodness and be lightened by the light of your face, and ever live to bless your holy name.

PSALM 35: Calling for the Divine Warrior

Of David.

1   Contend, Lord, with those who contend with me;
    fight with those who fight against me.
2   Lay hold of shield and buckler;
    rise up and come to my help.
3   Draw spear and javelin against my pursuers;
    say to my soul, I am your salvation.
4   May those who seek my life be put to shame and confusion;
    may those who plot evil for me
        be turned back and confounded.
5   May they be like chaff before the wind,
    with the angel of the Lord driving them away.
6   May their path be dark and slippery,
    with the angel of the Lord pursuing them.
7   For without any cause they have hidden a pit for me;
    without cause they have dug their trap for my soul.
8   May ruin come suddenly upon him,
        and the net which he hid catch him;
    may he fall to destruction in it.

9   And my soul shall be joyful in the Lord;
    it shall rejoice in his salvation.
10 All my bones shall say, Lord, who is like you,
    delivering the afflicted from one too strong for him,
        the poor and needy person from one that despoils him?
11 Cruel witnesses rise against me;
    they put to me things of which I know nothing.
12 They repay me evil for good,
    to the desolation of my soul.
13 Yet when they were sick I put on sackcloth;
    I afflicted my soul with fasting.
    And when my prayer returned empty to my bosom,
14 it was as though I grieved for friend or brother.
    I went about as if mourning my own mother,
    and I was bowed down with grief.
15 But when I stumbled, they rejoiced and gathered,
        they gathered against me;
    smiting me unawares, they tore at me without ceasing.
16 When I tripped, the circle of mockers
    all gnashed their teeth at me.
17 Lord, how long will you look on?
    Restore my soul from their ravages,
        my precious one from among the lions.
18 I will give thanks to you in the great congregation;
    in the multitude of the people I will praise you.
19 May those who accuse me falsely not rejoice over me;
    may they not wink the eye,
        those who assail me without cause.
20 For they do not speak of peace,
    but devise deceitful words
        against those that are quiet in the land.
21 And they have opened wide their mouth against me;
    they say, Aha, our own eye sees it!
22 But you see it, Lord – do not keep silence;
    O Lord, do not stay far from me.
23 Stir and awake for my judgement,
    for my cause, my God and my Lord.
24 Judge for me according to your goodness, Lord my God,
    and let them not rejoice over me.
25 May they not say in their heart, Ha, we have our desire.
    May they not say, We have swallowed him up.
26 May those who rejoice at my trouble
        be put to shame and confusion,
    and those who swell against me
        be clothed with rebuke and dishonour.
27 But may those who desire my right rejoice and be glad;

>   let them ever say, Blessed be the Lord,
>   who desired that his servant have peace.
> 28 And my tongue shall sound with your goodness,
>   and all the day long with your praise.

This passionate prayer mixes urgent appeals for help and vows of praise with depictions of the evil conduct of enemies and petitions for their overthrow. Three parts can be distinguished, each concluded with a vow of praise: vv. 1–10, 11–18, and 19–28. That the psalmist is the people's leader may be seen in vv. 20 and 27; and that he is a king faced with military threats appears from his call to the Lord to come in warrior fashion, wielding the weapons of battle and giving an oracle of victory. The depiction of relations with the enemies and of their conduct can be explained in a context of interstate treaties. The neighbouring rulers should have been as brothers, being bound by covenant (cf. 2 Kings 20.12). The Lord is invoked as witness of the treaties, and threats such as were commonly attached to these agreements are summoned into effect.

1–3 The context shows that 'contend' here has a sense wider than that of lawsuits, and is indeed linked with warfare (cf. Isa. 49.25). The psalmist calls to the divine Warrior, the unseen victor in the holy wars (Ex. 15.3; Ps. 68) to take up his weapons and fight for him. In such a prayer he surely speaks as the Lord's anointed 'Servant' (v. 27), responsible for the Lord's people. The two shields mentioned in v. 2a will be the smaller hand-shield and the body-length shield carried by an aide. 'Javelin' is the likely sense of *segor*, for which RV has 'stop the way' (but RV margin has 'battle-axe'). The psalmist asks in v. 3b for an oracle which will express God's will to grant protection and victory, saying 'I am your salvation' (cf. 27.1; 62.2, 6; 89.26; Isa. 12.2; 62.11).

4–10 He prays against the foes that would take his life, and asks that the angel of the Lord should rout them (cf. 2 Kings 19.35), or that they fall into their own traps (cf. 7.15; 9.15). The singular pronouns in v. 8 may refer to a leading figure among the enemy. The psalmist affirms his innocence in the strife, and knows that only as innocent can he expect his prayer to be answered by the just Lord. The images of defeat in vv. 5–6 may reflect the language of the sanctions written into treaties, penalties to be called down on those breaking faith. The section concludes with the promise of praise when victory is given (vv. 9–10). The incomparability of the Lord above all the gods of the nations will then be the theme (cf. 18.31; 71.19; 89.6f.), especially as saviour of the oppressed. The king, and his people too, are sometimes represented as 'afflicted' or 'poor' (*'ani*), lowly and humble, to stress dependence on the mercy of God (cf. 10.2, 9; 18.27; 22.24; Isa. 51.21; 54.11; Zech. 9.9).

11–18 The psalmist now portrays to the Lord the evil behaviour of his adversaries, and so builds up to his appeal (v. 17): 'Lord, how long will you look on?' The opponents are pictured first as violent or cruel witnesses, intent on destroying him. Their false accusations would in fact be part of the propaganda of war. Appealing to the righteous Judge, he relates how they are repaying evil for good, for he had in the past behaved in a brotherly way to them. Verses 15–16 contain difficulties of language. The picture seems one of spells and sorcery, as though he felt in time of weakness that these adversaries had circled about him, striking with evil words.

19–28 Renewed prayer against the adversaries denies any justification for their hostility, which is also directed against 'the quiet in the land', the innocent people represented by the psalmist. The speaking of peace (*shalom*), so far from the adversaries' behaviour, would reflect obligations of covenant. The winking eyes and gaping mouths seem to mean an evil gloating, but may have a background of sorcery. The portrayal of these encircling and sinister foes, the appeal to the Lord not to stand far off and silent, and the promise to give praise in the great festal assembly resemble verses in Psalm 22. The reference to eyes in v. 21b seems again to refer to gloating, a theme continued also in vv. 25–6. Earnestly the psalmist prays for the defeat of these foes and for the time of rejoicing and praise. Against the scenes of malice he can here set the goodwill of those who stand with him, those who desire for him a good outcome, and who will then exalt the Lord 'who has desired the peace of his servant' – desired that all should be well for his king. So the psalmist will have that *shalom* which treacherous allies denied him, and live to speak and sing continually of the justice and glory of the Lord.

The psalm expresses the horrible experience of finding former allies turned to malevolent foes, deadly enemies who use any deceit or sinister means to deprive their victim of peace and of life itself. Not only for himself, but for the sake of all his innocent and loyal people, and indeed for the divine kingdom which he serves, the suppliant prays for salvation, with the rout of the malevolent forces. The prayer acknowledges that only the Lord can deliver from the overwhelming might of these foes, and passionately urges that he should come swiftly through the great distance and silence that seem at present to hide him.

In Christian tradition this is one of the Passion Psalms (with 22, 55, 69, 109), prophetic of Christ's sufferings at the hands of false and malicious foes. The connection is already made with the citation of v. 19 in John 15.18–25: Christ is 'hated without a cause' by a hostile world, and with him the Father, and in turn his disciples. While the story of the passion brings to the fore a spirit of forgiveness towards the adversaries, there remains the need for persistent and passionate prayer for the defeat of the oppressors who pervert truth and rejoice in their cruelty. The church hears in the psalm the voice of Christ ever praying for 'the quiet in the land', and for all who make cause with him; he prays for the evil ones to be routed by the angel of the Lord, by the divine warrior himself, yet in the end to be reconciled in his kingdom of peace (cf. Int. 6k).

Fight, Lord, against those that with lies and cruelty assault your little ones; be not silent and far off when they would abuse and destroy your creatures; and hasten the time of salvation, when all alike will bless you for the peace you have willed and established through your Son Jesus.

PSALM 36: The Light Shining in the Darkness

For favour.   Of the Servant of the Lord.   Of David.

1   Sin whispers to the wicked man in the depth of his heart;
     there is no dread of God before his eyes.
2   For he flatters himself in his own eyes
     that his hateful wrongdoing will not be found out.
3   The words of his mouth are harm and deceit;
     he has ceased to act wisely and do good.
4   He devises harm upon his bed;
     he sets himself on a path of wrong and refuses no evil.
5   Lord, your steadfast love is in the heavens;
     your faithfulness reaches to the clouds.
6   Your goodness is like the towering mountains,
          your justice like the great deep;
     mankind and animals alike, Lord, you will save.
7   How precious is your love, O God!
     And under the shadow of your wings
          the children of man take shelter.
8   They shall be satisfied with the good things of your house,
     and you will give them drink from the river of your delights.
9   For with you is the well of life;
     in your light shall we see light.
10   Continue your love to those who know you,
     and your goodness to the true of heart.
11   May the foot of pride not come upon me,
     nor the hand of the wicked drive me away.
12   See how the evildoers shall fall;
     they shall be thrust down, unable to rise.

The psalm opens with a characterization of the evildoer, a kind of lament to move God to intervene (vv. 1–4). There follows the contrasting praise of the Lord's goodness, a trustful statement in support of a prayer (vv. 5–9). The supplication at last becomes explicit – a prayer for the Lord's help against the wicked (vv. 10–11). Then all is rounded off with an expression of confidence in the downfall of the evildoers (v. 12). Such use of lament and statements of

praise and confidence in support of a supplication is found elsewhere (cf. 9–
10, 14 etc.). That the entreaty is kept implicit for much of the psalm can be
seen as part of the skill of intercession, balancing tact with the sharpness of
prayer. Especially in the depiction of the evildoer there are features of the
Wisdom tradition, with which psalmists were no doubt at home from ancient
times (cf. above on 34). The praise of the Creator's universal care and provision uses themes prominent in the autumn festival, where also there were
ceremonies symbolizing the overthrow of evil, such as may be reflected in v.
12. The psalmist sings as the representative of the people (vv. 9–10), who are
carried as it were in his own person (v. 11); he may be the king, the servant of
the Lord, as suggested also by the title, which is found elsewhere only with
royal 18.

1–4 An evil figure is portrayed, one that represents a threat to the psalmist
and his people (cf. vv. 9–11). It is the figure of a ruthless oppressor, having no
respect for God, and taking guidance only from the wicked impulse within
him; v. 1a actually pictures him as it were receiving an oracle in his heart from
'sin' (or 'rebellion'), the only god that he worships. Even in resting he does
not desist, but lies thinking out new deeds of evil.

5–9 Addressing the Lord now in direct praise, the psalmist expresses confidence in his good rule of the world. He portrays this rule with a brilliance
that should more than counter the preceding image of evil. High as the
heavens, firm as the mountain-pillars of the cosmos, inexhaustible as the
cosmic ocean is the goodness of the Lord, as known in committed love and a
justice that upholds the right and defends the little ones. This God is Saviour
of humans and of animals (v. 6c). Under his wings there is shelter for all
humankind, for he is wonderfully faithful in his care for his creatures. The
thought of salvation here has a focus in the sanctuary of Zion (the 'house', v.
8), where the high moments of worship brought the vision of the Creator's
presence, radiant with the light of life, and a world made perfect as the garden
of Eden (*'edanim*, 'delights'), nourished and made fruitful by the fountain and
river flowing from the holy presence.

10–12 To this God, celebrated as Saviour of all the world, the supplication
is raised: may his *hesed*, his pledged love, not cease towards those who do take
heed of him and sincerely trust in him. The psalmist, in the royal manner,
speaks of himself as the adversary's target: may he not be overcome by the
trampling foot or the smiting hand of the aggressor. The confidence expressed
in v. 12 supports the prayer, and may reflect a symbolic action for the
worshippers to witness, a prophetic demonstration of the eventual doom of
those that work harm (cf. 48.9; 68.1–2; the first word, *sham*, 'there', seems
sometimes to be used like 'behold', cf. Dahood).

While the fluctuation of good and evil prospects, the alternation of hope and
fear, is a common experience, the psalm sees the contrast at a deeper level.

Through fellowship with God along a way of reverence and truth, the servants of the Lord perceive clearly and with horror the ravages of those who follow only the prompting of evil in their hearts. Against this sad perception, the worshippers cling to a vision born in the holy place, a light from God's presence, a vision of the divine wings that would shelter earth's peoples and animals, and a fountain that gives life to all his creatures. This good vision, with assurance of the Creator's faithful love, is nourished in the faithfulness of worship and persistence of prayer, and it will not surrender to the apparent dominance of the arrogant and cruel heart. The New Testament has many echoes of our psalm to show both the oppression of sin (Rom. 3.18; 6.12f.) and the immeasurable grace of God known in Christ, the light and the river of life (John 1.4f.; 4.10f.; 8.12; Rev. 21.6; 22.1–5), the heights and depths of love (Rom. 11.33; Eph. 3.18f.). In this new context, the psalm still makes its contribution of prayer to sustain the good vision.

O God, the Saviour of all your creatures, shelter your little ones in the covering of your wings, that they may be safe from cruel hearts and hands, and live with joy in the light of your face.

PSALM 37: To Dwell on God's Land

Of David.

1   Do not be resentful at the evildoers,
     and do not envy those who do wrong;
2   for like grass they will quickly wither,
     and like the green herb fade away.
3   Trust in the Lord and do good;
     dwell on the land, and feed on his truth.
4   Let your delight be in the Lord,
     and he will give you your heart's requests.
5   Put the burden of your way on the Lord;
     trust in him, and he will act.
6   And he will make your goodness shine out like the dawn,
     and your just dealing as the midday sun.
7   Be still in the Lord, and wait for him;
     do not be resentful at one who prospers
         while following evil schemes.
8   Leave off from wrath, and let go your anger;
     do not grow resentful and so be led to do wrong.
9   For evildoers shall be rooted out;
     it is those who wait on the Lord that shall possess the land.

10 In a little while the wicked one shall be no more;
    you will search his place, and he will not be there.
11 But the humble shall possess the land,
    and delight in abundance of peace.
12 The wicked man schemes against one who is just,
    and gnashes his teeth at him.
13 The Lord shall laugh at him,
    for he sees that his day is coming.
14 The wicked draw the sword and bend their bow,
    to strike down the poor and humble,
      and slaughter those who are true in the way.
15 Their sword shall pierce their own heart,
    and their bows shall all be broken.
16 A little that a good person has
    is better than great riches of the wicked.
17 For the arms of the wicked shall be broken,
    but the Lord sustains those who are true.
18 The Lord knows the days of the pure,
    and their heritage remains for ever.
19 They shall not be put to shame in evil times,
    and in the days of dearth they shall have enough.
20 But the wicked shall perish, and the enemies of the Lord
      wither as the glory of meadows;
    and like smoke they shall vanish away.

21 The wicked must borrow and cannot repay,
    but the good person is ever giving to those in need.
22 For those whom God blesses shall possess the land,
    but those he curses shall be uprooted.
23 When someone's steps are guided by the Lord,
    and they delight in his way,
24 though they fall, they will not be flung from the path,
    for the Lord has hold of their hand.
25 I have been young, and now am old,
    yet I never saw a good person forsaken,
      or his children searching for bread.
26 All day long he shows kindness and lends,
    and his descendants also shall be blessed.
27 Turn from evil, and do good,
    and so abide for ever.
28 For the Lord loves the thing that is right,
      and will not forsake his faithful;
    they shall be guarded for ever,
      but the brood of the wicked shall be cut off.
29 The just shall possess the land,
    and shall dwell on it for ever.

30   The mouth of the just utters wisdom,
     and their tongue speaks what is right.
31   The teaching of their God is in their heart,
     and their footsteps do not falter.
32   The wicked man spies on the just,
     and seeks occasion to kill them.
33   The Lord will not leave them in his hands,
     nor let them be condemned when they are judged.
34   Wait for the Lord and keep his way,
         and he will raise you up to possess the land;
     when the wicked are uprooted, you will see it.
35   I have seen a wicked person in great power,
     flourishing like a green tree in the forest.
36   Again I went by, and he was gone;
     I sought him, but he was nowhere to be found.
37   Keep innocence and heed the thing that is right,
     for that will bring you peace at the last.
38   But sinners shall all perish together;
     the continuance of the wicked shall be ended.
39   The salvation of the just comes from the Lord;
     he is their stronghold in time of trouble.
40   And the Lord shall help and deliver them;
     he shall deliver them from the wicked and save them,
         because they have sheltered in him.

In this alphabetic psalm each letter in turn introduces usually two verses. The main thoughts recur at the prompting of the alphabetic requirements, but for each quarter of the psalm a leading theme can be discerned: vv. 1–11 counsel against indignation; 12–20 the fate of the wicked; 21–31 blessing for the good; 32–40 reiteration of the contrast. The psalmist throughout is teaching (not praying or praising), and in the style characteristic of Wisdom schools from ancient times; it is like the voice of an experienced, indeed elderly, sage (vv. 25, 35–6) addressing a single pupil, as we often find in Proverbs. He warns against envy of the prospering wicked and insists that it is the faithful who will possess and dwell on the land – themes that could apply in any period, but possibly suggesting a time of foreign oppression and internal corruption, with dispossession or exile. Comparison can be made between the piety of God's 'law' in vv. 30–31 and that in 1.2, and it is Ps. 37 which seems to have the older conception. L. Delekat, who studied asylum procedures extensively, suggested that our psalm was a priestly exegesis of an oracle given to a group who planned to flee the land, but were counselled to remain; but a more general purpose seems likely. The psalm shows again the link between the Wisdom schools and the musical psalmody of the temple (cf. already 1, 32, 34, 36).

1–11 The opening counsel is against a bitter rage, a hot resentment arising when unscrupulous villains seem to fare better than oneself. They will fade away soon enough, the psalmist urges, and he uses the favourite image from that climate of fierce summer drought – the flowers and grass so fine in the spring, so soon withered in summer's heat. The counsel soon becomes positive: to trust and be still in the Lord, to centre one's happiness in him; and (lit.) to 'roll' one's way on him – unburdening oneself to him, letting him take charge of one's way. The promise is that soon you will lose that sense of personal injustice, and a happy light of contentment will shine from your heart. The wicked will vanish, but those who wait for the Lord, the humble, the poor, will live to enjoy the good things of God's land. This last image (vv. 9, 11, 22, 29, 34!) may go back to the idea of good land promised to the people in the wilderness, a heritage given by God and most pleasant through his blessings (Deut. 8.7f.; 11.9f.). There, according to v. 3b, you feed upon (his) faithfulness, having rich sustenance from his faithful love (less likely are the dubious translations 'feed securely' and 'follow faithfulness').

12–20 The evildoer now appears more clearly as an aggressor, scheming and savage against a good person, murderous indeed against the innocent that stand in his way. The psalmist teaches that such evil brings its own destruction. The might and wealth of the wicked is as nothing in the eyes of the Lord (he 'laughs' at it, cf. 2.4). The good may have little wealth, but having communion with the Lord, they have all. The Lord 'knows' their days, watching with care over all the daily events of their lives.

21–31 The rich in the end turn out to be caught in debts, while a good person is ever giving, and yet able to give again. There are stumblings for those who are guided by God, but they will not be hurled from his way, for his hand holds them. The specific claim of v. 25 brings the questionable side of all this teaching to the fore. Many indeed can testify to the wonders of help that come to the pure and good, the gentle and the kind, but this 'never' ('I never saw a good person forsaken') is hard to accept. The psalmist's testimony will surely have to be qualified and balanced with other scripture (cf. above on 34). In vv. 29–30 the picture is not so clearly that of a student of scripture such as we met in 1.2; more broadly, the reference is to those who have taken the guidance and commandments of God deep into their hearts, so that their action and their words alike flow from the divine will.

32–40 The murderous character of the 'wicked' in this psalm is again apparent (vv. 32, 35) – persons of power, ruthless to those in their way. The counsel of trust is repeated: wait for the Lord, keep the heart whole in devotion to him, and so in the end find peace. In v. 37a our translation assumes vowel changes in line with the ancient versions; the Hebrew gives 'Mark the pure person and see the true'. Verse 37b can be rendered 'there is posterity for a peaceable person', contrasting with 38b 'the posterity (/continuity) of the wicked shall be ended'; 'posterity' (*aḥarit*) would refer to an earthly life continuing through descendants.

The psalm is from one of those times when holding to what is good and true seems to bring disadvantage, and even suffering or death. The rising generations look eagerly for models, and many are impressed by worldly success, rather than by quiet virtues which seem unrewarded. The psalmist earnestly engages with this situation, and would have the young recognize the transience and vanity of the evil course, and the true satisfaction and delight of humble trust in the Lord. Taking delight in him, having his teaching in one's heart, putting burdens on him, being still to him, having him know one's days and guide one's steps, cherishing kindness, humility and purity – this is to find peace and to dwell on his land amid the harvest of his faithfulness. Knowing the fundamental truth of all this, the psalmist has struggled to assert it warmly against all the contradictions of what can be observed, and in v. 25 especially has come to sound like the hurtful counsellors of Job. But the thrust of his advice, his pointing to the only way of peace, this gives the psalm its lasting value and accounts for its echoes in the New Testament (especially Matt. 5.5).

Merciful and generous Lord, grant us to know that in you alone we shall find true delight and peace; and so may we commit our way to you and come to dwell on your good land for ever.

PSALM 38: A Prayer from the Edge

Psalm.   Of David.   For remembrance.

1   Lord, do not rebuke me in your anger,
     or chasten me in your wrath.
2   For your arrows stick fast in me,
     and your hand has fallen upon me.
3   There is no health in my flesh because of your indignation,
     and no peace in my bones because of my sin.
4   For my offences have risen over my head;
     like a great burden, they are too heavy for me.
5   My wounds reek and fester,
     because of my foolishness.
6   I am bowed down and brought very low;
     all day long I go about mourning.
7   For my bones are full of burning,
     and there is no whole part in my body.
8   I am utterly feeble and crushed;
     I cry out at the disquiet of my heart.
9   Lord, all my longing is before you,
     and my groans are not hidden from you.

10   My heart throbs, and my strength has left me,
     and even the light of my eyes has gone from me.
11   My friends and companions stand away from my misfortune,
     and my neighbours stay far off.
12   Those who seek my life lay snares,
     and those who would harm me speak evil,
         and mutter falsehood all the day long.
13   But I am like the deaf who do not hear,
     like the dumb who cannot speak.
14   Yes, I am like one who does not hear,
     in whose mouth are no reproaches.
15   Truly, I wait for you, O Lord;
     you will answer, Lord, my God.
16   For I have prayed that they should not rejoice over me,
     those who exult over me when my foot has slipped.
17   For I am ready to fall,
     and my pain is ever with me,
18   though I confess my wrongdoing,
     and am sorry for my sin.
19   Those who are my enemies without cause are strong,
     and those who hate me wrongfully are many.
20   Those who repay evil for good are set against me,
     in return for my seeking their good.
21   Do not forsake me, Lord;
     my God, do not stay far from me.
22   Hasten to my help,
     my Lord and my salvation.

In this lamenting prayer, the supplicant appears as grievously sick, the symptoms including skin disease, palpitations and burning pain; to this distress is added the sense of God's remoteness, with friends also withdrawn and enemies acting and speaking their hostility. Such comprehensive distress has suggested to some scholars that the psalm was intended as a typical lament, into which various sufferers could enter. Others have gone further and taken the psalm as voiced by the representative of the nation; and certainly such a national interpretation seems to have been established by the time of LXX (*c.* 250 BCE), which adds the heading 'for the Sabbath'. The heading 'For remembrance' or 'To remind' (also Ps. 70) gives the aim as to 'remind' God – to make vivid before him the distressing situation, appealing for his action. Some suggest a link with offerings made for such 'reminding' (Lev. 2.2f. etc.). The 22 verses may deliberately conform to the total of letters in the Hebrew alphabet (cf. above on 33). The tone remains dark throughout, with no expressions of confidence or anticipations of praise; lamenting depiction of the sufferings fills most of the psalm (vv. 2–20), while direct petitions are made only at the beginning (v. 1) and end (vv. 21–2). Related psalms are 6 and 39.

1–8 As often in supplication, the first word uttered is the holy name, 'Yahweh'; so the sorrowful psalm is launched from the outset as a direct appeal to the one who has made himself known in power and care. The opening prayer for the moderation of his 'rebuke' is almost the same as that of 6.1. It acknowledges that the affliction is in a sense intended by the Lord as a corrective response to some wrongdoing. At v. 2 the lament begins, depicting the suffering to move God to pity. His arrows and blows are seen in outward wounds and inward burning and throbbing. The sufferer is feeble and bowed low, and relates the ordeal to his sins, which he does not specify but sees (especially in their consequences) as a flood passing over his head, or as a massive burden.

9–14 The Lord is invoked afresh, this time with the name 'Adonay', the master and sovereign (Int. 6c). Before this almighty one nothing is hidden, and he must know how the sufferer yearns and sighs for his help. The distress is further held up to his pity – the throbbing heart, the weakness, the failing eyes, and more especially now the isolation. While those that should be close move away, reluctant to endanger themselves, enemies whisper harmfully and would have the sufferer done away; yet he makes no retort.

15–22 Again the plea is pressed with the name 'Yahweh' (v. 15a); all hope is centred on him; he, 'Adonay, my God' (v. 15b), will surely answer. The concluding verses allude again to those who are enemies without reason, and to the sense of an imminent fall to destruction; and again there is admission of sinfulness and penitence. Then at the last, a series of direct calls for help gives a glimpse of the foundation of the sufferer's hope; the Lord has been his companion and his saviour, and so the last words can call to him: 'Do not forsake me ... hurry to my help, Adonay, my salvation.'

The voices of the sufferers in the Psalms rise from various situations. In the present case the voice is that of one with extreme physical ailments, deserted by friends, reviled by adversaries, and admitting to a sinful past which has led to this condition. That the sufferer believes he is wounded by the arrows of God's wrath is in the end a hopeful aspect, in that he is not helpless before blind forces, but can appeal to the just and compassionate Lord, whom he can call his God and his salvation; and he can pray and know that a good outcome may yet await him. To this Lord he can yet say, 'All my longing is before you ... truly I wait for you ... do not forsake me or stay far from me ... hurry to my help, my Lord, my salvation.' And through the voice of this ancient sufferer many since have raised a 'reminding' prayer, making vivid before God their need and their faith, opening a way for deliverance.

With the later use 'for the Sabbath', the echo of v. 11 in the passion story (Luke 23.49), the addition in the old versions of phrases pointing to the suffering of God's Beloved, and the Lenten use as a Penitential Psalm, the voice of our psalmist is heard as the voice of the suffering people of God, and of him who entered into their ordeals that he might be their salvation. In this way the psalm can still plead for those in terrible sufferings, expressing also the prayer of the Beloved One who bore the sins of many that he might fulfil all their longing.

Almighty Lord and Saviour, behold with pity the wounds of your people; do not forsake us, sinful as we are, but for the sake of the passion of your Beloved One, Jesus, come quickly to our aid.

PSALM 39: A Passing Breath

For favour.   For confession.   Psalm.   Of David.

1   I said, I will watch my ways,
    that I may not sin with my tongue;
  I will keep a guard over my mouth,
    while the wicked are before me.
2   I kept still and silent;
  I held my peace, to no avail.
  For my pain increased,
3   my heart grew hot within me;
  through my sighs the fire has blazed up,
    and I have spoken with my tongue.
4   Lord, let me know my end,
    and what is the measure of my days,
  that I may know how short is my time.
5   See, you have appointed my days as hand-breadths,
    and my time is as nothing in your sight,
  for even in the prime of life man is but a fleeting thing.
  [Pause]
6   Each walks about like a shadow,
    and they are in turmoil for nothing;
  they heap up, but do not know who will gather.
7   And now, for what do I wait, O Lord?
  My hope is only in you.
8   O deliver me from all my sins;
  do not make me the scorn of the fool.
9   I was silent and did not open my mouth,
  for surely it was your doing.
10   Take away your plague from me;
  I am worn out by the force of your hand.
11   You chasten man with rebukes for wrongdoing,
    and like a moth you consume his beauty;

> all mankind is but a breath.   *[Pause]*
> 12 Hear my prayer, Lord, and give heed to my cry;
>   do not be silent at my tears.
>   For I am but a visitor with you,
>   soon passing on, like all my fathers.
> 13 Look away from me, that I may have cheer,
>   before I depart and am no more.

This seems to be the supplication of someone in grave sickness, a long ordeal
which has brought near the reality of death. It is a distinctive and very moving
prayer, but all its elements, as usual in lamenting supplications, can be seen as
intended to give force to the cry for help; they are not autobiographical or
philosophical ruminations, but considerations to move God. The psalmist
seems to have been at home in an ancient Wisdom tradition, which sounds
also in Job and Ecclesiastes. There are a number of similarities with the
preceding psalm. The second phrase in the heading (found again, but with a
different preposition, *'al* 'over', in 62 and 77) is often taken as a name, 'for
Jeduthun', explained as a psalm-guild father (Int. 2a); so the psalm would be
from his tradition. Mowinckel (*Psalms* II, p. 213) argues rather that it means
'for confession' (*y-d-h* as in 1 Kings 8.33, 35), indicating ceremonies of which
the psalm was a part.

1–3   This unusual introduction is an indication of the extremity of the
suffering. The psalmist had held to the ideal of suffering patiently (cf. 38.13–
14), acknowledging the hand of the Lord (cf. v. 9), and being careful not to
seem to question the justice of God in the hearing of the ungodly. But his
condition grew only worse, and the inward fires, as though fanned by his
sighs, have blazed up and caused him now to cry out to God.

4–11   The resultant prayer is still controlled by humility It begins without
reproaches; the sufferer simply asks that he may be helped to accept the
brevity of his life, as of all human life (v. 4 therefore not, as in BCP, asking to
know how many days remain). The thought is developed as a consideration
to move God – so short is human life, even at its best; so insubstantial, with
any wealth and achievements quickly snatched away; then (it is implied) may
not the little time that this sufferer has be more happy (cf. v. 13), especially as
all his hope is in the Lord alone? Again in humility, he does not claim to be
blameless, but asks to be saved from his sins (from their consequences),
recognizing that God chastens man 'with rebukes for wrongdoing', eating
away his vigour and health as a moth consumes a garment. With this readiness
to accept God's justice, the sufferer pleads also that time of silent acceptance
(v. 10, cf. 1–3), and prays for God to take away his 'stroke' or 'blow' of
sickness (v. 10).

12–13   The concluding prayer is that God, for his part, should not stay
silent, but speak the word of comfort and salvation. The brevity of life is

urged again. As 'sojourners' (*ger*, 'resident alien') without rights of possession, so human beings are granted a little stay on God's land, before passing on to their abiding home in the abyss of silence, Sheol; but sojourners and guests, because of their weak position, were specially protected and honoured, and so the comparison makes an appeal to the Lord's faithful kindness. The concluding verse is full of pathos – that a little cheer might return if God but looked away from the sufferer (cf. Job 7.19; 14.6). But again, there is the note of humility; it is the judging eye of God which should look away, for the psalmist does not claim the merit to satisfy its searching purity.

This touching prayer reflects the dominant religious outlook of most of the Old Testament, an outlook which did not expect real life for the individual beyond death. Even the hope of a kind of continuance through children is not mentioned here. In due course, the hope of God's good purpose for the future of his creatures was to develop in several ways, but in the meantime, for many centuries, the old austere outlook encouraged a keen appreciation of the light of life while it was given, and of the reality and glory of God. Eternity was his alone, and humans were a quickly passing phenomenon best occupied (so our psalm teaches) in looking to him with humility, patience and hope, and certainly not in heaping up wealth and self-importance. The theme is taken up in the New Testament in the new context of the resurrection: this fleeting life is a pilgrimage to the true home in God's eternal bliss (Heb. 11.13–16; 1 Peter 2.11).

Eternal Father, see the tears of those who suffer, and in your compassion deliver them; give us wisdom at all times to know that we are pilgrims passing soon through earthly life, and may all our hope be in you.

PSALM 40: The Self-Offering of the Lord's Anointed

For favour.   Of David.   Psalm.

1   I waited, waited for the Lord,
    and he inclined to me and heard my cry.
2   He brought me up from the raging pit, up from the miry clay,
    and set my feet on the rock, and made my steps secure.
3   He put a new song in my mouth, a song of praise to our God,
    that many should see and fear, and come to trust in the Lord.
4   Happy the person who makes the Lord his trust,
    and has not turned to false gods and evil spirits.
5   You have multiplied your wonders, Lord my God,

and in your thoughts for us you are beyond compare;
    if I declare and recount them, they are too many to tell.

6   Sacrifice and meal-offerings you did not want,
        so you revealed in my ears;
    burnt and sin offerings you did not require.

7   Then I said, See, I come,
    as it is written for me in the scroll.

8   To do your will, my God, I delight;
    your law is within my heart.

9   I proclaimed the good news of salvation
        in the great congregation;
    see, I did not withhold my lips, Lord, you know well.

10   I did not hide your just work within my heart,
        but declared your faithfulness and your salvation;
    I did not conceal your fidelity and truth
        from the great congregation.

11   So you, Lord, will not withhold your compassion from me;
    your faithful love and truth shall ever guard me.

12   For troubles without number have come about me,
        my offences have overtaken me so that I cannot see;
    they are more than the hairs on my head,
        and my heart fails me.

13   May it be your will, Lord, to deliver me;
    Lord, hasten to my help.

14   May those who seek my life, to sweep it away,
        be altogether put to shame and confusion;
    and those who desire my hurt be turned back and disgraced.

15   Let them be desolate with their shame,
    that say of me, Aha, aha!

16   But let all those who seek you be glad and rejoice in you;
    and those who love your salvation ever say,
        The Lord be praised.

17   As for me, I am poor and needy – may the Lord think of me;
    you are my help and my deliverer; O my God, do not delay.

This is one of several psalms which begin with thoughts of praise and salvation (so vv. 1–10) and end with lamenting supplication (vv. 11–17; cf. Pss 9–10, 27, 89). Most of the second part appears again as 70, but its genuine connection with the first part is shown by links of thought and wording. The two parts complement each other. By beginning with reference to former salvation and to the consequent testimony to God's faithfulness, the psalmist establishes a ground from which to launch his present supplication; surely this God, whose grace he has so openly celebrated, will not fail him now. There are remarkable features in the first part – a dramatic rescue from the mouth of Sheol, the 'new song' (at the new revelation of God), the witness in the full

festal assembly, with announcement of the divine victory, and the solemn
'entry' or self-presentation of the psalmist, in accordance with a document
and more pleasing to God than the sacrifices. A good explanation of all this
can be given if the psalmist is taken to be a Davidic king. We have already met
the themes of the rescue from Sheol and the subsequent witness in the royal
18 (cf. 9.13), and a document of God's words for the king featured in 2. The
second part of our psalm also suits a royal interpretation as a prayer against
many fierce assailants; in such a case kings came before God as *'ani* – humble
and afflicted, poor and helpless (v. 17, cf. above on 35.10). He especially is the
target of the enemies (vv. 14–15), but the interest of a whole people is at stake
(vv. 5, 16).

1–5   The psalm begins as testimony – how the Lord delivered the singer
from the mouth of Sheol, that great pit beneath the subterranean waters
imagined as the land of the dead (cf. 18.4–5, 16; 69.2). The reference could
be to a deliverance from some mortal danger, but it may be preferable, in
view of vv. 6–10, to see already here allusion to the symbolic ceremonies of
the great festival (Int. 5b, cf. above on 18). There it seems to have been shown
how God saves his 'Son' from the waters of death, establishing anew the
kingdom of life. Such a symbol was full of promise and hope, and gave
ground for the kings' pleas in times of need. The Hebrew idiom for the
'waiting' in v. 1 suggests a testing ordeal where hope and trust had to be
sustained (the verb has also been explained as 'I called, called', cf. Dahood).
The 'rock' is an image with echoes of the summit of the temple hill and of the
Lord himself (cf. above on 27.5). The 'new song' inspired by God belongs to
the moment that shines in the festival, when the Creator appears in full
majesty and makes all new (cf. above on 33.3). Likewise the 'many', who see
the deliverance with awe, represent not only the vast concourse of pilgrims,
but also the world's multitudes (cf. Isa. 53.11–15). One by one they learn to
trust; happy each one who so believes in the Lord and not in false, deceitful
'gods' (v. 4; the rare expressions are sometimes translated '. . . have not turned
to the proud and those that stray after a lie'). The testimony to God as saviour
declares his incomparability; none in heaven or on earth is the like of this
almighty and all-merciful Lord (cf. 18.31; 71.19; 77.13; 86.8; 89.6, 8).

6–8   From ancient times warning was sometimes given that ritual sacrifices
might not be God's chief desire from his worshippers; it was the dedication of
heart and conduct which pleased him best. In Egypt before 2000 a king taught
his successor 'More acceptable is the character of one upright of heart than the
ox of the evildoer' (*ANET*, p. 417). A similar message was given to King Saul
(1 Sam. 15.22f.), and the theme recurs in the Prophets (Hos. 6.6 etc.). These
were not proposals to abolish sacrifice, but corrections of motive, advice on
priorities (cf. 50.7–15; 51.16–19; 69.30–1). The present passage appears from
its context to be another reference to the symbolism of the royal ceremonies.
The rolled document of v. 7 is then the record of words of the Lord bestowed
at the enthronement and its renewals; these granted the king the divine

'sonship' and all its blessings (2.7f.), but also included God's requirements (hence it is called 'the testimony' in 2 Kings 11.12, cf. the 'covenant and testimony' in Ps. 132.12; comparison can be made with a 'protocol' presented to the pharaohs at their coronation, my *Kingship*, p. 204, n. 22). It seems that, in response to the bestowal of this oracular scroll, the king 'entered' before the Lord ('See, I come / enter') and declared his readiness to do God's will, having his teaching in his inward parts (*me'im* 'intestines'). This self-dedication of the Lord's Anointed is given a rich significance by its comparison with the sacrifices that would have been offered in the festival. His ears have been profoundly opened ('dug') by the Lord – he has received a word of the Lord (to judge from a similar idea in Mesopotamian kingship, such opened ears further signify a continuing grace to know and do God's will): the royal self-offering is more valued by God than all the sacrifices. The contrast puts the king's obedience and presentation of himself in a sacrificial light; in a sense it is the supreme sacrifice, from which many will be blessed (cf. Isa. 53.10f.).

9–10   Allusion to the king's duties in the great festival is here especially clear. Standing before the vast assembly, he proclaimed the divine victory which the ceremonies had signified; it was a 'gospel' (*bissar* especially of announcing victory tidings) which the Lord's Anointed announced to the humble (cf. Isa. 61.1f.). Such witness was a great royal duty, a proclaiming of Yahweh's faithfulness and salvation to all the world (see above on 18.46–50).

11–17   Having referred to all this service before the great congregation and indeed in the eyes of the world, signifying his dedication and his public testimony to God's faithful love, the singer now begins his supplication. Shall he not himself be guarded by the faithful love which he has openly praised, of which he has been appointed, as it were, the champion? He describes to the Lord how innumerable evils have befallen him, coming at him from every side, and he freely admits them to be consequences of his sins. He prays for the defeat of enemies who seek to sweep him away (with vv. 14–15 cf. 35.4, 26; 71.13), and for the joyous relief of the Lord's loyal people. He presents himself, not with any glory, but as one poor and afflicted (cf. above on 35.10; also 86.1; 109.22). May the Lord, his help, his deliverer and his God (cf. 18.2, 48; 27.9) hasten to his aid.

Those who divide this psalm into two separate compositions are right in appreciating the difference of tone. But the tension is not between two independent psalms, but between the ideals given in worship and the sufferings which can overwhelm the worshipper in the days that follow. Where now the divine salvation and faithfulness celebrated in the drama of worship, now that troubles encircle and death threatens? The psalm accepts the difference frankly, and makes it the basis of a prayer to move the Lord. The poetry of worship, that revealed the faithful Saviour and taught the way of dedication to him, is still accepted as profoundly true; but it leads to a powerful and penetrating prayer that the divine glory and salvation should act upon the current troubles. The sacrament and gospel of worship are the mighty foundation for the sufferer's appeal to the Lord.

In the New Testament vv. 6–8 are given an application to the 'offering of the body of Jesus Christ', a sacrifice better than the temple offerings, sanctifying believers and giving them entry into the holy presence (Heb. 10; the citation of our psalm follows LXX, giving at v. 6 'but a body you have prepared for me', which may be an interpretative rendering of the Hebrew 'ears have you dug for me'). With a special use on Good Friday, the psalm has been fruitfully applied to the raising of Christ from the place of death, the new song for the new kingdom, the countless miracles of grace, and the gospel of the divine faithfulness. Above all, it has illumined the cross as the true sacrifice, the self-offering which by the Father's will brings the salvation of the many. And in all sufferings which still beset the poor and the seekers of God, the gospel and the sacraments of that royal sacrifice give the strength to pray and to hope with the psalm, and in the end to rejoice in the Lord the deliverer.

O Christ, who took for us the royal way of sacrifice, deliver us from our innumerable offences; and graft your teaching within our hearts, that we may live to rejoice in you, and ever declare the good news of your salvation.

PSALM 41: Who Makes the Bed of the Sick?

For favour.   Psalm.   Of David.

1   Happy the one who attends to the needy;
     on the day of trouble the Lord will rescue him.
2   The Lord will guard and restore him,
          and he shall be blessed on earth,
     and you will not give him up to the will of his enemies.
3   The Lord will support him on his sickbed;
     you will turn over all his bed in his illness.
4   So now I say: Lord, be gracious to me;
     heal my soul, for I have sinned against you.
5   My enemies speak evil against me:
     When will he die and his name forever perish?
6   And if they come to see me they speak falsely;
     their heart gathers mischief,
          and they go out and speak it abroad.
7   All my adversaries whisper together against me;
     against me they think out what would harm me:
8   Let a fatal pestilence, they say, take hold of him,

and once laid low, let him never rise again.
9   Even one who was my ally, one whom I trusted,
        and who ate of my bread,
     has lifted his heel against me.
10   But you, Lord, have pity on me,
        and raise me up, that I may reward them.
11   By this I shall know that your delight is in me:
        when my enemy does not triumph over me,
12   while as for me, in my integrity you hold me fast,
        and set me before your face for ever.
13   Blessed be the Lord, the God of Israel,
        from everlasting and to everlasting, amen and amen.

This has sometimes been taken to be a psalm of thanksgiving, with vv. 1–2 drawing out the lesson from the healing that has been experienced, vv. 4–10 citing the prayer that had been offered in the time of sickness, and vv. 11–12 referring to the answering of the prayer. However, thanksgiving is not clearly expressed, and the supposed citation of a former prayer and lament would be taking up most of the psalm. More convincing are those who understand the psalm as a prayer actually in sickness. The introduction, vv. 1–3, alludes to a divine promise, which the sick person hopes will be applied in this case; the main section, vv. 4–10, is a lament depicting the evil behaviour of enemies, but beginning and ending with prayer for healing; the conclusion, vv. 11–12, looks forward to restoration in the favour and support of the Lord. The line of thought and a number of details become clearer if the sufferer is recognized to be a king. Royal duty was epitomized as care of the needy, and it would be thought a vital requirement if a king were to be healed. It is also understandable that a king in weakness should be preoccupied with suspicion of whispering, plotting and treachery. The expressions for Yahweh's delight, embrace, and setting his servant before his face for ever (vv. 11–12) relate best to the Lord's Anointed, as also does the hope to punish the traitors (v. 10). The formula of praise in v. 13 lies outside the original psalm, and serves to mark the end of Book One of the Psalter (Int. 7b).

1–3   The intercession begins somewhat indirectly by quoting authoritative teaching in the form of a beatitude, which holds up to emulation a kind of conduct and describes its reward from the Lord (for other examples see 1.1; 2.12; 40.4). The blessing here is for one who considers and helps a poor or needy person (*dal*; Rashi takes it to be a sick person; LXX has an additional term, probably *ebyon*, and so BCP 'the poor and needy'). When such a benefactor is himself in trouble, the Lord will deliver him, saving him from the evil desire (or perhaps 'throat') of his enemies. In particular, in sickness he will have the Lord to hold him up and 'turn over all his bed' (i.e. as a nurse remaking the bed; but some explain as 'transforming the condition'). By now it is clear that here is a traditional and trustworthy promise which the supplicant hopes will be applied in his case. For a sick king the promise was especially relevant, since royal duty was epitomized in the obligation to care for the poor and defenceless (72.12–14; Jer. 21.12; 22.16; and in the more ancient Ugaritic text *Keret* it was time for the king to be removed when he no longer protected widow and orphan).

4–10   The phrase which introduces the direct supplication is taken by some to announce citation of a past prayer (NRSV 'As for me, I said'). But the sense is rather to make a present application (cf. 82.6; 2 Sam. 19.29; Jer. 10.19): 'In my case, I say'; thus a link is made from the general promise to the particular application. The request for healing (v. 4b) links with the reference to sickness in v. 3b (cf. restoration of life in v. 2a) to show that the supplicant's suffering is indeed an illness, although in vv. 5–11 the concern is with enemies. The sufferer seems to feel that, in spite of his general faithfulness (v. 12, cf. v. 1), some sin has brought on him the sickness (v. 4b) and given an opening to enemies. The large part that these adversaries take in the lament is understandable in the case of a ruler; misfortune and vulnerability are quickly exploited, and former allies begin to reposition themselves. Even in sleep a king was at risk; whom could he trust when he was very ill? (An ancient pharaoh had warned his son: 'Even when thou sleepest guard thy heart thyself, because no man has adherents on the day of distress', *ANET*, p. 418). Our supplicant portrays to the Lord how even those who purport to visit him in his sickness are at that moment preparing harm, if only to spread the report that he cannot recover – almost a signal for revolt! Even 'a man of my peace', an ally or trusted friend, bound in the fellowship of hospitality, 'has lifted his heel against me' – perhaps meaning 'has spread great slander against me' (so Dahood). The jarring prayer in v. 10 is surely that of a ruler who is bound to act against such adversaries.

11–12   Some render as NRSV 'By this I know', and think the following passage refers to an accomplished deliverance or to a happy prospect now assured by some sign or oracle intervening after v. 10. The simpler course is to render as a future, expressing hopeful faith in support of the prayer: 'By this I shall know' (so *LP*); he will know that the Lord's choice still rests on his Anointed when the enemy is unsuccessful and he reigns again before the face of God. That the Lord 'holds' or 'grasps' him may refer to the clasping of the hand, a sign of the divine choice (as elsewhere in near-eastern kingship; it is combined with an embrace in a striking example from the Hittites, my *Kingship*, p. 144). It is especially the destiny of the Lord's Anointed to be 'set' or 'stationed' before God's face for ever (cf. above on 16.10–11; 21.4; 23.6). His 'integrity' (*tom*) is probably his wholehearted adherence to his God despite faults (v. 4), though the rendering 'in my health' (BCP) also fits well.

13   Added to the original poem is this formula of warm praise, responded to by the congregation's affirmation: 'Truly / Surely!' or, as LXX has it, 'So be it.' The Lord is to be praised and thanked through all the length of eternity.

Thus is marked the end of the first division of the Psalter (Int. 7b), and the worshippers are led into a view of the ultimate meaning.

The psalm reflects the ancient insistence on the duty of regard and care for those in adversity – suffering, poor, unprotected. For the most powerful it was their prime duty, and only those that respected it could look for God's care when they themselves were in trouble. The psalm also gives a glimpse of the treachery that permeates society, where supporters and friends so easily become enemies; how often do those in power experience it, and those less exalted too will taste some of its bitterness. The people of the New Testament, no less than those of Qumran (Int. 7d), saw in the psalm reference to the events of the epoch's last days. Especially it was the treachery of the table-fellow that foreshadowed Christ's passion (John 13.18; 17.12; Acts 1.16). The church finds also in the psalm prophecy of Christ's work for the poor and sick, and of his being raised up to be set at God's right hand for ever, the fulfiller of divine retribution and compassion.

Eternal Father, grant us healing of soul and body, as we put our trust in the passion and resurrection of your Son Jesus, and seek to follow his way of compassion for all in need; raise us up above all adversity, that with a whole heart we may join in your everlasting praise.

PSALMS 42 and 43: The Hind that Gasps for Water

For favour.   Poem.   Of the Sons of Korah.

1   As a hind pants for rills of water,
      so pants my soul for you, O God.
2   My soul thirsts for God, for the living God;
      when shall I come and see the face of God?
3   My tears have been my bread by day and night,
      while all day long they say to me, Where is now your God?
4   Yet I remember, as I pour out my soul before me,
      how I passed through the crowd,
         and led the procession to the house of God,
      in a tumult of praise and thanksgiving,
      as the pilgrim throng rejoiced.
5   How you are bowed down, my soul
         and how you moan before me!
      Wait still for God, for I will yet give him thanks,
         my saviour and my God.
6   My soul is indeed bowed down before me;

       for I remember you, Lord, from Jordan's source,
         from Hermon's slopes and Mount Mizar.

7   Deep calls here to deep with the roar of your waterspouts,
       and all your breakers and billows sweep over me.

8   O that the Lord would command his faithful love
       in the day-time,
    and that his song would be with me in the night,
       praise to the living God!

9   But I say to God my rock, Why have you forgotten me?
    Why must I go about mournfully,
       while the enemy oppresses me?

10 As though to crush my very bones,
       my adversaries speak cruelly against me,
    as they say to me all the day long, Where is now your God?

11 How you are bowed down, my soul,
       and how you moan before me!
    Wait still for God, for I will yet give him thanks,
       my saviour and my God.

43.1 Give judgement for me, O God, and take up my cause
       against an unfaithful people;
    deliver me from the deceitful and wicked man.

2   For you are God my refuge; why have you rejected me?
    Why must I go about mournfully,
       while the enemy oppresses me?

3   O send out your light and your truth, that they may lead me,
    and bring me to your holy hill and to your dwelling,

4   that I may come to the altar of God,
       to God my joy and gladness;
    and with the lyre I will praise you, O God, my God.

5   How you are bowed down, my soul,
       and how you moan before me!
    wait still for God, for I will yet give him thanks,
       my saviour and my God.

In many manuscripts these psalms are joined as one, while in those which divide them, 43 usually lacks a heading. That the psalms belong together appears from the refrain which they share (42.5, 11; 43.5), but 43 is distinguished as a more direct prayer, and this may have caused it to be sometimes separated, and even to acquire a heading in a few manuscripts and in LXX. The heading of 42 is the first of a series referring to the sons of Korah, one of the psalm-guilds (Int. 2a); for 'Poem' (*maskil*) see above on 32. We notice also now the special usage of the names of God, which will continue until 83; here 'Elohim' ('God') is the most common term, while 'Yahweh' ('Lord') is much less frequent (Int. 7b).

The two psalms together form a supplication of great beauty, the first part being chiefly a lament portraying and holding up to God the dire situation, while the second part brings the climax of direct petition. The refrain, concluding each of three equal sections, takes the form of the singer's exhortation to his own soul, which he pictures as a penitential mourner before him. He is 'remembering' (invoking) God 'from the land of (River) Jordan' and 'the Hermons', but since he is there overwhelmed by breakers amid the roar of the two 'deeps', it seems that the geographical allusion is metaphorical for a situation near to death, such as is often pictured as the watery mouth of the abyss (18.4f., 40.1; 69.1–2). (Dahood interestingly translates 'Descent' rather than 'Jordan', 'nets' for 'Hermons' and 'mountain at the rim' for 'Mount Mizar', all as references to the abyss; but the evidence seems slight.) That the singer is not a private sufferer appears from his having a dispute with a *goy* ('nation / people') that has broken covenant (43.1). Furthermore, the taunt 'Where is your God?' is elsewhere levelled at Israel (79.10; 115.2; Joel 2.17; Micah 7.10). Psalms 44 and 45 are definitely psalms of the king and nation, and if the singer of our psalms is the royal figure, we can well understand his leading of the festal procession (42.4), attended by heavenly emissaries (42.8; 43.3), as the festal role of the king. In a time of suffering, king and people are here plunged into mourning and penitential rites, remote indeed from the joyous scenes of festal celebration.

1–3 The soul's longing for God is here a matter of concrete circumstances – political and social calamity. The singer brings it before God with a striking image: in a drought-stricken land, a hind or doe (perhaps with young) is wandering desperately, straining upward to catch the scent of water. The verb for 'pants / gasps' occurs elsewhere only in Joel 1.20, where wild animals in a drought stretch upwards as if imploring God (related Arabic words mean 'ascend', 'incline toward', BDB, but some argue, from a different Arabic word, for 'cry out', Dahood, and this is the sense found by Rashi). The words 'living God' suggest the phrase for 'living water', fresh water from a spring (cf. Jer. 2.13). To 'see the face of God' meant to meet him in his sanctuary, especially in the high moment of his gracious appearing in the festivals (see Int. 6d for this phrase, which was later toned down by a change of vowels). Verse 3 indicates a time of penitential fasting; also to move God comes the report of mockery regarding his care, the mockery of foreign peoples (see above). The nation's mourning is a challenge to God's name (Ezek. 36.20f.).

4–5 The lament continues by drawing the contrast between the present state of mourning and past scenes of festal worship. The psalmist himself seems to have led the procession with dancing step up the sacred hill and into the house of God. Such processions were a climax of the drama of worship, not just ceremony for ceremony's sake. God's victory and new creation, his self-manifestation in light and life – such were the meanings of the solemn entry, and the pilgrim throngs danced also and shouted thunderous acclaim to their God and saviour. But how different now! In dialogue with his soul, the singer exclaims 'How you are bowed down' – how deeply you mourn, with gestures of crouching, rolling in the dust and moaning! But hold on in faith, he continues, and the time of thanksgiving will surely come again. In v. 4 some follow LXX and render 'I passed into the glorious tabernacle'. The verse ends (lit.) 'a throng dancing the festal dance / celebrating the festival'. The refrain of vv. 5, 11, 43.5 is usually rendered with the rarer sense of *ma*, 'Why do you ...', but it seems inappropriate as it were to question the point of a rite of mourning; more likely the singer calls God's attention to the depth of the mortification. One should not think, in modern terms, of the singer summoning himself out of a state of depression.

6–8   Now in direct address to God, the singer tells of his mourning soul, and how he is 'remembering' God – calling upon his name – from the mouth of the abyss (cf. 9.14; 18.3f.; 40.1f.; 61.2); the waves and billows of the death-land sweep over him. The poetry of his appeal is heightened as that dreadful situation is pictured in terms of the place where the Jordan begins. Down the slopes of the mighty massif of Hermon cascade the results of winter's rains and snows, and the turbulent waters roar together. 'Mount Mizar' ('Mount Littleness') is unknown – presumably one of Hermon's heights. The awesome scene gives a powerful image of the dire situation that is now lamented. In v. 8 the references to 'day' and 'night' are perhaps an example of a set phrase divided over two lines, a favourite poetic device: the wish is that both day and night the Lord will command and send his steadfast love to save the sufferer and give him the song of deliverance, 'praise' (so a few manuscripts; others 'prayer') to the 'living God' (or with some manuscripts 'the God of my life').

9–10   The lament is resumed with full force: God in bond with the sufferer ('my rock'), and yet 'forgetting' him, leaving him to the mockery of the enemy (cf. 22.1f.)! This reviling is 'as a crushing / slaying in my bones'; its constant theme plays on the psalmist's bond with his God (cf. above on v. 3). The refrain ends the lament with a note of trust, which carries its own appeal, as the soul is exhorted to wait for this one claimed as its champion (lit. 'the salvations of my face and my God').

43.1–5   Our poet's skill continues to be evident, as direct prayer (v. 1) passes into lament (v. 2), returns to petition (v. 3), then passes into a vow of thanksgiving (v. 4), to conclude with the beautiful refrain that is lament and trust and vow (v. 5). The 'unfaithful nation' is one that has not kept covenanted loyalty with the psalmist; the 'deceitful and wicked man' may be their leader. God's 'rejecting', like his 'forgetting' of 42. 9, again is in stark contrast with the various phrases throughout the composition for the very close bond that had existed. The 'light' and 'truth', like the 'faithful love' of 42.8, are to be sent on a mission of salvation from God's presence, angels that personify his fidelity and his will to save (cf. 23.6; 85.10–13). They are imagined as leading the rescued sufferer to testify of his deliverance in the temple. Some have thought, in view of 42.8 and 43.4, that the sufferer is someone from the musical orders of the Levites; but the Davidic kings, in the pattern of David, were especially supposed to give the lead in processions and in the song of testimony and thanksgiving (cf. 9.2; 18.49; 57.7f., 144.9 etc.).

This is the supplication of one oppressed by great suffering, yet in recollection and in hope glimpsing the light of salvation, and gathering all the resources of soul and faith to call it into the present darkness. One picture of distress succeeds another to move the divine compassion: the thirsting hind that cries to heaven; the overwhelming waters of the abyss; the bowing and moaning of the mourning soul. Can it be that 'my God', 'the God of my life', 'my rock', 'the salvation of my face', should now forsake and reject? Where now all that joy in worship, that light of his face, that grace for one that led others in his praise? Wait, wait, hold on to your trust – so the sufferer's own heart speaks; the saviour will again appear in all his light of faithful love. The lament is echoed in the words of Jesus when in the shadow of death (Mark 14.34; John 12.27). His way to the altar of sacrifice was in the end to be shown as the supreme way of light and truth and gladness. So down the centuries his followers have approached the eucharist with the prayer for the Lord's light and truth to lead them to the holy mountain and the music of joy and thanksgiving, to lead them up the way from the waters of death to the beauty of God's face.

God of our life, our rock and our salvation, when we feel forsaken and rejected and our soul is bowed down, send forth your light and your truth to lead us to your holy dwelling, where we may see the beauty of your face, and at your altar give thanks for your salvation.

PSALM 44: Crushed in the Place of Desolation

For favour.   Of the Sons of Korah.   Poem.

1   O God, with our own ears we have heard,
         our fathers have told us,
      all that you did in their time, in days of old.
2   By your hand you planted them, driving out peoples;
      you spread them abroad, where you had broken nations.
3   Not by their sword did they take the land,
      nor did their own arm save them;
      but it was your right hand and your arm,
         and the light of your presence;
      for you delighted in them.
4   You are my king, my God,
      who commanded salvation for Jacob.

5   By you we drove back our foes;
    by your arm we thrust down those that rose against us.
6   For I did not trust in my bow,
    nor could my sword deliver me.
7   But you saved us from our adversaries,
    and put our foes to shame.
8   We gloried in God all the day long,
    and were ever praising your name.   *[Pause]*
9   But now you have rejected us and brought us to shame,
    and have not gone out with our armies.
10 You have made us turn our backs to the foe,
    and our enemies have despoiled us.
11 You have made us as sheep to be slaughtered,
    and have scattered us among the nations.
12 You have sold your people for a pittance,
    and made no profit on their sale.
13 You have made us the taunt of our neighbours,
    the scorn and derision of those that are round about us.
14 You have made us a byword among the nations;
    among the peoples they shake their heads over us.
15 All the day long my dishonour is before me,
    and the shame of my face has covered me,
16 at the noise of the taunter and reviler,
    at the sight of the enemy and avenger.
17 All this has come on us though we have not forgotten you,
    and have not been false to your covenant.
18 Our hearts have not turned back,
    nor our steps gone out of your way;
19 yet you have crushed us in the place of desolation,
    and covered us with the shadow of death.
20 If we had forgotten the name of our God,
    and to some strange god spread out our hands,
21 would not God have searched it out?
    For he knows the secrets of the heart.
22 But for your sake we are killed all the day long,
    and counted as sheep for slaughter.
23 Arise – why sleep, O Lord?
    Awake, do not reject us for ever.
24 Why do you hide your face,
    and forget our grief and oppression?
25 For our soul is bowed down to the dust;
    our belly cleaves to the earth.
26 Arise, Lord, come to our help,
    and redeem us for the sake of your faithful love.

In this lamenting supplication God is addressed for the most part by a collective voice ('we', 'us', 'our'), but in vv. 4, 6, 15 by a singular voice. It is a lament of the covenanted people (v. 17), defeated in war (vv. 9–10), and consequently in some areas much ravaged and uprooted (vv. 11, 22). The psalmist is the representative who can embody his people, appearing also as the individual who wages the war and personally bears the shame; most likely it is the king who here exercises the supreme responsibility of carrying the burden before his God (as in the day of intercession in 2 Chron. 20.4f.). There are several links of wording and imagery with Psalms 42–3, and affinity with 60, 80, 83, 108. Reference to God's past salvation (vv. 1–8) precedes the lament, a pattern which may be compared with 9–10, 27, 40, 85, 89, 126. The Talmud (Sota 48a) tells how in Maccabeean times Levites known as 'Awakeners' daily ascended a pulpit in the temple and sounded the cry of v. 23a, until the practice was ended by the High Priest John Hyrcanus (135–107 BCE) as no longer appropriate.

1–3 As a foil for the coming lament, God is first addressed with a recollection of the salvation he gave of old (cf. Deut. 6.20; Ps. 78.3–4). Tradition had been solemnly passed down the generations, teaching that the nation's possession of her land was the work of God. If battles were won and older nations dispossessed, it was the action of his right hand on behalf of a people he had chosen for a special office. It was he who planted this his vine and caused it to grow well and widely (cf. 80.8f.).

4–8 To this teaching the supplicants have said Amen. They too, in solidarity with the former generations, testify to the royal care of God in sending salvation and granting victories. The image of a bull that 'gores' and 'tramples' (so, literally, the verbs in v. 5) was used for divine or divinely given strength to rout and subdue the foe (cf. Deut. 33.17; 1 Kings 22.11; Micah 4.13). They acknowledged that God had so given their victories, and they had duly offered praise and thanksgiving.

9–16 Against that former story of salvation and praise, the lamenting account of the present stands out in shocking contrast. With great poetic eloquence, the singer puts the situation to God. He has not gone out with the nation's armies and has left them to be defeated, resulting in slaughter, pillage and depopulation, no doubt in territories nearest to the enemy country. God was their shepherd – yes, but has allotted them not for care and preservation (as sheep might be kept for breeding, milk and wool), but for death and devouring. He is compared to an owner who was so little concerned that he did not hold out for a good price, but got them off his hands for a trifle. Even foreigners are appalled, shaking their heads. With defeat comes shame, a heavy reality especially on the king, for it undermined his position even at home.

17–26 The lament rises to an exceptionally forceful climax as the singer asserts that they are afflicted, not because of disloyalty to their covenant with God, but rather because of him, or for his sake (*'aleyka* 'as your responsibility / for your sake / on account of you'). No doubt the matter has been 'deeply searched' (*hqr*, v. 21), and no national fault that could account for the reverses has been found. King and nation truly feel, as Job did in his case, that the suffering cannot be the result of a turning away from God; on the contrary, their folk are being killed all the day on account of him. The thought here may be that their sense of a special calling in devotion to Yahweh marked them out as liable to the hostility of other populations; and the more strictly they kept to the covenant laws, the greater that hostility. In v. 19 the reading of the main tradition has 'in the place of jackals' (*tannim*), animals that settle in ruined places (Isa. 13.22 etc.) or scavenge among the corpses on a battlefield (Ps. 63.10), and so represent desolation and death, as is clear in the following phrase, 'covered with the shadow of death' (cf. 23.4). But Gunkel and others prefer another reading, '. . . dragon(s)' (*tannin*); the allusion would be to the place of the chaos monster as also associated with death, or the sense might be 'in place of the monster you crushed us' (cf. 74.13–14).

The psalm then concludes with urgent cries for God's saving action. From an ancient poetic tradition come the calls for God to awake and arise, to throw off the slumber of this apparent neglect. The 'forgetting' and 'rejecting' remind us of 42.9 and 43.2, and another link is the allusion to ritual mourning (v. 25, cf. 42.5, 9, 11; 43.2, 5), which no doubt was part of the day of prayer. The last word of the eloquent intercessor is the most telling: 'your-faithful-love'. With this he invokes the covenant, the bond with the Lord that meant everything to this people, and he rests his plea on the Lord's commitment and faithfulness.

The tension between the traditional affirmations in worship and subsequent devastation in personal or national experience are illustrated here, as in other psalms (cf. above on 40). Against the common interpretation of disasters, whether personal or communal, as divine displeasure due to sin, this psalm speaks for another situation: 'For your sake we are killed all the day long.' It has a tale of great national suffering to pour out before the Lord, but its last word is an appeal to his fidelity, the love that will not fail. Paul (Rom. 8.36f.) gathered much from the psalm in a new context; he too knew of the killing all day long 'for your sake' and came to rest on the divine love that does not fail: 'No, in all these things we are more than conquerors, through him that loved us. For I am persuaded that neither death nor life . . . nor any other creature shall be able to separate us from the love of God which is in Christ Jesus our Lord.'

O God, our king, we have heard with our ears and believed in our hearts all that you have done for the salvation of your people; rise up now for the help of those that are killed all the day and crushed in the place of desolation; and save them by the light of your countenance and the flame of your faithful love.

PSALM 45: The Lord's Anointed and the King's Daughter

For favour.   Over lilies.   Of the Sons of Korah.   Poem.   Song of love.

1   My heart is astir with a gracious word;
    I speak my poem for the king,
        my tongue like the pen of a rapid writer.

2   You are fair above the children of man;
    grace is poured on your lips, for God has blessed you for ever.
3   Gird your sword on your thigh, O mighty one,
    gird on your majesty and glory,
4   and in your majesty ride on victorious,
    because of truth, humility and justice.
5   Your right hand shall teach you dread deeds
        with your sharpened arrows;
    peoples shall fall under you, amidst all foes of the king.
6   Your throne is of God, for ever and ever;
    the sceptre of your kingdom is the sceptre of justice.
7   As you have loved right and hated wrong,
    God, your God, has anointed you
        with the oil of gladness above your fellows.
8   Myrrh, aloes and cassia are on all your garments;
    from halls inlaid with ivory, stringed instruments delight you.
9   Kings' daughters are among your noble women;
    at your right hand stands the queen in gold of Ophir.

10 Hear, O daughter, consider and incline your ear,
    and forget your own people and your father's house.
11 And the king shall delight in your beauty;
    since he is your lord, give honour to him.
12 Then the fair city of Tyre shall make gifts;
    the richest of peoples will seek your favour.

13 The king's daughter is all glorious within;
    her clothing is enwrought with gold.
14 She shall be led to the king in raiment of needlework;
    her companions, the maidens that follow her,
        shall also be led to you.
15 With joy and gladness shall they be led,
    and shall enter the palace of the king.
16 In place of your fathers shall be your sons;

you will make them princes throughout the earth.
17   I will make your name remembered through all generations;
so the peoples shall praise you for ever and ever.

This 'song of love' (so title) and 'poem for the king' (v. 1) comes from the heart of the royal wedding ceremony. The singer tells of his inspiration (v. 1), addresses praise and blessing to the Lord's Anointed (vv. 2–9), speaks counsel and blessing to the bride (vv. 10–12), depicts the bride in her beauty and her entrance into the king's palace (vv. 13–15) and concludes with promise to the king of enduring life through children and name (vv. 16–17). The references to ivory (ornamental inlay such as was found at Samaria, v. 8) and to Tyre (v. 12) have inclined some to think of the wedding of Ahab and Jezebel, when northern Israel was prosperous; and others again to think of Solomon's marriage to an Egyptian princess (1 Kings 3.1). These particulars are not by any means decisive. Failing any strong indication to the contrary, the psalm is best taken as another composition preserved from the ceremonies of the Davidic dynasty. Its strong and extended presentation of the royal calling has indeed raised the question whether the wedding was joined to other royal rites in the autumn festival (Int. 5b), contributing especially the theme of dynastic continuance. Distinctive is the heading 'Over lilies' (also 69, and cf. 60 and 80) and 'Song of love'. The budding of lilies may have been used to give an omen (cf. Num. 17.6f.); the flower (*shoshan*, perhaps waterlily or even lotus) is often mentioned in the other great love-poem, the Song of Songs.

1   The singer's introduction describes his inspiration (cf. Num. 24.3–4; 2 Sam. 23.1–3) and indicates that it is a poem for the king which he is now to utter. So he tells how his inspired heart seethes, driving up to his tongue 'a good word', a gracious message from God (hardly as *LP* 'fine phrases'). His tongue will dart swiftly and surely like the pen of an expert scribe. Here then is no poet reciting from a carefully composed script; rather he appears as one now inspired, whose poetry flows freshly and abundantly from his heart and through his lips. Gunkel compares the introduction of a Finnish epic, *Kalewala*: 'Words melt in my mouth; one presses upon another; they hasten over my tongue, on to my lips, over my mouth.'

2–5   Directly addressing the king, the psalmist declares and confirms the divine blessing which gives him beauty beyond that of mankind and inspired grace of speech; and it is a blessing 'for ever'. In this eternity is the thought of an enduring dynasty, but probably also of the king's personal bond with God (cf. above on 16.10–11). Still as bestowing blessing, the singer uses the imperative, 'Gird . . . succeed . . . ride.' So God will enable his Chosen One to ride forth in majesty and conquer for the cause of (or 'because of') faithfulness, humility and right ('humility-righteousness' seems to be a compound expression, like 'nakedness-shame' in Micah 1.11; the two roots occur in Zech. 9.9, where the mounted king is 'humble' and 'just'; Dahood suggests reading the consonants as 'and give justice to the poor'). The strong language of conquest bestows divine power to succeed against evil on behalf of God's kingdom (see above on 8.6; 18.42; for 'midst', lit. 'heart', cf. 2 Sam. 18.14; Jonah 2.3).

6–7 The context shows that v. 6 continues the address to the king, so 'Elohim', 'God', is best understood to describe the significance of the throne: the throne of the Lord's Anointed is the very throne of God and so eternal – his reign serves and expresses God's reign (cf. 1 Chron. 29.23; 28.5; Ps. 110.1). Likewise his sceptre, symbol of the rule, is the very sceptre of God, the sceptre of eternal justice. The Anointed One who is true to this justice, devoted to right, opposed to corruption, he is truly raised by God's anointing above all his companions (including other kings).

8–9 Thought now turns towards the union of king and bride. The oil of the anointing, from the very hand of God (v. 7), contained precious aromatic spices (cf. Ex. 30.23–5) and flowed down from the head to the garments (133.2). The myrrh, aloes and cassia on the garments are now seen as preparation for the royal love (cf. Song 3.6; 4.14; Prov. 7.17). From rooms adorned with ivory inlay the music of plucked strings sounds out to delight the king, being perhaps started now for a procession, and hence the reference to the king's 'precious ones' or 'jewels', noble and royal women. Among these wives of the king (as they seem to be) distinction now belongs to the new bride who takes her position at his right hand, the *shegal*, queen and consort, adorned (perhaps crowned) with gold from Ophir (thought to be in Arabia or Somalia).

10–12 The singer now addresses her, beginning with phrases like those of a Wisdom teacher. She is beginning a new life, and he bids her apply herself to her new role and not be distracted by recollection of what had been familiar in her life hitherto. She is to give her devotion ('make obeisance') to her royal husband, her 'lord'. But if much is asked, much will be given. The maritime city of Tyre may be mentioned as an example of great neighbours; even such peoples, wealthy from world trade, will come to honour her with gifts and seek her favour.

13–15 The singer describes what is probably a development in the ceremony. The bride has gone 'within' and is now clothed in beautiful raiment, enwrought with gold and embroidered. Followed by her train of virgin-companions, royal maids of honour, she is led into the king's residence.

16–17 In conclusion the singer returns to direct address to the king, a kind of blessing: by God-given destiny he will have children for the extension and continuance of his reign. The 'name' in v. 18 is not given, for what is meant is the dynastic life; there will always be a 'David' to serve and express God's kingdom. That the singer himself (rather than God, speaking in an oracle) will cause this eternal remembrance is perhaps not quite fitting, but reference to his song complements v. 1; LXX has 'They shall make mention ...'

While details of the wedding ceremony remain uncertain, the main lines of thought are clear and striking. The prophet-poet, conscious of a mighty inspiration, delineates a royal figure chosen and empowered by God to effect his reign; to this Anointed One is promised power to conquer, by way of and for the sake of justice, humility and faithfulness. The extension and everlasting continuance of this royal ministry is the aspect which then comes to the fore. A 'daughter' from another kingdom offers herself in humility and love, and from the union will come the blessing of continuance.

In the course of time, long after the overthrow of the Davidic kings, Jewish interpreters related the psalm to the Messiah and his people. The Targum (Int. 7c) takes the 'lilies' (probably via a change of vowels to *she-shonim*) as 'those who sit in the sanhedrin of Moses', and renders v. 2: 'Your beauty, King Messiah, exceeds that of the children of man; the spirit of prophecy is given upon your lips.' For v. 10 it has: 'Hear, O assembly of Israel, the law of his mouth, and consider the wonders of his works.' In the New Testament such an interpretation is assumed to be shared, and vv. 6–7 are used to show Christ's superiority to angels (Heb. 1.8). The psalm became a fountain of poetic meanings. The Jewish scholar Rashi, following the Targum's title verse and other rabbinic tradition, takes the 'king' to represent sages of the Tora, whose sharpened arrows were their students. For Christians the 'good word' of v. 1 was the Word (John 1.1) and the 'king's daughter all glorious within' could be expounded as the true church, simple and loyal, as against outward show of wealth (so Chrysostom). Most enduring are applications which stem from the psalm's own theology. Where this fidelity has been maintained, the warm poetry has led the soul of individual or community towards the everlasting throne of God by way of love for Christ. Adoring him, and forsaking all other, the soul finds in him all the meaning of God's eternal kingdom.

Eternal Father, lead us into the love of the Lord Jesus, that our hearts being ever stirred by this love, we may live in the cause of faithfulness, humility and justice.

PSALM 46: God With Us

For favour.   Of the Sons of Korah.   At the mysteries.   Song.

1   God is our refuge and stronghold;
     our help in troubles, and very ready to be found.
2   Therefore we shall not fear though earth sways,

and mountains reel in the depth of the sea;
3   though its waters roar and foam,
      and the mountains quake at its rearing pride.   *[Pause]*
4   But there is a river
          that gladdens with its streams the city of God,
      the holy dwelling of God Most High.
5   Since God is in her midst, she shall not be shaken;
      God helps her as morning breaks.
6   When the nations rage and kingdoms reel,
      he utters his voice, and earth melts in consternation.
7   The Lord of Hosts is with us;
      the God of Jacob is our stronghold.   *[Pause]*
8   Come, see the acts of the Lord,
      the destructions he makes on earth.
9   He makes an end of wars to the bounds of the earth;
      he breaks the bow and snaps the spear,
          and the shields he burns in the fire.
10   Be still and know that I am God;
      I will be exalted over the nations,
          I will be exalted over the earth.
11   The Lord of Hosts is with us;
      the God of Jacob is our stronghold.   *[Pause]*

This is one of the splendid psalms that reflect the sacramental drama of the autumn festival (cf. above on 24). Some of these centre on a symbolic deliverance of the city where God dwells (48; 76), and among them is the present psalm. With statements of praise and thankful confidence it combines exposition of what the drama signifies: the chaotic forces represented by the primaeval ocean and by rebellious nations have been subjugated, life and peace have been secured from the holy city to the ends of the earth. While this great sacrament bore in the first place on the need for rains, growth and social revival at the beginning of the (autumnal) new year, it opened such visions of a perfected world that it had an eschatological character – the worshippers were caught up in an experience of God's ultimate purpose. The three occurrences of 'Pause' (vv. 3, 7, 11), perhaps originally all following the refrain (now only 7, 11), mark the three sections: the first envisages the chaos forces evident in tottering mountains and raging ocean; the second tells of God's salvation for his city; the third points to the shattered weapons of rebellion, and brings God's own voice, as he is manifested in royal exaltation. The psalm well illustrates the way in which themes general in the Near East were worked into a thoroughly Israelite form; the Most High, Creator and renewer of the earth, king in his holy city at the source of the river, is also the Lord of Hosts, Yahweh, God of Jacob (cf. Int. 6c). The third phrase of the title (found also in 1 Chron. 15.20) is rendered by LXX 'over the secrets / mysteries', and perhaps refers to the festal rites (cf. on 9–10, and Mowinckel,

Psalms II, pp. 215f.). An earlier proposal was as a musical instruction, 'according to young women' and so 'for high-tuned instruments'.

1–3 The opening is a kind of exclamation in response to the coming or manifestation of God as saviour. He is praised as a stronghold amidst perils and as answering the prayer of distress – he 'lets himself be found', hearing and intervening (cf. Isa. 55.6; 2 Chron. 15.2, 4, 15; the familiar rendering 'a very present (help)' hardly conveys the sense, and in the Hebrew the word, *nimsa'*, does not qualify 'help'). Underlying the thought of vv. 2–3 is the idea that the Creator mastered and made serviceable the primaeval waters and fixed the earth over them on mountain-pillars (cf. 24.2); when the world's good order is threatened, the waters rage as of old and the mountains and earth rock, until the Creator renews his first work (cf. 75.3; 82.5; 93.3–4). This work of renewal was the theme at the heart of the festival.

4–7 The 'city of God', the place of the temple and the festival, is seen in such psalms in transfigured glory. It is the earthly counterpart of God's heavenly throne, and is seen as the Eden-like place from which the river of life flows out to give life to the world. The humble fountain of Gihon (if Zion is indeed the place in question) and its channels that run under the city and along the Kidron valley, are a glimpse of this poetic ideal (cf. Ezek. 47). This 'river' now is a sign of the cosmic waters made serviceable, and so of the life with which God will 'gladden' city, people and world. (In v. 4b LXX reads well: 'the Most High has sanctified his tabernacle' – God by his re-entry and his living stream re-consecrated temple and city at the new year.) The dramatic ceremonies, reflected and expounded in vv. 5–6, represented a time of peril, a war against the holy city; and then, with the break of morning, the manifestation of God's presence, his salvation of his city, his word that routs the chaotic powers (cf. 29.3f.). The refrain (v. 7) is a victory chant, ascribing the glory to the Lord alone (for the 'God of Jacob / Israel' cf. 24.6 and comments on that psalm).

8–11 The worshippers are summoned to see for themselves (cf. 48.12f.; 66.5) the results of the Lord's victory, probably symbolized in some way (cf. 48.8; 68.24, and the many symbolic representations done by the prophets). A vision arises of weapons in piles across the earth, broken up and burned – a beautiful destruction, for the Lord has ended wars, as only he could. (Burnt in the fire, v. 9, are probably 'shields', *'agilot*, as LXX, Targum and Jerome, rather than 'wagons', still less 'chariots', *'agalot*.) And his voice sounds out to all peoples: he bids them to 'desist' from their schemes and their rebellious and divisive ambitions, and to recognize where true power lies. The choral song of victory and thanksgiving (as v. 7) rounds off the psalm.

With economy and powerful imagery, the psalm has testified of the Lord who is ready to be found, to answer and make himself known in times of trouble. When it seems that the world is falling apart and evil breaking loose, he is a refuge and stronghold. The night of fear is banished by his rising sun; his presence is known in the midst of the troubled ones. He sends his life-giving streams into the desert places. Such is the testimony from ceremonies that distilled the experience of many generations, people who suffered much and lived precariously, and yet witnessed to the divine faithfulness. The ceremonies also projected an ideal. Entering through worship the timeless moment when God is manifestly supreme, the pilgrims see war destroyed and a world made glad for ever. Their 'God with us' was to be the church's theme. In Christ, Immanuel ('God-with-us'), the morning had broken, and the river of life flowed to the thirsty. Through him, God let himself be found, the stronghold of salvation. Not yet the completion on earth, not yet the end of hatred and killing; but with new force the psalm's vision of peace shines out, inspiring and sustaining until the day of fulfilment.

O God, our refuge and strength, grant we may not fear though troubles rage around us; send into our hearts your river of peace, and rise upon our darkness; so may we know that you are with us always.

PSALM 47: The Ascension of the King of all Nations

For favour.   Of the Sons of Korah.   Psalm.

1   Clap your hands, all you peoples;
      acclaim God with joyful voice.
2   For in dread majesty has appeared the Lord Most High,
      Great King over all the earth.
3   He has subdued peoples under us,
      and nations under our feet.
4   He has chosen for us our heritage,
      the pride of Jacob whom he loved.   *[Pause]*
5   God has gone up with the shout of praise,
      the Lord, with the sounding of the trumpet.
6   Sing praises to God, sing praises;
      sing praises to our King, sing praises.
7   For God is King of all the earth!
      Sing praises with a psalm.
8   God reigns over the nations!
      God has taken his holy throne!
9   The princes of the peoples are gathered,
          the people of the God of Abraham;
      for the shields of the earth belong to God,
          and he is very highly exalted.

This is a hymn surely from a high moment of worship. The calls to praise in
vv. 1 and 6 are each followed by reasons introduced by 'For', vv. 2–5 and 7–
9. The excitement in the praise runs high, and responds to a triumphant event
depicted in the reasons. While attempts have been made to explain the event
as a processional ascent and entry to the temple in celebration of a military
victory, it seems better (following the work of Mowinckel, Int. 71) to see here
dramatic moments from the annual celebrations at the autumn festival.
Through the symbolic movements of worship (probably involving the ark),
the Lord is shown to have subdued foes and ascended his holy mountain in
triumph (v. 5), there to take the throne of his world-reign (v. 8). Similar
ceremonial is reflected in 93, 96–9, and also 24, 29, 68, 132. Later Jewish
sources tell of the psalm being used on (autumnal) New Year's Day, when it
was chanted seven times before the blowing of trumpets.

1–5 Rhythmic clapping, concerted formulas of praise and the blare of the
ram's horn acclaim the returning victor (for the jubilant acclamations known
as *teru'a* cf. 89.15; 150.5). The vision of God ascending to his throne, v. 5,
will have been signified by processional ascent and entry, probably including
the ark (cf. above on 24. Striking is the call addressed to 'all peoples', and
indeed the psalm is remarkable for combining militant Israelite tradition with
much stress on the universality of God's reign and the consequent joy of all.
In line with this, God is called both 'Yahweh' and 'Elyon' ('Most High', Int.
6b–c). He has revealed his dread holiness (*nora'*, v. 2a), asserting his godhead
against all rebellion, and is manifest 'Great-King', sovereign over all powers.
In vv. 3–4 the voice of Israelite tradition seems in tension with the universal
theme; the reference to subdued nations, the land taken in possession and the
'pride of Jacob' (perhaps the holy place, cf. Ezek. 24.21), may allude to the
entry into Canaan and to the Davidic empire. The bridge between this
national strain and the worldwide celebration can only be found in that all is
of God: he 'loved' and chose a people, and made all provision for them – but
not for their sake alone, since the good purpose of the 'Great King' must
embrace all his world.

6–9 The renewed call to praise has an ecstatic quality, as the same verb (*zmr*,
'to sing praises / make music of psalmody') is repeated five times. The last
word in v. 7 is *maskil*, which may be a noun, as found in psalm titles and
denoting some type of sung poem; or it can be taken adverbially, 'skilfully'.
Verse 8 declares the beginning of God's reign – 'God (now) reigns' or 'has
become king', and 'has sat down upon his holy throne'. In prophetic visions
of the perfect kingdom replacing the present age, the idea of God 'beginning
to reign' fits well (cf. Obad. 21; Zech. 14.9; Rev. 11.15; 19.6). But in our
psalm our understanding has to begin from the poetry and drama of festal
worship; it is a moment as it were above time, with something of the first
beginning in it, and something of the final consummation. Translated into
prose, the poetry of this worship declares that the God who is eternally King
has here revealed his power, renewed the forces of life, and given an over-

whelming conviction of the perfection that will be (cf. Int. 5b). The 'princes of the peoples' may have been represented by guests from other states; but in any case it is a visionary ideal that all peoples will become the people of the God of Abraham, and their 'shields' (rulers) will belong to God in loyalty and service. Such will be the 'exaltation' of God, already experienced in the sacrament of worship: he is high above all, and the world is one in peace under him (cf. 46.10). The title 'God of Abraham' seems to have been chosen here because of universal features in the traditions of Abraham (Gen. 12.2–3; 17.4; it seem unnecessary with some translators to emend the text into the awkward 'im 'am, 'with the people of').

Of all biblical themes, that of God's 'kingdom' or 'kingship' is probably the most important. The New Testament's proclamation that the kingdom has drawn near is foreshadowed by Old Testament prophecies that the Lord would at last become king over all. But in a number of psalms there is reflected a present experience of the Lord's kingship – and with peculiar intensity. From the heart of festal worship is mirrored here an encounter with the Lord in his triumphal ascent. In victory and glory his reign begins, and the whole world trembles and rejoices before him. In the present psalm we do not hear (as in others) of the seas and mountains, the animals and trees as subjects in the new kingdom; the focus is all on the nations. No doubt it is through a development of tradition lying behind the psalm that we have the appearance of contradiction: Israel granted victory over the nations, and yet the context is of universal rejoicing. Through this tension the message emerges: God triumphs in his victory for his covenant people – but in fuller revelation it transpires to be for the good of all. All nations clap their hands and acclaim him as their king; all are now the one people of the God of Abraham. With its ideal vision and its immediacy of experience, the psalm replenishes hope and the springs of action in the political world. Those who would honour the King of all nations will yearn and work, inspired, for the peace and unity of all the world. In Christian use the psalm is especially appointed for Ascension Day, and there enriches the understanding of Christ's ascending to the Father.

O Lord Most High, who in the ascension of Jesus Christ have given us assurance of the triumph of your good kingdom, we pray you to put beneath our feet all that makes for strife and cruelty, so that all nations may be joined in gladness under your everlasting reign.

PSALM 48: The Parable of Faithful Love

Song. Psalm. Of the Sons of Korah.

1 Great is the Lord and most glorious
   in the city of our God.
2 His holy mountain is the fairest of heights,
       the joy of all the world;
   Mount Zion is the mountain of heaven,
       the city of the Great King.
3 God is her citadel;
   he has shown himself to be a tower of refuge.
4 For see, the kings assembled;
   together they swept on.
5 The instant they saw, they were dumbfounded;
   they were filled with terror and dismay.
6 Quaking seized them there and then,
   writhing, as of a woman in labour.
7 With a mighty wind from the desert,
   you broke up the galleons of war.
8 We have both heard and seen in the city of the Lord of Hosts,
       in the city of our God
   that God has established her for ever.   *[Pause]*
9 We have enacted your faithful love,
   in the midst of your temple, O God.
10 As your name, O God, so also your praise
       reaches to the ends of the earth;
   your right hand is full of justice.
11 Let Mount Zion rejoice and the daughters of Judah be glad,
   because of all your judgements.
12 Walk around Zion and encompass her,
   and count up her strong towers.
13 Mark well her rampart, and study her citadels,
   that you may tell the next generation:
14 This is our God, our God for ever and ever;
   it is he that shall lead us out from death.

Like the two preceding psalms, this is best understood in connection with ceremonies of the autumn festival. It responds to a symbolic act of salvation, and at the same time conveys its meaning. It is the salvation of Zion, God's holy place, which has been 'enacted' or 'represented' (v. 9), and the praise of God for this assurance is joined with praising appreciation of his holy place (cf. 46, 76, 87). This is another striking example of the adaptation of more ancient poetic and religious tradition; several threads can be traced back to older

Syrian culture, but all is re-created as a resounding tribute to Yahweh, Lord of Hosts, and his temple in Jerusalem. The structure of the psalm throughout reflects the festal ceremony. Already the opening praise of God (v. 1) involves his city. The praise of the city (vv. 2–3) then adumbrates the symbolic deliverance. The exposition of the ceremonial action then follows (vv. 4–7), with concluding affirmation of its meaning (vv. 8–10). The conclusion of the whole is a call for joyous praise (v. 11) and for a procession to be made around the city wall, reflecting on the meaning of all that has been done (vv. 12–14).

1–2 Praise of the Lord, present in a revelation of his glory, continues into praise of his city and temple hill; this continuation is a fitting introduction to what the psalm is about to unfold – God's work of salvation in and through his sanctuary-city. An ancient and widespread conception is here applied to Zion: she is given a rich role and meaning – centre of blessing for the world, a mystery where the heavenly throne of the King of all creation is known on earth. In the light of such a faith, the humble hill of Zion is seen indeed as 'the fairest of heights', and she can be called 'mountain of heaven' (literally 'the recesses / heart / summit of Zaphon', this being the Canaanite name for the mountain of the gods; cf. Isa. 14.13 and see further *TWAT* VI, cols 1093f.).

3–7 The singer now recounts an act of deliverance, and the indications are that this was not a historical event but a symbolic or sacramental action. Just as the prophets Jeremiah and Ezekiel were later to enact the destruction of Jerusalem, so the festal ceremony could enact salvation for this 'city of God'. The singer's task is to fill out the meaning of the symbolic action with his poetic word and song. He begins with the essence: God has himself been her citadel or stronghold (rather than 'is in her citadels', see Dahood); he has made himself known as her impregnable tower (v. 4). Now comes the detail: the worshippers are prompted to imagine how the world's kings consorted together (cf. 2.1), and joined forces to sweep on like a flood against Jerusalem. But coming into view of that glorious citadel and tower, the glorious presence of God, on the instant they were struck down with awe and trembling. In v. 8 one could translate (as clearer in a few manuscripts) 'like the east wind which breaks the ships of Tarshish'; but it may be better to keep the more obvious sense as above: with his east wind God has broken the mighty fleet of the attackers. The poetry here will have passed down from ancient use in the Lebanon, where devastating winds from the eastern desert sometimes blow across the lofty mountain ranges and pour down on to ships near the coast. In the symbolic ritual, even at land-locked Jerusalem, the picture was eloquent of shattered human arrogance. The 'galleons of war' are literally 'ships of Tarshish', probably large and splendid vessels like those developed for distant trade, and perhaps in particular their escort of fighting ships (cf. 1 Kings 22.48; Ezek. 27.26, and *TWAT* VIII, cols 778f.).

8–10 In choral style there comes a response of summary and affirmation: the worshippers have both heard and seen the sacrament of deliverance and know its meaning, namely that God has secured his city for ever. In v. 9 the first verb (basically 'to make a likeness') is taken abstractly by some translators, 'We have imagined / reflected on'; but the direct concrete meaning fits the context well: 'We have represented / mimed'; the acted parable, the sacred drama (done in the centre of the temple, perhaps the main court) has shown forth God's *ḥesed* – how in faithfulness and love he defends his city. For this his love even more than for his power, God's name and glory (cf. 8.1) shine from Zion to the ends of the earth, and his right hand, representing his deeds, is seen to hold the sceptre of justice (cf. 45.6).

11–14   The concluding call to praise summons both the holy hill and also the 'daughters of Judah' – either the young women who would take the lead in victory celebrations with tambourines, chants and dances, or perhaps the daughter-towns of Judah. Finally the worshippers are invited to make procession around the city, noting her defences and so being inspired to hand on the testimony to this Saviour God. (The last phrase of the psalm has also been rendered 'against / unto / away from death', or 'for ever', or even transferred to the title of 49 to be like the third phrase of the heading of 46, but leaving the psalm's ending rather abrupt.)

As one of the great 'Songs of Zion', this psalm has brought forward one of the richest biblical images – the holy city of God, that sanctuary where heaven is disclosed, and the presence and powers of the sovereign Creator are encountered. As an embodiment of the meaning of worship, this 'city' and 'fairest of heights' ever stands for humble pilgrims to come and see, hear and know. But the wonder of such psalms is that originally all this meaning was woven as one with the need for daily bread, for the defence of the realm, and for social justice. How great the tension for faith, then, when Zion was destroyed! Some looked for a future vindication, while some found Zion to be an image only for the church, the eternal home in God's presence. This latter interpretation has been immensely meaningful to Christians down the ages, but all the better when the relation to the worlds of nature, politics and community is strongly maintained. In this spirit the sacrament of God's love can still be celebrated with joy, and so there can be given the assurance of his defeat of the assaults of evil, and his leading of his world (as the Upanishad has it) from delusion to truth, from darkness to light, from death to life.

Lord, in our hymns and preaching, our prayers and sacraments we make a likeness of your conquering love, and believe you are at work in all this our worship; grant us so to stand in your fair and holy city that we may be able to carry forth your redeeming power and kindle the faith of generations to come.

PSALM 49: Ransom for a Soul

For favour.   Of the Sons of Korah.   Psalm.

1   Hear this, all you peoples;
    listen, all you that dwell in the world,
2   people of every kind,
    both rich and poor together.
3   My mouth shall speak of wisdom,
    and the utterance of my heart shall be discernment.
4   I will strain my ear for a parable;
    I will open my riddle with the lyre.
5   Why should I fear in days of evil,
    when the wickedness of my foes surrounds me,
6   such as trust in their goods,
    and glory in the abundance of their riches?
7   For no one can by any means ransom himself,
    or give to God his price.
8   The ransom of his soul is too costly;
    he would never have enough to pay it,
9   so that he could live for ever,
    and never see the abyss.
10 For one sees that the wise die also;
    with the foolish and ignorant they perish,
      and leave their goods to others.
11 Their tomb is their home for ever,
      their dwelling through all generations,
    though they made themselves owners of many estates.
12 A person in splendour, but without understanding,
    is like the cattle that are killed.
13 This is the way of those whose boast is in themselves,
    the end of those
      who are pleased with their own mouths.   *[Pause]*
14 They are taken like a flock to the great darkness,
      and death is their shepherd;
    and the true-hearted shall rule over them in the morning.
    Their beauty shall waste away,
    and the darkness shall be their dwelling.
15 But God will ransom my soul;
    from the power of the darkness
      truly he shall take me.   *[Pause]*
16 Do not fear if some one grows rich,
    and the glory of his house increases.
17 For he will carry away nothing when he dies,

nor will his glory go down with him.
18   Though he blesses himself while he lives,
     saying, They will praise you as you do well for yourself,
19   yet he will enter the company of his fathers,
     who will nevermore see the light.
20   A person in splendour, but without understanding,
     is like the cattle that are killed.

Although there are some links with the immediately preceding psalms – the title, the call to all nations (cf. 47.1), the references to inspiration (cf. 45.1), to death (cf. 48.14) and the hope of morning (cf. 46.5) – this psalm is generally of a very different character. It is in Wisdom style, where a teacher or sage addresses thought on life's enigmas to a human audience; it contains no praise, prayer or obvious oracle. The theme concerns the vanity of this world's wealth, but through the darkness of the universal fate of death some light is seen. The message can be seen as a warning to those ruthless in acquisition, and as as encouragement for those who are their victims. The structure appears as (1) introduction, vv. 1–4; (2) the end of the oppressive wealthy, vv. 5–12; (3) the contrast in the destinies of those trusting in wealth and one whom God will ransom, vv. 13–20. The two main sections are each concluded with a refrain.

1–4   The impressive introduction lifts the message beyond any study-circle, beyond the nation, to the ears of all that inhabit this passing world (*ḥeled*), both rich and poor; it will be an inspired message of universal importance (cf. Micah 1.2). The psalmist's very body is an instrument of wisdom revealed from beyond: his mouth expresses what his heart murmurs (cf. above on 45.1); his ear strains for a divine voice; his fingers through his lyre gain access to a hidden world (cf. 2 Kings 3.15), where the riddles of life may be unlocked.

5–12   This 'Why should I fear –' can be taken naturally as representative; here is a 'Fear not' for all who come upon 'days of evil', especially times of suffering when, pressing in from every side, come 'supplanters' (*'aqeb*, BDB 'over-reacher', seeking to take insidious advantage, rather than AV, BCP 'my heels'), who would take over all they have and are. Such predators are boastful of their great wealth, and trust in the power it gives them. But no amount of money will ransom them when God decrees their death. They cannot escape, be they wise or ignorant (v. 10); naked they go to their 'eternal home', the tomb, though they boasted of vast properties. The refrain sums it up: in riches and pomp man finds no stay (so the Hebrew in v. 12a), or (with the reading of LXX and Syriac, followed above) man in splendour but without discernment is comparable to cattle to be slaughtered. This latter reading gives an easier line of thought and matches the Hebrew in v. 20.

13–20 The singer now unfolds a contrast. The destiny of those that are god to themselves is to be herded by the grim shepherd death into Sheol, the dark underworld, where their opulent forms soon waste away. 'In the morning', the hour of God's salvation (cf. 46.5), the 'true of heart' are found to have the dominion; he puts down the mighty from their seat, and exalts the humble and meek (cf. Mal. 4.3; Wisd. 3.7–8). But some translators, with a little emendation (as *BHS*), obtain a simpler conception in v. 14: '(Death shall be their shepherd) and they go straight down to the tomb'.

In v. 15 the contrasting fates are brought out sharply; the singer expresses faith that God will indeed ransom and rescue him from the hand of Sheol. Only from the context and from related Old Testament passages can scholars seek to define the conception here. Is it the thought of deliverance from present peril? Or is it rather a rescue into a life beyond death (cf. Gen. 5.24; 2 Kings 2.9f.; Luke 16.19f.)? Could it be the royal hope of eternity (cf. above on 16.10)? Most have concluded that it is a salvation which delivers from final death, and certainly this is the way the psalm came to be read (the Targum says David speaks here by the spirit of prophecy, referring to his deliverance from the judgement of Gehennah). The end of the arrogant and all their wealth is further spelt out in vv. 16f.: in vain do they seek to create prosperity for themselves. The refrain again summarizes: the man of spendour, but lacking discernment to know the vanity of wealth, is comparable in the end to cattle taken for slaughter. In v. 16 some change the vowels to give 'Do not look (with envy)', but 'Do not fear' better answers the 'Why should I fear' of v. 5, and perhaps echoes an oracle which the singer received for himself and passes on as general counsel.

The differing interpretations of this psalm's hope, like those we shall meet for the comparable 73, call attention to the peculiarity of classical Old Testament religion, in that it mostly sees no clear hope of life beyond death, yet ever returns from sorrows to trust and contentment in the goodness of the Lord of life. However a full faith in a resurrection-life beyond death was at last attained, it was not found easily. In the present case there is a context of 'days of suffering' and the ruthless greed of 'supplanters', ever depriving others and outwardly successful in this world, trusting in their own wealth and con- gratulating themselves. But our psalmist, with his precious lyre, is inspired with a vision from beyond; he sees the utter futility of trust in wealth, and he finds the redeeming love of God. His vision is lit by the darkness of death; in this weird and inescapable light is seen the rotted pomp of the arrogant, and the wonder of the one who alone can ransom a life from the abyss. The New Testament often resumes the warning against trust in riches (Mark 10.23; Luke 12.16f. etc.), and proclaims the gospel of the ransom beyond human means (Mark 10.45; 1 Tim. 2.6).

Inspire us, Lord, by the music of your Word, that through all the darkness of death we may discern that our hope is in you alone, and know that you have ransomed our soul from the grave, to dwell with you for ever.

PSALM 50: Vision and Word in Worship

Psalm. Of Asaph.

1   The Mighty One, God, the Lord, has spoken,
    and called the world from the rising of the sun to its setting.
2   From Zion, perfection of beauty, God shines out;
    our God has come and will not keep silence.
3   Fire devours before him,
    and tempest rages about him.
4   He calls the heavens above,
    and the earth, to the judgement of his people:
5   Gather to me my pledged ones,
    who have sealed my covenant with sacrifice.
6   And the heavens declare his righteousness,
    for he truly is the God of justice.   *[Pause]*
7   Hear, O my people, and I will speak;
    heed, O Israel, and I will admonish you,
        for I am God, your God.
8   Not for your sacrifices would I reprove you,
    nor for your burnt-offerings, that are ever before me.
9   I will take no bullock from your house,
    nor he-goats from your folds.
10 For all the creatures of the forest are mine,
    and the beasts that roam the great mountains.
11 I know every bird of the hills,
    and all that moves in the wild is with me.
12 If I were hungry I would not tell you,
    for the world is mine, and all that fills it.
13 Do I eat the the flesh of bulls,
    or drink the blood of he-goats?
14 Sacrifice to God in thanksgiving,
    and so fulfil your vows to God Most High.
15 Then call to me in the day of trouble,
    and I will deliver you, and you shall give me the glory.

16 But to the wicked person God says:
        What do you mean by reciting my statutes,
    and taking my covenant upon your mouth,
17 when you have rejected discipline,
    and have cast my words behind you?
18 When you saw a thief you gladly joined him,
    and with adulterers you made common cause.
19 You have loosed your mouth for evil,

and have yoked your tongue with deceit.
20   You have sat and spoken against your brother,
and wounded with words your own mother's son.
21   These things you have done, and should I keep silence?
Do you think I am even such as yourself?
I will then reprove you,
and set your faults before your eyes.
22   You that forget God, consider this,
or I shall pluck you away, with none to deliver you.
23   One who sacrifices in thanksgiving gives me the glory,
and to one mindful of the way
I will show the salvation of God.

An introduction (vv. 1–6) tells of God coming and shining forth at Zion, but also preparing to speak words of judgement to his gathered covenant-people. There follows his speech of admonishment, in two parts (vv. 7–15, 16–22), concluding with a summary of both parts (v. 23). The first part gives teaching about sacrifices, and the second part about moral requirements. The warnings are given in a lively, even ironic fashion, and each topic is concluded positively with promise. As psalms come to be seen as often reflecting and expounding action in the festivals, so this and similar psalms (especially 81 and 95) are seen to set forth that moment vivid to faith when the Lord, having come afresh to Zion and taken his seat in glory, speaks to the world and his covenanted people. In part the tradition can be traced back to the ancient tribal days when, at such sanctuaries as Shechem and Shiloh, there would be held festivals of covenant renewal (cf. Deut. 31.10–11; Josh. 24). This seems to have later become an element in Jerusalem's autumnal festival, combined with thoughts of the Creator, the Most High, reigning anew over all his world. The situation in worship reflected in this psalm, where God addresses world and people through a prophetic spokesman, shows a tradition from which much of the prophecy in the prophetic books will have arisen. There, as here, eloquent words of criticism and encouragement are voiced for God to a gathered nation, assessing especially their faithfulness to the covenantal bond. For the heading see below on 73.

1–6   In prophetic role, the psalmist depicts the appearing of God, and his purpose and commands. He is expressing the visionary meaning of the present festal ceremony for renewal of the covenant. All the weight falls upon the presence and action of God, and the first words, in emphatic position, are three names of God: El, Elohim, and Yahweh (cf. Josh. 22.22, Int. 6b–c; we could otherwise understand 'The God of gods, Yahweh'). He has 'spoken'; this first action to be mentioned suits a psalm which is chiefly the conveying of his words. He has summoned the world from utmost east to west; indeed, heaven and earth themselves are called to the assessment of his people; they attend as witnesses to the covenant, as question is raised regarding its faithful keeping (cf. Deut. 31.28; Isa. 1.2). The prophet-psalmist sees the very presence of God, awesome and resplendent. God has come anew to his sanctuary on Zion, itself thereby transfigured in supreme beauty (see above on 48.2); beams of light shine out from him, fire and storm-wind rage about him, all signifying his divine majesty and holiness. A command to his messengers is now given in his direct speech: they are to gather his *ḥasidim*, his covenanted people, those who have ratified the covenant with sacrifice (or are about to do so – Craigie). In v. 6b the text has 'For God himself is judge', but a redivision (as *BHS*) gives the more probable sense as above. The 'Pause' falls appropriately at the end of this prelude.

7–15   God's speech begins in the ancient style of the Covenant-Lord present to his gathered people, powerfully present especially in the words of self-revelation and identification: 'I am Yahweh, your God', uniquely the One Who Is, yet 'your God', revealed and pledged to this people in grace and authority (cf. Ex. 20.2). Wonderful in itself is the living situation of the speaking and hearing, the 'I-thou relationship' of God and people. The first topic of the speech is introduced directly. The Lord has no fault to find in the quantity and constancy of sacrifices offered at his temple, but shows concern about the motivation or attitude of those that bring them. It was all too easy to feel, as a generous giver, that you were obligating God in some way. In vivid and ironic style, the speech reminds the worshippers that all is God's, an 'all' that is vast beyond their comprehension, and for his existence he has no need of the sacrifices they bring. He will be no tyrant coming to take from their houses or folds (cf. 1 Sam. 12.3–4). The idea, surviving from primitive antiquity, that the deity actually needed the sacrifices as food may well have had force for some worshippers, as it had abroad; in others the fault was a more subtle tendency to magnify oneself or seek to control the Lord of all. Nevertheless, this part of the speech ends with strong endorsement of sacrifices fulfilling vows made in time of need (cf. Lev. 7.12). These were the occasion of 'thanksgiving' (*todah*) – thankful praise and testimony, acknowledgement that the Lord had saved and the glory was his. (The idea that 'sacrifice of thanksgiving' was a sacrifice consisting only of thanksgiving, and so replacing material offerings, was surely not intended here, but came to have a rich history in Judaism without the temple and in Christianity, cf. Heb. 13.15.)

16–20   The psalmist-seer introduces the second part of God's speech with notice that the wicked person is now to be warned; some have suggested this clause is a later addition, but it seems a necessary transition to the sharp rebuke which immediately follows. The renewal of the covenant seems to have involved the recital by the worshippers of God's fundamental statutes, such as the Ten Commandments (Ex. 20; Deut. 5). The speech now bears sharply against those who publicly profess, but do not keep them. Examples given here echo three of the commandments. Again the speech has vividness and subtlety. In v. 18 we recognize those who may not be bold leaders in wrong-doing, but can be drawn to consent and participate. In v. 19 we meet the mouth 'set loose' – unrestrained by good feelings; also the tongue 'yoked' to deceit – close partner of lying, working as closely as two yoked animals. In v. 20 the 'sitting' suggests the temptations of bad company, and the malicious words that might be approved of there. But if such an offender consents or drifts with evil tides, then, as the speech asserts, not for the Lord such acquiescence! Now his word of warning, and soon his retribution! Such is the message for those who, despite participation in the public commitments of the covenant, yet in daily living 'forget God', do not reckon with him as the constantly decisive factor.

23 The final verse of the speech seems to summarize each part in turn, but positively: the one who faithfully fulfils vowed sacrifices for thanksgiving glorifies God; and the one firm in the way, loyal in practice to God's laws, will see divine salvation along that way. (In the Hebrew of v. 23b a word seems to be understood – 'one who sets (heart / foot) on the way'.)

The two themes of God's speech will have related to activity in the festival – the fulfilment of vows and the recital of the covenant laws. The psalmist, with his gift of music, poetry and prophecy, plays a vital part in the worship, mediating vision of the presence of God in beauty and terrible holiness, and then hearing of the word of God to purify the worship and the living that must follow it. This Asaph, or descendant of Asaph, is the prototype of all who, in gatherings for worship, are able by the Spirit to draw the people into the reality of the vision and word of God, into the confrontation with his holy presence and mind, his judgement and his grace. The message, too, is ever relevant for the community that would meet with God face to face: in worship and in daily life you must acknowledge God as God, the Lord as the Lord, and nothing less. This still is the way on which will shine the rising beams of God's salvation.

Most mighty God, grant us in worship to see the bright beams of your presence, and hear the searching words of your voice; that we may learn both in worship and in life truly to honour you, and to keep the way of your commandments; through him who is your Light, your Word and your Way, our Saviour Jesus Christ.

PSALM 51: My Sacrifice

For favour.   Psalm.   Of David.   When Nathan the prophet came to him, as he had come to Bath Sheba.

1   Be gracious to me, God, in your faithful love;
    in the abundance of your compassion blot out my offences.
2   Wash me thoroughly from my wickedness,
    and cleanse me from my sin.
3   For well I know my offences,
    and my sin is ever before me.
4   Against you only have I sinned,
    and done what is evil in your eyes,
    so you will be justified when you speak,
    and in the right when you give sentence.
5   Truly I was born in wickedness,
    a sinner when my mother conceived me.
6   Yet you desire truth in the inward parts,
    and in the heart's depths you will teach me wisdom.
7   Cleanse me with hyssop and I shall be clean;
    wash me and I shall be whiter than snow.
8   Cause me to hear joy and gladness,
    that the bones you have broken may rejoice.
9   Hide your face from my sins,
    and blot out all my misdeeds.
10 Create for me a pure heart, O God,
    and renew a steadfast spirit within me.
11 Do not cast me out of your presence,
    or take your holy Spirit from me.
12 Bring back to me the joy of your salvation,
    and uphold me with your gracious Spirit,
13 that I may teach the rebellious your ways,
    and sinners to return to you.
14 Deliver me from guilt, O God, the God of my salvation,
    and my tongue shall sing of your goodness.
15 Lord, open my lips,
    and my mouth shall proclaim your praise.
16 For you have not required a sacrifice;
    if I gave a burnt offering, you would not accept it.
17 My sacrifice, O God, is a broken spirit;
    a heart that is broken and crushed, O God,
        you will not despise.
18 Do good to Zion in your favour;
    build up the walls of Jerusalem.

19   Then you will accept the offerings of fellowship,
        sacrifice burnt and whole;
     then indeed shall they offer up bulls on your altar.

This prayer for forgiveness and restoration is distinctive in the depth and
persistence of its confession of sin. A common view is that it was an individual's prayer, which was later adapted to become a prayer for the community, especially by the addition of vv. 18–19. The last part of the heading
indeed connects the psalm with the best-known instance of sin and penitence
in David's life (2 Sam. 11–12), but this may well be only a deduction from the
character of the psalm (Int. 2b). We may, however, consider whether the
psalm could be the utterance of a king in his representative capacity; speaking
in individual terms, he would be leading the penitence of the people
incorporated in him, and so could naturally conclude with prayer for the
well-being of Zion. There are a number of similarities to phrases in the
Prophets concerning purification of the nation. Along these lines, as we shall
see, it is possible to trace a consistent development of thought to the end of
the psalm, and so to dispense with the theory that vv. 18–19 are a later
addition. The reference to Zion's walls in v. 18 is often connected with the
condition just prior to Nehemiah (Neh. 2.11f.), but again, this may be to
misunderstand a prayer of ancient type for the strengthening and prospering
of a holy city. At all events, the use of the psalm in later Jewish worship on the
Day of Atonement and in the church on Ash Wednesday (as one of the
Penitential Psalms; see above on 6) shows how it can speak for the community. It has indeed been used in the church more than any other psalm,
having been included in each of the seven Hours of the daily Office (NL).

1–4   The first word in the Hebrew, *honneni*, is the plea for grace; on nothing
else can the prayer be founded but the gracious compassion of God. May he
then be gracious according to his pledged and faithful love (*hesed*) and the
abundance of his tender pity, and so act to put away the supplicant's rebellion
and wrongdoing, expunging them as from a heavenly record, and washing
clean the sinner as clothes were pounded in water. The rebellious offences
had been deliberate, and the penitent one confesses to well knowing them
and having them ever before him. So clearly does he see that his wrongdoing
was an affront to God, a rebellion, a breach with him, that he says 'Against
you, you only, have I sinned' – surely not denying harm to others, but
expressing the overwhelming sense, the terrible insight, that the wrongdoing
was first and foremost against the Lord. Thus the supplicant 'gives God glory'
(Josh. 7.19) by confessing guilt and declaring that God would be just and
justified to condemn him.

5–8   Verse 5 gives (lit.) 'Behold, in iniquity I was travailed with, and in sin
did my mother conceive me', but the thought is of his own radical way-
wardness, a sense of being so profoundly unworthy of God that he yearns to
be purified and created anew, so that faithfulness and spiritual wisdom may

possess his deepest being. Such profound purification is the divine act signified in a rite of sprinkling water from a sprig of the hyssop shrub (cf. Ezek.
36.25; Num. 19.18); the word for 'wash' in v. 7 also is often applied to ritual
(Ps. 26.6; Ex. 30.19f.). Under the symbol, God's work, and that alone, can
make the sinner 'whiter than snow' (cf. Isa. 1.18). Then will come the time of
joyous festival, when the people, no longer like 'broken bones' (cf. Lam. 3.4),
in wholeness sing and dance their thanksgiving.

9–13 Prayer is renewed that God will put away and expunge the sins, create
for the penitent a pure heart, and renew a firm spirit within him (cf. Ezek.
36.25–7) – renew the inner life with all the firmness and strength to keep
God's way. In v. 13 it may be especially the ideal of the Lord's Anointed
which is in mind – serving in the near presence of God, empowered by the
Holy Spirit (the only other occurrence of this phrase in the Old Testament is
for the angelic presence in Israel, Isa. 63.9–14; but cf. the Spirit bestowed on
the king, 1 Sam. 16.13; Isa. 11.2 etc.). Verse 12b may also refer to the Spirit
bestowed on the king, and 'gracious' may rather signify 'royal' or 'noble'
(LXX 'ruling'; cf. *ndb* in royal names, and *nadib* in Prov. 25.6b, parallel to
'king'). Re-established before God, with all the strength given by the Spirit,
he will be able and glad to fulfil his duty of teaching, witnessing and
admonishing (cf. 2.10f.; 4.3f.; 62.9f.; 75.5f.).

14–19 This begins (lit.) 'Deliver me from blood / bloodshed', and is perhaps best understood to refer to guilt deserving death (cf. Isa. 1.18; Tate
'deadly guilt', while Dahood explains radically as tears of death). Relieved of
such guilt, the psalmist will sing of God's 'rightness', which clearly denotes his
grace and mercy. 'Open my lips' implies the act of salvation, which fills the
mouth with the song and power of thankful praise (cf. 40.3). Some have
understood vv. 16–17 to state absolutely that God does not want ritual
sacrifice, but a more qualified interpretation seems suitable. For such deliberate and extensive sins as are confessed in this psalm, ritual expiations were
not thought adequate (Num. 15.22–31; Ezek. 45.20); hope rested only in
God's grace, appealed to by one truly penitent, 'broken' and 'crushed' in heart
and spirit, the antithesis of the arrogant heart of the rebellious sinner. In v. 17a
the Hebrew gives 'The sacrifices of God are . . . ', but it is widely agreed that
the consonants are more suitably read as 'My sacrifice, O God, is . . .' (so
BHS).

Verses 18–19 are often considered a later addition, made while Jerusalem
was in ruins after 587, or still with ruined walls before 444; reacting to the
thought of vv. 16–17, the addition would affirm that when the walls are
rebuilt, God will again accept the offerings favourably. However, no reference is made to the most essential ritual need after 587, the rebuilding and
reconsecration of temple and altar, and it must be preferable to interpret the
text as a whole if reasonably possible. Particularly if the singer has a representative capacity (as king, or like the voice in Lam. 3), he can actually
conclude his Penitential Psalm with the prayer of v. 18 for the holy sanctuary

and city; prayer for the 'building' of the walls can well refer to their strengthening, repairing and prospering through divine care (cf. 147.2, 13; Isa. 26.1; also the Babylonian new-year prayer, 'the bolt of Babylon, the lock of the [temple] Esagila, the bricks of the [temple] Ezida restore thou to their places; O Lord, be appeased, may the gods of heaven and earth say to thee' – *ANET*, p. 390). Verse 19 then implies a vow: when the atonement which can only be made by repentance and grace is effected, leader and community will offer sacrifices, costly and in abundance, in thanksgiving for the restoration of right relationship or fellowship (*ṣedeq*). The thought resembles that of the preceding psalm, with its guarded approach to sacrifice, and its prizing of offerings for the occasion of thanksgiving.

To understand the voice in this psalm as representative or collective was, according to Gunkel, only to destroy the depth of the prayer; he prized rather the individual who so personally and profoundly recognized his unworthiness in the presence of God, and, rejecting the external ritual of sacrifice, hoped only in the re-creative grace of God. But the psalm, especially when taken as a whole, may rather arise from a proper integration of the inner, individual impulses with the public ceremony of the worshipping community. Here the leader would speak with all the penitence and longing of an individual heart, 'broken' and 'crushed', and the assembly would fully enter into his prayer, both one by one and as a group. He confesses offences, misdeeds and sins, and a sinfulness in the depth of his being; but all is put in general terms which a contrite people can apply to themselves, as they join in ceremonies of the temple. All the wrongdoing is focused as an alienation from God, no more, no less ('against you only'). And from this most miserable condition God alone, in his faithfulness, grace, tender love and pity, can deliver. So the supplication rises for his thorough washing, purifying, creating, renewing of the whole person in the springs of thought, being and action. When the representative singer, head of his people, is granted the new 'heart' and 'spirit' and is filled with the power of the Holy Spirit, he will joyfully proclaim the saviour's praise and celebrate it in public thanksgiving, ever renewing prayer for the prosperity of the holy city (cf. 122.6–9). And so it has continued in all the innumerable repetitions of this treasured psalm in Jewish and Christian worship. Led by the psalm into profound penitence, trusting in the one offering that fulfils all sacrifice, Christians to this day turn again to the Lord who creates and re-creates, while the visible sacraments still convey the deep purposes of his grace.

Gracious Lord, grant us true penitence, that you may be pleased to wash us from our sins and make our hearts anew; and do not take your Holy Spirit from us, that our tongue may ever sing of your goodness.

PSALM 52: The Destroyer and the Olive Tree

For favour.   Poem.   Of David.   When Doeg the Edomite came and told Saul and said to him, David has come to the house of Ahimelek.

1   Why do you glory in evil, you mighty one,
    while the goodness of God continues daily?
2   You plot destruction, you deceiver;
    your tongue is like a whetted razor.
3   You love evil rather than good,
    falsehood rather than true speaking. *[Pause]*
4   You love all words that destroy,
    and the tongue skilled in deceit.
5   But God shall bring you yourself to ruin;
    he will snatch you and pluck you out of your tent,
    and root you out of the land of the living. *[Pause]*
6   Then the just will see it and fear,
    and they will laugh at him and say:
7   See the one who did not make God his refuge,
    but trusted in the abundance of his wealth,
        and sought strength in his work of destruction.
8   But I shall be as a green olive tree in the house of God;
    I will trust in the goodness of God for ever and ever.
9   I will ever give you thanks for what you have done,
    and before your faithful I will declare
        how gracious is your name.

This denunciation of a powerful, deceitful and destructive person has prophetic force and authority, and has been compared with Isaiah's tirade against
the king's chief minister (Isa. 22.15f.) and Jeremiah's against the chief temple
officer (Jer. 20.3f.); the prophetic singer has been seen as representative of the
poor who are victims of this oppressor. Behind the picture of such an
oppressor, however, may lie a national danger from a foreign tyrant (just as a
great empire is condemned under parables of social wickedness in Hab. 2.6f.).
The psalmist, in a prophetic style traditional in worship, would then be
defending the faithful people of God with words of divine judgement. The
voice indeed may be that of the king, confronting the enemy of God's order
(cf. 2.10f.; 75.4f.), dwelling for ever in God's house (v. 8, cf. 23.6), anointed
with God's oil to be rich in the divine gifts of life (v. 8), and in his person
representing all God's people (vv. 6, 9). Comparison may be made with Ps.
58. The title connects the psalm with Doeg, butcher of the priests of Nob (1
Sam. 21.7; 22.6f.); this will be one of the expansions based on deductions
from the psalm (Int. 2b) and in this case not very appropriate, even if the
psalm is thought to be directed against Doeg's master, Saul.

1–7 The adversary is addressed directly with caustic question and damning description. He is doubtless not present, but the singer's words are like prophecies that can carry the power of judgement to the ends of the earth. The portrayal in vv. 1–4 exposes the sin so sharply that the condemnation of v. 5 is hardly needed. This 'mighty one', hero and champion in his own eyes, glories in his own wickedness, oblivious of the daily evidences of God's faithful love (*ḥesed*, but many emend v. 1b for a more expected sequence; the Hebrew consonants possibly intended 'reviling God every day', *ḥassed* as infinitive absolute, cf. BDB, p. 340a). The wickedness is specified almost entirely as deceitful, harmful speech, so injurious that the tongue is compared to a freshly sharpened razor; the psalmist seems to evoke all the power of God's justice to counter the deadly words, and perhaps, as Mowinckel suggests, the crisis has so far reached only to the preliminary barrage of curses and cunning propaganda from the aggressor. In vv. 5–7 the tyrant is promised the fate he planned for others, and the prophecy is strengthened by the depiction of joy at its fulfilment, when the loyal people of God will recognize the fate of one who made his own wealth and power his god and strength. (Gunkel prefers the possible sense 'May God bring you to ruin, may he snatch you … may the just see …', and similarly Dahood.)

8–9 Supporting the foregoing words, the singer expresses confidence in the *ḥesed*, the enduring goodness and love of God, whereby he will live joyously in the presence of God, and have cause to give thanks and testimony in the assembly of worshippers. The olive tree growing in the sacred courts, well tended and luxuriant, is here a symbol of one who will enjoy life close to God, able also to mediate the rich gift. The sudden emergence of this figure, so distinct and standing over against the evil 'mighty one', suits a royal interpretation, where the Anointed of the Lord, made rich in life and gifts of the Spirit by his holy oil (cf. Zech. 4.11f.), dwells in the house of the Lord for ever (23.6), and brings life and blessing to all the faithful (cf. 92.10; 72 etc.). Pre-eminently too, the Anointed proclaims the name of the Lord before the assembly of the covenant-people (v. 9b; for the sense of *qwh* as 'declare, proclaim', rather than 'wait for, trust in', see Dahood).

We have seen the psalmist confronting one who exults in earthly power and wealth, and attacks first with deceit and words deadly as razors. At every point of choice, this self-vaunting person chooses evil rather than good and proceeds to his glory through falsehood. To counter this evil the psalmist brings the word of God in judgement (cf. Heb. 4.12), and points to the only sure defence, the faithful love of God. So there arises confidence – a vision of rich life sustained for ever in the presence of God. The psalm encourages the church ever to address the follies of human power, and in particular the ruthless use of words, deceiving and destroying; it is for the church also to pray for and pronounce God's judgement on such evil; and by showing also the alternative – the beauty of life in God – to work for the repentance of the self-worshippers and the strengthening of the faithful. The green olive tree in the house of the Lord brings the thought of the tree of life, the cross of the Saviour, that gives eternal life to all who trust in the faithful love of God rather than in earthly glory.

Lord of faithful love, grant that your people be ever vigilant in prayer against the vaunting of evil and the deployment of words to deceive and destroy; defend us with your mighty Word, and plant us to grow in your house, that we may enjoy your truth and your goodness for ever.

PSALM 53: O for the Great Turning to Salvation

For favour.   *With music of flutes.*   Poem.   Of David.

1   The fool says in his heart, There is no God.
    They are corrupt and vile *in wrongdoing*,
       there is no one that does good.
2   *God* has looked down from heaven upon earth's peoples,
    to see if there is anyone acting wisely and seeking God.
3   But *every one of them has gone back*, all alike corrupted;
    there is no one that does good, no not one.

4   Are the evildoers without understanding,
    that they eat up my people as though they ate bread,
       and do not call on *God*?
5   There shall they fear with *fear such as never was*,
    for God *will scatter the bones*
       of him that is encamped against you.
    You will put them to shame,
    for God has rejected them.
6   O that the salvation of Israel were given from Zion!
    When *God* turns the life of his people,
       let Jacob rejoice, let Israel be merry.

In a different collection and with some variations, this psalm has already appeared as 14. The italic type above shows phrases that differ. 'Elohim' ('God') stands instead of 'Yahweh' ('the Lord'), as generally in this part of the Psalter (Int. 7b) and, in all, some 22 words are different. The substantial differences are between 14.5–6 and the corresponding 53.5, the latter giving a more specifically military picture (Kirkpatrick connects it with Sennacherib's withdrawal in 701, 2 Kings 18.13f.; but 'the bones of him that is encamped against you' is not well expressed in the Hebrew, and some emend to 'the bones of the impious' – so *BHS*). In the title the first of the two extra notes occurs also over 88. As the possible sense 'over sickness' is not very appropriate here, it may be best to render 'with flute / flute-playing' (cf. 5), an accompaniment of sorrowful nature (Mowinckel, *Psalms* II, p. 210). For commentary, see above on 14.

PSALM 54: The Name Gracious in Salvation

For favour.   With stringed instruments.   Poem.   Of David.   When the Ziphites came and said to Saul, Is not David hiding himself with us?

1   O God, save me by your name,
     and judge for me by your might.
2   O God, hear my supplication;
     give heed to the words of my mouth.
3   For strangers have risen against me,
     and the ruthless seek after my soul;
        they do not set God before them.   *[Pause]*
4   But God is my helper;
     the Lord is the upholder of my soul.
5   May the harm return upon those that lie in wait for me;
     in your truth put them to silence.
6   Freely will I sacrifice to you;
     Your name will I praise, Lord, for it is gracious.
7   For it shall deliver me from every trouble,
     and my eye shall see the downfall of my enemies.

This is a short prayer for salvation from enemies that are sinister and cruel, and lying in wait. It includes a lamenting description of the danger (v. 3), a statement of trust in the Lord (v. 4), and a vow of abundant sacrifice when the enemies are seen defeated (vv. 6–7). Prominent is the thought of salvation effected (as in 20) through the mighty name of the Lord. The psalm thus appears to be the prayer of a king troubled by armed foes, striking hard against them with the weapon of prayer, and promising sacrifices on a royal scale in the time of victory. The 'legal' expression in v. 1b is hardly enough to support the theory that the psalmist is a persecuted individual seeking justice or asylum in the temple (cf. such language along with warfare in 35). The title contains one of the expansions that theorize about a setting in David's life (1 Sam. 23.19f.; cf. Int 2b); the use of 'stringed instruments' (the plucking of lyre and harp) is appointed also for 4, 6, 55, 67, 76, and Hab. 3.19.

1–3   As usual in supplications, the name of God is the first word, and here at once the prayer is explicitly for salvation 'by your name'. The parallel term is 'by your might', and the thought is of God revealed and acting through his 'name' (see above on 20.1–5). The deliverance is seen as God's saving judgement (cf. 7.8; 9.4; 26.1; 35.24; 43.1). After the invocation and petitions of vv. 1–2, v. 3 presents to God the situation of need. The main text, with good support (LXX, Syriac, Jerome), describes the assailants as 'strangers' (*zarim*) who are 'ruthless / terrible' (these terms are combined in Ezek. 28.7; 31.12) and who do not respect the just will of God; it is altogether a sinister and fearsome prospect. (Many translators follow some manuscripts and the Targum in reading 'arrogant ones', *zedim*, instead of 'strangers', as in 86.14.)

4–5 A statement of trust in the Lord as supreme helper and sustainer prepares for the central petition in v. 5. The manuscripts vary as to whether v. 5a is indeed a petition or rather a prediction, but in view of v. 5b petition is probable; so God is asked to 'silence' or do away with the foes (pictured as ambushers), in accordance with his 'truth' (faithfulness), and so the harm they purposed will have returned upon themselves.

6–7 The singer ends with a vow to bring thanksgiving-sacrifices in abundance (*bi-nedaba*, on a generous, noble scale befitting a king; cf. the 'royal' spirit in 51.12). There he will praise and testify to the saving 'name', which will have delivered him and overthrown the aggressors. The reference to God's presence and saving power in his name, the form in which he gives himself to his worshippers and is open to their prayers, ties in with the first line of the psalm.

Faced with terrifying enemies that have no scruples and strike from hidden places, the psalmist defends his 'soul' and his people by calling on the holy name. In his name God has made himself known, has entered into a bond of faithful friendship, and ever comes in salvation. Through his name his people are mightily helped and sustained. The pattern of their life is ever to call upon this name, walk in its power and protection, and give themselves freely in thanksgiving for all that God bestows through it. The supplication strikes against the evil foe; but beyond the imminent peril, the triumph of the name in the end must mean the enemy's new life in the family of God (Int. 6k), and in this spirit the church has sometimes specially appointed this psalm for Good Friday.

O God, who in the name of Jesus has given us a strong salvation, help us with faith to call upon the holy name in every danger and adversity, and freely to give thanks and testify to its gracious help.

PSALM 55: Spectres in the City

For favour. With stringed instruments. Poem. Of David.

1   Listen to my prayer, O God,
    and do not hide from my supplication.
2   Give heed to me and answer me,
    for I am restless in my complaining.
3   I am alarmed at the voice of the enemy,
    at the clamour of the wicked;
    for they would bring down evil upon me,
    and are set against me in fury.
4   My heart is in turmoil within me,
    and the terrors of death have fallen upon me.
5   Fear and trembling have come upon me,
    and a horrible dread has overwhelmed me.
6   And I said, O that I had wings like a dove,
    that I might fly away and be at rest!
7   Then would I flee away far off,
    and make my lodging in the wilderness.   *[Pause]*
8   I would make haste to escape
    from the stormy wind and tempest.
9   Confuse their tongues, Lord, and divide them,
    for I have seen violence and strife in the city.
10 Day and night they go about upon her walls;
    and in her midst stalk mischief and trouble.
11 Ruin walks in her streets;
    deceit and guile linger in her square.
12 For it was not an open enemy that reviled me,
    for then I could have borne it;
    it was not my adversary that swelled so against me,
    for then I would have hid myself from him.
13 But it was you, one like myself,
    my companion and my familiar friend.
14 We took sweet counsel together;
    we walked as friends in the house of God.
15 May death come suddenly upon them;
        may they go down live into the darkness,
    for evils are in their dwelling and in their heart.
16 As for me, I will cry to God,
    and the Lord indeed shall save me.
17 Evening, morning and noonday,
    I will pray and make my supplication.
18 He shall hear my voice, and redeem my soul in peace

from the battle that is upon me,
where many have come against me.
19 God shall hear and bring them down,
even he that reigns from of old. *[Pause]*
For they will not repent,
and have no fear of God.
20 Against those at peace with him he stretched out his hands,
and thus he defiled his covenant.
21 His mouth was smoother than butter,
but his heart was set on war.
His words were softer than oil,
yet they were naked blades.
22 O cast your burden upon the Lord, and he shall sustain you;
he will never let the faithful one be overthrown.
23 But those who are murderous and deceitful, O God,
you will bring down to the pit of destruction.
They shall not live out half their days;
but as for me, I shall trust in you.

This is one of the most passionate and urgent supplications. It is voiced by one who is restless, alarmed, and shuddering with dread of death from furious enemies. It sometimes shows the singer individually facing a former ally who has turned traitor, but in other verses it seems that two communities are opposed in a situation of war. Hostile forces may have already ringed the city, and spectres of ruin seem to circle about it and haunt the streets. We may well see the psalm as the prayer of a beleaguered king, who makes special intercession at the temple thrice daily (v. 17) and calls for doom on the traitors, a doom such as tradition ascribed to those who had turned against the leadership of Moses. In keeping with the alarming urgency of the danger, the psalm swings to and fro between invocation of God, lament, imprecation of enemies and statements of trust.

1–8 The opening invocation is followed by portrayal of a terrible situation. The singer appeals for God's urgent intervention by depicting the disturbance and alarm, the turmoil and deadly horror from which he suffers. He is wrapped in a mantle of shuddering (v. 5b) because of the fury of enemies; the noise of their malevolent voices (v. 3) perhaps includes cursing and evil propaganda prior to outright assault (cf. 52.2–4). The hostility and tempestuous alarm are emphasized all the more by description of the longing to flee to a remote place of peace and silence. The rock dove, ancestor of our pigeons, provides a vivid image; she nests on ledges of cliffs far into the wilderness, but with her long wings and rapid flight, she can find food afar and return to her remote 'lodging'.

9–11 Against the hostile tongues the psalmist prays that they may be made ineffective; as in the story of Babel (Gen. 11.9), they are to be confused and set against each other. The shadow of evil is seen to have fallen on the city (probably Jerusalem); instead of the good angels of peace, righteousness and faithfulness that should be known in the holy city (cf. 43.3; 85.9–13), the demonic forms circle about it and penetrate its defences – the seven spectres of violence, strife, ruin, mischief, trouble, deceit, guile.

12–15   The lamenting description here includes an accusation. Among the adversaries is one who had been friend and ally, a person of like rank; the two had enjoyed 'counsel' (*sod*), conferring together as trusted companions, and had walked together in the temple (either 'in concord', so LXX; or 'in the throng' at festivals). The hostility of such a person is felt as extreme treachery, and so there follows a prayer for doom upon him along with the other enemies. That they should go down 'live' into Sheol, the underworld, is the thought of a sudden destruction like that recounted in Numbers 16.30f. as having befallen opponents of Moses.

16–21   Already there is a battle come upon him and the foes are numerous. All his effort is centred on prayer; the three main daily occasions of prayer (cf. Dan. 6.10) may here indicate gatherings for penitential supplication in the temple. The supplication is supported by statements of trust: 'The Lord indeed shall save us ... he shall hear my voice ... God shall hear.' In vv. 20–1 the treachery of the former ally is again set before God; this 'defiling' of covenant was felt so keenly, and the person concerned now so dangerous, that the grief must be expressed again – O the contrast of the oily words and the murderous intentions!

22–23   The address of v. 22a is to a masculine singular, and in a different tone, so that it seems like a word addressed to the psalmist; some indeed take it as an oracle given to him, but the wording (with 'Lord' in the third person) and the continuance in v. 24, favour an exhortation from the psalmist to his own spirit (cf. 42.5) and to the assembly (which could be addressed in individual fashion). One might otherwise think of a choral contribution in v. 22, with the solo voice resuming in v. 23. The word translated 'burden' is found only here and is usually explained as 'what is given, lot' – the burden of care or suffering which God lays upon you (so Kirkpatrick; LXX, followed by 1 Peter 5.7, has 'care', while Jerome has 'love', *caritatem*). The 'faithful / just one' (*saddiq*) may here refer especially to the Lord's Chosen One, his king (cf. 5.12; 11.3; 75.10; 92.12; Zech. 9.9). The renewed word against the deceivers (v. 23) matches the thought of a sudden and premature end in v. 15. The last sentence is of trust, and is a final appeal to the faithfulness of the Covenant Lord.

Facing deadly hostility, the psalmist wishes he could flee far off and rest like the dove in the inaccessible cliffs of the wilderness, in quietness and peace. But there can be no such escape, and all his trust is placed in the Lord. To God he unfolds the extent of his fears and alarm, putting before him the horrible dread and terror of it all. He recounts to him his dreadful vision of destructive forces that surround and penetrate the city, the evil angels of violence and deceit. He pours out to him the most bitter story of the trusted companion who, behind pleasant words, intended to destroy him. And he calls for a sudden destruction to come upon all these enemies of his own and his people's life. In all this supplication, repeated at the solemn hours of prayer, he is 'casting his burden on the Lord', who alone can sustain his trusting one, his *ṣaddiq*.

The New Testament recounts how a horrible dread came upon Christ (Mark 14.33; Luke 22.44), who also knew the pain of the friend's betrayal (Mark 14.44). With penetrating eye he could see the forces of destruction and the sentence that would suddenly fall. The church has sung this psalm in remembrance of Christ's passion, trembling at the depth of evil in the 'city', but trusting in the Saviour, and with him seeking the forgiveness and conversion of those that would only deceive and destroy.

Lord, in all times of fear and dread, grant that we may so cast our burden upon you, that you may bear us on the holy wings of the Spirit to the stronghold of your peace.

PSALM 56: Tears Treasured in Heaven

For favour.   Over the dove for the Far Ones.   Of David.
Atonement.   When the Philistines seized him in Gath.

1   Be gracious to me, God, for man tramples over me,
     all day long fighting and pressing upon me.
2   My foes trample over me all the day;
     many are those that fight against me, O Most High.
3   Yet in the day when I fear,
     I will put my trust in you.
4   In God whose word I praise, in God I trust and will not fear;
     for what can flesh do to me?
5   All the day long they wound with words;
     their every thought is to do me harm.
6   They band together and lie in wait,
     watching my heels as they eagerly seek my life.
7   Shall they escape for all their wickedness?
     In anger bring the peoples down, O God.
8   You have counted all my groans,
        my tears are laid up in your bottle;
     are they not noted in your book?
9   If my enemies turn back on the day when I call,

> then I shall know that God is with me.
> 10   In God whose word I praise,
>   in the Lord whose word I praise,
> 11   in God I trust and will not fear;
>   for what can man do to me?
> 12   Gladly will I render the vows to you;
>   fully will I bring you the offerings of thanksgiving.
> 13   For you will deliver my soul from death
>   and my feet from falling,
>   to walk before God in the light of life.

This supplication has two main parts, each concluded with the distinctive refrain (vv. 4 and 10–11); a conclusion for the whole looks forward to the time of salvation, the singer promising fulfilment of the votive offerings (vv. 12–13). Although he seems to speak as an individual, 'trampled' by enemies, assailed by cruel words, in danger from lurkers who are eager for his life, a national dimension appears in the expressions for the foes; these are warring and numerous, peoples or nations to be cast down or routed in the fury of the Warrior-God. The sufferer can therefore be well understood to be a king, bearing in his own soul hostilities against his land and nation from other peoples. He appeals to God to bring down the pride of human armies, and he especially praises the 'word' or covenant-promises to the dynasty; and he looks forward to serving in peace before the face of God, in all the abundant light and life granted to the Lord's Anointed. In the title we may (with Mowinckel, *Psalms* II, pp. 213f.) see the setting of the psalm on a day of penitence and intercession, which included ceremonies of 'atonement' (*miktam* as 16; some explain as 'inscription' – Dahood, Tate); the 'dove' may be one released to fly far into the desert, symbolically bearing away sin, rather as did the scapegoat (cf. Lev. 14.4–7; 16.20f.; Zech. 5.5–11); the 'Far Ones' probably occur in 65.5, spirits at the entrance of the underworld, comparable to 'the most distant of gods', *rhq ilm, rhq ilnym*, in the Ugaritic texts. The last part of the title will be another of the theorizing additions (Int. 2b); the episode mentioned is not otherwise recorded (cf. 1 Sam. 21.10f.).

1–4   The lamented situation may be the raiding of territory by foreign enemies; it is as though they trampled on the king's own person. The frequency of the attacks, the great number of the assailants – here are details that call for God's speedy help. Professions of trust also give point to the appeal; how could such a one be disappointed? God's 'word' (the sum of his commitments and promises) is praised as wholly trustworthy. 'Man' (v. 1) and 'flesh' (v. 4) represent the arrogance of earthly power, which the true power of God will surely demolish (cf. Isa. 31.3).

5–11   As often, it is malevolent words which the psalmist laments; they are words meant to bring ruin, and in ancient warfare they might take the form of ritual cursing and deceitful propaganda. The ambushes (v. 6) may have been a reality especially for outlying populations, attacks which the king feels in his own person. The prayer is that the aggressive peoples should be 'brought down' – down from their pride, down to the dust. Verse 8 refers to the mourning, penitential style of the national intercession; the Lord will have seen the extent of the king's abasement – his lamenting gestures and sighs, the many tears he has shed. Indeed God does not despise such tears, but as it were treasures them up in a heavenly water-skin as precious signs of penitence and faith. The section ends with statements of trust, including the refrain, expanded a little from v. 4. (In v. 9, for the construction with 'If', *az*, cf. Dahood, Tate.)

12–13 The singer willingly undertakes responsibility for the community's thank-offerings when deliverance shall be given, and he promises they will be brought in full without stinting (cf. 50.23; 51.19). He will give praise and testimony for the salvation that will have delivered him and his community from death and the abyss, and enabled him to serve once more in the presence of God, the source of light and life (for 'walking before God' cf. Gen. 17.1; 1 Sam. 2.30; 1 Kings 2.4; 2 Kings 20.3).

Against the wounding words, our psalmist sets the word of God; praising that word, he is enabled to trust and to cast out fear, perceiving the emptiness of human might in comparison with the power of God. At the same time he brings his grief to God, and penitence for sins; and he knows that every tossing of a supplicant's head, and every tear, is taken up and treasured by God, who does not despise the broken heart (51.17). Feeling in his own soul the suffering of vulnerable people who are daily trampled on, he is a type of all true pastors, a prefigurement indeed of Christ who 'offered up prayers and supplications with loud cries and tears' (Heb. 5.5f.).

Defend us, O God, from the false words of man by your eternal Word; and may the tears and prayers of Jesus deliver our souls from death and our feet from falling, that we may walk before you in the light of his eternal life.

PSALM 57: A Heart That is Ready

For Favour. Do Not Destroy. Of David. Atonement. When he fled because of Saul into the cave.

1   Be gracious to me, God, be gracious,
      for my soul takes shelter in you.
      In the shadow of your wings I take shelter,
      until the storm of ruin is passed.

2   I will call to God Most High,
     to the God who does great things for me.
3   From heaven he will send and save me,
         deriding those that trample upon me;   *[Pause]*
     God will send out his faithful love and truth.
4   I lie in the midst of lions,
     that breathe fire and are greedy for human prey;
     their teeth are spears and arrows,
     and their tongue a whetted sword.
5   Be exalted, O God, above the heavens,
     with your glory over all the earth.
6   They have laid a net for my feet, my soul is bowed down;
     they have dug a pit before me,
         but shall fall right in themselves.   *[Pause]*
7   My heart is ready, O God, my heart is ready,
     that I may sing and raise a melody.
8   Awake, my glory, awake, harp and lyre,
     that I may awaken the dawn.
9   I will give you thanks, Lord, among the peoples;
     I will sing your praise among the nations.
10   For your love reaches to the heavens,
     and your faithfulness to the clouds.
11   Be exalted, O God, above the heavens,
     with your glory over all the earth.

Beginning as supplication in a situation of great peril (vv. 1–5), the psalm culminates in confidence and morning praise (vv. 6–10), though a concluding verse reiterates the basic prayer (v. 11). There is much in the ideas to indicate that the psalmist is a king, and that the danger and anticipated deliverance are on a national scale (the refrain in vv. 5, 11 is here especially significant). There are links with surrounding psalms, especially 56. A night ceremony may be the occasion of the supplication, with transition to the theme of praise as dawn approaches (v. 8); one might think of incubation (the king sleeping in the sanctuary in quest of a visitation of God, Int. 6e) or more generally of a national vigil of intercession. The passage in vv. 7–11 is used again as 108.1–5. In the title, 'Do Not Destroy' (found also with 58, 59, 75) may refer to a type of intercessory service, pleading that God should not destroy this people (cf. Deut. 9.26), and perhaps in particular that he should spare this 'vine' for the sake of some good part that is in it (cf. Isa. 65.8). The reference to David as fugitive (1 Sam. 22 or 24) seems to be another of the later speculations (Int. 2b).

1–5   Petition, lament, and declaration of trust mingle in this opening passage. The troublous situation is pictured as a storm of ruin, 'trampling' by enemies (cf. above on 56.1–2), and attacks of dragon-like lions, an image which alludes to harmful words (cf. above on 56.5). The grace that is sought is like that often pictured in royal prayers – a nestling under God's wings (cf. 17.8; 61.4; 63.7; more generally 36.7), a mission of the angels that embody the covenant-blessings (v. 3b, cf. 18.16; 20.2; 23.6; 43.3; 144.7), the accomplishing by God of his covenant-promises (v. 2b), and the great 'appearing' of God as Sovereign to right the world (v. 5, cf. 7.6; 9.19; 18.46; 21.13; 46.10).

6–11 At the beginning and end of this section it is apparent that the thought of danger is still sharp; with hunter's net and pit the enemies work to destroy, and the final word is renewal of the prayer for the righting of the world. But there is also here a surge of confidence. The enemy will trap themselves (cf. 7.15f.; 9.16), and the psalmist is ready to stir the dawn with praise in anticipation of God's wonderful help. The dawn is pictured as a winged angel, to be awakened by the music of praise for the flight across the heavens; the mention of two kinds of instrument shows that a group participate in the prayer. It is especially in the royal psalms that we hear of the testimony sung out to all nations, a witness to the faithful goodwill and salvation of God (cf. 18.50, *Kingship*, pp. 182–7; in Egyptian texts also we hear of praise that awakens divine beings and parts of the temple with cosmic significance, *BRJL*, vol. 37, p. 179). The singer's 'glory' which is also to be awakened (v. 8) can be understood as his soul glorified by the grace of God (cf. 3.3; 4.2; 7.5; 16.9; 30.12; some prefer to revocalize as *kebedi*, 'my liver', seat of emotions). For the beautiful praise of God's *ḥesed* and *emet*, his boundless and utterly trustworthy love and truth (faithfulness), compare v. 3 and above on 36.5.

We seem to follow the singer through night to approach of dawn. At the outset of the night, enemies assail in terrible forms – a ruinous tempest, the flames and swords of malicious words, the concealed traps of the hunter. O to hide in the shadow of God's wings, or to see his bright angels of love and truth hastening to the rescue! O to see God manifest in glory over all the world, and the deeds of evil banished at last! As the night of prayer wears on, the sheltering wings and the might of the divine love have brought new hope. The heart is ready to praise the saviour in the new dawn, ready to bear witness to all the world. Already for the wonder of his love the music for God must begin, though not yet is seen that final victory of good. So the psalm corresponds to the pilgrimage of every worshipper, who, troubled and fearful, yet finds strength in God to defy the cruel shapes of evil and, before the night is ended, to begin the song of joyful thanksgiving.

Send out, O God, your faithful love to defend your little ones from those who assail them with cruel words and traps; and give us courage to awaken with our songs the dawn of hope, until you bring the full day of your glory over all the world.

PSALM 58: The Powerful Prayer of the Oppressed

For favour. Do Not Destroy. Of David. Atonement.

1 Do you mighty ones indeed speak justly,
   do you rule earth's children fairly?
2 With unjust heart you act throughout the earth,
   and weigh out the violence of your hands.
3 The wicked are estranged, even from the womb;
   speakers of falsehood, they went astray from birth.
4 They have venom like the venom of a snake;
   they are like the deaf viper that stops its ear,
5 which does not heed the voice of the charmers,
   and is deaf to the skilful weaver of spells.
6 O God, break their teeth in their mouth;
   the fangs of these lions, Lord, destroy.
7 May they dwindle as water that runs away;
   may they have no strength to aim their shafts.
8 May they be as a snail that melts away,
   and as one lost from the womb, that never saw the sun.
9 Before ever your pots feel the heat of the thorns,
   green and blazing alike, may he whirl them away.
10 But may the faithful one be glad when he sees retribution,
   and knows beyond a doubt the downfall of the wicked.
11 So people will say,
      There is a harvest for the one that is faithful;
   there is indeed a God who governs on earth.

The four phrases of the title are the same as in 57 and 59, a sign of a close relationship. The form, however, is reminiscent of 52, with an address to the mighty (vv. 1–2), followed by condemnation (vv. 3–5) and imprecation (6–12). The forceful passion of these dooming prayers suggests that, as in the surrounding psalms, there is a situation of communal suffering, in which a leading figure, with the power of prophetic intercession, utters the strong psalm as defence against a ruthless tyranny.

1–2 'Do you indeed speak righteousness?' – so far the opening words are clear; but an additional word comes second in the Hebrew. It has been vocalized by the tradition as *elem*, apparently the noun 'dumbness / silence'; this scarcely gives sense (Rashi: 'Should right be silent? You must speak'), and what is needed is a designation of those addressed. Hence most moderns re-vocalize as *elim*, 'gods', and either explain it as God's heavenly ministers, such as are condemned for maladministration in 82, or take it as ironic for earthly rulers, the 'powers that be'. As heavenly servants, these *elim* would be in league with earth's 'wicked' described in vv. 3f.; but as earthly tyrants, the ironically termed *elim* would more simply be referred to throughout the psalm. At all events, the crisis that concerns the singer is presented as universal injustice (cf. 10, 11, 14). The controlling powers are corrupt in heart, and the hands that should give just measure are violent in cruelty.

3–5 If not identical with the 'mighty' of vv. 1–2, the 'wicked' depicted here are at least their earthly counterparts. The particular oppression is still presented in general terms. Evil seems so inherent in their ways, that they are thought of as 'estranged' from goodness ever since they came into being. The image of the snake's venom seems especially to indicate harmful speech (cf. 57.4), and the horned viper, being deaf, cannot be trained by the voice of the charmer to be harmless.

6–9 The foregoing description of the cruel tyrants has prepared the way for their condemnation. Hence there follows a series of imprecations which use the style of ancient treaty-curses, similes of destruction which hang a threat over those unfaithful to the treaty. After prayer that the Lord would break the teeth of these voracious 'lions' (cf. above on 57.4), the similes are piled on: may these tyrants lose their strength like water that flows away, wither like snails in drought, pass away like a miscarriage, be blown away like twigs in a tempest. This last image (v. 9) seems to be of thorn–bush cuttings placed under a cauldron in the open, the dry branches for quick blaze, the green for sustaining the fire; but all in vain when the wind whirls in from the desert.

10–11 The conclusion looks forward to the time when God will have brought retribution on the oppressors and shown that true and faithful conduct has its good 'fruit' or harvest. Twice mentioned is the *ṣaddiq*, the just or faithful one, used collectively, or perhaps referring in the first place to the king (cf. above on 55.22). The language of v. 10b (lit. 'he shall wash his steps in the blood of the wicked one') involves an idiom 'to wash in' (cf. Gen. 49.11; Job 29.6) and the grim experience of hand-to-hand warfare; our translation seeks to elucidate the meaning in terms of vivid and irrefutable evidence of the defeat of injustice.

There are particular situations of oppression when it seems that the whole world lacks moral government, and that events are only in the hands of tyrants full of venom and deaf to entreaty. Our psalm responds to such a situation with a prophetic power, an intercession to call down the just salvation of God. The evil is first exposed, then prayed against with passionate vigour. Faith in the justice of the ruler of the world no doubt underpins the prayer, but to the end the intercessor leaves a reproachful edge on his words – at present people can hardly see that there is a God justly governing all. The primitive force of the imprecations makes the psalm unwelcome to many, but the forcefulness will be understood by those who have experienced the cruel reign of the wicked. In the church's tradition such fearsome psalms convey the word of Christ that in the end will shatter the forces of evil, and which at present serves to warn and to encourage (cf. Int. 6k).

Just and merciful Lord, see how your creatures are despoiled by the wicked; hasten the time when the power of evil shall melt away, and all your creation shall rejoice in your holy kingdom.

PSALM 59: Fears at Nightfall

For favour. Do Not Destroy. Of David. Atonement. When Saul sent and they watched the house to kill him.

1   Rescue me from my enemies, O God;
    set me on high above those that rise against me.
2   Save me from the evildoers,
    and from murderous foes deliver me.
3   For see, they lie in wait for my soul;
    the fierce ones band together against me.
    Not for any fault or sin of mine, O Lord;
4   for no offence, they run and make ready for war.
    Arise to meet me and to see,
5   for you are the Lord God of Hosts, the God of Israel.
    Awake to visit all the nations;
    do not spare any evil traitors.   *[Pause]*
6   They gather at nightfall and snarl like dogs,
    and circle about the city.
7   They pour evil words from their mouths,
      swords are in their lips;
    for who, they say, can hear?
8   But you, Lord, will laugh at them;
    you will deride the boasts of all the nations.
9   O my strength, I will watch for you,
    for you, O God, are my strong tower.
10   My God will hasten to me in his faithful love;
    God will show me the downfall of my foes.
11   Do not slay them, lest my people forget;
    shake them with your power, and bring them down,
      O Lord, our shield.
12   For the sin of their mouth, the words of their lips,
    let them be taken in their pride.
    For the cursing and falsehood they have uttered,
13   consume in wrath, consume till they are brought to nothing.

> And they shall know that God rules in Jacob,
> to all the ends of the earth. *[Pause]*
> 14 And still they gather at nightfall and snarl like dogs,
> and circle about the city.
> 15 Though they roam for something to devour,
> and howl if they are not filled,
> 16 yet I will sing of your strength,
> and every morning praise your faithful love,
> since you have been my stronghold,
> my refuge in the day of my trouble.
> 17 O my strength, I will make melody to you,
> for you, O God, are my refuge, my God of faithful love.

The heading suggests affinity with the surrounding psalms (for 'Do Not Destroy' see above on 56; for 'Atonement' see above on 57; for 'When Saul . . .' see Int. 2b and 1 Sam. 19.11f.). The national responsibility of the singer appears especially in vv. 5, 8, 11, 13. That enemies of nation and city should seek especially his 'soul' is understandable if he is the king. It seems that external foes threaten his city (Jerusalem), gathering around it at dark like scavenging jackals, and hurling curses and abuse. So he calls for God's saving action in accordance with the covenant promises and in terms of the heavenly King's judgement on the nations, at whose pretensions God mocks (cf. 2.4). In an urgent situation, the king is thus using his grace of prayer (2.8), his mighty weapon to defend people and city.

1–5 The singer calls for God to rescue him from his evil and murderous foes, and claims that he has not given them any justification for their hostility, yet they are intent on war (v. 4). His kingly office seems especially apparent as he calls for God to come to meet him, coming moreover as Lord God of Hosts and of Israel, judging the nations, dealing with those who have been treacherous (breaking treaty obligations).

6–10 The intercession develops with depictions of the situation and affirmations of trust. The description of harmful words resembles a prominent feature of preceding psalms (52.2f.; 55.3, 9; 56.5; 57.4; 58.3f.); it takes a special form here with the comparison of the enemy to wild dogs or jackals that scavenge near a town at night, barking and howling like demons. It seems from this that enemies approach the city walls as darkness falls, and assail the defenders with curses and threats – the swords of the lips (v. 7; v. 7c means 'as though there were no God to account to'). But the Lord's Anointed trusts in the promise given at his installation (2.8–9), invoking the Lord his fortress (cf. 18.1–2) and faithful saviour (cf. 18.35), who will give him victory over all foes (cf. 18.43).

11–13 The defeat of the foes is to serve God's glory. The prayer is therefore that they shall be brought down from the high pride of rebellion against God's good order, their pomp consumed to nothing, so that they acknowledge the rule of God in his covenant-people and in all the world; and so that, in their humbled state, they will serve as a reminder to his people of his power and faithfulness (cf. Ex. 9.15–16).

14–17 The concluding vow to praise God when salvation comes is expressed with a warmth of repetition. Every morning (*labboqer* as Amos 4.4) he will raise the psalmody that testifies to the Lord's power and faithful love, wonderfully known in the day of trouble. But this conclusion is introduced by a recalling of the weird scene already lamented – the terror of the voices in the night. These sinister sounds are clearly a great distress to the people of the city, and with fervour they cling to the hope of refuge in God's faithful love.

Bearing in his person the life of his city and people, the singer, in all probability a royal figure, prays for protection from fierce enemies determined to make war. Their evil intent is especially felt when, as night falls, they come close and circle about the defences, pouring out incantations against the city and its defenders. The singer mentions no other defence than that of God. He calls upon him as Lord of the heavenly hosts and as the God bound to this people in mutual promise and commitment. He calls on him as king and judge of the nations, upholding right; and he calls with trust in God's *ḥesed*, the love that faithfully uphold God's Anointed and the destiny of his people. His prayer for deliverance and the downfall of the arrogant foe is supported by his promise to raise every morning the melody of thankful praise and witness. The church has found here a prayer to enter into corporately and individually. Not least against words of falsehood and malice, she has this defence – a prayer that trusts only in the faithful love of the Lord, and sincerely expresses the intention to dedicate every day to testimony of his salvation.

Grant, Lord, that the people of your city may never forget that you, in your faithfulness, are the only sure defence against every enemy; and may the prayers of your Son Jesus and of all your saints protect us from the hidden foes, that our hearts may ever sing with the melody of your praise.

PSALM 60: Trouble Like an Earthquake

For favour.   Over the lily of testimony.   Atonement.   Of David.   For
reminding. When he strove with Aram-naharaim and Aram-Zobah, and Joab
returned and smote twelve thousand of Edom in the Valley of Salt.

1   O God, you have spurned us and thrown us down;
     you were angry – O restore us anew.
2   You made the earth shudder and rent it apart;
     heal its wounds, for it is shaking.
3   You have filled your people with a bitter drink;
     you have given us a wine that makes us stagger.
4   You have made those who fear you flee,
     to escape from the reach of the bow.   *[Pause]*
5   That your beloved may be delivered,
     save by your right hand and answer us.

6   God has spoken in his holiness:
         In triumph I will portion out Shechem,
     and share out the valley of Sukkoth;
7   Mine shall be Gilead, and mine Manasseh;
     Ephraim shall be my helmet, and Judah my sceptre.
8   But Moab shall be my wash-bowl,
         over Edom I will throw my sandal;
     acclaim me, O Philistia.

9   Who will bring me to the fortress city;
     who could lead me up to Edom?
10   Have you not spurned us, O God,
     and will you not go out with our hosts?
11   O grant us help against the enemy,
     for earthly help is in vain.
12   Through God we can do mighty things;
     it is he that will tread down our foes.

As in the case of Psalm 44, military defeat here occasions lamenting supplication, expressed partly as the voice of the people and partly as that of king or
other leader (v. 9); but this psalm differs in containing also an answering
oracle, greeted with renewed supplication, for which we may compare 12.
Though the occasion given in the title may, as usual in such cases, be a later
deduction (Int. 2b, cf. 2 Sam. 8; 10.13f.), a date in David's reign is possible;
but confrontations with Edom often occurred later, and most scholars look for
a period when much of the Davidic territory had been lost. There was
particular hostility after the end of the southern kingdom in 587, but the

psalm, like 44, fits better in the royal period when there was still a national
army. The 'lily of the testimony' in the title (so also for 80) may refer to the
use of flowers for obtaining omens (cf. above on 45). 'For reminding' may
refer to the aim of the intercession – to arouse the action of God (the root
lmd, like *zkr* in the comparable phrase above 38, originally meant 'prod').
After lament and petition (vv. 1–5), the oracle is uttered (vv. 6–8), giving
assurance of God's sovereignty over the land. Lament and supplication are
then briefly renewed (vv. 9–11) and pass finally into a declaration of confidence (v. 12). This sequence of worship may as usual have been held in
Jerusalem, but it is also possible that in urgent circumstances of war such
intercession took place at a mobile altar on campaign.

1–5 Prayer for restoration and salvation is accompanied with a vivid picture
of the people's plight. It is all put as the result of God's anger. To judge from
later verses, the language of earthquake is not meant literally, but expresses the
sense that their world has collapsed; not actual buildings have been 'demolished' (v. 1a), nor has the earth been 'made to quake' and 'split' (v. 2a), and
left with 'fissures' and 'after-shocks' (v. 2b). But severe defeat has demolished
morale and shaken the ground of their existence. The Lord has given them a
cup of judgement to drink (cf. 11.6; 75.8; Isa. 51.17f.), and they stagger
almost senseless from its force. As in 44, there is no expression of guilt, but the
people are depicted as faithful worshippers, fearing God and beloved by him.
In v. 4a the traditional vowels yield: 'You have given a banner to those who
fear you' – yet it only led flight! Our translation is perhaps more likely
(revocalizing *nes*, 'banner', to *nus*, 'to flee', 'flight').

6–8 To the prayer 'answer us' comes a response, a word of God. The
psalmist may have the prophetic gift both to intercede and to mediate answers
from God; such a dual role is often apparent in the prophetic books (e.g. Hab.
1.2–2.5). Or it may be that the oracle comes through another voice (cf. 2
Chron. 20.14f.). The picturesque oracle, which is used also in 108, may have
been a traditional one, formulated perhaps in the early days of David's kingdom. It is cited now to affirm that God remains sovereign over the holy land
and still gives this people supremacy. In triumphant song, God depicts himself
as a conqueror sharing out territory both east and west of the Jordan (Sukkot
on the east, Shechem on the west, linked by important valley routes, key-
points in Jacob's journey, Gen. 33.17f.). For himself he takes Gilead on the
east, and the tribal areas chiefly on the west, Manasseh, Ephraim and the
southerly Judah. That other tribes are not mentioned inclines some scholars to
date the oracle to the later years of the kingdom (around Josiah), but the
intention may be to mention representative and core areas, not least the rich
and central Ephraim and the royal Judah, home of David (cf. Gen. 49.10).
Surrounding lands are then mentioned as also owned by God, no longer
hostile, but subdued. Moab's role, by comparison with that of Ephraim and
Judah, seems a lowly one; the image of God's 'wash-bowl' may have been
suggested by the striking views as one looks east from the Judean hills, the line

of Moab's mountains forming a misty rim above the vivid blue waters of the Dead Sea. The sandal cast over Edom betokens God's ownership and lordship (cf. Ruth 4.7f.). The coastal territory of Philistia is to hail God as victor and Lord (in 108.9 a slightly different text, which may be more accurate, gives 'Across Philistia I will shout in triumph'). The note of subjection in these images is understandable in a context of warring neighbours, but with the main idea of a united kingdom under God there is hidden a seed of peace and amity.

9–12 It seems from v. 9 that the defeat has been suffered in war with Edom, and part of the oracle will have spoken directly to this calamity. But the triumphant mood of the old poem must have seemed a long way from the present dismay. The response of king and people therefore begins tactfully in question form: will God really lead me successfully through and up the for-midable cliffs of Edom, whose capital city is virtually inaccessible? A blunter question follows: Have you not spurned us and deserted our armies? The conclusion asks again for God's salvation, owning that human help alone is useless. And the final words, giving force to the supplication, express high confidence in the enabling power of God. The image of 'trampling' (v. 12b, cf. 44.5) reflects wonder at the might of the wild bull, a common near-eastern image of divine strength.

Disaster has struck the worshippers of the Lord like an earthquake. Their world, it seems, has fallen about them. The ground beneath them has parted, and still sways ominously. They lament that God has given them a cup of destiny that has sent them staggering. Their petitions are short gasps: 'Restore us, save us.' An answer comes, but one that takes them back to the beginning of the life in the holy land. They hear again the joyful song of the Lord, as he was set to establish his kingdom there, with happiness and strength for his people. Resounding again, the song means that God's purpose still stands, defeat will be overcome, the enemy subdued. This message, however, is received with some reserve. It has not actually referred to the present affliction, and the old vision of glory only points up the present misery and dismay, though the psalmist's last words are of trust and hope.

All through history there have been such situations. In tragic circumstances, believers can be reminded of God's classic promises and purposes, but may wonder all the more how they are to ascend from their present depths to the strong city and the lofty goal. The psalm would have them listen afresh to the old oracles, the promises, the gospel of the kingdom; and though, as prayer is renewed, doubts still linger, yet the sense of the only true help will grow. The wounded earth will come to be known as his possession, and his beloved will be led over every rock and chasm to his city of salvation.

O Lord Jesus, the conqueror of evil, help us in all our troubles to hear afresh your gospel words; that our faith may be rekindled, and by your Spirit we may do mighty deeds of love.

PSALM 61: A Cry from the End of the Earth

For favour. On stringed instruments. Of David.

1   Hear my crying, O God,
      and listen to my prayer.
2   From the end of the earth I call to you with fainting heart;
      lead me up the rock that is too high for me.
3   For you shall be a shelter for me,
      a strong tower against the foe.
4   May I dwell in your tent for ever,
      and shelter in the covering of your wings.   *[Pause]*
5   For you, O God, will hear my vows;
      you will grant the request of those who fear your name.
6   You will add days to the days of the king,
      that his years may be throughout all generations.
7   May he dwell before God for ever;
      bid faithful love and truth to guard him.
8   So shall I ever make music to your name,
      day by day fulfilling my vows.

A special feature of this supplication is that in vv. 6–7 the prayer is explicitly for the king and in the third person (similarly in 28 and 63). Some have thought these verses must be a later addition, clumsily positioned; and others a kind of dutiful courtesy to the chief authority of the sanctuary. But there are several indications in the other verses that the supplicant is a king, and one can well suppose that at v. 6 prayer for him is taken up by a choir, until he resumes in v. 8. A still simpler explanation is that he changes to the third person at v. 6 in accordance with a common oriental style (so King Zedekiah in Jer. 38.5, and King Yeḥawmilk in a Phoenician inscription quoted by Dahood); the effect here would be to plead the promises given to him as king (cf. 89.50–1) – the enduring life, closeness to God, protection by the angelic graces. The nature of the danger is not made clear; the 'enemy' may be of military character – in the comparable 63, a battle is evidently in prospect. For the heading 'on stringed instruments' we can compare 4 and Hab. 3.19.

1–5   Prayer rises from a dire situation. The 'end of the earth', like the miry pit of 40.2 and 69.2, or the overwhelming waves of 18.4 and 42.7, will be at the mouth of the underworld; it is the experience of being almost gone from light and life. The 'heart' has almost lost all strength, and the supplicant can only cry to the Lord to lead him from the dark waters up to the 'rock' of safety, which he cannot reach alone. 'Rock' suggests the holy mountain, or even God himself (18.2; 19.14); he indeed will be a shelter and high tower for his king against 'the enemy', the forces of evil (cf. 8.2). He will let him reside for ever in the holy 'tent' and will cover him with his wings (cf. 17.8; 23.6; 27.5; 63.7; 91.1–4); with such phrases was expressed the closeness and love of the Lord towards his Anointed (my *Kingship*, pp. 142–6). And the prayer is supported by reference to the far-reaching vows of service when life is restored (cf. v. 8) and to the prayer of all the loyal people (cf. 20.1–5).

6–8   The theme of the desired royal blessings continues – to dwell close to God, to have the guardian angels of *hesed* and *emet*, faithful love and truth (cf. 23.6; 43.3), and most characteristic of all, life 'for ever', 'throughout all generations' (see above on 16.10–11). The translation is best kept as petition, especially in view of v. 7b (where, however, some manuscripts and versions omit 'bid', *BHS*). The third person reference to the king may be a clue that a choir sings vv. 6–7, expressing the people's 'request' just mentioned; or it may be a matter of style, and bringing out the hopes associated with the royal calling. The line of thought continues consistently through the psalm, with the vows mentioned in v. 5 appearing again at the end – vows of obviously royal proportions, to be offered every day. With such offerings will sound the psalmic songs of testimony and thanksgiving, and they will especially praise the holy name in which the power and presence, the grace and salvation of the Lord is made known to his king (see above on 20.1; *Kingship* pp. 155–6).

In this prayer from 'the end of the earth', the extremity of human endurance, there come to expression the hopes based on God's promises to his king – the salvation found in the mighty rock, high above the evil tides; the safety in the embrace of the divine mother-love; the constant care of the angels that represent the divine faithfulness; eternal life in the home of God. In the ancient world the expression of such hopes for the royal soul was not meant to exclude the general people. They found light and breath in their king (2 Sam. 21.17; Lam. 4.20); the blessings focused on him were yet of benefit to all. So their 'request' for him, made in the fear and faith of God, was an act of solidarity; they would make with him the ascent on the great rock of God. Likewise in the church's use of this psalm, the worshippers cry with Christ from the edge of endurance, from the mouth of the abyss; with him they ascend the rock which they cannot climb alone; with him they dwell with the Father. Day by day they offer their lives, and make music to praise the name by which they have been given true life.

Father, hear us when we pray from the limits of our endurance; and as you brought up your Son Jesus, so lead us upon your rock, to abide with you for ever in praise and thanksgiving.

PSALM 62: Secrets of Stillness

For favour.   At confession.   Psalm.   Of David.

1   For God alone my soul waits in stillness;
    from him comes my salvation.
2   He alone is my rock and my salvation,
    my stronghold, so that I shall not be utterly shaken.
3   How long will you assault a man, all of you intent to destroy,
    as you would a leaning wall or damaged defence?
4   They consult only how to thrust me from my height,
        and have delighted in falsehood;
    they blessed with their mouth,
        but in their heart they cursed.   *[Pause]*

5   To God alone be still, my soul;
    from him comes all my hope.
6   He alone is my rock and my salvation,
    my stronghold, so that I shall not be shaken.
7   In God is my salvation and my glory;
    my mighty rock and my refuge is God.
8   Trust in him always, O people;
    pour out your heart before him,
        for God is our refuge.   *[Pause]*
9   The children of earth are but a breath, the peoples a delusion;
    on the scales they all are lighter than air.
10 Do not trust in oppression or be deluded by plunder;
    if power abounds, give it no regard.
11 Once has God declared it,
    twice have I heard the same,
    that power belongs to God,
12 and yours, Lord, is faithful love.
    For you reward each and all
    according to their deeds.

The psalmist faces opponents that would thrust him from his eminence; they are like an assaulting army that has damaged a city wall and now moves in to bring it down. The indications, then, are that a king is under attack, threatened in his eminent position above his people and as their wall of defence. His many descriptions of God as his fortress and refuge will have the military associations clearer in royal 18.1–2, and the position between Psalms 61 and 63 (both mentioning the king explicitly) is seen to be appropriate. A striking feature is that there is no direct address to God until the final verse; the address otherwise is to the self, the enemy, and the people. The general tone is of trust, and this amounts to an indirect appeal to God – may he vindicate this trust declared so openly and repeatedly. The exhortation to one's soul may be compared with 42.3f., while the combination of rebuke to adversaries and counsel to the supporting people is found also in 4, which also shares the expressions 'lies', 'children of (lit.) man', 'how long', 'my glory', and 'be still'. For 'confession' in the title, see above on 39, which has other links with our psalm, especially in the frequency of the word *ak*, 'only, but'.

1–4   The opening is immediately a statement of trust in 'God alone', the only source of salvation. Towards him the soul (lit.) 'is stillness', acknowledging that it is God's action that will be decisive, and opening the way for it. The combination of 'my rock', 'my salvation' and 'my stronghold' is also found in the royal 18.2. As the appeal to God is indirect in this statement of trust, so the lament depicting the danger is conveyed indirectly through an address to the enemies, who are then described. It seems that there have been outward courtesies (v. 4b), but concealing plots to oust him from his position of eminence. The hostility of the enemies in fact is felt as a continuous assault to destroy him; some insecurity or weakness in his position spurs them on to finish his downfall. (In v. 4a our Hebrew has 'to thrust from his height / honour'; the sequence is clearer in LXX, 'to set at nought my honour'.)

5–10   As though to counter the disturbing portrayal of the enemies, the psalmist resumes his opening testimony of trust, but with a significant heightening. It is now an exhortation to his soul, in defiance of the alarming situation, to be still before God; and additional statements of trust in God's protection are made in v. 7, where 'my glory' can be taken as a reference to the majesty bestowed by the Lord on his Anointed (21.5; 45.3–4) and now under threat (cf. 4.2). Then in v. 8 the address turns to the people (LXX: 'all you congregation of the people'). They are the psalmist's loyal people, who with him should trust in the protection God has promised. It seems they are in danger of being overawed, even seduced, by the enemy's power with all its violence and ill-gotten wealth; such human might, counsels the psalmist, is a delusion, nothing to weigh against the power of God. They should 'pour out' their heart before God, unburdening themselves of anxieties and counsels of despair, confessing all their weakness (102 title; 142.2; 1 Sam. 1.15; 7.6), allowing him to make them a pure and steadfast heart (Ps. 51.10).

11–12   In conclusion, the fundamental theme – God the only hope – is repeated as counsel for the people and for his own soul, and as a pleading testimony before God. Now, however, it is presented in another aspect – as revelation, spoken frequently by the mouth of God himself, and so of the utmost solemnity and reliability. 'Once . . . twice': such mounting numbers in the ancient poetry indicate numerous occurrences; this was the burden of many oracles given to king and people, that their salvation was in his might, faithful love, and justice.

What a contrast between the battering assault of the enemy and the stillness of the soul toward God! It is precisely because of the acute danger, and indeed the beginnings of disaster, that the theme of trust is sung out with such emphasis and repetition in this psalm. The singer has to contend not only with a conspiracy of foes determined to bring him crashing down from his eminence, but also with his own people's temptation to change sides, in view of the enemy's power and growing success. His testimony to salvation in God alone is made to strengthen his own soul, to fortify and guide his people, and implicitly to appeal to God to vindicate the declarations of trust.

There are 'deeds' enough from all the human participants in this drama (v. 12) – activity of self-defence on the one hand, conspiracy, treachery, lies and plunder on the other; and in the midst of it all the psalmist finds a stillness towards God. Before the almighty Lord, his soul is a still centre. And the meaning of this silence of the spirit is trust – profound and decisive acknowledgement that power belongs to God, and in him alone is salvation; he is faithful, and the source of all true hope. Perhaps it is on the way to this stillness that the wavering people are counselled to 'pour out' their heart before God. As they lay all their fears and doubts at his feet, they too will be granted that stillness which is the best prayer for the mighty deeds of the Saviour.

O God, in whom alone is our hope and salvation, help us amid all the blows of life to confess to you our failures and fears; and help us to pour out our hearts before you, until we find that stillness where we are sure that you alone will make all things well.

PSALM 63: A Love Better than Life

Psalm.   Of David.   When he was in the wilderness of Judah.

1   O God, you are my God, eagerly I seek you;
      my soul is thirsting for you.
      My flesh longs for you,
      as a barren and weary land that has no water.
2   Therefore I seek vision of you in the sanctuary,
      to see your power and your glory.
3   Your faithful love is better than life itself,
      and my lips shall sing your praise.
4   So shall I bless you all my life,
      and lift up my hands to your name.
5   My soul will be satisfied as with choicest fare,
      and my mouth will praise you with joyful lips,
6   when I remember you upon my couch,

and meditate on you in the watches of the night.
7   For you shall come as my strong help,
    and in the shadow of your wings I will rejoice.
8   My soul will cleave to you;
    your right hand will hold me fast.
9   But those who seek my soul to destroy it
    shall enter the depths of the earth.
10 They shall be delivered to the sword,
    and become a portion for the foxes.
11 But the king shall rejoice in God,
        and all who swear by him shall glory;
    for the mouth of those who speak falsehood shall be stopped.

As with Psalm 61, so here the reference to the king in the third person is best taken as to the psalmist himself, either from his own voice using a royal style, or as a contribution from a choir expressing the people's solidarity with their leader. The two contrasting elements in the psalm – tender spirituality and a lurid glimpse of warfare – then fit together; a king expects war, and prepares by seeking communion with his God, probably by sleeping in the holy place; if he is so blessed and the aggressors defeated, it is they who will be left on the battlefield (v. 10). The expressions of loving piety, numerous and beautiful, are such as were used especially of the close bond between the Lord and his Anointed (*Kingship* pp. 169–72). In the title a connection has been made with David's time in the harsh wilderness (1 Sam. 22f.), probably by deduction from v. 1 (cf. Int. 2b).

1–4 From a situation of utmost need, the psalmist calls to his God; the emphatic 'my God' expresses the covenantal bond with all its assurances. He seeks him urgently, comparing his need to the desperate situation of land without life-giving water; so he needs the living God (cf. above on 42.1–3). He has therefore come to the sanctuary to be replenished by vision of the divine glory, if God so wills. The verb in v. 2a, *ḥazah*, is often associated with visions and oracles, and here will refer to his approach to God in quest of such an encounter. If in some way, perhaps in a dream, God will reveal his glory and speak a word of comfort and guidance, the psalmist will be able to face what the day will bring. He will be replenished in all the vitality of 'life', the height and fullness of all God's gifts. Yet, better even than life is God's *ḥesed*, his everlasting and unfailing love; this remarkable tribute in v. 3 strives to express the inexpressible wonder of one who experiences that love. And perhaps it gives another glimpse of the royal destiny beyond this earth (cf. above on 16.10–11). But more immediately, if the Lord draws near in salvation, then the danger will be overcome, and the psalmist will devote his life on earth to praise and warm thanksgiving.

5–8 The longed-for encounter in the watches of the night now fills the supplicant's thoughts. These are expressed with a trustful confidence that, as it were, presses the Lord not to disappoint. 'Remembering' and 'meditating' here may refer to murmured praise and prayer; the names and attributes of God and other words of holy tradition would be repeated, driving out the anxieties of the world, allowing the divine being to become all in all and very near to the humble and longing heart. So the soul will be replenished with goodness; God will come as saviour; there will be shelter under his wings (cf. 17.8; 61.4; my *Kingship*, p. 143); he will embrace his clinging child with his right hand (*Kingship*, p. 144).

9–11　The conclusion looks confidently to the impending battle. Replenished by his Lord, the king will have success. He foresees the defeat of those who meant to destroy him, their bodies a portion for wild animals. With the thankful king will stand those who invoke or swear by God's name and life – all his loyal people. The enemy, in contrast, are characterized as uttering falsehood (a common feature in the portrayal of the king's enemies, 59.6f.; 62.4; 64.2f.).

In peril of destruction by relentless enemies, the psalmist seeks communion with his God. The danger and all its weight of cares has made God seem far off, and so body and soul thirst for him and the joyful life that he gives; they thirst like a drought-stricken land, barren and exhausted. One aim, therefore, fills the singer's heart: to come close to God, close enough to see his glory, to be hidden under his wings, to feel his embrace. Then the thirst would be broken, and the soul replenished with choice fare. Eagerly the psalmist seeks for this. He comes to the holy place. In the night-watches he recites the holy words of 'remembrance' that set heart and mind on the Lord alone. And confidence grows that his Lord will indeed come, fill him with joy, and ensure the defeat of the attackers. It is a confidence grounded in the faithful love of God, that love perceived as so wonderful that it is better than life itself. The expressions used here for communion with God are especially warm and intimate, and in the first place depict the ideal of God and his 'Son', his Beloved, his Anointed. The faithful people are near, however, and will glory with their king in God's grace and salvation.

The psalm strikingly shows how contemplation and communion relate to life in all its dangers, perplexities and struggles. To 'see' God, to hear his voice, to know his embrace, this is to receive fresh life, and more than life – to overcome fear of the enemy, to have strength for the crisis, and assurance that God will deliver. Christians have seen the church as the holy place where Christ draws his followers into the communion he has with the Father; he gathers them under the holy wings, the arms of his cross. Being found in him, they know the faithful love that surpasses life.

Teach us, good Lord, the way of meditation and holy remembrance; that in all the barren places of life we may be able to find the fountain of your presence, and so be replenished for your service.

PSALM 64: Against Evil Words

For favour.   Psalm.   Of David.

1   Hear my voice, O God, in my prayer;
    preserve my life from dread of the enemy.
2   Hide me from the plots of the cruel,
    from the gathering of evildoers,
3   who have sharpened their tongue like a sword,
    and aimed their bitter words as arrows,
4   that they may shoot at the innocent from their hiding-place;
    suddenly they shoot and are not seen.
5   They encourage themselves in mischief;
    they talk of laying snares, saying, Who shall see us?
6   They search out wickedness and lay a cunning trap,
    for deep are the inward thoughts of the heart.
7   But God will shoot at them with an arrow,
    and suddenly they shall be wounded.
8   They will bring him down on them because of their tongue,
    so that all who see them will shake their heads.
9   All people will fear, and tell of the work of God,
    and they will ponder what he has done.
10 The faithful one will rejoice in the Lord and shelter in him,
    and all that are true of heart shall glory.

This is a prayer for protection from enemies who plot together and strike through words like swords or poisoned arrows. After the plea for a hearing and lamenting description of the danger (vv. 1–6), the judgement of God is envisaged, and the time of thanksgiving for deliverance (vv. 7–10). This latter section can be related to the prayer as a supporting statement of trust and confidence: one who so testifies will surely not be disappointed. The nature of the supplicant and the enemies is not clearly revealed. The counsel of enemies has echoes of the hostile nations in 2.1–2 (in common are the roots *sod*, 'counsel', and *ragash*, 'tumult, gathering'); their deadly words and traps are reminiscent of hostile forces in the preceding psalms (52.2–4; 56.5–6; 57.4; 59.6–7). The effect of the salvation is envisaged very widely (vv. 9–10). It seems fair, then, to understand the psalm as continuing the series where the national leader laments of national foes, who target him especially. The hostility appears to be in the early stage of conspiracy and launching attacks of false propaganda and cursing.

1–6 The opening words convey the sense of urgent and sustained appeal. The enemy is able to cause terror and threaten life. The psalmist's 'prayer' (some translate 'complaining') is a stream of murmured or chanted sound.

The 'cruel', intent on harm, confer together; they are a horde of evildoers, mischief-makers, creating hurt by the evil of their tongue, wounding with poisonous words, operating stealthily and with cunning. They are ambushers and hunters of the soul, and have no regard for the Judge on high (v. 5b), as they devise schemes in the hidden depths of their heart.

7–10 At first sight the Hebrew here seems like a narration of what God has done, so some make slight adjustments to the vowels to make more definitely a prayer: 'May God ...' (so Gunkel). The context is best suited, however, if the verbs as they stand are taken as statements of confidence in future judgement (so RV etc.). Verse 8a is obscure and often emended to 'And he shall make them fall because of their tongue' (*BHS*). The judgement will be heeded far and wide; 'all mankind' (*adam*) will tremble with awe, testify to God's work and contemplate its meaning. The just one (*saddiq*, v. 10a), perhaps the psalmist as faithful king (cf. above on 58.10), will rejoice in the salvation and in the safety of the Lord's shelter (cf. above on 63.7), and all his people (v. 10b) will share in the thankful praise.

One who has great responsibility is here beseeching his Lord for his protecting power. While his own life is especially hunted, there is danger too for all that are true of heart towards God. The 'voice of the constant praying', therefore, is a supplication for all the innocent that are threatened by the sudden arrow and the hidden pit of evil words. And for all these, the prayer expresses faith that God's justice will defend them, turning the destruction back to the would-be destroyers. But if it is thus a prayer for the work of God against the stealthy deceivers and creators of harm, it is a prayer also that becomes a channel for the divine work, becomes as it were a creator of good.

Lord Jesus Christ, who for our sakes endured the plotting and poisoned arrows of the evildoers, defend us with your ever-flowing prayer from dread of the enemy; may we find shelter in you, and ever rejoice in your faithful love that redeems all creation.

PSALM 65: For the Dear Earth

Psalm.   Of David.   Song.

1   Praise is hushed for you, O God, in Zion,
       and for you the vow is fulfilled, you that answer prayer.
2   To you come all the children of earth, confessing wrongs;
3   though our sins prevailed against us,
       you have purged them away.

4 Happy the one you choose and bring near
      to dwell in your courts;
    we shall be satisfied with the goodness of your house,
      your holy temple.
5 With dread deeds in justice you will answer us,
      O God of our salvation,
    O hope of all the ends of the earth
      and the sea where the far ones dwell,
6 you that set fast the mountains by your might,
    having girded on your strength,
7 who stilled the raging of the seas,
    the roar of their waves, and the tumult of the peoples.
8 Those who dwell at the farthest bounds
      trembled at your wonders;
    the gates of morning and evening sang your praise.
9 O tend the earth and water her, and greatly enrich her;
    with the heavenly stream full of water
      you will prepare her corn,
      yes, so you will prepare her.
10 Soak well her furrows and settle her ridges;
    soften her with showers, and bless her springing.
11 O crown a year of your bounty,
    and let your tracks flow down with goodness.
12 May the pastures of the wilderness flow with your goodness,
    and the hills be girded with joy.
13 May the fields be clothed with flocks,
    and the valleys stand so thick with corn,
      that they shall laugh and sing.

In festal assembly at Zion, the community prays for God to send the vital rains, and so prepare a year of good growth and harvests. After introductory praise and acknowledgement of God's mighty deeds of creation (vv. 1–8), thought turns to the present need for creation's renewal – God's saturation of the earth, his inauguration of a year of his bounty, his preparation for abundant flocks and corn. One may wonder if the psalm was sung in connection with a ceremony of procession with the ark and sprinkling of the earth (cf. vv. 10–11). In any case, the festival will be that of the autumn, when the new agricultural cycle was about to begin, but where ceremonies had to include fulfilment of vows of thank-offerings and confession and atonement of sin (vv. 1–3). It is not known just what the heading 'Song' signified; perhaps there was a connection with the offerings or reference to a style of music (Mowinckel, *Psalms* II, pp. 207f.).

1–4 The opening words are literally 'For you praise is stillness / silence, O God, in Zion'. A slight change of vowel (*BHS*) would give a participle: 'For you praise grows still'. The tumultuous acclamation of God dies away; a quiet awe of his nearness prevails at the time of sacrifice (v. 1b, cf. Zeph. 1.7; Hab. 2.20). The vow of sacrifice made in time of need is fulfilled at the festival, with testimony to the faithful God who answered the prayer (the Hebrew singular 'vow', usually translated as plural, may refer to a communal vow and offering). For 'all flesh', all the human race especially, only God can truly grant expiation of sins that are 'too strong for us' alone. The psalm is probably not prophesying here some future transformation when 'all flesh shall come', but rather expressing the present ideal of God manifest in Zion as Creator and ruler of all. The element of atonement (*kpr* v. 3b), prominent on the Day of Atonement (*kippur*) in the later calendar, will always have been an important aspect of the festal season, a fundamental part of the theme of renewal for individuals, people, and world. But within that universal work of the Creator, those actually gathered in the temple courts, so near to the holy manifestation, were conscious of a special grace. They attribute their peculiar happiness to the gracious will of God, who has chosen each of them and brought them into the very aura of his sanctuary-presence, to drink deeply of his holy fountain of life (cf. 36.6–9).

5–8 Prayer is now raised that God will answer the worshippers' cry for rains and all that earth needs in her new cycle of life. By 'dread deeds in justice' is meant a renewal of the mighty work by which he first founded life and healthful order (*sedeq*, 'right'). The recital of these mighty deeds in v. 6f. is again, implicitly, a prayer for their renewal, making firm earth's mountain-pillars, subduing the waters to serve life (the stilling of rebellious peoples is part of the Creator's work in his ongoing rule). The universality of his work is emphasized by reference to the involvement of the farthest bounds of the world – the trust or hope in God even where the 'far ones' dwell (mysterious spirits at the borders of the underworld, cf. above on 56 title); such dwellers at the world's edge, indeed the very gates of light on the horizon in farthest east and west, responded to the work of creation with awe and praise.

9–13 This whole passage fits together as the main point of the psalm, when we recognize that the perfect tenses at the beginning of vv. 9, 11 and 13 are 'precatives', expressing prayer (so Dahood after Buttenwieser in the light of the other tenses and the context, and note already Jerome *visita terram et inriga eam* 'Visit the earth and irrigate her'). The Creator is implored to soak the land, at present parched from the long summer drought. The rains may fail in Palestine, and starvation and impoverishment were well-known experiences. The prayers and ceremonies of the autumn festival were so much the more earnest. The poet here beautifully expresses the marvel of good rains, which lead the barren earth through the orderly stages of cultivation and growth, until the hillsides and valleys are clad with crops and healthy flocks, themselves appearing to laugh and sing for joy in God. In v. 11 the crowning of a 'year of your goodness' (so the Hebrew) will refer to the inauguration (not completion) of a year of abundance. The 'tracks' are wagon or chariot routes, and the imagined journey of God over the fields may have been symbolized by procession of the ark, with asperging to represent the blessing he gave.

This great psalm discloses moments of the annual climax of worship. Following the loud acclamations of God with voices and instruments, there is a dramatic hush as the sense of his close approach fills the people with awe. There is offering in fulfilment of the vow made in time of need, a gift in acknowledgement that he had heard the prayer and was strong to save. And there is penitent confession of wrongdoing, so that God may take away the sins which make a burden too great for human bearing. How profound, then, the happiness that God in grace has brought this people to his house at this time! They are replenished in the springs of life, quickened by the light of his holy presence. From a people so 'brought near', cleansed and renewed, a great prayer then arises: may this God, this mighty Creator who formed and ordered the vast cosmos, may he renew his mighty deeds and grant a year blessed with his gifts of life. The prayer is full of sympathy for the good earth and her needs, which God will lovingly attend to; and there is warm feeling too for the hills and valleys that will wear the garments of praise, the clothing of green and gold, and contented flocks and herds.

The cycle of growth and the life it supported were precarious. The ancient worshippers felt that all was in the hands of the mighty Creator, and that happiness was to be right with him and near to him; so the fields and flocks would be bound in the circle of blessing, and the prayer of life would be heard. But can the song from the gates of morning and evening still be heard, the trust of farthest spaces still be known? Yes, surely it will be so, when the secret of worship is grasped.

O God, whose work of creation embraces all that exists, grant us to know what it is to be brought near to dwell in your courts; cleanse and replenish our souls, that our prayer for the earth may be a song in tune with the trust of the distant seas and the music of the gates of morning and evening.

PSALM 66: Through Fire and Water to the Place of Thanksgiving

For favour. Song. Psalm.

1   Sing aloud to God, all the earth;
2   sing praise to the glory of his name;
      ascribe glory in his praise.
3   Say to God, How awesome are your deeds;
      through the greatness of your power,

4   your enemies are humbled before you.
    All the earth shall worship you,
    make music for you and sing of your name.   *[Pause]*
5   Come and see the deeds of God,
    who is wonderful in his work over all the children of earth.
6   He turned the sea into dry land;
        they crossed through the river on foot;
    come, let us rejoice in him.
7   He rules with his power for ever,
        and his eyes watch over the peoples,
    that the rebellious should not exalt themselves.   *[Pause]*
8   Bless our God, you peoples,
    and make the voice of his praise to be heard,
9   who has set our soul again among the living,
    and kept our feet from stumbling.
10 For you, O God, have proved us;
    you have tried us even as silver is tried.
11 You brought us into the net,
    and bound us about with trouble.
12 You let men ride over our heads,
        we went through fire and water;
    but you brought us out to a pleasant place.
13 I will come into your house with whole offerings;
    I will fulfil to you my vows,
14 with which my lips opened wide,
    and which my mouth spoke when I was in trouble.
15 I will offer up to you whole offerings of fatlings
        with the smoke of rams;
    cattle and goats I will prepare for you.   *[Pause]*
16 Come and hear, all you that fear God,
    and I will tell you what he has done for my soul.
17 I cried out to him with my mouth,
    yet praise was ready under my tongue.
18 If I had cherished evil in my heart,
    the Lord would not have heard me.
19 But God did hear me,
    and heeded the voice of my prayer.
20 Blessed be God, who has not turned aside my prayer,
    nor his faithful love from me.

In this psalm of thanksgiving, some recent deliverance of people and leader is seen as a fresh instance of the power and grace of God shown in the Exodus. The deliverance of one people, however, is seen as revelation and blessing for the whole earth. After calling to all the world for praise of God (vv. 1–4), the psalm gives vivid remembrance of the Exodus as illustrating God's rule over the peoples; then testimony to his salvation after severe trials, though expressed in a general way, seems to relate to recent experience (vv. 5–12). Finally the recent deliverance is clearly celebrated, as one representative figure, most likely the king, brings thank-offerings on a national scale, and testifies to God's answering of prayer and to his faithful love (vv. 13–20). The psalm thus holds together several 'poles': the nation and the world community; the classic past and present experience; the people and the single figure who carries his people in his soul.

1–4   The time of festal worship was experienced as a time of God's self-revelation; he was powerfully present, and the glory of his name shone out over all the earth (cf. 8.1). It was for all in heaven and earth to confess that his alone was the royal glory (cf. 29.9; Isa. 42.12). Our psalm calls first for joyful acclamation, the concerted shouts that greet the victor (v. 1a), then the ascription of glory (v. 2b), then direct words of praise (vv. 3–4). Whatever dread deeds the Lord may have done against nations – so the underlying thought – it was all for the establishment of what is just and good; and so the joy is worldwide, as is the goodness of God's reign.

5–7   A fundamental example of God's salvation is now brought to mind – how at the Exodus he led his people safely through the sea and the river (the Reed Sea and the Jordan, unless 'river' also refers to the Reed Sea – so Dahood). The solemn 'remembering' of that ancient salvation made it seem so present that the singer can call 'Come and see . . .' , and 'we' are the ones who rejoice in that great experience (v. 6b, for *sham* as 'behold / come' see Dahood). The deliverance of the one people is seen as part of the universal reign, with its vigilance against any that set themselves up in rebellion.

8–12   The peoples are summoned again to thank and praise God for his saving work. The worshippers praise him as having delivered them from death; after proving them with much affliction, he restored their life (v. 9a). The suffering is graphically described in a series of images – silver in the furnace, the hunter's net drawn sharply round the body, trampling cavalry, an ordeal of fire and water (cf. Isa. 43.2). And after it all, God brought them out to a pleasant place, like a well-watered valley (*rewaya*; the ancient versions may have read *rewaha*, 'wide place'). The reference is not clearly to the ordeals associated with the Exodus and may refer to some recent experience, the same that will be expressed as personal to the people's leader in vv. 13–20. At all events, it was part of the world reign of God, for which all peoples are to bless the Lord.

13–20   The thanksgiving now takes on the characteristic form of an individual's testimony, bringing the offering vowed in the time of trouble, relating to the festal assembly ('all who fear God') how God heard the prayer in his committed love (*hesed*), and drawing out a lesson (v. 18). There is, however, one distinctive feature – the character of the sacrifices (vv. 14–15). These appear to be on a great scale, and in the first place are mentioned sacrifices wholly burnt (wholly devoted, as it were to the heavenly realm) rather than the usual votive offerings shared with the worshippers in a meal of communion. Reviewing the terms used here, Kirkpatrick remarks, 'Hence it may be inferred that the psalm refers to sacrifices offered by the nation or its leader, not by an ordinary private individual.' We have the impression of a great national celebration, similar in external details to those Isaiah saw in a negative light (Isa.1.11), and focused in the person of the king, whose prayer and integrity were regarded as vital for people and indeed the world.

The thread of salvation runs through this psalm of thanksgiving without a break – through all the earth, the ancestral people, the present community, to the representative individual. It is a salvation which has been preceded by trials of affliction and humiliation; all the more wonderful, then, is the coming to a place of space and delight, a garden of life for the rescued soul. The world is not too wide for the song of testimony and thanksgiving, sung with costly offerings that signify the new dedication of the worshippers' own selves. The psalm thus leads the sufferers of all generations to link their situation with the classic stories that are given to illumine the way of faith. They will be helped to recognize the pattern of trial and deliverance in their own experience, and to take to themselves the song of praise and re-dedication. In some Greek and Latin manuscripts the psalm carries the additional heading 'Of the Resurrection', an interpretation probably based on v. 9. Christ's passion and resurrection are in this case the fundamental salvation, shedding light on the experiences of both society and the individual. When the cry of distress is made to him, there may indeed, by his strengthening, be praise ready under the tongue for the time of risen life.

Almighty God, whose eyes ever watch over all your world, help us to bring both our troubles and our joys into the light of the passion and resurrection of your Son Jesus; grant us trust in the time of affliction, and in deliverance enable us to give you thanks and to offer up our lives to your service.

PSALM 67: For the Blessing of Earth

For favour. ˇWith stringed instruments.   Psalm.   Song.

1   May God be gracious to us and bless us,
     and make his face to shine on our path,   *[Pause]*
2   that your way may be known on earth,
     your salvation among all nations.
3   Then the peoples will praise you, O God;
     yes, all the peoples will praise you.

4   The nations will rejoice and sing,
         that you govern the peoples justly,
            and guide the nations on earth.
5   The peoples will praise you, O God;
         yes, all the peoples will praise you.
6   May earth give her increase;
         may God, our God, grant us his blessing.
7   May God give us his blessing,
         that all the ends of the earth may fear him.

Much turns on the understanding of v. 6a. At first sight, the Hebrew here seems to mean 'Earth has given her increase', and some therefore take the psalm to be a thanksgiving at harvest. However, this phrase contains the only occurrence of a 'perfect' tense in the entire psalm, which therefore is oriented rather towards the future, in prayer and hope. The tense of v. 6a will therefore express either confidence ('Earth shall give', so AV, BCP) or a prayer ('May earth give', Dahood). Like 65, then, this will be the community's prayer for rains and good growth, the divine blessings that alone sustain life.

1–2 Prayer is raised that God should act in grace and goodwill – that his face should give light or shine towards his creatures; the literal here is to shine 'with us' (*ittanu*), the sense being perhaps that his presence and power should ever assist the worshippers on their path. That he should 'bless' means especially that he should grant healthy life and increase, not least by sending good rains. It is characteristic of this psalm that the worshippers see such blessing, with all the good rule of God, as for all the world. His 'way' (*derek*) may mean here his path as he moves through the earth in his mighty work to provide for life; more succinctly Dahood argues for the sense 'your dominion'. 'Salvation' here involves God's conquest of chaos and his securing of life.

3–5 The thought continues in its universal scope. Rather than a vow of praise from the Israelites, there is declaration that all earth's peoples will give thanks for such salvation, rejoicing in the good reign of God. The theme is emphasized with much repetition and serves to add strength to the supplication for blessing. (Many translate 'Let the nations praise you ... let the nations be glad ...', but such summons to praise would be more suitable if the psalm were a thanksgiving.)

6–7 It becomes clear now that the desired blessing concerns especially the good things for life that earth 'gives', the plants that grow for man and beast. For these indeed there will be thanks raised to the Creator across all the world, with awe at his power and goodness. (Some translate these verses as expressing confidence that the preceding prayer will be answered: 'Earth shall give ... God shall bless ...' Less satisfactory in the context is the rendering of REB, 'Earth has yielded its harvest; may God, our God, bless us'.)

The sight and sound of strong rain made the people of the Psalms think directly of blessing from heaven; the rising green of earth told of the shining face of God, bright with favour. Good crops and flocks and herds spoke of his passing through the earth, the victor over chaos, the Creator who wrought the miracle of life. But the joy of all the earth was to be not so much in the gifts themselves, as in him, the saviour, 'God, our God'. The glad song was a thanksgiving, a testimony to the ruler and guide of all creation. And to him, at every stage of the year's growth, prayer was raised, as to the one who alone could so give and sustain life. The psalm thus summons to deep reflection a generation that sees cultivation as only a matter for human science and economic power.

Creator and saviour of the world, grant us in our generation to know that we live only by the light of your face, and flourish only through the pouring down of your blessing; may we respect the good earth, and value all that you enable her to give, until all peoples fear your majesty and sing to you the song of thanksgiving.

PSALM 68: When They Saw the Procession of God

For favour.　Of David.　Psalm.　Song.

1　As God arises, his enemies are scattered,
　　and those who hate him flee before him.
2　As smoke is driven, so they are driven;
　　as wax melts at the fire, so perish the wicked
　　　　at the presence of God.
3　But the faithful are glad and rejoice before God,
　　making merry with songs and dances.
4　O sing to God, make music to his name,
　　　lift praise to him who rides the clouds;
　　with his name Yah, rejoice before him.
5　Father to the fatherless, defender of widows,
　　such is God from his holy dwelling.
6　God gives the lonely a home, and brings out the prisoners
　　　to songs of welcome;
　　but the rebellious inhabit a desert.
7　O God, when you went out before your people,
　　when you marched through the desert land,　*[Pause]*
8　earth shook, the heavens dropped rain
　　before God, the Lord of Sinai, before God, the God of Israel.
9　You poured down generous rain, O God;
　　you renewed your own land when it was weary.

10 There your people settled;
    in your goodness, O God, you provide for the poor.
11 The Lord gives the word;
    the women who bear the tidings are a mighty host.
12 The kings of the armies flee, they flee,
    and women at home will share the spoil.
13 Though you have tarried among the hearth-stones,
    see now the dove's wings covered with silver,
        and her feathers with green gold.
14 As the Almighty scatters the kings,
    it is like a snowstorm on Black Mountain.
15 O mighty mountain, great hill of Bashan,
    O high-peaked mountain, great hill of Bashan,
16 why look with envy, you high-peaked mountain,
    at the hill that God has desired for his dwelling,
        where the Lord will abide for ever?
17 The chariots of God are twice ten thousand,
        and still thousands on thousands;
    the Lord is among them, Sinai's Lord in holy splendour.
18 You ascend on high, leading your captives;
    you have received as tribute those who rebelled,
        that you may reign as Lord and God.
19 Blessed be the Lord who daily bears our burdens,
    the God who alone is our salvation.
20 God truly is to us the God of all salvation,
    and the Lord God is able to deliver even from death.
21 But God will smite the head of his enemies,
    the savage head persisting in its wickedness.
22 The Lord says, From Bashan's heights,
    or from the depths of the sea, I will bring them back,
23 that you may dash your foot in blood,
    and the tongue of your dogs have its share of the foes.
24 They see your procession, O God,
    the advance of my God and King in holy splendour.
25 The singers go before, musicians follow after,
    in the midst of maidens playing timbrels.
26 In your companies bless God, the Lord,
    on the way from Israel's fountain.
27 See, Benjamin, the smallest tribe, is leading them,
    then Judah's princes in joyful array,
        princes of Zebulun, princes of Naphtali.
28 Command, O my God, according to your power;
    confirm, O God, what you have wrought for us.
29 At your temple above Jerusalem,
    kings shall bring to you their gifts.
30 Thunder with your rebuke at the beast of the marshes,

> the monstrous crowd, the bull-like hordes;
> pound them like fragments of silver,
>   scatter the people that delight in war.
> 31 From Egypt shall come gifts of bronze;
>   Ethiopia will stretch out hands to God.
> 32 Sing to God, you kingdoms of the earth;
>   make music in praise of the Lord,   *[Pause]*
> 33 to him who rides the ancient heaven of heavens,
>   and utters his voice, a mighty voice.
> 34 Give the glory to God, whose splendour is over Israel,
>   and his glory in the clouds.
> 35 God shines out in dread majesty from his holy dwelling,
>   the God of Israel
>   who gives strength and increase to his people.
>   Blessed be God.

This grand processional hymn falls into nine sections as shown below, reflecting stages in the progress of the festal procession. Following Mowinckel, we may conclude from the content that the procession in question was part of the ceremonies at the autumn festival in Jerusalem. Just as the procession had a sacramental character, signifying the entry of the victorious Creator and saviour into his temple, so also the psalm contributed to the sacrament, setting forth its meaning and its joy. Language and content indicate an early date, and it may have descended from the period of the Judges before reaching its present form in Jerusalem under the early kings (there are links with Deborah's song in Judges 5, and some think our psalm may have originated at the sanctuary of Tabor among the tribes of Zebulun and Naphtali, v. 27). Several resemblances to Isaiah 40 will be due to the exilic prophet having drawn on tradition; processional scenes from the pre-exilic festival live again in his inspired poetry, as the prophet envisages the new procession of the Lord across the desert to Jerusalem.

1–3   The beginning resembles the ancient chant sung at the lifting of the ark for its journey: 'Arise, Lord, let your enemies be scattered and your foes flee before you' (Num. 10.35). The likelihood is that this festal 'procession of God' (v. 24) includes the ark as symbol of his presence, the column moving off as the ark is taken up (cf. 132.8 and above on 24.7). Ancient versions, and many since, translate our passage as an invocation, similar to that in Numbers: 'Let God arise and let his enemies be scattered.' But it may be better to keep strictly to the traditional vowels: 'God arises / shall arise.' The singer is thus not only expounding the rite, but (as in the symbolic acts of the prophets) speaking with the power of God's action, mediating his work of justice.

4–6   A short hymn now marks the sense of God's nearness. It begins with the usual call to praise (v. 4) followed by reasons for praise (vv. 5–6). The call to 'lift (praise)' can otherwise be understood 'cast up (a highway)', meaning to restore and clear the holy route (Isa. 40.3–4; 62.10). As 'rider of the clouds' he is master of the rains and all growth; this is an ancient Canaanite title of deity (rather than 'rider of the deserts', which the Hebrew at first sight seems to mean – see Dahood). 'Yah' is a short form of 'Yahweh' (Int. 6b); in this name he is revealed among his people, and with much chanting of it they know his nearness. The reasons for praise ascribe to God the characteristics of the good king according to the ancient ideal – primarily protector of the vulnerable and powerless, concerned for the deprived, such as orphans, widows, the solitary, the homeless, the imprisoned. But the arrogant and cruel he treats as rebels, to be expelled to a fierce desert.

7–10   The festal procession probably ascended to Jerusalem from the eastern side, symbolizing a march through the wilderness. Over the years traditions were combined and transformed, and so we have in this passage recollection of how God led the ancestors through the wilderness from Sinai to the promised land, combined with the notion of his annual coming to give rains and turn the dry hills to green. As the psalm presents this dual 'remembrance', it brings out the significance of God's present work in the festival – ancestral saviour and renewer of earth's life through the rains. As of old, so now also, he leads the poor and humble through the wilderness to the place of living water.

11–14   At various stages in the Lord's procession, the ceremonies signified the rout of his foes. In the present passage the psalm pictures such victory in a scene where God commissions the tidings-bearers. Although we hear else-where of athletic men running great distances at speed to take news of battle (2 Sam. 18.19f.), there was also a role for women to spread the good news with songs and dances (cf. Ex. 15.20f.; Isa. 40.9). In the present case this latter role is represented in the procession by the young women with tambours (v. 25). It is a kind of prophesying, proclaiming God's salvation at the prompting of his 'word'. The burden of their songs is echoed in the psalm: the hostile kings have taken flight, and there will be much spoil to bring home; those who have stayed at home (cf. Judg. 5.16) may look up now and see the homing doves that have been released in sign of victory, wings iridescent in the morning sun (even perhaps adorned for the occasion with spangles of silver); God has scattered the kings as a storm drives snow on basalt mountains ('Zalmon', 'the Dark One', being perhaps Jebel Hauran).

16–18   The thought of the great mountains on the north-eastern borders (v. 14) seems to prompt this new section, with its address to Mount Hermon above the plain of Bashan. It is immense (literally 'Mountain of Elohim') and has several lofty heads. It might well be vexed that the honour of the Lord's central shrine was given to the modest hill of Zion, to which the procession draws near. But it is the paradox of grace, the choice of the lowly; here God has set his 'desire' and will 'abide' for ever. (cf. 132.14). Mysteriously, Zion gives a glimpse of the Creator's heavenly residence, and her processions reflect

the heavenly ascent of the Lord of Hosts, with all his fiery legions, his captives
and his tribute-bringers.

19–23   Thankful praise is offered to God as his people's salvation. Daily he
bears their burdens and gives deliverance from the assaults of 'death' – from
evil and suffering and all that would injure true life with God. The enemies
luridly pictured in vv. 21–3 are again death and his agents. The 'savage head'
(literally 'hairy skull') has a demonic echo in the Hebrew. These foes will not
escape (cf. Amos 9.2–3) and will be seen to perish without a doubt (v. 23).

24–27   The poet now passes to the appearance of the procession, perhaps
because it is now clearly visible to those watching for it from the holy city (cf.
Isa. 52.8). Emphatically he describes it as the procession (or 'goings') of God
himself, advancing in holy revelation (cf. Isa. 40.5; we could otherwise render
'into the sanctuary'). As 'King' he is the Creator and power above all powers
(cf. 24.7). The poet describes the marching singers as followed by players of
portable lyres and harps, and all about them (or possibly, between the two
groups) are the young women who tap hand-drums (like tambourines) as they
dance. The people in their 'companies', the well-ordered festal groups, are
summoned to respond with the formulas of blessing. Warmly they praise the
Lord 'from Israel's fountain' as the procession ascends from the last station of
the holy way, the spring of Gihon below the eastern wall (though some take
the phrase to mean '(you that are) from Israel's fountain', the descendants of
Jacob – rather a stretch of the given words; Dahood explains the phrase as 'in
the convocation of Israel'). The appearance of the ascending column is further
depicted: to the fore are the representatives of the small tribe Benjamin (from
which the pioneer monarchy of Saul had come); 'at the head' is literally
'ruling /? leading them', but LXX's rendering is striking: 'in ecstasy' (the root
being taken as *rdm*). Then comes the greater throng of Judah's princes. For the
other tribes there is just mention of two from the north, Zebulun and
Naphtali.

28–31   As the procession nears its end, prayer is raised that God will confirm
and carry through into the new year the salvation that has been symbolized;
God indeed has acted in the sacrament, but the prophetic reality has yet to
unfold in the continuing circumstances of life. So may he carry through his
victory over the forces of chaos and death (personified as the monster of the
marshes and her allies of bull-like demons) along with their human agents.
God's good kingdom will then be established over the earth, and great rulers
will come to Jerusalem to do homage.

32–35   The conclusion of all is a summons to praise. To all the kingdoms of
the earth the call goes out to raise the music of praise and to acknowledge the
Lord's unique glory. With the call is woven depiction of the revealed God,
carrying knowledge of his mighty and active reality into the hearts of all the
pilgrims. His utter supremacy is expressed in his riding the ancient heaven of

heavens, and in the thunder-voice that masters the cosmic waters (cf. v. 30; 29.3f.), and so gives life, strength and increase to his world. Here is the Creator, the Lord of all, yet knowledge of him radiates from that humble place and people of his choice. The last words are therefore this people's cry of thankful praise and devotion: 'Blessed be God.'

Such great Hebrew hymns were full of encouragement and help to know and respond to God; with the promptings and invitations to thank and praise him are given poetic glimpses of his power and justice, the unique sources of life. The present psalm, moreover, was combined with a sacramental procession, so that underlying all the service rendered by priests and people was 'what you have wrought for us' (v. 28). Through the action and through the song itself, the Lord was believed to be at work. His splendour is touching his people and his sanctuary, but also his whole world; his work, renewing life, is for all kingdoms, all families, all identities in his creation. He asserts his mastery over death and all the agents of chaotic harm; the poet here draws on the fearsome imagery of ancient battles to convey the certainty of the Lord's conquest of the cruel forces. It is one aspect of the divine upholding of justice and true life; another aspect which appears is his defending of the poor, his kindness to the lonely, and his taking upon himself his people's burden, day by day. The consummation of all his work of salvation is expressed in a vision of ascension; the ascending column betokens the Lord's going up to his throne in victory with his great train of captives and tribute-bringers. The vision was reborn in St Paul's application to the rising of Christ, who triumphed over the rebellious powers that he might give the abundance of his grace (Eph. 4.7f.; Col. 2.15).

The psalm is outstanding in its flashes of poetic imagination – the wind that drives the smoke, the blaze that melts the wax; the stampede of once-proud kings, the snowstorm on the black mountain, the monster of the marshes, the hairy skull, the tyrants fallen in their blood, the desert of godlessness; the rain in the wilderness, the envious mountain, the God who rides the clouds, father to the fatherless and home-maker to the lonely, carrying the loads daily for the little people; the musicians and dancing maidens that go up with God, the drudge who sees the dove's wings with their sheen of silver and green gold. This was a poetry united with song and sacred drama, ancient arts that brought knowledge of God. And still today they can serve the true and the holy, sacraments, no less, of the one who dispels chaos and renews the life of creation.

O Father of the fatherless, protector of the bereaved, we bless your name for all your daily care, and for the ascension of your Son Jesus; we pray you to bring us from the deserts of our own making to be his captives, and so gain true life and freedom.

PSALM 69: Will No One Have Pity?

For favour.   Over lilies.   Of David.

1   Save me, O God,
    for the waters come in up to my soul.
2   I sink in the mire of the great deep, and have no foothold;
    I have come into the depths of the waters,
        and the flood overwhelms me.
3   I am weary with crying out, and my throat is burning;
    my eyes fail with looking so long for my God.
4   Those who hate me without cause
        are more than the hairs of my head;
    many are those who would destroy me,
        enemies without reason,
    for how should I return what I have not seized?
5   But you, O God, know when I am foolish;
    when I am to blame, it is not hidden from you.
6   May those who look to you not be shamed through me,
        O Lord of Hosts;
    may those who seek you not be disgraced because of me,
        O God of Israel.
7   For your sake I bear reproach,
    and shame has covered my face.
8   I have become a stranger to my brothers,
    an alien to my mother's children.
9   Zeal for your house has devoured me;
    the reviling of those who revile you has fallen on me.
10 I afflicted my soul with fasting,
    and that was made a taunt against me.
11 When I made sackcloth my clothing,
    I became a byword to them.
12 Those who sit in the gate,
    and the drunkards also, make songs about me.
13 As for me, my prayer is to you,
    at the time of your favour, O Lord.
    O God, in the abundance of your faithful love,
    in the truth of your salvation, answer me.
14 Save me from the mire, before I sink for ever;
    may I be saved from my foes
        and from the depths of the waters.
15 May the water-flood not overwhelm me,
        nor the abyss swallow me up;
    may the pit not shut its mouth upon me.

16 Answer me, Lord, for your faithful love is gracious;
  in the greatness of your pity turn to me.
17 And do not hide your face from your servant,
  for I am in trouble – be quick to answer me.
18 Come near to my soul to redeem it;
  ransom me in face of my foes.
19 You know the reproach I bear, my shame and dishonour;
  all my enemies are before you.
20 Reproach has broken my heart;
  I am full of heaviness.
  I looked for some to have pity on me, but there was no one,
  and for comforters, but I found none.
21 They gave me poison for my food,
  and for my thirst they gave me vinegar to drink.
22 Let their table become a snare before them,
  and what was meant for fellowship become a trap.
23 Let their eyes be so darkened that they cannot see,
  and make their thighs to shake continually.
24 Pour out your indignation upon them;
  let the heat of your anger overtake them.
25 Let their camp be desolate,
  and let no one dwell in their tents.
26 For they have persecuted one whom you smote,
  and added hurt to those you pierced.
27 Charge them with sin upon sin,
  and let them not receive your vindication.
28 Let them be wiped from the book of the living,
  and not be recorded with the just.
29 As for me, though I am poor and in heaviness,
  your salvation, O God, will set me on high.
30 I will praise the name of God with a song,
  and glorify it with thanksgiving.
31 This will please the Lord more than the sacrifice of an ox,
  or a bull perfect in horn and hoof.
32 The humble shall see it and be glad;
  yes, you who seek God, may your heart live.
33 For the Lord listens to one brought low,
  and does not despise his bound ones.
34 Heaven and earth shall praise him,
  the seas and all that moves in them.
35 For God will save Zion, and build up the cities of Judah;
  and they shall dwell there and possess her.
36 The seed of his servants shall inherit her,
  and those who love his name shall abide in her.

Most of this psalm has the appearance of an individual's lamenting prayer (vv. 1–29), including depiction of a perilous situation (pictured as virtually in the jaws of the underworld) and an extended imprecation against the enemies (vv. 22–8). But the tone lightens in the conclusion (vv. 30–6), the theme of thanksgiving including the prospect of world praise for the salvation, building and occupation of Zion and Judah's cities. Some are therefore inclined to separate the first part as the prayer of an individual accused of theft (v. 4) and perhaps also ill; the concluding part is then considered to be, at least in part, a later addition to apply the psalm to the prospect of restoration for Jerusalem and Judah from the exilic destruction. It remains possible, however, to maintain the original unity of the psalm, especially by considering the sufferer to be a representative figure. As king or similar leader, God's servant (v. 17), he bears in his own person, as his own sufferings, the troubles of the community – probably assaults of national foes who allege against him acts of pillage (v. 4); against them he wields his weapon of prayer; and trusting in the covenanted fidelity of the Lord, he has confidence to envisage the salvation of the holy city and provinces as an event of importance for all the world. In its pattern and in several phrases, the psalm has resemblance to 22 and 102. For the (oracle-bearing) lilies of the title, see above on 45 and 60, both royal or national psalms.

1–3   The cry of 'Save me' rings out from a situation of extreme distress and danger. It is as though the sufferer were sinking into the watery jaws of the underworld beneath the subterranean waters; we hear of mire, ocean depths, cosmic flood, and the sense of sinking towards the extinction of life (cf. 18.4f.; 40.2; Jonah 2.2–6). In v. 1, therefore, the expression 'waters come in as far as (my) *nephesh*' seems best taken in the traditional understanding – the danger has almost overwhelmed the 'soul' or 'life'; some prefer the possible sense 'up to my neck', but this may be thought inadequate for the experience of the underworld's mouth. In v. 3 the picture changes to the plight of someone who has cried out for God till the throat is burning, and watching for him till the eyes can see no more.

4–5   To the foregoing depictions of extreme need, the psalmist now adds further considerations to move the Lord to intervene. If this cause were lost, worshippers of 'the God of Israel' would be humiliated. The suppliant seems indeed to speak as a ruler appointed by God to represent his kingdom: it is for the Lord's sake (v. 7) that he has taken the path which now brings such suffering. The picture of a loneliness which even means alienation from the closest kin has an archetypal character, an extreme of humiliation (cf. 38.11; 41.9; 55.13); a Canaanite king in political distress before 1300 BCE makes a similar complaint in the Amarna letters (Birkeland, p. 93). Like all pious rulers, he has been zealous in the care of God's temple (v. 9a), and perhaps here too, with all the costly requirements, there was opportunity for those bent on hostility (v. 9b); a traditional motif can be traced here, for an Assyrian lament runs 'I have longed for (the temple) Ezida; I constantly thought of all its fine things; the fire of Ezida has burnt my heart' (*Kingship*, p. 211). In vv. 10–12 the point again is the mocking of piety; adopting penitential fasting and clothing as an appeal to God in misfortune, he was taunted as one supposed to be in the Lord's favour, but now evidently forsaken (as we may fill out from 22.6–8).

13–21 Direct prayer is now renewed, the appeal from the deadly peril of the abyss. The 'time of your favour' refers to a time propitious for gaining acceptance, such as the hours of daily sacrifice or, as likely here, the special day of national penitence (cf. Isa. 58.5). There is repeated appeal to the Lord's *ḥesed* (vv. 13, 16), his covenanted support for his servant (v. 17). And the prayers are backed again by lamenting portrayal of suffering (vv. 19–21) – the numerous enemies, the reviling, the isolation in distress, the 'poison' and 'vinegar' instead of food and drink. This last feature will be an image for an extreme of unkindness, indeed treachery.

22–28 A fierce invocation of divine judgement now calls for God to bring the enemies' deeds back on themselves. As in 35.4–6, 58.6–9 and 109.6–20, we have to reckon with the prayer of a representative figure; the Davidic kings in particular felt it was part of their office to pray against oppressors. There is a curse-like quality in such passages, but the thought throughout is that of a pleading for God's retribution. So the enemies will themselves taste treachery, and know the dimmed eyes and shaking limbs that come with extreme consternation, the ruin of their settlements, exclusion from the roll of those living in God's light. This last phrase may refer to a heavenly book of destinies (cf. Ex. 32.32; Isa. 4.3; Dan. 12.1; Rev. 3.5), or may be based on the thought of registers of citizens (Jer. 22.30; Ezek. 13.9). In v. 26 the object of 'smote' can be rendered as singular or plural, while in v. 26b the singular is found in one Hebrew manuscript and the Syriac, the other witnesses having plural; this majority reading in the plural points to the representative character of the psalmist.

29–36 Though at present in affliction, the psalmist concludes with promise and indeed anticipation of thanksgiving for deliverance. The pattern is thus like that of the related 22 and 102. If Psalm 22 was giving expression to succeeding phases of a ritual, the present psalm, probably arising from a historical crisis, may intend the hopeful conclusion to strengthen the intercession; the readiness to trust and to give thanks will be pleasing to the Lord (cf. above on 66.17). (Some suppose that the change to a hopeful tone follows some word or sign of acceptance received after v. 9; so Johnson, *Prophet*, pp. 393f., and cf. above on 20.6). As in 50.14–15, 23, the offering of thanksgiving is especially prized; the song of testimony means more to the Lord than animal sacrifice. In v. 32 there is, however, anticipation of the sacred meal linked to votive offerings, when the blessing was spoken, 'May your heart live' (cf. 22.26). The joy will flow from the hoped-for deliverance; the Lord will have heard the afflicted, and not rejected his 'bound ones' –

captives of sorrow, bound also in covenant with the Saviour. The world, all nature, is one in such joy, and we may sense in v. 34 the cosmic significance of the Lord's Anointed and Zion. Many interpret vv. 35–6 as prophecy of the restoration of Jerusalem after the exilic destruction: Zion will be 'rebuilt'. But 'build' here may mean 'build up, make strong' (cf. above on 51.18), and 'possession' may simply refer to happy occupation through many generations.

We have traced through this psalm the prayer of the royal leader who, with his people, has come to a time of peril and sorrow. He feels to be in the jaws of the chaos-figure, a place of bottomless mire and overwhelming floods; and to be there for God's sake, bearing the hostility meant for the Lord himself. The psalm lent itself to messianic applications and, next to 22, is the most frequently cited psalm in the New Testament, where especially the zeal for God's house, the mockery, the bitter drink and the judgement on the adversaries were related to Christ (John 2.17; 15.25; 19.29; Matt. 27.34; Acts 1.20; Rom. 11.7f.; 15.3). In Christian worship the latter part of the psalm would be taken of the resurrection (v. 29b), the consequent universal joy, and the building of the church, 'Zion'. The imprecation of vv. 22–8 would of course seem contrary to the spirit of Jesus, but was taken, as in the New Testament, as prophecy of divine judgement. Today it can serve to remind worshippers of the work of passionate prayer ever needed against oppression of the poor and of all helpless creatures, but the ultimate desire must remain for the rebirth of the wicked beyond the cessation of their present course. The spirit of Jesus, stern against the harmers of his little ones, surely says Amen to the vision of all in heaven, earth and seas rejoicing in God, their Creator and saviour.

Lord Jesus, you who know the lowest depths of sorrow and the reproach that breaks the heart, come to the help of the suffering, and frustrate the forces of cruelty; may the poor see it and be glad, and their hearts live again, and the song be prepared for the day when all shall be made well.

PSALM 70: O That the Lord Would Hurry!

For favour.   Of David.   *For remembrance.*

1   [. . .] O *God*, to deliver me,
        to my help, O Lord, make haste.
2   May those who seek my life [. . .]
        be put to shame and confusion,
    and those who desire my hurt be turned back and disgraced.
3   Let them *turn back* on account of their shame,

that say [...] Aha, Aha.
4   But let all who seek you be glad and rejoice in you,
      and those who love your salvation ever say, *God* be praised.
5   As for me, I am poor and needy; O *God, hasten to me*;
      you are my help and my deliverer – *Lord*, do not delay.

Italic type indicates differences from 40.13–17, most of the material being the same. The chief variations are found in the title (for which see above on 38), in the divine names (vv. 1a, 4b, 5a, b), in the different wording of v. 3a (40.15: 'Let them be desolate') and v. 5a (40.17: 'poor and needy, may the Lord think upon me'); also in the absence of 'to sweep it away' (40.14) in v. 2a, and of the opening phrase 'May it be your will / Be pleased' (40.13) in v. 1a. This last 'omission' is striking, giving the beginning a fragmentary character; as the text stands, the verb in v. 1b has to govern the whole verse, adding to the effect of urgency (as also does the variation in v. 5a). Whether this psalm was extracted from 40, or was an independent psalm that had been incorporated into 40, is not agreed. But in some way it was available to the compilers of this collection, and came to be positioned between 69 and 71 to form a lamenting series. Some have thought that the collectors intended it to be united with 71, which in the Hebrew surprisingly lacks a title; these psalms are in fact united in many manuscripts. As it stands, the little psalm is notable for its urgency. If psalmists knew what is was to wait on the Lord, they also knew a suffering which cried out to him to make haste and not delay. (For further comment, see above on 40.)

O God, our help and deliverer, look with pity on those who are at the edge of endurance, and make haste to save them; that all who seek you and love your salvation may rejoice in you and bless your holy name.

PSALM 71: When Strength is Failing

1   In you, Lord, I have put my trust;
      may I never be put to shame.
2   Deliver me in your goodness and rescue me;
      turn your ear to me and save me.
3   Be for me a rock of refuge, a stronghold to save me;
      for you are my rock and my defence.
4   My God, rescue me from the hand of the wicked one,
      from the grasp of one who is evil and cruel.
5   For you, Lord, are my hope,
      my trust, Lord, even from my youth.
6   By you I was held at birth,

    when you loosed me from my mother's womb;
    my praise has ever been of you.

7   I was a sign to many,
    for you were my strong refuge.

8   My mouth was filled with your praise,
    and with your beauty all the day long.

9   Do not cast me away in the time of age,
    or forsake me when my strength is failing.

10   For my enemies speak against me,
   and those who lie in wait for my soul take counsel together,

11   saying, God has forsaken him;
   pursue and take him, for there is none to save him.

12   O God, do not stay far from me;
   my God, hasten to my help.

13   Let those set against my soul be shamed and confounded,
   and those who seek my harm
      be covered with scorn and reproach.

14   But as for me, I will hope continually,
   and praise you more and more.

15   My mouth shall tell of your goodness
      and of your salvation all the day,
   for I know no end of them.

16   I will enter and declare the mighty deeds of the Lord my God,
   and recount the goodness that is yours alone.

17   O God, you have taught me from my youth,
   and to this day I have proclaimed your wonders.

18   Do not forsake me, O God, now I am old and grey,
   until I have told the work of your arm to the next generation,
      your power to all who are to come.

19   Your goodness, O God, reaches to the heavens;
   in the great things you have done, who is like you, O God?

20   Though you have shown us great troubles and ills,
      you will turn and revive us,
   and bring us up again from the depths of the earth.

21   You will restore my strength,
   and turn about to comfort me.

22   Then I will thank you on the harp
      for your faithfulness, O God;
   I will make melody for you on the lyre, O Holy One of Israel.

23   My lips will sing out as I play to you,
   and so shall my soul, which you have redeemed.

24   My tongue also shall recount your goodness,
   for those who seek my harm
      shall be put to shame and confusion.

In this supplication the psalmist laments the hostilities of those who take advantage of his growing old, but he looks to the Lord to 'increase (again)' his 'greatness' (*gedullati* v. 21). The likelihood already that he is a king is supported by several other considerations, such as the close relationship with the God who at his birth acted as father and birth-nurse, was then his instructor and military defence ('crag', 'fortress'); the psalmist's prominence as a sign before multitudes and witness to God's goodness and power. There is good textual support for the reading of three plural pronouns in v. 20, which would indicate the psalmist's representative character. There are several close parallels of wording with other psalms, showing that this psalm comes from the same circle or tradition as 22, 31, 35, 40 especially; one should not conclude, as some do, that it is the work of a post-exilic author quoting from older psalms. There is no title in the Hebrew, perhaps because the psalm was sometimes treated as a continuation of 70. In LXX, however, we find the title 'By David, of the sons of Jonadab (cf. Jer. 35) and the first that were taken captive' – a Davidic title, but expanded with an interpretation that David had spoken prophetically about the Exile.

1–6 The suppliant cries to the Lord for rescue as one already 'in the hand ... in the palm' of one that is wicked and cruel (v. 4). Stressing that he trusts and hopes in the Lord alone, as all through his life, he pictures the divine salvation in the military terms common in the prayers of kings – the stronghold on a rocky summit, the fortress, the fortified defence. The translation of v. 3 above follows LXX, agreeing with 31.3, and likely to be the original. The present Hebrew gives: 'Be to me a rock to dwell in, where I may ever resort; send out (/'you have commanded') to save me, for you are my crag and my fortress.' The thought of his lifetime of trust leads to the striking image of v. 6: God had received him from the womb as father and birth-helper, owning him and supporting him, freeing him by severing the navel cord; how close and profound then the relationship! (This may be especially a theme of the sonship of the Lord's Anointed; see further on 22.9–10.)

7–13 His plea is that he has been prominent as one ever praising God for his 'beauty' or glory, and as his sure refuge; indeed he was a 'sign' or portent to the multitudes, one through whom the light of God's salvation shone out. (Some take the portent to be a signal example of God's punishment as in Deut. 28.46, but this is not so suitable for the context; in BCP 'I am become as it were a monster to many', 'monster' meant 'portent, wonder', Latin *monstrum*. For people as portents, cf. Isa. 8.18; Ezek. 12.6, 11; 24.24, 27; Zech. 3.8, and for the king's role as witness in God's praise before the multitudes, see above on 40.9f.) After this life of witness, how should he be forsaken in the weakness of old age? Certainly this time of weakness is the enemies' opportunity (cf. 1 Kings 1 and the Ugaritic example, *ANET*, p. 149a), and they are quick to say his incapacities show that God has withdrawn the favour with which he had once chosen and raised him up (cf. 3.2); they think he can now be pursued and destroyed, having lost his divine champion. So he prays for God not to remain aloof from his plight (v. 12, cf. 22.1), but to cover his adversaries with the shame of defeat.

14–24   The continuation of the prayer is more and more supported by the theme of praise, in essence a vow to testify all the more to the mighty deeds of God in salvation. He will tell of God's 'rightness' or 'goodness', faithful in saving acts beyond all counting (v. 15b lit. 'I know not numbers'). He will 'enter with' these mighty deeds, making solemn entry as God's witness in the great congregation (though some take the phrase as 'enter upon, begin to recite', which is less appropriate). It will be the renewal of his lifetime's service, and he resumes the plea from v. 9, that such a witness should not be at last forsaken. Typical of the royal testimony is v. 19 – the surpassing goodness of God (cf. 36.5; 57.10) and his incomparability (cf. 35.10; 86.8; 89.6, 8). While now he suffers as though in the grip of death (v. 20, cf. above on 69.1–2), he hopes for renewal of life and the royal 'greatness' he knew as ruler in God's cause. He vows to play and sing the psalmody of thanksgiving, and we may see a David-like figure in the one who can so promise to sing to his own playing of harp and lyre. If the reading 'us' rather than 'me' (three times in v. 20, *BHS*) is preferred, the solidarity of king and people is evident.

In this moving prayer, a David-like figure, perhaps even David himself, beseeches the Lord to help him as his strength declines in old age, and enemies see the opportunity to sweep him away. Again and again he appeals to the 'rightness' or goodness of the Lord, the divine readiness to right wrongs and save the ill-used. He draws on a lifetime of discipleship, trust and hope in the Lord, and on the innumerable instances when he has known God's help. He promises to make resound the music of thankfulness, with fingers, tongue, lips and soul.

At first sight, the psalm seems difficult for modern readers to appropriate. Their situation is probably not that of an ageing warrior-king; nor does the figure of the elderly psalmist lend itself to serve as a type of the youthful Jesus. Yet many know what it is to lose strength once possessed, to have colleagues then cooling, even becoming opponents, or to know such adversities that it seems as if many forces are out to destroy them. And the faithful are still a sign or portent; their very existence, their passing through the stages of life, all is a sign of God, a light or a word from him, which has its effect. If the church sees the cross especially as God's sign for the many, yet all who carry it in their hearts become part of its witness, their very existence eloquent of its grace. And as apparent also in 66, so once again the afflicted psalmist is longing for the time of praise; it is a lead that sufferers still follow when they pledge every fibre of their being to offer the music of thankfulness.

O Lord, be our rock in time of weakness and when adversities take hold upon us; remember what you have wrought in us from our very birth, and bring us up again from the depths, that we may sing with all our souls the music of your praise.

PSALM 72: The Saviour King

Of Solomon.

1   O God, give your judgements to the king,
    your justice to this son of the king.
2   Then he shall judge your people aright,
    and your afflicted ones with justice.
3   The mountains shall bear peace,
    and the little hills goodness for the people.
4   He shall judge for the poor of the people;
    he will save the children of the needy,
        and crush the oppressor.
5   He shall prolong his years with the sun,
    and before the moon, for all generations.
6   He shall come down like rain on the crops,
    like showers that water the earth.
7   In his days shall justice flourish,
    and abundance of peace, till the moon be no more.
8   And he shall rule from sea to sea,
    and from the great river to the ends of the earth.
9   Wild creatures shall kneel before him,
    but his enemies shall lick the dust.
10 The kings of Tarshish and the isles shall give presents;
    the kings of Arabia and Saba will bring gifts.
11 And all kings shall bow down before him,
    all nations do him service.
12 For he shall deliver the poor one who cries out,
    the needy one who has no helper.
13 He will have pity on the helpless and needy,
    and save the lives of the poor.
14 From falsehood and cruelty he will redeem their soul,
    and their blood shall be precious in his eyes.
15 So they shall live, and bring him more than Arabia's gold,
    as they pray for him continually,
        and bless him all the day long.
16 The corn shall be abundant on the earth and hilltops,
        its fruit heavy as on Lebanon.
    and from their cities they will flourish as the grass of the earth.
17 His name shall live for ever, and continue as long as the sun;
    all nations shall bless themselves by him, and call him blessed.
18 Blessed be the Lord God, God of Israel,
    who alone does wonderful things;
19 and blessed be his glorious name for ever,

> and may all the earth be filled with his glory.
> 20 Ended are the prayers of David, son of Jesse.

This prayer and prophetic blessing for the king has such a fundamental and idealistic character, that it probably belonged to the ceremonies of royal installation, and perhaps also to services of renewal. By prayer and prophetic word, the king is to become a true channel of the heavenly justice, above all defending the poor and vulnerable; and then will follow heaven's gifts to the land, and indeed the whole earth – a harmony of nature, health and abundance. Such royal installations were probably integrated into the autumn festival, with its overall theme of God's reign, centred at Zion, channelled through his royal servant, the Lord's Anointed (cf. Int. 5b; also above on 2, 21, 110). The heading 'Of Solomon' (missing in a few manuscripts; elsewhere only 127) might suggest the psalm originated at Solomon's coronation, or it could be a deduction from the phrase 'son of the king' in v. 1.

1–4   The whole psalm flows from the prayer of v. 1. This asks God, understood as the true king of all, to enact his just rule through the human king who is his viceroy and chief servant. The 'judgements' are more than legal decisions; they embrace all the work of government, but especially (as made clear in vv. 4, 12–15) the care of the poor. The king is also referred to as 'son of (the) king', which, spoken at a time of installation, might seem to allude to his status hitherto; more likely, however (in accordance with the parallel v. 1a) the expression is equivalent to 'king', and so means the Davidic heir, the dynastic representative. Some then take the verbs of vv. 2f. as jussive: 'May he judge ... may the mountains bear ...' But it may be better to keep strictly to the Hebrew spelling, with '(Then) he shall judge ... the mountains shall bear.' Undergirded by the opening prayer, the prospect of consequent blessing opens out. When the Davidic Son is truly the channel of God's rule, these wonderful things will follow. God's people will be ruled with honesty and fairness; the afflicted, lowly, poor and needy will be helped and defended, and oppressors crushed (cf. 101.8). Such rightness of rule is seen as one with the good order God wills for all the world of life. The 'peace' and 'rightness' borne by the hills mean good crops and fruit, but as part of a total harmony of society and nature.

5–11   The Hebrew text here begins: 'They shall fear you with the sun (while the sun endures)' – the king's good reign will lead the people in worship of God. Our translation, however, follows LXX (*ya'arik* instead of *yira'uka*), which is probably the original reading: 'He will prolong (years) with the sun' (on a par with, as the sun – Dahood). The thought can be understood of dynastic continuance, but as it stands expresses the ideal of a ruler wholly true to God in his compassionate justice; such a ruler would live and reign for ever. In such a vision of the ideal, the psalm is profoundly related to the later hope of a Messiah. The wonder of such a prospect is further developed. The effect on the natural world is resumed from v. 3. The king enabled by God to be thus just and compassionate would be like good rains bringing good harvests, and again 'rightness' (v. 7, so the Greek; Hebrew 'the righteous man') and 'peace' comprehend the health and happiness of both nature and society. The seas and 'river' of v. 8 are probably both cosmic terms, referring to forms of the cosmic waters that surround and penetrate the earth (cf. 24.2; 89.25, and for relation to Zion, 46.4; 87.7; others take the terms geographically, and refer to 1 Kings 4.21). In v. 9, 'wild creatures' are desert animals (*siy*, BDB, p. 850b), and their kneeling or crouching before the truly just king is again a sign of harmony in creation, with reconciliation of 'the Man' and the creatures (cf. Isa. 11.6–9; Jer. 27.6). Former enemies will come to make lowly obeisance before him, kings from afar bring gifts and tribute (Tarshish represents the far west, perhaps Tartessus in Spain; in v. 10b 'Sheba / Arabia' and 'Saba' may be along the coasts of the Red Sea).

12–17 All this glory, it is reaffirmed, is for the king who is the channel of God's justice, and its focus – defence of the vulnerable and needy – is set out even more strongly than in vv. 2, 4. He will be their 'redeemer', alongside them as if his own nearest kin, holding their blood precious, and so ever eager to save them from hurt. Those that he so 'redeems' will then 'live' (restored to good life and freedom) and will give a better gift than the rich potentates offer, for they will pray for their king and bless him all the day long. With such a king, the fruits of the earth and the populations of towns will flourish and abound. The royal name and line will endure, to the blessing of all.

18–19 The psalm proper has ended, and now is added a typical formula of worship to round off the second book of psalms (42–72, Int. 7b). Such a blessing (cf. v. 17) is the creatures' response to the Creator's blessing. It is all that in the end can be offered – fervent thanksgiving and praise. The divine 'name' is, as often, associated with the radiant glory of God, the revelation and gift of his holy being, and a splendour enough to fill all the world (cf. 8.1; Isa. 6.3). 'Amen' ('truly, surely') will be the response of the congregation to the cantor or choir, making the thoughts their own (cf. 106.48; Neh. 8.6).

20 A final notice states that here are concluded the prayers ('supplications') of David (cf. Job 31.40); presumably the notice was appropriate in a smaller collection of psalms than the present Psalter, which has further 'psalms of David' to come.

The psalm can lead people of our times to hold up their rulers in prayer, that they may be mediators of divine goodness; that all their policies and decisions may flow from the great eternal justice, to defend the defenceless and to crush oppression; and to know that this is the path to the health and harmony of earth and all that lives in her. Following from the insights of the collectors of the psalms and other Jewish interpreters, such as the Targum, the church has gained through the soaring poetry of the psalm a messianic vision. She has related it all to Jesus, Messiah and mediator of God's reign, and prayed that his work for the helpless and for the restoration of the world of goodness and peace may come to full fruition. And there is also an application of this prayer to each disciple, for each one in Christ becomes a channel of the divine compassion and justice in their own realm of influence, and each comes down there like rain to the crops and helps restore earth's peace. To the benediction of vv. 18–19, the people of the church then also say 'Amen and Amen'. For they give thanks that in answer to all the prayers of this book of psalms there has been given the vision of the Messiah and kingdom of the Lord, where the poor find true life, the wild creatures come to their Saviour, and earth has her springing of God's peace and goodness.

O God, eternal King, who caused the hope for the Messiah to arise, and answered it in your Son Jesus, we bless you for his care of the needy, and for the peace and salvation which he brings to those who love him; and we ask that his work be completed, and all the earth be filled with your glory; Amen and Amen.

PSALM 73: Drawing Near to God

Psalm.   Of Asaph.

1   Truly God is good to Israel,
    to those who are pure in heart.
2   But as for me, my feet were almost gone;
    my steps had all but slipped.
3   For I was envious of the proud;
    I saw the prosperity of the wicked.
4   For them there are no sharp pains;
    their body is well and fat.
5   The common sufferings are not for them;
    they are not smitten like other folk.
6   Therefore pride is their necklace,
    and cruelty covers them like a garment.
7   Their iniquity comes from within them;
    the conceits of their heart overflow.
8   They scoff and speak only evil;
    they pronounce oppression from on high.
9   They stretch their mouth to the heavens,
    and their tongue licks through the earth.
10 So their people gather round them,
    and drink in their doctrine to the full.
11 And they say, How should God know it?
    Is there knowledge in the Most High?

12 See, such are the wicked,
     and being ever at ease, they increase their wealth.
13 Did I then cleanse my heart in vain,
     and wash my hands in innocence?
14 All day long have I been stricken,
     and every morning chastened anew.
15 But if I had said, I will speak thus,
     I should have betrayed the company of your children.
16 When I thought to understand this,
     it seemed too hard for me,
17 until I came into the sanctuary of God;
     and then I discerned their end.
18 For you will set them in slippery places,
     and make them fall to destruction.
19 O how suddenly they will come to ruin,
     be overcome by terrors and perish!
20 As when one awakes from a dream,
     so, Lord, when you arise, you will dispel their image.
21 When I was bitter in heart,
     and consumed with grief within me,
22 I was but simple and ignorant,
     even as a beast before you.
23 But I am always with you;
     you keep hold of my right hand.
24 You will guide me with your counsel,
     and afterwards receive me in glory.
25 Whom have I in heaven but you?
     And there is none that I desire on earth beside you.
26 My flesh and my heart shall fail;
     but God is the rock of my heart and my portion for ever.
27 Those who go far from you shall perish;
     you will silence those who forsake you for false gods.
28 But it is good for me to draw near to God;
     in the Lord God I will make my shelter,
          that I may tell of all your works.

This psalm begins the third book of psalms (73–89, Int. 7b) and also the series headed 'Of Asaph' (73–83, also 50; Int. 2a). Tradition saw Asaph as one of David's chief leaders of psalmody, and these psalms will have come from his family down the generations. Kirkpatrick (pp. 427f.) gathers useful details and remarks that they are almost entirely national psalms; and though 73 and 77 have a more individual character, the psalmist there speaks as representative, the afflictions being not personal, but social and national. It is indeed helpful to bear in mind the position of psalms, and in the present case we come upon this distinctive psalm after one from the great royal ceremonies (72) and before a national lament over the devastation of the temple (74). Our psalm has been classed by some as an instructional poem, by others as a thanksgiving and testimony; but it scarcely accords with these types. God is the only party explicitly addressed (vv. 15, 18, 20, 22–5, 27, 28), and it may be best to see the psalmist as throughout concerned with what he calls *qirebat elohim*, 'drawing near to God' (v. 28). In a time of suffering, both personal and national, he seeks shelter, communion, and reviving grace in the sanctuary. Hence the warm appreciations of communion, comparable to those in 16, 17 and 63. Much of the psalm (especially vv. 1–19) is then a kind of preparation – a meditation and confession, composing the heart for communion (cf. 139) and trustfully resting an agonizing situation in the hands of the Lord. The arrogant and flourishing troublers described at such length (vv. 3–12) may be foreign tyrants of great power (cf. v. 9), in contrast to suffering 'Israel ... the pure in heart' (v. 1), 'the congregation of your children' (v. 15). The psalmist appears to represent and be responsible for the latter (v. 15), and several phrases in vv. 23f. suggest he is the king – clasped by God's right hand, led by his counsel, taken to glory. The theme of the problem of divine justice is found in the national context in other psalms (9–10, 12, 14, 58) and notably in Habakkuk.

1   The beginning and concluding statements of the psalm are like a frame enclosing the account of doubt and reviving faith. However it may seem, God is indeed loving and gracious to his faithful people. The phrase 'pure in heart' makes clear that 'Israel' is understood as the people sincerely devoted to God. A concern with injustice between nations is already apparent; the psalmist has been wrestling with the problem of his nation's suffering. In the interest of poetic balance and context, some prefer to change word-division and vowels to give as NRSV, 'Truly God is good to the upright, to those who are pure in heart', although there is no ancient support for this; but even then the reference could be national (cf. 'the righteous' for the nation in Hab. 1.4, 13; 2.4).

2–14   The psalmist now begins a confession of foolishness which almost led to a fatal fall from God. Bitter indignation had welled up (cf. 37.1) when he saw how the *holelim*, boastful, cruel (5.5; 75.4), prospered in comfort, while he himself, taking God's way in innocence, was continually afflicted. The extended description of the wicked serves to keep them exposed to the divine judgement; there seems to be an implicit appeal for action. The oppressors are typified as wealthy folk become arrogant and insensitive. They have leisure to devise evil, and they grasp and devour far and wide (v. 9 seems to use an ancient motif of voracious monsters or gods, see Dahood). Because of their power they are admired and emulated. Their attitude (but not their actual speech, v. 11) is that a just God can be left out of the reckoning.

15   One consideration helped to steady the sliding feet. The psalmist knew he must not betray the 'generation' or 'congregation' of God's children. It seems that he had a prominent responsibility. The people of the Lord looked to him and drew strength of faith from him. From this solidarity he too was strengthened.

16–20   But still the aggravation was a sore burden; to his eyes it was all perplexity and grief. Then relief came to him when he was in the temple (or perhaps 'in the holy rites'). Through some enlightenment (perhaps mediated in an oracle, vision or symbolic action) he saw how illusory was the stability of the wicked. Over them hung the threat of sudden ruin. He saw the certainty that God would act against them.

21–26   The psalmist confesses to God that it was through ignorance of his mystery that he had become so bitter, letting jealous indignation gnaw at his inward parts (v. 21b). But now he is renewed in the surpassing joy of the Lord's constant companionship and can affirm 'I am always with you.' God's hand–clasp expresses both his choice and support (often of king or Israel, cf. 18.35; 63.8; 80.17; 139.10; Isa. 41.10; 45.1). The reference of the phrases to the situation of God's king seems even clearer in v. 24. Such 'counsel' shows the way amid the problems of government; only the counsel of God will suffice (cf. Isa. 11.2 and on Ps. 16.7; my *Kingship*, p. 205, n. 43). So guided, the Lord's Chosen One will at last ('afterwards', cf. BDB, p. 29b) be 'taken' or 'received' into glory; although this could be understood of eventual victory on earth, a heavenly destiny is more probably in mind (cf. on 16.10 and 49.15, and for such 'taking (up)' cf. Gen. 5.24; 2 Kings 2.9f.). And the psalmist affirms his loyalty to this Lord alone (cf. 16.2–3). In v. 26 again, some understand the failing of flesh and heart as a temporary suffering within earthly life; but, as in v. 24b, the prospect could be of an eternal bliss beyond the body's death (for God as 'my portion' cf. above on 16.5–6).

27–28   In concluding appreciation of the blessing of nearness to God, the psalmist draws a contrast: forsaking God is the way to ruin (v. 27b is lit. 'whoring' from God; cf. 16.4), but 'drawing near' to God (especially in communion in the sanctuary, cf. Isa. 58.2) yields the supreme good, the divine shelter and salvation.

We have seen in this psalmist one who is concerned to draw near to the Lord. Before attaining the goal of communion, he had to prepare mind and soul, and in particular he needed to make a kind of confession. So he recounts before the Lord how he was consumed with such bitter indignation at the apparent unfairness of life that he almost concluded that service of God in purity was all in vain. Confessing and meditating further, he recounts how, in the sanctuary, it has been granted him to see further and deeper, to know the ruinous end awaiting the oppressors, and to acknowledge the shallow folly of his previous bitterness. So the way into the longed-for communion is cleared. To be always with God, to know the clasp of his hand, the salvation of his guidance and counsel through every peril, to be taken up at last into the glory of his nearer presence – these hopes begin to be realized; God becomes ever more surely 'rock of my heart, my portion for ever'. Moving on from his preparation in meditative thought and confession, the psalmist begins to attain his goal under the sheltering wings. He has not raised open supplication or lamentation, but will have confidence that, through his nearness to God, his needs and unspoken prayers will be answered, and a time for thankful witness will soon come.

To what extent the psalmist may have looked beyond this life for the bliss of salvation remains disputed. Certainly he does not theorize about an after-life. All the weight of hope is carried by the relationship with God. Given nearness to him, no other good is to be desired. As is further unfolded in the New Testament, eternal life is already bestowed on one who knows God; the failing of flesh and heart only makes clearer the true nature of that life as the enjoyment of God, 'my portion for ever' (John 6.54; 17.3).

Be our shelter, Lord God, in all the perplexities that assault our faith; guide us with your counsel, and bring us so close to you, that in this communion we come to know the fulfilment of all our hope and desire.

PSALM 74: Prayer Amid Utter Ruin

Poem. Of Asaph.

1   Why, O God, have you so utterly rejected us,
     why does your anger burn against the flock of your pasture?
2   Remember your congregation which you purchased long ago,
         and redeemed as the tribe for your own possession;
     remember the hill of Zion where you dwelt.
3   Lift your steps to the utter ruins,
     to all that the enemy has vilely done in the holy place.
4   Your foes roared in the place for your worship;
     instead of its signs they set up their standards.
5   They were like woodmen with axes,
     swinging them on high in a thicket of trees.
6   And then her carved work altogether
     they forced down with bars and hatchets.
7   They set fire to your holy place;
     to the very ground they defiled the dwelling of your name.
8   They said in their heart, Let us crush them altogether;
     they burnt all the sacred places in the land.
9   There are no signs for us to see, and no longer any prophet,
     not one among us, who knows how long.
10   How long, O God, shall the adversary taunt,

and the enemy utterly revile your name?
11 Why have you withdrawn your hand,
and held back your right hand in your bosom?
12 O God, my King of ancient time,
who did deeds of salvation in the midst of earth,
13 it was you that cleft the sea by your power,
you that broke the dragons' heads on the waters.
14 You alone crushed the heads of Leviathan;
you gave him as food for creatures of the desert.
15 It was you that cleft fountain and river,
you that dried up ever-flowing rivers.
16 From you came day, from you the night;
you alone established the sun and all the lights of heaven.
17 It was you that set up all the edges of the earth,
you that fashioned both summer and winter.
18 Remember, Lord, how the enemy derides,
how a foolish people scorns your name.
19 Do not give to wild beasts the soul of your turtle-dove,
or forget the life of your suffering ones for ever.
20 Look upon your covenant,
for the dark places of earth are filled;
filled with victims are the fields of violence.
21 May the oppressed not return ashamed,
but let the poor and needy praise your name.
22 Arise, O God, take up your own cause;
remember how the fool reviles you all the day long.
23 Do not forget the voice of your enemies,
the din of your foes that ascends continually.

The community here raises a lamenting supplication, pleading for God to exert his power in his own as well as his people's interest. The distress pictured in the lament centres on the devastation wrought by invaders in the sanctuary on Mount Zion; there are many dead, and instead of the daily offerings and praises it is the blasphemy of the foe that rises up to heaven. Characteristic elements that make up this tragic plea are petitions (vv. 2, 3, 18–23), lamenting questions ('Why', 'How long', vv. 1, 10, 11), portrayal of the outrage (vv. 3–10, 20, 22, 23), and more distinctively, invocation of God's power as Creator (vv. 12–17). It is widely agreed that the most likely occasion was the destruction carried out by the Babylonians in 587 BCE. The assault on temple and city by Antiochus in 167–4 seems too late for consideration (cf. Int. 5a, 7d,). Of destructions in the Persian period, for which some argue, very little is known. It has been objected against the Babylonian period that the psalm does not speak of exile, laments an absence of prophets, and refers to a plurality of sacred places, suggestive of synagogues. However, we may answer that the supplication concentrates on one decisive point, the outrage to God's habitation; the reference to prophets indicates a time of bewilderment and lack of oracles of salvation; and it is likely that there existed various sacred sites and stations, notwithstanding Josiah's attack on rival sanctuaries 34 years earlier (2 Kings 23). The psalm may have been voiced in lamenting worship which continued on the site of the ruined temple (cf. Zech. 7.3; 8.19; Jer. 41.4f.; Ezra 6.3). Other laments from this situation may be found in Lamentations (note ch. 2) and Psalm 79.

1–3 The intercessor at once begins to wrestle with the one who is Lord and shepherd of this people, and in whose will and power lies all their fate. The present disaster is not felt in the first place as caused by the enemy, but to be due to the Lord's displeasure with his people. So to this God, so personally conceived, is directly put the remonstrating question 'Why' and the urging to 'remember' the people he had once saved from oppression and made his own, and also the mountain where, in the temple, he had 'dwelt' through the mystery of his name and glory. This 'presence' has been withdrawn (cf. Ezek. 11.23; 43.1–5), but let God lift up his steps, marching with martial purpose and speed, to intervene on this holy place, now in utter ruin.

4–11 The evil situation is now portrayed with the aim of stirring God's intervention. The focus, therefore, is on the appalling affront to his honour and majesty perpetrated by those who assailed his temple. They roared like lions in the pride of their strength; they put their military standards, connected with their gods, in place of the signs or symbols of the Lord's worship. With hatchets and crowbars they forced down the precious panels in the temple – of gold, ivory, fine wood – and then burnt it to ruins (cf. 2 Kings 25.9f.). Further, they burnt down every sacred place they could find in the land. With such disruption of the sacred orders, but even more because of God's wrath, no oracles or omens of hope are given. Neither prophets nor any other mediators can say when the turning will come. The lament is rounded off with the imploring questions, 'How long, O God ... Why', and the situation is tellingly summarized – the enemy mocking God's name, and God unresponsive, his mighty right hand hidden and at rest in the folds of his garment.

12–17 In contrast to this right hand held back in the bosom, there follows an account of the mighty deeds it did in creation. The purpose of this recital is to beseech and indeed to move God to conquer the present manifestation of chaos. The imaginative poetry has its roots in ancient lore of creation stories evidenced among older near-eastern peoples. For Israelite faith, it was the Lord who in the beginning, the most ancient time, established his kingly supremacy, vanquishing the monsters of chaos in direct combat. Such monsters were embodiments of the untamed, destructive waters, and the victory meant that these were now subdued, divided and made to serve the cosmos, the order of life. Chief of the monsters here is Leviathan (probably 'Twisting One'), with seven heads (so Ugaritic texts, Mesopotamian seals, and Rev. 13.1; cf. Dahood). His body becomes food for 'a host of desert creatures' (this latter phrase is somewhat dubious, but perhaps the point of the detail is that the sea was dried up and so desert-life promoted, cf. Isa. 50.2; 51.10). From v. 15 the fundamental work of creation is followed further. The cleaving of fountain and river opened up passages down through the earth; whether the thought here is of draining away water from the earth (cf. v. 15b) or of providing springs, the purpose is to evidence the Lord's mastery over the waters (cf. again Isa. 50.2). By the same power were made the day and the night and all the lights of heaven (our translation takes *ma'or*, 'luminary' as collective; others take it just as 'moon'). Earth's 'edges' or 'bounds' are probably the rims of higher ground that hold back the sea. The last item of creation mentioned is the making of summer and winter, so concluding the account of how God's power established the conditions for life and growth. All has been recounted as what the Lord alone could and did achieve; seven times the Hebrew uses the pronoun 'You (alone)' to sustain the emphasis; more than enough for the seven heads of chaos.

18–23 With a sharp change we are back to the present situation: 'Remember, Lord, how the enemy derides.' The suffering people is pictured as a turtle-dove once dear to God's heart but now cast to wild beasts (one manuscript and LXX, instead of 'soul of your turtle-dove', have 'a soul that praises you', a difference of one Hebrew letter). Only now does the depiction of suffering widen to count the human cost; the caverns and fields of the land of death are filled with the slain. But the conclusion in vv. 22 and 23 returns to the theme of God's own cause and honour; may he act for this. The blasphemy of the enemies rises continually, where once praises and continual offerings had ascended to heaven.

Thus the psalm reflects a time of terrible disaster in the life of the ancient people. The many deaths are mentioned only after the principal outrage, the destruction of the temple. The invaders, vaunting the names of other gods, have been allowed to revile the name and dwelling of the Lord. He, the Creator, who clove the waters of chaos to establish the life of the world, he has chosen in his hidden purpose to allow this. His mighty arm has been kept back in his bosom. It can be seen as the Old Testament's own passion story, when that which bore the name and presence of God on earth was delivered into cruel hands to strip, mock and destroy. The scene reflected in our psalm is indeed very dark, for there was given as yet no word or sign of hope. But we know that the light of prophecy was in fact not far away. Through Jeremiah, Ezekiel and the Isaiah disciples (Isa. 40f.), meaning and hope would be rediscovered. As then, still today it is utterly perplexing when the Creator holds back his right hand while his dove is cast to the beasts. Yet the church sees the cross as embodying all such agonies from the beginning to the end of time; to faith and silent contemplation its enigma becomes the greatest of all the revelatory signs.

God, who alone in your power established the world of life, look with pity upon your
suffering ones and hasten to their help, as you raised the Lord Jesus from the fields of
violence, to the glory of your name for ever.

PSALM 75: The Horns of Arrogance and the Cup of Judgement

For favour.   Do Not Destroy.   Psalm.   Of Asaph.   Song.

1   We give you thanks, O God, we give you thanks,
     for your name is near, and your wonderful works are told.

2   I will seize the time appointed,
     and I myself will judge with justice.
3   The earth shakes, with all that dwell in her,
     yet I will set right her pillars.   *[Pause]*

4   To the boasters I say, Boast no longer,
     and to the wicked, Do not lift up your horn.
5   Do not lift up your horn on high,
     or speak with an insolent neck.
6   For neither from the east nor from the west,
     nor yet from the south comes exaltation.
7   But God alone is the judge;
     he puts down one and raises up another.
8   For in the hand of the Lord there is a cup,
     and its wine is foaming and fully mixed.
     When he pours from it, all the wicked of the earth
     shall drink it down to the very last drop.
9   But I will rejoice for ever,
     and make music to the God of Jacob.
10   I will break all the horns of the wicked,
     but the horns of the faithful one shall be exalted.

In this psalm there appear to be changing 'voices', even if all are carried by
one cantor. First comes the voice for the assembly of worshippers (v. 1); then,
to judge from the content, that of God (vv. 2–3, with 'Pause' at the end of the
section); and at greatest length there follows the voice of an authoritative
leader responsible for executing judgement, most likely the king (cf. 101.8).
Not of common type, the psalm is related to those which convey an assurance
of God's rectifying judgement (82; cf. also 12; 14), a suitable setting being the
autumnal festival with its theme of renewed order. The collectors may have

seen the psalm as responding particularly to the pleading of 74. For the heading 'Do Not Destroy' see above on 57.

1 The introductory verse gives a context for what will follow. The community here gives praise and thanks to God for his nearness in this time of worship, a presence which has shone upon them as the holy name of God has been proclaimed (cf. above on 68.4) and his mighty deeds of old have been recited and made contemporary (cf. above on 66.5).

2–3 The voice seems now to come from God's side, declaring to the festal gathering and to the world his purpose of judgement. He affirms that, at the time of his appointing, he will 'judge'; he will seize that moment and begin a reign of manifest justice. The present unjust world is pictured as though its physical supports were tottering; but God will set right these pillars, and the good world order, physical and moral, will be restored (cf. 24.2; 82.5). It is possible that the word rendered 'time appointed' (*mo'ed*) alludes to the heart of the festival, the solemn time, climax in the sacred calendar, when God purges and restores all for the new year. Such ceremony was seen as a time of God's saving action indeed, and yet also a prefiguring of his ultimate salvation.

4–10 That a fresh 'voice' is heard, developing the oracles just given, is likely from the 'Pause' (end of v. 3), from the introductory 'I say', and especially from the fact that while there is no break between vv. 5 and 6, God is not the speaker in vv. 6–7 (so Kirkpatrick). The authoritative human speaker, so fearsome to the wicked (v. 10), is likely to be the king, whose duty was to effect God's will for justice (72; 101). His admonition is directed to the mighty on earth, whose gods in practice are their own desires, ambitions, wealth and power. The 'horn' (especially of the wild bull) is symbol here of such arrogance and aggression. The psalmist warns that it is God who alone exalts and abases. His judgement or rectifying act is symbolized by a cup of heady mixture that makes the drinker reel and fall; God is seen holding it ready, and the wicked will have to drink it right down (cf. 11.6; 60.3; Isa. 51.17f.; Jer. 25.15f.). For his own part, the psalmist will ever be the Lord's witness, leading his praise, the one who has acted for the Lord in bringing down the oppressors. The last word in the Hebrew, *saddiq*, may allude especially to the Lord's Anointed as 'the faithful / just one', raised to glory (cf. 5.12).

The psalms 'of Asaph' have been sounding a counterpoint on the theme of divine justice. There has been perplexity and lament over its apparent absence (73; 74), announcement of its imminence (50; 75), and insight into its certainty given in God's 'nearness' (73; 75). It all reflects the tensions of experience – the times of violence and oppression when the arrogant seem to have a clear field for their deeds, and the times of sudden retribution when they fall in a ruin of their own making; and times also, through a divine grace, where, still in the midst of suffering, assurance is found in the nearness of the

Lord. Such assurance in 75 has arisen in a time of worship, when the united people praise and give thanks and there is recital of God's great works. The relationship with God has fresh immediacy as his name is called upon; the power of his presence falls upon the gathered people. And so the message is heard, bringing assurance that the Creator will not abandon his world to chaos, but willl restore and establish the order that is healthful and good in his eyes. God's servant, guide and protector of the people, draws out the message in warning to those who exalt themselves and their own desires, and in confidence that the time of goodness and joy will be shown to be the true and eternal time.

The church has related the execution of judgement (v. 10) to the role of the Messiah; in his coming and work God puts down the mighty from their seat and exalts the humble and meek (O that great *Deposuit* in Bach's Magnificat!). Through all time of apparent contradiction she has the task of confessing the goodness and glory of the Lord, recounting the story of salvation, making resound his name, and so entering and holding the experience of his nearness. In that holy place is granted the visionary conviction of the judgement that sets right earth's pillars and exalts all that is good.

O God, grant us to follow the way of humility and to know that your name is near; so may we not despair when the world reels with the evils of the arrogant, but know the certainty of the judgement at your appointed time, when you will set right earth's pillars and cause the music of your kingdom to resound for ever.

PSALM 76: Rage that Turns to Thanksgiving

For favour. With stringed instruments. Psalm. Of Asaph. Song.

1 God has made himself known in Judah;
   his name is great in Israel.
2 In Salem he has made his abode,
   and his dwelling is in Zion.
3 There he has broken the flaming arrows,
   shield, sword and line of battle. *[Pause]*
4 In brightness you appeared,
   glorious from the hills of prey.
5 The mighty ones were plundered and slept their sleep,
   and none of the men of war could find their hands.
6 At your thunderous word, O God of Jacob,
   both chariot and horse fell still.
7 In your dread majesty you appeared,

and who could stand before your face
    in the time of your wrath?
8   You sounded doom from heaven;
    earth trembled and was still,
9   when God arose for judgement,
    to save all the poor of the earth.   *[Pause]*
10   Truly, the raging of the peoples shall turn to your praise;
    the remnant of their rage you will gird on.
11   Vow and fulfil to the Lord your God;
    let all around him bring gifts to the awesome Lord.
12   He cuts down the pride of princes,
    and is fearsome to the kings of the earth.

This appears to be another of the psalms announcing and expounding symbolic action in the ceremonies of the autumnal (new year) festival (cf. 46 and
48, and more generally 24, 29, and 68). The meaning of the sacramental
worship is unfolded in the song: God has manifested himself in awesome
glory at Zion, and so he has overwhelmed all who would assault his holy city.
Terrible as he appears to the mighty and arrogant, he has come to save the
humble, and to him are now to be brought votive offerings and tribute. The
psalm aptly follows 75, reinforcing the assurance that tyrants will be overthrown. Already in the heading of LXX (which adds 'concerning the
Assyrian') the psalm was interpreted in connection with the invasion of
Sennacherib (2 Kings 18.13f.), a connection favoured by Kirkpatrick and
others.

1–3 The heart of the event to be recounted is announced at once. God has
'made himself known', making his coming experienced in the climax of the
dramatic festal worship. In the midst of 'Judah' and 'Israel', the two com-
ponents of his people united in the rule from 'Salem' (Jerusalem, cf. Gen.
14.18), his 'name' (his presence) is experienced afresh as 'great'. He has
renewed his mysterious dwelling in his temple on Mount Zion. This manifestation is here given a special significance: enemies of God, imagined as
assaulting his sanctuary, have been rendered powerless, their weapons broken
(cf. 46.9; 48.4f.).

4–9 The poetic imagination contributes much to what may have been a
relatively simple processional ceremony. The psalm, addressed now to God in
praising style, tells how he shone out in terrible glory and uttered the thunder
of his battle-roar (as once against the waters of chaos, cf. above on 68.30). The
foes fell helpless into deathly coma. It was like a sentence of judgement
pronounced from heaven, bringing relief to the oppressed and humble of all
the earth. The 'hills of prey' may reflect imagery of the divine Judge as a lion
(cf. v. 2 where 'abode' and 'dwelling' could be rendered 'covert' and 'lair',
also Amos 1.2; some emend with LXX to 'hills of eternity' and suppose that
ṭerep 'prey' has been substituted for *'ad* which can mean 'booty' or 'eternity').

10–12 Praise and homage are the themes of this concluding section. Our text of v. 10a gives lit. 'Truly the wrath of man shall praise you' (or 'praises / thanks you'); mankind is won from rebellion to worship God in thanksgiving. Verse 10b then follows with the thought that God girds on the saved people as a garment, in closeness to him (cf. Jer. 13). The offerings mentioned in v. 11 are signs of allegiance; with prayers in time of need, offerings are promised to the Lord, and these are fulfilled at pilgrimage feasts. The final words of praise bring out a central aspect: when the Lord appears in majesty, the powers of this world, in all their bluster and ruthlessness, are deflated and abased (cf. 75.4–7, 10).

If it is right that the psalm was originally intended to accompany symbolic actions in the festival, unfolding and projecting their meaning, other understandings still have value. Those who have looked for some historical assault on Zion as the topic of the psalm have rightly seen connections with narratives of deliverance. The great sacrament of Zion's salvation in the festival will have sent a light upon all the practical perils of the nation's life, and the stories of wars and deliverances took shape and meaning in this light. And others who took the psalm to refer to the Last Days have also seized a truth. For the sacrament of God's great judgement and salvation not only brought present knowledge of him, near and powerfully renewing life, but also gave vision of the ultimate, the perfection of the Lord's kingdom, an aspect which the prophets developed. The immediate contribution of our psalm, however, is as part of worship that affords present experience of God in his ultimate majesty. It can still take its part in those high moments of worship where the Lord makes himself known. Here still the psalm shows God as terrible to the mighty impostors, saviour to the meek of the earth, defender of the holy place.

Great Lord, we thank you for the vision of your appearing, when you break the flaming arrows and all the weapons of aggression, and we thank you for your sanctuary where the vision is given; we pray you to sustain all who love peace and justice, and hasten the time when the raging of the peoples shall turn to your praise.

PSALM 77: The Intercessor's Strongest Plea

For favour.   Over confession.   Of Asaph.   Psalm.

1   With my voice I cry to God,
      with all my voice to God, that he may hear me.
2   In the day of my trouble I seek the Lord;
      by night my hand is stretched out and does not tire,

and my soul refuses to be comforted.
3   I think upon God and I groan;
     I ponder, and my spirit faints.   *[Pause]*
4   My eyelids are held open;
     I am so stricken that I cannot speak.
5   I consider the days of old,
     and remember the years of long ago.
6   I commune with my heart in the night;
     I ponder, and search my spirit.
7   Will the Lord for ever be spurning,
     will he not once again show favour?
8   Has his faithful love ceased for ever,
     and his promise come to an end for all generations?
9   Has God forgotten to be gracious,
     has he in anger shut up his compassion?   *[Pause]*
10   But I say, this shall be my entreaty:
     to recite the deeds of the right hand of God Most High.
11   I will celebrate the acts of the Lord;
     I will recall your wonders from of old.
12   I will recite all your work,
     and tell out all your deeds.
13   Your way, O God, was in holy splendour;
     what god is so great as the Lord?
14   You are the God who does marvels;
     you made known your power among the peoples.
15   With a mighty arm you redeemed your people,
     the children of Jacob and Joseph.   *[Pause]*
16   The waters saw you, O God,
          the waters saw you and trembled;
     and the depths also were shaken.
17   The clouds poured out water, the skies uttered their thunder;
     your arrows flashed on every side.
18   The voice of your thunder was in the whirlwind,
          your lightnings lit up the ground;
     earth trembled and shook with dread.
19   Your way was in the sea,
          and your paths through the great waters,
     and your footsteps were not known.
20   You led your people like a flock,
     by the hand of Moses and Aaron.

In this lamenting prayer, the singer tells of personal grief and distress (vv. 1–9), but it becomes clear in vv. 10–20 that his concern is on behalf of his people. He seeks the Lord on behalf of all, bearing their sufferings in his own bosom. Following the 'Pause' in v. 9, v. 10 can be taken to introduce the recital of God's ancient deeds in the Exodus (vv. 11–20). This section is an implied prayer for the renewal of such salvation; it is almost as if the prophetic intercessor calls the ancient deeds into present effect. The end seems abrupt, but it gives the last lines a special force: will the Lord again shepherd his people by the hand of his chosen ones? The nation's ordeal seems to have been a protracted one, but is not clarified. Though some scholars point to ancient features in the language, others think of the use of ancient tradition in or around the Exile (cf. above on 74). For the title's reference to 'Confession' as a possible clue to the setting in public worship, see above on 39.

1–9 The lamenting entreaty is uttered to God with full voice, that he may indeed heed it (cf. GK 112q for the Hebrew as a clause of purpose). The singer portrays protracted distress to move the Lord – the hands stretched out in hours of supplication, the groaning of spirit night and day, the wakeful eyes, the force of grief, like a stroke that makes it hard to speak. It is perplexing to think of God's faithfulness of old; can he really have abandoned that enduring love, has he forgotten grace and compassion? Putting these sharp questionings in the form of a narrative, the intercessor avoids hurling them directly at God; but their force is unmistakable.

10 This pivotal verse has been rendered in widely differing ways, the Hebrew being ambiguous. NRSV has: 'And I say, it is my grief that the right hand of the Most High has changed.' *LP* has: 'And I say, Has the right hand of the Most High lost its strength, has the arm of the Lord changed?' However, the preceding occurrence of the 'Pause', and also the force of 'And / But I say', make it more probable that this verse introduces the hymnic section, countering the preceding questions. As in the Asaph psalm 74, the ancient work of God is to be recounted as plea for its renewal.

11–20 It is declared accordingly that the ancient miracles done by the Lord are now to be commemorated. The verbs 'celebrate', 'recall', 'recite', 'tell out' all refer to the devout rehearsal of sacred tradition which brings the light of the ancient salvation to bear upon the present. It is the deliverance of the people from bondage in Egypt which is recalled. The practical details are passed over; only the glory and wonder of God's action are mentioned, and their marvellous and life-giving nature is brought out by use of imagery drawn from traditions of creation and the annual renewal of life (cf. 18.7–16; 29.3f.; 68.7–9; 93.3–4; 104.6f.; Hab. 3.3–15). Clearly the recital is not a question of historical record, but of evoking the saving power and mystery of the Lord. The waters are especially prominent because of their symbolizing chaos, destructive power which only the Creator masters and makes to serve life. Through the deepest waters trod the saviour, where none could see his footprints, and so he came to rescue his flock and tend them all through the wilderness through his servants Moses and Aaron. Perhaps indeed a continuation of the psalm has been lost. Or perhaps in the flow of the liturgy of 'confession', other compositions took up the strain here. Yet as it stands, the ending is eloquent. The silence after v. 20 would itself be a moving entreaty.

May the Holy One, the mysterious and faithful saviour that deepest waters cannot hold back, may he come again to save his people, leading them by the hand of his anointed ones.

The psalm is an example of the strenuous work of the intercessors. Taking all the trouble of their people upon themselves and into their own heart, they cry for them to the Lord with outstretched hands and grieving soul; and through many an hour they ponder deeply on the absence of God's help. Their entreaty finds its full force as they address to God the recollection of his ancient salvation, the foundation of present life and hope. This remembrance is full of awe at the unique power, the marvel, mystery and faithfulness of the Lord. In the silence that follows, the voiceless prayer for renewal of that work of love rises with inspired strength. It is surely heard, though the saviour's footsteps through the deep waters of sorrow are not known. 'Thy purposes thou wilt accomplish, but the means are often concealed, indeed they are in themselves too vast and mysterious for human understanding' (Spurgeon).

Lord, who can come through the deepest waters to rescue your suffering ones, strengthen those who watch and suffer in prayer for others; inspire them to grasp with faith the salvation which gave birth to your world and your people, and to rest their plea upon it.

PSALM 78: The Mystery of Salvation

Poem.   Of Asaph.

1   Listen, my people, to my teaching;
      incline your ear to the sayings of my mouth.
2   I will open my mouth with a parable,
      and pour forth mysteries from of old.
3   The things we have heard and known,
      which our parents recounted to us,
4   we will not hide from their children,
        but recount to the next generation –
      the praises of the Lord and his power,
        and the wonders he has done.
5   For he laid solemn charge on the people of Jacob,
        and made it a law in Israel,
      commanding our ancestors
        to teach these things to their children,
6   that the next generation might know,
        even children yet to be born,

and arise and recount them to their children,
7   that they might put their trust in God,
     not forgetting the deeds of God,
         but keeping his commandments;
8   not being like their forebears,
         a stubborn and rebellious generation,
     a generation which did not set its heart aright,
         and whose spirit did not keep faith with God.
9   The children of Ephraim, best equipped of bowmen,
     yet turned back on the day of battle.
10   They did not keep God's covenant,
     and refused to walk in his laws;
11   and they forgot his deeds,
     and the wonders he had shown them.
12   For in the sight of their ancestors
         he had done marvellous things,
     in the land of Egypt, in the plain of Zoan.
13   He split the sea, and let them pass through it,
     while he made the waters stand still in heaps.
14   He led them with a cloud by day,
     and all through the night with a light of fire.
15   He split open rocks in the wilderness,
     giving drink in abundance as from the deeps.
16   He brought streams out of the rock,
     and made water pour down like rivers.
17   And still they sinned yet more against him,
     and defied the Most High in the desert.
18   They tested God in their heart,
     and demanded food for their craving.
19   They spoke against God and said,
     Can God furnish a table in the wilderness?
20   He struck the rock indeed, and water gushed out
         and streams overflowed,
     but can he also give bread, or provide meat for his people?
21   When the Lord heard this he was angered;
     fire was kindled against Jacob,
         and wrath went up against Israel.
22   For they did not have faith in God,
     and would not trust in his salvation.
23   So he commanded the clouds above,
     and opened the doors of heaven.
24   He rained down on them manna to eat,
     and gave them the grain of heaven.
25   So mortals ate the bread of the mighty ones;
     he had sent them food enough!
26   He brought out the east wind from the heavens,

and led the south wind from his stronghold.
27 He rained flesh upon them as thick as dust,
   and birds like the sand of the sea.
28 He made them fall into the midst of their camp,
   and round about their dwellings.
29 So they ate and were well filled,
   for he had brought them their desire.
30 But they had not given up their craving,
   their food was yet in their mouths,
31 when the anger of God rose against them,
   and slew of their strongest, and felled the choicest of Israel.
32 But for all this, they sinned yet more,
   and put no faith in his wonderful works.
33 So he consumed their days with trouble,
   and their years with sudden terror.
34 Whenever he slew among them, they would seek him;
   they would return and eagerly search for God.
35 They remembered that God was their rock,
   and God Most High their redeemer.
36 Yet they only flattered him with their mouth,
   and lied to him with their tongue.
37 For their heart was not fixed on him,
   and they were not true to his covenant.
38 But he, being compassionate, forgives wrongdoing,
      and does not destroy,
   and he often turns back his wrath,
      and does not rouse up all his anger.
39 So he considered that they were but flesh,
   a wind that passes by and does not come again.

40 How often they rebelled against him in the wilderness,
   and grieved him in the desert!
41 Again and again they tested God;
   they pained the Holy One of Israel.
42 They did not remember his hand,
   and the day he redeemed them from the foe,
43 how he set his signs in Egypt,
   and his wonders in the plain of Zoan.
44 For he turned their rivers to blood,
   and they could not drink from their streams.
45 He sent swarms of flies which devoured them,
   and frogs also that brought them ruin.
46 He gave their produce to the creeping locust,
   and to the flying locust the fruits of their toil.
47 He destroyed their vines with hailstones,
   and their sycamore trees with frozen rain.

48 He gave up their cattle to the hail,
    and their flocks to fiery lightnings.
49 He let loose on them the heat of his anger,
        wrath, indignation and trouble,
    a troop of destroying angels.
50 He made a way for his anger,
        and did not spare them from death,
    but gave their life over to the plague.
51 So he smote all the firstborn of Egypt,
    the first-fruits of strength in the tents of Ham.
52 But he led off his people like sheep,
    and guided them in the wilderness like a flock.
53 He led them on safely, and they were not afraid,
    but the sea covered over their enemies.
54 So he brought them to his holy mountain,
    to the heights which his right hand took in possession.
55 He drove out nations before them,
    and shared out to them their heritage,
        settling the tribes of Israel in their tents.
56 Yet still they tested and defied the Most High God,
    and did not keep his testimonies.
57 They turned back and fell away like their ancestors,
    starting aside like a bow not true.
58 They vexed him with their hill-shrines,
    and provoked him with their idols.
59 God heard and was greatly angered,
    and utterly rejected Israel.
60 He forsook his dwelling in Shiloh,
    the tent where he dwelt among mankind.
61 He gave his glory into captivity,
    and his beauty into the enemy's hand.
62 He delivered his people to the sword,
    and dealt angrily with his heritage.
63 The fire consumed their young men,
    and their maidens were not given in marriage.
64 Their priests fell by the sword,
    and their widows could make no lamentation.
65 Then the Lord awoke as out of sleep,
    like a warrior exultant with wine.
66 He smote his enemies backward,
    and put them to enduring shame.
67 But he rejected the tent of Joseph,
    and did not choose the tribe of Ephraim.
68 He chose the tribe of Judah,
    and the hill of Zion which he loved.
69 And he built his sanctuary like the heavens,

and like the earth which he founded for ever.
70 He chose David his servant,
     and took him from the sheepfolds.
71 From behind the ewes with their lambs he brought him,
     to feed Jacob his people and Israel his heritage.
72 So he shepherded them with devoted heart,
     and with skilful hands he led them.

Unlike the recitals of ancient lore in the Asaph psalms 74 and 77 which were addressed to God, this great retrospect is directed to 'my people', probably the festal assembly. Rather like Moses in Deuteronomy, the psalmist looks back to the people's early history, interpreted as an interaction with the Lord in patterns of divine election, salvation and judgement. He inculcates deep truths ('parable', 'riddles / mysteries') from this history – a teacher of wisdom, we might say, but also a prophetic figure. The particular use he makes of the general patterns concerns the overthrow of an older order, where the sacred authority had been centred at Shiloh, located in the tribal area of Ephraim; it was now replaced by the pre-eminence of Zion and its temple, Judah, and the house of David. The concluding perspective, appreciative of the great temple and the work of David, could indicate a date in Solomon's reign, though it can otherwise be argued that the psalm reflects hostility to the northern kingdom after Solomon's death, but before Jerusalem's own doom in 587 (yet some even think of the post-exilic period). The lengthy discourse falls into the seven sections expounded below. Comparison may be made especially with 105 and 106 and Deut. 32.

1–8 Addressing the great assembly as 'my people', the psalmist appears as a figure of much authority, the nation's teacher and guide. 'Parable' and 'mysteries / riddles' are terms that indicate that interpretations and applications are to be given for the otherwise puzzling events of the past. True, the accounts of the Lord's miraculous deeds, received from parents and passed on to their grandchildren (vv. 3–4), are clear enough; but the psalmist is going to search out deep levels of truth; mysteries will 'pour forth' from his mouth as wisdom given by inspiration. In v. 5 the 'solemn charge' (*'edut*) and 'law' (*tora*) are taken by some to refer to the covenantal laws, which are to be taught and transmitted down the generations (cf. NRSV in v. 5b, 'which he commanded our ancestors to teach to their children'). It may be better, as above, to understand the reference as being to the specific command to hand down the story of the wonders (so resuming vv. 3–4, cf. Ex. 10.2; 12.26, 27; 13.8f., 14; Deut. 4.9; 6.20f.; less likely is that v. 5b refers to the handing down of this requirement itself). The purpose of this solemn transmission is clearly stated and is broadly that also of our psalm: to foster a relation of trust and obedience with God, avoiding the fickleness of the earlier generations.

9–16 At the beginning and end of the long retrospect, the tribe of Ephraim is picked out unfavourably (vv. 9, 67). The strongest of the tribes for centuries, they had at Shiloh the main Israelite sanctuary, long the home of the ark. Their defeat by the Philistines and the capture of the ark are at the climax of the psalm's argument (vv. 56f.), and this early reference to that shameful defeat indicates that the traditional story of the nation's early experiences is going to be given a particular application. Fine bowmen as they were, they were untrue to God and so were defeated (cf. the image of the twisted bow in v. 57). The failure of this leading part of Israel is traced to their not living according to the laws and teachings of the covenant, and this in turn is traced to their losing the sense of what God had done to save their ancestors at the Exodus and in the wilderness.

17–31 In lively style the psalmist draws out the significance of the incidents we find reported in Exodus 16 and Numbers 11. They illustrate attitudes of defiance or rebellion, and of a disposition to 'test' God, querulously demanding, and yet unbelieving. The 'fire' and 'wrath' (v. 21) go out from God like punishing angels. The 'manna' (v. 24, perhaps fine flakes of a honeydew produced by insects) is taken here to be the bread of heavenly beings (*abbirim*), and so 'the corn of heaven' (it was later taken by the rabbis as food of the world to come, and by the New Testament as prefiguring Christ, John 6.31f.; 1 Cor. 10.3). The wonder and abundance of the provision, vv. 23–9, should have been received as grace, but the churlish and greedy conduct of the people turned grace into judgement.

32–39 The psalmist now characterizes the further years of wandering in the wilderness, following the incident of the spies whose report was greeted with alarm (Num. 14). Sufferings would induce repentance, but the heart would not stay fixed on God, and they would soon swerve again from the way of the covenant. Only through God's pity and forbearance were they given new chances; for he considered how frail and fleeting a thing was man. (The sombre v. 36, according to the calculation of the ancient Jewish scholars, is the middle verse of the 2527 in the Hebrew of the Psalms.)

40–55 The recurring departures from trust and obedience are again traced to a forgetting of God's 'hand', the great deliverances of the past. To show how shocking this is, and to help the assembly keep their own eyes steadfastly on God's great works, the psalmist reviews the 'plagues' in Egypt, the strokes of God against the oppressive kingdom to persuade it to let the Hebrews go free. The survey has fewer plagues than given in Exodus, and in a different order, perhaps representing an earlier form of the tradition. (For the rivers as blood cf. Ex. 7.17f.; for the flies Ex. 8.20f.; for the frogs Ex. 8.1f.; for the locusts Ex. 10.1f.; for the hail and ice Ex. 9.13f., 28; for the destroying angels Ex. 12.23, and more generally 2 Sam. 24.16f.; 2 Kings 19.35; Job 33.22.) The plagues had to reach their climax before the liberation was conceded (for 'Ham' as ancestor of Egypt see Gen. 10.6; Ps. 105.23, 27; 106.22). Then the shepherd got his flock on the move and led them through desert and water; the warmth of this shepherding image (common in the Asaph psalms – vv.

70–2; 74.1; 77.20; 80.1) contrasts with the preceding account of Israel's rebelliousness. There are resemblances to the song of Exodus 15: the sea 'covers over' the pursuing army (Ex. 15.10), the people arrive at last at the mountain-land, which is all virtually seen as the mountain-sanctuary where God will put his 'presence' (Ex. 15.17). The conquest is taken to be the work of God alone (cf. 44.1f.), as also the allotting of territory to the tribes (cf. Josh. 23.4; Ps. 105.11).

56–64   The story moves on through the times of the Judges and of Samuel. The settlement in Canaan brought temptations and deviations; hill-shrines (*bamoth*) in Canaanite style and idols were effects of the 'fertility' religion, contrary to the covenant laws. Israel, with Ephraim at its centre, was defeated by the Philistines, the ark itself was captured (1 Sam. 4), and its temple at Shiloh 'forsaken', probably demolished (cf. Jer. 7.12f.). The events are seen as resulting from God's rejection of Israel. He himself forsook Shiloh, where he had bestowed his earthly 'presence' (i.e. the chief centre of communion and worship). He himself had given his 'glory / strength' (*'oz*) and 'beauty' (*tip'eret*), the presence signified by the ark (1 Sam. 4.21–2; Ps.132.8), into the enemy's hands. And he himself had given his people to the sword. In such terrible conditions even the customary mourning for the dead was not carried out (cf. Job 27.15; Ezek. 24.15f.).

65–72   Attention is still fastened upon the amazing significance of the capture and recovery of the ark. The Lord willed to give his 'glory', his presence, into the power of the enemy. But now comes the time when he arises. It is like the arising of the divine champion of ancient mythical poetry, who puts off the deathly sleep and rises to triumph (for the phrase 'exultant with wine' the sense is uncertain, and some prefer 'throwing off the stupour of wine', and others again, with the ancient versions, 'overcome with wine'). So he smites his foes back (some render 'in the back', as an allusion to the piles that afflicted the Philistines, 1 Sam. 5.6f.). The 'tent of Joseph' could allude to the sanctuary at Shiloh, or to the pre-eminence that had belonged to the 'Joseph / Rachel' tribes, Ephraim, Manasseh and Benjamin. The reign of Saul the Benjaminite is not mentioned; it falls away silently with the rejected leaders. The story continues rather to the great positive act of the Lord in establishing his presence on Zion, and choosing David of the tribe of Judah to be his Servant for the shepherding of his people Jacob / Israel. Still the events are not strictly chronicled; the peaks of significance are presented. God 'loves' Zion (cf. 47.4; 87.2) and there himself built his temple, high as the heavenly heights and deep as the foundations of the earth; it has thus a cosmic significance, centre of the divine rule on earth. Solomon, the human builder, is not mentioned, and the psalm comes to rest with an extended reference to David, ideally portrayed as taken by God from devoted and tender care of his father's flock to be royal shepherd of God's people (cf. 1 Sam. 16.11; 2 Sam. 5.2). Such is the concluding image of the long survey: David's shepherd-care of God's people (lit.) 'according to the wholeness of his heart' and 'with the wise skills of his hands'.

Mysteries from of old have been poured forth; a story, familiar but hard to grasp, has been rehearsed to give a parable. The hearers can receive this parable as they compare their own situation. What a mystery, what an enigma, that the people rescued from slavery should turn against their saviour! What a mystery that, beyond all the afflictions and punishments, he should persevere in his care and love, setting up at last his presence in the world's centre and, through the person of his Anointed, selflessly shepherding his flock with tender devotion!

The parable, poured out like prophecy, is at its deepest in this matter of the enduring love of God; his own 'glory' must be exposed to the hate of the enemy. Even the rejection of the former elect is not the last word; according to the New Testament they can be grafted in again and all Israel saved, 'for the gifts and the calling of God are irrevocable ... O the depth of the riches and wisdom and knowledge of God' (Rom. 11.23–36). But the psalmist's parable throws light also on the enigma of human behaviour towards the Lord. Alienation from the saviour, it teaches, creeps in when the people's eyes are set only on their own needs and desires, pleasures and ambitions. They come to lose the sense of the wonders that gave them life and freedom, and easily wander down the ways of rebellion. Remember, remember, urges the psalmist, and hand on the remembrance unfailingly, how the Lord came to save his people, and ever be their shepherd; let your eyes and your heart be fixed upon him, and so you will be kept in trust and faithfulness; you yourselves will know how he cleaves the rock to give you the water of life, and sends down the bread of heaven, that you may eat, and hunger no more.

Lord our shepherd, we thank you for the story of faith that has been passed down to us; enable us also to hand it down, having ourselves been filled with the truth of your judgement, grace and everlasting love.

PSALM 79: Prayer in a Time of Devastation

Psalm. Of Asaph.

1   O God, the nations have come into your heritage;
    they have defiled your holy temple,
       and made Jerusalem into heaps of stones.
2   They have given the bodies of your servants
       to be food for the birds of the heavens,
    the flesh of your faithful to the wild beasts of the earth.

3   They shed their blood like water all around Jerusalem,
     and there was no one to bury them.
4   We have become the taunt of our neighbours,
     the scorn and derision of those that are round about us.
5   How long, Lord, will you be so greatly angered,
     and your zeal blaze out like fire?
6   Pour out your wrath upon the nations that do not
     acknowledge you,
     on the kingdoms that do not invoke your name.
7   For they have eaten up Jacob,
     and laid waste his dwelling-place.
8   Do not remember against us the sins of former times;
     let your compassion hurry to meet us,
          for we are brought very low.
9   Help us, God our Saviour, for the glory of your name;
     O deliver us and put away our sins for your name's sake.
10   Why should the nations say, Where is their God?
     Make known among the nations before our eyes
          requital for your servants' blood that was shed.
11   O let the groaning of the prisoner come before you;
     by the might of your arm save those condemned to die.
12   And return to our neighbours sevenfold into their bosom
     the taunts with which they have taunted you, O Lord.
13   But we, who are your people and the sheep of your pasture,
     will give you thanks for ever,
          and tell your praise to all generations.

The sequence of the psalms is especially striking here. Immediately after the final scenes of 78 – the temple surely founded by God and the people shepherded by his servant's skilful hands – comes this lamenting supplication that portrays the holy city in ruins, the temple defiled, people slain and left unburied. The piece is best understood as from the same situation and usage as 74, from lamenting worship on the ruined site of the temple during the Exile. It does not provide a balanced survey of the situation, and does not name the assailants or enlarge on the fate of the captives. Its aim is to move God to come in salvation and so brings to him a few piercing glimpses of the violation of his holiness and covenant care. Fittingly, the Talmud (Sopherim 18.3) has this psalm, along with 137, used annually on the 9th of the month Ab in commemoration of the destructions of the first and second temples (587 BCE and 70 CE). A citation from vv. 2–3 in 1 Macc. 7.17 (cf. also 1.37) suggests how the psalm was seen in the second century BCE as prophetic scripture.

1–4 After the invocation of God's name, 'Elohim', the singer immediately presents to him features of the tragic situation which should rouse him to intervene. All that lies under such abuse is his – his heritage, his holy temple, his servants, his faithful; and the city's name itself, Jerusalem (vv. 1, 3), so full of hope and identified with the glory of the Lord, carries its own plea. The 'heritage' is his special possession, and refers sometimes to the people (74.2; 78.62, 71), but here to the holy land (cf. Ex. 15.17). The violence against the temple and city (v. 1), if we allow for the poetic structure, is all of a piece: both are desecrated and both reduced to heaps. The horrendous scene of the unburied dead all about Jerusalem not only indicates the scale of the disaster, where the survivors could not perform the burials, but also the depth of the tragedy, since great store was put upon burial as a last kindness for the peace of the dead. The scorn of neighbouring peoples is not detailed here, but assumed to be an affront to God (cf. v. 10; 74.10).

5–12   For all the evil of the foe, the harm is traced more fundamentally to the Lord's displeasure with his people. It could not be that he was unable to prevent the disaster, but must all result from his anger. His 'zeal / jealousy' is kindled when his unique holiness and sovereignty are affronted; the sins of former and of recent times must be to blame (vv. 8–9). So the plea is for God to put from his mind, cover over, treat as expiated, all such offences, through his compassion and his care for his name (as pledged to this people). The groaning of the prisoners, many under sentence of death, is especially brought to his pity. With passion the plea is raised that the blasphemous taunts should rebound on the mockers with sevenfold force (representing a case for exceptional severity of divine retribution, Gen. 4.15; Lev. 26.18f.).

13   The supplication concludes with promise of unending praise and thanksgiving if God will turn his people's fate. Then will be manifest, what is yet true in this terrible time, that they are a people specially chosen and brought near, tended and guided by the divine Shepherd.

The community's lament rises from a situation of bitter tragedy, and beats on the doors of heaven with appeals to God's honour, faithfulness and pity. One can understand the desire that the punishing anger be diverted to those who despise his name and sanctuary and slaughter and torment his worshippers, or that the blasphemous derision of neighbours be turned back upon them in fullest measure. An important aspect of such vehement supplications is that they are directed to God; the perplexity is with his present anger, not with his power or his ultimate faithfulness. Even in the time of ruined homes and unburied dead and captives awaiting a cruel death, the community knows that all is in God's hand, and that it is to him they must ever turn. Another profound significance, still somewhat hidden in the prayer, is that God himself shares in the suffering; the violence and hate are directed against his holy place and people, the bearers of his presence on earth; his commitment with these is such that he must suffer with them.

And still today, in many a tragic scene, the psalm leads worshippers to speak out their indignation and passionate sorrow to God, and acknowledge that salvation is in his will and power alone. As for the sevenfold retribution, the comment of fifth-century Cassiodorus (noted in NL) gives a lead. He would have us pray down for the enemies an ultimate good: the work of the Spirit, bringing his sevenfold gifts into their bosom, will lead them through deep remorse to reconciliation with God.

Almighty and merciful God, whose name and glory are daily reviled in the cruelty done to your creatures, let the groaning of the captives and the bloodshed of your servants come before you; turn the hearts of the destroyers, and through the sevenfold gifts of your mighty Spirit gather all into your flock, to your everlasting praise.

PSALM 80: The Vine of God Laid Waste

For favour.   Over lilies.   Testimony.   Of Asaph.   Psalm.

1   Hear, O Shepherd of Israel,
    you that led Joseph like a flock.
    You that are enthroned above the kerubim,
    shine out before Ephraim, Benjamin and Manasseh.
2   Stir up your mighty strength,
    and come to our salvation.
3   O God, restore us again;
    let your face shine upon us, that we may be saved.
4   Lord God of Hosts,
    how long will you be set against your people's prayer?
5   You have fed them with the bread of tears,
    and given them abundance of tears to drink.
6   You have made us a mockery to our neighbours,
    and our enemies deride us.
7   O God of Hosts, restore us again;
    let your face shine upon us, that we may be saved.
8   You took out a vine from Egypt;
    you drove out nations, and planted it again.
9   You made room about it,
    and when it had taken root, it filled the land.
10 The hills were covered with its shade,
    for its boughs were like the cedars of God.
11 It stretched out its branches to the sea,
    and its tendrils to the river.
12 Then why have you broken down its walls,
    so that all who go by pluck off its grapes?
13 The wild boar from the forest roots it up.
    and all the beasts of the field devour it.
14 O God of Hosts, return again;

> look down from heaven and see.
> 15 Care for this your vine,
>   and guard what your right hand has planted,
>   for the sake of the son you made so strong for yourself.
> 16 It is cut down and burnt in the fire;
>   they perish at the rebuke of your face.
> 17 Let your hand be upon the man at your right hand,
>   upon the son of man whom you made so strong for yourself.
> 18 And so we shall not go back from you;
>   let us live, that we may proclaim your name.
> 19 Lord, God of Hosts, restore us again;
>   let your face shine upon us, that we may be saved.

The sequence is again notable. Psalm 79 ended as a plea of 'your people, the flock of your pasture', and now another communal lament begins its supplication to 'Israel's shepherd, who led Joseph like a flock'. The representative singer is supported by choral voices, sounding their refrain three times and with a climax of invocation (vv. 3, 7, 19). The suffering of the nation is represented in the figure of the vine, planted by God, but now abandoned and ravaged. The quest for identifying the period turns on the references in v. 1 to 'Joseph' and 'Ephraim, Benjamin and Manasseh' (as tribes from the sons and grandsons of Rachel). The first impression we may have is that these are the present worshippers who seek the light of God's sanctuary-presence for their salvation, and the period could then be the last years of the Northern Kingdom, as it goes down under Assyrian invasion towards 721, and the place perhaps Bethel. But taking account of the Jerusalem connections of the preceding Asaph psalms, we could rather think of an intercession on behalf of these tribes but in the Southern Kingdom, perhaps in Josiah's time around 620, or in the Exile (in view of Jer. 3.11–13; Ezek. 37.15–28). LXX points to the earlier periods with its heading 'concerning the Assyrian'. For our headings 'Over lilies' and 'Testimony' see above on 45 and 60.

1–3 God is called upon as shepherd of Israel in a plea that his care be now manifest. Reference is made to the sacred tradition that told how he had led his people through the wilderness (cf. 77.20; 78.52). 'Joseph' strictly should denote the two tribes from his sons Ephraim and Manasseh, but the tribe of Benjamin will be included since he, with Joseph, was the other son of Rachel. Strong centre of the Northern Kingdom, these tribes can be mentioned as representative of that kingdom (cf. Jer. 31.15), indeed of 'Israel'. The title of God as the one 'enthroned on / over the kerubs' reflects the idea of God as king in heaven on a throne supported and borne by celestial creatures, a conception represented by kerub-figures in the sanctuary. These figures were probably like the winged animals with human faces found in ivory panels at Samaria. At Jerusalem the ark was associated with this conception (cf. Ex. 25.22), and this seems to have been the case previously at Shiloh (cf. 1 Sam. 4.4; 2 Sam. 6.2; 2 Kings 19.15). God's salvation is sought with two expressions: that he should rouse his strength and come (cf. 78.65; 35.23), and that he should shine forth (cf. 50.2). Such 'shining' is the request also of the choral refrain (v. 3), which asks God to 'bring back / restore' his people; if he 'makes bright' his face, they will indeed be saved, the bright face signifying his presence and favourable attention (cf. above on 4.6), the very light of life (cf. 36.9).

4–7   But it is the Lord himself – so the prayer continues – who has brought about the afflictions. Towards the pleas of his people he is unyielding (so the verb '*-sh-n* can be understood from the Aramaic, *TRP*; otherwise the sense is 'fumes' – he angrily rejects the prayer). For their daily portion he gives them tears (cf. 42.3; 102.9), and tears again as copious drink (lit. as from a *shalish*, a large bowl, a 'third' of some big measure). It is he who makes them the butt of 'mockery' (*madon*, after Dahood; otherwise 'strife'). And again the choral prayer for light arises, but with fuller invocation of God's name (v. 7, cf. v. 3).

8–19   The intercession now gathers strength from the use of an image that recalls God's former grace and vividly depicts its present opposite. It is the image of the vine, so readily meaningful in this land (cf. Isa. 5; 27.2–6; Hos. 10.1; John 15). God has taken up his people as a vine from Egypt, taken every care to plant it well in the holy land, tended it so that it grew mightily and filled the land (the boundaries of 'sea' and 'river' may be the cosmic terms, cf. 72.8, or more prosaically the Mediterranean and the Euphrates). But now he has broken down her walls and allowed passers-by and beasts to snatch, devour and destroy. So the plea sounds out for God to return to his former care. (In v. 15 'guard' is for a word of uncertain meaning, *kanna*, the root *k-n-n* being perhaps a variant of *g-n-n*; but some take it as a noun, 'the stock which your hand planted'.) Verse 17 probably refers to the king (rather than to the nation), a child of man indeed, but raised up to be at the Lord's right hand and made strong by the gifts of his Spirit. Verse 15b will have the same reference, but awkwardness in the Hebrew has led some to conclude that the line has come in here by error from v. 17. If the hand of God, with blessing and support, so rests upon the king, the people will be renewed in their bond with the Lord, enjoying true life in his light, worshipping him as they proclaim his holy name. The concluding refrain invokes this name with the fullest form of three elements, 'Lord, God of Hosts' (cf. vv. 3, 7), and for the third time pleads for restoration in the light of the Saviour's face.

In spite of uncertainty about the original place and time of this supplication, it is clear that the suffering is to be connected with the destruction of the Northern Kingdom by the Assyrian armies. The prayer for restoration in the light of life is thus for the salvation of a whole people whose towns, shrines, farms and homes are laid waste, while families are uprooted and suffering many dead. The prayer in such a situation clings to the Lord's commitment of old: God our shepherd, God who took us up as a young vine, planted us again with great care, nurtured us to great strength and fruitfulness – can he abandon his vine to be devoured, uprooted, burnt? Again and again the people's prayer rings out: O to be restored, to have life and salvation in the light of God's face! Such salvation, they believed, would essentially involve the hand of God upon the one he raised up as royal head, his servant who binds the people in faithfulness and worship. The Targum found here a prayer for the coming of the Messiah, and the church in her turn sees Christ as the bearer of life and salvation; through him may be known already the blessing of the face of God (cf. Num. 6.25); the light of the knowledge of the glory of God is given in the face of Jesus Christ (2 Cor. 4.6), and in him shall be made perfect the restoration of the suffering world.

Lord God, you reveal to us that the vine of your church is one with the vine of all your creation, one in the sap of life, in health and in suffering; we pray you to care for this your vine, that is so plundered and harmed; stir up your mighty strength and come and save us by the light of your face, through the Son whom you raised in power to your right hand.

PSALM 81: Rejoicing and Trembling in Worship

For favour.   Over the Gittith.   Of Asaph.

1   Sing aloud to God our strength;
     with joyful praise greet the God of Jacob.
2   Make melody and sound drums;
     sweet lyres, together with the harps.
3   Blow the ram's horn as for new moon,
     and as for full moon, on our festal day.
4   For this is a law for Israel,
     a commandment of the God of Jacob,
5   a charge which he laid on Joseph,
     when he came out of the land of Egypt.

     I hear a voice of mystery, saying:
6   I released their back from the burden;
     their hands went free from the basket.
7   In the oppression you called to me and I delivered you;
     I answered you from the hiding-place of thunder,
         and proved you by the waters of Meribah.   *[Pause]*
8   Hear, my people, and I will admonish you;
     O Israel, if you would but listen to me!
9   There shall be no strange god among you;
     you shall not bow down to any alien god.

10 I am the Lord your God,
      who brought you up from the land of Egypt;
    open wide your mouth and I shall fill it.
11 When my people did not listen to my voice,
      and Israel would not obey me,
12 I sent them away in the hardness of their heart,
      to walk in their own counsels.
13 If only my people would now listen to me,
      if Israel would but walk in my ways,
14 I would quickly subdue their enemies,
      and turn my hand against their foes.
15 The adversaries of the Lord would become small before him,
      and their submission would be for ever.
16 I would feed you with the best of wheat,
      and with honey from the rock I would satisfy you.

This impressive psalm reflects a situation in a great pilgrimage festival. The coming of God into his sanctuary is acclaimed with the jubilation of voices and instruments, and then followed by God's speech to his people through a singer of prophetic character. The speech includes warning, but also sustains and renews the covenant bond. From the Targum onwards, the main Jewish sources (and practice also down to the present) link the psalm with the autumnal new year or Tabernacles, holy days of the month Tishri. This is generally accepted as a true indication of the original setting, though some scholars argue for the Passover because of the references to the Exodus. The structure is the same as that of the related 95: after a prelude of acclamation and reasons for praise (vv. 1–5ab), there comes a line of introduction to God's speech (v. 5c), then the speech itself (vv. 6–16). As with 77 and 78, the ending is rather abrupt; it is a style which likes to end with a pregnant thought for reflection. The psalm reflects the tradition of early Israel, such as was revived in Deuteronomy. (The obscure heading 'over the Gittith' has been discussed above on 8 and occurs also for 84. Related are 50, 95 and 99.)

1–3 The pilgrims assembled at the great festival could be described as 'those who know the *teru'a*', the acclamation of the Lord present in glory; such worshippers walked 'in the light of his face' (89.15). When our psalmist begins by calling for the concerted shouts and music of such acclamation, it will be in response to the coming or showing forth of God as now signified in the ceremonies. In the light of his new presence, the pilgrims are to hail him as glorious Lord, with all the accompaniment of the temple musicians and probably dancers. Instruments mentioned are the tambours or hand-drums used especially in dancing, the lyres characterized as 'sweet, lovely', and the deeper but still portable harps. Important especially for the acclamations was the ram's horn trumpet, the shofar (cf. 47.5 and 2 Sam. 6.15 at the Lord's ascension). The exact meaning of v. 3, however, is uncertain. The 'new moon' may indicate the autumnal new year's day (so the Targum; the first day of the month Tishri); it was a day for special *teru'a* (Lev. 23.24; Num. 29.1f.). The 'full moon', two weeks later, would then be the commencement of Tabernacles, 15 Tishri (Num. 10.10 appoints the blowing of silver trumpets on such days). But it seems that only one day, the present day, is indicated by 'the day of our festival', and our translation (taking the Hebrew preposition before 'new moon' and 'full moon' as Beth Essentiae) accordingly implies that at this high point of the long festival, when the Lord comes in glory, the greatest forms of acclamation are to be combined.

4–5ab The call for praise is now supported by a reason – the divine will. The Lord himself has appointed the festival; his is the initative in all that is done. His institution of it is traced back to the period of the Exodus, the fundamental salvation, leading to the revelations at Mount Sinai (cf. Ex. 23.14f.; 34.22; Deut. 16.13f.). 'Joseph' will denote the Israel of the Exodus, a usage found in other Asaph psalms and probably favoured at the ancient sanctuaries of the central tribes that were especially traced to Joseph (cf. 77.15; 78.67; 80.1).

5c Some have connected this clause with the preceding line; thus AV 'where I (Israel) heard a language I understood not'. But it is widely accepted now as introducing the following speech of God; such statements indicated to the hearers that the singer, in the manner of a prophet, was about to mediate God's words (cf. Num. 24.3–4, 15–17; 2 Sam. 23.1–3; Isa. 5.9; 22.14; Job 4.12–16; Pss 62.11; 85.8). Thus our singer refers to a 'lip', a language, which he did not know, but now hears (/understands). (Less likely is the translation 'I hear the speech of one I did not know' – the experience of a prophetic disciple, 1 Sam. 3.2f.). Our singer has heard a mysterious, other-worldly voice, and can now recount the message of God. It seems that such inspirations gave rise to the first presentation of an oracular psalm, but could subsequently be re-presented as ever valid messages of God.

6–10 As though to continue the note of mystery, the words where the Lord announces and identifies himself (used before the Commandments in Ex. 20.2) are here held back to v. 10. It is clear, however, that the God and Saviour of this people speaks, as he recalls the deliverance of the Exodus. From their oppressive fate as building slaves, bearing loads and the baskets of clay or bricks, he had rescued them. In v. 7 the worshippers are dramatically identified with the slaves: 'you called to me ... I answered you.' The commemorations of the festivals heighten the sense of unity through the generations. These present worshippers, as a saved people, are in the presence of the deliverer, who claims their loyalty and spells out now his fundamental laws. (The 'secret place of thunder' suggests the cloud which veils the divine presence, cf. Ex. 14.19f., 24; the reference to the desert halt at Meribah seems to assume another form of the tradition found in Ex. 17.1–7, cf. Ex. 15.25; Num. 20.1–13). Their worship must be for him alone (cf. Ex. 20.3). He, Yahweh, alone is their God, who bound them to him through the Exodus, and does so now again, and undertakes amply to give them the gifts of life (v. 10, perhaps the image of the parent bird with its young).

11–16 Identification with the ancestors is not carried right through. They are not held up for emulation; tradition told of their misdeeds and consequent judgement (cf. 78.10f.). In this respect the present generation was to stand apart and take warning. So the Lord's speech recalls that hardness of heart, that walking after their own counsels, deaf to his voice. But (v. 13f.) he tells also of his persevering love, his longing still to save his people from their foes, who would soon 'become lean', deflated, humbled, before him. The direct address is resumed at the end. The Lord longs to care for these his worshippers: '. . . I would satisfy you'. (In v. 16a the Hebrew has 'And he fed him', which is usually emended as above to suit v. 16b.)

The psalm is like a cameo of ancient Israel's worship. By the Lord's decree the people have come from far and wide to his sanctuary, at the time he has appointed and signalled in the rhythm of the seasons and the wondrous movements of the moon – a covenant people set in harmony with the created order. The Lord too has come; the glory of his presence shines out, and the worshippers have to acknowledge him with praise of voice, instruments and dancing feet. He is powerfully present, and has come to renew the relationship of Lord and covenant-people; he proceeds therefore to speak, expressing through the prophetic singer words of salvation, warning and promise. The Holy One is truly terrible; the joyful praise is fitting in its place, but the encounter must soon mean awe, humility, penitence. The people are indeed on a threshold of new opportunity. They must anew renounce false idols, and choose the Lord alone. In a new year of belonging to him, they will find true life, for the Lord longs to give them his choicest gifts. The ancient experience is relevant to worshippers of all times. The encounter with the Holy One always arouses fear and shame; and always there is his claim, the claim of the saviour, and his will to restore, renew, and bless with his wonderful gifts.

O God our strength, who have brought your people from slavery into the freedom of your service, forgive our sins of unfaithfulness, and renew us as your people, who shall live daily by the gifts of your hand and the words of your mouth.

PSALM 82: Injustice that Shakes Earth's Foundations

Psalm. Of Asaph.

1   God stands in the assembly of heaven;
     in the midst of the holy ones he gives judgement:
2   How long will you govern unjustly,
     and show favour to the wicked?   *[Pause]*
3   You were to rule for the weak and orphan,
     defend the right of the humble and needy,
4   rescue the weak and poor,
     deliver them from the hand of the wicked.
5   They have no knowledge or wisdom;
     they go about in darkness, while earth's foundations shake.
6   Therefore I decree that, though you are of heaven,
     and all of the household of the Most High,
7   yet you shall die like the people of earth,
     and shall fall like one of their princes.
8   Arise, O God, and govern the earth,
     for you shall take all nations as your possession.

So much in 58 Hebrew words! The visionary psalmist depicts a scene in heaven. God is presiding over his convocation of divine ministers and angels, and stands to denounce and sentence those present with responsibility for government of the nations. They have not upheld the right of the oppressed, and so have violated the essence of the divine order and must die. In response to this revelation, the singer pleads for its realization, when God himself will directly rule all the nations and so ensure good order and justice. The point about justice for the oppressed is amply made, but all else is terse. One may suppose that the vision was given in the course of worship in response to lament about evil conditions. The issue of justice for the poor seems intended here to apply to the suffering of the nation, assailed by foreign powers (cf. v. 8). The background of thought has parallels among older Syrian societies – conceptions of a company of gods in heaven, subordinate to the Most High as his 'sons'; duties are shared among them, and affairs of the world are reviewed and decisions made at an annual assembly on the divine mountain. Among a number of similar references in the Old Testament, we can compare especially the divine assembly in 1 Kings 22.19f. and Job 1–2; of particular relevance also is the conception in Deut. 32.8–9, where the Most High appoints for each nation a divine patron, but reserves Israel for his own direct rule. In some respects we can compare also 58 and 75, and more broadly 12 and 14.

1 The introduction is brief, preparing swiftly for the speech of God which is to form the bulk of the psalm. 'God' (originally probably 'Yahweh') is presiding at the divine assembly (*'edat el*), thought of as the solemn event where affairs of the world are reviewed and decisions of destiny made. It is a question whether to translate in v. 1a 'stands' (Tate) or 'has taken his place / presides' (see Dahood); for the former, nearer the usual sense of the verb, the point would be that the enthroned God now stands to announce his verdict, while the latter rendering has him seated in majesty throughout before the standing servants. These underlings are indeed 'holy ones / gods', but the psalm will vividly illustrate the limits of their power (cf. 29.1; 95.3; 96.4). In v. 1b the verb 'he judges / will judge' probably refers to the conclusion of his judging, the verdict which will now follow.

2–4 The address of God's question is not specified, being directed to the divine beings just mentioned. The conception is that the government of earth's nations has been delegated to them as ministers of the supreme King, the Lord. As generally in the Near East, the acid test of good government is held to be the care of the vulnerable and afflicted, such as widows, orphans, the poor and migrants (cf. 72.2f.). The four clauses of vv. 3–4 are actually imperatives, 'Rule for the weak ...' As we can see from the string of imperatives in Obadiah 12–14 (AV 'But thou shouldest not have looked ... '), the original duties are echoed ironically, for the chance to obey has now passed; the words only pinpoint the wrongdoing.

5 In distinction from the address to 'you' in vv. 2–3, 6–7, this verse refers only to a 'they'. The simple course of making it apply to the wicked on earth mentioned in v. 4b is taken by some (thus Johnson, *Sacral Kingship* p. 99: 'Deliver them from the hand of the wicked, who have neither knowledge or understanding, but live persistently in darkness.'). But the Hebrew itself hardly suggests this, and the verse may rather reflect a legal style, where a case is summarized; God here concludes that these authorities have not shown the wisdom required for their high office (cf. 14.4), but on the contrary have proceeded about their work without the light of justice and compassion, so that the very foundations of the cosmic order shake (cf. 75.3).

6–7 The Hebrew begins emphatically, 'I, for my part, I say ... ', which can be taken as the announcement of a decision or verdict (cf. 2 Sam. 19.29f.); this continues, literally, 'you are gods, and all of you sons of Elyon (the Most High), but you shall die like man and fall like one of the princes (/ governors).' (On another view, the sentence begins ironically, 'I had thought you were gods,' cf. 31.22; Isa. 49.4, Dahood.) The immortality of these heavenly beings (cf. Gen. 3.5, 22) is forfeit; they will be cast down from office like any human minister who has betrayed his king (cf. the myth of the fallen star or angel reflected in Isa. 14.12f.; Ezek. 28.16f.; Rev. 12.9).

8 In response to the visionary account, the singer concludes with a compact prayer for the realization of the hope it has stirred: may God indeed arise (cf. 3.7; 7.6; 9.9 etc.) and take up direct rule of all nations; may his will as seen in the vision of heaven be done on earth (cf. 12.5f.; 14.7). The final clause seems to mean that, as the Lord has 'possessed' and directly ruled Israel, so he would do for all peoples, and so ensure a world of justice and peace (cf. Dahood, but Tate prefers 'for you have patrimony among all nations').

The psalm gives vivid expression to the belief that the crucial duty of the ruler is to prevent the exploitation of the weak by the strong. Only too common was the situation where the strong, by dint of their strength and wealth, were able to secure the ruler's connivance or tolerance as they defrauded, dispossessed and enslaved those who were easy prey. To such a ruler it would appear advantageous to 'lift the face of the wicked' (so lit. v. 2b) – to flatter, favour and justify them in their oppression, for these strong ones had the means to reward the friendly ruler. The immediate concern of the psalmist seems to have been a national aggression, and indeed it is often the case that in such invasions, with settlements burnt down, people fleeing to the mountains or deserts, and many slaughtered, it is the poor who bear the brunt of it all. In the traditional interpretation of the psalm such moral chaos, disturbing the very earth, is blamed on the human rulers and mighty, and the vision is of a divine sentence already prepared for them. The psalmist would not altogether quarrel with this; such corrupt rulers are indeed responsible for their abuses of justice and will have to fall a great fall. But the psalmist saw further. He was aware of a corruption beyond the individual princes of this world, something indeed that came between the good and righteous God and the daily experience of so many of his creatures. He draws on the symbolic imaginings of an ancient poetry to express this, and from his vision two insights endure. First, that all the might of the Creator is on the side of justice and compassion; he has decreed their triumph through all reaches of the cosmos. And second, that there is a work of intercession to be done for the realization of this decree; 'hallowed be your name, your will be done, your kingdom come' is the theme which is daily to be particularized with all the intercessor's heart and vision.

O Lord, eternal King, who have commanded the care of your little ones, grant us both the faith that sees the certainty of your kingdom, and also the perseverance that ever prays for your will to be done on earth.

PSALM 83:   A Prayer of Flame and Storm

Song.   Psalm.   Of Asaph.

1   O God, do not be still;
     do not be silent or at rest, O God.

2   For see, your enemies make tumult,
     and those who hate you lift their heads.

3   Against your people they plan with cunning;
     they scheme together against your treasured ones.

4   Come, they say, let us finish them as a nation,
     that the name of Israel be remembered no more.

5   With one accord they conspire together,
     and against you they make a covenant,

6   the tents of Edom and the Ishmaelites,
     Moab and the Hagarenes,

7   Gebal, Ammon and Amalek,
     Philistia and those who dwell in Tyre.

8   Assyria also is joined with them,
     becoming a strong arm for the children of Lot.   *[Pause]*

9   Do to them as you did to Midian,
     and to Sisera and Jabin by the river Kishon,

10 who were destroyed at En-dor,
     and became as dung for the earth.

11 Make their princes like Oreb and Zeeb,
     and all their kings like Zebah and Zalmunna,

12 who said, Let us seize the pastures of God,
     and make them our own possession.

13 O my God, make them like rolling thistle-balls,
     like chaff before the wind.

14 As fire that blazes through the forest,
     as flame that devours the mountains,

15 so drive them with your tempest,
     and rout them with your storm.

16 Fill their faces with shame,
     that they may seek your name, O Lord.

17 May they be ashamed and dismayed for ever;
     may they be put to confusion and perish.

18 And they shall know that you, whose name is the Lord,
     are alone the Most High over all the earth.

While the preceding psalm implied that God's people were suffering under the assaults of the nations, this one openly shows them facing a coalition of foes. It is a supplication of the community, voiced by one (cf. v. 13) who can represent them and on their behalf doughtily wield the weapon of prayer. Invocation and plea for action (v. 1) are followed by 'lament', presenting to God a situation which must move him (vv. 2–9); then come direct petitions for God to deal with the enemy, imprecations that gather force from use of similes (cf. 58), but including the thought that the foes should turn to seek and acknowledge the Lord. The last verse in fact touches on praise and confidence, and again has resemblance to 82. Though the enemies are listed in unusual detail, it is hard to deduce the historical context. No event involving this coalition of ten is recorded elsewhere, and it is possible that the list of surrounding aggressors is, at least in part, a schematized formulation to represent encompassing danger. The reference to Assyria, however, points to the period of its expansive power in the eighth and seventh centuries. While it is possible that the psalm came from the Northern Kingdom to Jerusalem, an origin in Jerusalem might best accord with the localities of the foes.

1–8   The intercessor calls upon God not to remain inactive in the present danger (cf. Isa. 62.1, which may be a response to a prayer of this kind; for the 'silence' of God cf. Pss. 28.1; 35.22; 39.12). Verses 2–8 then lament the situation, stressing features that should spur divine intervention – these are foes of God himself, making covenant against him; it is against his people that they conspire, to blot out the very name of Israel. His 'treasured ones' are the people he specially owns and protects; some manuscripts and versions read 'your treasured one', which would denote Zion as in Ezek. 7.22. There is a rumble of rebellion against the Lord (v. 2) and much conferring (vv. 3, 5), a pattern like that of Psalm 2. A traditional scheme is reflected also in the list of ten surrounding nations which are said to form a league. On the east are Ammon and Moab ('children of Lot', Gen. 19.37f.) and, further south, Edom. Beyond these are the nomadic tribes of the Ishmaelites (Gen. 16.15; 21.18f.), Hagarenes or Hagrites (1 Chron. 5.10, 19f.; 27.30, perhaps like Ishmael claiming descent from Hagar) and Amalek (Ex. 17.8). Gebal may be another tribe of the area, there being a similar place-name near Petra; the ancient Phoenician port of this name, later known as Byblos, is probably too remote to be intended (though advocated by Dahood, and cf. Ezek. 27.8–9). A threat from the west and north is represented by the coastal towns of the Philistines and of Tyre. Assyria ('Ashur') as the 'arm' of Ammon and Moab is the source of their power (cf. Isa. 33.2; Jer. 17.5); when, as often the case, the Assyrian army was engaged elsewhere in the vast empire, vassal states could be used to discourage rebels. (Gunkel, thinking of the Persian period, preferred the identification of 'Ashur' with the Ashurite tribe of Gen. 25.3, 18; Num. 24.22, 24; 2 Sam. 2.9, but this would hardly be the 'arm', the main strength, of Ammon and Moab.)

9–18   The lament now gives way to vigorous prayer against the power of all these enemies. May God defeat them as once he did the ancient enemies of Canaan. The intercessor thus invokes that power of God which, as tradition related, had repulsed the nomadic hordes of Midian and brought down the

Canaanite leaders Sisera, Jabin, Oreb, Zeeb and Zalmunna (Judg. 4–8; cf. Isa. 9.4; 10.26). The prayer is intensified by use of images from nature: may God blow the foes headlong as wind drives the light chaff and thistle-balls (which have dried and broken off, and spin along the ground); may he blaze upon them as flame runs through the dry vegetation and forests on the mountain slopes; may he drive them away with his storm-wind. The aggressive coalition will thus perish in the shame of defeat (v. 17); but the peoples concerned may then 'seek the name' (become worshippers) of Yahweh, the Lord. They will acknowledge that he is the supreme, the only true God of all the earth. The intercessor thus knows that destruction itself is not a cause to move the Lord; but rather the prayer must take its greatest strength from this hope of God's own glory and his purpose for the world and all its peoples.

In a time when it seems that God is silent and inoperative, while enemies plan attack from every side, a singer leads the assembly at the temple in urgent and passionate prayer, the only true weapon of defence. It is put to God that this people and sanctuary are his treasured possession, dependent on his promised protection. Will he not save them as he did of old, when the early tribes were delivered from military might and fierce nomadic hordes? Prayer is strong that he should show his power again, active indeed as hurricane and forest fire. O that he would come with such force! Yet the intercessor knows that the appeal will do best to rest on the motive of God's glory and universal purpose. So for all the vehemence of the prayer against the agents of the gathering danger, there shines out a hope of presently hostile peoples turning to seek the Lord and acknowledge that he is the Most High over all the world. Users of the psalm, themselves familiar with the ordeal of God's silence, are led to call on that salvation which appeared so mightily in the past, to pray with passionate faith for new acts of God; but also to bring all their pleas into the one desire for his kingdom, for that time of return and restoration when all shall be at peace under his universal rule.

O God, when the mystery of your working seems to us as a silence of indifference, inspire us to pray all the more for the wonders of your salvation, and to desire that those who are in league against your treasured ones may be swept by the wind and fire of your Spirit, until they turn to seek you, and with us worship you as Lord of all.

PSALM 84: Travelling to God

For favour.   Over the Gittith.   Of the sons of Korah.   Psalm.

1   How lovely is your dwelling,
     almighty Lord of Hosts!
2   My soul longed and fainted for the courts of the Lord;
     my heart and my flesh cried out for the living God.
3   But now the bird has found her home, the swallow her nest,
     where she may lay her young near your altars,
          Lord of Hosts, my King and my God.
4   Happy those who dwell in your house,
     for they are ever praising you.   [Pause]
5   Happy those whose strength comes from you,
     for the ascent to your house is in their heart.
6   Passing through the driest valley,
          they make it a place of springs,
     and the autumn rain will cover it with blessings.
7   They will go from strength to strength,
     until they see the God of Gods in Zion.
8   Lord God of Hosts, hear my prayer;
     give heed, O God of Jacob.   [Pause]
9   Look with favour on our shield, O God;
     regard the face of your Anointed.
10   Better indeed a day in your courts,
     than any thousand I could choose.
     Better to touch but the threshold of the house of my God,
     than to abide in the tents of wickedness.
11   For the Lord is both sun and shield, giving grace and glory;
     the Lord will not withhold good from those who walk in truth.
12   O Lord of Hosts,
     happy the one who trusts in you.

Praise of God fills much of this psalm, though expressed indirectly through appreciation of his sanctuary on Zion and the communion which he grants there. But the main point may lie in vv. 8–9, an earnest supplication for the king, for which the praise would be preparatory and then supportive (along with the statement of trust, vv. 11–12). At all events, the thoughts of the psalm (including God as renewer of life and giver of rains) make it probable that it expressed praise and prayer at the outset of the festal celebrations in the autumn. A singer, representative of the great assembly, catches the spirit of pilgrims on their journey and their satisfaction on arrival, and so fittingly leads them all in a fundamental prayer for the king, the Lord's Anointed, the channel of God's blessings. (For the heading 'Gittith' see above on 8, and for 'Korah' on 42, which has much in common with this psalm.)

1–3 Praise is expressed in an exclamation of wonder (cf. 8.1, 9), which reflects the emotion of pilgrims who have come across the hilly country from their villages and towns and at last see the beauty of the holy city and temple. The depth of the love and joy is in the knowledge that here is the abode (Hebrew plural, for a place of many features) of Yahweh Sebaoth, the almighty Lord of Hosts, the 'living God'; it is the place where the Lord of heaven and of all creation receives his worshippers and bestows on them new life. On behalf of the pilgrims, the singer recalls that sense of longing and need far from the holy place and time, the weariness and thirst that cried out for the fountain of life (cf. 42.1–3; 69.1). But now the pilgrim soul has come with deep satisfaction to her true home; she is the swallow that nests happily in the peace of the sanctuary. (This metaphor reflects the ideal of not doing harm on the holy mountain, Isa. 11.9, and the widespread reverence for birds that nested around temples. Only one kind of bird is specified, the *deror*, 'swallow', since the first term, *sippor*, is a general term.)

4–7 The praise now takes the form of declaring the good fortune of those who enjoy the communion God grants in worship at his sanctuary. First are mentioned those who 'dwell' in the holy place (v. 4) – the sacred ministers, from the king, priests and musicians to the humble cleaners and porters. All these servants of the household of the Lord have constant opportunity to praise him in that blessed place of his name and presence. But there is a special happiness, an enviable good fortune, also given to the pilgrims. Appropriately for the occasion, this is dwelt on at some length. Already in the preparation and beginning of their journey (v. 5), when the *via sacra*, the final ascent up the holy hill, is still only a sincerely longed-for goal in heart and imagination, they begin to be touched by the Lord's grace, and receive from him strength to face the difficulties and persevere. Then they are pictured in mid-course. Some particular valley, noted for its dryness, represents the hot and dusty route before the long summer drought is broken. How dead everything seems! But the pilgrims keep hope, holding to the Lord's power to work the miracle of transformation. Where their faithful feet tread, there especially the Lord will send the blessing of water and the green of new life (v. 6). Sometimes, indeed, the first rains already begin, forming pools on the rock-hard earth; but in other years, they have still to be waited for. In any event, the power sent out from God helps the weary feet ever more and more; 'from strength to strength' the pilgims go, until they come to see God's glory in Zion.

8–9 Prayer for the king (v. 9) is introduced with special earnestness (v. 8; the 'Pause', perhaps involving obeisance and phrases of reverence and assent, adds to the solemnity of the prayer). Brief as this petition is, it may well be the heart of the psalm. The Lord's Anointed is king and 'shield', titles also of the

Lord (vv. 3, 11); the point is that he mediates the royal work and protection of God. Light and salvation are from God alone, and he has made his Anointed the channel of such blessing. The earnest desire of the pilgrims is that their Davidic ruler should remain in the favour of the Lord, and so pass on the blessing to all the society (cf. 72); the prayer is also in accord with the festival's great theme of God's kingship, with attention naturally given to the calling of his royal Servant (Int. 5b).

10–12 Words appreciating the grace of God in temple and life now resume the opening praises, but serve also to support the preceding prayer; God will surely hear those who so trust and rejoice in him! Though the pilgrim's stay in the holy place is all too short, it is valued above long residence elsewhere. The Lord is praised as the light of life and the royal defender, the giver of grace and glory – thus the source of all the blessings that will come upon and through his Anointed – and also as one who will not withhold 'good' from a people whole in loyalty. This 'good' (as Dahood often shows) may allude especially to rain and the health of a new year of growth (cf. 4.6a). The final thought (v. 12) is again a kind of praise, but implies a hope that the Lord of Hosts will hear the prayer of the one who now trusts – the king and each pilgrim at the festival.

The psalm's prayer for the Lord's Anointed is set in a context of praise, which is especially that of thankfulness for all God gives in the place and time of worship. The Creator, who is in every place and moment, has yet given an order of worship related to the seasons and having its yearly climax; and he has chosen a place where his presence may be especially revealed and a life-restoring communion granted to sincere and trusting worshippers. The psalm reflects the excitement of the annual gathering and the importance felt in another of God's dispensations, the office of his Anointed, through whom the light and protection of God's own rule are sent. The journey which the pilgrims have made is beautifully reflected. At the outset, when the road leading up to the holy place was still but a hope in their hearts, strength came to them from God. In mid-course, treading on the parched land, their faithful steps were preparing the blessings of water and new life. Arriving, their soul found its home with the contentment of the swallow that nests in the holy precincts.

The picturesque praise still speaks of the beauty and joy that are found in the appointed time and place where communion is given. The pilgrim's journey is still a parable of the way to God: the first aspiration, already nurtured by his grace; the long, hard way where the fruits of faithfulness will only be seen in his good time; the coming at last into his courts as to the true home, to be made new in the light of his face. The prayer of vv. 8–9 has been taken up by the church to offer Christ's work, asking that the Father will behold his Son in his people, and be gracious to them for his sake.

O Lord of Hosts, by your might may the hope of travelling to you be born in our heart; bless our steps through the dry places, that fruit may in time be gathered there for you; and may our soul at last take wing to your holy dwelling, where we shall see you face to face.

PSALM 85: The Kiss of Peace

For favour.   Of the sons of Korah.   Psalm.

1   Lord, you once showed favour to your land,
     and restored the life of Jacob.
2   You forgave the offence of your people,
     and covered all their sin.   *[Pause]*
3   You took away all your indignation,
     and turned back from the heat of your wrath.
4   Restore us again, O God of our salvation,
     and let your anger cease from us.
5   Will you for ever be angry with us,
     will you stretch out your wrath for evermore?
6   Will you not turn again and revive us,
     that your people may rejoice in you?
7   Show us your faithful love, O Lord,
     and give us your salvation.

8   I will hear what the Lord God speaks:
        truly he speaks peace,
     peace for his people, the folk of his covenant –
        only let them not turn back to folly.
9   Even now his salvation is near to those who fear him,
     that glory may dwell in our land.
10 Love and truth have met together;
     right and peace have kissed each other.
11 Truth springs up from the earth,
     and right looks down from heaven.
12 The Lord shall indeed give blessing,
     and our land shall give her produce.
13 Right goes on before him,
     and prepares the way for his steps.

An intercession for God to restore the life of his people (vv. 4–7) is grounded on past experience of his grace (vv. 1–3) and answered by a divine message of assurance (vv. 8–13, cf. Pss 12, 14, 60). The language of appeal for the great restoration and renewal, as well as the assurance of order and fertility in nature, may indicate a setting in the autumn festival, but a special time of intercession in a crisis of natural disaster is also a possibility. Some have felt that the opening of the psalm looks back on the restoration from the Exile, but the phrases probably have a more general reference, so that the psalm may be centuries older, when such highly poetic and visionary psalmody flourished. Though some imagine that a prophetic figure comes forward in vv. 8f., we can otherwise reckon that the one psalmist bears two roles – inspired intercessor, and also mediator of God's response. When the psalm was first uttered, the divine message, coming perhaps after a silence, will indeed have come as a relief, good news which was not a foregone conclusion. Such vivid inspirations were readily remembered, and in subsequent singing the total composition will have served to express the grace of God that was surely prepared for a penitent and trusting people – an interchange of prayer and assurance like that still set out in liturgies today. For the 'Korah' heading see above on 42.

1–3 The supplication opens with reference to former experience of the Lord's favour, transforming grace, atonement, forgiveness and removal of wrath; it is a former experience which is needed again (see v. 6). The expression in v. 1b gathers all such work of grace into one phrase: God 'turns the great turning' or 'restores with a great restoration' – he restores his people to wonderful life (see above on 14.7). There is no specific indication of the occasion of the renewal, which indeed characterized many times of grace.

4–7 Restoration as known in the past is prayed for now. The people have long lain under the shadow of affliction (v. 6), and earnestly seek that wonder of salvation and faithful love which will restore them again to true life (v. 7).

8 The singer here, in prophetic manner, introduces the Lord's response to the foregoing petition. After listening for the divine message (v. 8a, cf. above on 81.5c and cf. Hab. 2.1), he is able to sum it up as 'peace', *shalom*, comprising all the blessings of the covenant, including harmony, health and increase in field, flocks and family. A cautionary note is sounded in the last clause – to have such *shalom*, they must not return to folly, a foolish self-sufficiency, insensitive to the Lord's will. (The clause is different but also suitable in LXX: 'and to those who turn their heart to him'.)

9–14 The response of God is not quoted directly, but his good purpose is reported. The faithfulness and grace of his character and actions are seen by the visionary singer as angelic forms, cooperating and hurrying forward to dispense his blessings. These 'angels' are seen in pairs that work in harmony. 'Salvation' and 'glory', representing the saving power and presence of the Lord, are near; they will dwell in the land, a transforming power centred in the temple. 'Faithful love' (*ḥesed*) and 'truth', representing God's constant and enduring commitment, have come together in close embrace. 'Right' and 'peace', right order in creation and the consequent health and plenty, kiss in loving alliance. As in a vision, the singer sees 'truth' springing up in the green shoots from the happy earth, and 'right' leaning out from heaven to look down benevolently, as will be apparent in the good work of rain and sun. So the Lord will give 'good' (v. 12a), the blessing of rain especially, and the earth will respond with all her produce. The Lord himself is seen to advance, as sacred processions used to signify, touching the fields with living grace, entering his sanctuary to renew his good rule; and 'right', the angel of cosmic order and harmony, is the herald who prepares his way, the angel that signifies his good purpose.

Prayer is offered for a people suffering severe deprivation. It seems that conditions for harvests have been very adverse, and there has been a long period of impoverishment and starvation. The very life of the people has faded away. The intercessor asks for the great turning, the transforming and reviving touch of God to make the people truly live again; and the prayer draws strength from the recollection that in times gone by such miracles of restoration were known. Can it be that, dark as the scene is, the light is not far away? As the singer waits upon God, eager to hear what is his word, the conviction is given that the turn to good is near at hand. Angelic powers, reflecting God's heart, are already at work to heal and reconcile, to bless and make fruitful. The Saviour himself is hastening to his people, and they and the good earth will soon be bright with his glory.

The psalm reflects a sense of the connectedness of the spirit and the earth; the world of prayer and faith is also the world of nature. Love and faithfulness, right and goodness are ultimately the divine powers emanating from the Creator which make the order of life. The modern age has moved far from this ancient wisdom, but in our deepest reflections we begin to glimpse again that cosmic unity of spirit and earth, of right and health. It may be that in long afflictions we too, through prayer, may be shown that salvation is near, and we too may have vision of love and truth embracing, right and peace kissing each other, truth springing in the green of earth, and right leaning out of heaven in the fall of sweet rains. Then we shall know that life is the blessing of the Creator, and nothing else.

O God, who through your Word sent pardon and peace to restore your creation, cause your people to see afresh your love and be revived by your salvation; and so may we rejoice in the knowledge that you are redeeming all things in your faithfulness.

PSALM 86: A Prayer for a Sign

Prayer.   Of David.

1   Turn your ear, Lord, answer me,
    for I am poor and needy.
2   Guard my soul, for I am steadfast;
    you who are my God, save your servant who trusts in you.
3   Be gracious to me, O Lord,
    for all day long I call to you.
4   Gladden the soul of your servant,
    for to you, Lord, I lift up my soul.
5   For you, Lord, are good and forgiving,
    abounding in faithful love to all who call out to you.
6   O Lord, hear my prayer,
    and listen to the voice of my entreaties.
7   In the day of my distress I call to you,
    for you will answer me.
8   There is none like you among the gods, O Lord,
    nor any deeds like yours.
9   All nations you have made shall come
       and worship before you, Lord,
    and shall glorify your name.
10 For you are great and do wonderful things;
    yes, you alone are God.
11 Teach me, Lord, your way, that I may walk in your truth;
    compose my heart to fear your name.
12 I will thank you with all my heart, O Lord my God,
    and will glorify your name for ever,
13 that your love is great upon me,
    and that you have delivered my soul from the lowest pit.
14 O God, the arrogant have risen against me;
    the horde of the terrible seek my soul,
       and have not set you before their eyes.
15 But you, Lord, are God the compassionate and gracious,
    long-suffering, and abounding in faithful love and truth.
16 O turn to me and be gracious to me;
    give your strength to your servant,
    and save the son of your handmaid.
17 Make for me a sign of favour,
       that my adversaries may see and be ashamed,
    because you, Lord, have helped and comforted me.

This is the only psalm in Book Three to have the heading 'Of David', and its expressions have particular affinity with 25–8 and 54–7. While parallels can be found for many of its statements, it has an eloquence of its own and several unique features and phrases (e.g. the adjective 'forgiving' applied to God, v. 5, and the prayer 'unite my heart', v. 11). Its structure also is not without artistry, and a concentric order can be traced, pivoting around vv. 10 and 11 (cf. Tate). In 'a day of distress' the singer appeals to the Lord for help (vv. 1–7), supports his prayer with praise and promise of thanksgiving (vv. 8–13), and then returns to supplication, supported by lament and further praise (14–17). The psalm is expressed by an individual voice, but there are several indications that this 'Of David' composition may be the prayer of the leader; as in related psalms, it may be right to think of a king, in view of the strong expressions of covenant bond, the enemies as a horde of terrible assailants, the scale of the future hope (a fulfilment of God's kingship), and the request for a sign or omen. The 'day of distress' may then relate to a day of penance and intercession in face of some military threat.

1–7 On this 'day of distress', prayer and entreaty are raised 'all the day long', that the Lord should favourably hear, respond with pity and grace, and so gladden the supplicant with salvation. The petition is supported by various considerations: humility that acknowledges poverty and helplessness (cf. 35.10; 40.17; 69.29; 140.12); the bond that God himself has made, so that the psalmist is his 'servant' (vv. 2b, 4a, 16) and steadfast covenant-partner (*hasid* v. 2a, and hence also the frequent phrases of relationship, with *adonay*, 'Lord', occurring in the psalm seven times and *atta*, 'you', six times); the trust (v. 2b) and the traditional confession of the Lord's faithfulness and readiness to forgive (v. 5, cf. 130.4; Ex. 34.6f.).

8–10 The petition is also supported by praise of the Lord as the only true God, able to do mighty deeds of salvation (cf. 35.10; 40.5; 71.19). He is creator of all nations and to be worshipped by them all (cf. 22.27f.; 47.8f.; 66.4; 68.32f.). The 'gods' are the subordinate heavenly beings that serve and worship him (cf. 29.1; 82). The scale and spaciousness of this praising witness are typical of royal prayers (e.g. 18.31; 89.6) and seem to say, 'How could this one who so testifies be left unanswered?'

11–13 Further support for the prayer now takes the form of an expression of willingness to obey and fear the Lord, and of readiness to give thanks in the hoped-for time of deliverance. The psalmist would be guided in the Lord's way, to live in a loyal bond with him (cf. 27.11; 26.3); may God unite or knit together his heart, so that with an undivided heart he may constantly attend to God's will (cf. Deut. 6.4; Jer. 32.39; with weaker parallelism LXX and Syriac have in v. 11b 'may my heart rejoice', a difference of vowels, producing the root *hdh*). Verses 12–13 can be read as general praise, supporting the prayer, like vv. 8–10 and the strand of praise in Psalms 9–10. But it may be better to find here a vow of thanksgiving, anticipating the theme that the Lord will have shown his love and brought him from the deep hold of death (i.e. a most deadly peril).

14–17 The nature of the distress is indicated briefly in v. 14: a company of fearsome enemies has risen against the psalmist, looking to take his life, and in his appeal he stresses that they are 'arrogant' – ambitious and self-willed, disregarding God. The depiction is similar to that of 54.3 and may indicate a military threat. Appeal is made to the promised love of the Lord in a traditional testimony to his faithfulness and pity (v. 15, cf. Ex. 34.6). The covenant bond also underlies v. 16, which may best be related to the king as the Lord's adopted son (2.7; 89.26) and royal servant. The phrase 'son of your handmaid' (also 116.16) may arise from the idea of a servant born in the household (Gen. 14.14) and so all the more at home in it. In v. 17 the 'sign' (*ot*) which the Lord is asked to make or do is taken by some to be an omen or oracle to signify God's favour (so Johnson, comparing 74.9 and the change of tone in 28.6f.), and by others to be a striking act of deliverance (so Dahood, cf. 78.43; 105.27; 135.9). At all events, the context indicates a divine action which will signal God's support of the psalmist so clearly that the foes may be abashed (cf. above on 23.5).

Facing a horde of terrible foes, the psalmist lifts up his soul to God and continues long in prayer. His plea is grounded in the relationship which binds him to the Lord, a bond where he, the servant, is in himself poor and needy, but his faithful and compassionate Lord is the sole God, able to do marvels. It is a further strength to his prayer that he seeks to be guided in the Lord's way and to have his heart made single in devotion and alertness to God; also that he is ready to give thanks and testimony. The psalm still speaks for those exposed to horrible enmity. It leads them to rest in the recollection of the sovereign Adonay, the Lord, who guards those bound in his love, and is able to deliver them from the lowest pit. It prompts them with many cries of prayer, most notably that the Lord should make the heart single in devotion, with all the faculties united.

Compose our hearts, good Lord, to fear you alone, and guard us with the sign of your cross; that we may fear no foes, nor the deepest darkness, but may ever walk gladly in your way, giving thanks for your forgiveness and the abundance of your faithful love.

PSALM 87: The Rebirth of the Nations in Love

Of the sons of Korah.   Psalm.   Song.

1   On the holy mountains is the city he founded;
2   the Lord loves the gates of Zion
        above all the dwellings of Jacob.
3   Weighty things are spoken
        for you, O city of God: *[Pause]*
4   I enrol Egypt and Babylon as those who know me;
        Philistia and Tyre with Ethiopia, each as born there.
5   Yes, of Zion it shall be said, Each one was born in her,
        whom the Most High has established.
6   The Lord shall record, as he writes up the peoples,
        each one as born there.   *[Pause]*
7   And as they dance they shall sing,
        All my fresh springs are in you.

This song in praise of Zion may be grouped with 46, 48, 76, 84, and 122; it presents Zion as the Lord's dwelling, destined to be the mother-city of all peoples. In its present position it takes up the thought of 86.9. It may have originated in the part of the autumn festival when thought centred on the temple as purified and reconsecrated, glorious with the new advent and epiphany of God. An introduction declares the Lord's love for Zion (vv. 1–2) and announces a momentous oracle (v. 3). God's pronouncement follows in direct speech (v. 4), and is then developed by the prophetic singer (vv. 5–7). The weighty and visionary content of this psalm is expressed abruptly, especially in vv. 1 and 7. Perhaps this abruptness is connected with its prophetic character, shafts of meaning emerging from mysterious depths. At all events, it is wiser to accept the text as it is, jagged and forceful, than with many scholars to reconstruct it as a text we might have expected. The ancient versions confirm its general form, though they have difficulty with some phrases. The theme of Zion's universal significance is very ancient, but the particular selection of nations mentioned has been taken to indicate some date from the later monarchy onwards, Assyria being eclipsed; but if the 'dwellings of Jacob' (v. 4) are sanctuaries, an earlier date is required, and one may think of an optimistic period before the incursions of Assyria.

1–3 It is a transfigured city that is described, Zion according to her meaning in God's purpose. That he himself founded her, and on the mountains that reach into heaven and bear the very traffic of heaven – all this is to say that she is one with the heavenly sanctuary. She is the place on earth where heaven is disclosed and the Lord of all makes himself known (cf. above on 48.2). The founding is itself full of meaning: here is a bulwark for life and goodness against the vengeful tides of chaos (cf. above on 8.2). For Zion, that also personifies all his worshippers, the Lord has the utmost love and devotion (cf. 78.68; 132.13, 14); her very gates are dearer to him that all other 'dwellings' (or perhaps 'shrines') of his people 'Jacob', beautiful as they are (Num. 24.5). And now for this Zion, so meaningful in the Lord's loving purpose, an oracle is to be pronounced, a word and vision from the Lord, glorious, heavy with rich significance for her destiny. The prophetic singer addresses her directly as 'city of God' or 'divine city'.

4–7   The inspired message begins with God's own words (v. 4) and continues as the singer's exposition, giving the fuller picture of the visionary scene (cf. 75.4–8). The Lord is seen recording the names of those who know him, and it is whole peoples that he is inscribing in this book of life (cf. 69.28; Isa. 4.3). He writes them down, moreover, as having been born in Zion (cf. Ezek. 13.9). But it is, we might say, a new birth, a wonderful transformation, for these had worshipped other gods and were sometimes enemies of Israel. In particular, Egypt here is denoted as 'Rahab', the name of the hostile chaos-monster (89.10; Isa. 30.7; 51.9); but this oppressor of the Exodus is now forgiven. God 'Most High', the Creator and supreme ruler of all, has established his city as embracing a fellowship of all peoples (cf. 47.9; 82.8; 86.9; Isa. 19.23–25; Zech. 2.10–11). And the singer concludes by picturing them united in festal worship, dancing with joy in the Lord and singing of the fountains of life, the spring of living grace, that they have found in Zion ('you', a feminine form; cf. 36.9; 46.4; Isa. 12.3; Ezek. 47).

The psalm shows how the worshippers at the temple in Jerusalem might see through to an immense meaning; because they encountered there the Lord, the Most High, maker of all peoples, they saw in Zion a summit carrying them into heaven. Around this throne of the Creator all peoples must gather; his pleasure must be in the songs and dances of all. With a visionary leap beyond all historical divisions and enmities, the psalmist sees the Lord enrolling all the peoples as natives of Zion. How this could come about is not explained; only that it has been 'spoken', created beforehand by the divine word.

The little poem lived on when Jerusalem was cruelly destroyed, and is still sung in a world where murderous deeds between ethnic groups are common. Seeing beyond such hatreds, it prefigures a spiritual city where all nations will be born again as fellow citizens, a temple where they will meet with God in his love, a heavenly garden where together they will drink of the fountain of life. The New Testament teaches that something of this wonder is already to be experienced – the citizenship that is in heaven (Phil. 3.20), belonging to a Jerusalem that is above, the mother of many children (Gal. 4.26).

O Lord, the Most High, in love you have founded a place where heaven and earth meet, and by your Word you have prepared a new birth for all nations that they may belong to that place; we beseech you to strengthen us in this vision, prepare our spirits in forgiveness and reconciliation, and so bring to pass the time when all shall rejoice together at the wells of your salvation.

PSALM 88: A Plea from the Land without Memory

Song. Psalm. Of the sons of Korah. For favour. With music of flutes for grieving. Poem. Of Heman the native.

1   Lord, God of my salvation,
       I cry day and night towards you.
2   May my prayer come into your presence;
       turn your ear towards my crying.
3   For my soul is full of torments,
       and my life has come to the land of death.
4   I am counted with those gone down into the pit;
       I am like one whose strength has departed.
5   My couch is among the dead,
         with the slain that dwell in the tomb,
       whom you remember no more,
         and they are cut off from the help of your hand.
6   You have set me in the lowest pit,
       in a place of darkness in the mighty deeps.
7   Your anger lies heavy upon me,
       and you have afflicted me with all your waves. *[Pause]*
8   You have put my friends far from me,
       and made me to be abhorred by them.
       I am imprisoned and cannot go free;
9   my eyes fail through all my trouble.
       Lord, I call to you daily;
       I stretch out my hands to you.
10   Will you do marvels for the dead,
       will the shades rise up to praise you?
11   Shall your love be told in the tomb,
       your faithfulness in the land of the lost?
12   Will your wonders be known in the darkness,
       your goodness in the land without memory?
13   But as for me, Lord, I cry to you;
       even in the dawn my prayer comes early before you.
14   Why, Lord, do you spurn my soul;
       why do you hide your face from me?
15   I am brought low and my strength ebbs away;
       I bear your terrors and am almost gone.

16 Your wrath sweeps over me;
    your horrors bring me to destruction.
17 All day long they come about me like water;
    they close me in on every side.
18 Lover and friend you have put far from me;
    my best companion is now the darkness.

In this supplication the appeal for a hearing (vv. 1–2) is followed by lamenting description of suffering 'in the lowest pit' (vv. 3–9a). The appeal then takes the form of rhetorical questions, as often in such supplications (vv. 9b–14), and the psalm concludes with a further description of the suffering – ebbing strength, horrors, loneliness, darkness. The lack of hopeful statements usual in prayers of distress (assertions of trust, promises of thanksgiving) gives the psalm an especially tragic character, and there is not even the variety of any reference to guilt, innocence, or enemies. Much of the imagery for suffering comes from ancient poetic tradition depicting Sheol, the universal tomb or home of the dead, imagined as a place of darkness, silence and utter weakness beneath the subterranean waters. Similar poetic elements are found in some more ancient Mesopotamian laments and in Job (e.g. Job 3.17f.; 10.21f.; 14.10f.; 17.11f.). A date in the early monarchy is possible, and the psalm may be the expression of prayer in severe sickness. It was taken by the Targum as a prayer of Israel in the Exile. Some have argued indeed that it was always meant to speak for the nation, while a few have sought a symbolic usage in national rites of abasement. The title makes a connection not only with the sons of Korah (see above on 42), but also with Heman, a psalmist-sage apparently from the pre-Israelite population of Jerusalem (cf. 1 Kings 4.31; 1 Chron. 15.17f.; 25.5). 'Music of flutes' (so also the title of 53) was sometimes a feature of lamentations (Jer. 48.36; Matt. 7.23).

1–2   The opening plea for a hearing is especially significant in the context of this sombre psalm. The first word is 'Yahweh', the name God gave specifically for 'invocation', for calling down the saviour into the encircling darkness (Ex. 3.15, *zikri*). The name of God so used encapsulates an immense tradition of faith and experience, and at once sets the suffering and the cry to heaven in the context of a relationship, a mutual knowledge which should prove stronger than all affliction. The next phrase fills out the name itself: 'O God of my salvation', that is, 'God my saviour'; again the bond, the commitment of goodwill, the experience of grace. The prayer to this saviour rises night and day, a cry and a supplication which strives to rise from the depths to reach his holy throne. This is the nature of all that will follow. Utterly tragic as it seems, it is all directed to him who alone can save. Underlying all is a hidden but massive foundation of faith and hope.

3–9a   The plight of the sufferer is now depicted to move the divine compassion. The soul is sated with harms or injuries, and the sufferer can therefore be depicted as having already made the descent into Sheol, the land of the dead. He is like one of the shades, finally at rest in this universal tomb. An ancient instinct was that Sheol was an 'unclean' place, the antithesis of the living realm of the Lord, and so cut off from him, a place then without the communion of praise. The idea is not consistently maintained; in some texts we hear of the Lord's power to break into that farthest region. Nevertheless, our psalmist's thought is how near he is to being finally lost. He feels to be in the remotest part of Sheol, or again, to be battered by the deadly waves in the jaws of Sheol. It is through the Lord's action, he says, because of the divine anger, that friends keep far off, avoiding the contagion of misfortune. The sufferer feels shut in by walls of misfortune and unable to find a way out.

9b–12 The prayer takes a fresh beginning, invoking again the saviour by name. Pleading questions, as often in lamenting psalms, give poignancy to the appeal. The rhetorical questions assume a negative answer; once finally consigned to Sheol, the dead see no wonders of salvation and have no occasion or cult in which to raise thanksgiving and testimony, for all there – such was the ancient belief – lay in the silence of oblivion. The questions take the place of the promise, common in other supplications, to give thanks and praise when deliverance comes. We might say that such a promise is implicit. But to match the extremity of the situation, the psalmist confines himself to showing the terrible danger that he may soon be beyond the possibility of salvation and consequent praise.

13–18 The prayer takes its third beginning, again depicting the perseverance of the pleading and the eagerness of a plea that is already at heaven's gates as dawn appears. In this section the question and laments express the belief that it is with the Lord alone that the sufferer wrestles, for it is his will and action that cause the affliction. Implicit is the vital thought that it is therefore God who can change the situation. But the one he cherished he appears now to reject, hiding his face of love. Emissaries of his wrath hem the sufferer in. God has caused all friends to flee away, and the one that can be relied on to stay is the deadly shadow of Sheol.

The psalm gives a voice to all who are in the depths of suffering, without light, unable to express hope, almost at the end of their strength. It leads them to direct their supplication – or it directs it for them – again and again to the Lord, the only saviour. It is a voice also for those who, in loving sympathy, would pray on behalf of any in such extremity of suffering. But further, the poetical nature of the psalm, filled with metaphor, has long encouraged imaginative applications; it became the voice of a whole people in captivity, and then again the ever-renewed prayer of the royal one who suffers in the darkness for the healing of the many. In these many meanings, its plaintive tones, joined with the flutes that express the sorrows that surpass words, have often risen from the great deeps of suffering and pleaded early at the gates of heaven. Such prayer that invokes the holy name of the saviour, so the psalmist believed, does not rise up in vain.

Lord, God of our salvation, hear the cry of those who are full of torments and imprisoned by terrors; have pity on those who have fallen into the land without memory and are cut off from lovers and friends; and by the passion of your Son Jesus, in the mystery of your eternal purpose, raise them up into the light of your face where all is made well.

PSALM 89: Witness and Prayer When All Seems Lost

Poem.   Of Ethan the native.

1   I will sing always of the loving deeds of the Lord;
    with my mouth I will make known your faithfulness
        throughout all generations.
2   I declare that your love is built firmly for ever,
    and your faithfulness you have established like the heavens.
3   For you said: I make a covenant with my chosen one;
    I make a pledge to my servant David.
4   I will establish your seed for ever;
    for all generations I will build your throne.   *[Pause]*
5   O Lord, the very heavens praise your wonders,
    and in the assembly of the holy ones
        they praise your faithfulness.
6   For who among the clouds can be compared to the Lord?
    Who is like the Lord in all the host of heaven,
7   a God fearsome in the council of the holy ones,
    great and terrible above all that are round about?
8   O Lord, God of Hosts, who is like you,
    so strong, Lord, with your faithfulness all about you?
9   You alone rule the raging of the sea;
    you still its waves when they rise up.
10 It was you that smote the chaos-storm with piercing blow,
    and scattered your enemies with your mighty arm.
11 So to you belong the heavens, and also the earth,
    for you alone secured the world and all that fills it.
12 You created the mountains of north and south;
    Tabor and Hermon rejoice in your name.
13 Yours is an arm of might;
    glorious is your hand, supreme is your right hand.
14 Right and justice are the foundation of your throne;
    faithful love and truth go before your face.
15 Happy the people who know the praises of your glory,

and walk, O Lord, in the light of your face.
16   With your name they rejoice all the day long,
and are exalted in your goodness.
17   From your beauty alone they have strength,
and by your grace you lift up our horn.
18   Truly the Lord is our shield;
our King is the Holy One of Israel.

19   Of old you spoke in a vision,
and affirmed to your faithful one:

I have set a youth above the warrior;
I have raised a young man over the people.
20   I have found David my servant;
with my holy oil I have anointed him.
21   My hand shall hold him fast,
and my arm shall strengthen him.
22   An enemy shall not deceive him,
nor an evil man overcome him.
23   His adversaries I will strike before him,
and beat down his bitter foes.
24   My faithfulness and love shall be with him,
and through my name shall his horn be exalted.
25   And I will set his hand upon the sea,
yes, his right hand upon the rivers.
26   He shall cry to me, You are my father,
my God, and the rock of my salvation.
27   And I will make him my first-born,
most high above the kings of the earth.
28   The love I have pledged him I will keep for ever,
and my covenant shall stand fast with him.
29   I will also make his seed endure for ever,
and his throne as the days of heaven.
30   If his children forsake my law,
and cease to walk in my judgements,
31   if they despise my statutes,
and do not keep my commandments,
32   I will punish their offences with a rod,
and their wickedness with blows;
33   but I will not take from him my promised love,
nor betray my faithfulness.
34   I will not defile my covenant,
nor alter what has gone out from my lips.
35   By my holiness I have sworn once for all,
that I will not prove false to David.
36   His seed shall endure for ever,

and his throne as the sun before me.
37 As the moon he shall be established for ever,
an enduring witness in the clouds.

38 Yet now you have spurned and rejected your Anointed;
your anger has risen against him.
39 You have despised the covenant of your servant;
you have defiled his crown in the dust.
40 You have broken down all his walls,
and laid his strongholds in ruin.
41 All who pass by despoil him;
he has become the scorn of his neighbours.
42 You have lifted up the right hand of his foes,
and made all his enemies rejoice.
43 You have turned back the edge of his sword,
and have not upheld him in battle.
44 You have put an end to his lustre,
and hurled his throne down to the dust.
45 You have cut short the days of his youth;
you have covered him over with shame.   *[Pause]*
46 How long, Lord, will you hide yourself so utterly,
how long will your anger burn like fire?
47 O remember how short my time is,
how frail you have made all the children of earth.
48 Which of the living shall not see death,
and save their soul from the hand of darkness?
49 Where, Lord, are your loving deeds of old,
which you pledged to David by your faithfulness?
50 Remember, Lord, how your servant is mocked,
and how I carry in my bosom all the many peoples,
51 while your enemies mock, O Lord,
while they mock the footsteps of your Anointed.
52 Blessed be the Lord for ever,
amen and amen.

The climax comes at last in vv. 38–51, where a king of David's house (note vv. 49–51) appeals to the Lord from a situation of defeat and humiliation. The preparation for this appeal unfolds in full and measured style, praising God for faithfulness in his covenant with David, in the exercise of his supreme power as Creator, and as saviour of his worshippers. The exposition of the covenant with David (vv. 19–37) is especially full, and resembles the narrative prose version of the tradition, Nathan's oracle for David in 2 Samuel 7. The effect of the preparation is to achieve the maximum contrast between God's promises and the present situation. The king who witnesses to the Lord's fidelity and universal power is now apparently spurned by him and thrown down from glory into the dust.

Although such sharp contradictions are commonly used in intercessions, the measured fullness of the foil to the lament in this psalm is exceptional. The three main themes in this preparation – the covenant with David, the supremacy of the Lord in creation, and the blessedness of his festal worshippers – point to a connection with the great autumn festival. So much is easily agreed. But the explanation of the king's humiliation is not so obvious. Various defeats in history have been proposed, but without really matching the text, which tells of utter humiliation (with some phrases that seem to echo Mesopotamian mythological texts of Tammuz in the underworld) but gives no historical information. A few have therefore taken the humiliation to be symbolic, part of dramatic ceremonies that showed the calling of the king as the Lord's Anointed (Int. 5b, and cf. above on 18, 101, 118, 144). The 'Ethan' of the title, like Heman (see above on 88), will be another leader of psalmody from the older population of Jerusalem. The positioning of the psalm at the end of Book Three may have had special significance for the arrangers; a messianic hope having been indicated by the placing of 2 at the head of Book One and 72 at the end of Book Two, that hope becomes at the end of Book Three a matter of urgent intercession. One may note also how terms in 88 for God's pledged love, faithfulness, justice and wonders, are matched in 89.

1–4 To judge from the conclusion (vv. 47, 50), the voice is that of the king. Not only does he begin with the theme of the Lord's pledges to the dynasty of David (cf. 132.11; 2 Sam. 7.8–16; 1 Chron. 7.17f.; Jer. 33.17–21), but he also witnesses in hymnic style to the Lord's fidelity to this covenant. Thereby he fulfils before all the world the Davidic duty of testifying through the generations to the only God, supreme and faithful (see above on 18.46.f.; 40.9–10); would the Lord forsake such a witness? We hear of the 'covenant' (*berit*) the Lord made with David his 'chosen one', binding himself to establish the dynasty for ever; and repeatedly the words for commitment and constancy ring out – *ḥesed* and *emuna*, 'faithful love' and 'faithfulness', and the plural form of *ḥesed*, 'faithful deeds' or perhaps 'promises' (cf. Isa. 55.3), words that will be echoed throughout the psalm (vv. 5, 8, 14, 24, 28, 33, 49).

5–18 The kingship of David and his descendants is seen in essence as a channelling of the true kingship, that of God. In the autumn festival the theme of the kingdom was principally the proclamation of the Lord's own sovereignty, supreme over the natural world and the nations alike; subordinate to this, though still of vital significance, was the exposition of the role of the Davidic king. The psalm continues accordingly with the praise of the Lord as mighty and faithful Creator. With echoes of ancient mythology, Yahweh is envisaged in the assembly of the 'gods', the divine beings seen as a council, but still, only servants of the one heavenly King (cf. 82.1f.). The hymn stresses his unique godhead (cf. 18.31; 71.19; 86.8; 1 Sam. 2.2), which was manifest in his mighty deeds at creation. The crucial act of creation is pictured in the old poetic style as victory in a combat with 'Rahab', a monster personifying the wild and stormy chaos-waters (cf. 29.3f.; 74.12f.; 87.4 where Egypt is called 'Rahab'; 93.3f.). These had been pierced through and divided into waters above and below the earth, made to serve the purpose of life. So followed the ordering of the heavens and earth and all living things, and the firm establishment of the great mountains, the pillars of the cosmos. In v. 12a the names of two great mountains may be alluded to; in v. 12b, Hermon is by far the greatest mountain seen by Palestinians, but Tabor is also impressive as it rises steeply from the plain. Incomparable in power, this heavenly King is also praised as utterly just and faithful (vv. 8, 14). How great the bliss of those who are his worshippers, familiar with the festal acclamations (*teru'a* v. 15, cf. above on 47.5) and the light of his revealed presence in Zion, the people that have the Lord as shield and king!

19–37 The force of the preparation for the lament now intensifies as the Lord's promise to David is spelt out. The opening word (*az*), 'then', sometimes has a nuance of reference to a foundational time, when God gave shape to the present order. The 'vision' was an inspired message sent for his covenant-partner David ('faithful one', *hasid*); another reading gives 'faithful ones', the people or the dynasty). The oracle begins by recalling the rise of David, when he replaced the warrior king Saul. This was the work of the Lord, who himself (in effect through a prophet) poured upon him his holy oil, making him sacred, in bond with the holy God. Along with this went promise of protection and victory, the king being attended by the angels of God's faithfulness and love and the name of God like a warrior-presence (cf. 20). His 'horn' would thus be exalted and his supremacy on earth would correspond with that of the Lord in heaven, 'most high', with world dominion (vv. 25, 27b). Many kings might claim to represent divine rule, but of all these 'sons', David would be 'first-born' and senior. Essential to his power would be his 'prayer-privilege', the invitation from the Lord to call to him in all needs, the cry of son to father. In v. 26b we see the force of such expressions as 'my God', 'rock of my salvation' – expressions of the closest relationship. Particular stress is laid on the everlasting nature of God's promise. Through the line of descendants, David's 'seed', the 'throne' or reign of the dynasty will continue for ever. Punishment there will be for kings who do not keep their side of the obligation, the Lord's commandments. But the fundamental promise will not be cancelled; the Lord's *hesed* will remain, enduring love in accordance with his most solemnly sworn promise to David. In v. 37b the 'enduring witness in the clouds' has been understood as the moon or the rainbow, but perhaps it refers to the Davidic throne (see above on 45.6 and 87.1) and to the calling of the king to be God's witness (see above on v. 1).

38–45 In sharpest contrast to all that has been said of the Lord's irrevocable promise and faithfulness, the psalmist now laments to the Lord that he has spurned and in overflowing anger rejected his Anointed, despising his covenant and defiling his crown in the dust (lit. 'earth' here and in v. 44, but almost as an allusion to the place of death). He has broken down his walls and places of defence, so that he is pillaged and abused. The Lord has made him fail in battle, taking away the lustre or splendour which should have routed his foes, casting his throne, his kingly power, into the dust. The Lord has cut short his days of health and strength and covered him with a garment of shame; truly he is in the shadow of death.

46–51 The appeal comes to its climax with lamenting questions and calls for the Lord to 'remember' – to return to his love of old. The plea of human frailty (similar to that of the king in 144.3–4; cf. 39.6, 11; 90.3–10) points to the transience of human life; so little time on earth – must it be wasted in suffering? Where now those promises to David? Here is the anointed Servant of the Lord, appointed as shepherd for all the many peoples, to carry them as lambs in his bosom – here he is derided by those who hate God, and mocked at every step.

52 The arrangers of the psalms have here concluded their Book Three (73–89) with a formula of praise (cf. above on 72.18–19). It stands here as a brave expression of faith that, despite all that shows the contrary, the Lord is true, and in his mystery will prove true to David.

Whatever the origin of the psalm, whether in the sharp experience of military disaster or in a rite that interpreted age-long experience with prophetic insight, it came nevertheless to express the perplexity felt for centuries after the Davidic crown and throne had been thrown in the dust, and to lament the 'slowness of the steps' of the hoped-for Messiah. With the church's use of the psalm on Christmas Day, the whole context of worship proclaims that the faithfulness of God is vindicated in the mystery of the incarnation (cf. Luke 1.32f.; Acts 2.27f.; 13.22f.); nevertheless, the psalm can also be heard to warn of the suffering that will be known in the new era, the sword that ever pierces the Mother's soul. Still God's little ones are exposed to the ravagers and despisers, and still it is in a world of anguish that worshippers hold on to praise and blessing of the Lord for his goodness and wonders; still it is through darkness that those who know the festal praises walk by the light of his face, draw strength from his beauty, and rejoice in the name that brings his presence. Still the claim of their supplications is based on the *ḥesed* and *emuna*, the steadfast love and faithfulness, of his Word. Gathered into the bosom of the anointed Son, the first-born, they too can say 'my Father' and find answer in the rock of the divine salvation.

O God, creator and ruler of heaven and earth, by the coming of your Son Jesus you kept faith with your creatures and made out of his sufferings the rock of our salvation; help us in all our afflictions to hold on to the praise and blessing of your holy name, that we also may be guided and gladdened by the light of your face through all the shadows of this world, until with him we come to your eternal glory.

PSALM 90: Harvesting a Heart of Wisdom

Prayer.   Of Moses, the man of God.

1   Lord, you have been our refuge
    from one generation to another.
2   Before the mountains were born,
        or earth and world brought forth,
    from everlasting and for ever you are God.
3   You turn man back to dust
    and say, Return, O children of earth.
4   A thousand years in your eyes are but as yesterday;
    they pass like a watch of the night.
5   You carry them away, as though but a dream.
    In the morning they grow up like the grass,
6   early they blossom and flourish;
    by evening they droop and wither away.
7   Truly, we are consumed by your anger,
    and troubled by your wrath.
8   You have set our misdeeds before you,
    our secret faults in the light of your face.
9   All our days decline in your wrath;
    we spend our days like a sigh.
10 The days of our years may reach seventy years,
    or eighty if strength is great.
    Yet their span is but toil and trouble;
    quickly it passes, and we fly away.
11 Who knows the power of your anger,
    and your wrath, as you should be feared?
12 So teach us to number our days,
    that we may harvest a heart of wisdom.
13 Turn again, Lord; O how long?
    Have pity on your servants.
14 Satisfy us in the morning with your faithful love,
    that we may sing and rejoice through all our days.
15 Gladden us for all the days you have afflicted us,
    and for the years we have seen adversity.
16 Let your work be revealed to your servants,
    and your glory be over their children.
17 May the beauty of the Lord our God be upon us;
    and prosper the work of our hands for us,
        O prosper the work of our hands.

Headed as a 'prayer' (so also 17, 86, 102, 142; 72.20; Hab. 3.1), this is a supplication of the community in some long affliction. The main section of direct petition (vv. 13–17) is preceded by a preparatory statement of grounds for a hearing (vv. 1–6) and a lament (vv. 7–12). The affliction is understood to be due to the wrath of God in view of sin, but it is not specified. It seems to be a long period of economic hardship when the labour of the hands goes to waste (cf. v. 17). The hope for help 'in the morning' (v. 14) is possibly an indication that the worshippers are keeping a night vigil and looking for an answer at the break of day. Book Four of the Psalter begins here, but there is still a link with the preceding psalm in the theme of frail mortality (cf. 89.46f.). The naming of Moses in the title may have arisen from some linguistic resemblances to Deuteronomy or from the strength of an intercession that calls on God to 'turn' (v. 13). Many think of a post-exilic date for the completed psalm, though often allowing for older elements.

1–6 The psalm first calls on 'Adonay', the sovereign of all. And the first thought is then of the help with which he has sustained his people in time past. Shall it not be so again? In vv. 2–6 the consideration put before God is the brevity of human life – how fleeting against the eternity of God! An ancient conception of creation is reflected in v. 2 – earth as giving birth to mountains and living things (cf. Gen. 1.11–12; 2.4; Job 38.8, 28f.; in our Hebrew 'brought forth / travailed with' is active, the subject being either 'the earth and world' or, with RV but less likely, God; but some alter a vowel, as *BHS*, to obtain with LXX a passive, 'were brought forth'). Made from the earth, humans return to it as fine dust (cf. Gen. 3.19), such is God's ordinance (v. 3b). What slight duration this must seem to the Lord for whom a thousand years are but a flicker! People are transient as Palestine's green things – fresh in the cool of the morning, but finished by a day of burning wind or sun. Should such a brief life be spent in suffering? So the psalmist would stir the pity of God.

7–12 The present distress of the worshippers is now laid before God. It seems to be a protracted period of hardship; they interpret it as sent by God in anger at their sins, which he is not covering or forgiving, but keeping exposed to his judgement. So the days pass away without apparent fruit or value, like a mere breath (v. 9b 'sigh / moan'; BCP 'we bring our years to an end, as it were a tale that is told' is a wonderful translation, but not quite suiting this verse's reference to the particular situation). At v. 10 the thought turns again to the general human lot, its transience being a consideration to move God's compassion (cf. vv. 3–6). The average lifespan was probably scarcely half the seventy or eighty years mentioned; even the few people granted such fullness of days found them fleeting and hard. (In v. 10 'span', *roḥbam*, is a reading with support in the ancient versions; our Hebrew, with a similar word, gives 'pride'.) Who can fear God with the fear due to him? This grave thought of v. 11 prompts a prayer in v. 12 that God will teach his people so to realize their transience that they may 'bring in' (as harvest) a heart of wisdom (cf. the sober reverence, not without joy, taught by Ecclesiastes.).

13–17   The main prayer now unfolds in the form of several petitions. May the Lord return to his loving dealings with his people. How long till he have pity? Verse 14 may refer to the hope of a sign or word given as morning breaks (cf. 5.3; 46.5; 130.6), a signal of a new time of salvation. May there be joy enough to make up for the days of affliction. May the Lord's saving work appear, with the splendour of his favour, the light and beauty of his face. So the work in fields and home will be founded in his grace, proving fruitful once more.

As in some countries still today, adverse conditions for cultivation could quickly devastate the society. Impoverishment, starvation, slavery – from such consequent evils there might be a long entail. The prayer of this psalm seems to rise from an experience of such troubled years. O that the Lord would again show the beauty of his face; O that his light would shine upon the toiling hands and establish all their work in fruitfulness! The prayer rests not upon any claim to merit, but on hope of the Lord's compassion. In pity may he regard his people, so fleeting in their stay among the living, and grant them days of joy. And with his compassion, there is also his *ḥesed*, the commitment he made as Creator and revealed Lord. May the morning be a daybreak of this faithful love.

The psalm is set within the boundaries of a faith which humbly accepted only life on earth as God's allotment to the human race. If we truly recollect our mortality, it says, we may harvest a wise heart that finds peace within the boundaries God has made. When a greater hope became general, the old wisdom such as we see in this psalm and in Ecclesiastes still had its value. The hope in God's compassion and steadfast love, a hope sustained in sad realism and humility, was a precious heritage for ever.

Eternal Lord, help us to take to heart the brevity of our time on earth, and so gain wisdom to live here in reverence and humility; prosper the work of our hands, and satisfy us with the morning light of your faithful love, through your son Jesus, who is the fulfilment of all our hope.

PSALM 91: The Mystery of Protection in the Shadow of God

1   You that sit in the shelter of the Most High,
    and nest in the shadow of the Almighty,
2   saying to the Lord, My refuge and my strength,
    my God, in whom I put my trust –
3   he shall deliver you from the fowler's trap
    and from the word that would destroy.
4   He will cover you with his pinions,
        and you will shelter under his wings;
    his faithfulness will be your shield and rampart.
5   You shall not fear the terror of the night,
    nor the arrow that flies in the day,
6   the pestilence that walks in the darkness,
    nor the plague that destroys at noon.
7   Though a thousand fall at your side,
        ten thousand at your right hand,
    yet it shall not take hold of you.
8   You need only look with your eyes,
    and you will see the reward of the wicked.
9   Since you have made the Lord your refuge,
    and God Most High your stronghold,
10 no evil may befall you,
    no plague come near your tent.
11 But he will command for you his angels,
    to keep you in all your ways.
12 They will carry you on the palms of their hands,
    lest your foot should strike a stone.
13 You shall trample on dragon and cobra,
    on lion and sea-dragon you shall tread.
14 Because he loves me, I will deliver him;
    I will set him on high, because he knows my name.
15 When he calls to me, I will answer him,
        and be with him in danger;
    I will deliver and glorify him.
16 With days unending I will satisfy him,
    and fill him with my salvation.

Throughout vv. 1–13, as translated above, the singer pronounces blessings, a kind of prophetic promise, assuring the person addressed of the protection the Lord will give (the person concerned becomes plural in some translations for the sake of inclusive language). Then in vv. 14–16 the Lord's words on this theme are quoted directly, referring to the person concerned in the third person. The two forms of speech have the same purpose: with prophetic force, assurance is given to this person that the Lord will defend him from curse, plague, and weapons of war, and will grant him conquest of the forces of chaos, glorify him and give him enduring life. Who then is the person receiving such assurance? Though without title in the Hebrew, the psalm is headed in LXX 'Song, Psalm, Of David'. The Syriac, connecting with the Assyrian invasion, heads the psalm as 'Of David, but concerning King Hezekiah, that he should be called the son of David'. The Targum understands David to be speaking in converse with Solomon. The New Testament (Matt. 4.6; Luke 4.10f.) seems to presuppose a messianic interpretation. Such royal and messianic interpretations match the content of the psalm which consistently fits the office of the Davidic king – one who is seated or enthroned close under the shelter of the Lord, one who must also go out to battle and put down evil forces, and who may hope for years without number, glory and salvation from the hands of the God who has chosen him, invited his prayers and required of him trust. The situation may be imagined as either the encouragement of the king before battle (cf. 20) or part of the representation of the royal calling in the recurring festivals (cf. 21).

The arrangers of the psalms no doubt saw a link between 90.1 and 91.1–2, and this sequence has encouraged those who relate the promises of 91 to the collective person Israel. While the Talmud (b. Sheboth 15b) shows how the psalm might later be used to avert the power of demons, modern interpreters have often taken the promises more generally as addressed to any trusting person and assume that any royal elements have been taken up into a democratized usage. Nevertheless, we may feel that the psalm as a whole, as well as in many details, is most meaningful when understood in the context of kingship.

1–8 The great promises that will be unfolded are made within a close relationship. The one described as so close to the Lord has pleased him with trust (vv. 2, 9) and love (v. 14). That he 'sits' in the shelter and shadow of God can already be taken as the designation of a king (the participle *yosheb*, 'sitter', can denote one enthroned, cf. Amos 1.5; Ezek. 27.8; and often of the Lord enthroned in Zion). With the Lord he dwells on Zion (cf. 2.6), sits even with him on the holy throne (cf. 45.6), closely sheltered as the young of a bird (cf. 17.8; 57.1; 61.4; 63.7; wider use in 36.7 and Ruth 2.12). The protection of God is pictured especially as defence against secret and sudden assaults. In v. 3 the 'trap' may be imagined as the kind depicted in Egypt, where birds were enticed into a basket that was closed by a hidden fowler operating a cord; the 'word' that destroys might be a spell or a falsehood (this is the reading of LXX; the Hebrew has different vowels to give 'pestilence'). In v. 6 'pestilence' and 'plague' are seen as angels of destruction going about their grim work. The 'thousands' of v. 7 may be troops struck down by plague (cf. Dahood).

9–13 The theme is reiterated: trust and protection. Military situations are again indicated – defence from strongholds, campaigns with tents, and always the danger of plague. The Lord sends his angels to guard even against stumbling on a stone; the picturesque idea of them carrying the precious one on the palms of their hands is reminiscent of the symbolic bearing of seated kings in enthronement ceremonies in Assyria and Egypt (my *Kingship*, p. 58) and of the Lord's throne in Ezekiel's vision (Ezek. 1–3). Royal symbolism appears also in v. 13; the animals are mythical shapes (cf. Tate, p. 449) that embody the storms of chaos, which God and his king conquer to establish the kingdom of life.

14–16 The foregoing assurances, so wonderful and absolute, were obviously intended as given on the authority of the Lord. All the same, the present passage forms an arresting climax as the psalmist carries the voice of God himself speaking of his beloved one in the third person, as though to a congregation. The promised salvation is given 'because he loves me' (cf. 18.1; 116.1) and 'because he knows my name' (he is a devoted worshipper, calling with the name in prayer and praise, cf. 9.10; for 'set on high' cf. 20.1 where the name is the subject). Prayer is the explicit theme in v. 15; by prayer the king overcomes the many dangers (see above on 3.4) and is delivered and glorified. He is given life and salvation with divine fullness; 'length of days' in this context probably means 'for ever and ever' as in 21.4 and probably 23.6. It is a cup from God's hand that truly runs over (*r'h* in v. 16b probably as *rwh*, 'I will satiate').

Two features stand out: the closeness to God of the person addressed, and the strength of the Lord's promises of protection to this person. Here is one who abides in the shadow of the Almighty, like a young eagle hidden under the protecting pinions of the parent. And in so sheltering, this person is governed by trust in the Lord and by devoted love; he 'knows the name' of the Lord, living by the strength of a communion of prayer and praise. The promises of God are poured out with warmth and abundance. Even against the most deadly things, attacks often invisible or sudden, the Lord will protect. Angelic powers are commanded as it were to carry this trusting one. He will be set on high, glorified, given to drink deeply of the cup of eternal life. In the pattern of the Creator, he will be master of the forces of chaos, as the Lord himself will scatter the hosts of wickedness.

From an origin in the ideals of the Davidic kings, this poem of human trust and divine promise came to be understood of the Messiah. The story of Christ's temptations has the tempter suggesting a test of the promise in v. 12. Such testing of God is rejected by Christ. It would not accord with full trust, nor with a humility of following rather than leading God. In Gethsemane also, Christ does not look for the legions of angels (Matt. 26.53). The wondrous protection is hidden in mystery. The Messiah is utterly exposed to the evil ones. But in the end the triumph is manifest, the promise of God redeemed. Who will want to join this Christ? Who will rejoice with him in the closeness to the Lord, the sheltering in the shadow of the Almighty? Who will claim with him the protection of the holy angels, the victory over evil foes? The invitation is indeed to the many, and they can take the psalm to themselves. But they must be ready for the mystery of a protection seemingly absent when needed most, winning its victory in a paradox of suffering. Their joy will be, not in evident power, but that their names are written in heaven (Luke 10.19f.).

Grant us, Lord, the faith to believe in your unfailing love and protection even in the way of suffering; that, holding on to Christ, we may know at last with him the glory and salvation of your eternal life.

PSALM 92: The Trees that are God's Witnesses

Psalm.   Song.   For the day of the Sabbath.

1 It is good to give thanks to the Lord,
   and to make music to your name, O God Most High,
2 to tell of your love early in the morning,
   and your faithfulness in the watches of the night,
3 with the ten strings of the harp,
   and the music that sounds from the lyre.
4 For you, Lord, have caused me to rejoice in your work;
   with the tale of the deeds of your hands I will sing aloud.
5 How great are your works, O Lord!
   Your thoughts are very deep.
6 A senseless person does not perceive,
   the fool does not consider,
7 that when the wicked sprout like grass
   and all the evildoers flourish,
   they will soon be destroyed for ever,
8 while you, Lord, are exalted evermore.
9 For see, your enemies, Lord,
      for see, your enemies shall perish,
   and all those who do evil shall be scattered.
10 High as the horn of the wild ox, you have lifted up my horn;
   I am anointed with flowing oil.
11 My eye has seen the flight of my foes;
   my ears have heard the rout
      of the wicked who rose against me.
12 The just shall flourish as the palmtree,
   and shall grow mighty like a cedar in Lebanon.

13   Well planted in the house of the Lord,
     they shall flourish in the courts of our God.
14   When old they still bear fruit;
     they are healthy and full of life,
15   to proclaim that the Lord is true,
     my rock, in whom there is no wrong.

A link with the preceding psalm can be found in v. 11 (cf. 91.8). But this is the only psalm designated in its Hebrew heading as for use on a particular day of the week; we learn from the Talmud that it came to be sung with the morning offering at the temple. Psalms for the other days are specified in later sources, and we may conclude that this one for the Sabbath was the first to be so appointed. It may be that its seven occurrences of the name 'Yahweh' suggested its suitability for the seventh day, and certainly the praise of God's work (vv. 4–5) and triumph (v. 9) was appropriate there. The Targum's title shows how the individual singer might also be understood: 'A psalm of praise and song which the first man uttered on the day of the Sabbath.' Because of references to future triumph, some early interpreters related the psalm to the Sabbath at the end of the world. What the original setting of the psalm was can only be surmised from the contents and with some respect for its position in the sequence of psalms. It is not in the style of the usual individual thanksgiving (e.g. 30), and it blends thankful statements with more general praise. While there is broad praise of the Lord's 'work', his deep purposes and the destruction of his foes, the singer also rejoices over being granted victory over martial enemies and given rich life in the house of the Lord. Commentators who have thought of the singer as leader or representative of the people are surely justified. If he is further taken to be the Davidic king, a number of details fall into place – the ample provision of music, the role of witness to the divine work, the images of the horn, the oil, the lordly trees, the residence in the temple precincts. The evildoers are enemies of God and of himself, and he rejoices at their defeat as befits the representative of God's kingdom. One may think of thanksgiving after some particular victory, but the reference may be rather to the divine work and salvation symbolized in the festal ceremonies (cf. 18, 48). The psalm may be quite early; the style of v. 9 resembles that of ancient Canaanite poetry.

1–4   Instead of the usual hymnic opening ('I will praise' or 'Praise ye'), we have the variation 'It is good / sweet to . . .' The reason given for the praise is as usual introduced by 'For', but then takes a personal form, 'you have caused me to rejoice.' The joyful praise is especially a testimony to the Lord's faithfulness according to his promises (v. 2), and is to be rendered at daybreak and through the night-watches (lit. 'in the nights') as psalmody with harps and lyres. The introduction thus fits the royal tradition, where the king would appoint music with the daily and nightly temple services and himself be chief witness to the faithfulness of the Lord.

5–9 The 'works' that give rise to the praise are now indicated a little more fully. They concern the judgement of the evildoers – judgement hidden, mysterious, sometimes apparently long delayed, but yet sure and inevitable. Perhaps, as apparently also in 73.16f., the psalmist responds to truths embodied in ceremonies of worship. Festal rites showed the Lord as Creator and ruler of all, defeating and judging the destroyers of his good order; also as saving his faithful king (Int. 5b). The poetic pattern of v. 9 (A+B+C, A+B+D, E+F+G) is reminiscent of ancient Canaanite poetry (Dahood).

10–11 Linked to the thought of the downfall of the Lord's enemies comes now depiction of the psalmist as made victorious by the Lord. If indeed the psalm is responding to the festal rites, the thought is of the assurance they have given. The king, through God's help, will be a triumphant figure, like the great aurochs or wild bull, once common in the Syrian mountains, that raises high its horn in supremacy (cf. 75.4; 89.24; 132.17; 1 Sam. 2.10). The very rite of anointing with holy oil fills the king with power from God (cf. 23.5; 45.7; 89.20; 133.2). The rendering 'anointed' would more literally be 'I am moist' (Delitzsch); and the oil is described with a word usually applied to trees as fresh and luxuriant.

12–14 The 'just / faithful one' (*ṣaddiq*) has reference here in the first place to the psalmist – the anointed one, in accord with the will of the Lord, and therefore destined to blossom and grow mighty like the palm and cedar, the kings of the trees. In vv. 13–14, however, the subject becomes plural, and the thought is perhaps of the blessing on all those who stand with their king. They are like the well-tended trees in the sanctuary (cf. 1.3; 52.8). Rooted in the springs from God's presence, they have abundance of fruitful life, that with their king they may bear witness to the Lord so faithful and just. (For God 'my rock' cf. 18.2, 46; 28.1; 62.2, 6; 144.1.)

Often indeed evildoers sprouted like weeds favoured by rain and warmth. It was easy then to conclude with the foolish that this was the way to success. The psalmist, probably a royal figure, stood out for a different view. Heartened by the revelation of God in worship, strengthened by sacraments of grace, he would fill his whole existence with testimony to the Lord's faithful and just power. The music of the temple, at night and at break of day, was the music of his testimony. Right would prevail, the way of wickedness would perish for ever, because the Lord was true and without corruption. The church has seen this royal witness as fulfilled in Christ, the Lord's Anointed, victorious over death and evil. When society is led by fools who seek success along ruthless ways, the disciples of this greater Anointed are also called to make their existence, day and night, a witness to the truth and righteous power of God, which alone will prevail. Nourished by gifts and revelations of God in worship, they too will find the strength and health of spirit to live out the poems of his praise.

Lord, Most High, when base teachings are strong all about us, enable us to make music to your name night and day; and grant that as we are nourished by your grace, we may ever declare the greatness of your works and your truth.

PSALM 93: Proclaiming the Kingdom

1   The Lord is King! He has robed himself in majesty;
    he has robed himself, yes, girded himself with glory.
    So the world is established;
    it shall not be overthrown.
2   Your throne was established of old;
    you are from everlasting.
3   The rivers lifted, O Lord, then lifted the rivers their voice;
    the rivers lifted up their din.
4   More than the thunders of the mighty waters,
        than the glorious breakers of the sea,
    more glorious was the Lord on high.
5   Your commands are very sure;
    holiness adorns your house, O Lord, for evermore.

It is now widely acknowledged that this an ancient psalm, dating from the early monarchy, as both style and content indicate. Its rich significance is probably to be found in the context of the autumn festival, indeed at its very heart. We have already met psalms which celebrate the kingship of the Lord as new – 29 relating it to his mastery of the waters, 47 to his mastery of the nations, and 68 to a blend of both. Psalm 93 is closest to 29, and proclaims the new reign of the Lord, with the establishment of the world, as the consequence of his mastering the chaos represented by the water-powers. In the mysteries of worship, where the long line of time is dissolved or transcended, the first founding of the world is present again, and the Lord's reign begins (a theme to be resumed in 95–100). The worshippers find assurance that creation, growth, life and blessing will be known in the coming year, as the glory of the Lord, the King, now shines from his newly sanctified temple. LXX has the heading 'For the day before the Sabbath, when the earth was peopled; a praise-song of David' (cf. above on 92). Thus it maintains the sense of commemorating the creation.

1–2 The singer proclaims the meaning of the dramatic moment in worship. In movements with processions, acclamations, obeisance, incense and fire, the supremacy of the Lord as Creator and ruler is shown, and the psalmist brings out this essential meaning in terse, ancient phrases. The name 'Yahweh' comes first, as though to say 'He and no other'; unworthy contenders for the throne have been routed. Proclamation is therefore made that the Lord begins his reign, taking the throne in the robes of his unique majesty and power. The new reign means that an order of joyful life is established; chaotic forces have been subdued, the earth has been made firm in all the conditions for life. The singer addresses praise to the Creator (v. 2) as the One whose sovereignty was destined from eternity, from the unimaginable and ultimate beginning.

3–4 Continuing his tribute of praise, the singer recalls the Lord's victory over the chaos-waters, the victory seen in poetic traditions as crucial to creation, the waters being made to serve the economy of life (cf. 29.3f.; 74.12f.). The style here is especially reminscent of the very ancient poetry from Ugarit on the north Syrian coast (cf. Dahood), and it reflects the tradition of personifying the water-powers with titles. We might render more literally: 'More than the thunders of their majesties the waters, of their lordships the breakers of the sea, more lordly on high was Yahweh.' The effect is ironic. These would-be kings rose up to do battle, proud waters that reared and dashed with thunderous voices. But the outcome proved that it was to Yahweh, high above them, that the true majesty belonged.

5 The singer's praise moves on to the consequences of the creation-victory – the joyful present and its prospect. The 'commands' of the Lord are especially his mighty words that constituted and ordered the living world and ever sustain it (cf. 29.3f.; 33.4–9); they are 'sure' in that they are effective and also a source of confidence and gladness. The 'house' of the Lord is his heavenly abode, but also its earthly manifestation in Zion; the rites of new year will have included the cleansing of the temple for his re-entry. Its beauty of holiness is its reflection of the glory of the Lord in his new presence as victorious King; it is itself a sign of his established reign.

This small but highly significant song shares in the paradox of all the psalms that proclaim the reign or kingdom of God – a wondrous new event, yet established of old and sure for evermore. We have followed those (especially Mowinckel) who explain that in the drama of festal worship, the founding acts of God could be celebrated year by year as present and new; here was an experience that filled the present with joy and cast beams of light into the days to come. When read outside this original context of worship, the texts might seem to depict a scene at the end of the present age, a world beyond evil and suffering, where only the good reign of God, finally triumphant, is known. But we should hold on to the special contribution of these psalms as texts of worship – their ability to lead into a present experience of the Lord's triumph and perfect reign. Psalm 93, with its vision of the Creator in glory, thus brings a mighty recollection of the fundamental purpose and destiny of creation. Those led to see this vision are replenished in hope and granted a joy which the upsurgings of evil cannot kill; they live already in the certainty of the kingdom. This and related psalms accordingly have something of peculiar value to offer in the way of spirituality. Let other texts exhort and promise. In these psalms the gates are open to a celebration already begun. Even now they invite to a time-transcending experience of the great intervention, the world's transformation (cf. my *Psalms of the Way*, p. 126).

Open, O Lord, the eyes of our heart, that we may already see you as victor over all evil, the eternal King of peace; may we love your commands, and adore you in the beauty of your house for ever.

PSALM 94: The Vengeance of God

1   O Lord, God of vengeance,
     O God of vengeance, blaze out in majesty.
2   Rise up, judge of the earth;
     turn back the deeds of the proud upon themselves.
3   How long shall the wicked, O Lord,
     how long shall the wicked triumph?
4   How long shall they pour out words of arrogance,
     how long shall the evildoers boast?
5   It is your people, Lord, they crush,
     and your heritage they afflict.
6   Widow and stranger they slay,
     and orphans they put to death.
7   And they say, The Lord will not see;
     the God of Jacob will not heed it.
8   Consider, most stupid of people;
     O fools, when will you understand?
9   He who planted the ear, shall he not hear?
     He who formed the eye, shall he not see?
10 He who instructs the nations, shall he not rebuke?
     He who teaches the peoples, shall he lack knowledge?
11 The Lord knows the thoughts of the heart,
     that they are but a breath.
12 Happy the person you instruct, O Lord,
     and teach from out of your law,
13 giving quietness in days of trouble,
     until the pit is dug for the wicked.
14 For the Lord will not fail his people,
     and will not forsake his heritage.
15 For government shall turn again to justice,
     and all the true of heart shall follow it.
16 Who will rise up for me against the cruel,
     and who will take my part against the evildoers?

17   If the Lord were not my help,
       my soul would soon dwell in the land of silence.
18   And if I say, My foothold is gone,
       your faithful love, O Lord, shall hold me up.
19   In the multitude of cares within me,
       your comfort will gladden my soul.
20   Shall the throne of wickedness be allied to you,
       as it fashions mischief through its law?
21   They gather against the soul of the just,
       and condemn the innocent to death.
22   But the Lord is my stronghold,
       and my God the rock of my trust.
23   And he will turn against them their own evil,
          and silence them in their malice;
       the Lord our God shall put them to silence.

The psalmist utters lamenting supplication (vv. 1–7), warning to the foolish wrongdoers (vv. 8–11), encouragement to God's people (vv. 12–15), and a conclusion that combines renewed lament with assurance that God will destroy the evildoers (vv. 16–23). For such a pattern of elements we can compare 4 and 62. The oppression is on a national scale. The singer calls for the glorious manifestation of the Lord as ruler of the world (v. 2), chastizer of the nations (v. 10); God's kingship over the world is appealed to in the lament for the slaughter of the defenceless (v. 6); world order and government is awry (v. 15a) and a 'throne of destructiveness' reigns unchecked as though with God's support (v. 20a). Against this evil and on behalf of God's people stands the individual figure of the psalmist (vv. 16–19, 22), looking to the Lord to be his stronghold and rock. Representative and leader of the people, he can well be seen as the king – the Lord's witness, the admonisher of peoples and invoker of the Lord's uprising (*Kingship*, pp. 59f.). The community seems to be suffering from the cruelty and injustice of a world power, as was the case in the Assyrian period; it was an oppression which also corrupted some within Israel. The Talmud (b. Sukka 53a) recollected use of the psalm in the feast of Tabernacles; like several of the surrounding psalms, it may well have been composed for the autumn festival, but brought to that celebration of the Lord's kingship a lamenting appeal reflecting current sufferings. Several links can be seen with 92 and 93: the repetitive pattern of vv. 1, 3, 23 (cf. 92.9; 93.1, 3), expressions for the fools in v. 8 (cf. 92.6) and for oppression in v. 16 (cf. 92.7, 11; note also the contrast of v. 11 with 92.5). The position of this lamenting psalm inside the celebratory series 93–100 is striking and significant.

1–7   The opening call to the Lord is strong and urgent. It echoes the ancient tradition that acknowledged the Lord as the God who, in the cause of justice, would defeat and punish his adversaries; he would not be frustrated by any other power, but would avenge, recompense, requite (Deut. 32.35, 41; Jer.

51.36; Nahum 1.2). The cruel despoilers of the weak would not be able to get away with their crimes. But already in this invocation (vv. 1–2) it is evident that the actual situation is quite the contrary. The God ablaze against the wicked is not to be seen; the Judge of all the earth has not risen up. So the psalmist calls, 'Shine forth' (the verb used in the festal revelation of 50.2) and 'Lift up yourself' (so also 7.6). The lament then depicts the evil situation to arouse the divine concern. The wicked have long been triumphant, vaunting themselves with arrogant and harmful words. The people covenanted to the Lord are their victims. The widows, residing aliens and orphans (the special care of kings, see above on 41.1) are killed, and the murderers act as though the heavenly king did not see it.

8–11 The singer now addresses the perpetrators of the oppression, admonishing them for their folly in supposing their deeds unregarded by the heavenly ruler. In v. 8a some find a reference to fools within Israel (cf. NRSV 'O dullest of the people'), but the phrase may rather denote 'the most stupid / brutish of people' and be aimed primarily at foreign tyrants; they should have sense to know that the creator of sight and hearing sees and hears them, the instructor of all the nations has knowledge and understanding of their intentions. Such admonition of foreign rulers was a feature of the king's psalms, along with his general witness to the unique power of the Lord and exhortation to his own people (cf. 2.10–12; 4.2–5; 52.1–5; 62.10; 75.5–8; my *Kingship*, p. 181); in its own way it still presses upon God to vindicate the psalmist's words.

12–15 The singer's witness now passes to encouragement for the oppressed. Using the form of teaching which holds up an ideal and its happy reward (*asherey* ... cf. above on 1.1), he commends willing acceptance of the Lord's discipline and instruction from his *tora*, his treasury of guidance and wisdom; the patient disciple of God will be quiet in heart amid all the disturbing evils of the time, until justice appears. The suffering nation, the singer witnesses, may trust their God; he will not abandon his people. The government of the world's affairs (*mishpat*, cf. Hab. 1.4) will return to right order (*sedeq* – the picture is reminiscent of the harmony of angel-forms in 85.9–13) with the glad support and adherence of all the true of heart.

16–23 The singer continues to support his supplication with evidence of his faithfulness and trust. The force of vv. 16–17 is to say that he has no hope of salvation but in the Lord. When all seems lost, he trusts still in the promised love of his Lord (v. 18). When anxieties fill his breast, he hopes still for the reviving comfort with which the Lord will bring delight again to his soul. In vv. 20–21 the evil situation is again brought sharply before the Lord. Earthly government was supposed to be on God's behalf; foreign rulers too were seen as his servants (Isa. 10.5; 45.1; Jer. 27.6). But the present tyrants, slayers of the innocent, must surely have lost his friendship and support. The conclusion returns to expressions of confidence in the defence of God and in his justice that will exact retribution. In royal style, the trust is expressed in terms of a single figure facing all the evildoers and having a fortress in Yahweh. But the last phrase gathers in the nation – 'our God'.

As his people are plundered and murdered, the singer invokes the Lord as 'God of vengeance' and calls on him to blaze forth out of his present hiddenness and silence. The characterization of God as avenger may have a primitive ring, but it was precisely this aspect which prompted Paul to teach a forgiveness that renounces retribution into the hands of God (Rom. 12.19). In similar spirit, an ancient collect based on this psalm prays for the guilty to find mercy (see NL). In the first place, however, the psalm stands as an example of the forthright and powerful prayer that the anointed leader raises against a cruelty which was also a contempt of God as world-ruler. It is a prayer full of urgency and indignation, but passing on to expressions of faith. These expressions show an underlying concern to convert the evildoers, victims of their own folly, and to hearten the oppressed. Even while troubles rage, the psalmist knows of a submission to the Lord's teaching which gives a quiet spirit of trust; he knows of the Lord's 'comforts', his strengthening angels which gladden the soul. He testifies that the government of the world will indeed return to right; the avenging God will not leave evil to triumph. The church has seen the praying figure as the Christ who was not abandoned by the Father to the land of silence (v. 17). Christ prays for the comforting of his 'little ones' with all the force of his 'Shall not God avenge . . .' (Luke 18.7–8), and his bold and powerful intercessory prayer must ever be renewed for the exploited and tormented creatures of each generation. And with the prayer goes all the underlying strength of the faith that Christ imparts, comforting the troubled and calling the foolish to repentance.

Hardly has the great series of psalms (93–100) proclaiming the kingship of the Lord got under way, when this psalm intervenes with its picture of a world subjected to a 'throne of destructions', a reign of mindless cruelties. So the harsh context for faith in God the King is acknowledged. The Talmud tells of the psalmists in 587 who stood at their posts singing this psalm as the destroying army stormed the temple, until in the last verse they were struck down. It is a story which matches the depths and heights of the faith in God's reign.

O God, who made ear and eye and gave knowledge to all the peoples, you hear the cries of the abused, and see the deeds of cruelty, and know the arrogance of earth's powerful ones; comfort your people with tranquillity of faith, until you come in your terrible majesty to avenge the evil deeds and turn earth's government to right.

PSALM 95: Joy, Awe and Listening in the Presence of the Lord

1 Come, let us sing out to the Lord;
   let us acclaim the rock of our salvation.
2 Let us come before his face with thanksgiving;
   let us acclaim him with psalms of praise.
3 For the Lord is the great God,
   the great King over all the gods.
4 In his hand are the depths of the earth,
   and his also are the peaks of the mountains.
5 The sea is his, for he made it;
   the dry land also, which his hands formed.
6 Come, let us worship and bow down;
   let us kneel before the Lord our maker.
7 For he is our God,
   and we are the people of his pasture,
       the flock tended by his hand.

   O that today you would hear his voice:
8   Do not harden your hearts as at Meribah,
   on that day at Massah in the wilderness,
9   when your fathers tried me;
   they tested me, though they had seen my work.
10 Through forty years I was sickened by that generation,
    till I said, These are a wayward people,
        for they do not know my ways.
11 So then I vowed in my anger:
    They shall not enter into my rest.

The first part (vv. 1–7ab) is in hymnic style. The worshippers are summoned to acclaim the Lord as they come before his face. They are to kneel in obeisance and acknowledge him as King above all, the Creator of all, but also the Covenant Lord, the shepherd of Israel. In the second part (vv. 7c–11) they are bidden to hear God's voice, as the singer proceeds to give God's words of warning. The pattern is then like that of 81 (cf. also 50), but here the kingship of God as Creator is explicit, and the contrast of mood between the two sections is starker. The resemblance with 81 and the theme of kingship support the likelihood that the psalm comes from the heart of the autumnal new-year celebrations. The great procession is entering the temple courts, and the manifestation of the 'face' of the Lord in his royal glory is proclaimed. This holy effulgence is acclaimed with joy, but then follows a speech from the throne. The ascended Lord has now to address his people. In such a solemn moment there may well be cause for trembling. Such prophecy in worship was often seen by commentators as a consequence of the work of the radical prophets and so probably post-exilic. But it may rather be the root from which those prophets grew, and so the date could be much earlier (cf. above on 50 and 81).

1–5 In a customary pattern, the singer calls for praise (vv. 1–2) and gives reasons (vv. 3–5). The verb in vv. 1b and 2b (corresponding to the noun *teru'a*, 33.3; 47.5; 89.15) refers to the acclamations with voice and instruments for the God manifest in triumphant glory. With joyful songs and thanksgiving, he is hailed by the worshippers as rock of their salvation, their mighty and faithful saviour. They are 'coming' or 'entering' before his face, and we may think of a procession entering the temple courts, conscious of coming into his holy presence. Such acclamation is fitting because he is revealed as high above all the powers of heaven (cf. 29.1; 82.1f.; 89.6; 96.5), owner and Lord of earth and sea to their utmost limits – such is his supremacy as the Creator who with his own hands shaped and moulded the land (cf. the 'fingers' in 8.3).

6–7ab Advancing a little, the procession must now make obeisance before the Holy One, and the singer calls on them all as one to fall down and kneel with head to the ground. His words themselves evoke a wondering reverence, for this King and Creator is '*our* Maker', '*our* God'; for them especially he is their Covenant-Lord, their Shepherd (cf. 74.1; 80.1).

7c A prophetic voice, perhaps that of the previous singer adopting the role of God's spokesperson, utters an introduction to the oracle (cf. 81.5c and 85.8a). Implicit in the 'O that today you would hear' is the world of blessing which could be theirs (cf. 81.8b, 10b, 13–16); but the message itself will concentrate on warning. The 'today' here is a traditional and significant expression, common in such a context especially in Deuteronomy (Ex. 34.11; Deut. 4.40; 6.6; 7.11; 8.19; 9.3). It summons up all the tradition of the Lord's dealings with his people; as he now appears before them with all his grace and all his claim, it is for them, the present generation, to hear and respond and this very day to enter into the true life with him, their Lord and saviour.

8–11 Now comes the oracle, the direct speech of the Lord. He calls on the people not to harden their hearts; not to close their hearts away from trust, patience and love, yielding readily to grumbling and disbelief. The 'hardened' heart is one without living relationship to the Lord, no longer hearing, attentive, trusting, centred on his will, but rather awake only to immediate desires and impulses. The bulk of the oracle, as a warning, recalls the story of the wilderness generation which, having hardened its hearts in particular incidents and also throughout the 40 years, did not live to enter the promised land, God's 'rest', his blessed abode (Deut. 12.9; Num. 14.30; Ps. 132.8, 14). The sudden ending of the psalm at this point gives the warning great solemnity; a whole generation can lose its living relationship to the Lord and so miss the goal of its life-journey – what then of the present generation? The traditions about the places Meribah ('Dispute') and Massah ('Trial') took various forms; Ex. 17.1–7 tells of an incident early in the Wandering, Num. 20.1–13 one at the end (cf. above on Ps. 81.7, and for the vow of God Num. 14.26.f., Deut.1.34f.).

The psalm shows the test of true praise as the readiness to hear. Joy in worship is here complementary to willingness to hear God's voice, even in stern warning. The rich significance of this psalm is shown not only by its ample use in the New Testament (Heb. 3.7–4.13; cf. 1 Cor. 10.1–13), but by its daily use in the church down the centuries (in the East usually vv. 1, 3, 6, 7, in the West in its entirety). Morning by morning it has invited God's people to pass through the sacred gates and kneel before the face of the Lord; to rejoice in acclaiming him our rock, our saviour, our shepherd, our creator, in whose hand rests the world, even to its most mysterious depths and heights. And morning by morning also it has placed great importance on this present moment of encounter, the 'today' in which the Lord of the church binds his people to himself and sets before them his way – the way of the responsive heart, open to him in love and trust, in patience and hope. His 'rest', his beautiful country, lies before them, but every day the psalm has voiced his earnest warning against the hard heart that would keep them from it.

O Lord our maker, send, we pray, your Holy Spirit into our hearts, that they may not be hardened towards you or our fellow creatures; and bring us every day to worship before your face and hear your voice, that we may enter into your rest, and know you as the rock of our salvation.

PSALM 96: A Song of the New Kingdom

1   Sing to the Lord a new song,
      sing to the Lord, all the earth,
2   sing to the Lord, bless his name;
      tell the tidings of his salvation from day to day.
3   Declare his glory among the nations,
      his marvellous deeds among all peoples.
4   For great is the Lord and very glorious,
      terrible in majesty over all the gods.
5   For the gods of the peoples are feeble,
      and it was the Lord who made the heavens.
6   Splendour and majesty are before him;
      power and beauty are in his sanctuary.

7   Give to the Lord, O clans of the peoples,
     give to the Lord the glory and the power,
8   give to the Lord the glory of his name;
     take up your offerings and come into his courts.
9   Bow down to the Lord in the beauty of his holiness;
     dance at his presence, all the earth.
10   Proclaim among the nations: The Lord is King!
     So the world is secured, it will not be overthrown,
         and he will rule the peoples with justice.
11   Let the heavens be merry and earth rejoice,
     let the sea thunder and all that it holds,
12   let the highland exult and all that is on it,
     the very trees of the forest sing out in joy
13   before the Lord, for he has come,
     he has come to rule the earth.
     He shall rule the earth in justice,
     and the peoples in his faithfulness.

Like 47 and 93, this rapturous hymn acclaims the Lord as King-Creator, and will have belonged to the autumnal festival and its proclamation of the Lord's new reign (cf. also 29, 68, 95, 97–100). The Chronicler is in harmony with this judgement in placing it in the foundational ceremony of the bringing in of the ark, symbol of God's glory and presence (1 Chron. 16.23f., cf. below on Ps. 132). In the nature of the case, the songs from the heart of the festal drama resemble one another in themes and phrases, and prophets also who contributed to the festal worship would draw upon the same tradition of expression. It would thus be inappropriate to think this psalm's similarities with kindred psalms and with Isa. 40–66 were evidence of a late author dependent on earlier texts. The psalmist has given vibrant expression to a well-established theme of worship, and in fact complements the ritual action most effectively, carrying his fellow worshippers into a wonderful vision of worldwide rejoicing before the Lord. The poetic style has several ancient features (as noted by Dahood), and the psalm may well belong to the royal period; the exilic prophets of Isa. 40f. were then concerned to make such former festal joy live again, with its message of atonement, its glad tidings of the Lord's salvation and his great procession into Zion. The structure has a double character: call to praise (vv. 1–3), reasons (vv. 4–6), renewed calls to praise combined with reasons (vv. 7–13). LXX has the heading: 'When the house was built after the Captivity; a song by David.'

1–3   For the Creator who makes all things new a 'new song' is fitting (see above on 33.1). The call to sing praise is repeated excitingly, and it is addressed to 'all the earth'. The ceremony of worship has a meaning beyond its apparent space and time. The Creator is manifest in his cosmic victory, and the congregation represents the whole world of his creatures. They are to 'bless his name', acknowledging his revelation of himself with thankful joy.

From this day forth they are to tell the good news, the victory tidings, the story of his saving deeds which subdued chaos and made the world of life. Peoples who once worshipped other powers are to hear this gospel and to recognize the supreme glory that belongs to the Lord alone. (In the phrase 'from day to day' a vowel change may be considered, giving 'from sea to sea' – Dahood.)

4–6 The songs of praise are a response to the manifestation of the Lord signified in the actions of worship and expounded by the psalmist. He depicts the Lord as radiant in majesty (*nowra* as in 47.2; 76.12), supreme over all the powers of heaven, the 'gods' or 'gods of the peoples' which must recognize him as the only true God and serve him in awe (cf. 29.1; 95.3). They are 'feeble' (*elilim*, a word of obscure origin but sounding like an echo of *elim* and *elohim*, 'gods' and often applied in scorn to idols or their deities), whereas Yahweh, the Lord, has shown his unique power in creation. His glorious attributes, like attendant angels, now shine before and beside him in his temple – the splendour, majesty, power and beauty before which all must bow.

7–10 The ancient repetitive style of vv. 1–2 is resumed in vv. 7–8 to summon every tribe and clan of the world to acknowledge in worship the unique glory of the Lord now revealed in his 'name' and his holy epiphany (v. 9a, where with *BHS* I have added 'his' for clarity, cf. 29.2; 68.17). Represented by the festal pilgrims, they will take up their offerings (cf. 68.29, 31), enter the temple courts and make obeisance (cf. 95.6). Indeed, the present pilgrims represent 'all the earth', all living things which dance and whirl (*hyl*) in joy at the revelation of God's new reign. Across the wide earth the good tidings are sent, that the Lord is victorious, he is 'become king' (cf. 29.10; 47.7; 93.1; 97.1; 99.1) and the world of life is established, to flourish in the peace and goodness of his reign.

11–13 In the ecstatic conclusion, the call to the joyful praise is especially directed to the world of nature – the skies and the soil, the sea and its myriad inhabitants, the 'field' of steppe and wilderness and all their animals and birds, the great forest trees (cf. 98.7f.; 148.1–10; 150.6). Healing and health will be theirs, as the Lord who has now 'come' (entered his temple and taken his throne) rules his created order and all nations with 'right' – all the goodness of his faithful heart.

An inspired poetry, with music and dance, here leads the worshippers up through the gates of God, to stand in his heavenly courts and behold his beauty, power and majesty as newly triumphant king. The courts and temple of Zion have become the holy dwelling on high, the throng of pilgrims has become the living circle of created things, and the praises are one with the rejoicing of the fields, forests and oceans and all their hosts. To all the bounds of the cosmos the gospel resounds, that the Lord has overcome the false powers, the many forms of chaos and corruption; he has won salvation for the good order of life, and has come in as victor, to rule his world in faithfulness.

The visionary experience that so transfigured the new-year celebration of the ancient pilgrims had an abiding significance. Though it had gathered force from the conditions of that particular society – especially the relation to the earth and the traditions of the divine purpose – it was able to surge up in later centuries. For Christian worshippers it has brought its transforming light upon their own encounter with the drama of salvation. In individual hearts and in the great cycle of the liturgy, the poem still invites them through the gates of God, to kneel before the ascended Lord, and to begin to hear the thunder of praise from the circle of all that he has made.

Lord, we thank you for the moments of vision where we see for ourselves that yours is the kingdom, the power and the glory, yours the victory of salvation and the reign in faithfulness over a healed creation; may we thus be inspired to pray with all our hearts that this your kingdom come, and this your will be done on earth as it is in heaven, when the fellowship of all living beings shall join in the thunder of your praise.

PSALM 97: Glory Wrapped in Thick Darkness

1   The Lord is King! Let earth rejoice,
    and the hosts of islands dance for joy.
2   Cloud and thick darkness are all around him;
    right and justice are the foundation of his throne.
3   Fire went before him,
    and burnt up his foes on every side.
4   His lightnings lit up the world;
    earth trembled at the sight.
5   Mountains melted like wax before the Lord,
    before the Lord of all the earth.
6   The heavens told of his justice,
    and all the peoples saw his glory.
7   All who served idols were ashamed,
       all who sang the praises of mere nothings;
    the gods themselves bowed low before him.
8   Zion heard and was merry,
       and the daughters of Judah danced for joy,
    because of your saving deeds, O Lord.
9   Truly, Lord, you are the Most High above all the earth;
    you are highly exalted over all the gods.
10 The Lord loves those who hate evil;
    he keeps the souls of his faithful ones,

and delivers them from the hand of the wicked.
11 Light is sown for the one who is just,
    and joy for the true of heart.
12 Rejoice, you right-hearted, in the Lord,
    and give thanks with the remembrance of his holy name.

Like 93 and 99, this is the unfolding of an initial proclamation of the Lord's new reign (v. 1). As in 93, the scene of the Lord's present exaltation (vv. 1–2, 9f.) is supported by a retrospect, telling of the preceding rout of his foes and the effects on beholders (vv. 3–8). After the retrospect, thought returns to the present exaltation (v. 9) and good rule (vv. 10–11), and all is concluded with a call to praise (v. 12). The setting will have been the triumphant heart of the autumn festival (cf. above on 93 and 96). The reference to 'the daughters of Judah' is possibly an indication of a date after Solomon and the separation of Judah. LXX has the heading: 'By David, when his land is established.'

1–2 The ascent of the Lord is accomplished. The festal worshippers have now to acknowledge him in the fullness of his glory. Proclamation is made that he and no other now reigns, and the call goes out for praise and joy. It is a new era for all the world to its utmost bounds (the 'islands' being suggestive of coasts reached by distant voyages). The words for joy and gladness here, as often, denote an excitement such as would be expressed in dance, or indeed denote dance itself (my *Psalms*, pp. 102f.). Earth and islands themselves are alive to this joy, one with all the creatures that inhabit them (cf. 96.11f.). The Lord's throne is seen as founded on right and justice, attributes of the ideal order which were often symbolized by kerub or sphinx-like figures at the base of thrones (cf. 89.14). Though such a manifestation of the Lord is often depicted in effulgent glory (cf. v. 6; 50.2; 96.3, 6), here it is the encompassing cloud and storm-darkness that are portrayed, a reminder of the mystery veiling his holiness even in revelations (Ex. 19.16; 20.4) and of the storms which convey his power to give life (Pss. 18.9f.; 29.3f.).

3–5 The singer now describes the terrible warfare of the Lord which led up to his new reign. His march against his foes, the enemies of life, is depicted in the traditional imagery of the thunderstorm (cf. 29.3f.). The bolts of lightning blazed across the world, and the mighty elements of earth and mountains, streaming with water, seemed to melt in consternation; it was a time for the mightiest to renounce pride and melt in awe before the fearsome Creator (cf. Micah 1.3f.; Hab. 3.5f.; Ps. 77.16f.).

6–8 The immediate effect was to make clear his divine supremacy. The heavens rang out with testimony to his establishment of right order (his 'justice'), and his godhead (his 'glory') was manifest to all peoples, so that those who had worshipped unworthy powers were now ashamed, and these lesser powers themselves fell down in obeisance to acknowledge his supremacy (cf. 29.1). Zion's reaction to the tidings was joyful, and the 'daughters of Judah' perhaps represent the way the returning victor would be greeted (cf. Ex. 15.20; Ps. 68.11, 25).

9–12 The singer returns to the present scene before the victorious Lord, and he emphasizes its immediacy with a direct address to him as 'Elyon', the Most High, supreme above all in heaven and earth (cf. 47.2, 9). The essence of the psalm's joy is that this supremacy is the victory of right and goodness; the concluding verses therefore bring home to the worshippers that the happiness of the new reign is for those that 'hate evil', those that are *ḥasid*, faithful and trusting, those that are *ṣaddiq*, just and true, all in bond with the Lord. Such is the way of joy and light; and the final words, calling for praise and chanting of the name of God, show how the happiness centres in knowing him.

The psalm resounds in a scene of worldwide rejoicing, following the Lord's victorious battle against the false powers of chaos. It sounds a note of awe, portraying this Lord, for all his glory, as still surrounded by storm-cloud and darkness. It cautions also that to live with this God, whose throne rests upon right and justice, his followers must themselves turn away from evil and keep faithfully to all that is good in his sight. Only thus can they hold this present happiness, which is knowledge of him, communion with him, wholly taken up with his will, his goodness, his holy being.

O God Most High, whose conquering glory is yet veiled in thick darkness, create in us good and faithful hearts, that we may ever rejoice in the salvation you have sown and in the memorial of the death and resurrection of your Son, our Lord Jesus Christ.

PSALM 98: The Marvellous Circle Won by God's Holy Arm

Psalm.

1 Sing to the Lord a new song,
    for he has done marvellous things.
  His own right hand and holy arm
    have wrought salvation for him.
2 The Lord has made known his salvation;
  before the eyes of the nations he has shown his justice.
3 He has remembered his love and faithfulness
    to the house of Israel;
  all the ends of the earth have seen the salvation of our God.
4 Acclaim the Lord, all the earth;
  break into singing and make music.

5   Make melody to the Lord with the lyre,
    with the lyre and the voice of song.
6   With trumpets and the voice of the horn,
    sound praise before the Lord the King.
7   Let the sea thunder and all that fills it,
    the round earth and all its creatures.
8   Let the rivers clap their hands,
    the mountains also join the praise,
9   before the Lord who has come to rule the earth;
    he will rule the world with right,
      and the peoples with his justice.

This has much in common with 96, especially the beginning and the ending, and no doubt comes from the same setting in the autumn festival. Prophecies from the Exile (Isa. 42.10; 51.3; 52.9f.; 55.12) sometimes use similar phrases as they re-create in imagination the joyous scenes of the old festival to body out the expected turn of history. The psalm itself is then likely to be pre-exilic; in a great sacrament of renewal, the Lord has come to his people as Creator-King, and the worshippers see about him an ideal world, which we can interpret as both a hope for the new year and an earnest of the ultimate new creation. LXX has the heading: 'A psalm by David'.

1–3 The call for a 'new song' reflects the sense of a new order, the new reign of the Lord (vv. 6, 9, cf. above on 96.1). The originative marvels, fundamental to the society, embrace both the whole earth (as creation, establishment of living order) and 'the house of Israel' (as the grace of the Exodus and Covenant 'remembered', made new). Such marvellous work, victorious deeds, salvation – all is seen as having preceded his ascent to his temple and his glorious presence now proclaimed before his worshippers.

4–9 After the 'reasons for praise' given in vv. 1b–3, the call to praise is resumed more fully. The acclamations are for the victorious King, ascended to the sound of trumpets and ram's horn (cf. 47.5), hailed also in psalmody with voice and music (especially of the lyre, the chief instrument of the psalmists). To this glorious Creator must also be given praise from the great elements and from all living beings, thanksgiving for the victory over chaos and for the reign that creates and sustains the order of life. In the chorus of praise the great oceans contribute their thunder, the bounding streams clap their hands, and the mountains sing to the rhythm; all creatures in their own way offer up the movements and sound of thankful joy to the giver of their life. The conclusion (v. 9) restates the reason for praise: the Lord is revealed in his temple, victorious and supreme, faithful and bearing salvation, at the outset of a reign of right, the inauguration of the kingdom of all that is good.

This thrilling psalm has represented again the culmination of the ancient society's religious experience, an experience which yet gathered up all their life. The church appointed it for daily uses and for several festivals, including Christmas Day. In Evening Prayer (BCP) it comes as an alternative to the Magnificat, bridging the readings of Old Testament and New Testament. In such usage it calls upon all the world of creation to sing, play and dance to the Lord who in Christ has 'gotten the victory', wrought and made known his salvation, fulfilling the promise given to the house of Israel, establishing the good kingdom over all that he has made. Very precious is the psalm's vision of worship as far transcending the praises of one nation and indeed of all nations. Reconciled to each other as worshippers must be, bound in a new mutual respect and love, these myriad creatures of God find joy in being wholly centred on their Creator. The scene is as ultimate as ultimate can be, involving a drastic revolution in our ways; but it is nothing if not a present reality, more real than what passes for reality, and the true worshippers of God, those who know his salvation, must enter it now.

We thank you, Lord, for poets and artists who lead us into love of your creatures, and for the psalms which reveal the fulfilment of such love in your kingdom; help us to respond without delay and enter the circle of praise, that in the fellowship of earth and waters and all that lives in them, we may give thanks for your marvellous salvation, through Christ the Word by whom all things were made.

PSALM 99: The Dread Holiness and the Forgiving Heart of God

1   The Lord is king! The peoples tremble;
     he has taken his seat above the cherubim,
       the earth is shaking.
2   The Lord is great in Zion,
     and high above all peoples.
3   They give praise to your name,
     for it is great and awesome. Holy is he!
4   You that command good rule and love good government,
      you yourself have established justice;
    good government and right in Jacob
      you yourself have fashioned.
5   Lift high the praise of the Lord our God,
     and bow low before his footstool. Holy is he!
6   Moses and Aaron, chief of his priests,
      and Samuel, chief of those that call on his name,
    these would call to the Lord, and he would answer them.
7   From the pillar of cloud he spoke to them;
     they kept his testimonies and the statutes that he gave them.

8   O Lord our God, you answered them;
     a forgiving God you were to them, pardoning their offences.
9   Lift high the praise of the Lord our God;
     bow low before his holy hill. Holy indeed is the Lord our God!

Like 93 and 97, this unfolds from the initial proclamation that the Lord has
entered upon his new reign. As in 93, the 'holiness' of God is here a theme of
great significance. But in some ways the closest resemblance is with 95; both
psalms share reference to old Israelite tradition and both convey a sense of
dread and solemnity. The refrain 'Holy is he' (perhaps an example of the
teru'a, the acclamations for the Lord as victorious king, 47.5) is repeated in vv.
3 and 5 and with a variation in v. 9, giving a threefold structure to the psalm.
First comes announcement of the Lord's ascent and description of its effects
(vv. 1–3); then a tribute to the Lord as founder of just governance (v. 4) and a
call to praise and obeisance (v. 5); and finally, the longest section, an allusion
to the mercy won by great intercessors of old (implying a request for mercy
now, vv. 6–8) and another call for praise and obeisance (v. 9). The setting, as
generally in this sequence of psalms, will have been the celebration of the
Lord's reign in the autumn festival. A pre-exilic date is likely; v. 4 seems to
allude to the establishment of Davidic rule, the references to earlier leaders
reflect an early form of the tradition, the 'footstool' may indicate use of the
ark, and the refrain illustrates worship like that echoed in Isaiah 6, also a vision
of the Lord as King.

1–3   The psalmist fills out the meaning of the most solemn moment of the
festal worship. The ascent of the Lord has probably been signified with
procession of the ark (cf. on v. 5; 47.5). He now sits in the majesty of his new
reign above ark and kerubs in the Holy of Holies, the inmost shrine of the
temple (cf. above on 80.1). The symbols convey the cosmic reality of the
Creator, ascended as victorious and supreme over all; and the trembling of the
peoples and of earth represents the dreadful power and impact of the event.
What is manifest 'in Zion' is a glimpse of the universal: the Lord reveals his
greatness over all. His 'name' or presence is known in awesome glory, and
creatures above and below respond with the acclamation 'Holy is he' – true
divinity, fullness of godhead, belongs to him alone.

4–5   The Lord is praised as having established just rule in the world (cf. 98.9)
and in the people of Jacob. Such establishment of true kingship, the reign of
the Lord himself, also embraces the idea of its mediation through God's
chosen dynasty, the house of David, to which the psalmist perhaps intends to
allude (cf. above on Ps. 2). In v. 5 the call to 'exalt' the Lord continues as a
summons to fall down in obeisance towards his 'footstool', an image applied
to the ark (1 Chron. 28.2; Ps. 132.7) and perhaps primarily so intended here;
the broader applications – to the temple (Isa. 60.13), Jerusalem (Lam. 2.1) and
indeed the earth (Isa. 66.1) – show the scope of the temple's symbols.

6–9 As many as three verses are now devoted to recollection of the role of Moses, Aaron and Samuel as great intercessors. The Lord had communed with them from the pillar of cloud and they had been loyal to his commandments. He answered their pleading on behalf of their people, showing himself as a God who forgives and pardons (v. 8b will relate especially to the offences of the people). There is an element of teaching in the passage, but the main purpose is probably an implied prayer that present-day intercessors may likewise find such grace. In the dread revelation reflected by the psalm, the need for forgiving grace comes to be keenly felt, but in humility and tact the request for mercy is put indirectly, implied. Some take v. 9b to indicate that the worshippers are still at the foot of the hill; more likely they are in the court, looking towards the temple itself, where ascending steps symbolize the summit of the divine mountain.

The last of the psalms to quote and unfold the proclamation that the Lord is now king, this has conveyed especially the impact of 'the holy', the manifestation of the dread godhead. It is an event of overwhelming awesomeness, at which all tremble, cast themselves down, and confess in praise that 'He', Yahweh, the Lord, he alone is holy. A kindred spirit of the psalmist, the prophet Isaiah, likewise saw 'the King', the ascended Lord, and likewise felt the earth trembling and witnessed the heavenly worship of incense clouds and antiphons of 'Holy, holy, holy'; for Isaiah it was prelude to a terrible sentence pronounced against his people (Isa. 6, cf. Jer. 15.1). From this we can well understand our psalmist's earnestness, as he carefully introduces into this dread situation the theme of intercessors who stayed the divine wrath and found forgiveness for their people. Hardly will he dare to ask now, but he has said enough to rest his hope upon the forgiving love of this mighty king. The revelation of God's holiness must ever evoke in his worshippers the knowledge of their unworthiness, their need of a mediator. The church (cf. Heb. 3–10) has seen in Jesus the supreme mediator and intercessor, through whom the unworthy can find life in communion with the holy and righteous God.

Exalted Lord God, terrible in your holy majesty, grant to us the help of those strong to call upon your name, and pardon our offences through the mediation of your Son, our Saviour Jesus Christ.

PSALM 100: The Lord is God and We Are His

Psalm. For thanksgiving.

1   Acclaim the Lord, all the earth;
    worship the Lord with dancing,
       come before him with songs of joy.
2   Know that the Lord alone is God;
    he made us and we are his,
       his people and the flock of his pasture.
4   Enter his gates with thanksgiving, his courts with praise;
    give thanks to him and bless his name.
5   For the Lord is good, his love endures for ever,
    and his faithfulness throughout all generations.

Although not making explicit reference to the Lord's kingship, this psalm is clearly related to the preceding series (93, 95–99) in its main features. Thus it begins with a call for the *teru'a*, the acclamations of the Lord as victorious king; this is addressed to 'all the earth', the created order; the festal procession comes into the temple courts before his glorious manifestation of 'face' and 'name'; the reason for praise is the assertion of the Lord's supremacy as sole God and Creator. As regards structure, the pattern is the same as that of 95.1–7: call to praise (vv. 1–2) and reason (v. 3); further call to praise (v. 4) and reason (v. 5; cf. also 96 and 98). Our psalm will thus have belonged to the same context in the autumn festival as its immediate predecessors. The title (which could also be translated 'For the occasion of a thank-offering') perhaps reflects a later usage or interpretation based on the word *toda*, 'thanksgiving / thank-offering', in v. 4; thank-offerings featured in festal worship (cf. 66; 116.14; 2 Chron. 29.31; 33.16), but the content of our psalm, lacking a narrative of deliverance, does not suggest this was its original intention.

1–3   The singer calls on the whole created community to sing and play the acclamations for the glorious Lord, Creator and king (cf. above on 47.5f.). The worshippers are to pass through the gates into the temple courts, and their rejoicing will have been expressed in dancing step as well as in music (cf. above on 97.1, 8). Although the expressions 'his people' and 'the flock of his pasture' focus on the covenant-community, there is no break with the initial address to 'all the earth'; the representative character of the assembly is thus maintained throughout. The climax of the festival is well expressed in the acknowledgement that Yahweh, the Lord, alone is true God (cf. 46.10; 48.14; 95.3; 96.5; 97.7–9; Deut. 4.35, 39), Creator and shepherd (cf. above on 80.1). For 'we are his' there is another reading, 'not we ourselves' – not quite so appropriate.

4–5 The renewed call for praise clearly reflects the procession through the gates. The terms used for thanksgiving, praise and blessing are all related in sense; the songs and responses are in acknowledgement of the Lord's glory and goodness, but the first and third have a note of grateful warmth, a consciousness of having received salvation from the Lord who is kind and gracious, committed in his love, faithful and true for ever.

The psalm is widely known as 'the Jubilate' (in BCP an alternative to the Benedictus after the New Testament reading in daily morning prayer), and in traditional translations begins 'O be joyful in the Lord' or 'Make a joyful noise to the Lord'. However, the Hebrew refers to acclamation, particular formulas of homage before the Lord who has ascended in victory and supremacy. Joy there is, but it is focused as response to his mighty work of creation and salvation. It acknowledges that he is sole God, Creator and king over all, but also expresses the loyalty and love of worshippers who know profoundly that he is *their* maker and *their* shepherd. The acknowledgement of his godhead would be empty without the sense of relationship and devotion. This thread continues into the call for thanking God and blessing his name; again, it is all in heartfelt response to his deeds and revelation, his making himself known, his coming forth as saviour, and it is taken up in joyful testimony to his everlasting love and unwavering faithfulness. Significant also is the implicit transition from the greater circle of universal praise to the inner, representative group of worshippers, an assembly of 'his people, the flock of his pasture'. There is no break. The love and faithfulness, cherished in the representative few, is seen in the fullness of vision to be for all that he has made.

O God, our maker and shepherd, inspire in us the joy that is unfeigned response to your work of salvation; and grant that with thankful hearts we may ever serve before your face, you who have come to us in the name of Jesus.

PSALM 101: Integrity in Government

Psalm.   Of David.

1   Of faithful love and justice I will sing,
        making music to you, O Lord.
2   My song shall be of the way that is pure –
        O when will you come to me?

        I will walk in purity of heart
        within the walls of my house.

3   I will not set before my eyes
     a counsel that is evil.
     I will abhor the deeds of unfaithfulness;
     they shall not cling to me.
4   A crooked heart shall depart from me;
     I will not know a wicked person.
5   One who slanders another in secret
     I will quickly put to silence.
     Arrogant eyes and a greedy heart –
     I will not suffer them.
6   My eyes shall be on the faithful in the earth,
     that they should dwell with me.
     One that walks in the way that is pure
     shall come and be my servant.
7   There shall not dwell within my house
     one that practises deceit.
     One who utters falsehood
     shall not stand before my eyes.
8   Morning by morning I will silence
     all the wicked of the earth,
     to banish from the city of the Lord
     all those who practise evil.

Although the psalm contains no designation of the king, the content shows that it is a king's utterance, as is generally agreed. In the main part (vv. 2c–8) he affirms his adherence to the Lord's requirements of a ruler (it can be translated either as a vow of future conduct or as a claim regarding the reign hitherto), and it seems that the affirmation is in support of his lamenting cry that the Lord should come to him (v. 2b). The metre (3+2 beats per line) is one especially favoured for laments, and all in all the psalm can best be understood as a supplication from distress. The measured rehearsal of royal duty, however, along with the lack of some typical features of laments (depictions of sufferings, enemies etc.), points to a formal, ceremonial setting, and this would most likely be in the part of the autumn festival where the calling of the Anointed was set forth – rites of enthronement or their renewals. It is in fact generally agreed that the king responds to the duty there laid on him to uphold justice and purge corruption. But the aspect of need and lament is more controversial. Some feel obliged, against the evidence, to treat v. 2b as a textual error or gloss; but the fairer conclusion seems to be that the prayer arises from an element in the ceremony with the character of an ordeal, a symbolic humiliation (cf. on 18, 89, 118, 144). Comparison for this has been made with foreign royal ceremonials, especially in Babylon where the king, early in the new year festival, was humiliated and buffeted until he made a similar protestation of just rule pleasing to the deity and beneficial to the holy city (my *Kingship*, p. 92, *ANET*, p. 334a). The structure of the psalm can be taken as an introduction (vv. 1–2b) and a conclusion (v. 8) framing ten lines or couplets that express the royal duty (cf. above on Ps. 15).

1–2b   Addressing the Lord, the king undertakes to raise to him a psalm, as he pleads to him to come to his help. He will sing of *ḥesed* and *emet*, the basic covenantal values of committed goodwill and faithfulness; though the style resembles the opening of lamenting royal 89, we may judge from the sequel that now it is the king's faithfulness which is in mind, rather than the Lord's. He is to sing a moving poem (v. 2a 'I will render a *maskil*-poem') about the way he takes, the way that is pure or 'whole' in loyalty to the Lord. When, O when will the Lord come?

2c–3   Not only in public display, but in the midst of the palace, in the counsels and decisions arising there, and in the inner world of his home, he must conduct himself in 'the wholeness' of his heart – consistently in accord with God's requirements. He undertakes to banish from his mind any evil purpose (v. 3b 'any word / thing of Belial', an embodiment of evil) and not to let deeds of unfaithfulness ('swervings' from God's way, v. 3a) stick to his hands or heart.

4–7   However much the ideal of sovereignty was focused on a single figure, the Lord's Anointed, an immense amount of administration and rule was in the hands of ministers and officials. These verses therefore concentrate on the need for a just king to govern through honest servants. Those of crooked heart, those who use slander to advance themselves, the arrogant and those intent on gathering wealth and power for themselves, all such corrupt characters who in fact gravitate towards the opportunities of government, and might have the means to ingratiate themselves and even to make themselves seem indispensable — all such the just king must exclude from his service. He must be ever alert to find the reliable and faithful (true in the way of 'wholeness' towards God) to serve in the palace and other centres of power. In vv. 6a and 8b 'earth' is more commonly rendered here as 'land', the king's domain, but in the ideal the Lord's Anointed is responsible for the world.

8   As the sun rises day by day, with its all-seeing eye, purity, healing and majesty, so the ideal ruler would rise with it, hear the appeals of the oppressed, discern the truth in the accusations and crimes, and by righteous firmness check the forces of oppression and corruption that would else swamp the society (cf. 2 Sam. 15.2; 23.1–7; Jer. 21.12; Ps. 75.10). So the king now concludes his avowal of loyalty to the duty given him by the Lord with a commitment to such daily jurisdiction, for the protection of the holy city and the earth which it represents. The severe language for the king's judicial action has to be seen in the light of 72; it is above all an uncompromising action against the powerful who would prey on the defenceless.

On king and people this psalm and its accompanying ceremony impressed the Lord's requirement of faithful love, truth and sincerity. Only to a king so minded would the Lord come as partner in rule, furtherer of policies, giver of victories. Both in his private and his public life the king should follow the Lord's way with a whole heart and exert himself to employ only those true in this way. It was above all a disposition of humility and trust that was required, making way for the Spirit; for it was recognized that only by God's Spirit could the ruler carry the immense burdens of his office. The prophet Isaiah (11.1f.) expressed this ideal in a prophecy of one that should come, one filled with all the gifts of the Spirit, slaying the wicked by the breath of his mouth, creating a harmony of people, animals and nature where none would hurt or destroy. The ideal is carried forward in the New Testament and focused in the Christ who has pleaded from his ordeal, and is made king and judge to establish the community of faithful love in the city of God; Paul declares him the man ordained to judge the world in righteousness (Acts 17.31), and visionary John sees him with seven stars in his hand, a sword proceeding from his mouth, and his face like the sun in his strength (Rev. 1.16).

Integrity in government is a heavy subject, but it is striking that here it is expressed in a song, a poem to be sung and played to the Lord. Justice indeed must rise above rules and codes of practice and deeply breathe the air of the arts; only so does it engage the imagination, the heart, the very soul, and find the way of wholeness. What music indeed is this song for the Lord, for its melody is the union of *mishpat* and *hesed*, just government and faithful love!

Help us, Lord, to sing to you of faithful love and justice as we take our way through community and home, work and leisure; and may the music of humility and kindness ever resound in our hearts, that we may be accepted for the service of our king, your Son, Jesus Christ.

PSALM 102: The Sufferings of the Intercessor

Prayer.   Of a sufferer, fainting and pouring out a plea before the Lord.

1   Lord, hear my prayer,
    and let my crying come before you.
2   Do not hide your face from me
    in the day of my distress.
    Turn your ear to me;
    in the day when I call, be quick to answer me.
3   For my days are consumed in smoke;
    my bones burn as in a furnace.
4   My heart is smitten and withered like grass,
    so that I forget to eat my bread.

5 I am weary from the noise of my groaning,
   and my bones cleave to my skin.
6 I am become like an owl of the wilderness,
   like the owl that haunts the ruins.
7 I watch and am like the bird
   that sits alone on the rooftops.
8 My enemies revile me all the day long;
   those who rage at me are sworn together against me.
9 Ashes I eat for bread,
   and I mingle my drink with my tears,
10 because of your indignation and wrath,
   for you have taken me up and cast me down.
11 My days are like a shadow that declines,
   and I wither away like grass.
12 But you, Lord, sit as King for ever,
   and your name shall be invoked through all generations.
13 You will arise and have pity on Zion;
   it is time to have pity on her,
     surely the appointed time has come.
14 For your servants love her very stones,
   and feel compassion for her dust.
15 Then the nations shall see the name of the Lord,
   and all the kings of the earth your glory,
16 when the Lord shall have built up Zion,
   and shown himself in his glory,
17 when he has turned to the prayer of the destitute,
   and has not despised their plea.
18 This shall be written for those that come after,
   and a people to be created shall praise the Lord,
19 that the Lord has looked down from his holy height,
   and out of heaven regarded the earth,
20 to hear the groaning of the prisoner,
   and set free those condemned to death,
21 that the name of the Lord be told in Zion,
   and his praises in Jerusalem,
22 when the peoples are gathered together,
   and the kings, to serve the Lord.
23 He has brought down my strength in my journey,
   and he has cut short my days.
24 I pray, my God, do not take me in the midst of my days,
   you whose years are throughout all generations.
25 In the beginning you founded the earth,
   and the heavens were the work of your hands.
   They will perish, but you will remain,
26 and they will all wear out like a garment.
   You will change them like clothing and they will be changed,

27 but you are he, and your years shall have no end.
28 The children of your servants shall abide,
     and their seed shall be established before you.

For much of this great prayer we seem to hear the supplication of an individual sufferer (vv. 1–11, 23–4). Yet in the remainder, where the plea is urged in forms of praise (vv. 12–22, 25–8), the concern is only for the fate of Zion. This all makes sense if the solo voice is that of a representative, such as the king or his successor in exilic times. All the community's sufferings are borne by this single figure, the representative and penitential intercessor, who first cries out as a lonely sufferer, and then expressly seeks to stir God's pity for the city and people (cf. Lam. 1.12f.; 3). The reference to Zion's pitiable stones and dust and to prisoners expecting death may reflect conditions after the destruction of 587 (cf. Pss 74 and 79), but this is not certain. The unique heading, although sounding quite general, may refer to a leader undertaking such a role as representative 'sufferer' (*'ani*, cf. 22.24); the word for 'faints' can otherwise be rendered 'when he wraps himself' – puts on sackcloth (so Bentzen). One of the church's seven Penitential Psalms (see above on 6), its use has included Ash Wednesday. Verses 25–7 are strikingly quoted in Heb. 1.10–12 as address to Christ the creative Word. There are resemblances especially with 22 and 69.

1–11 The supplicant first implores the Lord's attention (vv. 1–2), his first word being the holy name (cf. above on 20.1f.). The 'day' of distress, the 'day' of his crying to the Lord, may be the special day of national penitence and intercession (cf. Joel 2.15f.). The distress depicted in vv. 3–11 is in part a reflection of the penitential rites – fasting, vigils, sackcloth and ashes (cf. 42.5), but this in turn is a manifestation of the distress of the soul that represents a tormented community. In vv. 6–7 the comparison may be with one bird throughout, a solitary owl that sits on the skeletal tops of ruined buildings in the wilderness, its weird voice echoing through the night as it were the moan of the dead. The sufferer likewise feels that he sinks in the land of death; his days are like the lengthening shadow that will soon be lost in the total dark (cf. 109.23). The circle of enemies closes round, reviling, raging, a malicious alliance; such are the enemies never absent from the afflicted king or nation, and in final extremity appearing as demonic, mocking shapes of death (cf. 22.12f.).

12–22 The wider significance of the sufferings now begins to appear. The praise of the Lord as everlasting King ('one who sits') is meant to make the contrast with the nation's prince, whose days are so pathetic (vv. 3, 11). Throughout all generations stands the Lord's name (*zeker*, his memorial, as invoked in praise and prayer; another reading has 'throne'). The words of trust in v. 13 still press the plea: surely the Lord will come in compassion, surely the appointed time of salvation for Zion has come! In v. 14 the Lord's love of Zion is taken for granted, and it is the pity of this praying people for the very stones and dust of Zion which is held up in plea; they keep faith with the city of the Lord (cf. 137) and he will count it in their favour. The thrust of the prayer is further strengthened with the thought that an answering salvation would serve the Lord's glory. Salvation for Zion will be a revelation for all the world; his name will be 'seen' (cf. Isa. 59.19; another reading gives 'feared') and all nations and kings will worship at his glorious epiphany. (The Hebrew of v. 17 refers first to the 'prayer of the destitute man' and then treats it as 'their prayer', fitting the interpretation of vv. 1–11 as the voice of a representative.) The singer undertakes that when the Lord indeed hears the groans of the prisoners and frees those condemned to death, a written record will be made of the salvation, to evoke God's praise among a generation yet to be created (cf. Isa. 30.8); and the prospect brings again the vision of a salvation that will spread to all the world.

23–28   The lament returns abruptly; the whole crisis of suffering is expressed as the Lord's blow against this one sufferer, a blow that has struck down his strength in mid-course and cut short the days of normal life. He gathers up his plea into a final petition: 'I say (/pray): O my God (*eli*, cf. 22.1), do not take me away at the half of my days.' And he repeats the contrast of vv. 11–12 – his days in any case so few in comparison with the eternity of the Creator, for whom even the earth and heaven are but as perishable, replaceable garments. 'You are He' – the unique sovereign Reality, the eternal Holy One (cf. Deut. 32.39; Isa. 41.4; 43.10, 13; 46.4; 48.12). The concluding verse sounds a note of confidence, but it is in effect a plea that the everlasting Creator will save his servants, his worshippers, from this peril of oblivion, and establish before his face their life and its continuation in generations to come.

Sympathy has its degrees. The intercessor in this psalm has taken the agony of his community wholly into his own heart. His own days are consumed in the fires of tribulation and his bones burn in its furnace. The loneliness of the forsaken, the helpless, the abandoned, hangs like a shroud upon him. With his people, he knows what it is to be taken up by God, only to be cast down. Little is said directly about the love or goodness of God, but much is implicit. The enduring Creator-King does not rule without the aim of blessing his world and people. His 'memorial', his name invoked through all generations, embodies his utter commitment and care. In the mystery of his appointed time he will come in pity to save his 'Zion', building her again, making her radiant with his presence.

   The psalm leads those who pray for the church to the deepest level of sympathy, where they themselves bear the afflictions and forsakenness of this 'Zion' of God that is the heart of his world, the emblem of the family of all creatures. They will be speaking with the voice of the one who gathers all this suffering into his own, and who in his own person binds it to the everlasting love of the Creator. For he himself, the intercessor, is also the name of God and the Word through whom he created all (Heb. 1.10–12). The suffering, the compassion and the salvation are joined in him; fire and rose are one.

Eternal Lord, let our crying come before you for the ruined places of the earth, for captives and those condemned to death; have pity on the stones of your holy place and fill her with your glory, that all your creatures may worship you together in gladness and in peace, through him who is our intercessor, Jesus your Son and your Word.

PSALM 103: The Soul that Finds God's World

Of David.

1   Bless the Lord, O my soul,
     and all that is within me, bless his holy name.
2   Bless the Lord, O my soul,
     and do not forget all he does for you,
3   forgiving all your wrongdoing,
     healing all your sicknesses,
4   redeeming your life from death's hold,
     encircling you with faithful love and compassion,
5   satisfying you daily with good things,
     so that your youth is renewed as an eagle's.
6   The Lord does deeds of salvation
     and justice for all the oppressed.
7   He made known his ways to Moses,
     his deeds to the children of Israel.
8   Compassionate and gracious is the Lord,
     patient and plenteous in faithful love.
9   He will not always be contending,
     nor for ever be displeased.
10   He has not dealt with us according to our sins,
     nor rewarded us according to our offences.
11   For as the heavens are high above the earth,
     so great is his love over those who fear him.
12   As far as the east is from the west,
     so far has he removed our sins from us.
13   As a father has pity on his children,
     so the Lord has pity on those who fear him.
14   For well he knows how we are formed;
     he is mindful that we are but clay.
15   Man's days are but as grass;
     he flowers like the flower of the field;
16   when a wind passes over him he is gone,
     and his very place will know him no more.
17   But the faithful love of the Lord is from of old and for ever

> upon those who fear him,
>   and his goodness upon children's children,
> 18 for those who keep his covenant,
>   and remember his commandments and do them.
> 19 The Lord has established his throne in heaven,
>   and his kingship rules over all.
> 20 Bless the Lord, you his angels,
>   you mighty ones who do his bidding,
>   and obey the voice of his word.
> 21 Bless the Lord, all his hosts,
>   you servants who do his pleasure.
> 22 Bless the Lord, all that he has made,
>   in all places of his dominion;
>   bless the Lord, O you my soul.

This beautiful psalm takes the form of a hymn, consisting of calls to praise and reasons for praise. But a distinctive feature, imparting a heartfelt warmth, is the casting of the opening lines (vv. 1–5) in the form of exhortation to the singer's own soul, resumed only in the final phrase (v. 22b). In the rest of the psalm the expressions are those of the usual congregational hymn, with references to 'we/us/our', to Moses, Israel, the covenant, man's frailty, God's kingship and the universal circle of worship (angels and all created beings joining the praise). Although the tone of gratitude to God for all his goodness is strong throughout, the hymnic form gives a general testimony, not focused on some particular event as in the psalms of thanksgiving. We may imagine the psalm as intended for the assembly at the autumn festival, when the ceremonies have signified atonement and forgiveness, renewal of the springs of life, and the proclamation of the Lord's kingship over all. The 'individual' form of the opening would then be a variation of the usual calls to praise, the singer giving the lead and example for every one present to engage their whole heart. A late date is favoured by many in view of several apparently Aramaic touches in the language and resemblances to Second Isaiah and Job. However, the dialectal forms could be of any period, and the relevant poetic traditions are no doubt ancient. The relationship to the possibly ancient 104 cautions against very late dating, and some weight also can be given to the royal heading.

1–5 The summons to praise the Lord takes the form of self-exhortation (so also 104.1, 35, and more generally 42.5; 146.1). Of several words that might have been chosen for praise, 'bless' is our poet's choice, moreover three times here and four times at the end. It is the word for praise most warm with gratitude. By the 'soul' and 'all my inward parts' is meant the very core of one's being, with all the powers of heart and mind; with God's 'name' is meant the form of his making himself known, giving himself in power and grace. Alas, when relief is given, the heart easily comes to take it for granted; so 'do not forget' urges the singer, 'do not forget all his deeds' (of salvation; cf.

2 Chron. 32.25). These acts of grace are then depicted in general terms; in a hymnic style, five participles describe the Lord in his constant, ever-repeated work of care. He, and none but he, is the one who forgives, heals from sickness, wins back from the abyss, encircles with tenderness and faithfulness, constantly nourishes with good things. The comparison with the eagle (or griffon-vulture), similar to that in Isa. 40.31, may refer to the great bird's renewal of feathers after moulting, or simply to its amazing flight as it soars effortlessly to great heights on currents of warm air.

6–18 The reasons for thankful praise are now continued in the more usual style, cataloguing the Lord's saving deeds on behalf of the oppressed, and so for the enslaved people of Israel. Ever since their deliverance he has been proclaimed as the compassionate and faithful one, slow to anger (cf. Ex. 34.5f.). The divine forgiveness is especially dwelt upon. His is a love which will not give up; its persistence is compared to that of a father for his children. Moreover, the Lord is eager utterly to remove the sins, with all their guilt and entail. He is mindful of human frailty and transience, and through his faithful love he gives an enduring meaning to human life, expressed here as the continuity of life running through the generations (cf. 102.28) – a blessing for those who fear him and endeavour to keep the way of his covenant laws.

19-22 The skilful psalmist now moves into his widest perspective. He echoes the great proclamation of the festival that the Lord has established his throne and kingdom (93, 96-99), his reign breaking with new light and glory over all the world. The great circle summoned to bless him now extends to his servants in the heavenly sphere (cf. 29.1) and indeed to all he has made, all his creatures (cf. 96.11f.; 98.7f.). All the 'places of his dominion' can be understood as comprehending the wondrous places remote from our experience, but ever open to the presence of God the King. And the round of praise returns at last to its starting point, the overflowing gratitude of the singer's inmost being.

Here is a small key that opens to mighty spaces. From the warm response of a single soul, the way leads to the fellowship of the people that fear God, to all who have known deliverance from oppression, on to the ministers of the heavens, and so to all created beings. In the thankful sincerity of the one soul lies the capacity to love God as he is and the world as it will be. The thankfulness centres in the experience of forgiveness; it is the knowledge of God as the awesome One who upholds all that is just and good, and yet is full of pity and mercy, patient, and wonderful in his tenacious and abundant love. His forgiveness delivers from the dark abyss, and gives new life as the redeemed soul rises on the breath of his Spirit. Against the fleeting nature of life is set the enduring love of God. Belief will grow that, blessing God, the soul in its turn is blessed with a place in the heart of God that will never be lost.

Father, grant us the heart to bless you with such sincerity that we are drawn ever deeper into your forgiving love and your renewing grace; may we rejoice to keep your covenant and do your commandments, as you have removed our sins far from us by your mercy in Jesus Christ.

PSALM 104: A Sweet Song of Adoration for the Creator

1 Bless the Lord, O my soul.
   O Lord my God, you appear in glory.
   You have put on majesty and splendour,
2 and wrapped yourself in light as in a garment.
   You spread out the heavens like a curtain,
3 and in their waters laid the beams of your high dwelling.
   You make the clouds your chariot,
   and ride on the wings of the wind.
4 You make the winds your messengers,
   and fire and flame your servants.
5 You founded the earth upon its pillars,
   that it should never be overthrown.
6 The deep covered it like a garment,
   the waters stood high above the hills.
7 At your rebuke they fled;
   at the voice of your thunder they hastened away.
8 They went up the mountains, they went down the valleys,
   to the place which you appointed for them.
9 You set them their bounds that they should not pass,
   nor turn again to cover the earth.
10 You send the springs into the brooks,
   to run among the hills.
11 They give drink to every creature of the field;
   the wild asses quench their thirst.
12 By the brooks dwell the birds of the heavens,
   and give voice among the branches.
13 From your high dwelling you water the hills,
   and the earth is replenished through all your work.
14 You make grass to grow for the cattle,
   and crops for the labour of the people,
   to bring forth food from the earth,
15 and wine that gladdens their heart,
   oil that makes their faces to shine,
   and bread to sustain their heart.

16 The trees of the Lord are well nourished,
    the cedars of Lebanon which he himself has planted,
17 where the birds make their nests,
    while the stork has her house in the fir-trees.
18 The wild goats have the highest mountains;
    the rock badgers find refuge in the cliffs.
19 You made the moon to mark the seasons,
    and the sun that knows his time to set.
20 You made darkness that night may fall,
    when all the beasts of the forest creep forth.
21 The lions roar for their portion,
    and seek their food from God.
22 The sun rises and they are gone,
    to lie down to rest in their dens.
23 Then the people go out to their work
    and to labour until the evening.
24 How many are your works, O Lord,
        and all of them done with wisdom!
    The earth is filled with your creatures.
25 Yonder is the sea, great and wide,
    and there move creatures beyond number,
        both small and great.
26 There go the ships, and there is Leviathan,
    whom you formed to play in the waves.
27 These all look to you,
    to give them their food at the proper time.
28 When you give it them they gather it;
    you open your hand and they are filled with good.
29 When you hide your face they are troubled;
    when you take away their breath,
        they die and return to their clay.
30 When you send out your Spirit they are created,
    and you renew the face of the ground.
31 May the glory of the Lord be for evermore,
    and the Lord ever rejoice in his works,
32 who but looks on the earth and it trembles,
    or touches the mountains and they smoke.
33 I will sing to the Lord as long as I live;
    I will make music to my God while I have my being.
34 So shall my song be sweet to him,
    while I rejoice in the Lord.
35 Let sinners be taken from the earth,
        and the wicked be no more;
    bless the Lord, O you my soul.

The alleluia placed at the end of this psalm in the Hebrew should probably with LXX be taken as the beginning of 105. Our psalm then begins and ends with the self-exhortation 'Bless the Lord, O my soul' (cf. above on 103.1) and maintains the character of an individual's utterance throughout. However, the theme of praise for the Lord as manifested Creator, ruler, carer and renewer of the world and all its creatures suggests, as many scholars have observed, a setting in the autumn festival; and the vow of constant psalmody and the offering of the composition as a sweet sacrifice (vv. 33–4) also point to a connection with worship at the temple. There are striking similarities with Egyptian materials from the second millennium, especially the great hymn of Akhenaton (Amen-hotep IV) to the Creator manifest in the sun-disk, the Aton (*ANET*, pp. 369f., *TUAT*, pp. 848f.; note also his smaller hymn, *TUAT*, pp. 846f.). While remaining entirely true to the Israelite faith in Yahweh and the Hebrew traditions of creation reflected in Job and Genesis, our psalmist seems to have inherited Egyptian influence, probably passed down from the pre-Israelite poets of Jerusalem who had lived under the Egyptian empire. The Akhenaton hymn is expressed as Pharaoh's adoration, and one may wonder if our psalm also was meant as specifically the king's act of praise, which of course would have significance for the people and the world, not least in defending them with prayer from the evil ones (v. 35). A heading 'Of David' is indeed found in a Qumran manuscript and in LXX.

1–4 The singer first calls his soul to thankful praise (cf. above on 103.1). Then, addressing the Lord directly (a style not so common in Hebrew hymns), he praises the present manifestation of the Lord, a revelation of his greatness (lit. 'how you have become very great'). God appears in royal splendour, the victorious Creator (cf. above on 93.1). The triumph of creation is recalled in several features – the spreading of the heavens like an arch or canopy above the earth, undergirding the heavenly ocean; the founding of the heavenly palace or temple in these waters; the riding of God across the heavens on clouds and the wings of the wind, attended by angelic servants of storm and lightning. All this is referred to in a construction (with Hebrew participles) that focuses not on the deeds as such but on the doer, the mighty one now revealed.

5–9 Tribute to the Creator continues with reference to the firm foundation of the earth upon its bases, the bottoms of the great mountains (cf. 24.2; 75.3; 82.5). Then reference is made to the vital work of mastering and organizing the waters. The great deep ('Tehom') that covered the earth was put to flight by the thunder roar of the warrior-Creator, then divided, with part driven up to become the heavenly ocean, and part sent down through the clefts to form the subterranean waters (cf. 74.12–15; Gen.1.7; some think of the ascending waters as simply becoming mountain springs, but this would fall short of the tradition of the division of the deep, and in Akhenaton's hymn also there is reference to the 'Nile of the sky' and 'the Nile from the underworld').

10–18   The tribute of praise now passes on to the present and continuing work of the Creator. From his kingship over the waters he is able to dispense the gifts of life. Out in the wilderness and remote mountains, where man's control is not known, the Creator's care of his creatures is a special source of wonder (cf. Job 38.39f.). He makes the brooks to provide for the onager or wild ass (cf. Job 39.5–8) and other animals. The flood-beds produce belts of trees and shrubs along the banks, where the birds nest happily and 'give voice' (in many kinds of utterance). From the waters imagined as stored in the roof chambers of his heavenly palace, the Lord pours down rains to saturate the earth, producing grass for the animals and crops to be turned by human labour into bread, wine and oil. Especially wonderful are the giant trees which only the Lord could have planted and tended, the cedars of Mount Lebanon. Here again is provision for birds, though it is in the fir trees that the huge nests, the 'houses', of the stork are prominent. The craggy mountains are there for the nimbly leaping ibex or wild goats, and also for the rock hyraxes. These latter animals, about the size of a rabbit and with round backs and no visible tail, can tread surely on steep rocky surfaces; they love to sit in groups in the sun, while one is posted to keep guard as a sentry (cf. Prov. 30.24, 26).

19–23   The Lord's care is further seen in the wonders of night and morning. He made the moon to mark the round of months and holy days; he made the sun, so regular to set and leave the world to darkness. Whereas in Akhenaton's hymn the night is a rather sinister time, when the face of the solar god is withdrawn, for the Hebrew poet it is a time wisely appointed and used by the Lord. In the darkness nocturnal animals have their proper turn, and the roar of lions is their prayer to God for their due portion. Sunrise again is the proper time for the commencement of human labour. So God makes provision for all.

24–26   The psalmist exclaims at the sheer multitude of creatures in earth and sea, and each one created with 'wisdom', that divine quality of understanding and skill which here, as in Prov. 8 and Job 28, may be envisaged as a being who shares and delights in all the Creator does.. The ships that float and make their way by the winds become part of the wonderful scene of the great open sea, and the sight of large marine creatures leaping and turning in the waves is reflected in the myth of Leviathan, the personification of the chaos-waters as a fearsome sea-monster that the Lord was able to control and make part of his benevolent kingdom (cf. Job 41).

27–30   Wonder extends not only to the creation, but also to the continuing care and sustenance of these myriads. There is not one that does not look to God for food from his hand. The time comes when he lets them be troubled and die, and turn again to the elemental material from which he had formed them. But then comes re-creation and renewal, when God sends forth his breath or Spirit, from which is derived the living spirit of every creature. So the face of the earth is renewed, and plants and animals live again.

31–35 The great survey of the created order has all been but a tribute to the Lord manifest in his glory. So now the conclusion returns to this glory of the Lord, and a blessing-wish is offered for the everlasting splendour and joy of the Creator in all his works, he who is so mighty that a look or a touch from him can bring earthquakes and volcanic eruptions (cf. 18.7; 97.2f.; 144.5). The singer undertakes to offer psalm-praise to this God as long as he has breath (cf. 61.8), offering it as an acceptable sacrifice (cf. on 19.14), expressive of delight in the Lord. Perhaps we discern the kingly character of the psalmist not only in the commitment to continual praise through temple music, but also in the prayer against the sinners and wicked of the earth. May those who would defile and ruin the good world of life be removed from it. Here we glimpse the responsibility of our race to guard the treasure of life, not least by strong and continuing prayer. The last word is the renewed exhortation to the singer's own soul, to bless, and bless again, this Lord of all. (The 'alleluia' is best taken to begin the next psalm; see above.)

Readily the soul may wonder at the curtain of heaven, the stores of water on high and below, the animals of the wild that find their places to drink, the birds that weave their nests and sing their countless melodies, the little animals that tread the rock-faces so surely, the seedtime and harvest, the constancies of moon and sun, dark and light, the width of the sea, the play of dolphins, the course of the ships through waves and wind. But for our psalmist, as for the poet of Job 38f., the real wonder is the wisdom and glory of God discerned in all these things. The world indeed is vast and multitudinous in its kinds, but the beginning and end of this meditation is the soul that recognizes and blesses the Lord in it all. Notable is the way the poet puts human beings within his list of the creatures that depend on the Lord; they appear humbly alongside their fellow creatures. Time was when the concluding prayer (v. 35) might be found jarring within the sweet meditation. But as human exploitation becomes ever more comprehensive, the prayer against the ruining of earth's order and species is seen as ever more important. Coming at the end of the psalm, it can appropriately be read as its climax. The sinners that exploit to ruination are many indeed, and the prayer for the removal of this cruel work from the good kingdom of life must burst from the soul that has loved and wondered at the creatures of God.

O glorious God, creating and caring for all that has being, help us to sing to you through all our life with the sweetness of joyful adoration; deepen our tenderness for all your creatures and take from the hearts of all people the callousness and greed which harm your world.

PSALM 105: Seeking the Lord through the Sacred Story

1   Alleluia.
     Give thanks to the Lord, proclaim his name;
     make known his deeds among the peoples.
2   Sing to him, make music to him;
     make songs of all his marvellous works.
3   Rejoice in the praise of his holy name;
     let the heart of those that seek the Lord be merry.
4   Seek the Lord and his strength;
     seek his face for evermore.
5   Recall the wonders he has done,
     his marvels and the judgements of his mouth,
6   O seed of Abraham his servant,
     O children of Jacob his chosen one.
7   He is the Lord our God,
     whose judgements are in all the earth.
8   He has remembered his covenant for ever,
     the word which he ordained for a thousand generations,
9   the covenant which he made with Abraham,
     the pledge which he gave to Isaac.
10   He confirmed it also to Jacob as a statute,
     to Israel as an everlasting covenant,
11   saying, To you I will give the land of Canaan,
     to be the portion of your inheritance.
12   When they were small in number,
     few indeed, and strangers in the land,
13   and they wandered from nation to nation,
     from one kingdom to another,
14   he suffered no one to oppress them,
     and reproved even kings for their sake:
15   Lay no hand on my anointed ones,
     and do my prophets no harm.
16   He called out famine against the land;
     he broke every staff of bread.
17   He had sent a man before them;
     Joseph was sold as a slave.
18   They afflicted his feet with shackles;
     his neck was ringed with iron.
19   Till all he foretold came to pass,
     the word of the Lord was testing him.
20   The king sent and released him;

the ruler of peoples set him free.

21   He appointed him lord of his household,
    the ruler of all he possessed.

22   to instruct his princes as he wished,
    and teach his elders wisdom.

23   Then Israel came into Egypt,
    and Jacob lived as an alien in the land of Ham.

24   The Lord made his people very fruitful,
    and made them more numerous than their foes,

25   whose heart he turned to hate his people,
    and craftily plot against his servants.

26   He sent Moses his servant,
    and Aaron whom he had chosen.

27   At their word he showed his signs,
    his wonders in the land of Ham.

28   He sent darkness and all grew dark,
    yet they did not heed his words.

29   He turned their waters into blood,
    and so brought death to their fish.

30   Their land swarmed with frogs,
    till they filled the rooms of the palace.

31   He spoke, and in came clouds of flies,
    swarms of gnats throughout the country.

32   He gave them hail for rain,
    and flames of lightning across their land.

33   Then he struck their vines and fig trees,
    and broke down the trees on their hills.

34   He spoke, and there came swarms of flying locusts,
    then creeping locusts beyond all counting.

35   They ate up every plant in their land,
    and devoured the produce of their soil.

36   Then he struck all the first-born in their land,
    the first-fruits of all their strength.

37   He brought his people out with silver and gold,
    and there was not one among their tribes that stumbled.

38   Egypt was glad at their departing,
    for a dread of them had fallen upon them.

39   He spread out cloud for a covering,
    and fire to light up the night.

40   They asked, and he brought them quails,
    and with the bread of heaven he satisfied them.

41   He opened the rock and the waters gushed out,
    and ran in the parched land like a river.

42   For he remembered his holy word,
    and Abraham his servant.

43   So he brought out his people with joy,

his chosen ones with singing.
44   And he gave them lands of the nations;
     they took possession of the labour of peoples,
45   that they might keep his statutes,
     and faithfully observe his laws.
     Alleluia.

The psalm appears to be a hymn for a festal occasion when the thought of the covenant was to the fore. The introduction has the usual calls to praise (vv. 1–6), followed by reasons (vv. 7–11). These reasons are then developed in a long review of God's grace to the ancestors (vv. 12–45, cf. Pss 78 and 106), all in illustration of how he kept his promise to Abraham for the settlement of his descendants in Canaan, 'that they might keep his laws'. The alleluias at the beginning (see above on 104.35) and the end reinforce the character of the psalm as primarily praise. The Chronicler puts part of this psalm into his account of David's bringing in of the ark (1 Chron. 16.8f.), which suits the psalm's festal character. It is commonly thought, however, that it was composed about the fourth century, being dependent on the Pentateuch. The considerable number of differences from the Pentateuchal narrative are then explained as due to poetic freedom. But others prefer to see the psalmist as drawing rather on a living tradition of recital in worship. In this case the question of date is more open, and the pre-exilic period need not be ruled out. The differences from the Pentateuch include the psalm's account of the testing of Joseph by the word of the Lord, the order and total of the plagues in Egypt, the absence of reference to Sinai, the benevolent purpose of the incident of the quails, and the cloud not as a pillar but as a covering. The only covenant is that with Abraham, on later occasions confirmed or remembered.

1–6   The most concentrated call to praise, 'Alleluia' ('Praise ye Yah'), is filled out with rich phrases. The congregation, heirs of Abraham and Jacob, are to testify to all the world of the faithful and wonderful deeds that founded and shaped their destiny as a people. In this joyful witness, it is the Lord himself that is celebrated; his name is proclaimed and praised, and so the power of his presence is felt. The witnesses turn ever and again to the Lord, seeking him in the manifestations of his 'strength / glory' and his 'face' that he gives especially in his sanctuary. And the special stress of the psalm, soon to be greatly developed, is that he is to be experienced ever anew through the recalling and reciting of the tradition of his marvellous deeds.

7–11   The reasons for praise centre on the covenant made with Abraham and confirmed to Isaac and Jacob, essentially a promise that their descendants should receive the land of Canaan as their heritage (Gen. 12.7; 26.3; 28.13f.; 35.9f.). But at the very heart of the praise is the person of the revealed Lord and the relationship with him; he is 'Yahweh our God' and at the same time the ruler of the world (v. 7). The covenantal promise which he gave he has 'remembered'; he has stayed true to his word. This statement will now be substantiated from the traditional story of the ancestors.

12–45 Few and vulnerable as were the nomadic patriarchs, the Lord faithfully protected them (for the 'kings' cf. Gen. 12.17; 20.3). They were his 'anointed ones' and 'prophets' in the sense that they were his intimates, specially called to his service and favoured with his converse and self-revelations (cf. Gen. 20.7). The 'staff of bread' is a metaphor for bread as mainstay, but it may arise from the practice of stacking ring-shaped loaves around a pole. The story of Joseph (Gen. 37; 39f.) is dwelt upon; his sufferings are interpreted as a testing and refinement before his great exaltation. (In v. 22a 'to instruct' is the plausible reading of LXX; our Hebrew seems to intend 'to bind', reversing Joseph's previous situation). The story proceeds to the oppression of the Hebrews in Egypt; the plagues here are fewer than the ten in Ex. 7.20f. and in a different order. The slaves were brought out laden with treasure (Ex. 12.35f.), as it were a payment for their enforced service. The joyful hymns in the story of the Exodus (v. 43) reflect the way it was commemorated down the centuries (cf. Ex. 15). The events at Mount Sinai are not mentioned, but the keeping of the Lord's commandments is said to be the purpose of the gift of the land (v. 45). The 'alleluia' (cf. on v. 1) encloses all the contents of the psalm in the community's praise of the Lord.

In this part of the Psalter we have seen a variety of ways for the individual or congregation to 'become immersed in the praise of God' (so the sense of the verb in 105. 3a). One may dwell on the experience of forgiveness, healing and life renewed (103), or on the marvels of light and rain, plants and animals, measureless sea and fertile earth (104). In 105 thought is directed to the Lord's faithfulness as evinced in the sacred story that ran from the call of Abraham to the settlement of the tribes in the promised land. The story is rehearsed simply to show that faithfulness and grace; other aspects, such as the people's frequent backslidings, are passed over. The heart of the story is that the Lord solemnly promised to the nomadic patriarchs that their descendants would be given land as a heritage and possession, and he fulfilled the promise 'so that they might keep his laws'. We discern here that the promise was fundamentally about life before the face of the Lord; the ever growing people would have a home with God, a place for the rich fulfilment of life with him, bound to him in loyalty and loving obedience. It is this fundamental purpose of the promise to Abraham which is taken up in the New Testament, as it recognizes the promised extension of Abraham's blessing to all the families of the nations. The ancient pledge is still vital, but it is now 'remembered' or kept by God in the coming of Christ (Luke 1.68–79). For through him is given that pleasant land, that heavenly country, where God's more multitudinous people can enjoy the true and abundant life according to his word and will (Heb. 3.7f.; 11.13f.). The church's praise will indeed remember the oath to Abraham and his seed, but also the unfolding of its deepest sense in Christ. Here are wonders enough to encourage the great congregation to seek the Lord's face evermore and praise him with a merry heart.

God of Abraham, grant that we may so hear the story of your work in ancient times, that we may recognize you now as the Lord our God, ever marvellous in power and love; and may we be strengthened by the example of those whom you tested, refined and found faithful in your service.

PSALM 106: Sinfulness of Centuries and God's Persevering Goodness

1 Alleluia.
   Give thanks to the Lord for he is good;
   his faithfulness is for ever.
2 Who can express the mighty deeds of the Lord,
   or tell out all his praise?
3 Happy those who treasure what is right,
   and always do what is just.
4 Remember me, Lord, in the time of favour for your people;
   consider me in the day of your salvation,
5 that I may see the happiness of your chosen,
      and rejoice in the gladness of your people,
   and glory with your inheritance.
6 We have sinned with our fathers;
   we have done wrong and acted wickedly.
7 In Egypt they did not consider your wonders,
      or remember the greatness of your faithful love,
   but defied the Most High at the Sea of Reeds.
8 Yet he saved them for the sake of his name,
   that he might make his power to be known.
9 He rebuked the Sea of Reeds and it dried up,
   and he led them through the deeps
      as through a land of pasture.
10 He saved them from the enemy's hand,
   and redeemed them from the hand of the foe.
11 The waters covered their oppressors;
   there was not one of them left.
12 Then they believed in his words;
   they sang aloud his praise.
13 But very soon they forgot his works;
   they would not wait for his counsel.
14 A craving seized them in the wilderness,

and they tested God in the desert.

15 So he gave them what they asked,
  but sent a wasting sickness into their souls.

16 They grew jealous of Moses in the camp,
  and of Aaron, the holy one of the Lord.

17 Then the earth opened and swallowed up Dathan,
  and covered the company of Abiram.

18 A fire was kindled against their party;
  the flame burnt up the wicked.

19 They made a calf at Horeb,
  and worshipped the molten image.

20 And so they exchanged God's glory
  for the likeness of a bull that feeds on grass.

21 They forgot God their saviour,
  who had done such great things in Egypt,

22 wonders in the land of Ham,
  awesome things by the Sea of Reeds.

23 Therefore he would have destroyed them,
  had not Moses his chosen one stood in the breach before him,
    to turn back his wrath from that destruction.

24 Then they scorned the pleasant land,
  and would not believe his word,

25 but murmured in their tents,
  and would not heed the voice of the Lord.

26 So he lifted his hand against them,
  vowing to overthrow them in the wilderness,

27 to cast out their children among the nations,
  and scatter them through the lands.

28 They yoked themselves to the god of Peor,
  and ate sacrifices offered to the dead.

29 They provoked him with their evil deeds,
  and plague broke out among them.

30 Then Phinehas arose in judgement,
  and so the plague was stayed;

31 and that has been counted to his credit
  throughout the generations for evermore.

32 They angered him also at the waters of Meribah,
  so that Moses suffered for their sake.

33 For they so embittered his spirit,
  that he spoke rashly with his lips.

34 They did not destroy the peoples,
  as the Lord had told them to do.

35 They mingled with the nations,
  and learnt to follow their ways.

36 Thus they worshipped their idols,
  and this became for them a snare.

37 They sacrificed their sons
   and their daughters to evil spirits.
38 So they shed innocent blood,
   the blood of their sons and daughters,
   whom they sacrificed to the idols of Canaan,
   and the land was defiled with their blood.
39 They were polluted by their acts,
   prostituting themselves by their evil deeds.
40 So the anger of the Lord was kindled against his people,
   and he abhorred his own inheritance.
41 He gave them into the hand of the nations,
   and their enemies ruled over them.
42 Their adversaries oppressed them,
   and they were subjected under their hand.
43 Many a time he delivered them;
   but they were rebellious in their counsel,
     and were brought low by their wrongdoing.
44 Yet he looked upon their adversity,
   when he heard their cry for help.
45 He remembered his covenant with them,
   and relented through the greatness of his faithful love.
46 He made them also to be pitied
   by all who had taken them captive.
47 Save us, O Lord our God,
   and gather us from among the nations,
   to give thanks to your holy name,
   and glory in your praise.
48 Blessed be the Lord, the God of Israel
     from everlasting to everlasting,
   and let all the people say, Amen.
   Alleluia.

The bulk of the psalm consists of a review of the experience of the ancestors. But whereas 105 kept rigorously to the citing of events as examples of God's faithfulness, 106 is as rigorous in presenting the incidents as illustrating the people's infidelity. No doubt such recitals were always adapted to a particular aim, and it is even possible that two would complement each other on the same occasion of worship (Weiser). The introduction strikes the notes of praise and hopeful prayer (vv. 1–5). The main section (vv. 6–46) then confesses sin, the worshippers admitting that their conduct is continuous with that of the unfaithful forebears. This sad tale, however, concludes with the recollection of God's pity, and a concluding verse (47) prays for the salvation and re-gathering of the scattered people. Verse 48 appears to be an addition to mark the end of the fourth book of the Psalter. Plausible is the common view that our psalm is from exilic or post-exilic worship at some annual occasion of penitence and intercession (cf. Zech. 7.3f.; 8.19; more generally Neh. 9;

Ezek. 20). But there remains some uncertainty as to whether the psalm depends on literature of this period or rather on preceding traditions, and Weiser's openness to a pre-exilic date is not unreasonable. The Chronicler combines vv. 1, 47, 48 with 105.1–15 and Psalm 96 in his account of David's festivity with the ark (1 Chron. 16.34f.). The familiarity of New Testament writers with the psalm appears in Luke 1.68, 71f.; Rom. 1.23f.; Rev. 19.4.

1–5 Initial and concluding alleluias orient the worshippers to an act of praise, in spite of the story of sin which fills much of the long psalm. The congregation is summoned to give thanks and testimony to the Lord because of his goodness or kindness. Verse 1b takes up one of the great congregational responses (cf. especially 136), a rhythmic cry of three stresses in Hebrew, *ki le'olam ḥasdo*, 'truly for ever his faithful love'. At v. 3 the theme of human response is introduced, its positive tone contrasting with what is to be unfolded. The prayer of vv. 4–5 is expressed as an individual's; the cantor sings earnestly for each worshipper. For each there is a challenge to respond to the Lord's grace, and so have part in the hoped-for time of restoration and favour and its fulfilment of joyful praise.

6–12 Verse 6a is often translated 'we have sinned as did our fathers', but the literal 'we have sinned with our fathers' may intend more. They confess indeed that they have sinned in fundamentally the same way as their forebears; but more than that, they feel that the unity of the people through all the generations means a shared responsibility, and so in the end a shared hope in the promises given to the first generations. It was the practice on great days of national lamentation for the worshippers to abase themselves in a confession that included both themselves and the 'fathers', an act of solidarity seeking the grace promised to the first patriarch on behalf of all (Lev. 26.39f.; Jer. 3.25; 14.20). At v. 7 the great narration of the ancestral sins commences. Already in Egypt (cf. Ex. 14.11–12) the lack of trust and the readiness to rebel were evident; how quickly was the significance of the acts of salvation put out of mind! But the counterpoint of grace is already heard. In spite of all, he brought them through the deadly waters and overthrew their pursuers 'for the sake of his name' – in the consistency of the revelation of his nature, supreme in faithfulness and power (cf. 23.3; Ezek. 20.9, 14). The 'rebuking' of the sea echoes the thunder-roar of the warrior Creator in combat with the water-chaos monster (cf. 29.3; 68.30; 74.13f.; 104.7; Isa. 50.2).

13–33 Soon losing the sense of wonder and trust, the people fell into incidents of lust and rebellion – the quails (Num. 11.4f.), Dathan and Abiram (Num. 16), the worship before a bull-image (Ex. 32.4f.), the rejection of the promised land (Num. 14.31). Through this conduct, it was as though a breach had opened in the people's defence; the divine wrath approached, and it was for Moses, the go-between of the covenant, to put his own life in the gap (Ex. 32.10f., Ez. 13.5; 22.30). 'Peor' was a mountain in Moab, east of the Dead Sea, where the cult of the god Baal proved a snare; the intervention of

Phinehas was remembered to the credit of the priests descended from him (Num. 25; for the trouble at the oasis of Meribah and Moses' 'rashness', see Num. 20 and cf. above on Ps. 95.8).

34–47 The scene moves on to the period of the settlement in Canaan. The summary account resembles the constant theme of Judges, resumed in Kings. Worship often swung towards the practices of the fertility cults of Canaan, with child sacrifice being a special abomination; practices of sacred prostitution gave a ready image of 'whoredom' for the infidelity of Israel to her 'marriage bond' with the Lord. Verse 34 reflects the harsh doctrine (for only once in the Psalter) that the idolatrous deviations resulted from failure to destroy the native peoples without pity as a religious duty (Deut. 7.2, 16). The description of the resulting adversities is quite general and meant to cover all the history from the settlement onwards. Even the captivity (v. 46) and need for gathering (v. 47) are not certain references to the Babylonian exile, though most think this likely. The long confession ends with reference to the compassionate relenting of God, which ever and again prevented total catastrophe. From this thought, the concluding prayer is launched that the people be gathered from among the nations, to the greater praise of the Lord.

48 Although this verse was attached already in the Chronicler's time (1 Chron. 16.34f.), it appears to be an addition that marks the end of the fourth book of the Psalter. It reflects a worship where through all adversity the blessing and praise of the Lord are faithfully sustained (cf. on 89.52).

Nations are selective in telling their histories. They dwell on successes. They have heroes with whom the people proudly identify. How different our psalm! Its story is of the persistent failures and offences of the former generations; only the Lord in his goodness could have persevered with them. These tales of the past were always a window into the present. The characterization of the ancient conduct always reflected the storyteller's insight into his own and his people's heart. In a solemn moment of assembly before the Lord, the singer makes confession of the unworthiness of the people to which the worshippers belong, the entire people throughout the generations. The ancient incidents in his song illuminate the lack of trust and devotion still prevalent. But they also reveal the perseverance of God. Beginning and ending with the praise of God, and finding a path through frankness of confession, the singer rests all his hope in the one known from ancient times, the God of mighty deeds, faithfulness and compassion.

O Lord our God, we confess that we, with all your people through the ages, are unworthy of your goodness, and especially that we do not live as those considering and remembering the instances of your grace; may we never scorn the pleasant land of trust and faithfulness before your face, and so may we truly rejoice in your praise and ever bless your holy name.

PSALM 107: When the Shackles of Misery are Broken

1   Give thanks to the Lord, for he is good;
     his faithfulness is for ever.

2   So let the redeemed of the Lord declare,
     even those he redeemed from the hand of distress,

3   and gathered from the lands,
     from east and west, from mountain heights and sea.

4   Some lost their way in the wastes of the wilderness,
     and could find no path to any settlement.

5   They suffered hunger and thirst,
     till their soul was fainting within them.

6   When they cried to the Lord in their trouble,
     he rescued them from all their distress.

7   He led them by the right way,
     till they reached an inhabited place.

8   Let them thank the Lord for his faithful love,
     and his wonders for the children of earth.

9   For he satisfies the longing soul,
     and fills the hungry soul with goodness.

10   Some sat in darkness and the shadow of death,
     bound fast in misery and iron.

11   For they had rebelled against the words of God,
     and despised the counsel of the Most High,

12   and he bowed their heart with heaviness;
     they stumbled and there was none to help them.

13   When they cried to the Lord in their trouble,
     he saved them from all their distress.

14   He brought them out of darkness and the shadow of death,
     and broke their bonds asunder.

15   Let them thank the Lord for his faithful love
     and his wonders for the children of earth.

16   For he has broken the doors of bronze,
     and struck through the bars of iron.

17   Some were foolish and took a rebellious way;
     they suffered because of their misdeeds.

18   Their soul abhorred all manner of food;
     they drew near to the gates of death.

19   When they cried to the Lord in their trouble,
     he saved them from all their distress.

20 He sent his word to heal them,
and deliver them from their perils.
21 Let them thank the Lord for his faithful love
and his wonders to the children of earth.
22 Let them offer sacrifice for thanksgiving,
and tell of his deeds with songs of joy.

23 Some went down to the sea in ships,
to do their work in the mighty waters.
24 These truly saw the work of the Lord,
and his wonders in the deep.
25 For he spoke, and the tempest came at his bidding,
and lifted up his waves.
26 They went up to the heavens and down again to the depths;
their soul melted away in the peril.
27 They reeled and staggered like a drunkard,
and all their wisdom was confused.
28 When they cried to the Lord in their trouble,
he brought them out of all their distress.
29 He made the storm be still,
and the waves of the sea were calmed.
30 Then they rejoiced to be at rest,
and he brought them to the haven they desired.
31 Let them thank the Lord for his faithful love
and his wonders to the children of earth.
32 Let them exalt him in the assembly of the people,
and praise him in the session of the elders.

33 He turns rivers into a wilderness,
and water-springs into thirsty ground.
34 Fruitful land he makes a salty waste,
for the wickedness of those who dwell there.
35 He makes the wilderness a pool of water,
and water-springs out of a land of drought.
36 And there he settles the hungry,
and they build a city to dwell in.
37 They sow fields and plant vineyards,
which produce the fruit of harvest.
38 He blesses them and they increase greatly,
and he does not let their cattle decrease.
39 When some are diminished and brought low,
through oppression, misfortune and sorrow,
40 then he pours contempt on princes,
and makes them wander in trackless wastes;
41 but he raises the poor from their misery,
and increases their families like a flock of sheep.

42   The true of heart shall see it and rejoice,
     and all wickedness shall shut its mouth.
43   Whoever is wise will ponder these things,
     and discern the faithful deeds of the Lord.

Although the fifth book of the Psalter begins here, this psalm has phrases in
common with 105 and 106, and indeed these three have been called a 'tril-
ogy' (Delitzsch). The psalm is nevertheless quite unique in form, having at its
core four examples of divine rescue (from being lost in the desert, from
prison, sickness and storm at sea); symmetrically constructed, these examples
all advocate the consequent duty of thanksgiving (note the refrains in vv. 6
and 8, 13 and 15, 19 and 21, 28 and 31). The introduction to this core is a
summons to thankful praise (v. 1), addressed to a festal assembly of pilgrims
gathered from far and wide, pilgrims who have experiences to give thanks for
(vv. 2–3). Following the core is a substantial piece in hymnic style, and
teaching of the Lord's sovereign power and his disposition to save the humble
and afflicted (vv. 33–43). It is likely that the psalm had its place in one of the
great annual festivals where many of the pilgrims, often from afar, had come
to fulfil vows made in time of distress. It might have served to introduce the
proceedings where the 'redeemed' came forward individually with their
offerings and testimony; or it might have served when thanksgiving was
arranged on behalf of large groupings of pilgrims (little is known of this, but
sometimes an individual would undertake the votive expenses of a number of
other pilgrims, cf. Acts 21.23f.). A rather late post-exilic date for the completed psalm (but not for the core) is widely favoured, suiting the period
when large Jewish populations resided abroad and the didactic style of vv. 33–
43 (thought to be an addition dependent on Job). Some also regard v. 3 (or
vv. 2–3) as an addition referring to return from exile; but this hardly fits the
cases that follow, which would then have to be interpreted metaphorically.
But such theories of expansion (which are very varied in detail) are perhaps
misleading. The psalm as we have it coheres well as belonging to the festal
thank-offerings of any period when the temple flourished, and concluding in
a wisdom style suited to its purpose of instruction.

1–3   The opening call to praise (v. 1a), with the echo of the mass response
(v. 1b), all exactly as 106.1, well introduces the theme of the psalm – the duty
to acknowledge instances of the Lord's faithfulness. We sense in v. 2 that the
gathering is particularly of those who have recent experience of this love to
acknowledge; here are those who have been 'redeemed', delivered by the
intervention of a faithful champion (cf. Isa. 62.12; Ps. 103.4 and on 72.14)
from the grip of 'anguish' (or 'the Enemy', the personification of suffering and
death). The Lord has freed them from their various distresses and now gathers
them as thankful pilgrims from far and wide, from various lands, from
remoteness (*sapon*, the mysterious highest mountain, also rendered 'the
north') and from deadly peril (*yam*, 'the sea', often emended to *yamin*, 'the
south', but the text is well supported and the phrase is found also in Isa.

49.12). The opinion that vv. 2–3 refer to the return from the Exile seems based on an unrealistic view of that somewhat meagre and gradual event, is too quick to assume dependence on Second Isaiah, and does not accord well with what follows.

4–9 In his first example of redemption, the singer pictures travellers in the fierce wasteland, perhaps traders, who have lost their way and almost died from hunger and thirst. Praying as never before, they experience a miracle; they are guided on a way that brings them to an inhabited place, where they are nourished and sheltered. The 'soul' in vv. 5 and 9 is the inner man, the sum of vital energy and being (hardly with Dahood in v. 9 'their throat'). The refrain in v. 8 calls for these redeemed ones to thank the Lord for the miracles of his faithful love shown, not just to one people, but (lit.) to the 'children of man', a phrase suggesting the frailty and transience of the race (cf. 90.3f.).

10–16 A second example pictures some who, having despised the Lord's counsel, had ended up in captivity, prisoners fettered with irons in a cavernous dungeon. They were virtually in the domain of death, remote from help (for death's shadow cf. on 23.4, cf. Luke 1.79). But their prayer was heard and the saviour shattered the prison doors of bronze and bars of iron to bring them out to freedom and the duty of thanksgiving (cf. on v. 8).

17–22 The next example also involves forgiveness for those who had offended. Here were some whose folly had brought on them grave illness, so that they could take no food. Their cry to the Lord was answered by the sending of his word or promise (perhaps a favourable oracle), resulting in healing and rescue from their terrible 'pits' (v. 20b). Their thanksgiving is clearly envisaged in v. 22 as a testimony sung at the fulfilment of their vows of sacrifice.

23–32 Such occasion of thanksgiving is pictured with further detail in this fourth example of deliverance; in the great festal congregation and before the seated array of dignitaries, they extol the Lord as their gracious saviour (v. 32). This case of redemption concerns some who had experienced the peril of storm at sea, sailors and merchants. They prayed, the sea was stilled, and they reached port in safety – a profound experience of miracle indeed, again to be acknowledged in open thanksgiving.

33–43 After the four specific examples, a more general hymnic passage moves to the conclusion by praising the Lord for his power to work trans-formations, particularly in abasing the proud and raising up the humble (cf. Luke 1.46–55). So good land becomes a waste through the wickedness of its inhabitants, and the erstwhile proud and mighty become vagabonds. But for the lowly, hungry ones God sends water, good land, homes, sustenance and blessing. In all this his *hesed* is at work, but not always evidently so. Through all the paradoxes of destiny, the wise, themselves humble and with a listening heart, ponder and are granted to discern the manifold instances of God's everlasting love.

Not denying the constant, everyday relationship with the Lord, the psalm focuses on moments of extreme crisis. Situations are pictured where one sinks in suffering to the very verge of death, far beyond any human help. When prayer in such a case is answered and the Lord is found to come as champion to redeem and restore, the rescued soul knows a wonder which can scarcely be shared. The tale can be told, but will the world discern there the faithful love of the Lord? In the transformation of the fate of mighty rulers and suffering populations, the working of the divine fidelity may also be hard to perceive. The great occasions of worship make their contribution, resounding with thanksgiving and testimony, a challenging opportunity for the redeemed of the Lord to make specific thanksgiving with sacrifice and with public acknowledgement. But perhaps what matters most is that this is all in sign of a profound and enduring response to the wonderful saviour, a new life dedicated to him. The life-music of those who know they live only because of the Lord's faithfulness will carry far its message.

O Lord, the redeemer of those who cry to you, grant us the wisdom to discern your faithful love in all the changes of the world; and may we give thanks for the wonders of your grace not only with our lips, but in the sacrifice of our lives, by giving up ourselves to your service.

PSALM 108:   When the Beloved seem Spurned

Song. Psalm. Of David.

1 My heart is ready, O God,
   that I may sing and make melody with all my soul.
2 Awake, harp and lyre,
   that I may awaken the dawn.
3 I will give you thanks, Lord, among the peoples;
   I will sing your praise among the nations.
4 For your love reaches over the heavens,
   and your faithfulness to the clouds.
5 Be exalted, O God, above the heavens,
   with your glory over all the earth.
6 That your beloved may be delivered,
   save by your right hand and answer us.

7 God has spoken in his holiness:

In triumph will I portion out Shechem,
and share out the valley of Sukkoth.
8   Mine shall be Gilead, and mine Manasseh;
Ephraim shall be my helmet, and Judah my sceptre.
9   But Moab shall be my wash-bowl;
over Edom will I throw my sandal,
over Philistia I will shout in triumph.

10   Who will bring me to the fortress city;
who could lead me up to Edom?
11   Have you not spurned us, O God,
and will you not go out with our hosts?
12   O grant us help against the enemy,
for earthly help is in vain.
13   Through God we can do mighty things;
it is he that will tread down our foes.

Two vivid passages found in other psalms are here joined to make a new composition; our vv. 1–5 correspond to 57.7–11, while our vv. 6–13 correspond to 60.5–12. The circumstances for this psalm may have been similar to those for 57 and 60, a king or similar leader facing a foreign threat to his community; but the present combination of elements must have seemed to fit the situation best. In the needs of worship, psalmists were not concerned about originality, and could draw on and rearrange traditional materials, just as the Chronicler did in picturing David's festival (1 Chron. 16.8f.). One might even think the time of crisis was the same for all three psalms (57, 60, 108), but most scholars judge 108 to be much later, thinking that it has drawn on the other psalms after they had been through a revision where 'Elohim' became the commonest name for God (Int. 6b, 7b).

1–4 In the style of the royal leader, specially called to be God's witness (cf. above on 89.1–4), the singer tells of his readiness to testify among the nations to God's faithfulness. Assisted by a number of musicians, he is ready to 'awaken the dawn', as though calling the angel of morning to begin her flight across the skies. There will have been a watching and praying in the darkness, and now there is hope of a sign of God's answer as morning breaks. ('My glory', the soul, is itself summoned to awake in 57.7–8, where also the phrase 'my heart is ready' is repeated.)

5–6 Prayer for the deliverance of God's 'beloved ones', his covenant people, calls for his appearing as glorious and powerful King of creation and all nations. The prayer is in the tradition of the Lord's Anointed, whose struggles are with the enemies of God's own kingdom.

7–9 The divine response, probably an ancient and classical oracle, affirms God's lordship over the Holy Land (cf. above on 60.6f.). But perhaps the oracle is cited here to sharpen the lament through the contrast of its bright promise with the present situation.

10–13 Following the triumphant tone of the oracle, supplication breaks out anew, ending with the appeal of those who would see their trust vindicated (see also on 60.9f.).

As the ancient oracle is heard again down the centuries of worship, it reveals further levels of meaning. Most solemnly God has promised here that he will establish and bestow a home where his beloved can live before his face; the enemies will be subdued, indeed brought in a new humility into the divine fellowship. The promise remains in all its certainty, even when the church seems to face overwhelming difficulties and feels spurned and deserted by the all-powerful God. The holy word remains, and the psalm would have God's servants hold to their prayer and their praises, ready for the dawn and for the risen sun of God's glory over all the earth. Through him they will do mighty things, and at last will see that he himself has subdued every evil force.

O God, who use the songs of your people to awaken your dawn over all the earth, grant us to hold on to your promises in all adversities, that we may not flinch from undertaking daunting tasks in the strength of your Spirit.

PSALM 109: The Curse – and the Seed of its Undoing

For favour.   Of David.   Psalm.

1   Do not be silent, O God of my praise,
2   for a mouth of wickedness and treachery
        they have opened wide against me.
    They have spoken against me with a tongue of falsehood;
3   with words of hate they have surrounded me,
        and made war against me without cause.
4   In return for my goodwill
        they have set themselves against me,
    even though I prayed for them.
5   Thus they have rewarded me evil for good,
        and hatred for my goodwill.
6   Appoint over him a wicked man,
        and let an accuser stand at his right hand.
7   When he is judged, he shall be condemned,
        and his prayer shall not avail.

8　Let his days be few,
　　and another take his office.
9　Let his children be fatherless,
　　and his wife become a widow.
10　Let his children wander to beg their bread,
　　let them seek it in desolate places.
11　Let the creditor seize all that he has,
　　and strangers plunder his labour.
12　May he have none to remain ever loyal,
　　none to maintain kindness to his fatherless children.
13　Let his line come soon to an end,
　　his name be blotted out in the next generation.
14　Let the offences of his fathers
　　　be remembered before the Lord,
　　and the sin of his mother not be put away.
15　Let them be ever before the Lord,
　　that he may root out their names from the earth.
16　For he was not minded to keep faith,
　　but persecuted the poor and helpless,
　　　and sought to kill the broken in heart.
17　He loved cursing and it came to him;
　　he had no delight in blessing, and it stayed far from him.
18　He clothed himself with cursing as with a robe,
　　and it came into his body like water,
　　　and into his bones like oil.
19　So let it be to him as the garment he wraps around him,
　　like the sash that he wears about him continually.
20　This shall be the recompense from the Lord
　　　for my adversaries,
　　and for those who speak evil against my soul.
21　But deal with me, Lord God, according to your name;
　　deliver me, as your faithful love is kind.
22　I am helpless and poor,
　　and my heart is wounded within me.
23　I fade like a shadow that lengthens,
　　and am driven away like a locust.
24　My knees are weak through fasting,
　　and my flesh is dried up and wasted.
25　I have become for them one to be mocked;
　　those that look upon me shake their heads in scorn.
26　Help me, O Lord my God;
　　save me according to your faithful love.
27　Then they shall know that this is your hand,
　　and that you, O Lord, have done it.
28　Though they curse, yet you will bless;
　　let those who rise up against me be put to shame,

>   but let your servant rejoice.
> 29   Let my adversaries be clothed with shame,
>   and cover themselves with confusion as with a cloak.
> 30   I will give great thanks to the Lord with my mouth,
>   and praise him among the multitude,
> 31   that he has stood at the right hand of the needy one,
>   to save him from those who would condemn his soul.

Though some take this to be the prayer of an accused person facing trial at the temple, it is better to explain it, like the preceding and following psalms, of the national leader, most likely the king. Fasting severely and in mourning rites before the Lord, he appears as a poor and afflicted figure. He appeals for the covenanted support of the Lord against adversaries set on war (v. 3) and assailing him with deadly words, the curses used in war and false accusations. His case before the Lord is that this hostility has no just basis; indeed it is unleashed against one who has shown them goodwill. The situation may then be compared with 27, 35 and 55. The opening appeal to the Lord is grounded on a lamenting depiction of the hostility (vv. 1–5). Prayer against the enemy and a leading figure in particular is especially fierce and extensive, drawing on the ancient style of cursing (vv. 6–20). Renewed appeal for help calls for God's covenant love and pleads the supplicant's weakness (21–9). The conclusion is a vow to give thanks and testimony when the Lord has supported his 'needy one' (vv. 30–1). NRSV freely supplies the words 'they say' before v. 6 and then takes the long imprecation (down to v. 19) as a quotation of what the enemies say against the psalmist. This is an old theory which has been judged artificial. As Gunkel notes, such a quotation would surely have needed an introductory phrase in the Hebrew; and it is unlikely that the psalmist would spell out such a lengthy and dangerous curse against himself. That the target in vv. 6f. is chiefly a single figure (though plural forms occur in vv. 13b, 15, 20) does not mean that the reference must be to the psalmist himself; the enemy becomes singular in other laments (35.8; 55.13), and in any case the traditional formulas could easily take on a collective sense.

1–5   In contrast to the clamour of the foes, God seems silent, inactive (cf. 35.22f.; 83.1); will he not prove again to be the saviour praised in the past? As often, it is the harmful words of the enemy that are especially lamented (cf. 52.2f.; 55.21; 57.4; 58.3f.; 59.6f.; 64.3f.), though warfare is also specified (v. 3b). The ritual cursing and malicious propaganda and accusations would feature especially in the opening stages of hostility, and seemed so deadly that only prayer could parry and turn back their darts. Appealing to God the upholder of justice, the supplicant affirms that he has not merited this hostility and indeed has shown goodwill and friendship ('love'); as friendly rulers sometimes did, he had prayed for them when they were afflicted (cf. 35.13; for v. 4b, lit. 'but I prayer', cf. 120.7, 'I peace').

6–20   So now the prayer takes a different turn, becoming an imprecation full of traditional cursing phrases. Against the enemy – perhaps one prominent foe in particular (in high office, v. 8b) or a collective figure – comprehensive doom is invoked. May the Lord bring on him the ill he has sought for the psalmist and quickly end his life. So the enemy will know what it is to find *ḥesed*, loyal friendship, withheld. His life will not be allowed to revive in his descendants; poverty, unrelieved by anyone to extend *ḥesed*, will be their lot, and his whole line, the expression of his life, will soon be lost and forgotten. The imprecation concludes with a summary in v. 20; not a magical force has been invoked, but 'requital from the Lord'.

21–29   Appealing prayer is renewed, grounded on God's 'name', his giving of himself as faithful saviour, and on his *ḥesed*, his enduring commitment. To move the Lord also, he stresses his total dependence; from the terrible situation and from his fasting, God's servant is weak and wounded, a veritable *'ani* and *ebyon*, a poor and vulnerable person such as the divine king loves to defend and help (cf. 35.10), weak as the last shadow (cf. 102.11), frail as a locust driven by the wind (cf. Ex. 10.19). The prayer against the adversaries (v. 29) is now more standard, but the terms can refer to total overthrow.

30–31   The concluding element in support of the prayer is a vow to give thanks in the great festal congregation, testifying how the Lord has stood by him in his need. Though the enemies, with their unjust accusations, would have him condemned, the Lord will speak and decide for him (cf. 16.8; Isa. 50.8f.; Rom. 8.33f.).

The extent and the vehement detail of the prayer against the enemy (vv. 6–20) make it impossible for us to take the psalm readily to heart. Some modern psalters for singing or recitation understandably put square brackets round the passage, a practice which accords with the liturgical freedom exercised by the composer himself in the preceding psalm. Even if we were persuaded that vv. 6–19 were a quotation of words aimed at the singer, we would be little better off, since in v. 20 he would still desire all the aforementioned ills to rebound on his foes. The contrast with the 'Forgive us … as we forgive them' of the Lord's prayer would still be violent. It is true that, on the explanation offered above, the motive is not an individual's vindictiveness; the ruler defends his realm and people, striking with the weapon of prayer given with his office. It is true also that the imprecation reflects the ancient apprehension that a person's life extends through the family, and hence the doom, to be complete, is invoked upon the descendants. But the difficulty is still forbidding.

Worried by the blandness of some worship today, some advocate a fresh appreciation of such harsh passages. They would hear in them the voice of the poor and afflicted, expressing the depth of their abuse and the natural vehemence of their cry for justice; this depth is to be thoroughly acknowledged before the virtue of the forgiving spirit is extolled. When the callous cruelties that abound in our own time are fully faced, can any cry for retributive justice seem too strong? In the church's tradition, however, the passage has been read with a transformation of meaning. After the example of the New Testament (Acts 1.15f.; Matt. 27.39 echoing our v. 25), it has been taken as a prophecy 'spoken beforehand' by the Holy Spirit concerning the treachery of Judas. The betrayal of Christ is the archetype of all betrayals, the consequence of which is a misery that engulfs the total life of the betrayer. The passage then brings a terrible warning. Yet the betrayed Messiah has another word to speak, and in his 'Father, forgive them' the power of his mighty redemption still perseveres, seeking the rebirth of the sinners and the fulfilment of the Father's *ḥesed* for all his creatures.

O God of our praise, help us to repent of malicious desires, acts of betrayal, and our share in the oppression of your little ones; forgive and restore us, for the sake of him who has undone the ancient curse, our Saviour Jesus Christ.

PSALM 110: The Son on the Throne of God

Of David.   Psalm.

1   A word of the Lord for my lord: Sit at my right hand,
      till I make your enemies a stool for your feet.
2   The Lord shall extend the sceptre of your power from Zion,
      so that you rule in the midst of your enemies.
3   Royal grace is with you on this day of your birth,
        in holy majesty from the womb of the dawn;
      upon you is the dew of your new life.
4   The Lord has sworn and will not go back:
      You are a priest for ever, after the order of Melchizedek.
5   The Lord at your right hand
      will smite down kings in the day of his wrath.
6   In full majesty he will judge among the nations,
      smiting heads across the wide earth.
7   He who drinks from the brook by the way
      shall therefore lift high his head.

Questions arising here are like those discussed for Psalm 2. Again we are led to a setting in the ceremonies enacting the installation of the Davidic king in Jerusalem. The prophetic singer announces two oracles of the Lord for the new king (vv. 1, 4) and fills them out with less direct prophecy (vv. 2–3, 5–7). Items of enthronement ceremonial seem reflected: ascension to the throne, bestowal of the sceptre, anointing and baptism signifying new birth as the Lord's son (v. 3), appointment to royal priesthood, symbolic defeat of foes, the drink of life-giving water. As mentioned on 2, 18, 89, 101, the rites may have involved a sacred drama and been repeated in commemorations, perhaps annually in conjunction with the celebration of God's kingship, for which the Davidic ruler was chief 'servant'. After the end of the monarchy, the psalm was understood to foreshadow the victory of the Messiah, the saviour-king at the end of the age. Verses 1 and 4 are often applied to Christ in the New Testament, making it the most quoted psalm there.

1–2 The psalmist-prophet declares to his royal lord a message from God. It is an invitation to share the throne and sovereignty of God (cf. above on 45.6), to enter the role of the Lord's Anointed, mediating on earth the rule of the heavenly King (cf. 2.2). But it carries also the promise of victory, for God undertakes himself to subdue the enemies. The position at God's right hand is the most honoured of all; the actual seat taken by the king, if it were (as the palace itself was) on the south side of the temple, would be thought of as on God's right (since Hebrew uses 'right hand' for 'south'). Exalted thrones always had a footstool, and there are Egyptian examples of such stools formed or decorated to symbolize subjected foes. The singer continues with reference to the king's sceptre, which may now have been presented to him. Symbolic of conquest and righteous rule, the sceptre will be stretched out by the Lord from Zion over all adversaries – a joint sovereignty indeed.

3 The singer may here interpret the rite of anointing and perhaps also baptism. The king is born anew, God's son (cf. 2.7). Grace has been given him, a holy beauty (cf. 45.2). As he came up at daybreak from the spring Gihon (cf. 18.16; 68.26; 1 Kings 1.33), an ancient myth lent its poetry to depict the king as it were born from the womb of the dawn, glistening with the life-giving dew (cf. Isa. 14.12; 26.19).

4 The psalmist resumes quotation of the Lord's words, an oath which he will never revoke. It appoints the king to be God's priest for ever. He will be priest-king. the supreme figure for whom all the other personnel of the temple were only assistants. It was a role of the highest significance in the ancient societies, treasured by the great kings of Egypt and Mesopotamia under their respective deities. There are indications in the historical sources that the role was indeed held by David and his successors, though opposed and obscured in the records by priestly clans after the end of the monarchy. The oracle gives a special aspect to the priesthood by linking it to the pre-Israelite king of Jerusalem, Melchizedek. David's dynasty are here recognized as heirs of Melchizedek, who was remembered in tradition as priest and king of El Elyon, God Most High, Creator of heaven and earth (Gen. 14.18f.). As Israel's God took the title of the Creator as worshipped in old Jerusalem (El Elyon), so David took over the city-kingdom and royal priesthood of the old dynasty.

5–6 The theme of victory returns, probably in interpretation of some symbolic representation (cf. 2.8–9). It is the Lord who slays the forces of evil, the 'kings' who represent chaos (cf. 2.2; 48.4); in awesome glory he conquers and restores right.

7   The conclusion seems to depict the warrior who refreshes himself with living water and so is renewed in strength. Some take this, as the passage reads naturally, to be a poetic description of the Lord in his warfare (so Johnson, 'a vivid glimpse of the heavenly King ... pausing to slake his thirst.'). But we might rather find an allusion to a symbolic drink, a cup of life and salvation, given to the king from the Gihon source, and so we could take the third person verbs as a proverbial style: 'One who drinks ...'; with this water of life, the Lord gives strength for victory, raising the head of his king (cf. 3.3).

The psalms from the royal ceremonies penetrate the meaning of the Davidic office with the eye of poetry and prophecy. Our psalm consists of oracles and prophetic declarations, and with strong images it depicts an ideal figure most intimate with God, mediating God's own kingship – his son, his priest, and his warrior against the world's evils. No less than such a figure indeed would be needed truly to represent and express God's reign, and in time this ideal person of our psalm was understood as the Messiah, the saviour-king who should come. The question Jesus put to the Pharisees (Matt. 22.41f. etc.) shows it was the common opinion that the psalm referred to the Messiah. The many citations and echoes of vv. 1 and 4 in the New Testament then show how it was found eloquent of the victory of Jesus the Messiah beyond his death – his resurrection, ascension (Acts 2.34f.; Eph. 1.20) and eternal priesthood (Heb. 5.5f.; 6.20; 7.17f.). From the dark night of trial he had come forth in the break of a new day, proved to be the true Son, bearing the dew of eternal life, powerful to atone, to intercede, and to bless.

   The fierce imagery of war in such royal psalms is the common coin of the sacral kingships of the ancient Near East. The earthly ruler, servant of the heavenly kingship, is endowed with no uncertain power to combat the abundant enemies who would destroy every good cause; word and picture strive for the utmost power against these terrible forces. But the church, following the New Testament, finds here the message of certainty for Christ's victory. For all the raging of the monstrous powers, it is this Lamb who will sit as victor on the throne of God.

Lord Jesus, divine Son and eternal priest, inspire us with the confidence of your final conquest of evil, and grant that daily on our way we may drink of the brook of your eternal life, and so find courage against all adversities.

PSALM 111: Redemption Renewed through Remembrance

1   Alleluia.
    I will thank the Lord with all my heart,
    among true-hearted friends and in the congregation.
2   Great are the deeds of the Lord,
    sought out by all who delight in them.
3   His work is in splendour and majesty,
    and his goodness stands for ever.
4   He appointed a remembrance of his wonders;
    the Lord is gracious and compassionate.
5   He gave sustenance to those who feared him;
    he remembers his covenant for ever.
6   He showed his people the power of his deeds,
    when he gave them the heritage of nations.
7   The works of his hands are truth and justice;
    all his commandments are sure.
8   They are upheld for ever and ever,
    being done in truth and right.
9   He sent redemption to his people,
        and commanded his covenant for ever;
    holy and awesome is his name.
10 The fear of the Lord is the beginning of wisdom;
        a good understanding have those who live by it.
    His praise endures for evermore.

This psalm, as also 112, is a skilful and well-preserved acrostic, the Hebrew beginning each half-verse with the next letter of the alphabet. Although this could make for a series of short, rather unrelated statements, in fact the themes are significantly ordered. The opening might lead us to expect the public thanksgiving of an individual, and indeed some take the psalm to be a late form of personal thanksgiving in a festal assembly, where a small group gathers round the singer to hear his testimony. However, the reasons or grounds for the praise (vv. 2–9) surely show that a more general hymn is intended, gratefully praising the Lord for his wonders in Egypt, Sinai and the Settlement in Canaan. This purpose of praise is gathered up in the conclusion (v. 10c), after the element of teaching in the psalm has been rounded off in v. 10ab. Some ancient witnesses head (also for 112): 'Of the return of Haggai and Zechariah'.

1   After the alleluia, the psalm proper begins the acrostic; the need for the first letter of the Hebrew alphabet may have suggested the individual form of the statement, the letter *aleph* beginning the singular verbal form. Although conveniently translated 'thank', the verb (*ydh*) signifies a praising acknowledgement close to other verbs for praise. The location of this act of praise is given in v. 1b; many take the whole expression to refer to one setting – the assembly of worshippers at a pilgrim festival, where the congregation (*'eda*) might also be seen as a company of trusted friends (*sod*, cf. Ezek. 13.9). Others take the expression more literally of two gatherings – the intimate circle (*sod*) of friends, perhaps studying around a sage, and the general congregation (*'eda*); these two in fact could interact in the many-faceted activity of the temple.

2–9   With a whole heart the singer unfolds the grounds and substance of his praise. He will allude to the great works of the Lord when the ancestors were led from Egypt – the Lord revealed his name and his holy splendour, he appointed for all time the duty of commemorating the deliverance (Ex. 12.14, cf. Ps. 78.5), he showed himself full of grace and compassion (103.8; Ex. 34.6), he fed his people in the wilderness, established his covenant and commandments, gave victory and settlement in the Holy Land. But all these works of long ago are still shining on the faithful and uplifting them. The deeds are 'sought out' by those who recite, study and meditate on them as their chief delight (cf. 1.2). In the rites and customs of 'remembrance' they dramatically become present, involving every generation in their wonder and power. So ever and anew the Lord is revealed and known in his authority and mercy, his holiness and his pity, his greatness and his faithfulness; ever and anew he sends that great redemption.

10   In the style favoured by the Wisdom teachers (cf. Prov. 1.7; 9.10), the singer teaches the fundamental lesson. The beginning and chief part of wisdom is to fear the Lord – truly to acknowledge his awesome reality; good understanding is seen only in daily response to this reality, 'doing' the fear of the Lord, living by it in every turn of activity and thought. The last letter of the Hebrew alphabet suitably begins the word 'praise', and so the psalm's end answers to its beginning; here perhaps the sense is close to 'glory', the wondrous majesty of the Lord that 'stands' for ever.

The question whether we have here an individual's thanksgiving or a hymn for the community leads to thoughts about the relation of the individual worshipper to the congregation. For the Psalms generally, the individual thanksgiving, made with all the heart, is shared with the assembly. The great moments of communal praise are given sincerity and passion as they draw on the experience of God's wonders which individuals have known. Our psalm inclines us further to value the small groups that foster a fellowship of meditation and study, and have a true and warm experience to contribute to the greater congregation. But the core of our psalm invites reflection on the wonders of the Lord's ancient deeds that are made present and active through the commemoration that he appointed. Such commemoration still has a major part in worship, not least in the eucharist or Lord's Supper. Here still the wonders alluded to in the psalm have their counterparts; still sought out and known with delight are the giving of the name above every name, the redemption from bondage, the new covenant with all it means for relationship and light of guidance, the sustenance in hardship, and the homeland of life in his presence. Through this continual remembering and re-experiencing, the fear of the Lord becomes natural and habitual and more than proves itself the beginning of wisdom, becoming known also as a fountain of life (Prov. 14.27).

O Lord and redeemer, increase in us that fear of your name which is found to be the beginning and chief part of wisdom; so that, sharing in the fellowship of praise and communion, we may ever delight in your wonders and be nourished with your sustenance.

PSALM 112: The Imitation of the Love of God

1 Alleluia.
Happy the one who fears the Lord,
and greatly delights in his commandments.
2 His seed shall be mighty in the land,
a true-hearted generation that will be blessed.
3 Wealth and riches shall be in his house,
and his blessing will stand for ever.
4 He will rise in the darkness as a light for the true of heart,
gracious, compassionate, and just.
5 How happy the one who lends in kindness,
and orders his affairs with justice.
6 For he will never be overthrown;
the just person will remain in everlasting remembrance.
7 He will not fear any evil tidings;
his heart is steadfast, trusting in the Lord.
8 His heart is sustained and will not fear,
until he sees the fall of his enemies.
9 He gives freely to the poor,
and his blessing stands for ever;
his horn shall be exalted in glory.
10 The wicked man shall see it and be vexed;
he will gnash his teeth in despair;
the hope of the wicked shall perish.

This is a 'half-verse' acrostic, the alphabetic scheme being exactly like that of 111. Moreover, the two short psalms have about eleven terms or phrases in common. But while 111 treats chiefly of the works of the Lord, 112 portrays the character and destiny of one who fears the Lord. Some see a complementary pair composed by the same author or at least from the same circle; others think of 112 as a somewhat later piece modelled on 111. There is also little to fix the original setting of our psalm. Some hold to the usual purpose of biblical psalmody and look for a setting in temple ceremony – teaching given on entrance to the temple or in rites of blessing, an ideal put before kings (noting especially vv. 2, 3, 4, 9c), or even the priest's response in the ceremony of thank-offering (cf. on 111). Others stress the Wisdom style and look rather to instruction and fellowship in the circles of scribal sages in the latest period. As for 111, some versions again head: 'Of the return of Haggai and Zechariah'.

1 The alleluia before the psalm proper brings all that will be said of the saintly life into the context of praise to the Lord, for all is of him. The *aleph* letter that must now begin the acrostic is conveniently provided by *asherey*, 'O the sheer happiness of . . .', introducing a portrait of character and action for emulation (cf. above on 1.1). A single person is pictured throughout (though altered in recent translations for inclusivity); the individual bears responsibility in the matter, and must even be ready to stand against the tide. The all-embracing characteristic mentioned first is fearing the Lord, having him in awe at all times (see below on 111.10). Flowing from this is a great willingness – that comes to be a holy joy – to consider and follow his commandments (cf. 1.2).

2–9 For the Old Testament generally, the continuance of life is looked for in descendants; the life of this fearer of God will be so blessed that it will flourish in such offspring, themselves true of heart. His 'house' may mean especially his continuing family, and through their wealth will be seen the blessing on him (lit. 'his rightness', meaning the reward for it, cf. 24.5b). His character begins to reflect that of the Lord he loves and reveres; so he shows a divine kindness, for he comes as a light into the darkness of suffering, full of pity and consideration. He is compassionate in lending (that would be without interest, cf. 15.5), and manages his business affairs without oppression or corruption. He is not ridden with anxiety, having a steadfast trust in God which gives strength when bad news comes. Enemies will assail, but he will in the end see their downfall. Generous to the poor (cf. 41.1), he will be granted victory (cf. 'horn' in 75.4; 92.10).

10 The conclusion is made with a contrast. The 'wicked' person is one not respecting the Lord, but having hope in evil schemes, which in the end must fail. The wicked life itself runs out in a desert, contrasting with the blessed continuance of the life in reverence for the Lord. This contrast is more developed in the comparable Psalm 1.

To 'fear the Lord' and take delight in his commandments involves a communion with him (cf. 25.14), which results in a reflection of the Lord's qualities in the disciple's soul. Here is a wealth and beauty that does not pass into nothing; a light that arises in times of darkness to give comfort, hope and courage to fellow pilgrims; here is kindness, compassion and generosity; here is a victory within the struggles of life that will ever be remembered and so bring grace. Of such things consists the 'sheer happiness' to which the psalmist invites all who hear his song; this is the wealth, the blessing, the goodness and rightness which he promises will be given to one who loves the Lord's will and delights in his guidance. This pilgrim will pass through darkness, blows of misfortune, the envy and hatred of enemies, but having the life-giving fear of God, will rise above other fears, sustained and finally exalted. In Christian experience the likeness to the Lord is the fruit of the Incarnation, the Word becoming flesh that those who receive him might become children of God (John 1.12f.). The disciple is called to be an imitator of God, a child who walks in his love (Eph. 4.32–5.2).

O Christ the light of all creatures, make new our hearts to fear you and delight in your commandments, that we too may walk in love, even as you loved us and gave yourself up for us.

PSALM 113: The Lord who Humbles Himself

1   Alleluia.
    Praise, you servants of the Lord,
    O praise the name of the Lord.
2   May the name of the Lord be blessed,
    from now and for evermore.
3   From the rising of the sun to its setting,
    may the name of the Lord be praised.
4   High above all nations is the Lord,
    and his glory is above the heavens.
5   Who is like the Lord our God,
    that has his throne so high,
6   yet humbles himself to behold
    the things of heaven and earth;
7   taking up the poor from the dust,
    lifting the destitute from the ash-heap,
8   making them sit with princes,
    with the princes of his people;
9   giving peace to the barren wife,
    making her a joyful mother of children?
    Alleluia.

This hymn eloquently uses elements characteristic of psalms of praise, especially the call to praise (vv. 1–3), reasons for praise (vv. 4f.), a rhetorical
question expressing the uniqueness of the Lord (v. 5), and a series of four
Hebrew participles expressing his characteristic and continuing actions. It is
likely to have been intended for a great occasion of worship, the congregation
being addressed as 'servants of the Lord' (v. 1). The Lord is praised as raising
the poor from the utmost degradation and as wonderfully changing the fortune of a barren wife. The Targum found allusion here to the salvation of
Israel, but one may judge that originally the literal, individual sense will have
been intended. This is the first of the group of praising psalms (113–18) which
came to be known as 'the Hallel' ('hymn of praise') or sometimes 'the
Egyptian Hallel' (cf. 114.1); it was sung in later times at Passover, Weeks,
Tabernacles, Hanukka and New Moons (except New Year). At family
Passovers 113–14 were sung before and 115–18 after the meal, and so perhaps
at the Last Supper (Matt. 26.20; Mark 14.26). While it has been regarded as
one of the later psalms, an earlier date is possible, and some have even thought
of it as an ancient victory song, comparing 1 Sam. 2.5f.

1–3 The singer's call goes out to the 'servants of the Lord' (cf. 134.1;
135.1f.); probably here the reference is wider than priestly servants – the
whole congregation of his worshippers. Indeed, those gathered at the temple
represent the whole world of his creatures (cf. 96.1, 11; 150). They are to
praise and bless his 'name' (specified thrice), the form in which he reaches out
to his creatures, making himself known in glory and accessible in grace (cf.
8.1, 9; 20.1f.; 96.2; 103.1).

4–9 The grounds for the praise (elsewhere introduced by *ki*, 'for') are given
from v. 4 on. At first it seems that they will consist of tribute to his exaltation
above all in earth and heaven. (The question in v. 5 is an ancient way of
praising the divine uniqueness, cf. 18.31; 35.10; 86.8.) But the thankful praise
unfolds further. The greatest wonder is that this king, who 'shows exalted
supremacy' in his throne above all that exists, 'shows lowliness' in taking heed
of the suffering of his little ones and acting to save them. This highest of all
lords thus comes to the heaps outside the town, where the community's
garbage and filth is collected and incinerated; here he finds the outcasts of
society scavenging to keep alive, homeless and friendless. He restores them to
honoured life, to sit indeed among the noblest (cf. 1 Sam. 2.8). Or again, he
takes note of the misery of a barren wife, an especially acute grief in that
society (cf. 1 Sam. 1; 2.5); he gives her a highly honoured place in the family
group, as she becomes the joyful mother of (lit.) 'sons' (cf. 127.3f.; Ruth
4.13f.).

The examples of salvation given in the psalm do not describe things hap-
pening with monotonous regularity; though they are indeed characteristic of
the Lord, many an outcast has remained at the refuse-tips, and many a wife
has had to carry her grief to the end. Worshippers ancient and modern have

always known this. But the examples represent the experience of grace which animates all true praise. When the rational mind could not expect it, when hope itself was running low, the saving power has come and transformed the situation of grief. The later Jewish worshippers, including the disciples of Jesus, would think of the nation that the Lord had saved and would save again, and of the mother–city that would be blessed with many children (cf. Isa. 54). But the individual reference of the psalm's examples remains important; that experience of a saving love beyond all expectation is known fully only by the one saved, who then contributes fervently to the world of praise (cf. above on 111). A special beauty of the psalm is its sense of the divine humility, the readiness of the highly enthroned one to care for the lowest and loneliest. The New Testament sees this grace embodied in the Lord Jesus, to be reflected in his disciples (cf. Mark 2.15f.; John 13.2f.; Phil. 2.5f.).

We bless your name, O Lord, the name above all names, and we thank you that from your high throne you have seen the wretched and humbled yourself to save them; grant that this mind be in us, that we also humble ourselves, and take our part as obedient servants in your work of salvation.

PSALM 114: The Holy One in his People

1   When Israel came out of Egypt,
     the house of Jacob from a people strange in speech,
2   Judah became his sanctuary,
     Israel the heart of his dominion.
3   The sea but looked and fled,
     the Jordan ran back in its course.
4   The mountains skipped like rams,
     the hills like lambs and kids.
5   What ails you, O sea, that you flee away,
     and Jordan that you run back,
6   you mountains that you skip like rams,
     you hills like lambs and kids?
7   Tremble, O earth, at the presence of the Lord,
     at the presence of the God of Jacob,
8   who turns hard rock into a pool of water,
     flint-stone into a springing well.

Although conveying a sense of the majesty and presence of God, this splendid poem does not have the usual hymnic form; here is no call for praise, no main sentence in which God is subject, no naming of God till near the end, where still neither 'Yahweh' nor 'Elohim' is used. Like 78, 105 and 106 it recalls the salvation of the Exodus, but how different the manner! Here so terse and dramatic! Perhaps due to a setting in an ancient tradition of worship where the old story was vividly relived in ritual and song, the force of the psalm is all for actualization; it moves swiftly from introductory reference to the Exodus (vv. 1–2) to the marvels and consternation in waters and mountains (vv. 3–4), and then deftly makes these upheavals seem present (vv. 5–6), concluding with a call for trembling now at the powerful presence of 'Adon', earth's master and the God of Jacob (vv. 7–9). Opinions on the date differ according to interpretations of the reference to 'Judah' and 'Israel' in v. 2; some look to a late period when Judah might be considered heir of the whole people, synonymous with Israel. But the verse may simply reflect the view of the nation as in two main parts, a view which already David had to take into account. The celebration of the Exodus would be in place at the Passover, but also in the autumn festival (which dominated in and around the royal period).

1–2 Just one feature of Israel's life in Egypt is mentioned – the language which seemed so strange (with its partly African character, Egyptian would differ sharply from the Semitic language areas of the Near East). With this one feature, the poet conjures up a place of discomfort, insecurity, hostility, a place which is not home. But at that coming out, that Exodus, there occurred the amazing event which founded the enduring mystery of Israel's significance. This people became the bearer of the divine presence; God was pleased to centre in them his holy power, his royal glory. The parallel statements of v. 2 are best taken as complementary, 'two sides of the same coin' (Mowinckel); 'Judah' and 'Israel' are the main blocks of the tribal people which together are the bearers of the one holy and royal presence of God. The lack of the naming of God makes no difficulty for the sense in such a well-known story, but the naming, when it comes at last in v. 7, will be all the more striking (cf. the play on the withheld name and title in 24.7–10).

3–4 A similar reticence is used in v. 3a. It is the glorious presence that the waters saw, but again this is not specified until vv. 7–8 (cf. 48.5, 'they saw – so were they dumbfounded'). The flight of the waters is an echo of the creation battle (cf. above on 29.3f.). The consternation of the mountains is a common feature of accounts of God's appearing (cf. 29.6; Ex. 19.18). With these reactions in nature to the fearful presence of God in his people, the psalmist sweeps on from the Exodus to the crossing of the Jordan (cf. Josh. 3.9–17) and the entry into Canaan; the years of wilderness wanderings, however, will be glimpsed in v. 8.

5–6 Taking up the very words of the preceding description, the psalmist asks the waters and mountains the reason for their consternation. The living personalities of sea, river, mountains and hills (as later also the earth) are brought out even more by his address to them; but his question further makes the transition from an account of ancient events to a present reality. It is the question of one who with amazement witnesses the fleeing waters and leaping hills.

7–8 The singer provides his own answer, implying 'Yes, you do well to be in consternation.' He calls to the whole earth to tremble before the manifest Master and sovereign Lord (*adon*, cf. Josh. 3.11, 13; Ps. 97.4–5), owner of all the lands, and Covenant-lord of this people 'Jacob'. In evidence of the power of this God, reference is made only to the wilderness miracle (Ex. 17.6; Deut. 8.15; cf. Ps. 107.33f.); here the positive aspect of the divine power is seized upon, the creation of the spring of life from the hard and barren rock. With this the psalm ends, having reached its goal of conveying the vision of the Lord present in all his power and salvation.

This is a song to bring the listening worshippers into an awesome scene. With the waves of the Reed Sea, the currents of the Jordan, the great mountains and the rolling hills, they too are to tremble in the presence of the King of creation, mighty in his purpose of redemption. The Christian use of the psalm at Easter and in the offices for the dying and the dead have continued the psalmist's work of actualization. The church here recognizes her Lord who has made his sanctuary within his people, leads them through the waters of death, and gives from the hard rock of his sufferings the water of life. The Exodus becomes real also for the individual, who is granted safe passage through death's waters and entrance into the land of divine rest. Down the centuries the psalm has been sung to Tonus Peregrinus, the pilgrim's tune, handed down from ancient psalmody; for church and individual it is indeed a good song of pilgrimage – arresting, dramatic, bringing the sense of the living world that responds to its almighty Lord, and revealing this Lord himself, ever present, ever active in redemption.

Make real to us, great Lord, the wonders of your ancient work, that we may know you present still as saviour and guide of your people; so may we also tremble and worship, and drink deep of the springing well of your salvation.

PSALM 115: Glorify your Name

1   Not to us, Lord, not to us, but to your name give glory,
     for the sake of your faithful love and truth.
2   Why should the nations scoff,
     and say, Where now is their God?
3   Our God, he is in heaven;
     whatever he wills he does.
4   Their idols are but silver and gold,

the work of human hands.
5   They have a mouth, but cannot speak;
    eyes they have, but cannot see.
6   They have ears, but cannot hear;
    a nose they have, but cannot smell.
7   They have hands, but cannot feel;
        feet they have, but cannot walk;
    they make no murmur with their throat.
8   Those that make them will grow like them,
    and so will all who trust in them.
9   O Israel, trust in the Lord.
    He is their help and their shield.
10 O house of Aaron, trust in the Lord.
    He is their help and their shield.
11 You that fear the Lord, trust in the Lord.
    He is their help and their shield.
12 The Lord will remember us, that he may bless.
        May he bless the house of Israel;
    may he bless the house of Aaron.
13 May he bless those that fear the Lord,
    both small and great together.
14 May the Lord give you increase,
    you and your children after you.
15 May you be blessed by the Lord,
    the maker of heaven and earth.
16 The heaven of heavens belongs to the Lord;
    the earth he has entrusted to the peoples.
17 It is not the dead who praise the Lord,
    not those gone down into silence.
18 It is we who will praise the Lord,
    from now and for evermore.
    Alleluia.

This is often classed as a 'liturgy' in the sense that its several sections may represent different voices and responses. At the same time it is basically a national lament, praying for help in a situation of protracted distress. The prayer is that the Lord should vindicate his own name by saving and blessing his covenant-people (vv. 1–2). This is supported by a statement of faith – the Lord is truly God and the idol-gods are nothings (vv. 3–8). The address is then directed to the worshippers, both people and priests, who are admonished to trust in the Lord (vv. 9–11). There follows, not quite an answering oracle from God, but a comprehensive benediction of people and priesthood, starting from assurance that he will think of them in mercy (vv. 12–15). Finally, the people for their part vow to bless the Lord evermore in thankfulness for the desired deliverance (vv. 16–18). The community seems to be humiliated and diminished, and will be praying for renewed blessing at an annual festival. The complex and responsorial structure of the psalm should not be made an argument for a late date, neither should the phrase 'you that fear the Lord' (which some take to mean proselytes); the possibility of a pre-exilic date may be left open. The solemn and comprehensive blessings, following the denunciation and rejection of idols, may indeed suggest a connection with the ancient ceremonies for the renewal of the covenant. The psalm is joined to 114 in many manuscripts, in LXX, the Syriac and Jerome; this will not be correct originally, but may reflect usage that developed in worship. Verses 4–8 will recur in 135.15–18.

1–2 A first impression of the opening words might suggest some sort of victory celebration (as for Henry V after the battle of Agincourt; in Shakespeare's play the king says 'Let there be sung Non Nobis and Te Deum'). But, as v. 2 confirms, the meaning is an appeal to God to glorify his name, extricating it from the derision of the heathen by truly showing his power and faithfulness in defending the people bound to him in covenant. They do not deserve glory and salvation, but may he act for the sake of his own honour (cf. Ezek. 36.20f.). At present the surrounding nations may well see cause to think them poorly served by their divine protector (cf. 42.3; 79.10).

3–8 The prayer is supported by a vigorous affirmation of faith – surely God will vindicate it. There is no mystery in the whereabouts of our God, they declare; he rules from heaven, accomplishing all that he wills, while the gods of the hostile nations are powerless. These inferior heavenly beings (cf. 29.1; 95.3; 96.4) are not referred to directly, but are scorned by association with the idols of their worshippers (an old tradition, cf. Isa. 2.20; 44.9f.; Jer. 10; Hab. 2.18f.). The Israelites' avoidance of making likenesses of God (Ex. 20.4) leaves them free to deride the foreign idols, made by human hands and unable to act; here was an incapacity that would soon characterize also those who trusted in such objects.

9–11 Exhortations to trust are sometimes found in lamenting psalms (42.5; 62.8f.; 130.7–8); like the more common statements of trust (3.3, 6; 4.7–8; 7.10), they reinforce the supplication as implicitly appealing to God for vindication. In the present case, the call to trust is directed first to 'Israel', the main assembly; next to 'the house of Aaron', the priestly orders; and finally to 'those who fear the Lord', which could cover pilgrims of other nationalities (not necessarily in post-exilic times, 1 Kings 8.41; cf. Acts 13.16), but may rather gather up all the worshippers in one great unity (cf. v. 13b; 22.23), even reaching to the farthest bounds (96.1; 150.6). To each call of the cantor it seems that a choir responds 'He is their help and their shield'. The dividing and uniting of the call to trust gives it all the emphasis of repetition, as will be the case also in the subsequent benedictions (vv. 12f.).

12–15 In response to the themes of supplication and trust come words of blessing. The singer is assured that the Lord takes notice of the people's plight

('He has remembered' or 'He will indeed remember', and that for blessing). These blessing-wishes of the authoritative singer go out with holy power; the goodwill of the Lord is active in them. Distribution again gives emphasis: blessing on the people, on the priests, on all, great and small. The essence of such blessing appears in v. 14: the Lord will 'add upon you', granting healthy increase of family, flocks and produce (cf. again Ezek. 36.29, 30, 35). It is all within the power of the one who is maker of heaven and earth (cf. 134.3).

16–18   The interchanges are brought to a close by a vow of thanksgiving on behalf of the assembly, a customary seal upon a psalm of supplication (79.13; 109.30 etc.). Verse 16a seems to mean 'The heavens are heavens for the Lord', but the grammar can be explained to give 'The heaven of heavens belongs to the Lord' (see Dahood), which in fact is the rendering of LXX. Verse 16b of course does not mean that God has 'given' (*ntn*) the earth to man, renouncing his own ownership (24.1; 50.12; 89.11); the Hebrew verb sometimes means 'entrust' (BDB, p. 679b, 1r), and in the present context the thought is that the Lord of all, supreme in the supreme heaven, has allotted man this sphere of life on earth, and this life is to be fulfilled in the praise of the Lord. The thought is enhanced by reference to the underworld, the land of death, generally imagined as silent, remote from the worship that is the essence of life (6.5; 88.4f.; Int. 60). The worshippers look forward to a continuance through their descendants in the sphere of life and thankful praise.

Several great thoughts emerge from the voices of this psalm. The suffering community asks for God's actions not for its own merit, but that he may glorify his name and vindicate his faithful love and truth. In a world where more prosperous and powerful communities worship their own manufactures and indeed trust in them, this people would hold fast to the one true God, alone worthy of worship, alone giver of life and salvation; they recognize that those who worship idols they have made grow to be like them in futility. In a worship where each encourages the other to trust, the community regains confidence that the Lord remembers them and prepares blessings for them; and so they pledge themselves to reflect that blessing in constant and thankful praise, the height of true life on this earth. So the psalm can still lead the church in difficult times to have hope and trust that rest on God's will to hallow his name and to bless the humble. The idols of earthly wealth and power, the blessings people would ever make for themselves, these continue indeed to be widely worshipped and highly exalted. Our psalm would see them still as degrading their devotees, and would direct trust only to the Lord of the heaven of heavens, in whose praise is the truest blessing of life.

O Lord, our help and shield, unite your ministers and people in the fear of your name; and bless us with the trust to look only to you for abundant life, and with thankful heart to praise and worship you alone.

PSALM 116: Raising the Cup of Thanksgiving

1   I am moved with love,
    for the Lord has heard the voice of my pleading.
2   He turned his ear to me
    on the day that I cried out.
3   The deadly cords entwined me;
    death's messengers of pain took hold of me;
        by grief and anguish I was seized.
4   Then I called on the name of the Lord:
    O Lord, I pray you, deliver my soul.
5   Gracious and good is the Lord;
    truly our God is full of compassion.
6   The Lord watches over the simple;
    I was wretched, and he saved me.
7   Return, O my soul, to your rest,
    for the Lord has shown you abundant grace.
8   You delivered my soul from death,
    my eye from tears, my foot from plunging.
9   I will walk before the Lord
    in the good land of the living.
10 I believed that I should perish,
    for I was sorely troubled.
11 So I said in my alarm,
    All earthly helpers fail.
12 How can I make return to the Lord
    for all the goodness he has poured on me?
13 I will raise the cup of salvation,
    and proclaim the name of the Lord.
14 My vows to the Lord I will now fulfil
    in the presence of all his people.
15 Costly in the eyes of the Lord
    is the death of his faithful ones.
16 O Lord, I am your servant;
    I am your servant, the child of your handmaid;
        you have loosed my bonds.
17 I will offer to you a sacrifice of thanksgiving,
    and I will proclaim the name of the Lord.
18 My vows to the Lord I will now fulfil
    in the presence of all his people,
19 in the courts of the house of the Lord,
    in your midst, O Jerusalem.
    Alleluia.

This is the thanksgiving of an individual, who expresses warm gratitude for being rescued from near-death. The testimony is made with the fulfilment of promised offerings in the temple at Jerusalem and in the sight of all the festal assembly. The person concerned thus seems to be a leading figure, quite possibly a king. In this connection we note that the warm opening and the imagery of rescue from death certainly resembles royal 18, and v. 16 could refer to the royal role as 'servant'; the psalm is akin to the thanksgiving of King Hezekiah (Isa. 38) and also, in ritual and phrases, to the stele inscribed for the Phoenician king Yeḥaw-milk (*ANET*, p. 502; *ANEP*, no. 477). Arguments adduced for a post-exilic date (supposed dependence on other psalms; Aramaic touches) are hardly valid. LXX divides into two psalms (vv. 1–9; 10–19).

1–4 The thanksgiving begins at once as a testimony, telling of the wonderful response to prayer. The first words have a peculiar emphasis in their abruptness: 'I love, for the Lord heard' (cf. 18.1; 1 John 4.19). This 'love' includes a commitment, a dedication. It has welled up in response to the experience of salvation. Like a terrible hunter, 'death', 'Sheol' (the underworld), had already caught the sufferer in his cords and sent the death-pains like hounds to the kill. There was but one defence, and it was enough. The prayer in the name of the Lord, the mighty and grace-filled name above every name, representing the self-giving of the Lord in readiness to save – the invocation of this name was heard and acted upon.

5–9 The thankful testimony continues with some general application, instructive to the hearers. Verse 5 indeed may be a choral response, acknowledging the pitying, caring character of the Lord, 'our God'. The 'simple' (v. 6) are often elsewhere the gullible, even foolish; but here are meant those who confess their weakness and their dependence on God's wisdom. The singer can exhort his own soul (cf. 42.5; 103.1; 131.2), that she may now come back into the place of peace; this 'rest' is like a promised land, a happy life before the face of the Lord. To 'walk before the Lord' may indicate a close service (elsewhere of the patriarchs, the house of the chief priest Eli, and the kings; see above on 56.13).

10–11 The singer returns again, as the rescued do, to that fateful moment, the confrontation with death and the realization that only One could help. In v. 10a we have obtained a natural sense, accepting the view that the Hebrew verb (*dbr*) has not the usual sense 'speak', but (as in the Arabic counterpart) 'be carried away, pass away, die' (cf. Hebrew *deber* 'pestilence'). More traditional renderings are somewhat strained: RV 'I believe, for I will speak'; NRSV 'I kept my faith, even when I said, I am greatly afflicted.'

12–19 Impossible as it is to give again to the Lord as he has given in his bountiful grace, yet he will be pleased with the thank-offering, which fulfils the promise made in the time of need and makes public witness to what he has done. So the saved one raises the cup that symbolizes the salvation (cf. 23.5, perhaps part of the sacrificial meal; or Num. 28.7, the cup raised and poured out at the altar), and he proclaims the holy name of the only Saviour. In the open court of the temple he presents his offering at the altar in the sight of the massed assembly of pilgrims. The psalm itself accompanies and fills out the meaning of these actions. And as the singer concludes his testimony to the gracious Lord, who does not lightly regard the suffering and death of those in his care (v. 15, cf. 72.14), he renews his dedication of himself as the Lord's lifelong servant, knowing in that service true freedom, loosed from the snare of death (v. 16; cf. 86.16; also Gen. 14.14 for house-born servants, wholly of the family, especially loyal).

We have heard here the song of someone rescued from a terrible confrontation with death. In the full earnestness of the realization that all human help was vain, this person cried to the Lord and was saved. Now the heart floods with loving gratitude, and the question resounds, 'How can I make return to the Lord for all the goodness he has poured on me?' It is beyond all repaying, but with fresh dedication the psalmist renews his work of daily serving the Lord, 'walking before the face of the Lord', ever ready to do his bidding. Further, he brings his thankful commitment to a focus in the place of worship, in the presence of the people; there he presents his promised gifts and raises the cup that signifies salvation, and chief of all, he proclaims the name of the Lord. The psalm thus lends thoughts and words to all who experience answered prayer and deliverance from mortal peril. For Christians here are words that correspond to their experience of salvation, their overflowing gratitude, their lifelong consecration, and the focal points of worship where they witness to God's goodness and take up the cup of the thanksgiving, Christ's eucharist.

Lord Jesus, our gracious redeemer who made the costly sacrifice to save us from destruction, help us in gratitude to walk daily before your face, to serve you with a heart of love, and gladly to raise the cup and proclaim your name in the worship you have appointed.

PSALM 117: The Seamless Robe of Creation

1   Praise the Lord, all nations;
    sing praise to him, all peoples.
2   For his faithful love rises mightily over us,
    and the truth of the Lord endures for ever.

There was plenty of scope for short psalms in the sequences of worship (cf. Ex. 15.21; Ps. 134). Brief calls and responses contributed as well as did the cantor's longer expositions, as each found its appropriate place in the dramatic flow of sacred action in the festivals. Even without knowing the original context, we can feel the force of the present tiny hymn. The singer calls for universal praise (v. 1), and gives reason in brief but rich terms (v. 2). In many manuscripts the psalm is joined to either 116 or 118 – understandably, but the main tradition is no doubt right to maintain its distinction. The post-exilic dating favoured by many is, as so often, open to question; arguments for dependence on Isa. 40–55 and for late language are frail. The worship of God as universal Creator and ruler seems to underlie v. 1 and could point to a setting in the autumn festival. In LXX the concluding alleluia begins 118.

1–2   The faithfulness of the Lord is bestowed on his covenant people indeed, but also wherever he has made commitment or holds responsibility – so upon all his creation, his kingdom (as clear also in 36.5–9; 96.13 etc.). It is therefore unnecessary to strain at an explanation of why the 'nations', and not Israel, are called to praise God's fidelity to 'us', taken to be Israel. The plain sense is that this 'us' is continuous with the peoples of v. 1. The festal assembly is the heart of a world adoring the manifest Creator (see above on 96); the call goes across this world that all should praise the Lord for his faithful rule of all, characterized by his *hesed*, faithful love, that reaches to heaven, and his *emet*, truth or faithfulness, that to all eternity never wavers (cf. 36.5; 103.11).

It is the wonder of the Psalms that – not as a late development but as something always essential in their worship – they find a bridge between the chosen people and the whole created order, a bridge so easily traversed that there sometimes seems no division to cross. Our psalm is one where no division appears, and so it came readily into Paul's exhortation to unity (Rom. 15.11). Christ, he says, was made a minister of the circumcision for the truth of God, that he might confirm the promises given to the fathers, and that the nations might glorify God for his mercy ('truth' and 'mercy' here echo our psalm's *emet* and *hesed*). So through Christ is realized the vision that lights our psalm, the vocation of a people that finds full meaning as the adoration of the Lord is taken up by all peoples.

O God of hope, fill us with the joy and peace of believing, and grant that with one accord we and all your creatures may glorify you, and give thanks for your faithful love and truth, made known in your Son Jesus.

PSALM 118: The Stone which the Builders Rejected

1   Give thanks to the Lord, for he is good;
     his faithfulness is for ever.

2   Then let Israel say,
     His faithfulness is for ever.

3   Then let the house of Aaron say,
     His faithfulness is for ever.

4   Then let those that fear the Lord say,
     His faithfulness is for ever.

5   From the grip of distress I called to the Lord;
     the Lord answered and set me in a wide place.

6   With the Lord beside me I will not fear;
     what can flesh do to me?

7   With the Lord by me as my saviour,
     I shall see the downfall of my foes.

8   It is better to take refuge in the Lord,
     than to put your trust in man.

9   It is better to take refuge in the Lord,
     than to put your trust in princes.

10 All nations surrounded me;
     with the name of the Lord I drove them back.

11 They surrounded me, they hemmed me in;
     with the name of the Lord I drove them back.

12 They surrounded me like bees,
      they blazed like fire among thorns;
     with the name of the Lord I drove them back.

13 You thrust me, you thrust me to the edge,
     but the Lord came to my help.

14 The Lord is my strength and my song,
     for he has become my salvation.

15 O the sound of singing and salvation,
     that rises from the tents of the just!
     The Lord's right hand does mighty deeds,

16   the Lord's right hand raises up;
     the Lord's right hand does mighty deeds.

17 I did not die, but found new life,
     that I might recount the deeds of the Lord.

18 The Lord sorely chastened me,
     but he did not give me over to death.

19 Open to me the gates of salvation;
     I will enter to give thanks to the Lord.

20 This is the gate of the Lord;
     only the just may enter by it.

21 I will give you thanks because you answered me,
   and you became my salvation.
22 The stone which the builders rejected
   has become the head of the corner.
23 This has come from the Lord;
   it is marvellous in our eyes.
24 This is the day that the Lord has made;
   we will rejoice and be glad in it.
25 Come, Lord, give salvation;
   come, Lord, give prosperity.
26 Blessed be he that comes in the name of the Lord;
   we bless you all from the house of the Lord.
27 The Lord is God and has given us light;
   with green boughs link the dance,
      up to the horns of the altar.
28 You are my Lord, and I will thank you;
   my God, and I will lift high your praise.
29 Give thanks to the Lord, for he is good;
   his faithfulness is for ever.

This is the last psalm of the Hallel, the chain of praise sung on festal occasions in later times (see above on 113). References in the Mishna (Suk. 3.9) and Talmud (Suk. 45a, b) further show this psalm well set in the ceremonies of Tabernacles. And no doubt the grand festal occasion mirrored in the psalm, including procession with green branches up to and through the temple gates and onward to the altar in the court, was part of the autumnal festival. The thanksgiving centres in the words and person of a leading individual (vv. 5–21, 28); the participation of the festal assembly is shown in the introductory calls to thankful praise (vv. 1–4) and various calls, blessings, responses and prayers (vv. 20, 22–7, 29). The individual singer tells of a time of distress, when he personally was surrounded by all nations, like a swarm of angry bees, like raging fire, till he almost plunged into the abyss of death. But with mighty hand the Lord delivered him. He had been sorely chastized, apparently rejected, but now was become the prized and vital chief cornerstone. This his day of deliverance brings light and salvation also to the community, which with dancing step and jubilant chants shares fully in his thanksgiving. No historical occasion is recognizable, despite many proposals, and the psalm is more likely to have been part of an annual ceremony, as Jewish tradition knew it. Post-exilic dating, based on the view that the 'fearers of the Lord' are proselytes in the late period and on supposed borrowings from other scripture, is not well founded. The obvious interpretation that the central individual is the king can therefore be accepted. His fate is the focus of the people's light and salvation, the great cornerstone of the society, the target for the mythically pictured hostile nations. His peril and rescue, his rejection and reinstatement, can be understood as scenes from the ceremonies that dramatized the royal calling (see above on 2, 18, 101, 110; my *Kingship*, pp. 61–3, 133–4).

1–4 As those who are rejoicing now in the experience of God's promised salvation, the worshippers are summoned to give the thanksgiving of praise and testimony, first the laity, then the priestly orders, then all together (the 'fearers of the Lord'; see above on 115.9f.); and each, then all together, respond with the rhythmic mass chant, no doubt with clapping of hands: 'Yes, for ever his faithful love' – we might render 'For ever he keeps faith.' This summons to praise may come from the solo singer of vv. 5f., or some choral leader; there will much vocal interchange later in the psalm (cf. the lively scene in Ezra 3.10–11).

5–18 The central figure, most likely the king, now recounts his deliverance, with all the lessons of faith that it holds. He begins in general terms, concentrating on testimony to the Lord's faithfulness and power. Through these teachings year by year, king and people are moved to ever deeper levels of trust in the Lord rather than in human power. The story begins in v. 10. The encircling attack by 'all nations', like that in 46.6 and 48.4 (cf. 2.1f.; 110.5f.), will be a poetic picture from the preceding ritual, an imaginary drama of a world of hostility against the bearer of God's cause. How fierce the enemy, how close the fatal plunge! But – so the rite signified – the Lord came to his rescue. On all sides now the calls of salutation and thanksgiving to God are sounding, and no doubt we hear some of the rhythmic and responsorial chants in v. 16. The rite signified suffering and humiliation (v. 18a), but all as prelude to the vindication of trust. Life was restored, that the rescued one should recount the deeds of the faithful Lord.

19–22 The procession (which may have ascended from the spring and caverns of Gihon, cf. above on 18; 68.26; 110.7) has now come to the temple gates. These gates signify *ṣedeq*, 'right, goodness, salvation'; the term points to the fitness, through due preparation, which entrants should have in order to pass through the gates, but also to the grace and salvation of God (cf. Isa. 26.2). In the present case the king and people would pass through as those wonderfully saved and accepted by the Lord; they are right and just in that they have been humbled by affliction and have learnt to put their trust in God (cf. Zech. 9.9, a king 'right, filled with salvation, and humble'). There seems to be a dialogue at the entrance (cf. 24.3f.), v. 20 being the response of the priests that kept the gates. The meaning of the king's ordeal and salvation is summarized picturesquely in v. 22; once scorned, rejected, he has now been taken up to be the cornerstone of the community. (It is not certain whether the crowning or foundation stone is meant, but the role at the junction of walls was crucial.)

23–29 The voices call and respond as the procession passes through into the holy court and towards its great altar. The essential belief in such ceremony is that all is of the Lord's appointing; the vital action is his. The very day of the celebration is of his making. Wonder and rejoicing fill hearts and voices. But all that has been done by the Lord is an earnest for days to come, and the chants take on the nature of short prayers for realization of the blessings: 'Hosanna (Save), prosper' (v. 25). The entering of the king is greeted with a blessing (v. 26a); he enters by the power of the name of the Lord (cf. vv. 10–12; 20.1f.; another view understands 'Blessed with the name of the Lord be he that comes'). The blessing, from priests within the sanctuary, is extended to all the procession ('you' plural in v. 26b). The cry goes up that the Lord has indeed shown himself to be the true God, and has this day caused the light of salvation to shine upon his worshippers (v. 27a). Then the word is given for the procession to move up to and probably round the altar; this movement, with dancing step, seems to be the sense of *ḥag* here (v. 27b, older versions render 'sacrifice'; elsewhere it means the festival as a whole). They are to 'connect' ('bind') it with the green boughs they carry (palm, myrtle and willow bound together), linking the worshippers and the altar itself in token of the new life that God imparts. (The 'horns' are the four spikes rising from the corners of the altar; instead of 'boughs' some render 'cords', but the branches are well attested at this festival.) One may imagine vv. 28–9 repeated in the circling of the altar, the thanksgiving first of the king, then of all the people.

The lively scenes and profound thoughts of this psalm are enframed in the community's thanksgiving for the faithful love of the Lord. An action of the Lord, centred in one person, has brought light and life to them all. Through a darkness of suffering and rejection, this person, bearing in his heart the cause of his God and the fate of his people, has been tested and tried; but trusting only in the Lord, and invoking his holy name, he has been granted victory over all the enemies of God's reign. The Lord's right hand has raised him up. He ascends the hill and passes through the gates into the holy presence, bringing his people also into that place of blessing and salvation. This sacred drama is expressed in movement and dance, poetic song full of imagery and bounding phrases, a music of thankful joy, and through it runs the conviction that it is all from the Lord; he has made this day and all that is shown forth in it. It is still a time of prayer, for the day is an earnest of salvation yet to unfold, the seed of what is yet to blossom. Much used in later Jewish worship, the psalm is prominent also in the New Testament and echoes constantly as the eucharist is celebrated. The stone rejected by the builders but made the chief cornerstone, the blessed one who comes in the name of the Lord – here is a figure readily found prophetic of Christ. From him is received the pattern of trust amid darkness, with him is made the ascent into God's light and the dance of life.

O God of faithfulness, whose right hand raised up the Lord Jesus from the power of death, grant that we also may trust in you and call upon your name in every peril, that we may recount your deeds in the time of singing and salvation.

PSALM 119: A Sustained Prayer for Life

1   Happy are those wholehearted in the way,
    who walk by the law of the Lord.
2   Happy those who treasure his testimonies,
    who seek him with all their heart,
3   such as do no wickedness,
    but truly walk in his ways.
4   For you have given command,
    that your precepts be carefully kept.
5   O that my ways were so firm,
    that I might keep your statutes!
6   Then I should not be put to shame,
    as I kept my eyes on all your commandments.
7   I will thank you with a true heart,
    as I learn your saving judgements.
8   I will keep your statutes;
    do not utterly forsake me.

9   How shall a young person keep to a pure way of life?
    By holding fast to your word.
10 With my whole heart I have sought you;
    do not let me stray from your commandments.
11 I have laid up your promise in my heart,
    that I should not sin against you.
12 Blessed be you, O Lord,
    for you will teach me your statutes.
13 With my lips I tell over
    all the judgements of your mouth.
14 In the way of your testimonies I rejoice,
    as beyond all manner of riches.
15 I meditate on your precepts,
    and contemplate your paths.
16 My delight shall be in your statutes,
    and I will not forget your word.

17 Do good to your servant that I may live,
    and so shall I keep your word.
18 Uncover my eyes that I may see
    the wonders of your law.
19 I am a stranger upon the earth;
    do not hide your commandments from me.
20 My soul is consumed with longing
    at all times for your judgements.

21 You have rebuked the arrogant;
   cursed are those who stray from your commandments.
22 Remove from me reproach and scorn,
   for I have treasured your testimonies.
23 Princes also sit and take counsel against me,
   but your servant meditates in your statutes.
24 For your testimonies are my delight,
   and I have them for my counsellors.

25 My soul cleaves to the dust;
   O give me life according to your word.
26 I have recounted my ways and you have answered me
   in teaching me your statutes.
27 Help me discern the way of your precepts,
   and I shall meditate on your wonders.
28 My soul melts away in tears of sorrow;
   raise me up according to your word.
29 Take from me the way of falsehood;
   be gracious to me through your law.
30 I have chosen the way of faithfulness;
   your judgements I have laid before me.
31 Lord, I cleave to your testimonies;
   let me not be put to shame.
32 I will run the way of your commandments,
   when you have set my heart at liberty.
33 Teach me, Lord, the way of your statutes,
   and I shall keep it to the end.
34 Give me understanding that I may keep your law,
   and I shall treasure it with all my heart.
35 Help me to walk in the path of your commandments,
   for in that way is my delight.
36 Make my heart incline to your testimonies,
   rather than to greed of gain.
37 Turn my eyes from gazing on worthless things,
   and in your ways give me life.
38 Confirm to your servant your promise,
   which you have given for those who fear you.
39 Turn away the reproach I dread,
   for your judgements are ever good.
40 See how I long for your precepts;
   in your goodness give me life.

41 And may your faithful love come to me, Lord,
   your salvation according to your promise.
42 And I shall answer those who taunt me,
   for I have trusted in your word.

43 And do not take the story of your truth
     utterly from my mouth,
   for my hope is in your judgements.
44 And so I shall always keep your law,
   now and for evermore.
45 And I shall walk in a wide space,
   for I have sought your precepts.
46 And I shall speak of your testimonies,
   even before kings and not be ashamed.
47 And my delight shall be in your commandments,
   on which I have set my love.
48 And I will lift my hands in praise for your commandments,
     which I love,
   and I will meditate in your statutes.

49 Remember your word to your servant,
   in which you have made me hope.
50 This is my comfort in my trouble,
   that your promise will give me life.
51 Though the arrogant have greatly derided me,
   I have not turned aside from your law.
52 Lord, I have remembered your judgements from of old,
   and so I have been comforted.
53 I am seized with horror at the wicked,
   for they have forsaken your law.
54 Your statutes have become melodies for me,
   my songs in the house of my pilgrimage.
55 I have recited your name in the night, O Lord,
   and so I have kept your law.
56 These blessings have been mine,
   for I have treasured your precepts.

57 Lord, you are my portion;
   I have promised to keep your word.
58 With all my heart I entreat you;
   be gracious to me according to your promise.
59 I have considered my ways,
   and turned back my feet to your testimonies.
60 I have made haste and not delayed
   to keep to your commandments.
61 The cords of the wicked have wrapped me round,
   but I do not forget your law.
62 At midnight I rise to give you thanks
   for all your saving judgements.
63 I am companion to those who fear you,
   to those who keep your precepts.

64   Lord, earth is filled with your faithful love;
     I pray you, teach me your statutes.
65   You will deal kindly with your servant,
     in accordance with your word, O Lord.
66   Teach me true understanding and knowledge,
     for I have believed in your commandments.
67   Before I suffered I went astray,
     but now I keep your saying.
68   You are kind and gracious;
     I pray you, teach me your statutes.
69   The proud have smeared me with lies,
     but with my whole heart I will treasure your precepts.
70   Their heart is gross and unfeeling,
     but my delight is in your law.
71   It is good for me to have been afflicted,
     that I might learn your statutes.
72   Dearer to me the law of your mouth,
     than hordes of gold and silver!

73   Your hands have made me and fashioned me;
     give me understanding that I may learn your commandments.
74   May those who fear you be glad when they see me,
     for I wait in hope for your word.
75   I know, Lord, that your judgements are right,
     and in faithfulness you have caused me to be troubled.
76   May your faithful love come to comfort me,
     according to your promise to your servant.
77   Let your pity come to me that I may live,
     for your law is my delight.
78   Let the proud be shamed, for they wrong me with lies;
     but I will meditate in your precepts.
79   May those who fear you return to me,
     that they may know your testimonies.
80   Let my heart be whole in your statutes,
     that I may not be put to shame.

81   My soul longs for your salvation;
     I wait in hope for your word.
82   My eyes fail with watching for your promise,
     while I say, When will you comfort me?
83   I have become like a bottle in the smoke,
     yet I do not forget your commandments.
84   How many are the days of your servant;
     when will you bring judgement on those who persecute me?
85   The proud have dug pits for me,
     for they do not heed your law.

86 All your commandments are true;
    help me, for with falsehood they persecute me.
87 They have almost made an end of me upon earth,
    but I do not forsake your precepts.
88 Give me life according to your faithful love,
    and so shall I keep the testimonies of your mouth.

89 Everlasting is your word, O Lord;
    it stands for ever in the heavens.
90 Your faithfulness remains through all generations;
    you have established the earth and it abides.
91 Your judgements also stand firm this day,
    for all things are your servants.
92 If your law had not been my delight,
    I should have perished in my trouble.
93 I will never forget your precepts,
    for by them you have given me life.
94 I am yours; O save me,
    for I have sought out your precepts.
95 The wicked wait for me to destroy me,
    but I will contemplate your testimonies.
96 I have seen an end of all perfection,
    but your commandment has no bounds.

97 Lord, how I love your law!
    All the day long it is my meditation.
98 Your commandment will make me wiser than my enemies,
    for it is ever with me.
99 Beyond all my teachers I shall gain wisdom,
    for your testimonies are my meditation.
100 Beyond all the aged I shall gain understanding,
    because I treasure your precepts.
101 From every evil path I hold back my feet,
    so that I may keep your word.
102 I have not turned aside from your judgements,
    for you have been my teacher.
103 How sweet your sayings to my tongue,
    sweeter than honey to my mouth.
104 From your precepts I get understanding;
    therefore I hate all ways of falsehood.

105 Your word is a lantern to my feet,
    and a light upon my path.
106 I have sworn, and will fulfil it,
    that I shall keep your saving judgements.
107 I am greatly afflicted;

Lord, give me life according to your word.
108 May the offerings of my mouth please you, Lord;
    I pray you, teach me your statutes.
109 My soul is ever on the palm of my hand,
    yet I do not forget your law.
110 The wicked have laid a snare for me,
    but I do not wander from your precepts.
111 Your testimonies I have claimed as my heritage for ever,
    for they are the very joy of my heart.
112 I have inclined my heart to fulfil your statutes,
    always, even to the end.

113 I oppose the double-minded,
    but on your law I set my love.
114 You are my hiding-place and my shield;
    I wait in hope for your word.
115 Get from me, you evildoers,
    that I may keep the commandments of my God.
116 Sustain me according to your promise, that I may live,
    and let me not be put to shame for my hope.
117 Hold me and I shall be saved,
    that I may ever gaze upon your statutes.
118 You reject those who stray from your statutes,
    for their deceiving is in vain.
119 All the wicked of the earth you will count as dross;
    therefore I will love your testimonies.
120 My flesh trembles for fear of you,
    and I am afraid of your judgements.

121 I have done what is just and right;
    do not leave me to my oppressors.
122 Stand surety for the good of your servant;
    may the arrogant oppress me no longer.
123 My eyes fail with watching for your salvation,
    and for your promise of deliverance.
124 Act for your servant according to your faithful love,
    and teach me to know your statutes.
125 I am your servant; give me understanding,
    that I may know your testimonies.
126 It is time to act, O Lord,
    for they do away with your law.
127 Truly I love your commandments
    more than the finest gold.
128 I hold dear all your precepts,
    but all false ways I utterly abhor.

129 Your testimonies are wonderful;
    therefore my soul has treasured them.
130 The opening of your word gives light,
    imparting wisdom to the simple.
131 I open my mouth and gasp,
    as I long for your commandments.
132 O turn to me and be gracious to me,
    according to your judgement for those who love your name.
133 Order my steps by your word,
    and may no evil have dominion over me.
134 Redeem me from man's cruelty,
    that I may keep your precepts.
135 Make your face to shine upon your servant,
    and teach me to know your statutes.
136 My eyes run down with rivers of water,
    because they do not keep your law.

137 You are good, O Lord,
    and your judgements also are true.
138 Rightly you have commanded your testimonies,
    and with great faithfulness.
139 My indignation consumes me,
    for my adversaries forget your word.
140 Your promise has been tried to the uttermost,
    and therefore your servant loves it.
141 Though I am small and despised,
    I do not forget your precepts.
142 Your goodness is ever right,
    and your law for ever true.
143 Though sorrow and anguish have found me,
    your commandments are my delight.
144 Your testimonies are for ever right;
    O give me understanding that I may live.

145 I call with my whole heart;
    answer me, Lord, and I shall treasure your statutes.
146 I call to you; O save me,
    that I may keep your testimonies.
147 Before the break of morning I cry to you,
    and I wait in hope for your word.
148 My eyes are open before the night-watches,
    that I may meditate on your promise.
149 Hear my voice in your faithful love;
    Lord, by your judgement give me life.
150 Those who persecute me from malice draw near,
    but they are far from your law.

151 You are near, O Lord,
       and all your commandments are true.
152 I have long known from your testimonies,
       that you have founded them for ever.

153 See my suffering and deliver me,
       for I do not forget your law.
154 Take up my cause and redeem me;
       through your promise give me life.
155 Salvation is far from the wicked,
       for they do not seek your statutes.
156 Many are your mercies, Lord;
       by your judgements give me life.
157 Many are those who pursue and oppress me,
       but I do not turn from your testimonies.
158 I am sickened with grief to see the treacherous,
       for they do not keep your word.
159 See how I love your precepts;
       give me life, Lord, in your faithful love.
160 The sum of your word is truth,
       and all your saving judgements stand for ever.

161 Princes persecute me without a cause,
       but my heart trembles only at your word.
162 I rejoice over your word
       as one who finds great spoil.
163 Falsehood I hate and abhor,
       but for your law I have great love.
164 Seven times a day I praise you
       because of your saving judgements.
165 Great peace have those who love your law
       and they shall not be overthrown.
166 Lord, I look for your salvation,
       and I follow your commandments.
167 My soul has kept your testimonies,
       and greatly have I loved them.
168 I keep your precepts and testimonies,
       for all my ways are before you.

169 Let my cry draw near before you;
       give me understanding through your word.
170 May my pleading enter your presence;
       O deliver me according to your promise.
171 My lips shall pour out your praise,
       for you will teach me your statutes.
172 My tongue shall sing of your promise,

for all your commandments are right.
173 Let your hand reach out to help me,
    for I have chosen your precepts.
174 Lord, I have longed for your salvation,
    and your law is my delight.
175 Let my soul live that it may praise you,
    and may your judgements come to my help.
176 I have gone astray like a sheep that is lost;
    O seek your servant, for I do not forget your commandments.

We met the ideal of constant preoccupation with the Lord's teaching (*tora*) in Psalm 1, and in 19.7–11 we met a thankful praise for his teaching, praise expressed in a pattern of statements using five or six equivalent terms for such divine utterance. The roots of such piety are ancient (cf. 18.22, 30; 25.4, 5, 8f.), but from the later monarchy onwards the ideal of devotion to the Lord's *tora* seems to develop in circles connected with Deuteronomy (cf. Deut. 6). It comes to fullest expression in Psalm 119, which can be understood as a supplication from a situation of distress, the prayer being supported by constant reference to the Lord's teachings – how much the supplicant loves them, endeavours to keep them, appreciates them as expressions of the divine faithfulness and compassion, longs to see deeper into them and to find their saving force fulfilled in his life. While some have imagined the psalm as reflecting the tensions of the Greek period around the third century, when the contrast between conservative and liberal factions was acute, others have looked for earlier settings, such as the sufferings of the young king Jehoiachin in the Exile (cf. Deut. 17.18f.). It is easier to describe the distinctive form of the psalm. We have already met acrostic psalms, each verse or half-verse beginning with the next letter of the Hebrew alphabet (Int. 4e). But here the scheme is much developed, since for each successive letter there are eight verses that each begin with that letter. For the 22 letters we thus have a total of 176 verses, by far the longest psalm.

The pattern has a further feature which strongly marks the psalm's character. Almost every verse contains one of a set of eight terms (virtually synonyms) that denote God's word or commandments. These are: *tora* (law, teaching, guidance), *dabar* (word), *imra* (saying, promise), *mishpatim* (judgements, ordinances), *huqqim* (statutes), *miswot* (commandments), *'edot* (testimonies, stipulations), *piqqudim* (orders, precepts). With such terms the tradition of the Lord who guides and commands his covenant-people is evoked – the one desirous to bless them with life by showing them the right path; and indeed words for 'way' and 'path' are also prominent. The repeated occurrences of so many terms brings out the importance and richness of the theme. Not the commandment itself, but the guiding, teaching Lord comes to dominate the mind of the one reciting the psalm; and here it is important to note that these terms for 'law' etc. are qualified by the added syllable meaning 'your', so there is no question of 'the Law', but always (lit.) 'law-of-you' etc. It is striking also that the psalm does not enable us to define what material is referred to by this *tora* of the Lord. Some feel a collection of covenantal laws is in mind, something dear to the circles connected with Deuteronomy; others, with later dating, speak for the Pentateuch, and others again add to this some other scriptural books. In fact no document and no particular law are mentioned in the psalm, and whatever the form of *tora* familiar to the psalmist, the object of his devotion is essentially the one who thus teaches, judges, promises, decrees and so saves and gives new life (cf. 19, where it is explicitly the Creator who illumines through his *tora*). The alphabet itself would be revered as the elements of scripture's written form. As a frame for composition and meditation it could give momentum, sustenance, and a sense of wholeness. Some have judged the pattern artificial, productive only of stilted thought and tedious repetition. But the psalm's great honour in Christian use, with daily recital in monastic prayer, points rather to a peculiar value. It has proved a precious aid to sustained meditative communion (after the introductory vv. 1–3, every verse is addressed to the Lord except v. 115 which rebukes enemies). We may say that the plan of composition has been vindicated as able to unfold a great prayer for help, which is supported by statements of praise, loyalty and love for the saviour's will – statements that seem simple, yet prove often to have immeasurable depth.

1–8   For the beginning of the alphabetic prayer, *asherey* ('O the happiness of . . .', beginning with *aleph*) offers itself readily (cf. 112.1 and on 1.1) and here leads two verses. Verses 1–3 amount to an indirect praise of the Lord, whose good guidance brings true happiness to those who value and follow it. They are 'whole' (*tamim*) in their way of life, 'all their heart' set upon him. That they 'seek him' indicates that the course of their life has become a pilgrimage into his presence. From v. 4 (with 'you' in emphatic position) the direct address to the Lord begins and is sustained to the end, except for v. 115. Already it is clear that this disciple is conscious of yet having much to learn (v. 7) and of needing to be made firm and constant in keeping the Lord's directions and in contemplating them with steady gaze. But at least he can plead that his intention is good, and so he comes to the climax and conclusion of the section with the petition which is the gist of the whole prayer of the psalm: 'Do not utterly forsake me.' The prayer, it is already clear, rises from a time of suffering.

9–16   Before the Lord the psalmist is a pupil learning from the mouth of a revered teacher. Like a youth or child (*na'ar*, cf. Jer. 1.6) he learns the secret of keeping to a pure way – it is by heeding the Lord's word. He remembers his teacher's saying, so full of promise; he stores it as treasure in his heart, where it strengthens him against sin. He can only bless him with thankfulness in return for his teaching (in v. 12b the Hebrew imperative, 'teach me', seems to be used idiomatically; cf. GK 110). From his teacher's mouth he recites aloud and learns all his directions. The teachings amount to a way of life which gives a joy beyond all that riches can give. Murmuring and meditating in the teachings, he comes to contemplate, to see with opened eyes, the paths of the

Lord. To delight in the Lord's statutes implies an eagerness to be engaged with them, a constant remembrance of his word (cf. 1.2).

17–24   More definitely now the shadow of suffering falls across the verses. From the bountiful goodness of the Lord the psalmist seeks new life. At present scorn and hostility weigh upon him, and rulers or high officials plot against him. Having but a short time on earth (cf. 39.12), he longs to see revelations of God's will. This longing (vv. 18, 19, 20) is both for the wonder and beauty of the revelations themselves but also for the saving force which shines from them, the will of the Lord for justice and the salvation of his servants (cf. 2 Kings 6.17; Eph. 1.17f.). If the princes confer and take counsel against him, he has still the comfort and delight of the Lord's testimonies, his words of guidance and assurance, which are 'the men of my counsel', the wise and trusted friends that stay with him to guide and console.

25–32   The suffering makes death seem near, and the psalmist's soul seems pressed down to the dust (or 'mire') of the underworld (v. 25) or dissolving in tears of sorrow (v. 28), so the prayer for new life rises again. All his troubles he has told over to the Lord and been answered and instructed (cf. on v. 1b). The prayer to be granted to discern (v. 27) perhaps includes the desire to see the application of the teachings to his plight. Humbly the psalmist asks to be preserved from falsehood and in God's law to find his grace. Rather than the way of falsehood he has chosen the way of faithfulness, of loyalty to his Lord, setting before his eyes all the Lord's utterances. Rather than cleave to the dust (v. 25), he would cleave to the Lord's testimonies. With joy he will run the way, as God takes from his heart the constriction of fear and anguish (or we could take the literal 'make wide my heart' to mean 'enlarge my understanding').

33–40   The singer sustains his plea for restoration of true life (vv. 37, 40) and for deliverance from malice and scorn (v. 39, cf. v. 22). Strongly he continues his prayer to be taught and guided by the Lord and to be given discernment and good inclinations. He longs for God's commandments in the sense of desiring deeper knowledge of them and the fulfilment of God's will for salvation (cf. v. 20). The humility of the prayer is apparent in the recognition of need: 'Teach me … give me understanding … cause me to walk … incline my heart.'

41–48   Lacking Hebrew words beginning with 'w', the psalmist attaches the prefix 'w-', basically meaning 'and', at the beginning of all these verses. This give a rather flowing sequence of thought, from God's faithfulness to the disciple's trust, and so to spaciousness, delight and thankfulness. 'Faithful love' (*hesed*) is shown clearly in its meaning of God's help in fulfilment of his commitment (v. 41). The 'word of truth' (v. 43a) seems here to refer to testimony to God's faithfulness; may there be cause for such testimony. Then he will walk 'in a wide space', freed from the painful pressures of affliction.

49–56 Prayer rises for the fulfilment of the divine promise to give true life again, a promise which in all the psalmist's trouble gives him hope and comfort. Derided by the powerful and shocked at their contempt for God's teaching, the psalmist has a hard pilgrimage; but like a traveller enjoying rest and music at an inn, he is refreshed by the music of holy words – the chanting of God's teachings (v. 54) and formulas praising God's name through the night (v. 55).

57–64 In ancient times it was said that, while other tribes had their allotted lands to live off, Levi, the landless tribe of priests, had the Lord for their 'portion'; in fact they lived from a share in the offerings at the temple (Num. 18.20; Deut. 10.9; Josh. 13.14). The expression came to mean satisfaction in the Lord alone, dependence on him alone; and to this ideal our psalmist aspires, promising also in gratitude to keep the Lord's word (another reading, 'words'). In v. 58 the basic plea of the psalm is expressed again; it is the Lord's promise which is fundamental to this hope of new life. The psalmist is always ready to admit that he may go astray (v. 59, cf. vv. 67, 176), but he eagerly seeks again the right path (v. 60). The enemies (like death in 18.4f.) are pictured as hunters that lay snares (v. 61). At the midpoint of night, the psalmist rises from his bed to give thankful praise. With all who revere the Lord he feels close fellowship. Earth can hardly contain the immense *hesed*, faithful love of the Lord (cf. 33.5; 36.5; 57.10); from such a teacher the psalmist must ever yearn for instruction.

65–72 This section seems to open with prayer for the goodness of God to transform the situation (though others render 'You have dealt'). The psalmist has 'believed' God's utterances, trusting their rightness and promise, and he asks further to be taught good judgement and knowledge. He sees gain in his suffering, through which he has been led back to the true path (vv. 67, 71). His adversaries, arrogant and eminent, have smeared him with false accusations, but in the word of the Lord he has beauty and inspiration to treasure and take delight in, better than thousands of gold and silver pieces.

73–80 As with potter's hands, the Lord made and shaped the one who now cries from suffering and who would be further shaped in the wisdom of obedience. May he become an example of salvation to gladden believers' hearts. He has already come far, for he recognizes God's faithfulness even in his suffering. He asks for the angel of *hesed* to be sent to comfort him, the love that fulfils all God's promise (cf. v. 41); and the fellow-angel also, the divine compassion. The arrogant men of power twist the truth about his character and deeds, and so devout folk forsake him; may they return and see for themselves the assurances of God proved true. (Another reading in v. 79b gives 'those who know your testimonies'.) But if God grants him to be whole in loyalty, with undivided heart, he will not be overthrown.

81–88   With this section the first half of the alphabetic scheme comes to an end. Accordingly, the lamenting prayer rises in intensity. The longing expressed in vv. 81–2 is the yearning of one whose strength fails, as he still watches and waits for the messenger of salvation. Indeed he can say that the enemies have almost made an end of him on earth. In his suffering he is 'like a bottle in the smoke', a skin bottle that is grimy from the smoke; either it is stored empty in the rafters, or (another theory) it holds wine and is set in the smoke escaping through the window to mature the contents; the blackened skin resembles that of the lamenter in mourning and penitential rites. So the prayer rises for judgement on the persecutors and for salvation and new life through God's faithful love.

89–96   As the second half of the alphabetic prayer begins, the plea for salvation (v. 94) is surrounded and supported by the thought of the faithful word of God that stands for ever (vv. 89–91, 96). At the source of his various utterances is the one Word that stands firm with him in heaven. Here is true faithfulness, of which earth's stability is but a sign. Through his Word was established the manifold order of creation, where all identities are but servants of the Lord. His Word is known also in his words, the teachings which give delight to the disciple who recites, searches out and contemplates them. All earthly perfection is seen to come to its end, but the Lord's 'commandment', his royal Word, continues beyond the bound of space and time (lit. as BCP: 'is exceeding broad').

97–104   It is the statements in support of the psalmist's plea, statements of appreciation for the Lord's teachings, that fill these verses. These words of the Lord he loves, and finds them sweet to his palate as he murmurs them to digest them (cf. 19.10). From their wonderful truth and grace he will become wiser than his foes, than his teachers, than the venerable sages. To think to surpass one's teachers and the aged would be a vain presumption, except that it is meant as a tribute to the teaching of the Lord, his teacher now (v. 102b).

105–111   Greatly afflicted, the psalmist walks through a vale of darkness, but in God's word he has a lamp to show where his feet should tread. The wicked have laid their snares, and he carries his soul, his very life, as it were on the palm of his hand, so open is he to danger. His songs of praise are offered willingly in thankfulness; the Lord's testimonies are a possession which no one can take from him.

113–120   In Hebrew to 'love' and to 'hate' often means to be 'for' and 'against', to adhere to the Lord and to reject evil. There are several statements here of this loyalty that is 'for' and 'against' (vv. 113, 115, 118, 119) and deprecation of insincerity, deceitful double-mindedness (vv. 115, 118). Alongside the comfort of God as 'hiding-place' (v. 114) there is the numinous awe of his reality, which causes the very flesh to 'bristle' (v. 120); this dread presence may even shine through his utterances, as human speech is stilled and the heart waits only on him.

121–128   As the arrogant oppress without restraint, the psalmist, protesting that he has not wronged them (v. 121a), prays not to be left to them. Is it not time for the Lord to act? Will he not go surety, giving a pledge with which he would make himself responsible for his servant's safety (cf. Gen. 43.9)?

129–136   Prayer to be rescued from oppression continues (v. 134) and is supported by a wealth of loving praise for God's words. They have a marvellous quality, like miracles. When by God's grace his word is opened, an inner depth is revealed, a light shines into the disciple's heart, and the humble or simple one is given a wisdom from above. In his suffering the psalmist, like an animal snuffing for water in the drought (cf. 42.1), opens his mouth and yearns for salvation to come by the word of the Lord. The wonder and beauty of God's words arise from his presence in them; he himself turns here to his servant in grace, and their light is the light of his face. As the psalmist praises God's revelations, so he testifies to his tearful grief that they are ignored by the proud. For himself however, the prayer of humility is fitting, with fallibility confessed: 'Make firm my steps by your saying; may no wickedness hold sway over me.'

137–144   The initial letter for this section prompts the thought of God's *ṣedeq*, his saving righteousness, compassionate justice – in a word, his goodness (vv. 137, 138, 142, 144). This quality therefore belongs also to his utterances, eternally faithful, tested and tried like oft-refined silver (cf. 12.6). In support of his prayer for renewal of true life, the psalmist praises this 'rightness' of the Lord and his words, and affirms his delight in his commandments and his horror that the enemies disregard them. In much suffering and treated with scorn, he can yet delight in the truth and beauty of the Lord's word.

145–152   Dawn and the beginnings of the night watches may have been set times of prayer. The psalmist affirms that when these rigorous times come round, they find him already awake, praying, meditating, and yearning for the Lord's answering word of salvation. When aware of the nearness of his persecutors, he is comforted to know that his Lord is also near. From his meditation in the Lord's testimonies, he perceives their enduring truth; against the malice of the transient wicked, he sets the everlasting faithfulness of God.

153–160   The section is led by an urgent cry for help: may the Lord see the suffering in all its pain and length, and so in his pity fight for his servant, deliver, redeem, and restore to true life. Supporting thoughts are of God's promise and of his compassion. This last word is plural in Hebrew, and so in v. 156a can be rendered 'mercies' to keep the contrast with v. 157a (the many troublers); originally the word (related to that for 'womb') referred to the love between those from the same womb, or indeed to a mother's love – warm, tenacious, merciful. Another contrast comes in the psalmist's love for the divine words and his sickening grief at their being scorned by those betraying God and man. In v. 160a the Hebrew word *ro'sh*, 'head', can also refer to a 'well-spring'; from source to sum, from first to last, the Word of God is sure and faithful; and here the sufferer may rest his hope and trust.

161–168 The emphasis in this next-to-last section is on the wonder and grace known in God's word, and there are no direct petitions. Sufferings are still present – unjust persecution by rulers. But the psalmist wishes to gather up all the affirmations he has been making in appreciation of the Lord's utterance. Arousing numinous dread, awakening joy with sudden disclosures, stirring love and praise, bestowing peace, the Lord's words of promise, guidance and command have become the centre of the psalmist's existence. The comparison with discovered treasure (v. 162b) arises from the experience of discovery, the sudden seeing of what had been hidden in God's word (cf. v. 18). The 'seven times' (v. 164) may be a zealous rule of prayer, times for praise and gestures of reverence (cf. vv. 147–8, and the threefold pattern of 55.17).

169–176 The concluding section finds the singer praying that his composition may ascend, 'draw near', and 'enter before' the Lord's presence, phrases that suggest an offering (cf. 19.14) or a messenger of supplication. The terms he uses for his great psalm (vv. 169a, 170a) bring out its central purpose; it is a cry from the heart (*rinna*, 'ringing cry') and a supplication (*tehinna*, 'plea for grace'). Like most supplications, it draws to an end with vows of praise (vv. 171, 172, 175). But the final words return to prayer. For all his love and delight in God's teachings, he confesses himself to have gone astray. He has wandered into hostile country, a wasteland of distress, and he implores the Good Shepherd to seek him and bring him home.

The huge psalm expresses a sustained work of prayer and communion. The address to the Lord continues virtually without a break from v. 4 on, and the majority of verses carry their own complete petition. These are brief and without complexity. Indeed, the long flow of statements that sustain the communion are simple in structure and extremely limited in range of topic; but it is a simplicity that proves to have wonderful depth, and the restraint in theme aids the concentration which is necessary in contemplation. As in most psalms of supplication, there is a wrestling with God where many con- siderations are urged for the changing of the lamentable situation. A person who has loved the Lord and treasured his guidance is now ill-used by powerful people and brought near to the borders of death. So the prayer for new life rises, supported by the great stream of affirmations about the Lord's word in promise, teaching and commandments – how the sufferer has loved and followed it and longs to know it better. These considerations are not urged in the spirit of one who is blameless. There is almost a contradiction between the claims to have kept the Lord's law and the readiness to admit inadequacy and erring from the path. If it is a contradiction, it is a common experience – years of devotion and loyalty, yet shot through with deviation, and perceived in deep moments to be quite inadequate. So the point often put to God is the desire to be taught by him, to be guided on the good path, to be given a better understanding, and to receive the wonder of revelation, when the eyes are uncovered and the beautiful, terrible wonder of the divine Word is beheld.

The psalm has been in daily use in the offices of the church down the centuries, and so has continued its work of sustaining communion and devotion while voicing prayer for deliverance from oppression and for new life – for the reciters themselves and those in their heart. The strengthening references to the Lord's word here become related to Christ the Word, and all the light of guidance and salvation given through him. He is the Word established for ever in heaven, the thought and true expression of God, eternal and boundless, yet close in his grace as teacher, counsellor, comforter, shepherd, lamp, fountain of hope and joy. The psalm becomes a prayer through this Word, built on him, and offered for all his suffering ones.

Lord, hear the cry of the souls that melt away for heaviness, those that cleave to the dust, the victims of the cruel, and all who long for your judgements; let their supplication enter into your presence, and give them life according to your Word, your Son, our Saviour Jesus Christ.

PSALM 120: Living with the Enemies of Peace

A song of the steps.

1   To the Lord I cry in my distress,
    and surely he will answer me.
2   Lord, deliver my soul from lying lips,
    and from the deceitful tongue.

3   What shall he give you, and what more besides,
    O you deceitful tongue?
4   The sharp arrows of a mighty one,
    and burning shafts of broom!
5   Pity me, that I am like a stranger in Mesek,
    or one who must dwell among the tents of Kedar.
6   Too long my soul has dwelt
    with the enemies of peace.
7   I am for peace, but when I speak of it,
    their mind is only for war.

The heading 'song of the steps' occurs over each of 120–34 and nowhere else. Some of the fifteen mostly small psalms are clearly pre-exilic, but a common view is that the present collection was made in later times in connection with the autumn pilgrimage festival; some think of the journey itself, others of ceremony at the sanctuary. The theme of Zion is prominent, but not in all the psalms. The 'steps' (plural of *ma'la*) are associated in Jewish tradition with steps leading up to the inner court of the temple; the fifteen steps there are said to correspond to the fifteen psalms, and on them Levitical musicians made melody in the festival (Mishna Sukka 5.4). LXX, Vulgate and Jerome all render the title 'Song of the steps', and it may well be that this collection of psalms was sung as the festal procession reached this richly symbolic ascent. The wider meaning 'ascents' is not so well attested, but is preferred by scholars who think either of worshippers ascending to Zion or of exiles returning from Babylon (cf. Ezra 7.9).

Psalm 120 is best understood as a supplication from distress (cf. on v. 1). The threat of war (v. 7) is, as often elsewhere, accompanied by a barrage of hostile words – curses, false accusations, propaganda (cf. above on 109.2). The prayer may thus be that of a king or similar ruler; in his own person he is the enemy's target. The references in v. 5 are to areas far apart, and so probably meant figuratively for quarrelsome and aggressive neighbours, 'enemies of peace' (v. 6).

1 This introductory verse establishes that the singer is in great trouble and depends on the Lord to whom he now cries. The sense given above is clearer in the Hebrew if the vocalization is adjusted (*we-ya'aneni*). The traditional translation, 'I cried ... he answered me', would have to be taken with some strain as either a testimony to experience before the present crisis, or the beginning of a psalm of thanksgiving, vv. 2f. quoting an earlier lament.

2 The petition now follows, beginning with the holy name. The enemy's false words threaten the psalmist's very life and are probably the beginning of military asssault (cf. above on 109.2).

3–4 In the form of question and answer to the enemy, there follows an invocation of divine judgement (cf. Hos. 9.14), a doom appropriate to the offence. For as the enemy's words fly like deadly arrows and flaming shafts (cf. 64.4; Prov. 16.27), so God, the mighty warrior, will recompense with the sharp arrows and fiery darts of judgement (cf. 7.11–13; 28.3–4). Broom (or juniper) was noted for the fierce and lasting heat of its brands.

5–7 The conclusion takes the form of a lament with declaration of innocence. The troublous situation is depicted, with the final trait that the psalmist's peaceful overtures are met only with the preparation of war. A more literal rendering of v. 5 is given by RV: 'Woe is me, that I sojourn in Meshech, that I dwell among the tents of Kedar.' But since these tribes lived far apart (Meshech in the Caucasus, Gen. 10.2; Ezek. 27.13; Kedar in the

Syro–Arabian desert, Gen. 25.13 etc.), a metaphorical sense is required; it as though the psalmist were among these notoriously ferocious tribes.

In terse, vivid fashion the psalmist conveys the situation of one who would make peace, but is answered only by hatred and war. Here is one who is assailed by piercing abuse and lies that will kindle a spreading fire. In this distress he cries to the Lord, and looks for the divine justice which will requite these shooters of deadly words. The style here, with address to the enemy, leaves open the possibility of repentance. Can the warning, mysteriously borne on the music of the prayer, yet reach the soul of the hitherto implacable foe? In Christian use, the psalm has inaugurated the steps of ascent to God; the one who begins this upward journey is at once beset by much antagonism and many hostile tongues. From the follies of his own tongue also he prays for deliverance, and would be taken into the peace of Jesus, to whom the words of v. 7a are appropriate (literally 'I am peace').

Good Lord, deliver us from lying lips and a deceitful tongue, and grant that we never weary of speaking peace to those intent on war, through him who is our peace and the true dwelling-place of our soul, Jesus Christ your Son.

PSALM 121: The Hills of Hope

A song of the steps.

1	I lift up my eyes to the hills;
	O from where shall my help come?
2	My help will come from the Lord,
	the maker of heaven and earth.

3	He will not let your foot be tripped;
	he who guards you will not slumber.
4	See, the guardian of Israel
	will neither slumber nor sleep.
5	The Lord himself is your guardian;
	the Lord at your right hand will be your shade.
6	By day the sun shall not strike you,
	nor shall the moon by night.
7	The Lord will guard you from all evil;
	he himself will guard your soul.
8	The Lord will guard your going out and your coming in,
	from now and for evermore.

The sequence in this collection of 'psalms of the steps' is striking here. The lament from the midst of trouble, 120, is now followed by strong assurances. A singer in need expresses trust (vv. 1–2), and is answered by divine affirmation. From the Creator, the guardian of Israel, protection is promised by day and night and for ever; he will be at this person's right hand, ever vigilant, defending from all harm. The weight of these assurances would be appropriate originally for the king, and reasons and conditions would have been treated in other moments of the worship. Here it is enough that the supplicant has expressed trust (cf. 91).

1–2 The worshipper (the community's head or representative) asks a question in order to give a resounding answer. Looking up to the heights, he asks where his salvation is to come from, and testifies that it will be only from the Lord, the Creator of heaven and earth (cf. 115.15; 124.8; 134.3; 146.6). His looking up to the mountains has been variously interpreted – hills as dangerous (robbers), as shrines of other gods, as symbols of God's protection of Zion (cf. 125.2), or as the route of the Lord's festal advent (cf. 68.7; 76.4; Isa. 52.7; Nahum 1.15). The positive explanations seem more probable, and for the thought of the Lord's longed-for coming we could compare 101.2, 'O when will you come to me?'

3–8 A singer now addresses the supplicant (with 'you' singular), unfolding assurances of the Lord's protection. It is like an indirect oracle, delivered with the authority of one inspired by God. The Creator (so v. 2) is now further entitled 'guardian of Israel' (cf. Gen. 28.15), and the verb 'to guard / keep' is used prominently – six times in six verses. Like a good shepherd or city watchman, he will not forsake his vigilance (a contrast may be intended with the gods supposed to 'sleep' in summer). At his beloved's right hand (cf. 16.8; 109.31; 110.5), he is 'shade' against the fierce sun; the word suggests the dominion of the heavenly king spread over his servant in closest care (cf. 91.1). Verse 6b reflects the widely held view that the moon also could strike with various maladies. The 'going out and coming in' means the beginning and finishing of any undertaking (cf. Deut. 28.6), and is especially applied to rulers (Num. 27.17; Josh. 14.11; 1 Kings 3.7) and to warfare (1 Sam. 8.20; 18.13; 29.6). A royal or national dimension is again suggested by the protection 'for evermore' (cf. 21.4, 6; 72.5, 17; 91.16; 115.18).

As though from a valley of suffering, a supplicant raises eyes to the hills. Whence shall come the light of salvation? He holds fast to his trust in the Lord; he believes that the angels of faithfulness and comfort will appear in a new dawn, heralding the Lord's own coming. A voice of assurance then sounds; the minister of God promises unceasing protection from all harm, and for ever. As with the promises in 91, there is a mystery in this divine protection. Again and again it is known in all its wonder and grace. But how often again it seems absent, and the eyes strain up to the hills in vain! The especially glowing promises here and in 91 seem to come from the royal ideals, and so their fulfilment is to be sought in the Messiah. The disciples of Christ expect to suffer with him, yet guarded by God in deepest mystery, until the secret of that faithful guarding is fully revealed.

Grant, Lord, that when we lift up our eyes to the hills in longing for your help, we may hear and take to our hearts the promise of your unfailing care; may we know that you are guarding us by day and night, as we go out and come in, and that whatever our share in the sufferings of the cross, you are our shade and our saviour, now and for evermore.

PSALM 122: Arriving in Jerusalem

A song of the steps.   Of David.

1   I was glad when they said to me,
     We will go to the house of the Lord.
2   And now our feet are standing
     within your gates, O Jerusalem –
3   Jerusalem, you that are built
     as a city bound in fellowship.
4   Here the tribes ascend, the tribes of the Lord,
     as is the law for Israel, to give thanks to the name of the Lord.
5   And here stand thrones for justice,
     the thrones of the house of David.
6   O pray for the peace of Jerusalem;
     may blessing abound on those who love you.
7   Peace be within your walls,
     tranquillity within your palaces.
8   For the sake of my brothers and companions,
     I will pray down peace upon you.
9   For the sake of the house of the Lord our God,
     I will seek good for you.

This can be seen as a 'Song of Zion' (Int. 4d), centring on appreciation of Jerusalem as the city of the Lord's house, the goal of pilgrims, where his name and presence are praised in the gathering of his people, and his justice effected by the house of David. The likely setting is the autumn festival, the greatest celebration of 'Zion' in the royal period. Especially in vv. 1–2, 8–9 the psalmist speaks as one who has made the pilgrimage with a party of companions, and is moved to utterance by the thrill of arriving. But rather than being an impromptu, individual song, which had somehow to find its way into the official collections, the psalm more likely is from temple ceremony, the poet making skilful use of the typical pilgrim's experience (cf. 84). Such openness to the genuine feelings of the heart, the very life of the people, is part of the greatness of the Psalms; we might compare the refreshment of formal music through the openness of the great composers to popular melody and dance. The psalm may be divided into two parts: praise of the Lord's city (vv. 1–5), and prayer for her (vv. 6–9). For the heading, see above on 120; the additional 'Of David' is found in this group also over 124, 131 and 133 (cf. 127 'Of Solomon').

1–2 The singer voices common feelings among the worshippers, beginning with recollection of the excitement at the outset of the pilgrimage. A party was formed to make the journey together (cf. Isa. 2.3; Zech. 8.21), and now, here they are, standing within the famous gates! (The construction can be understood: 'our feet have become standing, have come to stand', rather than 'were standing' as Dahood.) Love for the holy city leads the singer to address her as the living Beloved of the Lord (cf. 87.2; 132.14). Her name 'Jerusalem' ('foundation of peace') is pronounced three times in the short psalm, preparing for poetic use of its sound and sense in vv. 6–8.

3–5 The address to Jerusalem continues. The compact, walled city, nestling in the hills, a beautiful scene from the surrounding heights, is praised as well-suited to the gathered fellowship of pilgrims, representative of all the Lord's tribes. How wonderful she is as the place for all his people, as he has commanded (cf. 81.4f.), to acknowledge, bless and praise him in his name, his revelation from his temple! Moreover, she is the centre of justice, that good order given by the Lord through his Anointed and assistant princes, which brings health to society and all the living world (cf. 72 and 2.6).

6–9 The singer now calls upon all the worshippers to pray for this beloved Jerusalem. The remarkable play of sounds in the Hebrew here was probably felt to evoke deep realities of God, all the destiny that was inherent in this place through God's choice and purpose: *sha'alu shelom yerushalayim, yishleyu ohabayik.* The pilgrims are to ask peace, *shalom,* for her – tranquillity and all that is good; and the psalmist shows the way with his own example, undertaking to continue praying down peace and well-being upon her. He will seek good for her from God for the sake of all his people, the family of God, for God gives them life through her; also for the sake of the Lord's house, that it may continue in purity and peace as the vessel of the Lord's presence and grace.

From the inexhaustible meaning of the holy city, our psalm draws several great themes. It is the place of the fellowship, the loving unity of the Lord's worshippers. It is the place of the name of the Lord, his presence, his self-giving, where his people find their life renewed as they worship and sing praise. And it is the centre and source of justice, the good order sent by God through his anointed ones, bringing his law to bear on every aspect of life, rescuing, healing, and guiding. In her deepest meaning, Jerusalem is secure and eternally filled with God's peace and blessing. But the psalm would have prayer ever to call down this peace upon her walls, gates and stones, and all the servants of the Lord that serve her also. For at the edges of this Jerusalem there is a vulnerability, a divine poverty and exposure, and those who love her must pray for her in her weakness, seeking good for her from God, calling down his peace upon her. And in this work of love, they themselves will find blessing.

O Lord our God, may we ever be glad to go to your house, and in the power of the Spirit find ourselves before your presence, bound in the fellowship of all your worshippers, and renewed by the healing of your judgement and mercy; and grant us ever to persevere in prayer for the well-being of your holy church, the mother who would embrace us all in your new creation.

PSALM 123: Imploring Eyes

A song of the steps.

1   To you I lift up my eyes,
     you that sit enthroned in the heavens.
2   As the eyes of servants look to their master's hand,
     as the eyes of a maid to the hand of her mistress,
     so our eyes look to the Lord our God,
     until he take pity on us.
3   Have pity on us, Lord, have pity upon us,
     for we have had more than enough of derision.
4   Our soul is filled with the scorn of those at ease,
     with the derision of the proud.

The dialogue of supplication and promise continues in these 'songs of the steps'. Now we have lamenting prayer of the community voiced by a leading singer. The introduction expresses need and dependence on the Lord by depicting the eyes raised imploringly to heaven (vv. 1–2). Petition for the Lord's pity and saving action is brief and supported by a depiction of the wretchedness of the worshippers, the objects of scorn and mockery (vv. 3–4). There is no definite clue to the period of the psalm.

1–2 Leading the community's prayer, the singer looks imploringly up to heaven; the Lord enthroned as king of all has power to change the present situation of his people. (The conception of the heavenly throne is not contradictory to that of the throne in the temple; the latter is a mysterious

manifestation of the super-cosmic reality, cf. Int. 6f.) The comparison with
the eyes of family servants may allude to their watching for a signal of the
hand, but perhaps the thought is rather of the hand that distributes food (cf.
104.27). The reference first to male and then to female servants may reflect a
common situation, and also builds up the force of the comparison. The male
servants are more numerous for the work in the fields; the single maid
assisting her mistress in the house may have come with her at the marriage.

3–4 Following the theme of need and reliance on the Lord alone, direct
petition is made in brief but passionate style. In vv. 3b–4 it passes into lament,
presenting to God the picture of a people in great hardship and humiliation,
and so mocked by hostile neighbours, who themselves appear to prosper and
enjoy the ease of the arrogant.

The eyes lifted up to heaven express the prayer of longing souls and their
reliance on the Lord alone. To this king of creation they turn; he is the Lord
who provides for them and on whose compassion they depend. Their *Kyrie
eleison*, 'Lord, have mercy', has constantly echoed in the devotion of the
church, continuing the ancient recognition that the hope of prayer in the end
rests only on the compassionate heart of God.

*With our eyes and our voice, O King of heaven, we plead with you: Lord, have
mercy; on all your creatures that are abused by the arrogant, Lord, have pity, and by the
majesty of your power speedily deliver them.*

PSALM 124: Freed from the Snare

A song of the steps.   Of David.

1   If the Lord had not been with us,
      let Israel now say,
2   if the Lord had not been with us,
      when men rose up against us,
3   then they would have swallowed us alive,
      when their anger burned against us;
4   then the waters would have drowned us,
      and the flood gone over our soul;
5   right over our soul would have swept
      the proud and raging waters.
6   But blessed be the Lord,
      who has not given us up for a prey to their teeth.
7   Our soul escaped as a bird from the snare of the fowler;

> the snare was broken and we went free.
>
> 8 Our help is in the name of the Lord,
>   the maker of heaven and earth.

After the lamenting supplication of 123 there follows a testimony to help and deliverance granted by the Lord (there is no address to him). It is a thankful testimony for the whole people to join in (v. 1). There are vivid images of danger and escape, but not such as to reveal a particular historical event. Perhaps we have here a festal psalm which reflects many precarious situations in the people's history and rejoices that here they are still, by God's grace. Several features of the language (cf. Delitzsch, Allen) have been thought to indicate a late date, but it is also possible to think here of dialectal variations which could affect Hebrew speakers even in early times (as in Judges 5 and perhaps Job). The style is especially rhythmic and melodious, with effects of repetition and inner rhymes of vowels and consonants. Some suggest a popular song has been taken over for temple use, but we may rather think of the psalmist's skill in using a style suited to congregational participation. The first section envisages what might have been but for the Lord (vv. 1–5); the second, concluding section testifies directly to deliverance (vv. 6–9).

1–5 As the singer begins his lilting testimony, he seems to call on the assembly, representative of all Israel, to sing with him (cf. 129.1). If this understanding is correct, the song may have long been in use, v. 1 being added when the following words were already familiar. The threatening forces are designated first simply as *adam*, 'man', perhaps in contrast to the defence of God. But these men were like agents of death and chaos – the great swallower, the raging waters of destruction. What a terrible fate then, 'if the Lord had not been for us' (cf. 94.17; 119.92; Gen. 31.42)!

6–9 The Lord is 'blessed' in warm thanksgiving and praise. He has frustrated the weapons of the evil forces, which are pictured now as monster's teeth and bird-traps set for 'souls' (the essence of a person's life traditionally pictured as a bird, cf. above on 11.1; 102.6; some translate *nepesh* here in the primitive sense 'throat, neck', cf. above on 69.1). Even when the trap closed, it was not too late for the Lord; he broke the cage and at once the bird flew free. The concluding, summary testimony ascribes salvation to the Lord alone, the all-powerful Creator (cf. above on 121.2), revealed and present in his name (Int. 6b).

The attacks mentioned in the psalm were from human troublers who seemed allied to all the ancient forces of destruction. Their hostility sweeps forward like the great wave of winter flood-water that suddenly rushes down a wadi. Or their cunning malice entraps their victim in its snare. The song recognizes how evil the case would have been – except for the Lord. He defends his people that are under fierce attack; he sets free those that have been trapped. The ancient Aramaic Targum renders v. 2b: 'If the Word of the Lord had not been our support when the child of man rose up against us.' The church for her part ever thanks God for the saving help that has come in the name of Jesus, the Word of creation. He has shown himself with us and for us; who then can prevail against us (Rom. 8.31)?

O Lord, in whose name alone is our help, we pray you ever to defend us against the assaults that come suddenly upon us, and the unseen snare that may entrap our souls; so may we bless you and sing of you as the saviour who has set us free.

PSALM 125: Ringed by the Hills of God

A song of the steps.

1   Those who trust in the Lord are like Mount Zion,
       which shall not be overthrown, but stands for ever.
2   Jerusalem has mountains round about her;
       and so the Lord is round about his people,
           now and for evermore.
3   The sceptre of wickedness shall not rest
           on the portion of the just,
       lest even the just stretch out their hands to wrong.
4   Do good, Lord, to those who are good,
       to those who are true of heart.
5   Those who turn to crooked ways
           the Lord will lead off with the evildoers;
       peace be over Israel.

The prayer in v. 4 can be taken as the main point of the psalm, preceded by a supporting statement of confidence in God's care. The concern is with the community, where those loyal to the good way of the Lord have to stand firm against the pull of self-advantage along 'crooked ways'. The society lies under the shadow of an evil dominion, probably from a foreign empire, and as some turn aside to corruption, the singer seeks to strengthen his people in trust and loyalty and to pray to this end. The period might be any time from the seventh century on, many favouring the Persian era. The vivid use of Zion's aspect would fit with a festal setting, when the worshippers looked in awe and gladness at the holy place (48.12f.; 122).

1–3   The symbol of stability and continuance for 'those who trust in the Lord' is not expressly the city or temple buildings, but 'Mount Zion', which to faith represented the cosmic mountain, the centre of the divine kingdom (Int. 6f.). But in more earthly terms, even in Jerusalem itself there is a picture of God's guarding. The higher mountains ringing her give protection, and likewise around his trusting people the Lord sets his ring of defence. The 'sceptre of wickedness' means an evil dominion, which may be that of a foreign empire. We may suppose that the land (the 'lot' or 'portion' of God's people) was in bondage to such a power, but the hope was that it should not long continue so; it is urged that otherwise even some at present faithful may fall away.

4–5   Prayer is made for the Lord to strengthen and prosper those who still hold to him and his commandments. We can sense that temptation to fall away was proving strong. In v. 5 the warning is sounded in prophetic fashion, declaring the fate of those who make the corrupt ways their own (Hebrew 'their crooked ways'). The concluding wish of 'peace', perhaps from responding voices, provides a positive ending.

The psalm expresses a trust that the present 'sceptre of wickedness', the shadow of an evil dominion, will not lie for ever over the country given to the Lord's people. The singer, looking deeper than Jerusalem's historical sufferings, directs attention to the everlasting strength of the divine kingdom, the reign of good. But the contradictions of daily experience are sharp, and prayer must be raised that God 'do good' to his loyal people, strengthening them to hold to their faith. In the crooked paths of corruption lies doom, but for a faithful people there will be the overshadowing of 'peace', the fullness of divine blessing. It is not an easy message to convey in such a situation, when the crooked ways seem to prosper. But the singer in effect challenges his people to see through to the deepest truth, to believe in the Lord's steadfastness and so be made steadfast themselves (Isa. 7.9), a stronghold of good in the world, ringed by the saviour's power.

O God, our eternal King and mountain of strength, let not evil have the dominion over your people, but grant that as we are supported by your goodness, we may reject all crooked ways, and with steadfast hearts ever rejoice in your peace.

PSALM 126: Prayer for the Springing of New Life

A song of the steps.

1   When the Lord restored the life of Zion,
    we were like those who dream.
2   Then our mouth was filled with laughter,
    and our tongue with songs of joy.
    Then they said among the nations,
    The Lord has done great things for them.

3   The Lord indeed did great things for us,
     and how we then rejoiced!
4   Restore, O Lord, our life again,
     as you revive the brooks in the wilderness.
5   Those who sow with tears
     shall reap with songs of joy.
6   One who goes out bitterly weeping, bearing the bag of seed,
     shall come in singing for joy, bearing the harvest sheaves.

The main point in this beautiful song is best found in v. 4 – a prayer that the people's exhausted life be renewed. By way of support for this prayer, it is preceded by recollection of past renewal (vv. 1–3) and followed by proverb-style thoughts of suffering turned to joy (vv. 5–6). The repeated phrase for renewal of life (vv. 1a, 4a), the reference to winter rain (v. 4b), and to sowing and harvest (v. 6) join with the title and the trend of the collection in pointing to the autumn festival as the likely setting. The best comparison is with 85. Although the psalm is often thought to reflect post-exilic conditions of hardship and a retrospect to the return from exile (encouraged by a mis-translation of v. 1a), the reference throughout could be chiefly to agricultural conditions, and it is as well to leave open the question of date.

1–3   Lamenting psalms sometimes urge the Lord to consider how other nations will remark on a deity who so leaves his people (79.10; 115.2). But the present intercessor approaches the point another way. He recalls past salvation and points out how the nations were impressed by the Lord's saving power – and this could happen again. He beautifully portrays the happiness of that time resulting from the great and gracious deeds of the Lord; surely the Lord will desire to give such joy again. In v. 1a we have the phrase encountered in 14.7 and 85.1, traditionally rendered 'turned / brought back the captivity', but now recognized to mean 'turn the turning, restore with a great restoring', virtually 'bring back to life' (note v. 4b; the old renderings can suitably be read of release from the captivity of the death-powers). Verse 1b also has been variously rendered – 'as those comforted' (LXX and Vulgate), 'as sick men recovered' (Targum); but the commoner meaning of the verb, 'dream', gives a stronger comparison, more worthy of this poet. The restored people could hardly believe their situation was real (cf. Luke 24.41; Acts 12.9).

4   The phrase of v. 1a is used again now in a prayer, and its meaning is clarified for us by the comparison in v. 4b, literally 'as the wadies of the Negev'. These wadies are the gullies running down the arid country on the south of Judah. After the long drought of summer, the winter rains send floods of water down the parched courses, turning them to ribbons of green life. It seems then that the people pray from a death-like situation; their soul cleaves to the dust. Their prayer is for the transforming work of God to restore their life, just as with his rains he brings up grass and flowers in the wilderness.

5–6 The force of this picturesque conclusion may be to express trust in support of the prayer; or it may be that the singer, in prophetic manner, reports to the people his sense of God's favourable response (cf. 85.8f.). The 'weeping' and 'rejoicing' have ancient roots in the nature religions and related agricultural customs; but here we have proverbial sayings which declare how weeping or hardship turns to joy as deeds, faithfully done when all seems dead, bear happy fruit.

For a people largely consisting of subsistence farmers and peasants, life and happiness were closely bound up with the annual cycle of growth. The winter rains were vital, but sometimes failed; bondage and starvation then ensued. The psalm's recollection of a time of dream-like joy and the prayer for restoration of life may well relate to good seasons renewing life and joy. The unity of life in land and people was keenly felt. And still today, prayer for new life, for the transformation of dried-up souls and communities to living joy, should also envisage new life and health in earth and waters and a unity of peace among all creatures. The psalm's final assurance has many echoes in the New Testament, which especially tells of a self-giving service, a sowing in death, which brings forth much fruit and finds the great transformation into life eternal (John 12.24f.; cf. 1 Cor. 15.36f.).

Lord, as you send rain and flowers even to the wilderness, renew us by your Holy Spirit; help us to sow good seed in time of adversity, and so live to rejoice in your good harvest of all creation.

PSALM 127: The Fruitful Sleep

A song of the steps.   Of Solomon.

1   If the Lord does not build the house,
    its builders toil on it in vain.
    If the Lord does not guard the city,
    its guard is wakeful all in vain.
2   In vain you rise up early,
    and go so late to your rest,
    eating the bread of anxious toil –
    for he gives to his beloved in sleep.

3   See, children are a heritage bestowed by the Lord;

the fruit of the womb is given by him.
4   As arrows in the hand of a warrior,
       so are the children born of youthful strength.
5   Happy the one whose quiver he fills with them;
       they shall not be put to shame
           when they speak with adversaries in the gate.

The previous psalm had an ending resembling proverbs, and now we have a song wholly in such Wisdom style. It thus has the form of teaching (cf. Ps. 1), but if it were used in a festival, it could have also had a hymnic force, testifying to the Lord's decisive and generous action in human affairs. It falls into two parts (vv. 1–2; 3–5) united by the theme of the divine action as decisive. Some have argued that these parts are too different to have originally belonged together, but this view may be too severe; a much older Sumerian hymn to the goddess Nisaba (cited by Kraus) shows how one song might, in tribute to the divine work, cover house and city building, contentment of heart, and fertility of the womb. The psalm is judged by some to have been designed for an educational circle rather than for the great gatherings for worship, but its topics would have been relevant in the autumn festival – thoughts of toil and produce, of fertility and blessing in the family, and 'house' and 'city' perhaps echoing concern for the temple and Zion. Like 72, it is headed 'Of Solomon' (not well attested in LXX); this may be a deduction especially from the word 'beloved', v. 3, which in Hebrew is suggestive of a name given to Solomon (2 Sam. 12.25); the proverb-like style and the allusion to building might also have been factors.

1–2   The point is made strongly: not just help from the Lord is required as the house is built; it is the Lord himself who must build it. So the toiling builders must be as it were his hands, and their toil only expressive of his. To strengthen the unity of theme in the psalm, some take v. 1 to refer to building a household, a family (cf. Deut. 25.9), but the plural builders toiling on one 'house' hardly suit this, nor does the continuation, the guarding of the city (v. 2). The worshippers, however, might well have thought of the temple and its repair as a prime example. Again, the Lord must not only help guard the city, but actually guard it himself, the watchman serving but as the channel of his work. The singer maintains the striking emphasis as in v. 2 he addresses his people and declares that by their own efforts they can achieve nothing. However early the rising, however late the taking of rest, however hard the work to produce, without God it is all wasted. 'His beloved', one who trusts in him, is provided for – even as he sleeps! The thought here is the contrast between an anxious toil which supplants trust, and a life, no doubt dutiful, that rests in the knowledge of the Lord's presence.

3–5   The first word, *hinneh*, 'Behold', indicates that a fresh example will now be given. God's decisive role in human life is now illustrated by the family; children are a heritage and gift (lit. 'reward') that he bestows. Especially in the old Israelite society, children born when mother and father were young became a great support and strength as parents reached middle life. The comparison of the children to arrows and the thought of their value against enemies might suggest that it is the (more literal) 'sons' that are in mind, but old translators (BCP, RV) were justified in rendering 'children'; the daughters in themselves could prove an immense strength and comfort (cf. Ruth 4.15; Job 42.15), and in marriage might make valuable alliances. The city 'gate' was a complex that included space of social importance; here was much meeting, trading and legal business, and so there were occasions of confrontation with hostile folk. Armed with the children given by the Lord, the parents would not easily be abashed.

The first part of this song beautifully teaches its philosphy of work. Can the house-builder and the city's watchman, with the poet, the singer, and everyone at work, learn to do their work so that the Lord is doing it through them? Can they discover the happiness of work with the soul at peace with God, trusting him a day at a time, waking in the knowledge that he has already provided for the day? Our singer does not mince words; what is done without the Lord is futile (*shaw*) – so he says thrice (cf. John 15.5). The second part does not seem spiritually so profound, and one can understand why some have wanted to detach it. Granted that it speaks still of God's action, it still seems rather earthy – how those with a big family (sons?) can stand up to adversaries in the public arena. But it gives a deep appreciation of a fine family: such is seen as a heritage given by the Lord, which under the light of this recognition will be a source of happiness and strength. Later users of the psalm went beyond the concrete case: those who influenced others for good or made disciples for the Lord were indeed blessed with a spiritual family, bringing joy and comfort against adversity. But in any case and above all, the song will leave for everyone who hears its melody, whether or not they have sons or daughters, the mighty teaching of the sleep in God's arms, the resting in his love and care, in trust that he will give and do all that is necessary (similarly Jesus in Matt. 6.25f.).

Lord Jesus, who taught us to look at the birds and the raiment of the flowers, we thank you for all you give us as we rest in you; and we pray you to strengthen us by the angels of your love against all adversity.

PSALM 128: The Happiness of Fearing the Lord

A song of the steps.

1   Happy is everyone who fears the Lord,
      and ever walks in his ways.
2   You will eat indeed the labour of your hands;
      happiness and blessing will be yours.
3   Your wife will be like a fruitful vine within your house,
      your children like olive plants round about your table.
4   See, this will be the blessing
      for one who fears the Lord.
5   The Lord bless you from Zion,
      so that you see Jerusalem happy all the days of your life,
6   and see your children's children.
      Peace be over Israel.

The theme of the gift of children links this psalm with the preceding. Beginning as teaching (vv. 1–4), it reaches its main point as a blessing (vv. 5–6). Its concerns again suit the autumn festival (the year of toil and produce, fertility in the family, health and long life), and it will have been sung in blessing over the assembly of pilgrims, who would take the singular 'you' to themselves (a common usage in Deuteronomy).

1–4 The opening exclamation (cf. above on Ps. 1) gives the condition for the benefits described, and the essential point is repeated in v. 4. Such happiness is for the person who 'fears the Lord', taking account of God's reality at every point of life. The toil in the fields and other labour will then come to fruition and not be snatched away. The householder will be blessed in home and family. The wife is pictured safe within the home and happy with her many children. Gathered round the table at mealtime, the children are like a ring of young olive plantings, lively and full of promise.

5–6 As especially celebrated in the festival, new life for the people and the world is given from Zion, from the presence of the Creator signified there. The singer's benediction on the pilgrims is like a strong prayer that they may live to see the children of their children, and so see their life renewed down the generations; and also that they may all their days see Jerusalem have all that is good. The holy city is the centre of the society; from her peace will extend a peace over all the people (cf. 122.6–9).

For an assembly largely of subsistence farmers, the singer brought his message that profound and simple happiness would be granted them as they constantly revered the Lord and walked by his guidance. Their work would not be wasted; their family life would be richly blessed. And he added his prayer and benediction that with their own blessing they should see peace extend from the sanctuary to cover all the society. Especially today, the literal detail of the psalm is not always relevant. But those who hear the song can ever take from it the conviction that in the fear of the Lord and in daily walking with him lies the secret of happiness. Along this way, even in suffering, lies the blessing that shines into work and home, and out into the community.

O God, our Creator, bestow on us the happiness of fearing you and living in your paths, that we may know in work and home the fruits of the Spirit; and grant us to see good for your church and peace upon all your people.

PSALM 129: Where no Reaper can Fill his Hand

A song of the steps.

1 Many a time they have afflicted me from my youth up,
   let Israel now say,
2 Many a time they have afflicted me,
   but they have not prevailed against me.
3 Over my back the ploughers ploughed,
   and made their furrows long.
4 But the Lord is good and has cut in pieces
   the cords of the wicked ones.
5 All the enemies of Zion
   shall be confounded and turned back.
6 They shall be as the grass on the house-tops,
   which withers before it can grow up,
7 so that no reaper can fill his hand,
   nor a binder of sheaves his bosom,
8 and none that go by say, The blessing of the Lord be on you;
   we bless you in the name of the Lord.

The series of 'songs of the steps' continues with yet another short, powerful and distinctive poem. Opening with prompting for all to join in, rather as in 124, the singer testifies to the Lord's faithfulness in preserving his people through many afflictions (vv. 1–4). This section is a kind of communal thanksgiving, and is followed by an assurance with prophetic force – the enemies of Zion will not succeed. The psalm as a whole then, with elements of thanksgiving and prophecy, still apparently belongs to a situation of hardship; this is pondered before the Lord in recognition of past help, and with reception of his continuing promise. It is possible, however, to render

vv. 5–8 as an imprecation ('Confounded be . . .'); in this case the psalm more clearly takes on the aspect of a lamenting appeal, though one wonders then that it contains no address to the Lord.

1–4 The festal assembly of Israel is invited to take up the testimony. From Israel's 'youth', the time of slavery under Pharaoh, and all down the centuries, they have been assailed by enemies and cruelly afflicted; but the Lord, being 'right' (faithful and strong to save), has brought them through. The festival was near the time when, with the first rains, ploughing could begin, and the image came easily to mind; it is as though the people and land were one, and the enemy is pictured ploughing long furrows over Israel's back (cf. Micah 3.12). The enemy's 'cords', if the image is the same, would be the cords attached to the ploughing animals; the metaphor may, however, have changed, and the cords could be those of hunters, as with the great hunter death (18.4–5).

5–8 It seems that the prophetic element in psalmody now comes to the fore. The inspired singer declares doom on 'all the enemies ("haters") of Zion', adversaries, that is, of the Lord himself. Their rout is pictured with another striking image. The flat-roofed houses of Palestine, as still today, have packed earth on top, rolled out after rain to close cracks. In spring, greenery will grow there, but lacking good rootage and exposed to blazing sun and easterly winds, it soon perishes. Not here is there anything for the reaper to grasp, cut, and drop from his hand for the binder behind him to collect in the fold of a garment for tying. There will be no such harvesting here, and so no passers-by to wish them the Lord's blessing and receive a courteous blessing in return (cf. Ruth 2.4).

The servant-people of the Lord reflects here on her destiny to suffer and bear enmity. From the earliest days onwards, the ploughers have ploughed over her. And yet she can testify that her Lord is good and faithful; he has not let the wicked prevail. From the cruel and malevolent ones there will be nothing to reap and bind, but from the suffering people there will be a good harvest (cf. 126.5–6), when blessing indeed will be exchanged. How often it happens still that in those who have suffered long and deeply there can be recognized the blessing of God upon them, and from them others receive an immeasurable blessing in the name of the Lord!

Lord Jesus, who bore the sin of the world and gathered up the pain of all the ages, we thank you for all who have joined their afflictions to yours; and we ask that their blessing may fall upon us, so that we may rejoice with them in the harvest of your Holy Spirit.

PSALM 130: Longing and Looking for the Lord

A song of the steps.

1   Out of the depths, Lord, I call to you;
2   O Lord, listen to my voice.
     May your ears be attentive
     to the sound of my supplications.
3   If you, Lord, retained offences,
     who then, O Lord, could stand?
4   But with you there is forgiveness,
     so that you may be feared.
5   I wait for the Lord, my soul is waiting,
     and for his word I hope.
6   My soul looks for the Lord
        more than watchmen for the morning,
     yes, more than watchmen for the morning.
7   O Israel, wait for the Lord;
     for with the Lord there is faithful love,
        and with him is plenteous redemption,
8   and he will redeem Israel
     from the bonds of all his sins.

With the address to gathered 'Israel' (vv. 7f.) this fits well into the series that seems to have belonged to the pilgrimage festival of the autumn. In deepest sorrow and penitence the people are waiting and watching, perhaps at night, looking for the Lord and his word which was sometimes given at break of morning. The singer is best seen as a representative person, who can turn to address and encourage the people (vv. 7–8). No particular circumstances are revealed in the rather general expressions, but we may think the themes well suited to an annual occasion of penitence and expiation (cf. 51 and 102).

1–6   The appeal to the Lord rises 'from the depths', the deeps of trouble and affliction, which are pictured as subterranean waters at the mouth of Sheol, the land of death (cf. 69.1, 2). In support of the plea, the singer calls to the Lord as one who does not 'keep' offences, harbouring wrath against the guilty; rather he clears away the sin by forgiveness. This mercy is not to make light of wrongdoing, but to preserve for the Lord a people 'fearing' him, worshipping him, ever mindful of him (cf. Rom. 2.4). For without his forgiveness, who would remain? A further consideration urged by the singer is the expectant trust, a hopeful waiting for the Lord, in which no doubt all the worshippers share. They look for the word of salvation, indeed for the Lord himself, and even more eagerly than watchmen for the sunrise. The comparison may be, as the Targum has it, with the priestly watchers high on the walls, whose duty was to watch for daybreak and give the signal for the first offerings in the temple court. The comparison in any case supports the idea that the psalm was part of a pentitential night vigil, where all looked for a sign of God's salvation as morning broke (cf. 22 title; 46.5; 102.16).

7–8 The singer now turns to the people and urges them to continue the yearning but trusting watch for the Lord, in sure hope of his *hesed*, his faithful love, and his abundant 'redemption'. With prophetic assurance the singer concludes that the Lord will set Israel (the corporate personality, the ever-living ancestor) free from all the bondage that has resulted from 'his' sins. Both the faithful love and redemption are the work of the Lord as committed to his people; he has taken them into his protection, and in times of trouble will come to them as their nearest and dearest, determined to restore their life.

For all in profound suffering the psalm voices its appeal to the Lord. Conscious of their unworthiness, they are to ground their hope in the forgiving love of God and to watch in penitence, prayer and trust. And in the time of redemption they will tremble at the wonder of the saviour's love, and live their days in the light of his reality.

Father, we commend to your faithful love those who are crying from the depths; help them to watch and pray through their time of darkness, in sure hope of the dawn of your forgiveness and redemption.

PSALM 131: The Weaned Child upon its Mother

A song of the steps.   Of David.

1   Lord, my heart is not haughty, nor my eyes set high;
     I do not concern myself with grand things,
         or matters too marvellous for me.
2   But I have quieted and stilled my soul,
         as a weaned child upon its mother;
     like a weaned child is my soul upon me.
3   O Israel, hope in the Lord,
     from now and for evermore.

We saw in 46.10 how ideas of quietness before the Lord were not restricted to individual spirituality, but could be applied to nations (cf. also 62). In the present psalm also, the singer's theme of humility and quiet trust has national relevance (v. 3). As in the previous psalm, therefore, we best take the individual to have a representative role. He gives the lead in the attitude he describes (vv. 1–2) and can then turn to encourage the festal assembly in such trust. His song may have been inspired in circumstances of hardship for the people, and when little had come from the customary loud laments. But the period cannot be determined. The title 'Of David' may have been a deduction from the theme, thought to be true of David's piety; but a royal connection (as with the following psalm) is possible (cf. 101.5b).

1–2 The singer's address to the Lord leads all the worshippers to take the way of humble trust in seeking relief from present hardships. There was a time for loud cries of protest and even bitter argument with God, a time for giving vent to passionate feelings. But our psalmist has seen that now is a time for humility and restraint. He would pray without great demands and arguments; he would acknowledge that God's ways are great and wonderful beyond human understanding. There is much to endure, and his soul might well have clamoured to the Lord. But he has restrained and quietened it, just as a mother soothes and calms a child that makes the transition from breast-feeding; the child has struggled and cried in frustration, until at last it rests peacefully on its mother. The psalmist here sees his soul as a distinct entity that he can talk to and work upon (cf. 42.5; 103.1–2). So he has brought his soul through to peace and trust, and would let this trust alone be his appeal to the Lord.

3 He concludes his song by directly addressing his people, urging them likewise to wait for the Lord in trustful hope. However long they must wait, let them ever continue, and let them always look to the Lord and believe in his faithfulness.

The Psalms show various aspects of prayer. Like a child they may cry stridently and express their passion; and like a child, so our psalm has it, the Lord's people come humbly to trust in him and quietly wait. For both these kinds of praying, comparison with a child has come to mind, and here we find the heart of biblical prayer – a simple turning to the God who is mother and father (cf. Matt. 18.2f.). But this psalm is an example of prayer without any petition. Its quietness has not been attained easily. Beyond crying and complaining a wonderful rest has been reached, a deep trust that the Lord knows all that is needed and will provide it.

Grant to us, Lord, a quieted and patient spirit, that we may ever hope in you, and wait upon your wisdom and your goodness.

PSALM 132: When David Found a Place for the Lord

A song of the steps.

1 Lord, remember in David's favour
   all the hardship he endured;
2 how he swore an oath to the Lord,
   and made a vow to the Mighty One of Jacob:
3 I will not enter the dwelling of my house,
   nor get up into my bed,
4 I will not grant sleep to my eyes
   or slumber to my eyelids,
5 until I find a place for the Lord,
   a dwelling for the Mighty One of Jacob.
6 See, we heard of the ark in Ephrata,
   and found it in the woodland.
7 Let us enter his resting-place,
   and fall low before his footstool.
8 Arise, O Lord, to your resting-place,
   you and the ark of your glory.
9 May your priests be clothed with salvation,
   and your faithful sing for joy.
10 For the sake of David your servant,
   do not turn away the face of your Anointed.
11 The Lord swore an oath to David,
   a pledge from which he will not turn:
   One who is the fruit of your body
   I will place upon your throne.
12 If your children keep my covenant
   and my testimonies which I will teach them,
   then their children also
   shall sit upon your throne for evermore.
13 For the Lord has chosen Zion;
   he has desired her for his dwelling.
14 This shall be my resting-place for ever;
   here I shall dwell, for I have desired her.
15 I will abundantly bless her provision;
   her poor I will satisfy with bread.
16 Her priests I will clothe with salvation,
   and her faithful shall sing for joy.
17 There I will make a horn spring up for David;
   I will keep a lamp burning for my Anointed.

18   His enemies I will clothe with shame,
     but on him shall his crown be bright.

Here is an example of the rich symbolism expressed by processions in worship. The psalm was evidently sung as the ark was borne from an outlying station back to its resting-place in the inmost shrine of the temple. The procession commemorated David's first installation of the ark in Jerusalem, when he went dancing in the procession vividly described in 2 Samuel 6. The autumn festival is specified when Solomon brought in the ark again, to reside now in the newly completed temple (1 Kings 8; the parallel in 2 Chron. 6.41f. uses our psalm). This was no doubt the festival for the commemorating ceremony, for the religious and social foundations were then made new, including the temple and the royal dynasty as reflected in our psalm. There is a dramatic quality in vv. 6–7 as we hear the words of David's men; but we should probably think of the drama as sufficiently enacted by the procession itself, perhaps with some alternation of singing voices (cf. 24.7f.). After the Exile, when the monarchy was not restored, the psalm will have taken on a messianic meaning, looking for the saviour-king and the full glory of Zion.

1–5   The prayer is that the Lord should remember 'for David' – for the benefit of his dynasty – how he fulfilled an ascetic vow not to rest until he had brought the ark from obscurity to a fitting sanctuary, in effect Jerusalem, recently captured and made the capital (2 Sam. 5.6f.). This vow of 'hardship' (LXX, with different vowels, 'humility') is not mentioned in the historical accounts; perhaps it was remembered in worship because of some custom of later kings also to avoid sleep until the commemorative procession was completed. The ancient title 'Mighty One of Jacob' is rare (Gen. 49.24; Isa. 49.26; 60.16).

6–10   The worshippers in the procession relive the moments when David's men sought and found the neglected ark; news of it was obtained in Ephrata (linked in some way with Bethlehem, Gen. 48.7; Ruth 4.11; 1 Sam. 17.12; Micah 5.2), and then it was found in the 'woodland' (*ya'ar*), probably an allusion to Kiriat Ye'arim, 'the city in the woods' (1 Sam. 7.1f.). Verse 7 anticipates the moment when the ark ('his footstool', see above on 99.5) will be installed in its shrine and worshippers will make obeisance to the enthroned presence which it helps to signify. This moment is near, for the ark is being lifted towards its resting-place with a prayer that echoes its more ancient processions (v. 8, cf. above on 68.1). Verse 8 shows vividly how it symbolized God's presence and formidable 'glory' (*'oz*, cf. 8.2). Prayer is made for the priests to be clothed (as their festal garments will have signified) with 'rightness' (*ṣedeq*), which here is close in meaning to 'salvation' (cf. 2 Chron. 6.41); acceptable to God, may they mediate his blessings, and so all the covenant-people will rightly sing for joy. Linking with the opening petition, prayer rises for the present king to be acceptable to the Lord for the sake of David's pious deed.

11–18 To the prayers comes assuring answer. The singer, with prophetic authority, quotes and reports God's solemn promises. For the house of David the original promise is reaffirmed: after his successor, the dynasty will, if faithful, ever continue (cf. 2 Sam. 7; 1 Kings 8.25f.; Ps. 89.3f.). Bound up with this is the Lord's love for Zion, the hill he has chosen as his home for ever, the sanctuary for his ark. With this again is promise for city and people – bread and provision. The psalm's prayer for the priesthood and the faithful (v. 9) is granted (v. 16). Moreover, 'David', through his successors, will have strength and salvation, prevailing over foes. The imagery is expressive of divine power and blessing sent through the Anointed to people and world – the 'horn' of might and supremacy (cf. above on 75.4f.), the 'lamp' of life (cf. 18.28; 2 Sam. 21.17), the 'crown' of the divine reign. This 'crown' (*nezer*) is an emblem of consecration; some think that more strictly the word denotes an emblematic flower fixed to the front of the royal headband, and hence the promise that it will (lit.) 'blossom', manifesting divine life (so Noth, *Laws*, p. 236). If the promise was intended first for a continuing dynasty, the expressions could easily come to be taken of one great saviour-king, himself the divine horn, lamp and emblem of God's kingship. (The conditional element in the promise of v. 12 differs in expression from 89.30f., but the rest of our psalm suggests that the basic intention is the same.)

The procession of worshippers had in their midst the ark that was the sign of God's glorious presence. Their prayer recollected the anointed servant who had put that glory of God before all else. So the prophetic voice reaffirmed God's will to establish his kingdom through his chosen dynasty and his throne-centre on Zion. The psalm was preserved beyond the Babylonian destruction of Jerusalem and Davidic rule, and so through all the darkness continued to promise the coming of one who would be God's horn of strength, and his light and flower of life. The New Testament has a corresponding song of fulfilment; the Lord is praised that in Jesus he has raised up the horn of salvation in the house of his servant David and sent the day-spring from on high to give light to those who sit in darkness (Luke 1.68f.). Here is one who truly puts first the cause of God, accomplishing his task in hardship and humility. The church has continued to sing this colourful psalm, praying that God's ministers be clothed with salvation and his faithful sing for joy, for through Jesus they enter the dwelling-place of the Lord, bow low before his footstool, and are abundantly blessed with the gifts of eternal life.

Almighty God, grant that we may, before all else, seek a resting place for your presence in our hearts, so that from all our work and prayer your blessing may go out to comfort the needy, and bring light to those who sit in darkness; for the sake of him who by his humility and suffering established the sanctuary of your eternal salvation.

PSALM 133: Ointment and Dew for a Needy World

A song of the steps.   Of David.

1   See, how good and how pleasant it is,
    when pilgrims dwell together as one.
2   It is like the precious ointment on the head,
    that ran down upon the beard,
    ran down upon the beard of Aaron,
    and on to the collar of his garments,
3   as though the dew of Hermon
    ran down on the hills of Zion.
    For there the Lord has commanded the blessing,
    even life for evermore.

This picturesque song can be understood as a 'Song of Zion', praising the Lord's work of blessing through his chosen sanctuary. This theme is approached through appreciation of the great fellowship of pilgrims (lit. 'brothers'), no doubt at Zion's autumn festival, and two striking images are used in praise of the blessing that the Lord there sends down. The wording in v. 1b (lit. 'the dwelling of brothers together as one') may be connected with an old custom of brothers deciding to stay together on an undivided heritage; the psalmist may have deliberately reapplied the phrase to the 'brotherhood' of worshippers.

1   The gathering of innumerable pilgrims from far and wide in orderly and reverent unity made a great impact on those who experienced it, coming as most did from small communities (cf. 122.3–4). How good it was, so to be together for a week or more, how sweet this union in love of the Lord! (In v. 1b the psalmist may echo the phrase used for the old custom for brothers staying in the family home, referred to in Deut. 25.5.)

2–3   Upon such a united gathering 'on the hills of Zion', the Lord confers the height of blessing – life, and moreover, life that continues through the generations. This wonderful gift, for which the pilgrims longed (42.2; 84.2), is compared first with the sacramental oil (Ex. 30.23f.) used to install Aaron as the archetypal high priest (Ex. 29.7; Lev. 8.12); it was poured over his head and ran down his beard and over his vestments (themselves symbolic of the twelve tribes, Ex. 28.9f.). This aromatic oil was a sign of the holy power of God passing down upon the representative figure of Aaron. For good measure, the singer adds another comparison, the extremely heavy dew that runs down Mount Hermon, bringing life to parched places beneath. Taken literally, the singer seems to describe the dew as reaching the hills of Zion – a poetic licence; he certainly means to say that on Zion flows down God's most abundant blessing of life.

How good and how pleasant, how full of grace and sweet life, is the fellowship of those truly united in worship – so sings our psalmist. It is like a mountain towering into heaven, its sides running with the life-giving dew of God's blessing, which flows down upon arid lands. Or it is like the great high priest, carrying on his breast the needs of all society, and receiving the wondrous ointment from God's hand, a power of holy healing that flows down from his head and blesses all that he holds in his heart. 'There', in that united communion of worshippers, God sends the supreme blessing, the life that is before his face for evermore. 'That they may be one' is the prayer of Jesus, and he would have the disciples united in the mystery of God's own love, and so sanctified and sent out into the needy world (John 17.1–26).

Grant to your people, good Lord, the spirit of unity, that they may dwell together in your love, and so bear to all the world the ointment of your healing and the dew of your blessing.

PSALM 134: Blessings Given and Received

A song of the steps.

1   Come, bless the Lord, all you servants of the Lord,
      who wait at night in the house of the Lord.
2   Lift up your hands towards the holy presence,
      and truly bless the Lord.
3   The Lord, who made heaven and earth,
      give you blessing out of Zion.

This concluding piece for the 'songs of the steps' consists of two parts: a hymnic call to praise (vv. 1–2) and a blessing (v. 3). The division is all the clearer in the Hebrew, since 'you / your' is plural in the hymn and singular in the blessing. The occasion, as with the other psalms in the series, may be the autumn festival, some service being held at night in the court before the temple. It is possible to think that the 'servants' are priests or Levites on duty, but usage of the word and the general concern of the series favour taking the reference as to a congregation (cf. 135.1). The two parts can be taken to represent a dialogue; the cantor calls for praise (vv. 1–2), and the assembly, perhaps led by another voice or choir, respond with a blessing upon him (v. 3).

1–2 The call to praise is expressed as a call to 'bless' the Lord, a word of praise with a warm thankfulness; thus the little psalm will make a link between the blessing that is directed to the Lord and that bestowed by him (v. 3). His 'servants' are 'standing' – attending upon him. Night services were held in the festivals (cf. Isa. 30.29), and throughout the year priests and Levites had nocturnal duties around the temple. The worshippers are to raise their hands in a gesture of praise towards the sanctuary and especially its inmost shrine, where the invisible presence of the Lord was represented.

3 We may understand this benediction from the gentle social custom of responses that invoked a blessing (cf. above on 129.8). To the solo singer of the previous verses is addressed this answering blessing: may the creator who has chosen to be known in Zion give you life and health. From his presence in the sanctuary he sends out the gifts of life (cf. above on 133.3). (Some understand this blessing to be from the priests and upon the people as 'one body'.)

Not by day only, but even in the nights the Lord is to be praised, and his worshippers are to stand before him to serve. With body and soul, heart and hands directed to his presence, the Lord is to be blessed. And all is communion, an interchange of blessings; to the heart that looks thankfully to the Lord comes his blessing, the power of true life. Among the worshippers also, communion and interchange flourish, as they exhort one another to bless the Lord, and call down his blessings one upon the other. The little psalm has concluded the 'songs of the steps' in a darkness close to the presence of God; the ascent has come to a wondrous place of blessing, not in solitude, but in the mutual help of those who love the Lord.

O Lord, the maker of heaven and earth, help us to ascend the steps that mount to your presence, that we may stand before your holy place; and as by night and day we lift our hands to bless you, may we also receive blessing from you, even life in Jesus Christ, your Son, our Saviour.

PSALM 135: The Sweet Name and the Special Treasure

1   Alleluia.
     O praise the name of the Lord;
     praise it, you servants of the Lord,
2   you that wait in the house of the Lord,
     in the courts of the house of our God.
3   Praise the Lord, for the Lord is good;

make music to his name, for it is sweet.
4   For the Lord has chosen Jacob for himself,
    Israel for his own possession.
5   Truly I know that the Lord is great,
    and that our Lord is above all gods.
6   Whatever he wills, the Lord does in heaven and on earth,
    in the seas and in all the deeps.
7   He brings up the clouds from the ends of the earth;
    he makes lightnings with the rain,
        and brings the winds out of his treasures.
8   He smote the first-born of Egypt,
    of people and cattle alike.
9   He sent signs and wonders into your midst, O Egypt,
    upon Pharaoh and all his servants.
10 Then he smote great nations,
    and slew the mighty kings,
11 Sihon, king of the Amorites, and Og, the king of Bashan,
    and all the kings of Canaan.
12 And he gave their land as a heritage,
    a heritage for Israel his people.
13 Your name, Lord, is everlasting,
    and shall be called upon throughout all generations.
14 For the Lord will give justice to his people,
    and have compassion on his servants.
15 The idols of the nations are but silver and gold,
    the work of human hands.
16 They have a mouth, but cannot speak;
    eyes they have, but cannot see.
17 They have ears, but cannot hear;
    neither is there breath in their mouth.
18 Those who make them will grow like them,
    and so will all who trust in them.
19 O house of Israel, bless the Lord;
    O house of Aaron, bless the Lord.
20 O house of Levi, bless the Lord;
    you that fear the Lord, bless the Lord.
21 Blessed from Zion be the Lord,
    who dwells in Jerusalem.
    Alleluia.

This hymn consists of the regular calls for praise and grounds for praise. Developing the praise of the Lord's wondrous work is a section which by contrast decries idols and the powers they represent (vv. 15–18, similar to 115.5–8). The calls are addressed to the full assembly, distinguished as laity, priests and Levites, and gathered in the courts of the temple in Jerusalem. The setting will thus be one of the great pilgrimage festivals.

1–4   Those addressed as the Lord's 'servants', to judge by the psalm as a whole, are the full assembly in the courts; they 'stand' or 'wait' as worshippers before their Lord, wanting only to please and serve him. The 'name' is mentioned first, as the form of his revelation, the expression of his presence in the sanctuary. The 'music' is the praise and psalmody sung to the accompaniment of lyres and other instruments of the sacred musicians. General reasons for praise (v. 3) are developed with reference to the Lord's choice of 'Jacob', the ancestor and the descendants in whom his life continues, to be God's *segulla*, his specially treasured possession – a people that will be very close to him, but in order to serve his wider purpose (the term is found outside Israel of kings as chosen servants of a god or an overlord; cf. Ex. 19.5; Deut. 7.6).

5–12   The reasons for praise are further developed. The singer gains emphasis with a personal testimony; he tells of what he knows. The Lord is supreme, high above all the beings of heaven, able to do what he wills to do throughout heaven and earth, master of rains, storms and winds. He is to be praised also for the deeds remembered in the sacred traditions, the deeds to rescue his people from slavery – the plagues and the Exodus, the victories and settlement in Canaan (the battles with Sihon and Og are recorded in Num. 21.21f., 33f.).

13–18   Briefly the singer addresses the Lord himself, praising the 'name' as that by which for ever the Lord is called upon, and so the means of prayer and answering grace (cf. Ex. 3.15). This 'name' (lit. 'remembrance', *zeker*) is both invoked and proclaimed (cf. 6.5; 30.4; 97.12; 111.4). Through such interchange of prayer and answer – the singer is sure but also hopeful – the Lord in his pity and justice will right the wrongs his people suffer. The impotence of other 'gods' is ridiculed, heightening the sense of the Lord's sole true deity (so also 115.3–8).

19–21   The call to the divisions of the assembly goes beyond those of 115.9f. and 118.2f. in that the House of Levi is also distinguished, reflecting perhaps a later period when the Levites were more clearly demarcated as lower orders of the temple personnel. The 'fearers of the Lord' are sometimes taken to be proselytes, pilgrims from other nationalities; but the expression may rather be inclusive for all worshippers together. Verse 21 may reflect the responses that were made to the singer's call.

A lively scene of festal worship comes before us, resounding with the music of praise. Before the great array of pilgrims and sacred orders the leading singer urges praise. He calls to each section in turn and receives the response of blessings upon the Lord, while the instrumentalists also play with skill for the pleasure of the Lord. The song is a testimony to God's supreme power in nature and history; from personal experience of his mighty name, the contrast is drawn between his decisive acts of justice and pity and the utter failure of the idols that many worship. The Lord is blessed from Zion, from the people gathered in his presence as his special treasure, but gathered also as his servants ready to obey. The renewed knowledge of the Lord that is bestowed and built up in such worship strengthens the pilgrims against the temptation to worship the false goals of human devising.

O Lord above all lords, working your will in cloud and rain and in the strivings of the nations, we thank you that you have given us your name in Jesus Christ and made us your treasured people; and we pray you to help us wait before you as ready servants, and to bless you with the music of a faithful heart.

PSALM 136: The Lord who for ever Keeps Faith

1   Give thanks to the Lord, for he is good;
his faithfulness is for ever.
2   Give thanks to the God of gods;
his faithfulness is for ever.
3   Give thanks to the Lord of lords,
his faithfulness is for ever,
4   to the One who alone does great wonders,
his faithfulness is for ever,
5   who by wisdom made the heavens,
his faithfulness is for ever,
6   who laid out the earth upon the waters,
his faithfulness is for ever,
7   who made the great lights above,
his faithfulness is for ever,
8   the sun to rule the day,
his faithfulness is for ever,
9   the moon and the stars to rule the night,
his faithfulness is for ever,
10 who smote the first-born of Egypt,
his faithfulness is for ever,
11 and brought out Israel from among them,
his faithfulness is for ever,
12 with a mighty hand and outstretched arm,
his faithfulness is for ever,
13 who split the Sea of Reeds asunder,
his faithfulness is for ever,
14 and brought Israel through its midst,
his faithfulness is for ever,
15 but swept Pharaoh and his hosts into the Sea of Reeds,

>   *his faithfulness is for ever,*
> 16   who brought his people through the wilderness,
>   *his faithfulness is for ever,*
> 17   who smote the mighty kings,
>   *his faithfulness is for ever,*
> 18   and slew the famous kings,
>   *his faithfulness is for ever,*
> 19   even Sihon, king of the Amorites,
>   *his faithfulness is for ever,*
> 20   and Og, the king of Bashan,
>   *his faithfulness is for ever,*
> 21   and gave their land as a heritage,
>   *his faithfulness is for ever,*
> 22   a heritage for Israel, his servant,
>   *his faithfulness is for ever,*
> 23   who remembered us in our troubles,
>   *his faithfulness is for ever,*
> 24   and rescued us from our foes,
>   *his faithfulness is for ever,*
> 25   who gives to all creatures their food,
>   *his faithfulness is for ever.*
> 26   O give thanks to the God of heaven;
>   *his faithfulness is for ever.*

While the responsive or antiphonal style of Hebrew praise can be discerned in a number of psalms, only here is the method fully recorded. The first half of each verse, usually just three beats of rhythm, will have been sung by the leading or prompting singer, while the second half, a constant refrain, equally short, will have been the assembly's response. The cantor calls for praise, and gives reasons in the form of relative clauses that unfold the Lord's work in creation and history, in provision and salvation. The constant response gives the dominant note to the Lord's enduring *ḥesed*, his faithfulness to his commitments in creation and covenant. This theme came readily into the singing at the autumn festival – so in the Chronicler's account of the dedication of the first temple (2 Chron. 5.3; 7.3, 6; cf. Ezra 3.11).

1–3   The call is to 'give thanks' or 'make praising testimony' to the Lord, firstly 'for he is good' – generous, kind, gracious. The response may be translated also as a reason for praise, 'for his faithfulness is for ever'; but taking the psalm as a whole, we may better understand the first word not as 'for', but as the emphatic 'truly, indeed'. The rhythmic refrain testifies that the faithful love and goodwill of the Lord, once committed or pledged, is not just long-lasting, but everlasting (cf. above on 118.2). The cantor's words also are melodious with repetition and rhythm as he describes Yahweh as the true God, above all heavenly powers, the master of all forces.

4–9 The relative clauses prolong the sentence from v. 3 to v. 25, depicting the wonderful deeds of the Lord. Creation is the first theme. The Lord created 'by wisdom', his divine skill and understanding, which is seen almost as a personal being (cf. Job 28.20f.; Prov. 8). Almost every reference to the creation in the Old Testament has its own variation, and here the earth is said to have been (lit.) 'hammered out' on to the subterranean waters (cf. 24.2). In v. 9 the 'stars' seem to have been added later for completeness, the moon alone originally being mentioned as night's ruler (cf. Gen.1.16).

10–22 The Lord's deeds are further unfolded from the tradition of the Exodus and entry into Canaan (cf. above on 135.8f.). In v. 13 the cleaving of the sea is linked to the victory over chaos at creation, when the warrior Lord with a mighty blow divided the monster representing the chaotic waters (74.12f.).

23–26 The list of deeds is concluded with a summary which may refer especially to experiences after the Settlement. God was mindful of his commitment whenever his people were brought low, sunk in deep humiliation. The last of the relative clauses returns to the universal work of the Lord – the Creator is the provider, constantly feeding 'all flesh', his myriad creatures (cf. 104.27). The final verse, with a new sentence at last, resumes the opening calls. 'The God of heaven' is a title prominent around the fifth century (Ezra 1.2; Neh. 1.4 etc.).

The antiphonal form of this hymn vividly illustrates the mutual encouragement in the work of praise, a similar form having been widely used from ancient times for a group to encourage each other and gather strength in many a mighty task. So all the pilgrims were led to rejoice in the 'goodness' of the Lord; and here his power, his compassion, his generosity – all is crowned by his 'faithfulness'. In a world where on every hand is experience of suffering, destruction and death, how miraculous such trust in God's faithful love! This testimony is indeed a mighty work, well nigh impossible, except by the strength given and shared in the communion of those who gather before the Lord of all lords.

O God, you that have made us, given us our daily bread, and rescued us from many dangers, grant that in all times of deep trouble we may know still that your faithfulness is for ever, and give thanks for your goodness, through him who is your Wisdom and your Word, Jesus Christ our Saviour.

PSALM 137: Jerusalem Set Above All Joys

1   By the rivers of Babylon we sat and wept aloud,
     when we remembered Zion.
2   On the trees along the banks
     we hung our lyres unused.
3   Our captors asked us there for a song –
      those who had despoiled us, for music of joy:
     Sing us one of the songs of Zion.
4   How should we sing the songs of the Lord
     on the soil of a foreign land?
5   If I forget you, O Jerusalem,
     may my right hand forget its powers.
6   May my tongue cleave to the roof of my mouth,
     if I do not remember you,
     if I do not exalt Jerusalem
     above my highest joy.

7   Remember, Lord, against the people of Edom
      the day of Jerusalem,
     how they said, Down, down with it, right to its foundations!
8   O queenly Babylon, great destroyer,
     happy the one who requites you for all you did to us,
9   who seizes your children in your turn,
     and dashes them against the rock.

This passionate poem can be understood as an intercession for Jerusalem in the sorrowful services commemorating the Babylonian destruction of the city (Zech. 7.3), a use found in later Jewish worship. If the Exile has recently ended, Jerusalem's situation is still pitiful, while Babylon has passed peacefully into Persian control and, as evident in the prophetic books, bitterness against neighbouring Edom is sharp. The psalm begins its prayer by pleading the loyalty to Zion maintained in the Exile (vv. 1–4) and now reaffirmed (vv. 5–6). The climax is reached with the call for judgement on Jerusalem's murderers – the treacherous Edomites and the ruthless Babylonian conquerors.

1–4 The recollection of the mourning in Babylon may arise from the psalmist's own experience, or from a collective memory preserved in the guild of musicians. The scene is put vividly before the Lord to show the love and loyalty of the worshippers towards his sanctuary. The characteristics of the Babylonian plain, so different from Judah, are well recalled – the great river and its lesser streams and canals, the trees (Euphrates poplars, resembling willows) literally 'in her midst' – not in distant woods. The exiles are glimpsed sitting down by the waters, weeping and wailing – an act of mourning, perhaps a formal commemoration (sites by water were favoured for prayer-gatherings, Acts 16.13). The lyres, from which the devoted musicians would not be parted in all their hard journey, were hung silent on the trees in sign of the death-like mourning. The Babylonian captors (no doubt aware of the fame of Jerusalem's musicians, so Gunkel), asked for the merry music of Zion's festivals. Alas, what an irony there would be in citing the glorious promises to Zion! And how could the holy songs be rightly sung on ground not dedicated to the Lord (cf. 1 Sam. 26.19; 2 Kings 5.17; Hos. 9.3f.)?

5–6 The singer puts it personally for greatest emphasis (cf. 135.5) as he avows his present devotion. His words are appropriate to a lyrist (v. 5b) and a singer (v. 6a), and one dedicated to the Lord's service in Zion. He calls a curse upon himself (cf. 7.3–5; Job 31) should he ever forget Jerusalem, ceasing to delight in her above his highest joys. His hands could then no longer play and he would never sing again. In v. 5b the rendering 'forget its powers' preserves the Hebrew play on words, but 'its powers' is not explicit, and the sense may rather be 'fall limp / wither' (so Thomas and Dahood).

7–9 The vow of loyalty has prepared the way for the petition, a call for retributive justice against Jerusalem's destroyers. The neighbouring brother-people of Edom had deserted their allies and indeed assisted the enemy (Obad. 10f.), and had continued to take advantage of Judah's plight. But coming to Babylon's principal share in the outrage, the singer is taken with a prophetic force (cf. Isa. 13.16f.; 14.22). He addresses the personified capital city, and pronounces as 'happy' the one who will do to her what she did to Jerusalem, seizing the infants as she had done, and battering them to death against the rock. Not as deadly as the saturation-bombing of modern warfare, the ancient policies of hand-to-hand war were terrible enough (cf. 2 Kings 8.12). In a case like the Babylonian treatment of repeatedly rebellious Jerusalem, many adults might be spared to serve various purposes for the conquerors, but the infants were killed to end the community's future. The psalmist, from feelings of bitter passion, invokes a justice of retaliation (cf. Obad. 15); whoever carries it out, he declares, will have done well.

The first part of the psalm challenges worshippers to profound commitment to the 'Jerusalem' or 'Zion' of their faith – the forms and fellowship which convey the revelation of God. Against this zeal Christians may measure their mindfulness for the church, their setting her above other pleasures, and their consecration of gifts and skills. But how difficult the use of the concluding imprecations! Some praise the opportunity given here to the powerless to vent their indignation and turn to God for justice; certainly there is evidence here of the dreadful situations through which the biblical faith had to live. More traditionally, Christians have seen Babylon as an allegory of wickedness; her children are our evil thoughts, to be crushed at the outset. Again, some have found value in the prophetic aspect, which can be heard as a warning that evil deeds rebound upon the perpetrators. In the end, however, the terrible words serve best as a reminder that there must always be a discernment of the Spirit in the use of scripture. In the present case the bitter words must at last be washed over by streams of mightier teaching: 'Seek the peace of the city (Babylon) whither I have caused you to be carried away captive, and pray to the Lord for her (Jer. 29.7)'; 'If your enemy be hungry, give him bread to eat ... (Prov. 25.21)'; 'Love your enemies, and pray for those who persecute you ... (Matt. 5.44).'

Enable us, Lord, to dedicate our talents and love to the care of your holy church, and grant that in times of her humiliation we may be strong in prayer, both for her restoration and for the repentance and blessing of her adversaries.

PSALM 138: Thanksgiving in Time of Danger

Of David.

1   With all my heart, Lord, I will give you thanks;
      I will make music to you before all heaven.
2   I will bow down towards your holy temple,
      and will give thanks to your name,
      because of your faithful love and truth;
      for you have glorified your word above all your name.
3   In the day that I called, you answered me;
      you exalted me, with glory in my soul.
4   All the kings of the earth shall thank you, Lord,
      when they have heard the words of your mouth,
5   and they shall sing in the ways of the Lord,
      that great is the glory of the Lord.
6   For though the Lord is high, he watches over the lowly,
      and well he knows the proud from afar.
7   Though I walk in the midst of trouble,
      you will keep my life against the fury of my foes.
      You will stretch out your hand,
      and your right hand shall save me.
8   The Lord will accomplish his will for me.
      O Lord, your faithfulness is for ever;
          do not forsake the work of your hands.

This is usually described as a song of thanksgiving, but it is possible to regard the 'thankful' vv. 1–6 as preparatory to the following prayer. The grand style of several verses suggests the worshipper is a king, and we might then see vv. 1–6 as a typical royal testimony (cf. above on 18.49), leading to the prayer that develops in vv. 7–8. While the singer can witness to God's help in previous struggles, he is at present facing great trouble and the fury of (no doubt military) enemies. A royal link may be indicated by the fact that this is the first of a series (138–45) headed 'Of David'. Some Greek manuscripts add 'Of Haggai and Zechariah' or 'Of Zechariah'; there may be a reminiscence here of how appropriate the psalm was found soon after the return from exile.

1–3 The singer begins with a warm and thankful testimony. He lifts praise to the Lord (lit.) 'before the gods', the subordinate heavenly beings (LXX 'angels'; cf. 8.5; 29.1–2; 96.4). The scene of worship may well be set, as often, in the open court where the altar of sacrifice stood; so obeisance is made towards the divine presence signified within the nearby temple building. Especially praised are the name, the word, the faithful love and truth of the Lord – manifestations and emissaries of his gracious and faithful being. Though v. 2d reads somewhat awkwardly, the sense is strong: of all the gracious revelation of the Lord, his promise is especially prized, and it may be the promises to the house of David that are especially in mind (cf. 89.19f.). The 'faithful love' and 'truth', then, are the Lord's fidelity to this commitment. The singer testifies that the promise to hear his prayers (cf. 2.8; 89.26) has been kept, and God has (if our difficult text can be accepted) made him exult, with glory in his soul (cf. 3.3; 4.2; 57.8).

4–6 This testimony is before the world, and will move the kings of all nations to worship the Lord with thanksgiving (cf. 22.27f.; 47.9; 68.31f.; 102.22). These former foes of the Lord (cf. 2.2; 48.4) will come as pilgrims and ascend the sacred 'ways' to the temple, praising his glory. And the singer declares that the Lord so high yet loves the lowly and disdains the arrogant (cf. 113.5f.); it was an ideal for kings also to take to heart (cf. above on 35.10).

7–8 Statements of trust are often made in the Psalms to support petition (e.g. 3.3–6), and this seems to be the case here. Great danger is envisaged, furious foes seeking the life of the worshipper; as the 'work' or creation of the Lord's hands (an expression like some used of Babylonian kings, my *Kingship*, p. 63), he can well ask not to be forsaken. His trust is that the Lord has a purpose to accomplish in him, and that the Lord's *ḥesed*, his fidelity to those he has created and called (cf. above on 136.1b; the Davidic kings, 89.1f.), will indeed prove to be enduring. Deliverance will come through the Lord's right hand (18.35; 20.6).

Here is a worshipper who bows before the Lord, having much thanksgiving to render and trust to express; and yet, sensing much tribulation to come, he must appeal not to be forsaken. If indeed a Davidic king prays here, we see him fulfilling his calling to bear witness to the Lord who is faithful to his promise and purpose. His service is for the conversion of all kings and their peoples, and he praises the Lord to the bounds of the earth and the heights of heaven. Yet he is frail and in peril, and can count only on the faithfulness of the Lord, who made him for his service and will accept his humility. The psalm has been used by the church especially on the feast of St Michael and All Angels and other feasts of angels; also for Friday vespers, with thoughts of the passion and resurrection (v. 7b taken as 'you will revive me'). Her eucharists share the psalm's combination of thankful witness and intercession, and often carry the plea from tribulation raised by those already thankful for a surpassing salvation. And through the centuries the psalm has led worshippers to know that their praises, sung with a whole heart, echo far beyond the place of worship, mysteriously touching hearts in many lands, and rising to join the praises of heaven.

Almighty God, who glorified your Word in the resurrection of Jesus Christ, stretch out your hand and save us in all our troubles, that we may with all our heart bear witness to your salvation, with praises that go through all the earth and join the music of your heavenly host.

PSALM 139: Enfolded by God

For favour.   Of David.   Psalm.

1   Lord, you search me and know me.
2   You know my sitting and my rising;
        you discern my thought long before.
3   You know well my journeying and my halting,
        and are acquainted with all my paths.
4   For there is not a word on my tongue,
        but you, Lord, know it altogether.
5   Behind and before you enclose me,
        and lay your hand upon me.
6   Such knowledge is too wonderful for me,
        so high that I cannot grasp it.
7   Where shall I go from your Spirit,
        or where shall I flee your face?
8   If I climb up into heaven, you are there;
        if I make my bed in the depths beneath, you are also there.
9   If I take the wings of the dawn,
        and dwell in the farthest sea,
10   even there your hand shall lead me,
        and your right hand shall hold me.
11   If I could say, Let darkness cover me
        and the light about me turn to night,
12   even the darkness would not be dark for you;

dark and light are alike for you.

13 It was you that created my inmost parts;
   you wove me in my mother's womb.

14 I thank you that I am fearfully and wonderfully made;
   marvellous are your works, my soul knows well.

15 My frame was not hidden from you
      when I was made in secret,
   and wrought in the depths of the earth.

16 Your eyes saw my form yet unfinished;
   already my parts were all written in your book,
   as day by day they were fashioned,
   when not one of them was ready.

17 How many are your thoughts for me, O God;
   O how great is the sum of them!

18 If I count them, they are more in number than the sand;
   if I reached the end, I would still have you.

19 O that you would slay the wicked, O God;
   O that the murderous would go away from me!

20 For they speak of you with wicked purpose;
   against you they raise their voice for evil.

21 Those who oppose you, Lord, do I not oppose,
   and those who rise against you, do I not abhor?

22 I oppose them utterly;
   they have become enemies also for me.

23 Search me, O God, and know my heart;
   try me and know my thoughts.

24 See if there is any hurtful way in me,
   and lead me in the everlasting way.

The purpose of this distinctive and beautiful psalm is apparent in v. 19 – prayer against murderous men who threaten the psalmist's life. In a long preparation (vv. 1–18), he addresses the Lord with praise and thanksgiving, developing especially the theme that his heart and all his ways are known to God. He is thus approaching the Lord with the sincere belief that right is on his side. He invites the scrutiny of this all-knowing God and believes the wicked ones will be found to be God's enemies too. The psalm's heading and position in the series invite the idea that a king is the speaker, and comparison can be made with such psalms as 16, 17, and 63, where we found a kind of 'incubation', the king drawing close to God in the sanctuary to gain strength to confront enemies, and of necessity praying in this holy presence with a deep spirituality. Indications that the psalmist is a king can be found in the claim that the enemies who beset him are also God's foes; he claims merit in his total opposition to such; he would be led in the 'way of eternity' (cf. 21.2f.; 45.6; 61.7f.; 72.5; 110.4), and like Babylonian and other kings, he dwells on God's foreknowing and predestining him, and in every detail personally creating him (cf. my *Kingship*, p. 84). Resemblances of thought have been noted not only with the royal tradition of Egyptian hymns, but also with an Indian hymn to Varuna as omniscient and omnipresent (Atharva-Veda 4.16). Peculiarities of language, a kind of Aramaic colouring, need by no means entail a post-exilic date (cf. Dahood). But perhaps, as with the Book of Job, there may be a link with a Wisdom circle, learned in international poetry and open to linguistic influence from around the eastern borders.

1–12   As is often the case with supplicatory psalms, the first word is the holy name. Then, immediately and at length, the supplicant develops the theme of the Lord's searching knowledge of him; God will thus know whether his motives are pure and his cause just. He does not need to assert his integrity directly, but humbly acknowledges that the Lord will know. A tone of praise enters as he describes God's knowledge of him, a knowledge that constantly embraces all his activity, and too wonderful for him to understand. If he had reason to avoid the divine scrutiny, he could not escape it. In the remotest parts of the cosmos, God would still be with him and about him. And if he could conjure up thick darkness to hide in, it would make no difference; for the divine eye of judgement, the light and darkness are alike.

13–18   The Lord's knowledge of him rests even deeper – not just on God's omnipresence, but also on his role as Creator. The psalmist speaks not of the making of creatures generally, but of his own origin. One may wonder if his account here is related to the many references in other countries to the creation of kings – the special care of the Creator's hands, full of predestined meaning. Certainly we find a remarkable concentration on the theme of the Lord's forming, weaving, shaping, intricately working this particular wor-shipper in his mother's womb, and more mysteriously, in the depths of the earth. Though some take this last reference as only a metaphor for the hid-denness in the womb, it is more likely an ancient poetic tradition of human origin from the mother earth (cf. 2 Esd. 5.48; Job 1.21; Ecclus. 40.1). Thus, beyond even his origin in the womb, back into an ultimate mystery, the Lord knew him and formed destiny for him. For the terrible wonder of it all he must give thanks and praise. Beyond all his reckoning is the weight and abundance of God's thoughts for him; and if he could count them to the end, he would scarcely have begun to comprehend the wonder of God himself.

19–24   The singer's prayer against 'the wicked (man)' and the murderous 'men of blood' is blunt: O that God would kill them and rid him of them! Verse 19b suggests that the psalmist refers to particular foes who beset him and threaten his life. He presents them (vv. 20f.) as hostile to God himself, somewhat as the enemies of God's kingdom in royal psalms 2, 101, 144, planning rebellion, uttering arrogance. And like the Anointed in Psalm 2, the psalmist would make the Lord's cause his own, utterly opposing the enemies of the Lord. (The word-root often translated 'hate' occurs four times in vv. 21–2; the reference is to active opposition, rather than to an emotion, and hence the rendering above.) The conclusion connects with the beginning of the psalm, as the singer specifically invites God now to search his heart to see if he follows any 'harmful' (or perhaps 'idolatrous') way. The implication – out of humility not expressed – is that he claims integrity over against the enemies and so looks for God's support. He would be led in the everlasting way ('way of eternity') – granted a continuing life with God (cf. above on 16.11; 21.4).

Troubled by evil adversaries, the psalmist seeks God's help against them. But his prayer is like a meditation, and full of awe. Knowing that his heart must be cleansed, his motives pure, he contemplates the total knowledge that God has of him and all his doings, a knowledge that surrounds in time and space, that sifts, and sees through dark and light, and cannot be evaded in the heights or depths of the universe, a knowledge that is bound up with a loving care and purpose, going back to ultimate origins, continuing in the intricate working and weaving in the womb. What a deep and honest self-searching was needed before this worshipper could call, 'Lord, search me and see if there is any hurtful way in me'! Beyond all the strife of the wicked, he asked to be led on the everlasting way, the path of unbroken communion and life with the Lord. Church tradition has heard here the voice of Christ, but also of every one become part of him. To sing these words sincerely, they also will have searched their own conscience and called upon the Lord's name with awe. They acknowledge him as the reality that closely and always enfolds them, the one of penetrating knowledge, but also of caring thoughts without number for each one. Their prayer against the ruthless is a necessary opposition to his adversaries; but the death they call for is a death to cruel ways and a rebirth in the service of God. And as he leads them on the eternal way, they will at last come to know, even as they are known (1 Cor. 13.12).

Lord, you know well our journeying and halting, and the sum of your thoughts for us is beyond all our reckoning; help us ever to reject evil and live wholly for you, and lead us in the way everlasting.

PSALM 140: Prayer Against the Poisoners of Society

For favour.   Psalm.   Of David.

1   Rescue me, Lord, from evil folk,
    and guard me from the men of violence,
2   who think out harm in their heart,
    and daily stir up war.
3   They make their tongue sharp as a snake's;
    a viper's poison is under their lips.   *[Pause]*

4   Keep me, Lord, from the hands of the wicked;
    protect me from the violent, who plan to overthrow my steps.
5   The arrogant have laid a snare for me,
        and with cords have spread their net;
    along the way they have set their traps for me.   *[Pause]*
6   So I say to the Lord, You are my God;
    listen, O Lord, to the voice of my supplications.
7   Lord God, my glorious Saviour,
    you cover my head on the day of battle.
8   Do not grant, Lord, the desires of the wicked;
    do not let their evil purpose prosper.   *[Pause]*
9   When those who surround me lift up their heads,
    the mischief of their lips shall cover them.
10 Fiery coals shall fall upon them;
    they shall be cast into the depths, and shall not arise.
11 The slanderer shall not be established on earth;
    harm shall hunt the man of violence to overthrow him.
12 I know that the Lord will give justice for the poor,
    right judgement for the needy.
13 So the just shall give thanks to your name;
    the true-hearted shall sit before your face.

In headings, occurrences of *selah* ('Pause') and in content, 140–3 have contacts with lamenting psalms in the main collections headed 'Of David' (3–41; 51–70). In the present case, we are reminded of psalms which speak of warfare, but especially lament the evil words poured out by the enemy. It seems that a king or other national leader, one at the focus of all the hostility, seeks God's help in public prayer to counter the threat and bring down a just judgement on the foe (cf. 7, 10, 57, 64) for the relief of his people (vv. 12–13). The pattern is fairly typical of lamenting psalms: invocation and petition merge into depiction of the danger and appeals to a close bond with the Lord (vv. 1–8); doom is declared (or sought) for the foe (vv. 9–11); the conclusion adds its force by expressing confidence in God's justice, and by speaking of the thanksgiving that will be offered for deliverance (vv. 12–13).

1–5   Calling on the Lord for rescue and protection, the singer depicts the oppressors and their preparations for assault. He complains of their violence, their desire for war, their venomous words (slander, curses), their cunning traps (similarly in 9.15f.; 10.7f.; 31.4; 35.7; 52.1f.; 57.4, 6f.; 58.3f.; 64.1f.).

6–8   The plea is supported by reference to a bond with the Lord; with rich meaning he can say 'You are my God' and look for his prayers to be answered (cf. 89.26); the Lord by his glory ('*oz*) grants victorious salvation (cf. 28.8) and on the day of battle covers his head with the helmet of his protection. Such was the bond the Lord made with his Anointed (cf. my *Kingship*, pp. 170f.), and the psalmist is able to claim it for himself.

9–11 The passage is often translated as an imprecation: 'May the mischief of their lips cover them, may fiery coals fall upon them, may they be cast.' But LXX and Vulgate take it, as above, in the style of a prophetic judgement, which certainly seems more suitable in vv. 10b and 11. The psalmist thus assumes a prophetic role, conveying the Lord's power against wickedness. Judgement will fall in fire from heaven (cf. 11.6; 18.12f.) and in the opening of the earth (cf. 55.15).

12–13 An expression of confidence in the Lord's justice adds to the force of the supplication. It is a justice for the poor (in this case the humble and needy people dependent on God) which the heavenly king will not neglect. Finally, a vow of thank-offerings is implied. God's people will come to the temple to celebrate salvation, bearing witness to his faithfulness, sitting in the court before his temple to share in the meal of thanksgiving.

This is another example of prayer offered by an individual figure who turns out to have a representative character. He bears the whole community of God's poor and needy in his heart, and for their sakes is the target of sharp and poisonous words and many sinister traps. It is his calling to defend this people, using the weapon of prayer, the appeal to God's committed love, and the mediation of God's word of judgement. In the church's use of the psalm, the powerful intercession of Christ has been heard, defending God's poor from the cunning and violence that would stir up war and poison mind and spirit.

Glorious Saviour, rescue us from the subtle evils that are too strong for us, from poisonous words and the spirit of war; by your judgement overthrow the forces of violence, that all the world may join to worship you in thanksgiving and in peace.

PSALM 141: The Incense of Prayer

Psalm. Of David.

1 Lord, I cry to you, come quickly to me;
   give heed to my voice, as I call to you.
2 May my prayer be accepted as the incense before you,
   and the lifting up of my hands as the evening sacrifice.
3 Set a watch, Lord, before my mouth;
   keep guard at the door of my lips.
4 Let my heart not incline to any evil thing,
      to join in deeds of wickedness with evildoers;
   then I shall not partake of their pleasures.
5 Let the faithful rebuke me strongly in friendship;

> but let the oil of the wicked not anoint my head,
>   for my prayer is ever against their evil deeds.
> 6 They will hear my words and find them good,
>   when their rulers have been thrown down stony places.
> 7 As when the ground is broken and cleft,
>   so our bones are scattered
>   at the mouth of the cavern of death.
> 8 But to you, Lord God, my eyes are turned;
>   in you I take shelter – do not pour away my life.
> 9 Keep me from the grip of the snare they have laid for me,
>   and from the traps of the evildoers.
> 10 The wicked shall fall into their own nets together,
>   while I pass on in safety.

Interpretation must take into account the similarities between 140–3, and in the present case commentators rightly continue along the path they began with 140. The view that a national leader (most naturally a king) offers the prayer of 141 in a crisis for his people accords well with the text. The situation of war (cf. vv. 6, 9, 10), in which many have already died (v. 7), is mostly presented as a struggle borne personally by the psalmist, whose prayer and piety before the Lord will be a key factor in the (national) intercession. One might further infer from v. 2 that the prayer is offered on campaign away from the temple, and there may be a hint of war against Edom (as in 60) in the reference to 'rock' in v. 6 (*sela‘*, suggesting the cliffs of Edom and the capital city, Sela); but such circumstances are uncertain. The psalm opens with invocation and request for the Lord's attention (vv. 1–2); right motives are shown by requests for preservation from sin (vv. 3–5); prophetic assurance seems to prompt lament (vv. 6–8); prayers for safety are rounded off with fresh assurance (vv. 8–9, 10).

1–2   The singer first invokes the holy name, then asks that his prayer be readily heard, indeed received as favourably as the divinely appointed offerings at the temple. (For the 'hasten to me' in v. 1a we can compare 40.13 and 70.5, but from the context some have looked for a different sense, 'take note of me', root *ḥush* II.) The 'incense' may be the daily burning of incense on the small golden altar (Ex. 30.7f.), or the smoke of the memorial offering (Lev. 2.2) or other offerings (Ps. 66.15). The lifting of hands was an expressive gesture of prayer (28.2; cf. 63.4; 134.2; 1 Tim. 2.8). The 'evening sacrifice' would be either the daily meal-offering (Ex. 29.38f.) or the entire evening sacrifice, an occasion propitious for intercession (1 Kings 18.36). The request in v. 2 is that the prayer should be as acceptable as these regular offerings; it is possible, but not necessary, to infer that the psalmist is far from the temple. To take the verse as meaning that prayer is substituted for sacrifice in exilic conditions is unwarranted.

3–5 Such a supplicant against the wicked should himself be innocent, and the singer approaches this requirement by humbly asking the Lord to guard him from sin; may God set a guard at the doors of his lips that no evil be allowed through (cf. Micah 7.5); and may God grant him a heart firm against the temptations of fellowship with the makers of mischief (the 'pleasures' are an image from table-fellowship or cultic meals). The wicked are adept at corrupting others through flattery and bribery; something of this may have featured in the present crisis. By prayer the psalmist rebuffs such temptation.

6–7 In confident prophetic style, the psalmist seems to say that the rank and file of his opponents will be reconciled to him when their rulers are tumbled by divine judgement; echoing the word for the table-pleasures used in v. 4, he foresees his 'good' words now winning them back. But at present the situation is lamentable; many of the psalmist's supporters have been slain (in battle, it seems), and so he depicts 'our bones' strewn at the mouth of the underworld.

8–10 Pleading his reliance on the Lord (cf. 121.1; 123.1), he asks that his life be spared, and that the sinister plots of the foe may entrap only themselves (cf. 7.15f.; 140.5).

Here is a leader who not only laments many of his people killed and his own life ever in danger, but also is aware of temptation. While he is willing to take stern reproof from the faithful, he is aware that the enemy aims to undermine his position by flattery and the temptation of rewards. He is therefore urgent in prayer, and asks to be guarded and guided by the good powers of God. From early times the psalm was used by the church at evening services as sanctuary lamps were lit; prayer arose as incense, and hands and hearts were raised as once had been the evening sacrifice. Especially treasured was the prayer for pure speech, and countless worshippers have asked that the Lord set his guard of angels at the door of their lips, and that he would bless them through the incense of the prayers of all the saints (Rev. 8.3).

In all our dangers, Lord, as our eyes are turned to you, keep us from the corruption of evil temptations; set a watch before our lips, and help us by the lifting up of your Son Jesus, and by the incense of the prayers of all your faithful servants.

PSALM 142: Prayer when the Soul is in Prison

Poem.   Of David.   When he was in the cave.   Prayer.

1   With my voice I cry to the Lord;
    with my voice to the Lord I make my supplication.
2   I pour out my lament before him,
    and tell him my distress.
3   When my spirit faints upon me, you know my path;
    in the way that I walk, they have laid a snare for me.
4   I look to the right hand, but see,
    there is no one that will know me;
    I have no longer any refuge;
    there is no one to care for my soul.
5   I cry to you, Lord, and say,
    You are my shelter, my portion in the land of the living.
6   Give heed to my cry, for I am brought very low;
    save me from those who pursue me,
       for they are too strong for me.
7   Bring my soul out of prison,
    to give thanks, Lord, to your name.
    The faithful will gather around me,
    when you act for me in all your goodness.

Here we find a singer praying that his soul be brought out of prison (v. 7), but even this distinctive detail is probably figurative for a life in suffering and danger. Also, his spirit faints and foes have laid a snare on his path; he is deserted, without helpers. Interpreting such features from the group 140–3 and from several other psalms, we may trace the supplication of a Davidic king, portraying national enemies. His loyal people will celebrate his deliverance (v. 7) from enemies too strong for him (v. 6b, like royal 18.17), when the Lord bountifully rewards him (v. 7d, like 18.20). The various headings point back to an older collection (for 'Poem', *maskil*, see above on 32; for 'Prayer' on 90; for the 'cave' on 57).

1–2   Instead of launching into direct appeal, the singer portrays himself loudly calling in lamenting prayer. The depiction indirectly commends him to God, for it shows one in deep distress, but relying on the Lord (cf. 77.1–3).

3–4   But with sudden force comes the direct 'you'. Expressing trust, the supplicant is sure that his Lord will know how his spirit faints upon him (cf. 131.2) and the enemy assails with cunning. No advocate stands at his right hand to help him, nor anyone to acknowledge friendship (cf. Isa. 63.16); there is no refuge offered, and no one seeks him to bring help. That a leader can present himself to God as so abandoned and destitute is apparent from other psalms and from foreign texts (cf. above on 69.8).

5–7 Brought very low, the supplicant pleads his bond with the Lord and especially his sole reliance on him and his devotion (for 'portion' cf. above on 16.5; 73.26; 119.57). So he asks for deliverance, and that his soul be brought out from 'prison', this state of virtual death, to enjoy true life again. The conclusion looks to the hoped-for time of thanksgiving, when the Lord will have acted bountifully on his behalf, and his people, the 'just' or 'faithful' (*saddiqim*), circle about him in festivity. (For 'circle about' some render 'shall place a crown on me', so REB).

The rather general expressions of the psalm, along with the passion of its plea, have enabled it to speak for many a sufferer or afflicted community. They readily identify with the sense of lowness, the fainting spirit, the absence of helpers, the soul held fast in prison. The psalm leads them to direct their voice and heart to the Lord, pouring out their story of woe to him, recognizing in him their sure refuge and their true joy, hopeful for the time when they may serve him in thanksgiving. In Christian use the psalm has been much appointed in commemoration of the passion, when the prayer to be brought out from prison has led worshippers to join their suffering to Christ's, looking also for the thanksgiving of the resurrection.

To you, good Lord, who walked the way of the passion for our sakes, we lift our voice; we pray you, bring our souls from their prisons, that we may bear witness to your name, and know you as our portion in the land of life.

PSALM 143: An Appeal to the Faithfulness of the Lord

Psalm.   Of David.

1   Lord, hear my prayer, give heed to my supplications;
    answer me in your faithfulness and goodness.
2   Do not enter into judgement with your servant,
    for no one living shall be justified before you.
3   For the enemy has pursued my soul,
        and crushed my life into the earth;
    he has made me dwell in deep darkness like those long dead.
4   My spirit has fainted upon me,
    and my heart within me is desolate.
5   I call to mind the days of old;

> I meditate on all your work,
>   and ponder the deeds of your hands.
> 6 I spread out my hands to you;
>   my soul longs for you like a thirsty land.
> 7 Answer me quickly, Lord, for my spirit fails;
>   do not hide your face from me,
>   or I shall become like those gone down to the pit.
> 8 Let me hear your faithful love in the morning, for in you I
>   trust;
>   show me the way I should go, for to you I lift my soul.
> 9 Rescue me from my enemies, Lord,
>   for I flee to you for shelter.
> 10 Teach me to do your will;
>   lead me by your good Spirit into a pleasant land.
> 11 For the sake of your name, Lord, grant me life,
>   and by your goodness bring my soul out of trouble.
> 12 In your faithfulness you will silence my enemies,
>   and sweep away all the adversaries of my soul,
>   for I am your servant.

In this supplication the poet draws on many traditional phrases but still achieves some distinctive emphases. The underlying situation seems related to that of 142, while the indications that the worshipper is again a king are somewhat stronger. Thus, it suits this identification that he looks to God to dispose of his enemies because he is the Lord's 'servant' (v. 12); that he links his plight with ancient national salvation (v. 5); that he would be led by the angel Spirit (v. 10, cf. above on 51.11–13); that he lays such weight on 'you are my God' (v. 10, cf. above on 140.6), and desires guidance and instruction to carry out God's will (vv. 8, 10, cf. 27.11; 40.8; 86.11). As he seeks deliverance from cruel enemies, he may be undertaking 'incubation', a night in the sanctuary, for he hopes for a sign of acceptance in the morning (v. 8, cf. above on 139). LXX's heading shows how the link was made with David, adding 'when his son was pursuing him'.

1–2 Appealing to the Lord for a hearing, this 'servant' of his at once invokes the divine fidelity and goodwill pledged in covenant (v. 1b). He is not going to assert his own worthiness, but count rather on God's grace, for in common with all living, he could not be found wholly just by the eye of God's judgement (cf. 130.3; Job. 4.17; 9.2; 15.14; 25.4f.; Rom. 3.20).

3–6 His lament would move the Lord by depicting the effect of the enemy's attacks. It is as though he were already in the deepest caverns of the underworld among those 'long dead', those from whom the life-force had most utterly drained away. It is especially as bearing all his people in his heart that he can so depict himself (cf. Lam. 3.6); many may already have perished (cf. 141.7). His spirit faints 'upon him' (cf. above on 142.3), another picture of dwindling life-force. He tells of his recitals of the stories of ancient salvation; O that such salvation for king and people would again be seen (cf. 77.11f.)! His hands, spread out in appeal, express dependence on the Lord (cf. 44.20; 88.9); his soul pines with thirst for God and his salvation (cf. 63.1).

7–12 A series of petitions carry the supplication to its end. When morning breaks, he would 'hear' the Lord's faithful love (*ḥesed*) – perhaps an oracle giving assurance of help from the faithful Covenant-Lord (cf. 46.5; 90.14); perhaps also words of counsel, showing the right course of action. He would be taught to do God's will in this crisis, and led as it were into pleasant, fertile country by the angel-Spirit that enabled kings to bear their heavy tasks (see above on 51.10f.). The last verse sustains the appeal to the Lord's covenant with his servant; the enemies, seen as in effect opponents of the Lord's rule, are to be brought to nothing.

Rather than claim virtue to support his plea, this worshipper relies on the committed goodness of the Lord, his faithful love to his servants. Through a night of prayer, he tells the Lord of the evil situation, spreads out his hands to him, disposes himself to renewed obedience and guidance by the Holy Spirit, and trusts to hear the voice of faithful love at the first light of morning. As one of the Penitential Psalms (see above on 6), this prayer has led penitents to look to God's grace, remembered in scripture's great story of salvation, and ever known afresh in the mornings that follow the nights of trial.

God of faithfulness and goodness, we hold before you the sufferings that drain away your people's life, and the enemies that crush them into the earth; come quickly, Lord, to save us, and by your Spirit lead us into your just and pleasant land.

PSALM 144: Prayer from the Waters of Chaos

Of David.

1   Blessed be the Lord my rock,
      who trains my hands for war and my fingers for battle,
2   my sure help and my fortress, my castle and my deliverer,
      my shield in whom I trust, who subdues my people under me.
3   What is man that you know him,
      the child of man that you take thought for him?
4   Man is like a breath of wind;
      his days are like a passing shadow.
5   Lord, part your heavens and come down;
      touch the mountains and they shall smoke.

6 Hurl down your lightning and scatter them;
   shoot with your arrows and put them to flight.
7 Reach down your hand from on high;
   rescue me and pluck me out of the great waters,
      and from the hands of the aliens,
8 whose mouths speak but harm,
   and their right hand is a hand of falsehood.
9 O God, I will sing a new song to you,
   and make music for you with a ten-stringed harp,
10 you that give salvation to kings,
   and have delivered your servant David.
11 O save me from the evil sword,
   and take me from the hand of the aliens,
   whose mouths speak but harm,
   and their right hand is a hand of falsehood,
12 so that our sons in their youth
      may be like well-nurtured plants.
   our daughters like pillars well-shaped
      for the corners of the temple,
13 our barns filled with all manner of store,
   our flocks bringing forth thousands
      and ten thousands in our fields,
14 our cattle heavy with young and bearing in safety,
   and no cry of distress in our streets.
15 Happy the people for whom it is so;
   happy the people who have the Lord for their God.

After a praising testimony to the Lord as his castle and shield, a Davidic king prays for deliverance from enemies in terms like those of 18, seeking a dramatic intervention of God on cosmic scale. He asks to be thus delivered in order that his people may have health and plenty (conditions as in the royal ideal of 72). Victory over political enemies might indeed lead to prosperous times, but a fuller understanding of the connection of the blessings in vv. 12f. and the conflict in the main part of the psalm is possible if the conflict is taken as symbolic. In recurring festal rites, the king seems to have been shown in conflict with the forces of death and chaos, the comprehensive dangers to the society and the world. Deliverance for the Lord's Anointed was related to God's requirements of humility and loyalty, and to hope for the fruits of God's kingdom in peace and harmony with nature (cf. above on 18, and my *Kingship*, pp. 127–34). Echoes of other psalms (especially 18 and 8) will be due to a common liturgical tradition; arguments for a late date because of 'Aramaisms' have long been unconvincing (cf. *Kingship*, p. 208, n. 40, also Dahood). The form of the psalm is given by its liturgical purpose: testimony to the royal bond with God (vv. 1–2) and to the frailty of humanity represented by the king (vv. 3–4) is followed by the plea for deliverance (vv. 5–8) and vow of thanksgiving (vv. 9–10). A resumption of the plea (v. 11) leads into trustful expectation of consequent blessings for the people (vv. 12–14) and a concluding testimony to the goodness of the Lord (v. 15).

1–4 The king prepares for his plea by blessing God as his faithful defender (vv. 1–2, cf. 18.1–2, 46–7) and by urging the pathetic weakness of the human race that he represents (vv. 3–4, cf. 8.4; 62.9). Praise of God as committed (through the king's election, anointing etc.) to his protection implies an appeal that this commitment be now manifested. The covenant with the Davidic house is alluded to in v. 2a, where 'my sure help' is more literally 'my faithful love' (*hesed*), a forceful appellation. 'My people' in v. 2 may be very comprehensive – the subjects of one ideally set over the world (cf. 18.47 'the peoples', which is the reading also here in some manuscripts). The depiction of God as the king's teacher in the arts of war has parallels in Egypt (cf. 18.34).

5–8 The king's prayer for rescue depicts him as fallen into the chaos-waters and the hands of abhorrent foes; these are the forces of death, and the scene gathers up all the recurring threats to human existence and the health of the world of life. So the Lord's Anointed calls to him to bend back the solid firmament under the heavens and come flying to his rescue, drawing him out of death's tides and the evil hands (cf. 18.9–18). That the saviour's advent is pictured in terms of storm is probably connected with the country's round of growth (cf. above on 29).

9–11 The king promises new music of thanksgiving when he is delivered (cf. 33.2–3; the ten-stringed portable harp was much valued in psalmody, cf. Int. 3b). The Lord's goodness to David his servant is shown afresh in every faithful act for his continuing line (cf. 18.50). The plea of vv. 7b–8, the core of the psalm, is now repeated for due emphasis and to make a clear link to vv. 12f. The phrase 'from the evil sword / sword of harm' (probably to be attached to v. 11 as above, not as traditionally to the end of v. 10) is added, filling out the picture of the evil foes in the service of destruction and chaos.

12–15 The blessings that will come to society through the deliverance of the Lord's Anointed are now unfolded, adding notes of appeal and faith to the supplication, but also, in the manner of prophetic poetry, seeming almost to shape the future that will be given. The passage flows from the preceding, being linked by 'so that' (*'-sh-r* as in Deut. 6.3, BDB, p. 83, 8b). Society will rejoice in healthy children, cattle and crops, and justice for the poor ('no cry of distress in our streets'); it is an ideal linked to faithful kingship in 72 and characteristic of royal ideals in many countries (my *Kingship*, pp. 165–8). The closing words blend praise and appeal: O the happiness of a people so blessed because Yahweh, the Lord, is their God! In covenant with him, and true to him, they will know the fullness of life (cf. the conclusion of royal Ps. 2).

In this dramatic psalm we see the royal figure as the bearer of all his people, and indeed of the natural order with which they would live in harmony. He is consequently the target of the forces of destruction. The danger is acute, almost fatal, so overwhelming are these sinister forces. But because of his bond of faithful love with the almighty Lord and Creator, they are not to triumph. His strong prayer rises to the heavens and leads to hope of wonderful blessing – justice, health, beauty and peace – for people, animals and plants. The church readily applied the psalm to the salvation of the passion and resurrection, the source of true life for all God's creatures.

Lord Jesus, our exalted King, grant to your people the pure happiness of being ever bound to you in love, that through our prayer and constancy your blessings may flow to all peoples and creatures.

PSALM 145: The God who Cares for Every Creature

Praise. Of David.

1   I will exalt you, my God, the King,
       and I will bless your name for ever and ever.
2   Every day I will bless you,
       and praise your name for ever and ever.
3   Great is the Lord and very glorious,
       and there is no searching out his greatness.
4   Let one generation to another praise your works,
       and tell of your mighty deeds.
5   Let them speak of the splendour of the majesty of your glory,
       and I myself will sing of your marvellous works.
6   Let them speak of the power of your awesome deeds,
       while I too recount your mighty acts.
7   Let them pour out the story of your abundant kindness,
       and sing with joy of your goodness.
8   Gracious and compassionate is the Lord,
       patient, and great in faithful love.
9   The Lord is good to all,
       and his compassion is over all that he has made.
10   All your works shall give you thanks, O Lord,
       and your faithful ones shall bless you.
11   Let them speak of the glory of your kingdom,
       and tell of your mighty power,
12   to make known your power to the children of man,
       and the glory of the splendour of your reign.
13   Your kingdom is an everlasting kingdom,
       and your dominion shall endure through all generations.

The Lord is steadfast in all his words,
and faithful in all his deeds.
14 The Lord upholds all those who fall,
and lifts up all who are bowed down.
15 The eyes of all look to you,
and you give them their food at its proper time.
16 You open your hand,
and satisfy the wants of every living thing.
17 The Lord is good in all his ways,
and faithful in all his deeds.
18 Near is the Lord to all who call upon him,
to all who call to him in truth.
19 He will fulfil the request of those who fear him,
he will hear their cry and save them.
20 The Lord guards over those who love him,
but all the wicked he will destroy.
21 My mouth shall speak the praise of the Lord,
and let all creatures bless his holy name for ever and ever.

The sufferings of the Davidic figure and his people are over, and the book is brought to a conclusion with six resounding songs of praise (seven in LXX and Vulgate through their division of 147, and taken by Bede as symbolic of praise in the world to come). This is the only psalm to carry the title 'Praise', though the Psalms were eventually to be known in Hebrew as 'The Book of Praises'. It is a hymn consisting of calls and resolves to praise (vv. 1–2, 4–7, 10–12, 21) and grounds for praise (vv. 3, 8–9, 13–20). The verses begin with successive letters of the Hebrew alphabet (Int. 4e); although the letter N is missing in the main Hebrew tradition (to show the inadequacy of earthly praise, suggests Cassiodorus), it is supplied with an appropriate verse in one manuscript, in LXX, and now also in a Qumran scroll (as above, v. 13c, d).

The Lord is to be praised as eternal King of all (vv. 1–2, 21); his greatness is seen in his work as Creator (vv. 3–6); his goodness and pity are shown to all his creation (vv. 7–10); his kingship is glorious and everlasting (vv. 11–13b; he helps all in need, feeds all his creatures, answers the prayer of 'truth', but destroys the wicked (vv. 13c–20). The psalm is remarkable for its reiterated universalism; his caring kingship is for all that he has made, for all that lives. Although the poetry has been found wanting (repetitive, derivative, contrived because of the alphabetic scheme, cf. Gunkel), it is to be judged according to its purpose – to lead praise on some festal occasion. Here it is clearly effective, especially if a refrain was chanted by massed voices. Such a refrain is indicated by the closing words, 'for ever and ever', while a fuller one may be reflected in the reading here of some manuscripts, as 115.18; most remarkably however, a Qumran scroll has the refrain written out after every verse, 'Blessed be the Lord, and blessed be his name for ever and ever.'

1–12   An individual voice leads the praise representatively. Verses 1–2 are a kind of self-exhortation to praise (cf. 103.1), combined with the direct address to God frequent in the psalm and giving it its warmth. 'My God' combines the thought of God in his bond with his faithful worshippers with the absolute title 'the King', the Creator and ruler of all. Third person reference is used in vv. 3, 8, 9 and (so the Hebrew) 12, as commonly for grounds of praise, involving a testimony to others. In vv. 4–8 the thought seems to centre on the generations of worshippers at the temple rehearsing and giving thanks for the historic deeds of redemption, so eloquent of the faithful and compassionate qualities of God. But explicitly v. 10 draws into the work of thanksgiving all the Lord has made, all his creatures; these too are bound in his *ḥesed*, his faithful love, as his 'faithful' (v. 10b), embraced in the commitment of his care.

13–21   The praise declares the Lord's kingship to be everlasting, and passes on to describe its benevolent character. He is faithful, and ever concerned for those in trouble – stumbling on life's way, bowed down with afflictions; these he supports and raises up. All living creatures look to him; beyond all numbering they are, but he feeds each one at the proper time (cf. 104.27). Utterly kind and reliable, he is known as near and strong to save by those who cry to him in truth, fear him and love him – they are faithful to him, acknowledge his lordship in all their ways and cleave to him. The 'wicked', spreading evil and destruction in God's world, must themselves face destruction. The final verse takes up again the opening theme; the singer sets himself anew to praise, and calls for the thanksgiving of every living thing. The final 'for ever and ever' is additional to the metre of the last line and is probably a refrain (see above).

In a world where suffering and violence abound, knowledge of the kingship of God – almighty, eternal, benevolent – comes as a disclosure from beyond. Our psalm indeed follows in the tradition of the hymns from the great festival, where they celebrated the manifestation of God as King, the Creator and the saviour from evil. The pilgrim worshippers experienced a revelation like the breaking in of light from an ideal world, and by such an illumination our psalmist is able to depict the royal Creator and ruler, the everlasting God, raising those who are bowed down, satisfying the desire of every living creature, destroying the agents of evil, filling the whole created order with his goodness and glory. Well did the Talmud (Berakot 4b) declare that those who recited this psalm thrice daily are children of the age to come, for the worship fostered by such a recitation is present experience of a pure world from beyond. Its echo is in the Lord's Prayer: 'Your kingdom come . . . for yours is the kingdom, the power and the glory.' Rather as in 117, there is in our psalm an unhindered passing between the narrower circle of the faithful and the vast array of all living. Repeatedly it is said that the care of this God and King is for all he has made, and all creatures are destined together to love and bless him. Synagogue and church have made great use of this psalm (cf. Kirkpatrick), and it has sometimes been appointed for Pentecost.

O Lord, eternal King, lead us through moments of vision to a continuing faith in your kingdom, that every day we may bless you and, through all we do and are, pour out the story of your abundant kindness.

PSALM 146: Trust and Salvation

1   Alleluia.
    Praise the Lord, O my soul;
2   let me praise the Lord as long as I live,
        make music to my God all my life long.
3   Put no trust in princes, nor in any child of man,
    for there is no salvation from them.
4   When their breath is gone, they return to their earth;
    on that same day their thoughts will perish.
5   Happy those whose help is the God of Jacob,
    who set their hope on the Lord their God.
6   For he is the maker of heaven and earth,
    the sea, and all that lives in them,
    keeping faith for evermore,
7   doing justice for the oppressed,
    giving bread to the hungry,
    the Lord who sets the prisoners free,
8   the Lord who gives sight to those who are blind,
    the Lord who raises those bowed down,
    the Lord who loves the faithful,
9   the Lord who watches over the strangers,
    who upholds the fatherless and widow,
    but overturns the way of the wicked.
10 The Lord shall reign for ever,
    your God, O Zion, throughout all generations.
    Alleluia.

This song of praise has also an element of instruction, and we should understand the individual singer (vv. 1b–2) as leading an assembly of worshippers (cf. vv. 3, 10, and the alleluias), leading the praise by example, and testifying to the Lord's good reign in a way that teaches as it praises. The psalm begins a series of songs (146–50) where each is furnished with introductory and concluding alleluias, but it is also linked to 145 by similarities of wording and ideas. Although it is usually considered post-exilic, Dahood may be right to signal caution, pointing to some ancient poetic features, especially word-pairings. The theme of God's kingship would make it appropriate for the autumn festival. For each of 146–48, LXX, dividing as four psalms, has the title 'Of Haggai and Zechariah', suggesting how these psalms were sometimes related to the return from exile.

1–2   The alleluia, as usual, lies outside the psalm proper, as the metre shows. After this preliminary and general call to praise, the singer opens his song by exhorting his own soul to praise the Lord (cf. 103.1; 104.1). As long as he has the living breath, he would sing and make music in praise of the Lord.

3–5   The singer exhorts the gathered people not to look to human beings, even the most eminent, as though salvation was within their power; their limitations are apparent when they die and return to the 'earth' (*adama*) from which 'man' (*adam*) was made. But 'happy' (cf. above on 1.1) the one whose help is first and foremost the God of Jacob, the God known through all his revelation to his people, the Lord who binds the faithful to himself.

6–10   A series of hymnic clauses, extending to v. 9, depicts this Lord in all the wonder and goodness of his work. The kingship of the Lord (v. 10) is shown to involve his creating of all, his frustrating of the wicked, and above all, his salvation, healing and care of all the humble in their need. The oppressed, the hungry, the prisoners, those who are blind or bowed down, the vulnerable 'resident aliens', the fatherless and the widow – to all such, this mighty king is saviour.

The experience of such saving acts of the Lord is linked by our psalm with trust in him, and with not treating as god earthly wealth, power or wisdom. Those who take the Lord as their true help, founding their hope on him, will know that 'sheer happiness' (*asherey*, 1.1) of finding him come with power to break the prison bars, to open their eyes to his light. The stories of Jesus give examples of such kingly acts, showing the breaking through of the kingdom of God (cf. Luke 4.16–21; 7.18–23). Our psalm can give voice to all whom he so saves, as it ever reiterates the golden rule to found all trust and hope on the Lord, Creator, King, and only true saviour.

Lord God, Creator and King, help us in every need to put our trust and hope in you, that we may know the happiness of your salvation, and all our life long make music to your name.

PSALM 147: Lord of Stars and Fledglings

1   Alleluia.
    How good to make music to our God;
    how pleasant to make melody of his praise!
2   The Lord builds up Jerusalem;
    he gathers together the outcasts of Israel.
3   He heals the broken-hearted,
    and binds up all their wounds.
4   He counts the number of the stars,
    and calls them all by their names.
5   Great is our Lord and mighty in strength,
    and his wisdom is beyond all measure.
6   The Lord lifts up the poor,
    and brings the wicked down to the dust.
7   Sing to the Lord with thanksgiving;
    with the lyre make music to our God.
8   He covers the heavens with clouds, preparing rain for the earth,
    and he makes grass to grow on the hills.
9   He gives the beasts their food,
    and feeds the young ravens when they cry.
10 The Lord does not delight in the strength of the warhorse,
    and the warrior's strong legs he does not prize.
11 But the Lord delights in those who fear him,
    who trustfully wait for his faithful love.
12 Glorify the Lord, O Jerusalem;
    O Zion, praise your God.
13 For he strengthens the bars of your gates;
    he blesses your children in your midst.
14 He gives peace throughout your borders,
    and satisfies you with the best of wheat.
15 He sends his command to the earth;
    his word runs very swiftly.
16 He gives the snow like wool;
    he scatters the frost like ashes.
17 He throws down his hail like pieces of bread;
    before his cold the water stands still.
18 He sends his word and melts them;
    he blows with his wind and the waters flow.
19 He declared his word to Jacob,
    his statutes and his judgements to Israel.
20 He did not do so for any other nation;
    he did not make known to them his judgements.

The 'alleluia psalms' continue (cf. above on 146). In this song of praise, the fresh calls to the worshippers in vv. 7 and 12 give the impression of a sequence of worship divided into three parts (vv. 1–6, 7–11, 12–20; Greek, Syriac and Latin traditions take vv. 12–20 as a separate psalm). But the overall unity can be supported by structural analysis (finding 'inclusions' and pervading patterns, see Allen). The themes of God's care of creation, the afflicted and Zion, and the giving of his law would be at home in the autumn festival. The psalm is often said to be dependent on other texts (Isa. 40f.; Job 37–39; Pss 33; 104; Deut. 4.7–8) and so a late composition. The references to 'outcasts' and the building and strengthening of Jerusalem, moreover, are taken to be retrospects on the return from exile and on Nehemiah's walls. The 'dependence', however, may be more a matter of common tradition (Second Isaiah's own inheritance of the poetry of worship is so often overlooked), while the references to 'those driven out' and building may be quite general, having parallels in Babylonian texts. The question of date is therefore best left open.

1–6 Not an irksome task, but a sweet pleasure is the praising of God; through the music and poetry of praise one bathes in the light and glory of his revelation. Grounds of praise are unfolded with the use of many Hebrew participles for God's activity, conveying the impression of his constant and characteristic work. For his holy city he is the builder (cf. 78.69); for his wider people, he is the one who regathers those thrust out; for all broken lives and bodies, he is the healer, the bandager of wounds. And yet he, the Creator, controls all the bodies of heaven, with full knowledge of each one, a power and wisdom beyond all human reckoning. Such power, so high; such concern for the lowly, and indignation against their oppressors (cf. 113.5f.)!

7–11 A more direct summons heralds a fresh burst of thankful praise, sent up on the melody of the lyres (Int. 3b). By his powerful work, the Creator provides the rain, and so the greening, the fruits and the crops, and so the food for the animals and for the vociferous young ravens (cf. my *Circle of Creation*, pp. 36, 40f.). Not in the fierce pride of war (the warhorses, the well-muscled infantry), but in the faith and humility of his worshippers does the Lord take delight.

12–20 Central in the festival is the Holy City (cf. 48, 76, 87, 122). She is now addressed and called to praise her God. For she owes her strong defences to him, and the blessing of all her children. Here the sense widens, for she is mother of all the faithful (87). In all her 'border', wherever these children live, he sends *shalom*, the abundance that springs from the harmony of humble people and nature. By his swift word, he commands the forces of growth – the snow, frost, hail, ice, streams. The sequence here suggests tradition from the mountains of Lebanon and Hermon, from which the snow and ice melt to give cascades of pure water to replenish the streams and rivers. By his word also, he revealed his law in Israel, cause again for rejoicing in Zion's congregation (cf. Deut. 4.7f.).

The psalm gives rich impressions of an experience of worship. How good to take part in it, how sweet to join in the music of praise and thanksgiving! The sense of encounter with the Creator and revealed Lord cannot be ordered in compartments. Here is rather a mingled excitement of being close to the one who is at the same time Creator and saviour, Lord of the stars and healer of broken lives. So the joyful worshippers acknowledge him almost in one breath as builder of the Holy City, the one who brings home the outcast, who exalts the downtrodden and abases the oppressors, who has no pleasure in the arrogance of war, who sends clouds, snow, ice and rain, fills springs and streams, turns hillsides green, feeds beasts and young birds, and who gave to Zion's children the special treasure of his Word, his guidance on the way of life and service. It is indeed a manifold experience, this fulfilment of a pilgrimage, but all revolves around the glory and lowliness of the Lord.

O God, who declared your Word in Jesus Christ, and are ever building your Holy City by bringing home the outcast and healing the broken-hearted, strengthen us with the delight of your praise, and grant us to be at peace with all the wonders of your creation.

PSALM 148: Precentors and Priests in the Cosmic Praise

1   Alleluia.
    Praise the Lord from the heavens,
    O praise him in the heights.
2   Praise him, all his angels,
    O praise him, all his hosts.
3   Praise him, sun and moon,
    praise him, all you stars of light.
4   Praise him, heaven of heavens,
    and you waters above the heavens.
5   Let them praise the name of the Lord,
    for he commanded and they were created.
6   And he established them for ever and ever;
    he gave them a law which they might not transgress.
7   Praise the Lord from the earth,
    you sea-monsters and all ocean depths,
8   fire and hail, snow and mist,
    stormy wind obeying his word,
9   mountains and all hills,
    fruitful trees and all you cedars,
10 you beasts, both wild and tame,

you creeping things and birds of the air,
11 kings of the earth and all you peoples,
    princes and all rulers of the earth,
12 young men and maidens,
    old people and children together.
13 Let them praise the name of the Lord,
    for his name alone is exalted, his glory over earth and heaven.
14 And he has raised up the horn of his people,
       a cause for praise from all his faithful,
    the children of Israel, a people close to him.

Of psalms which call all creatures into the circle of praise (96.9f.; 98.4f. etc.), this is the most detailed. First, the call to praise goes out to all in the heavens (vv. 1–4), and the grounds are that the Lord created them all by his word and ensured their continuing functions (vv. 5–6). Then the call is addressed to earth, with her waters, weather, mountains, trees, animals and peoples in their kinds (vv. 7–12), and the grounds are that his name and glory are exalted over all (v. 13). Finally (v. 14), these grounds are developed to include the strength he has given this people assembled in festal worship at his temple, 'close to him'. Such orderly listing of creatures has been thought to reflect the contemplative study of the universe in the Wisdom schools; another example might be Job 38–41, and more elaborate listing is evidenced from the work of Egyptian sages (cf. von Rad, p. 286). The date is an open question, and an early period could well be considered. A magnificent counterpart in the late period is found in the Apocrypha, the Benedicite or Song of the Three Holy Children.

1–6 The singer's call for praise goes first to the heavenly region (so also 29, which likewise ends with the strength given to the Lord's people). The heavenly beings (angelic servants and fiery hosts), sun, moon, stars (perhaps especially the planets, visible still in the morning 'light'), the highest heaven itself, and the ocean thought to rest on heaven's floor, the sky-vault or firmament, are all to sing praise to the name of the Lord. The grounds for praise (vv. 5b–6) are that he created them, so marvellously too by his word, and through his 'statute' gave them the way of their happy existence in the harmony of his cosmos.

7–13 The pattern of calls for praise and grounds for praise is now applied to the earthly region, which also includes the oceans and great creatures of the waters (cf. 104.26; Gen. 1.21), and also the atmospheric elements, where 'fire' may refer to lightning. As to living beings, the singer calls to the mountains and hills (the main constituents of his landscape), and to their trees, which will include olives and figs and the mighty cedars of Lebanon. Each element has its own way of singing the creator's praise, and to this great chorus is added the music of the animals, the reptiles and the birds. People of all nations, too, are addressed – sturdy young men and women, the frailer elderly and children; all are summoned to praise the Lord's 'name', his glorious self-revelation, the splendour of his unique godhead and supremacy over all, the heart of the worshippers' vision (cf. on 8.1). To behold this glory is reason enough for praise.

14   For the great chorus there is a precentor, a skilled singer who calls for each contribution. And for the universal host that worships the holy name there is a central group, a people called to stand close to the Lord and minister for the benefit of all. The psalmist does not distinguish them for a summons of their own, but develops the final grounds for praise to rest at last on the Lord's grace to this people: the raised 'horn', an image from the wild ox, indicates the strength and vitality he has given them (cf. 75.4; 89.17, 24; 92.10; 1 Sam. 2.1); like priests, they are called so to draw near that they may mediate for all his creatures (Ex. 19.6; cf. Num. 16.5; Jer. 30.21; Pss 65.4; 73.28).

Often in the Psalms we have met the belief that the creator holds everything that he has made in a relationship to himself, with a commitment of his faithful love. In this relationship all created beings are called to look to him in trust and praise. In the high moments of worship, when drawing near to the creator and seeing his glory bring vision of the ideal, this praising universe is real to the pilgrims gathered in the sanctuary. The psalmist's list of beings who are to sing praise to the name of the Lord may be judged but a slight indication of the innumerable identities in God's cosmos, but it is enough to burst the confines of narrow-minded, imagination-less worship. His vision does not ignore the salvation known in the smaller circle of God's people, indeed this may be taken as its climax. But those brought specially near are led to see the ultimate reach of the creator's faithful love and the cosmic congregation of his worshippers; they are given his holy strength that they may serve him in this great array, and their praises will only truly delight him when they are reconciled to creatures they have wronged, and so can lead the praises of all in the full sincerity of love.

Almighty Father and Creator, make us so close to you that we grow close to all your creatures, and ready to join in the hymn of all creation, to the praise of your glorious name.

PSALM 149: The Sword of Praise

1   Alleluia.
    Sing to the Lord a new song,
    his praise in the assembly of the faithful.
2   Let Israel rejoice in their maker,
    the children of Zion exult in their king.
3   Let them praise his name in the dance,
    and with drums and lyres make music to him.
4   For the Lord delights in his people,
    and adorns the humble with salvation.

5   Let the faithful exult with glory,
    and sing praises from their ranks,
6   with acclamations of God in their throat,
    as a two-edged sword in their hand,
7   to bring requital on the nations,
    and rebuke upon the peoples;
8   to bind their kings in chains
    and their nobles with links of iron;
9   to do among them the justice that is written;
    that will be glory for all his faithful.

Skilfully positioned, this takes up the theme of 148.14, and almost at the end of the Psalter, gathers up thoughts of God's great self-revelation and of conflict in his cause. It is a hymn in two parts. In vv. 1–4 we have a customary structure, with calls for praise (vv. 1–3) and reasons (v. 4). The second part (vv. 5–9) begins with a fresh call (vv. 5–6), but ends by describing the mission of the worshippers as God's soldiers (vv. 7–9). The setting is a great assembly of the covenant-people at Zion's sanctuary, and the principal festival, in the autumnal new year, is indicated by the references to the 'new song', the kingship of the Creator, the time of 'acceptance' (v. 4a) and salvation of the poor (v. 4b), the dancing and music, the rows of pallets (v. 5b), and the triumphal acclamations of God (v. 6a). The peculiar ending is probably due to the particular dramatic purpose. We have met elements of sacred drama in other psalms (the victorious ascent of the Lord, 24, 47, 68, 93; the defence of Zion, 46. 48; the installation and destiny of the Lord's Anointed, 2, 101, 110). In the present case, the worshippers rejoice in the salvation already signified in the ceremonies, and as God's army, look forward to the full realization of his kingdom across the world.

1–4 The 'new song' is one appropriate to the sacred time when all is made new; it greets the vision of God's perfected kingship and new creation that shines over the festal worship (cf. above on 33.3). It is a response to this revelation from the vast congregation of the *hasidim*, the pilgrims bound in the Lord's *hesed*, his covenant and commitment. They are 'Israel', 'children of Zion', and their rejoicing acknowledges the Lord in his work as Creator and king. It is expressed in dance (cf. 68.24f.; 118.27; 150.4) to the rhythm of hand-drums (tambours) and lyres (cf. Int. 3b). The Lord's 'delight' is his favourable acceptance of his people, probably with reference to the rites of penitence and atonement already accomplished. The new year brought hope for restoration of the downtrodden, and the whole people, waiting on the Lord in humility and lowliness, might be seen as the poor whom he would now raise up (cf. 18.27; 22.26).

5–9 A fresh call to praise introduces the second section of the psalm, where more details of the scene emerge, and the praise takes a particular direction. This people bound to the Lord and pledged to him are to exult in the glory of his present revelation, no doubt with the responding cries of 'Glory' (29.9). Their praises ring out from their places in the orderly lines of the vast assembly; these 'places' are more literally 'couches / pallets / beds', the clothes or mats where they rest or kneel during the many days and nights of the festival (Hos. 7.14; Amos 2.8). Their cries of homage to God the King form the *teru'a* (89.15), where no doubt many a guttural consonant (as in the rich sounds of Arabic) sounded from their 'throat'. It seems unlikely that all the worshippers at this point were literally brandishing double-edged swords; v. 6b rather expounds v. 6a – the praise is a veritable sword or battle-axe to subdue God's foes (cf. on 8.2; for the rendering 'as' rather than 'and' in v. 6b, a '*waw* adaequationis', see GK 161a and Seybold after Tournay). Plausible, however, is the common view that the ceremony included a sword-dance by special dancers in symbol of God's victory. The 'nations' appear in the figure of foes of God's kingdom, agents of chaos (cf. 2.1; 47.3). The divine 'requital', with capture and judgement of the leaders, signifies their complete repulse and submission. That the judgement is 'written' may refer to destinies decreed by God at the new year, though some explain it of written prophecies.

The martial language concluding this psalm echoes the biblical tradition of the Holy War, where the real combatant is the Lord who wars against evil, and all is done by his power, at his will, for his purpose. In the setting of the great pilgrimage festival, the spiritual aspect of this warfare is all the clearer; there is rejoicing that an earnest of the great salvation, the new creation, is given, and with it a vision of the fulfilment. The worshippers respond to this revelation of their king with dance, songs of praise and mighty acclamations. But they are summoned also to play their part in God's continuing campaign by sustaining their praise. As Psalm 8 spoke of God's little ones, albeit mere babes in this world, making with their praise a bulwark against the enemy and the avenger, so this present assembly of the poor – the humble and lowly before God – are called to overcome evil by the sword of their praise. The New Testament turns the battle yet more thoroughly into a spiritual conflict; 'the weapons of our warfare are not worldly' (2 Cor. 10.4) but rather 'the sword of the Spirit' (Eph. 6.17; Heb. 4.12). The psalm continues to call the Lord's people to the song acclaiming his new creation, the dance that witnesses to its joy, and the praise that responds to its light and reflects it with saving power on all that hinders God's kingdom.

Help us, Lord, to grasp the power not only of prayer, but also of praise, that we may overcome evils by lifting our hearts and voices in thanksgiving for your salvation and the sure hope of your world to come.

PSALM 150: The Greatest Symphony of All

1 Alleluia.
  Praise God in his holy dwelling;
  praise him in the firmament lit with his glory.
2 Praise him in his mighty acts;
  praise him in the greatness of his power.
3 Praise him with the blowing of the trumpet;
  praise him with the harp and lyre.
4 Praise him with the drums and dances;
  praise him with the strings and pipes.
5 Praise him with the cymbals for proclamation;
  praise him with the cymbals for acclamation.
6 Let every living thing
  praise the Lord. Alleluia.

Following the hymn of 'the sword of praise' (which also mentions instruments and dances), comes this further hymn, so concise, yet so abundant. Ten main calls to praise (using the imperative *halelu*, 'Praise ye') are increased to twelve by the opening and concluding *alleluias* and summarized in the last line with a different form (jussive *tehallel*, 'let it praise'). There are no lines devoted to reasons for praise, but this element of hymnic style is economically covered by the briefest indication of God's glorious epiphany and of his might as creator and saviour (vv. 1–2). Worshippers in the heavenly and earthly temples are summoned to praise; then, with some fullness, the variety of sacred musicians and dancers, and finally all creatures. This colourful poem surely existed first in its own right as a psalm for festal worship, before it came to serve as the seal of praise for the joyful sequence 145–9, for the fifth division of the Psalter (107–50), and for the whole book. There are no adequate clues to the period of origin.

1–2 The first call for praise goes out to worshippers in God's sanctuary; to judge from the parallel call (v. 1b), this refers primarily to his heavenly dwelling. But with this and its heavenly company (cf. 148.2), the earthly worshippers readily feel joined (cf. 148.7f.). (Judging again from the parallel call, the translation of v. 1a as 'Praise God in his holiness' is less likely.) Then the call goes to those in the sky-vault (v. 1b), namely sun, moon and starry hosts (cf. 148.3f.). This vault is called 'the firmament of his *'oz*', perhaps defining it as his 'fortress' (cf. 8.2), but more likely as radiant with the out-shining of his 'glory' (132.8), the manifestation of 'El', 'God' as Creator-King (cf. above on 19.7). His creatures are to praise him because of (perhaps 'by telling of') his wonderful acts of power and wisdom in creation and beneficent rule.

3–5 Further calls to praise bear more definitely on the worship in the temple courts, envisaging the main resources of the sacred music. The first instrument mentioned, the ram's horn trumpet, was especially used for sacred signals (new moons, sabbaths etc.), but had also an important role in the festal salutations greeting the Lord manifest in glory (47.5; 81.3; 98.4–6). In these celebrations, which were mostly processional, the portable harps and lyres carried much of the music. The dancers, especially young women, moved in processional dance with rhythmic tapping of their hand-drums or tambours. The 'strings' may comprehend forms of instruments additional to those of v. 3b, while the 'pipes' may be a kind of flute or be intended comprehensively for the woodwind. The two kinds of cymbals are those for 'proclamation' (lit. 'hearing', in festal worship perhaps in proclamations like 'The Lord is King') and for 'acclamation' (the *teru'a*, greeting the victorious Lord, cf. above on 89.15). The combination of such instruments is noted in the festal procession of 2 Samuel 6.5, and similar groupings are found in Egypt and Mesopotamia (an Assyrian stone-relief shows an Elamite marching band of fifteen singers, male and female, seven vertical harps, two double oboes, one horizontal harp and one drum, while a great array of musicians is envisaged in 2 Chron. 5.12f.; for instruments see Int. 3b).

6 In keeping with the psalm's economy of wording, the summarizing conclusion says much in few words. Much indeed, for it summons every 'breath', meaning every creature given life by God, to praise him. Concluding a psalm that has addressed all in the heavens and in the temple, symbolic centre of the universe, this last summons will be meant with all the scope of 96, 98 and 148. Every being in which the Creator has breathed his life (cf. Gen. 2.7) is to direct that life to him, rejoicing to know and behold him, to trust him, to honour his will, to testify to him and to exalt him above all else. The final alleluia ('Praise ye Yah') appropriately ends all with the short form of the name 'Yahweh', 'He That Only Is'. God the Creator ('El', v. 1), so utterly beyond the understanding of creatures, has given himself to them in grace to be known as their constant guide and helper, ever present to them in the name above all names.

So terse, this last of the psalms, and yet with more words than any other for the musical instruments! Enveloped in references to God's servants in the heavens and to every being in his cosmos, the musicians and dancers here will have a representative role. At the heart of the worship before God's face, they represent every voice in earth, seas and heavens. As horns are blown, frame-drums tapped, strings swept and plucked, pipes breathed and cymbals shivered, the sounds of nature come together – the praise of the waters and the winds, grasses and leaves, lions and birds, goats and oxen, mothers and children, and the circling, turning dancers represent the movement of the world round God, from him and to him again.

But this scene of highest joy is not characteristic of all the ancient worship; it was not a standard procedure whenever people gathered in God's name. The dramatic course of the festival, itself reached by a hard pilgrimage, passed through penitential abasement, depths of fear and sorrow, vigils of silence and hope, before such joy prevailed. In the Psalter itself, our ecstatic psalm stands at the end of a long story of tears and complainings, outnumbering the praises. But still it stands as the final testimony. Through all the pain and conflict, by the way of humility, trust and hope, of prayer and praise, the open gates are found, inviting to the cosmic celebration before the face of the one who at last has made all well in peace and love.

Almighty and gracious Lord, lead us through all doubts and sufferings into the world lit by your glory, that we may join with full heart in the music of all your creatures, in praise and thanksgiving to your holy name.

Appendix

Introduction

3 Psalm Music
Details, illustrations and bibliography for this section can be found in my article, 'Music's place in worship', and more generally in my *The Psalms Come Alive*. Vantoura's theory is worked out with confidence and enthusiam in her book of 1978. Braun notes the dearth of evidence in Palestine 586–333 BCE; he thinks the *nebel* was a large lyre. Terrien (p. 930) is sensitive to the Psalms as music; the music gives to praise a reconciling quality, and theology that is chanted receives the power of hope.

5 The Ancient Situations of Psalmody
On the Psalter's date of completion cf. Mowinkel, *Psalms* II, pp. 198–201. Theories of the purpose of the psalms of individual supplication and also details of festal ceremonies may be conveniently approached through my *Kingship* and my 'The Psalms and Israelite Worship'.

7 The Psalms down the Ages
Lamb traces the use of the Psalter through Jewish and Christian worship. Holladay's outline includes theological consideration. Useful also is the handbook of interpreters edited by McKim.

7b Division and order
Important stages in recent research into the arrangement of the Psalter are seen in the works of G. H. Wilson and the volume edited by J. C. McCann. D. C. Mitchell argues that the psalms were arranged to indicate an elaborate messianic scheme, involving the coming of the messianic king, his first works and death, the final victory and consummation. J.-M. Auwers provides an excellent synopsis of the spate of works on the literary composition of the Psalter.

7d The Dead Sea Scrolls
J.-M. Auwers, pp. 198f., lists 36 works on psalms from Qumran, including fundamental treatments by J. A. Sanders and more recently P. W. Flint. For translation of the Hodayot and for general discussion see G. Vermes, especially the major work of 1997.

7e Midrash and synagogue
There are some 41 references to psalm-passages in the Mishnah; see the index and text of Danby's excellent translation. Some useful details on rabbinic interpretation are given by Mitchell, pp. 28–33.

Psalm 1

Various opinions on this psalm are presented and assessed in my *Psalms of the Way*, including the notable treatment by the Jewish scholar Nahum Sarna.

[1] The expression for 'Happy . . .' (*asherey*) is most common by far in the Psalms, and next in the Wisdom books. It is not strictly equivalent to 'Blessed . . .' (*baruk*), although the meanings can be close; the ideas are parallel in Ecclus. 37.24, while in Jer. 17.7 (related to Ps. 1) the term is *baruk*, 'Blessed'. With *asherey* there is usually stress on some human conduct or attitude which is required for attainment of happiness. The expression is never applied to God, as *baruk* often is (in the sense 'thanked and praised'). The root of *asherey* points to the sense 'steps' or 'walking', and so to the idea of a happy way or life. The expression is an exclamation, holding up a kind of person or people as an enviable model. It was thus useful in teaching devout conduct. Terrien (p. 799) remarks that it is a dynamic expression, a send-off wishing someone a *bon voyage*.

[3] The Egyptian 'Teaching of Amen-em-Opet (around the time of the Hebrew monarchy; *ANET*, p. 422), compares the heated person – noisy, impatient, aggressive – to a tree growing in open country, exposed to heat and drought; its foliage quickly falls, and the trunk ends in the shipyard or on the fire. But the silent, contemplative person is like a tree tended in a secluded garden, waiting before its lord with sheltering leaves and sweet fruit in double yield.

[6] A hymn to Shamash the sun-god (from the library of the Assyrian king Ashur-bani-pal, seventh century; *ANET*, p. 388) praises him as universal upholder of justice; he helps the just who travel on a dangerous road, sail through fearsome seas, or track along unknown ways, but he spreads his great net for the evildoer, who will find no saviours against his weapon.

Psalm 2

For the oriental background and the views of several scholars, see my *Kingship*, pp. 87–134. Craigie describes the piece as a coronation psalm crafted with power and elegance; he discusses at length its use in the NT.

[12] The word that RV renders 'Son' (*bar*) is normal in this sense in Aramaic, but rare in Hebrew (Prov. 31.2), and though this meaning is preferred by the Syriac Version and the mediaeval Jewish scholar Ibn Ezra and suits the context, the abruptness of the unqualified noun tells against it. Preferable is Jerome, following Symmachus (cf. Aquila 'choicely'), taking the word as from the root 'to be pure' (*br*) and as used adverbially: 'purely, sincerely'. Many modern translations follow an ingenious conjectural emendation, reversing and merging the two surprising words (*gilu* and *bar*) to yield 'at his feet' (*beraglaw*). *LP* has deleted *bar* and rendered, not 'kiss', but 'govern yourselves', following an Arabic sense.

Psalm 3

While some think the royal language has here been adopted for a private citizen, Mowinckel is among those who maintain the literal sense; he thinks of a king on campaign, praying in the morning before battle. Craigie gathers all in his suggestion that the prayer was first David's, fleeing from Absalom, then used by other kings in military crises, then more generally for other citizens in morning worship.

Psalm 4

Kraus detects here the plight of a poor man hounded by people of wealth; after a favourable oracle at a sacred trial, he can sleep safely in the asylum of the sanctuary. But Broyles thinks the issue is communal: to which deity should the people look for produce?

[3] 'Wonderfully answers' (lit. 'acts wonderfully') follows the usual sense of the verb *pl'*; this fits the context better than the possible 'sets apart', from the similar root *plh*.

[4] 'Tremble' is the most likely sense, though LXX has 'be angry' ('if you get angry'), echoed in Eph. 4.26.

[6a] 'O that we might see' is the sense of the idiom 'Who will show us?'.

[6b] The translation is based on a change of vowels, suiting the parallelism.

Psalm 6

Johnson (*Prophet*, pp. 237f.) sees the psalm as the work of a cultic prophet who both voices a sufferer's need and mediates an answer.

[8] The 'voice of my weeping' may be an idiom for 'my weeping voice', but the literal rendering is powerful. Spurgeon remarks : 'Is there a voice in weeping? In what language does it utter its meaning? Why, in that universal tongue which is known and understood in all the earth, and even in heaven above ... Is it not sweet to believe that our tears are understood even when words fail? My God, I will weep when I cannot plead, for thou hearest the voice of my weeping.'

Psalm 7

One of those who prefer non-royal interpretations, Kraus thinks of the psalm as a formula used by accused persons who have to swear an oath of innocence at the temple; martial phrases would be but distant echoes of older royal psalms.

[4a] The verse could be rendered, 'If I have repaid one who did me wrong'.

[4b] I have followed the Aramaic sense 'plundered'; the usual Hebrew sense could give as RV, 'Yea, I have delivered him that without cause was mine adversary'.

Psalm 8

[1] I have accepted the view that *tnh* (RV 'hast set') is to be pronounced *tunnah*, passive of *tnh* 'to recite, chant'. I have taken *asher* not as 'whose' but in its basic role as connecting word, hence 'while'.

[2] I have taken 'babes and sucklings' as a hendiadys; one could find another in 'enemy and avenger', but the literal translation has good resonance. Other interpretations of the 'babes' include reference to the first cry of a baby, the cry of life. Some take the expression, after Ugaritic mythology, as denoting heavenly beings (cf. Dahood). Seybold would get rid of the babes altogether with emendation of *yoneqim* to *yonim*: 'away from the mouth of evildoers and oppressors'.

Psalms 9 and 10

Those who would see the psalmist as an individual commoner have a difficult task with these psalms. Gunkel thinks of a late author stumbling into a variety of thoughts and traditional elements as he struggles with the alphabetic scheme. Kraus thinks of a didactic development of the form of individual thanksgiving perhaps about the sixth century. Mowinckel says the speaker is evidently Judah's king who represents the people.

[10.3] 'In his greed' represents *boṣea'*, 'a greedy getter'.

[10.5] 'Brazen' represents *yaḥilu* in the sense 'be strong, stout'.

[10.10] The reading for 'crouches' is either *wedakah* or *yidkeh*; some revocalize as *dakeh* or *yiddakeh* with the subject being the poor as 'crushed' (cf. BDB, p. 194a).

[10.17] Sometimes translated 'You have heard ...', but the context favours a future

reference ('perfect of confidence', so NRSV). 'Fullness' represents revocalization of the inappropriate verb *takin* ('you will establish') to the noun *token*.

Psalm 11

Kirkpatrick argues confidently for the situation of David in Saul's court. Kraus thinks of a fugitive seeking refuge at the temple. Girard also describes the situation as a fairly clear case of recourse to the right of asylum. But Mowinckel sees here a king or later ruler when the country suffers from invading neighbours or nomads, and prayers are held in preparation for the conflict (cf. my *Kingship*, pp. 65f.).

[1b] We read *nudi* and link the *-km* to *sippor* (*BHS*).

[6a] The Hebrew actually has 'snares' rather than the similar word for 'coals'.

[7] The Hebrew rendered 'shall see' can be accepted as an old form of singular, preserving the root-letter *w*.

Psalm 12

[1] Spurgeon is eloquent on the short prayer 'Save, Lord', or as he has it, 'Help, Lord'. It is 'a kind of angel's sword to be turned every way, and to be used on all occasions. As small ships can sail into harbours which larger vessels cannot enter, so our brief cries and short petitions may trade with heaven ... when the stream of grace seems at too low an ebb to float a more laborious supplication.'

[5] For the last phrase Seybold accepts a suggestion of P. D. Miller (*VT* 29, 19, pp. 495f.) that *yapia'* is a noun, 'witness'; hence: 'I set in freedom, I am a witness for him'.

[6] 'To the ground' (or possibly 'from the clay' (Dahood) – some prefer an emendation: 'gold (*harus*) seven times purified'.

Psalm 13

In his analysis, Girard finds that vv. 5–6, contrary to first appearances, are closely integrated in the whole balanced structure. The parallelism of the whole puts side by side the complaint (vv. 1–2) and the confident supplication (vv. 3–6).

[1–2] From Babylon comes a copy (*ANET*, pp. 383f.) of a long lament to Ishtar, 'Goddess of goddesses, Queen of all peoples, the light of heaven and earth'. The supplicant repeatedly asks 'How long': 'How long, my Lady, shall my foes look upon me ... How long, my Lady, shall the crippled and weak turn on me ... How long, my Lady, will you be angered ... How long, my Lady, will you be enraged?'

Psalm 14

[7] While some have regarded this verse as a later addition that changes the bearing of the psalm, Girard is emphatic that his analysis demonstrates the unbreakable unity of the seven verses.

Psalm 16

[3] The verse is commonly rendered, straining the Hebrew, as NRSV: 'As for the holy ones in the land, they are the nobles in whom is all my delight.' This hardly suits the context or the usual sense of 'holy ones'. My rendering assumes an ellipsis: '... and the lords (of whom men say), All my delight is in them.' Cf. *LP*: 'As for those who are held holy on the earth, the other gods in whom people delight.' There is a similar expression for idols in Isa. 44.9, 'those in whom they have pleasure'.

[10b] Older English versions follow the tradition from LXX: 'You will not give your holy one to see corruption.' 'Corruption' is here a rendering derived from a root of similar sound (*sh-ḥ-ṭ*) and meaning 'to decay', but the actual root here, *shuḥ*, indicates 'depression, pit', the abyss of Sheol.

[11] Terrien (p. 181] aptly counts the singer among those psalmists who, by way of love, grew into a consciousness of infinity.

Psalm 17

[3b–5] My translation follows the probable structure of the Hebrew lines. A slight change supported by LXX is used to give 'evil purpose of mine' (*zimmati*), and *pariṣ* (usually 'violent') is rendered 'commandment' (so G. R. Driver, *JTS* 24, 1925, pp. 172f.). The traditional division of lines might be rendered thus: 'You shall try my heart when you visit me in the night; test me and you shall find nothing, for I resolved that my mouth should not transgress. As for the deeds of man, at the word of your lips I have kept guard on the ways of the violent. My steps have held to your paths; my footsteps have not stumbled.'

[8] The 'little one of the eye' is applied to the people in Deut. 32.10 and to Zion in Zech. 2.8. The customary rendering 'apple' of the eye refers to the eye's pupil, but is perhaps misleading. The image of the sheltering bird was similarly applied to kings by the Assyrians, Hittites and Egyptians (cf. *ANEP*, nos 377, 389).

[12] The verse begins 'His likeness is as a lion', but LXX ('They laid wait for me') indicates a better reading (*BHS*).

[14] I have read the first phrase as *mumetey miyyadeka*, and later *mumatim*. The (lit.) 'among the living' would indicate abrupt departure to Sheol. But if we retained the received vowels we could render: 'From men, by your hand, Lord, from men whose portion in life is endless, and whose belly you have filled with your riches, who have children in plenty and can leave their increase to their young.'

[15b] The verse ends (lit.) 'I shall be satisfied with your form'; 'form' here represents *temuna* (BDB, p. 568; *TWAT*, cols 687–680). The word is used in the prohibition of images (Ex. 20.4; Deut. 4.12f.; 5.8) and is probably more comprehensive than the companion term *pesel*. It is used of the form or appearance of Yahweh's manifestation in Num. 12.8 (where seeing it is a privilege restricted to Moses) and (probably of Yahweh again) in Job 4.16, where it is an indistinct nocturnal revelation. LXX renders it 'glory' (*doxa*) in Num. 12 and Ps. 17, and as 'form' (*morphe*) in Job 4.

Psalm 18

In favour of the sacramental understanding is the mythic character, so expansive and often didactic. There are similarities with several other texts which may also have come from ceremonies of this kind (118, 144; Zech. 9.9–10). Johnson (*Sacral Kingship*, pp. 117f.) champions this approach, while Mowinckel was among those who preferred to explain the psalm as thanksgiving after a battle (*Psalms* II, p. 254). See further my *Kingship*, pp. 113f., 129f.

It is through the sacramental approach that the psalm can be accepted still as a spiritual treasure, which would hardly be justified if the original reference had been to human victory. As noted, some translators (e.g. NRSV) prefer to render with many past tenses in vv. 32–48, believing this to be the more literal account of the victory put mythologically in vv. 4–19.

[50] The role of the Lord's Anointed as evangelical witness to all nations can be traced through Isa. 55.4; Pss. 57.8–11; 89.1 etc., and is treated in my *Kingship*, pp. 182–5. A similar theme is found in the religion of Mesopotamian kings.

Psalm 19

Scholars who have not accepted the unity of the psalm include Duhm, Gunkel and Westermann. Mowinckel fully recognized the differences between the two parts, but saw important continuity and totality of meaning resulting from the psalmist's use of an ancient hymn as his starting point. Spieckermann stresses that the psalm is built of four parts, and he considers that it is the last of these (vv. 11–14) which is an expansion. Those appreciating the unity of the psalm include Delitzsch, Dahood and Girard (who after close analysis says, 'The two sections are inseparable; they correspond one to the other. It is exactly their being put beside each other which gives the psalm its unique and profound significance'). For a range of views, see my *Psalms of the Way*.

[1–4a] A quite different interpretation from this is represented by old versions from LXX onwards, hence AV: 'There is no speech nor language where their voice is not heard.' Commentators (including Delitzsch and Baethgen) have then thought of the glorious sight of the heavens as speaking of God's glory to all of every tongue. This revelation through nature paralleled that through the moral law or the Gospel (cf. Rom. 1.20). My preferred rendering, however, with its elements of mystery and paradox, seems truer to the Hebrew and has been widely accepted since Gunkel's expositions. In v. 4a my translation 'their music' is based on the context concerning hymnic praise, and on a possible development of *qaw*, 'line, string' to 'chord, musical note'. Gunkel and Kraus compare Isa. 28.10, 13 for a meaning 'ecstatic sound, overflowing speech' (root *qy'*). Dahood prefers a sense 'call' based on root *qwh* II 'to collect' and perhaps occurring in 40.1; 52.9. All these suggestions are in line with LXX and Rom. 10.18 *phthongos*, 'sound, cry'. But some still prefer the sense '(measuring) line', as AV, RV (cf. Jer. 31.39), suggestive of the wide reach of the witness, or the measure and fine proportions of the great elements, or their 'rule' as they regulate times and seasons; none of these, however, seems so suitable for the context.

Psalm 20

Gunkel, Mowinckel and Craigie are among those who picture here a day of prayer before a specific battle; likewise Johnson (*Prophet*, pp. 175f.) with detailed discussion of v. 6. Those who prefer to think of royal inauguration include Duhm, Schmidt and Weiser. Cf. my *Kingship*, p. 131. Among Aramaic texts written in demotic script on a papyrus roll in Egypt *c.* fourth century BCE, one prayer appears to be an adaptation of our psalm and may have originated near Tyre (*TUAT*, pp. 930f.).

[6] A less obvious but viable translation may be borne in mind as a possibility: 'Then I shall know that the Lord saves his Anointed, when he answers him ... ' Though the first word, '*atta*, generally means 'now', there are seven passages where the reference is to the future (BDB, p. 774, 1c). The verb 'I know' easily refers to future, as does the next verb, *hoshia'*. This translation agrees better with the continuance of petition, v. 9.

Psalm 21

[8–12] Johnson (*Sacral Kingship*, p. 133) takes the passage as addressed to the Lord, but the third person reference in v. 9 is against this.

Psalm 22

[12] 'Pierce' follows textual evidence (*BHS*) for a verb *k'rw* or *krw*, 'they dig, pierce, wound' or 'they bind'. The main reading, *k'ry*, gives 'like a lion (at) my hands and feet'.

[17b] 'They' may mean the bones, or else the undefined adversaries of v. 18.

[18] The sharing out of the garments may be an image from the plundering of the dead in warfare.

[19] 'Help' is the word that may be found in the heading, where it is associated with the dawn.

[20] 'My poor life' is literally 'my only one', RV 'my darling', a term of affection and pathos for one's soul.

[21] The last word in the Hebrew, a perfect tense, could be as RV 'you have answered me', or better suiting the context (as precative perfect) 'do answer me', or again (perfect of 'confidence') 'you will surely answer me', in any case something of a bridge to the next section. Some emend the word (after LXX and Syriac, and for parallelism) to 'my afflicted one', *'aniyati*. Girard, however defends the Hebrew as of the greatest significance, the pivotal point of the whole structure of the psalm, situated exactly between the two sections.

[29–31] Such an effect in Sheol, the land of the dead, is seen as the utmost marvel. The dead are usually pictured as remote from remembrance and worship of Yahweh (115.17). But there are in the Old Testament glimpses of other views. According to 139.8f. Yahweh is present in Sheol, and in a passage not necessarily very late, Isa. 26.19, the dead are called on to arise and sing. There may be an influence in our psalm from Egyptian ideas, which picture the joy of the departed when the sun-god passes through the underworld, and Sethos I is praised as king upon the throne of Re, giving joy to the underworld through his counsels, awakening those who slumber, giving light to those in darkness (my *Kingship*, p. 203, n. 9). It seems unwise to destroy the exceptional thought of v. 29 by conjectural emendation (cf. *BHS*). More feasible, but unnecessary, is redivision of the opening letters to give 'Surely all those who prosper on earth will bow before him, all gone down to the dust will do reverence before him ...' The common emendation of 'all the living (lit. fat ones)' to 'all that sleep' (*yesheney*) suits parallelism but is unnecessary. The last clause of v. 30 in the Hebrew seems to mean 'and he who has not kept his soul alive'; the better sense, as above, has two small changes supported by LXX (*napsho* to *napshi, l'* to *lw*).

Psalm 23

Delitzsch thinks of this as an expression of trust by David during Absalom's rebellion, looking to return to Jerusalem. Mowinckel pictures a king or later leader at a special day of prayer before setting out on a dangerous journey or expedition (cf. Ezra 8.21f.). Others have thought of someone testifying at a meal of thanksgiving for asylum in the sanctuary or for acquittal in a sacred trial.

[3] Recent translations often have 'right paths', but the older rendering, 'paths of righteousness' shows a spiritual sense supported by usage of this idiom; cf. Prov. 4.11; 8.20; 12.28 for the way characterized by 'righteousness', and Ps. 118.19 for the gates which stand for righteousness and salvation. The phrase in 23.3 properly speaks of 'roads' suitable for a wagon, and so could allude to the procession of the Anointed, righteous and endowed with salvation (Zech. 9.9).

[4] The 'shadow of death' is a compound word, as recognized by LXX and the Hebrew vowels, and there need be no grammatical objection (see D. Winton Thomas, *JSS* 7, 1962, pp. 198f.). 'Shadow', not in itself sinister, probably denotes 'dominion' (cf. Judg. 9.15), and the psalmist envisages going into the chasm where death holds dominion.

[6b] Most translations have 'and I shall dwell', but the Hebrew is (lit.) 'and I shall return', often explained as short for 'return and dwell', to fit the context. Some prefer to change the vowel (to *weshibti*) to give 'and my dwelling / sitting enthroned'. 'For ever' is probably a fair understanding of the (lit.) 'for length of days' (cf. 21.4; 91.16).

Psalm 24

[6b] My translation follows LXX and is partly supported by some Hebrew manuscripts and the Syriac and Targum (*BHS*). The main Hebrew tradition seems to mean 'seekers of your face, Jacob', where 'Jacob' is in apposition, defining the seekers; but Dahood argues for it meaning '(seekers of) the Presence of Jacob', a divine title.

Psalm 26

Some have connected this psalm with a national emergency such as pestilence (Kirkpatrick). Others think of an accused individual come to trial in the temple (Int. 5b). Craigie thinks of general use at the entrance of pilgrims to the temple with a rite of handwashing. Mowinckel, after Birkeland, thinks of a leader accused and summoned by a foreign overlord, and here keeping a day of prayer before setting out.

[6] We could translate 'I will wash', but an actual rite of washing need not be intended here, in spite of the parallel reference to going around the altar. The ritual washing of hands for duties in the temple was a strict requirement (Ex. 30.17–21), but the phrase used here and in 73.13 gives a different orientation.

Psalm 27

Kirkpatrick thinks the psalm may well be Davidic. The probability that it is at least royal (Birkeland, Mowinckel) is accepted by Craigie. But Kraus sees the psalm as a formula for use of accused persons as they pass into the temple precincts for a sacred trial.

Psalm 28

Delitzsch notes links with 26 and 27, and connects with David and Absalom's revolt. Kirkpatrick connects with 26 and a threat of pestilence. Gunkel finds the lament of an individual troubled by sickness and false friends, vv. 8–9 being probably an addition to adapt the psalm to royal use. Kraus sees these verses as the psalmist's appreciation of grace given in the royal temple. Mowinckel takes as a king's prayer in sickness, when enemies see their opportunity. For Girard, vv. 8–9 are an integral part of the psalm, inseparable from its structure; the psalm is a prayer of a king who, receiving answer for his own needs, persists in prayer for all his people – he is a model of the Atlas figures, blessed in their own freedom, but willing to bear the load of praying for all.

[9] The Te Deum, as familiar from BCP, follows the Vulgate in v. 9b, 'Govern them and lift them up for ever' (*et rege eos et extolle eos* . . .). Here and in Ps. 23 (*Dominus reget me*, 'The Lord rules / directs me') the Latin, while losing the force of the image of shepherd, well brings out the reference to the role of ruler or king.

Psalm 29

The setting and point of the psalm are well grasped by Mowinckel and a treatment on the same lines is given by Johnson (*Sacral Kingship*, pp. 62f.). Not so differently, Kraus thinks of a high moment in the festival when the Lord's kingship was proclaimed and honoured in general obeisance. But Briggs, like many before him, finds simply a description of the Lord's advent in a storm. Craigie suggests the storm is a metaphor for warfare, as the army returns from a victory. Gunkel is inclined to accept the view that v. 11 is a later addition, while Seybold goes further in detecting stages of growth. Girard champions the unity of the structure, a masterpiece of architectural skill.

Psalm 30

[5] An Egyptian thanksgiving to Amun says, 'If the servant is disposed to sin, the Lord is disposed to mercy; the Lord of Thebes is not angry a whole day long . . . it is but a moment, and nothing of it remains' (*TUAT*, p. 874, *ANET*, p. 386).

Psalm 31

Mowinckel joins those who interpret of a king (cf. my *Kingship*, pp. 67f.). Some older commentators thought of David in the wilderness (1 Sam. 23.25f.), while Kirkpatrick, because of certain phrases, opted for Jeremiah. Kraus suggests a general use for those seeking asylum and justice in the temple. Seybold finds stages of growth around the kernel, a sick person's prayer. But Girard insists on an original unity; all holds together as a perfectly crafted edifice.

[11a] 'Burden' may be the sense of a noun *ma'od*, instead of the received text *me'od*, 'exceedingly'; Dahood redivides to obtain *ed*, 'calamity'.

Psalm 32

Gunkel (taking vv. 8–9 as counsel from the psalmist) stressed the Wisdom elements, comparing Job's counsellors, who linked suffering with unconfessed sin. Kirkpatrick (who gives reasons for taking vv. 8–9 as speech of God) sustains the view that David composed the psalm to fulfil his promise in 51.13. Johnson (*Prophet*, pp. 296f.) thinks a cultic prophet speaks in the psalm, first for a successful suppliant, and then as the Lord's spokesman

[8–9] The untrained steeds do not 'heed' their owner; for this sense of *habin* cf. BDB, p. 107a. The deplorable rendering 'which have no understanding' is contrary to fact and the Old Testament's appreciation of the gifts of animals (cf. my *Circle of Creation*). Gunkel is perhaps too attached to his classification of Wisdom psalm when he accepts that vv. 8f. is a sage's address to his disciples (the 'eye' then suggests comparison with 2 Kings 8.11; Luke 6.10; Acts 3.4; 13.9). Such a sudden prominence of the relation of sage and disciple would seem to unbalance the psalm.

Psalm 33

[6] From *c.* 1300 comes an Egyptian hymn to the creator (*ANET*, p. 371); he 'spoke with his mouth, and there came to be all mankind, all gods, all large and small beasts, and all that flies and alights.'

Psalm 34

[8] Cassiodorus, relating 'O taste and see' to communion, explains that 'see' refers to contemplation; almost as if composed in Christian times, the psalm follows the order of the Mass – the hymns, the summons to communion, the invitation to those undertaking their first instruction.

Psalm 35

The legal nuance of some phrases disposes Kraus, but with misgivings, to follow the theory of a private individual slandered and persecuted, and seeking judgement in the temple. Kirkpatrick advances points favouring the traditional link with David, persecuted by Saul. My interpretation is like that of Birkeland and Mowinckel (cf. my *Kingship*, pp. 41f.); Craigie agrees and adds points about near-eastern treaties.

[15–16] The rendering 'smiting' (*nekim* or perhaps *nokim*) follows Jerome's *persecutientes*. 'Unawares' refers to the victim who cannot see blows coming; for the (lit) 'and I knew not' a disputed theory of D. Winton Thomas (*TRP*) about this verb would give an alternative: 'and I had no rest'. Some prefer to take *nekim* as passive, 'smitten ones, outcasts', but others emend to *kenokrim*, 'as strangers'. Craigie has 'oppressors', citing the Qumran reading

'*tkym*', which however may rather signify 'injuries', so LXX, *mastiges*. 'When I tripped' is based on an Arabic sense (*TRP*). For 'circle', *ma'og*, cf. Dahood.

Psalm 36

[1–2] In v. 1a 'his heart' is read by a few mss. The main tradition has 'my heart', and hence BCP 'My heart sheweth me the wickedness of the ungodly'. In v. 2b text and translation are dubious.

Psalm 37

[28b] ('They shall be guarded for ever'); many translators emend on the basis of LXX to achieve a clearer alphabetic sequence (*BHS*): 'wrong-doers shall be destroyed for ever'.

[36] 'I went by' (against the Hebrew 'He went by') is supported by LXX, Syriac, Jerome and a Qumran ms. (Craigie).

Psalm 38

[19] RV makes from the Hebrew 'my enemies are lively and strong', but instead of 'are lively', there is support from Qumran for the expected phrase 'without cause' (*hinnam*, as in 35.19; 69.4; see Craigie).

[22] Extra words occur before this verse in part of LXX's tradition, 'and they have cast me away, the Beloved, like an abhorred corpse', and Bar Hebraeus attests a Coptic reading, 'he has nailed my flesh'.

Psalm 39

Craigie sees this psalm as arising from 'the reflective consciousness of old age', any ailments being incidental. He describes some parts as 'meditation' and concludes the psalm is 'a private song of a literary, non-cultic nature.' Kirkpatrick thinks it is a sequel to 38, the psalmist being still near to death.

[6] 'They are in turmoil' (or 'they bustle about') is plausibly emended by some to 'wealth' (*hamon*): 'Surely in vain he heaps up wealth' or 'the wealth he heaps up is a breath'.

Psalm 40

Gunkel represents the view that two independent psalms have been joined together; the psalmist is a devotee of the Tora, read in the spirit of the great prophets, and v. 12 is a bridging verse composed when vv. 13–17 were added. Kraus indeed is so convinced of the original independence of vv. 1–11 that he does not treat vv. 12–17 till he comes to Ps. 70. Weiser has a strong feeling for the unity of the psalm and the significance of the tension between the two sections. Several scholars take the psalmist to be a king (my *Kingship*, pp. 42f.), not least Johnson (*Prophet*, pp. 399f.).

Psalm 41

Gunkel takes the psalm to be a thanksgiving, but finds it difficult to explain v. 1 and drastically emends it; he thinks it can only be described as a sin that some have taken the speaker to be 'Israel'. Seybold sees in the psalm the testimony of a healed person, who from the experience of recovery is now hopeful for a good outcome against the enemies; the citation of the earlier lament renews the prayer against the foes. For

Mowinckel the psalmist is a sick ruler, but post-exilic (cf. v. 9 with Neh. 5.17f.). Craigie thinks of a liturgy used when a sick person came to the temple for healing. Delitzsch maintains the view that David prays with reference to Absalom and Ahitophel.

[1a] *Maskil* sometimes means 'give attention to' (so Neh. 8.13), but the reference here must be to action; often it is used of the wise and ideal actions of kings (my *Kingship*, pp. 45, 204 n. 24). The expression is thus not as difficult here as Gunkel and others have found it.

Psalms 42/43

For Goulder (*Korah*, pp. 23f.) Pss 42–3 belong to a national pilgrimage of the Northern Kingdom to Dan by Jordan's springs; beneficent waters sweep 'by me'. Craigie inclines to the spiritual plight of some unknown individual. Kirkpatrick sees the author as a Korahite Levite yearning for the temple services.

Psalm 44

Kirkpatrick argues for the royal period, when the nation had independence and was accustomed to send out armies. Delitzsch, from resemblance to 60, favoured David's time. Gunkel rejects Maccabeean datings and favours the later Persian period.

Psalm 45

Kirkpatrick argues for the house of David, and thinks of Solomon's Egyptian marriage. Goulder (*Korah*, pp. 121f.) favours Ahab and Jezebel in the north, while Gunkel is not averse to Jereboam II. Baethgen argues in detail against a purely allegorical interpretation.

[6a] The verse by itself would more obviously mean 'Your throne, O God, is for ever and ever'; so LXX and consequently Heb. 1.8. But in this address to the king, it is improbable that he would be called 'Elohim', suggested parallels being inadequate. Dahood takes the word for 'throne' as a verb: 'God has enthroned you'. Seybold follows an old theory that 'Elohim' replaced 'Yahweh' which was a corruption of *yhyh*, 'shall be': 'Your throne shall be for ever and ever.'

[12] Some render 'daughter of Tyre' and think the queen is a Tyrian princess (Goulder: 'And do thou homage to him, daughter of Tyre'). But the phrase is better understood as (lit.) 'Daughter Tyre' (cf. 'Daughter Zion'), the city personified.

Psalm 46

Kirkpatrick affirmed that Psalms 46–8 could not be merely general expressions of confidence in God's protection of Zion; writing before Mowinckel's work, he sought the particularity in the withdrawal of the Assyrians from Jerusalem in 701 (2 Kings 18.13f.). Goulder (*Korah*) finds a festal setting at Dan.

Psalm 47

For the struggle over the years to understand psalms of this type, with their 'realized eschatology', see my *Psalms of the Way*, pp. 116–26. Craigie still thinks of victory hymns which have developed into general praise of God's kingship, while Seybold attempts to explain the new reign as on the model of a king's visitation. Girard regards the psalm as a jewel of the structural art.

Psalm 48

Some found here a historical deliverance of Jerusalem, and Sarna (pp. 151f.) still thinks that the most probable of the proposed situations is the withdrawal of Sennacherib in 701. Mediaeval Jewish scholars (Saadia, Rashi, Kimhi) took the reference to be to an eschatological event, and this is also the view of Gunkel. Among those following Mowinckel on lines as above are Bentzen and Johnson (*Sacral Kingship*, pp. 85f.); the latter well grasps the point of v. 9, rendering 'we have pictured thy devotion' but explaining that the context shows that what is meant is 'a ritual performance or acted picture of a piece with the prophetic symbolism but on the grand scale'. Goulder (*Korah*, pp. 159f.) argues for another psalm from Dan (cf. above on 42) and treats the references to Zion as clumsy alterations of the original. Seybold also is inclined this way.

Two passages in the Mesopotamian Epic of Gilgamesh suggest how ancient is the poetic tradition behind this psalm. When reference is made to the hero's building of the ramparted wall of the city Uruk and its pure and holy sanctuary, we are bidden, 'Behold its outer wall, whose cornice is like copper; peer at the inner wall, which none can equal; seize upon the threshold which is from of old; draw near to the dwelling of Ishtar, which no future king, no man, can equal; go up and walk on the walls of Uruk, inspect the base terrace, examine the brickwork' (*ANET*, p. 73, cf. p. 97).

Psalm 49

The psalm is difficult, both for its textual problems and its line of thought. Scholars generally discern a situation of oppression by the wealthy and take the teaching to be that, while these arrogant ones are destined for doom, the psalmist as representative of the faithful poor hopes for a better fate; according to most, the hope (v. 15) is beyond this life, but others restrict it to this life, as generally in the Old Testament. Gunkel prefers to treat vv. 10 and 15 as later additions. Goulder (*Korah*, pp. 181f.) stands apart as taking the psalm to be a continuation of the Korahite festal psalms; there is a national fear of invasion, and the psalmist on behalf of the king warns aggressors while hoping for salvation in this world for king and people. On this view, we might add, an apparently ethical discourse would have an implied political reference rather as in Hab. 1–2. Seybold takes the psalm as a thanksgiving-testimony, vv. 5 and 15 echoing the earlier supplication.

Psalm 50

Gunkel thought the author was a post-exilic disciple of the great prophets, boldly denouncing sacrifice as such, and he rendered v. 14 'Offer to the Lord a song of thanks'. From Mowinckel onwards the setting in worship has been more appreciated. Johnson (*Prophet*, pp. 24f.) sees here an example of the role of prophets in worship and also notes the symbolism of the rising sun 'which figured so prominently' in the autumnal festival during the monarchy. Craigie indeed suggests that the psalm was used at dawn on a day for renewing the covenant – 'the actual sacrifices and fulfilment of vows still lay before them (v. 14), as did the formal recitation of covenant statutes (v. 16)'; it was an occasional part of the Feast of Tabernacles (cf. Deut. 31.10–11). For comparable material in the Prophets see my *Vision in Worship*, pp. 40f.

Psalm 51

Theodore of Mopsuestia (Int. 7g) took the psalm to speak for Israel in the Exile. Baethgen was among several moderns who upheld the communal interpretation, and he took the whole psalm as a unity, verses which apply to the individual (6, 10 etc.)

being easily taken up by the individuals that make up the community. Against such collective interpretation, Gunkel portrays an individual pouring out his soul, seeking relief from sickness (v. 8) and a guilty conscience – a post-exilic psalm, with vv. 18–19 being a still later addition. Johnson (*Prophet*, pp. 412f.) advocates David's authorship in the crisis at Mahanaim with news awaited from the battle; highly individual, the psalm still alludes to features of the royal calling; vv. 18–19 are an addition, but harmonious with the preceding thought. Mowinckel (and cf. *Psalms* II, pp. 17f.) finds a unity throughout; he suggests it was written for Nehemiah as head of a community under judgement. Dalglish examined the psalm at length comparing Akkadian texts; he concluded for a king's prayer, probably Josiah's, vv. 18–19 being an exilic addition. A situation in rites of atonement led by the king is advocated in my *Kingship*, pp. 71f. Other views are mentioned in an expansive treatment by Tate. Goulder (*Prayers*) proposes links with David throughout 51–72; for 51 the heading is right.

Psalm 52

Gunkel classed this as a variation of the Laments of the Individual; so incensed is the psalmist that, rather than lament, he assails his adversary with imprecation; it illustrates party strife in the late period. Tate thinks of internal strife among the temple personnel, the psalm speaking for prophets or priests under attack from opponents. Bentzen (*Sakrale Kongedømme*, p. 87) pictures a king challenging and threatening his foe. Mowinckel thinks of a leader who, with prophetic force, counters cursing and war propaganda which the foreign foe has already launched.

Psalm 54

Kraus follows those who find here a setting in sacred trials for accused persons (Int. 5b). But Dahood is impressed by similarities with 20 and 86 and thinks the poem 'distinctly emerges as the supplication of a king for deliverance from his foreign enemies'. Johnson (*Prophet*, pp. 359f.) says 'the fact that so many works of this type have proved to be royal psalms makes it likely that here again we should think of the suppliant as a king.' Mowinckel sees here a leader of Israel facing foreign foes and uttering a 'protective prayer', a type directed against an imminent peril.

Psalm 55

An old view, found already in the Targum, that the psalm reflects Ahitophel's treachery (2 Sam. 15.31f.) is examined and rejected by Kirkpatrick, not venturing beyond this conclusion. Baethgen gives details of those who opted for the Maccabean period (cf. 1 Macc. 7.9–25) but he thinks the evidence insufficient; he affirms that the psalmist speaks not just for himself but also for companions. Gunkel thinks an original psalm, vv. 1–18b, 22, has been joined to a fragment from another, vv. 18c–21, 23; both pieces related to treachery but otherwise do not accord. Kraus follows, but puts v. 22 with the second piece. Mowinckel sees a king (or later leader) facing war or rebellion and representing his community on a day of prayer. Goulder (see above on 51) relates to David's flight from Absalom.

[18] Some revocalize the word for 'many' to give 'archers'.

[19] It is possible that the words of the first two lines should be read as designations of Arabian tribes: 'Ishmael, and the tribes of the desert, and the dwellers in the east' (Gunkel after Ehrlich emended the second phrase to give 'Yaalam', Gen. 36.5f.). If indeed such tribes are intended, the situation might have been like that reported in Assyrian records, when Hezekiah was deserted by contingents of auxiliary troops.

Psalm 56

Gunkel classifies the psalm as the lament of an individual, but having echoes of expressions in royal psalms; the psalmist was in the dispersion, oppressed by the heathen. The headings of LXX and Targum reflect a national interpretation, and Briggs saw here a late pre-exilic national prayer. Mowinckel takes the voice to be that of the community's ruler in a national crisis, the hostile words being curses and propaganda. Dahood describes the psalm as 'the lament of a king, who prays for deliverance from slanderers'. Johnson (*Prophet*, pp. 331f.) likewise sees a Davidic king, his rule threatened from across the borders.

Psalm 57

Kraus thinks royal elements have here been taken into common use; following Schmidt and Beyerlin, he pictures an accused person held with his accusers in the sanctuary through the night under ordeal, then acquitted at dawn; he also suggests the psalm was a formula often used in such cases. Mowinckel thinks of a leader turning to protective prayer as enemies approach. Dahood finds here the lament of a king harassed by slanderers, and he disparages the view of Kraus.

Psalm 58

Baethgen takes the psalm as sarcastically addressing overlords, whether Babylonians, Persians or Hellenistic Syrians. Kirkpatrick thinks human judges are addressed, but favours an internal situation in the royal period, such as concerned the great prophets. Gunkel, closer to 82, thinks the 'gods', heavenly powers in charge of foreign nations, are first addressed, and then in vv. 3f. reference is made to their human servants; finally, the action of the Most High is envisaged, when the intermediary gods will be dispensed with. Kraus develops this view.

Psalm 59

Many remark on the difficulty of relating the personal and international features, and Kirkpatrick wonders if a Davidic psalm has been adapted for 'liturgical use'. Kraus endeavours to envisage a fugitive seeking asylum, waiting through the night for God's verdict in the morning. Mowinckel takes the singer to be a king or similar leader facing invasion and threats against the capital. Dahood calls the psalm a royal lament complaining of national foes in battle array and of domestic defamers like prowling dogs. Goulder (*Prayers*) has David beleaguered on a hilltop by the rebels.

Psalm 60

Gunkel prefers a date after 587 and takes v. 9 to allude to a proposed flight to Edom; he thinks the oracle quoted from tradition and dating from about Josiah. Mowinckel dates the psalm to the monarchy, perhaps Joram's reign (2 Kings 8.20f.) or Amaziah's (2 Kings 14.7) or Uzziah's (2 Chron. 26.2). Johnson (*Prophet*, pp. 165f.) thinks of some defeat by Edom in the royal period and suggests the oracle is quoted as an appeal to God (cf. 89.19f.).

Psalm 61

Gunkel thought vv. 6–7 a badly positioned addition; the main psalm, uttered by an individual abroad, came into use at the royal temple and was adapted. Kraus suggests the intercession for the king is original even if a change of topic, and compares Babylonian usage. Seybold thinks of Persian times, with vv. 6–7 a prayer for the Persian king (though Gunkel ruled this out 'for a certainty'); otherwise we might emend *melek* 'king' to *mal'ak* 'messenger', a self-designation of the psalmist as priest. But Kirkpatrick sees David praying throughout, using third person in vv. 6–7 to claim promises of kingship as such; the reversion to first person in v. 8 is then natural, but otherwise would be harsh. Mowinckel also finds a king throughout. Likewise Dahood, illustrating the royal style. Johnson (*Prophet*, pp. 352f.) agrees and suggests the actual composer and singer is a cultic prophet. The Targum takes vv. 6f. of 'the King Messiah', while Rashi thinks of David throughout.

[5] NRSV 'heritage' follows the usual sense of *yerusha*, but here the sense is probably the same as that of the similar word in 21.2b, 'request' (*TRP*). The tenses in v. 5 could be rendered 'You have heard, you have granted', but the context may be better suited by sustaining the note of petition through vv. 5–7.

Psalm 62

Kraus, following Beyerlin, reads from the expressions for refuge the situation of an asylum-seeker; he thinks of a formulary used in the interval between the granting of asylum and the final oracle of acquittal. For Seybold also the psalm comes from the asylum situation, where a hunted person is reproaching the pursuers; but Seybold finds the present text to be the result of later changes. Kirkpatrick considers Davidic authorship, the enemies being Absalom's forces. Mowinckel, after Birkeland, thinks of a king or other leader troubled by hostile kings or by overlords and their officers; against the threat of a punitive expedition this is a protective psalm in that part of the fast-day's ritual called 'Confession'. For Goulder (*Prayers*), David is here besieged in Mahanaim.

Psalm 63

In a Qumran fragment the psalm is joined to 62. The series 61–4 certainly has inner links and is described by Tate as a sub-group within the Davidic collection (51–71). Gunkel could not see logical order in 63 and rearranged the verses, separating v. 11 as an addition. Oesterley, content with the text, thought of an exile in Babylonia ending with prayer for fellow-exile Jehoiachin. Kraus explains as he did for 61, and Seybold as for 62. Kirkpatrick declares that the connection at the end would be unintelligible unless the king there mentioned is identical with the psalmist whose enemies are to be destroyed. Mowinckel thinks the situation the same as he found for 62, the king now preparing for sleep at the sanctuary. Dahood finds a heavenly hope; a king longs to escape this life's troubles and have the beatific vision in the heavenly sanctuary. Johnson (*Prophet*, pp. 276f.) finds here 'a perfectly intelligible royal psalm' with cultic prophet as author and singer for the king; a theophany has already been given, and thanks are offered for its assurance of coming deliverance. Goulder (*Prayers*) remains with David in Mahanaim.

[10] 'They shall be delivered': I follow an emendation as *BHS*. Johnson renders the Hebrew text: 'Those who would hand him over to the sword will be left for jackals to share', but 'him' is awkward in advance of its noun 'king'.

[11] 'Swear by him': 'him' refers to God, to judge from the balance of the Hebrew (cf. Deut. 6.13; 10.20; Isa. 45.23; 48.1). But swearing by the life of the king is also possible (Gen. 42.15f.; 1 Sam. 17.55; 25.26; 2 Sam. 11.11; 15.21) and relevant as a sign of loyalty.

Psalm 64

Kraus takes vv. 1–2 as the prayer of one seeking asylum, and vv. 3–6 as description of the persecutors; but he translates vv. 7–10 as accomplished action – in thanksgiving the psalmist narrates God's intervention. Tate observes that there is little evidence for an asylum setting, but there are signs of a community-leader. Mowinckel sees the psalmist as 'a high-standing person' and Goulder (*Prayers*) links with David.

Psalm 65

Opinion divides over the tenses. Some understand from vv. 12–13 that the growth is present, and so think of first-fruits brought at Passover (Lev. 23.10f.). Others argue for the autumn and render as a mixture of thanks for the past year and hope for the new one. Dahood firmly takes vv. 9–13 as prayer for rain. Tate agrees that v. 10 (with imperatives) is a prayer and a key verse; he entitles the psalm 'Prayer for rain and the bounty of the year'. Some manuscripts of LXX and Vulgate add to the heading 'A song of Jeremiah and Ezekiel and the people of the sojourning, when they were about to set forth'. Another Latin heading is 'A song of Jeremiah and Haggai concerning the word of travel when they were about to set forth' – here the psalm has been taken as forward-looking, anticipating a coming to Zion and a time of salvation.

[1] Rashi explains: 'Silence is praise for you because there is no end to your praise, and whoever multiplies your praise, only, so to speak, detracts from it' (see Gruber). LXX renders 'Praise befits you' (cf. NRSV 'is due to you'), but this is a dubious sense (being derived from the verb *dmh* II 'to resemble').

Psalm 66

Between the two main parts (vv. 1–12, 13–20) Kirkpatrick finds a similarity of situation (vv. 9f., 14f.) and of style (vv. 5, 8, 16) which favours the unity of the psalm; perhaps Hezekiah here gives thanks at the Passover for the Assyrian withdrawal. Gunkel also appreciates the unity; the parts on their own would be torsos; he thinks of some wealthy figure who sets his personal thanks in a context of festal celebration. Kraus proposes that the first part originated at Gilgal commemorating the ancestral crossing of the Jordan; the second part is the thanksgiving of an individual after personal trouble, and it is not clear whether this individual or a redactor joined the pieces. Seybold considers the psalm an extract from liturgy at the fulfilment of vows; from v. 8 on we hear a variety of testimonies. Bentzen finds a king whose fate is bound up with the nation's. Mowinckel agrees and suggests the thanksgiving follows repulse of some national invader. Goulder (*Prayers*) continues his link with David.

Psalm 67

Spurgeon takes v. 6a as anticipatory, best rendered with future tense. Delitzsch thinks the psalm's mood is towards the future, though v. 6 indicates that growth has begun well ('Earth has given her fruit'). Kraus finds a prayer for fulfilment of the Aaronite blessing (Num. 6.24f.) heard earlier in the worship; vv. 6–7 are 'demonstrative', the desired blessing being already perceived. Tate agrees the psalm is more likely a prayer than a thanksgiving. Dahood consistently translates the psalm to express wish and prayer. Seybold takes vv. 6–7 to be an acknowledgement that earth has given its yield, and then prayer that something greater may follow, with the worship of all peoples.

Psalm 68

W. F. Albright showed the linguistic relation to older Canaanite poetry, but took our text to be only a catalogue of 30 'first lines' of poems – for this see Dahood, who continued the philological exploration, but was able to appreciate the unity of the psalm as a triumphal hymn in mythopoetic language. Coherent exposition in a festal context is given also by Johnson (*Sacral Kingship*, pp. 77f.). Basic bibliography is given by Seybold, who considers the psalm only the torso of an earlier acrostic.

[4–6] An Egyptian hymn from *c.* 1300 declares that widows say to the creator, 'You are our husband', and children say 'Our father and mother!' Rich and poor praise him; the sick cry to him. Plants turn towards him to be beautiful (*ANET*, pp. 371f.). A Hittite king's praise of the sun-god says 'You are father and mother of the dark earth' . . . of those hurt and orphaned; and he judges the cause of dog and pig and all animals that cannot speak with their mouth (*TUAT*, pp. 796f.).

[13] 'Hearth-stones' represents a little-known word which some render as 'sheep-folds', others 'donkey-panniers'. Other interpretations of the 'dove' see it as a figure for Israel (cf. 74.19) or a metal image as an example of the spoil. But the release of birds at festivals in sign of the divine sovereignty is known as an Egyptian practice (Lipiński, p. 446; Keel).

[17] Dahood follows Albright in explaining *shin'an* as 'archers' (rather than 'twice-over', BDB, p. 1041): 'God's chariots were twice ten thousand, thousands the archers of the Lord.'

[22] Lit. 'From Bashan I will bring back', and one may find here reference to the heights of Hermon and assume the object is the enemy. Dahood follows Albright in explaining *bashan* as 'the serpent', but this does not altogether suit the context.

Psalm 69

Kirkpatrick envisages Jeremiah as author in royal Jerusalem; he opposes the idea that the final verses are a liturgical addition. Mowinckel finds a king or later leader, defeated by invaders and made to pay indemnities; on a day of prayer and fasting, the 'time of favour', the psalm was recited over lilies from which an oracle was sought. Johnson (*Prophet*, pp. 386f.) sees a cultic prophet speaking for a defeated king. Tate reports many opinions and praises an analysis by Allen favouring the integrity of the psalm. Tillmann finds three stages of growth: a formula for the accused (vv. 1–4, 13b–18, 30–3; the prayer of a bitter invalid soon after the Exile (adding vv. 5–13a, 19–29); and the prayer and praise of the restored community (adding vv. 34–6).

[10a] 'Afflicted' represents, with change of vowels, a causative sense of *bkh*, so 'caused to weep'; Dahood proposes the root as *nbk*, like *npk* 'poured out'. For v. 12a he suits the context with a suggestion from Ugaritic: 'those who sit at a feast, feasters'; he sees that in the Hebrew syntax the verb is in v. 12a ('made, uttered') and its object ('songs') in v. 12b, while the double subject is divided between the two lines.

Psalm 70

Terse urgency is found also in a letter-prayer of King Zimri-lim of Mari (*c.* 1782–59 BCE): '. . . may my Lord not be neglectful in the protection of my life. May my Lord not turn his attention elsewhere. May my Lord not have need for any but me' (*TUAT*, p. 754; *ANES*, p. 627).

Psalm 71

Baethgen was among those taking the suppliant to be Israel. Mowinckel thinks of a king's protective prayer against political foes. Kraus sees here an asylum-seeker, old, sick, accused; but the piece is a formulary for use whenever appropriate. Tate has mistaken my view in *Kingship*, pp. 54–5, 130. Goulder (*Prayers*), uniting 70 and 71, has the aged David troubled in the rising of Adonijah.

Psalm 72

The Targum illustrates how such royal texts were applied after the end of the monarchy to the Messiah, future Saviour; v. 1 is rendered: 'O God, give the precepts of your judgement to King Messiah, and your justice to the son of King David.' An Egyptian hymn (*c.* 1300) celebrates Pharaoh's accession, which brings life, prosperity and health; right banishes wrong, the Nile's waters rise and the people live in laughter and wonder (*ANET*, p. 378).

[15] The Hebrew begins with a singular verb, but RV and others see this is best taken collectively, reverting to the collective singulars of vv. 12–13. The verse then continues with three more collective singulars, which can be translated quite naturally as above. Instead of 'more than Arabia's gold', we could understand a metaphor: 'and they shall give him of Arabia's gold indeed, for they shall pray continually for him'.

Psalm 73

Gunkel calls this psalm an instructional poem (*Lehrgedicht*) taking the form of a narrative of the author's personal struggle and using a theme developed in the later Wisdom teaching. Mowinckel found here a personal thanksgiving for insight, and from Wisdom circles. Engnell and Würthwein judged the psalmist to be a king, similarly Ringgren, while Birkeland thought of a post-exilic leader – for these refs, see my *Kingship*, pp. 75–8. Seybold says the psalm is built on the fundamental elements of a song of thanksgiving and is formed as a poem of great artistry, which has incorporated an older composition, vv. 3–12. Tate thinks the psalm is in type more a reflection than a thanksgiving; after the turning-point of v. 17 the thoughts mirror those of the earlier verses, only positive now and in reverse order. Goulder (*Asaph*) places the origin of this, and of all the Asaph psalms, in Bethel towards 720, a national crisis, and supposes later alterations to adapt to Jerusalem.

[4a] My translation follows a redivision (as *BHS*), instead of the traditional 'for there are no sharp pains in their death'.

[7a] 'Iniquity' has support in LXX and the Syriac, while the Hebrew has 'eye' – their eyes shine out from prosperously fat faces.

[10] RV more closely has 'Therefore his people return hither, and waters of a full (cup) are wrung out / drained by them.'

[13b] Cf. 26.6.

[13–14] Cf. Isa. 49.4; 50.6; 53.4–5.

Psalm 74

Gunkel preferred to think of some otherwise unrecorded assault on the temple in the later Persian period. Johnson (*Prophet*, pp. 131f.) provides a vivid translation and exposition without deciding between the Babylonian and Persian periods. Mowinckel and Kraus favour a time well into the Exile. Tate thinks a setting among the people left behind in Palestine after 587 is highly probable. A Hittite prayer lamenting ravages by invaders also stresses the affront to the gods themselves. The king and queen (Arnuwanda and Asmunikal, *c.* 1430) claim to have given great care to the temples and offerings, but now the invaders from the mountains have destroyed temples and smashed statues and carried off treasure and sacred personnel; the names of the gods are no longer invoked, the offerings no longer brought (*TUAT*, pp. 799f.; *ANET*, pp. 398f.).

[8] The term for 'sacred places', *mo'adey el,* has been much debated as a possible clue to the date. The sense seems basically to be of divine appointments, with reference to assembly and ceremony. The context shows that structures serving such appointments are intended here, and one can be sure that there were throughout the land places of prayer and of sacred association long before the institution of synagogues was developed (cf. A. Gelston, *VT* 34, 1984, pp. 83f.; Tate, pp. 249f.).

Psalm 75

Gunkel describes the psalm as 'peculiar, fantastic-baroque' and classes it as a 'prophetic liturgy'; he also takes vv. 2–3 as an oracle and vv. 4–10 as the response of a singer, who, in enthusiasm to join in God's judgement, adopts an old royal style (v. 10). For Mowinckel, with the same division of speech, vv. 4–10 are exposition from the community's leader – king or similar figure. Johnson represents another analysis (as also does Tate), taking the oracle to extend through vv. 2–5, resuming in v. 10; he imagines the whole psalm as delivered by a cultic prophet, able to speak to God, for God, and about God.

Psalm 76

Gunkel classes this psalm in his group 'Songs of Zion', celebrating the glory of God in his sanctuary; he has no doubt that it tells of judgement on the Last Day. Mowinckel (*Psalms* I, pp. 142, 151) says the epiphany depicted in this psalm is not a mere idea, but a reality vividly experienced through the symbols and rites of the feast and the emotional reaction of the congregation. Tate observes that 'the psalm has the generalized imagery of cultic celebrations and all efforts to relate it closely to a specific historical context should be avoided ... Mowinckel's theory ... is probable.'

[10] LXX, instead of 'wrath', has *enthumion,* 'inner thought, desire', perhaps a free rendering based on the sense of 'hot desire' in the Hebrew; and instead of 'you shall gird on', it has 'shall keep festival to you'. The Fathers then explain the verse of the Last Judgement, when every thought is disclosed, and the splendour of that day makes it a 'festival'. With change of vowels, other readings have been proposed. In one of these the southern and northern borders of the Davidic empire are mentioned: 'The wrath of Edom shall praise you; the remnant of Hamath you shall gird on (or with LXX, "shall keep your festival").' Another suggestion gives: 'You crush the wrath of man; the remnant of wrath you restrain' (cf. J. A. Emerton, *VT* 24, 1974, pp. 136–46).

Psalm 77

Gunkel thinks of the psalmist as a pious individual who counters his complaints with the triumphant tones of a hymn. Mowinckel speaks of a lamenting psalm with extensive hymnic motivation; it is however only a fragment, lacking the resumption of the lament, prayer for help, and confidence of having been heard; the situation may be a period of foreign domination. Kirkpatrick had rightly seen similarity with Hab. 3; he placed the psalm in the exilic situation, Israel being apparently rejected by God; the emphasis given by the abrupt ending is a mark of the poet's skill. Tate also looks to the Exile or its aftermath. Seybold relates the psalm to 73, both recording a process of enlightenment: the psalmist recounts how he lamented, but to no avail, and so fell into a crisis of faith; only recital of salvation-history brought renewal of trust.

[4a] The Hebrew text has: 'You hold the lids of my eyes', but as there is otherwise no address to God in this section, the vowels are best changed, with some support of ancient versions (*BHS*): 'Fixed are / I hold the lids of my eyes', more freely, 'I stare from sleepless eyes'. In vv. 5–6 I have again been guided by the ancient versions (*BHS*); the Hebrew runs:

'I consider the days of old, the years of long ago. I remember my song in the night, I commune with my heart and my spirit searches.'

[10] My translation takes the disputed words as infinitives of *hillah* 'to entreat, appease' and *shanah* 'to repeat, recite'. A similar sense can be inferred even with the common rendering of 10b as 'the years of the right hand of the Most High'.

Psalm 78

Kirkpatrick says the rebuke of Ephraim is not the main purpose; the intention is positive, to draw warnings from consideration of the past. He thinks the date uncertain, but inclines to the late eighth century – the southern kingdom is warned in view of the fall of the north. Gunkel looks to a much later period, seeing dependence on the great prophets and affinities with the perspective of Chronicles; various psalm types are merged together, and he wonders if a continuation dealing with the judgement of Judah has been suppressed. In contrast, Weiser denies such dependence and finds here a much earlier cultic tradition; in view of the problem dealt with by the psalm, the absence of Jerusalem's doom virtually proves a pre-exilic date. Johnson (*Prophet*, pp. 45f.) has a similar approach and argues for the time of Solomon, the sharpness against Ephraim being to combat disruptive elements such as broke away after Solomon's death; the psalmist brings earlier tradition (Ex. 15 etc.) up to date with reference to Zion and David. Tate still feels vv. 67–8 too sharp against the north to belong to the united kingdom of Solomon. Seybold looks for stages of growth before and after the Exile. Goulder (see above on 73) argues extensively for the priority of the psalm's tradition over the Pentateuch.

Allusions to this psalm in the New Testament can be found as follows: v. 2 in Matt. 13.35; v. 3 in 1 John 1–4; v. 18 in 1 Cor. 10.8; v. 24 in John 6.31; v. 37 in Acts 8.21; v. 44 in Rev. 16.4

[1–8] An Egyptian thanksgiving to Amun says, 'Tell of him to son and daughter, great and small; tell of him to children's children yet to be born; tell of him to the fish in the river and the birds in the sky; proclaim him to the one who knows him and the one who knows him not' (*TUAT*, p. 872, *ANET*, p. 380).

[9] The verse is regarded by some scholars as a later addition, surprising in the context and perhaps also in wording and metre. However, all the ancient witnesses have it, and its important function in the psalm is strongly defended by Johnson.

[12] 'Zoan', in Greek 'Tanis', also known as 'Avaris', was a royal city in north-east Egypt (cf. Num. 13.22); the name is not given in the accounts of the Exodus, one of the many signs of the independence of this psalm's tradition. For the incidents mentioned in the following verses cf. Ex. 13.21; 14.21; 15.8; 17.6; Num. 20.8f.; also Pss 105.39; 106.13; 114.8; 136.13.

[28] The Hebrew is literally 'his camp ... his dwelling(s)', probably a collective use meaning 'their camp ... their dwellings'; the collective occurs again in vv. 63–4. But Johnson, followed by Tate, is one of those who prefer to keep the literal 'his' in v. 28 – it is the camp and shrine of God.

[69] An Akkadian hymn to the city of Arbela, seat of Ishtar, says, 'Like heaven stands Arbela there; its foundations are as firm as those of the earth ... O exalted sanctuary ... gate of heaven' (*TUAT*, pp. 768f.).

Psalm 79

Scholars' views divide much as noted for 74. While Gunkel and Mowinckel think of some otherwise unknown attack in the post-exilic period, Kraus and Seybold look to services of lamentation in Jerusalem in the exilic period; Seybold finds later adaptations in some passages.

Psalm 80

Kraus inclines to an intercession in Josiah's time, Kirkpatrick to a prayer of Israel in exile for restoration of the whole people. Seybold is among those who see development in the psalm; a piece from Northern Israel in the Assyrian invasion has been adapted and damaged in later times. Hieke sees the origin in intercessions in Jerusalem for the Northern Kingdom in its last years; among later developments, v. 18 refers to Josiah.

Psalm 81

Delitzsch considers the unity of the psalm indisputable; he notes features suggesting a common authorship with 77 and 78, and he observes thematic continuity (the Exodus) with 80; though noting the new year connection made by Jewish tradition, he argues for an original setting in the Passover. Gunkel also favours the Passover, and finds the influence of the great prophets. Kirkpatrick is stout for the Jewish tradition and inclines to Josiah's time. Mowinckel also looks to the autumn and denies dependence on the great prophets. Kraus envisages a festival of early times stretching from 1 to 15 Tishri (cf. v. 3). Seybold regards the text as having originated in an exilic oracle, but now virtually in ruins from a series of alterations.

[3] LXX refers the whole verse to the new moon by rendering v. 3b 'in the glorious day of your feast' (cf. BCP, AV, and Targum); others again have referred the whole verse to the full moon day by translating 'new month' in v. 3a and supposing that at one time months began at full moon. This latter view is criticized in Mowinckel, *Psalms* II, pp. 235f. (note that on p. 236 lines 7 and 10 unfortunately have 'full moon' instead of 'new moon').

Psalm 82

The traditional view, theologically simpler, and found already in the Targum (cf. John 10.34f.), was that God here addresses and condemns corrupt earthly judges, who, it was thought, could be designated *elohim*, gods, as being representatives of divine law; so still Kirkpatrick. Gunkel strongly opposed this view, especially in the light of v. 7, and most now agree that the reference is to heavenly beings (cf. the Syriac, 'angels'). Dating is another matter, some even advocating a period earlier than the monarchy (cf. Dahood), and others around the fifth century. Mowinckel notes traditions in the Talmud that the psalm was sung with the offerings on the next to last day of Tabernacles, and he shows how it fits with the autumn celebrations of Yahweh's kingship – the heavenly assembly, judgement, restoration of world order; the need for 'realization' suggests to him a late period when Israel had long been under foreign domination. In a vivid exposition, Goulder (see above on 73) takes the psalm as the climax of the Asaph series, sung on the last day of a festival at Bethel. Tate has useful bibliography.

Psalm 83

Kirkpatrick notes possible connection with the war of 2 Chron. 20, but is inclined to see imaginative elements in the lament, striving to represent the danger forcibly. Weiser goes further in allowing for a theological pattern, but still thinks of the Assyrian period. Kraus essentially agrees. Mowinckel calls it a protective psalm on a day of intercession, forestalling an attack; seventh-century Judah, because of its moves towards independence, is harried by neighbours at Assyrian instigation. Tate inclines to the view that 'Assyria' is only symbolic of foreign empire in an exilic or post-exilic situation. Seybold, who thinks of the exilic period and in northern circles, notes readings of a Masada manuscript which contains most of the psalm.

Psalm 84

Gunkel takes the form to be that of a hymn though, like 122, especially related to pilgrimage; the singer is an individual experiencing the joy of arrival, and to take it collectively would be 'a painful tastelessness'. He takes vv. 8–9 to be a later addition and put in the wrong place. Mowinckel takes the 'I' to be the king in spite of v. 9, and thinks of the autumn festival in the late monarchy. Kraus thinks the psalm is part of the liturgy at the temple gates for Tabernacles. Goulder (*Korah*) suggests the singer is a Keeper of the Threshold, originally at Dan. Seybold sees the origin at Dan, the psalm then growing in stages until it became a 'many-coloured florilegium' of religious experiences.

[5b] Mesillot, 'raised ways', seems to allude to the paved processional route such as most temples had (cf. 68.4; 1 Chron. 26.16, 18; Isa. 35.8f.; 40.3; 49.11; 62.10).

[6a] Most manuscripts have 'valley of the *baka*', which may denote an arid place (cf. the Arabic word discussed by Johnson, *Sacral Kingship*, p. 104) or the site of balsam trees (cf. 2 Sam. 5.23) found in arid places, and may indeed be the name of a particular valley (e.g. Wadi el Meiseh running north from the Valley of Hinnom near Jerusalem). The idea of aridity suits the context and so this reading is preferable to that of a few manuscripts, *bakah*, more clearly the root for 'tears, weeping', a sense given in the ancient versions.

[7b] The bold phrase was later modified in pronunciation to give 'to appear before God in Zion' (Int. 6d).

[10] The word rendered 'I could choose' (*baharti*) is often taken with the next line as 'I would rather' (in v. 11 the 'Better to' of my translation, understood from v. 10, would then be omitted); another suggestion is to keep the word in v. 10 but revocalized to mean 'in my property' (*beheruti*), so L. Grollenberg, *VT* 9, 1959, pp. 311f.).

Psalm 85

For Kirkpatrick the psalm is from the difficult days attested by Haggai and Zechariah, and looks back to the salvation of the return from exile. Mowinckel similarly looks for a post-exilic situation and finds indications of worship at the autumnal new year in the idiom of v. 1b and the theme of God's advent, vv. 9–13. Kraus also thinks of this dating. Gunkel understands vv. 1–3 as 'prophetic' perfect tenses predicting final salvation; prayer for realization then follows. Johnson (*Prophet*, pp. 191, 199f.) sees intercessions in face of natural disaster; he thinks a pre-exilic dating a serious possibility in view of attacks in Jeremiah, Ezekiel and Lamentations against prophecies of 'peace' before the fall of Jerusalem. Dahood finds a prayer for rain, favourably answered, and considers that 'the intense and austere language points to a pre-exilic date'. Goulder (*Korah*) thinks of festal worship at Dan before 722, vv. 1–3 referring to salvation in Moses' time. Seybold also inclines to Dan, but in a 'diaspora' community.

Kirkpatrick comments on the traditional use of the psalm on Christmas day, noting as 'fulfilment' the message of peace (Luke 2.14), the nearness of the salvation (Matt. 1.21), the divine glory dwelling in the earth (Luke 2.32; John 1.14), the union of loving-kindness and truth, righteousness and peace (John 1.17; Rom. 5.1), and more generally the advent of God preceded by righteousness.

[1–3] Dahood supports the theory that the six verbs in vv. 1–3 are all precative perfects, hence 'Favour your land, Lord, restore ...' But this makes for a long and unduly repetitive prayer in vv. 1–7, while the plainer translation seems to give better balance and a typical ground of appeal (cf. Johnson's change of heart, p. 202, n. 1). We might think the 'Pause' more appropriate after v. 3, but a pause for gestures of adoration after v. 2 would well underscore the wonder of that forgiveness.

[13] This verse may also envisage a pair of angel-forms: 'Right shall go before him, and Beauty (shall follow) in the way of his steps.' The verb rendered as 'shall prepare' may originally have been intended as a noun, 'beauty / pleasantness' – so Dahood, after Ugaritic and Arabic.

Psalm 86

Very late dating by many was due to their understanding of the parallels with other scripture as anthologizing from older texts, rather than as sharing a common stock of liturgical poetry. Briggs thought of a composition for use in the synagogue and understood the voice as collective, the people as one before God. Baethgen also took the voice collectively, in view of the claim to be faithful, the messianic hope, and the scale of the enemies. Kirkpatrick speaks of the composition of some pious soul in the post-exilic period, whose mind was steeped in the existing scriptures. Kraus also regards the psalm as late, and adds it to his long list of pieces for fugitives or accused persons waiting in the sanctuary for Yahweh's oracular decision. Tate gives details of analyses which detect a chiastic or concentric structure, and inclines to post-exilic dating and 'literary composition for the use of any who found its content helpful'. Mowinckel sees the psalmist as a post-exilic leader, the enemies being foreign rulers and their associates. Dahood expresses surprise that commentators seem not to have noticed 'that this individual happens to be the Israelite king', and he compares style in the ancient Canaanite royal correspondence. Johnson (*Prophet*, pp. 226f.) also comes out firmly for a royal interpretation.

Psalm 87

Baethgen argues against a post-exilic date and favours *c.* 600. Kirkpatrick prefers a date after 'the Return', an utterance to raise the spirits in hard times. Gunkel confesses to a heavy heart in re-arranging the verses as 2, 1, 5c, 7, 3, 6, 4c, 4ab, 5ab, but he claims justification in the outcome, dispelling the confusion caused by some somnolent copyist. He thinks of a festal dance-procession in the Persian period and takes the psalm to refer to dispersed Jews, not to Gentiles. Bentzen disputes the need to re-arrange and inclines to the period of Josiah. Goulder (*Korah*) discovers a psalm from ancient Dan underlying a Jerusalem adaptation, and takes the birth in the holy city to have been originally that of a crown prince. Tate prefers to follow the received text, noting a concentric pattern.

[1] This has the appearance of only a half-verse, and perhaps the poet intended it to link with v. 2 for its parallel lines, (lit.): '(As for) his founded one on the holy mountains, the Lord loves (even) the gates of Zion more than all the dwellings of Jacob.' 'Weighty' or 'glorious' refers to weight of value and significance, and in Prov. 8.24 the word refers to abundant water from a spring.

[5] LXX begins 'Mother Zion a man shall say', a reading adapted into some modern translations.

[7] The laconic final verse is emended by some to ease the construction, giving e.g. 'And singers and dancers chant (*'oney* from *'nh*) of you' (so *TRP*).

Psalm 88

The communal interpretation (Israel in the Exile) found in early interpreters is pre-ferred by Briggs. St Jerome heads the psalm: 'The voice of Christ; he speaks con-cerning his Passion to the Father', and the church still appoints the psalm for Good Friday. Gunkel insists on the individuality of the sufferer – a case of severe sickness from youth upwards, but not necessarily leprosy; and this is the common approach. Among those who have suggested a connection with national rites of atonement Goulder (*Korah*) is most specific, picturing a priest at Dan as substitute for the king in bearing affliction; striking is Goulder's reading of the psalm alongside Isa. 53.

[5] 'My couch' is a suggested meaning (see Dahood). It is taken by others (including LXX) to mean 'free (among the dead)' – an irony, death bringing freedom of a kind.

[10–12] A Babylonian prayer to Marduk laments sickness, sleeplessness, anxiety, horror and dread, and asks, 'What profit is there in one returned to clay – only a living servant can honour his lord; what can dust avail the deity?' (*TUAT*, pp. 754f.).

[15b] Most render '(expiring) since my youth', but the sense may rather be '(expiring) away from my vitality' i.e. 'my strength ebbs away'.

[18b] 'My best companion' represents an intensive plural (cf. Dahood, 'plural of majesty'); NRSV 'my companions are in darkness' is an unlikely sense in the context. The consonants of 'darkness' are sometimes read, as in Jerome, to give the sense of the clause as 'restraining (*mehasseq*) my acquaintances'.

Psalm 89

The Targum relates to the delay in the coming of the Messiah, rendering v. 51: 'For your enemies reproach, Lord, they reproach the slowness of the footsteps of your Anointed.' Kirkpatrick considers the psalm exilic, reflecting the imprisonment of Jehoiachin. Gunkel dated the completed psalm to about the fifth century, when it was presented in public worship by the senior member of the surviving Davidic family; it incorporated a Northern Israelite hymn from about the time of Jeroboam II (much of vv. 1–18) and a poetic version of Nathan's oracle (vv. 19–37). Mowinckel thinks of the use of an ancient hymn and oracle as foils for the lament of one of the later Davidic kings on a day of prayer following a lost war or battle. Kraus thinks the setting could be the autumn festival soon after the defeat and death of Josiah, but with the use of older elements. Johnson maintains in *Prophet*, pp. 73f., the interpretation he gave in *Sacral Kingship*; the psalm was part of a dramatic ritual repeated annually in pre-exilic Tabernacles 'with a somewhat indefinite eschatological orientation'; he contrasts the historical allusions clear in such texts as the Song of Deborah, the lament of David over Saul and Jonathan, and Pss 74, 79, 137. Ahlström also argues for a ritual setting and gives details of the linguistic echoes of Tammuz texts. Goulder (*Korah*) endeavours to trace a development from a hymn at Tabor into a psalm for the autumn festival at Dan in the eighth century, then expanded and recast for use at Jerusalem soon after 597. Tate allows that materials from royal enthronement ceremonies have been incorporated, but looks for completion soon after 515 in the dismay at the demise of Zerubbabel.

[17] The lifting of their 'horn', an image from the great wild oxen, signifies victory over enemy armies.

[18] For the translation see Dahood; it can also be rendered 'Our shield belongs to the Lord, our king to the Holy One of Israel', the testimony of choir or people (cf. 84.9, 11).

[50b] In his shepherding the king was to mirror the work of the God who carries the lambs (Isa. 40.11). Hammurabi of Babylon is called 'Shepherd of great populations' (Seux, p. 248). Most translators, however, emend (*BHS*) or assume a severe abbreviation; thus NRSV 'how I bear in my bosom the insults of the peoples', RV 'how I do bear in my bosom the reproach of all the mighty peoples'.

[52b] Mediaeval comment on the double 'Amen' (NL): 'It teaches us that our own sorrows and troubles are no reason for omitting the praises of God, but rather a reason for doubling them, as is here done by the forcible repetition of "Amen", wherewith we welcome our returning Lord as he comes from the battle, with recovered crown and firmly established throne. Praised be the Lord Jesus by his twofold church of Jews and Gentiles, Amen, Amen; with the double service of soul and body, Amen, Amen; by all his saints in this world and the world to come, Amen, Amen.' Cf. also Thomas à Kempis: 'If thou willest me to be in light, blessed be thou; if thou willest me to be in darkness, blessed again be thou.'

Psalm 90

While the Targum understands Moses to have prayed this when the people sinned in the wilderness, most early Christian commentators took the reference to Moses figuratively – the psalmist spoke as it were in the character of Moses; v. 10 was thought especially to fit ill a man computed to be by then 120 years old (NL). Bede suggested that the name was prefixed to show the force of the supplication, for Moses often appeased the Lord's wrath through his prayer (NL). Gunkel thought vv. 1–12 probably an independent piece which was later expanded with v. 13f.; he admired the completed psalm as 'a whole history of Israelite religion in brief' and 'of indescribable nobility and force'. Dahood saw linguistic clues to an early date, perhaps ninth century. Johnson (*Prophet*, pp. 191f.) inclines to an early post-exilic date and finds good illustration of the ministry of psalmists who were prophets in the service of the temple. Tate takes note of structural studies and signs of an intricate 'envelope' structure. Goulder proposes that Book IV is the psalmody for 17 evenings and mornings of a fifth-century Tabernacles, responding to readings from the Law and Histories (*JTS* NS 26, 1975, pp. 269–89). Balentine (pp. 147f.) argues the collection is meant to summon the people back to the memory of Moses.

[11b] Some follow LXX (see *BHS*) to obtain 'or who considers the fierceness of your wrath?'.

[12b] For 'harvest', cf. Johnson, *Prophet*, p. 195.

Psalm 91

Gunkel judges most of the psalm to be didactic and suggests it originally began 'Happy the one who dwells'; it tells of God's care of those who trust, and comes from humble circles where the desire was to escape oppressors, not oppose them. Mowinckel thinks a king or similar leader is addressed. Dahood considers the psalm a royal text, full of characteristic royal phrases. Johnson (*Prophet*, pp. 184f.) thinks of a king about to depart for battle and compares the vocative beginning with 20; the change to third person in v. 14f. indicates the presence of a congregation. Starbuck (pp. 195f.) compares amuletic papyri sold to worshippers at Theban temples, promising protection from all ills in formulae originally used for the pharaohs; he is therefore inclined to consider the psalm also as 'fully democratized', directed to ordinary worshippers.

[1–3] Difficulties of translating these verses are resolved when the vocative is recognized in v. 1 (Johnson) and the participle restored with a change of vowel in v. 2 (this latter point with support from a Qumran manuscript and LXX). Assyrian kings speak of being covered by the deity's shadow, a Hittite king takes refuge with his lord as a bird hides in its nest and lives, and Egyptian kings are shown pictorially under the deity's wings or shadow (my *Kingship*, p. 143). That the person in the psalm 'nests / lodges' (*yitlonan* cf. Job 39.28) in the shadow of the Almighty suggests the picture of eagles that nest on a high cliff, here the rock of Zion.

Psalm 92

Kirkpatrick thinks it clear that this is not merely an expression of individual gratitude for personal mercies; he suggests thanksgiving of Israel at the end of the Exile. Gunkel is all for personal experience; to take the psalm collectively would be to cut the heart out of the song; finding the form to be mixed, he judges it rather late. Mowinckel bridges the gap by thinking of a leader who gives thanks perhaps for the overthrow of hostile neighbours. For Dahood it is a royal psalm of thanksgiving to be classified with 18, and he notes many elements with parallels in other royal psalms. Tate considers that the appropriateness of its language for a king should not be doubted, and it may come from a celebration of victory.

Psalm 93

Kirkpatrick speaks for many before the work of Mowinckel. He well grasps that the psalm reflects an event by which the Lord's sovereignty has been visibly declared – but a historical event, probably the return from the Exile; having seemingly left his throne, the Lord has now re-assumed his royal state, and so v. 1 declares 'Jehovah hath proclaimed himself king'. Gunkel finds eschatology: towards the end of the age the old chaos-forces will surge up again, but the Lord will defeat them and ascend the throne to reign over a peaceful world; in the manner of the prophets, the singer pictures the future as already accomplished. Gunkel seems more tentative here than in his earlier work (cf. my *Psalms of the Way*, pp. 70f.). For Mowinckel the psalm, at the heart of the new year festival, makes present the Creation victory. The Lord is hailed as the one who has taken the kingship and put on the glory which is his battle-armour; he then overpowers the chaos-waters, and the establishment of creation is indicated by his sure edicts and the new glory of his temple. For the worshippers this actualization of creation means renewal of life and blessing in the future. Kraus also thinks of worship at the autumn festival in the early monarchy; a procession into the temple is completed with obeisance and acclamation before God as the enduring, perpetual King. Dahood finds the arguments for a tenth-century date convincing, whereas Gerstenberger believes the psalm acclaims the Torah in a typically post-exilic fashion. Tate gives consideration to the sequence of psalms in Book Four and notes signs that 92 and 93 were intended by the collectors to be read together. Howard treats 93–100 as a sequence.

[1–2] This style of praise may be compared with tributes to Mesopotamian rulers, who were said to have been named for the kingship and established in their royal destiny at the foundation of the universe (Seux, pp. 135, 370–1; *ANET*, p. 104); thus was the surpassing significance of the new reign expressed.

[4] For the translation without emendation see my *Psalms of the Way*, p. 109 and note.

Psalm 94

The Talmud (Erachin 11a, Delitzsch) relates that Levites stood in their pulpits to sing this psalm as the temple was assaulted in 587 but could not complete the last verse; and it says that normally the psalm was sung with the offering on Wednesday mornings (cf. LXX 'Psalm of David, for the fourth day of the week', and see above on 90). Gunkel thought that the 'mixture' of forms or styles pointed to a late date. Mowinckel sees a leader ('most likely the king', *Psalms* I, p. 227) interceding on a day of supplication or perhaps in the autumn festival, seeking a turn of fate with the epiphany of the Lord. Dahood thinks the use of tenses points to the pre-exilic period. Tate, who inclines to a setting in the social strife of the post-exilic period, discusses the placing of the psalm in the series, favouring the view that 90–94 are an editorial unit with coherence of meaning and function.

[10a] The two verbs are similar in sense ('admonish / discipline') and so we are near to a tautology. The first verb (*yoser*) therefore should perhaps be taken as equivalent to *yoṣer*, 'he who formed'.

[10b] we read as *adam midda'at*, lit. 'Is the teacher of mankind without knowledge' (cf. Dahood).

Psalm 95

Gunkel opposes those who found here two independent psalms; he argues that the parallel in 81 shows that we have here a liturgical sequence, where the first voice sounds from the entering column, followed by the prophetic voice from the temple. The situation is post-exilic, like that in Isa. 56f. and Malachi; the prophetic psalmist is a worthy successor of the prophets, not needing to expand on God's requirements because that had all been amply done before. He cites parallels for the mass obeisance from ancient Egypt, Judaism, Islam and China. Mowinckel largely agrees, but develops the festival context, especially noting the combination of the Lord's kingship and covenant-renewal. Kraus, however, thinks the later monarchy more suitable; he thinks of the prophetic psalmist as a major figure with the traditional role of mediator in covenant ceremony, and he sees the obeisance and acclamation as the key moment in the celebration of the Lord's kingship. Johnson (*Prophet*, pp. 18f., cf. *Sacral Kingship*, pp. 68f.) also finds the setting in Jerusalem's autumn festival under the monarchy, but perhaps, with 81, descending from the time of the Settlement. He thinks of one singer who changes role to become spokesperson for God. The 'rest' is God's 'home', and the conception here is prior to Deuteronomy.

Psalm 96

For Gunkel the psalm is a late compilation drawing on older texts, and so not an organic whole in sense; the first part is a general hymn, while vv. 10f. borrow from eschatological psalms. Mowinckel explains that the new year corresponds to new creation, the new reign of the Lord, and so evokes a 'new song'; 'salvation' is the overcoming of chaos and making earth right for life. Kraus sets the psalm in a post-exilic resumption of the former autumn festival, and belonging to a processional entry on the first day; though it draws on its pre-exilic counterparts, it has acquired an eschatological perspective due to the influence of Isa. 40f. Dahood does not favour the idea of dependence on Isa. 40f. he notes ancient forms of parallelism and some archaic phrases, and thinks both the psalm and the prophecies heirs to a common literary tradition long existent in Canaan.

[13a] Whether taken as the perfect tense or the participle, the repeated verb *ba'* surely means 'he is / has come' as the context indicates, the psalm being dominated by the experienced presence of the victorious Lord.

[13b] Either 'He now rules ...' or as rendered above.

Psalm 97

Delitzsch, Baethgen and Duhm illustrate the old division of opinion. For Delitzsch the poet projects himself into the end-time, when God takes his reign; for Baethgen the Lord 'has become king' in the recent overthrow of Babylon; for Duhm God manifests his majesty in a thunderstorm, which is, however, a harbinger of world-judgement. Gunkel, beginning to take account of Mowinckel's work, describes the setting as an annual celebration of Yahweh's ascension to the throne, but in the post-exilic period when, he supposes, the ceremony will have been influenced by Second Isaiah's eschatology. Kraus takes the same view. Johnson (*Sacral Kingship*, pp. 95f.) places it in the pre-exilic festival. Lipiński devotes over 100 pages to the psalm and firmly rejects the common view that it is dependent on Second Isaiah; in its final form, he thinks it comes from the dedication of the temple in 164 BCE, the new reign of the Lord being the historical deliverance, but parts of the psalm are very ancient. For details of such views see my *Psalms of the Way*.

[6–8] Some take 'daughters of Judah' to mean the provincial towns. This whole passage is sometimes translated with present tenses, making it part of the present scene of homage rather than of the retrospect, but this seeing of glory and the remorse of shame are somewhat different from the scene of vv. 1–2.

[10] I have followed the emendation in *BHS*; the Hebrew gives 'Lovers of the Lord, hate evil'.

[11a] Some follow another reading to give 'Light is risen' as 112.4; but there are classical parallels for the idea of light as sown or strewn (Kirkpatrick; cf. also Milton's *Paradise Lost*

V.1), and the thought could be of salvation prepared for growth and flowering in God's time.

[12b] zeker, usually translated 'name' for convenience, is (lit.) 'remembrance', and various passages (135.13 etc.) and the Arabic equivalent show that the reference is to calling out the name of God in worship, sometimes in sacred dance.

Psalm 98

Kirkpatrick again represents the 'historical' interpretation of such celebration of the Lord's new reign: 'Another psalm of praise for the redemption of Israel from Babylon.' Kraus follows Gunkel in seeing the psalm in post-exilic worship, with elements of the old festal acclamation of the Lord as king, but also with an eschatological perspective derived from Second Isaiah. Johnson (*Sacral Kingship*, pp. 99f.) includes the psalm in his treatment of pre-exilic worship; it illustrates the autumn festival as concerned with celebration of the creation victory, but also making it a prelude to eschatological re-creation. Mowinckel more directly sees a celebration of a present, accomplished coming of the Lord, a renewal of the salvation of creation. Oesterley places the psalm in the festal celebration of Yahweh's kingship – a prophetic representation of his ultimate entering upon his world-dominion; 'the reign of universal peace and justice and happiness has begun in the psalmist's prophetic vision'.

Ancient comment tended to be human-centred. The 'rivers' denote those saints of various degrees of eminence, from the merest rill to the mightiest torrent, who flow from the Lord Jesus, the fountain of living waters; they 'clap their hands' in that they praise God with practical deeds of the hand. Others again saw these waters as representing all reborn in the sweet waters of baptism (NL).

Psalm 99

Gunkel, finding here a vision of the end-time, stresses the dynamic event of the Lord's taking his seat; the awe and the ethical themes show the influence of the prophets. Mowinckel (*Psalms* I, p. 117) becomes inclined to pre-exilic dating, which Bentzen too shows is most likely. Even Kraus dissociates the psalm from Second Isaiah and thinks of it as from the royal period, linked to the promulgation of covenant-law in Tabernacles. Johnson (*Sacral Kingship*, pp. 70f.) says it an obvious companion piece to 95, part of the pre-exilic liturgy in the autumn festival; the opening sounds an eschatological note. Lipiński thinks it could date to the era of Solomon and adduces ancient Sumerian and Akkadian parallels especially for v. 4. For details of such opinions see my *Psalms of the Way*.

[1–3] In v. 1b parallelism favours vocalizing as *yashab* 'he has sat down' rather than *yosheb* 'sitting' (so Gunkel, Lipiński). In v. 2b another reading is 'above all gods', but the parallel reference to Zion favours the reading 'above all peoples'. The verbs 'tremble', 'shake', 'praise' seem best taken as indicatives, describing effects of the dread theophany – so the Hebrew vowels in v. 1b (where the verb *nwt* will be like *mwt* in meaning, cf. the Ugaritic comparison in Dahood and Lipiński). Others take them as jussives: 'let the peoples tremble'.

[4a] The Hebrew is problematic. I have used a bold suggestion (*w'z* as participle of a verb *w'z / y'z* 'to command', *mlk* as a noun 'kingship', *Psalms of the Way*, p. 114) to obtain a well-balanced result. NRSV follows another route (cf. *BHS*) to obtain 'Mighty king, lover of justice'. The general sentiment is clear and is found already in the third and second millennia (Lipiński pp. 317f.).

[6–8] At the end of v. 8b the Hebrew seems to mean 'avenging for their (evil) deeds', hardly suiting the context. I have followed Buhl's suggestion in *BH3* to vocalize as *noqam* rather than *noqem*, assuming a transitive *qal* of *nqh* with suffix, 'acquitting them' (*Psalms of the Way*, p. 115). In the translation of v. 6a one should recognize the idiom that gives 'chief of his priests', not just 'among his priests' (cf. BDB, p. 88a). In v. 8b some unnecessarily take

the participle of present time, 'they are calling', and explain that 'a Moses . . . a Samuel' are present-day intercessors, while Lipiński more radically thinks of the ancient worthies still at prayer in Sheol.

Psalm 100

Kirkpatrick regards this as the conclusion of a series for the dedication of the temple in 515; he gives information on Christian usage and on the metrical version ('All people that on earth do dwell'). For Gunkel it is 'an entrance hymn at the thank-offering'. Mowinckel notes the 'royal homage' of the opening and links the psalm to the autumn festival with its predecessors, but as specially related to the community's thank-offering.

Psalm 101

Kirkpatrick adopts the view that David prays for the Lord to come as he renews his procession with the ark to Jerusalem; the placing after 93, 95–100 may have been to suggest how God's kingship could take effect through a second David. Gunkel and Kraus both adopt the emendation of v. 2b to 'Let truth come to me' (*emet tabo'lî*). Johnson (*Sacral Kingship*, pp. 113f.) sees the psalm, in a symbolic rite of humiliation, as pleading just rule hitherto. Kaiser (*ZAW* 74, 1962, pp. 195f.) notes features which support Johnson's approach. Dahood also takes the tenses as referring to past conduct. Allen likewise; he suggests that we have here a formula for use in times of political distress. Seybold describes the psalm as a 'palimpsest'; an old fragment from the monarchy can be descried under a rewriting by a post-exilic priestly leader. Gerstenberger also looks to post-royal times, where a congregation is instructed in the ideal of a righteous person who will take any measures to cleanse his community.

[2c–8] The tenses can be translated as 'future' (and so a promise) or 'past' (and so a claim about conduct hitherto). The future seems the more obvious grammatically, but strikingly LXX chooses the past, and this would fit renewals of the royal office and match the Babylonian parallel. In the original usage the tenses would have been understood as the context required.

Psalm 102

Kirkpatrick describes the psalmist as an individual who loses his personality in that of his people and speaks for fellow exiles. But others follow Gunkel's insistence that the supplicant is an individual sufferer who finds comfort in the hope of Zion's restoration. Thus Kraus thinks of a sick, persecuted person in the Exile who sets his plight in the context of hope for Zion; similarly Allen and Broyles, also Bruning who suggests the psalmist is the head of the Davidic house 538–515. Mowinckel recognizes the representative role, sees possible connection with the new year festival (the 'appointed time', the manifestation of God's glory, his creation and kingship), and begins to change from post-exilic dating to thinking of a royal psalm (*Psalms* I, p. 61). Dahood too finds a royal speaker and lists relevant phrases and motifs.

[5] 'I am weary' is supplied to suit the context, filling an apparent gap in the text. For another approach see Dahood who has: 'My jaws fester from my groaning'.

Psalm 103

Kirkpatrick takes the individual singer to be speaking for the nation, giving thanks for restoration from the Exile. Gunkel insists that we have here the hymn of an individual; the collective interpretation is a sin which could only be forgiven for a Wellhausen. Kraus likewise finds an individual who is giving thanks for his own healing and offering words of teaching to the attendant congregation. Mowinckel sees a union of the personal and communal in the psalmist's being a prominent person in the community; like Gunkel and Kraus, he assumes a late date, with dependence on Second Isaiah and Job, but he also notes a relation with the glad tidings of the new year festival. Allen thinks of a solo singer who would stimulate fellow worshippers to give thanks for their particular experience. Dahood is distinctive in declaring a postexilic date very unlikely; the 'Aramaisms' could be Canaanite archaisms, and the literary resemblances could be due to all parties drawing on a common stock.

[5] The sense may be 'satisying your (daily) course with goodness'; some revocalize to *'odeki* 'your continuance'.

[15–17] The poetry of transience is especially reminiscent of that in Isa. 40.7 and Job 7.10. The comparison with the green things of the Palestinian wilderness, which spring up so boldly after winter rains but are quickly withered by sirocco and sun, was a widespread poetic inheritance, and it would be unwise to assume that our psalmist was drawing on the writings of Second Isaiah and Job. His contrast of the fading flower with the enduring *hesed* of God is more basic than the Isaiah comparison with the word of God.

Psalm 104

Kraus is among those who can envisage a pre-exilic date and a setting in the autumn festival; he does not think the psalm dependent on Gen. 1. Craigie (1974) suggests it was composed for the dedication of Solomon's temple, expounding the temple's cosmic significance. The heading in the Syriac goes a step further back: 'Of David, when he was going to worship before the ark of the Lord together with the priests'.

Mays comments that usually we see the world in fragments, according to our interests as developers, scientists, artists, sportsmen ... we imagine ourselves as autonomous, disposing of earth and creatures at will. We are alienated from that to which we belong, and threaten the future of life. But 'praise of God puts us with our assumed identities in a quite different place, and opens up perspectives possible only from its vantage'.

[1–4] Akhenaton also begins with the manifestation of the Creator, which he sees in the rising sun-disk: 'You appear in beauty on heaven's horizon, O living Aton, the first to live ... filling all lands with your beauty. You are glorious and great, shining on high over every land.'

[10–18] Akhenaton illustrates the Creator's care with his soothing of the child in the womb and his help for the chick within the egg; at the right time of growth, he enables the chick to break the shell and come forth, to speak and to run upon its legs.

[19–23] Akhenaton envisages the night with death-like qualities; there are anxieties about thieves, creeping things that sting, and lions at large. So sunrise is especially joyful, when the Creator shines on his world. People are raised up, washing and dressing, lifting their arms in praise, doing their work. Trees and plants flourish, birds stretch their wings in praise; the creatures 'live when you have risen for them.'

[24–26] Akhenaton tells of ships that, with the Creator's appearance, can sail off north or south, while fish in the river dart before his face and his rays light up the depths of the green sea. He exclaims, 'How numerous your works which are hidden from the face. O sole God, like whom there is no other ... you created the world according to your desire while you were alone.' An earlier Egyptian hymn praises Amun-Re as sole creator; mankind came forth, tear-like, from his eye, and the gods came into being from his mouth; he made plants for the cattle and the tree of life for the people; he provides for fish and birds and gives breath within the egg; he nourishes the young of snakes, also gnats, worms and fleas, and he looks after mice in their holes and beetles in wood (*TUAT*, pp. 840f.).

Psalm 105

Gunkel thinks of a date between the completion of the Pentateuch and the writing of Chronicles. Mowinckel echoes these views, but adds a link with learned scribal circles. Kraus also follows Gunkel, but allows for the psalm's standing in an ancient cult-hymn tradition which still flourished in the Qumran community. Weiser thinks dependence on the Pentateuch improbable and links the psalm to renewals of the covenant. Allen sides rather with Gunkel; he looks for clues of structuring and finds four strophes (from vv. 1, 12, 24, 37). He also treats the Christian transformation of the geographical promise to that of the heavenly country. Broyles shows how the Chronicler might have seen a link with the ark from phrases in v. 4.

[*27a, 28b*] These verses are emended (cf. *BHS*). RV offers for the Hebrew 'They set among them his signs ... and they rebelled not against his words.'

[*30b*] The verse follows a plausible emendation in *BHS*; the Hebrew gives, as RV, 'in the chambers of their kings'.

Psalm 106

Kirkpatrick dates the psalm, with 105, to the years after the restoration from Babylon. Gunkel and Mowinckel broadly share this view. Beyerlin (1974) sees decisive significance in the opening call to praise; in the years after 597 there was great longing for a new era of praise (Jer. 33.10–11) and everything in the psalm is meant to pave the way for such a time. Weiser connects it with recitals of sacred history at the autumn festival, and he is open to a pre-exilic dating; he suggests that 105 and 106 may belong to the same covenantal liturgy; as in the Qumran community, separate recitals might be given to the gracious acts of God on the one hand and the sins of Israel on the other. Allen's structural observations lead him to find three strophes, vv. 1–12, 13–33, 34–47; he favours the exilic period (so also Broyles). Regarding the use of the psalm in Rom. 1.23f., he remarks that the apostle describes sin and its results in terms of Israel's experience, mirrored and magnified in the Gentile world.

[*7b*] 'The Most High' is an emendation (*BHS*); RV represents the received text thus: 'they were rebellious at the sea, even at the Red Sea'.

[*20*] 'God's glory' is based on the reading 'his glory', (*BHS*); the text has 'their glory', probably an alteration on grounds of reverence.

Psalm 107

Kirkpatrick thinks of returned exiles soon after 538; they are meant to see in the examples illustrations of their own experiences in the desert of the world, the prison of exile, sick from sin, tossed in a sea of nations. Gunkel regards the main composition as vv. 1–32, a song for the thanksgiving when grouping of pilgrims was adopted to relieve the pressure of the throngs, v. 3 simply referring to pilgrims gathered from residence abroad; vv. 33–43 have been added by another author, picking up some of the preceding phrases and wishing to end the celebration with an impressive hymn. Allen includes in his review of opinion a book on the psalm by Beyerlin, but is not drawn to his four stages of growth (1, 4–22; 23–32; 2–3; 33–43); he opts for three stages: first, vv. 1, 4–32, an exhortation to inaugurate the proceedings of individual thanksgiving; second, vv. 2–3, the imposition of an application to returned exiles; third, vv. 33–43, the addition of a didactic meditation weaving in elements from the preceding.

Psalm 108

The views of Kirkpatrick and Gunkel are close: a situation in post-exilic times made part but not all of 60 relevant, so a more suitable beginning was supplied from 57. Dahood protests that to call the psalm a compilation from two other psalms goes beyond available evidence; he prefers to say that a liturgical composition has been made by drawing on ancient poems which are also used in 57 and 60. Broyles thinks the later use of these materials carries an eschatological sense; the oracle foreshadows God's final kingship over the nations, which is prayed for in v. 5.

Psalm 109

The Syriac has the heading: 'Of David, when without his knowledge they made Absalom king ... to us it sets forth the sufferings of the Lord's Anointed.' Kirkpatrick and Davidson speak of the 'quotation' theory for vv. 6–19 as straining the natural sense; cf. Jeremiah's imprecations (11.18.f.; 15.15f.; 17.18; 18.19f.; 20.11f.). Kraus (like Allen and Broyles) accepts the view that an individual faces sacred trial and quotes the curse made against him. Jacquet restricts the quotation to vv. 6–15 and takes vv. 16–20 as the psalmist's rejoinder. Dahood judges the psalm early pre-exilic, by an elderly and skilful poet awaiting trial by 'a court filled with perjurors and presided over by a knavish judge', against whom vv. 6f. are directed. Mowinckel, following Birkeland, finds a king or similar leader, accused to the imperial overlord by neighbouring rulers or by commissars and perhaps already attacked; it is a national lament in the 'I' form for a special day of intercession. Bentzen remarks that vv. 6f., as a counter-curse, had to be stronger than the enemy's to ward it off.

[17–18] Many alter the vowels (*BHS*) to translate, '... let it come to him ... let it stay far from him ... let come into his body ...' But Kirkpatrick defends our text: the evil man welcomed cursing into his heart and banished blessing; he put on cursing as a garment daily; it was his refreshment and invigoration.

Psalm 110

Gunkel writes with fullness to rule out post-exilic or Maccabeean origin and to link with pre-exilic enthronement ceremony. Mowinckel takes the same line; he accepts that items of the ceremony are reflected throughout. Kraus thinks of the oldest royal period but doubts a close reflection of ceremonies; it seems rather to be a secondary putting together of oracles, wishes, and depictions. For Johnson (*Sacral Kingship*, pp. 130f.) the psalm is the conclusion of the annual ritual drama, a prophetic symbol of Yahweh's eschatological purpose; the king takes the role of 'the Messiah', the ideal king who is to come, and the psalm shows him reborn after his deliverance from the underworld and given his place of glory. Verses 5–7 recall how the Lord came to his aid against the armies of darkness, the Lord 'mighty in battle', pausing to slake his thirst; it is the deliverance Johnson found also in 18 and 118. The drama challenged each generation and their king, through faith and righteousness, to be instrumental in bringing near the fulfilment. Allen thinks the psalm may have celebrated David's conquest of Jerusalem and succession to Jebusite kingship; later use could have been in enthronements and other cultic settings showing the king's relation to Yahweh. Starbuck gives parallels with Egyptian and Mesopotamian royal texts; noting the lack of a king's name in Hebrew royal psalms, he doubts that we have actual texts used and reused in enthronements, but rather materials revised and rearranged after the end of the monarchy; the reference to Melchizedek may be the result of textual corruption and a post-Qumran interpretation.

[3] The Hebrew begins awkwardly 'Your people are nobility / willingness on the day of your might', but LXX with a slight difference of vowel begins 'With you is dominion'; hence our rendering here, adding another change of vowel (*hileka*, 'birth' rather than 'might'). For 'of your new life' some manuscripts and versions have 'with which I have begotten you', a difference of vowels and suiting the context.

[6] The Hebrew 'he is full / he fills (with) corpses' is not a plausible expression and different readings are found in some versions. I have followed the Samaritan psalter (*male ge'ut*), a difference of one letter giving 'full of majesty'; so also *LP*.

Psalm 111
Mowinckel finds here an individual thanksgiving with thank-offering; it is a late type where the personal story is replaced by testimony to the national redemption, but personal experience appears in glimpses of the studies of the wise (vv. 2, 10) and encounter with the divine compassion (v. 4). But Allen sees the psalmist intending to speak for the assembled people at an annual festival in the post-exilic period; he stresses the link with 103.17–18.

Psalm 112
Kirkpatrick judges this post-exilic, dependent on other psalms and Proverbs. Words applied to God in 111 are transferred in 112 to the godly person 'with startling boldness' to show how the godly character reflects that of the Lord. He lists the chief parallels of wording as v. 1a (cf. 111.10a), v. 1b (cf. 112.2), vv. 3b, 9b (cf. 111.3b), v. 4b (cf. 111.4b), v. 6b (cf. 111.4a).

Psalm 113
[5–6] some translators either adopt a conjectural emendation (cf. *BHS*) or assume what would be a very strained parenthesis, to obtain: 'Who is like the Lord our God in heaven or on earth, so high in his throning, so lowly in his looking?'

[7f.] Unlike Gunkel, Mowinckel accepts that these verses allude to national deliverance, even with hope for the final salvation; he suggests a setting in Passover. Kraus and Allen concur in leaving the date open.

[9] The concluding alleluia introduces 114 in LXX, 'perhaps rightly' (Kirkpatrick).

Psalm 114
Kirkpatrick, thinking of Passover in the period of the Return, sees this as a sequel to 113, perhaps by the same author; he notes Christian use in offices for the dying and dead – the Exodus of the soul. Gunkel prefers the time of the divided kingdom, after the Deuteronomic reform. Kraus finds reflection of worship at Gilgal near Jordan before the monarchy; from Josh. 3–4 it may be deduced that the worship involved actualization of the Exodus in a ritual fording of the Jordan.

Psalm 115
Allen inclines to agree with Gunkel and Kraus on a setting in a post-exilic festival, but does not close a pre-exilic possibility. Dahood inclines to the period of the monarchy, and Weiser thinks of covenant ceremony which might be pre-exilic.

Psalm 116
Kirkpatrick thinks this a post-exilic thanksgiving after sickness; he notes echoes of 18, 27, 31, 56, also that part has been used in the church's office for the thanksgiving of women after childbirth. Mowinckel sees the pointers to a 'leading figure', but suggests royal tradition has been democratized for some post-exilic person. Allen also thinks of the later period; the language is left unspecific to cover more than one occasion.

Dahood notes signs of royal tradition and thinks the language requires an early pre-exilic date.

[10–11] LXX rendered 'I believed, therefore I spoke, but I was greatly afflicted'; and this is followed by Paul in 2 Cor. 4.13, applied to the testimony of those who bear in their body both the death and the life of the Lord Jesus.

Psalm 117

Kirkpatrick connects the acknowledgement of God's faithfulness with the return from the Exile or some subsequent relief. Kraus notes the connection with the ancient worship of the creator, God Most High, but still supposes dependence on Second Isaiah. Weiser sees the psalm as the priest's call to the congregation to sing a hymn, all in response to the festal theophany. Dahood suggests a date in the sixth or seventh century on linguistic grounds. Broyles defends the psalm's distinction as functioning within a larger liturgy.

Psalm 118

For once, Gunkel is somewhat isolated in trying to explain this as an individual's thanksgiving; he pictures a private person, recovered from sickness, providing a sumptuous thanksgiving at the temple, entering in the midst of a procession of friends, restored to honour as evident in the fine feast; the repulse of nations and other elements are old royal phrases taken up metaphorically by the enthusiastic psalmist. Gunkel as usual is most concerned to reject outright a corporate interpretation of the individual speaker, but Kraus is clearly not comfortable with this 'private' emphasis and post-exilic dating. Kirkpatrick voices the widespread older view that the individual speaker is indeed Israel or a representative who speaks in her name, most probably at Tabernacles in 444 BCE in celebration of the completed city wall (Neh. 8.14–18). Mowinckel had thought of a communal celebration in the late period led by a representative leader; but in *Psalms* (I, p. 180, II, p. 254) he can envisage a pre-exilic king giving thanks for the long history of national salvation compressed into a single picture. Johnson (*Sacral Kingship*, pp. 123f.) describes the psalm as an obvious companion piece to 18 and expounds it as part of an annual ritual drama, the king being the main speaker; the drama is a *mashal* or parable of God's re-creative work. Weiser has a kindred view; the divine combat with chaos is developed with reference to Israel's historical conflicts, dramatically celebrated and represented by the king, an action mediating salvation for the community year by year. Anderson favours Johnson's view, while Dahood, Allen, Broyles and Davidson think of thanksgiving at the festival for some recent victory which cannot be identified. Seybold keeps alive the view that various individual cases of salvation are gathered in a collective thanksgiving (cf. above on 107).

Citations of the psalm in the New Testament include: v. 6 in Heb. 13.6; vv. 22, 23 in Matt. 21.42; Mark 12.10–11; Luke 20.17; Acts 4.11; 1 Peter 2.4, 7; vv. 25, 26 in Matt. 21.9 and 23.39, Mark 11.9; Luke 13.35 and 19.38; John 12.13.

Psalm 119

It has been thought that the eight terms originally all appeared without fail in each group of eight verses, and the more varied occurrence that we now find arose from centuries of chanting and copying. Certainly there are minor discrepancies in manuscripts and ancient versions, which show how variations could develop. But the evidence does not support the extreme view that the eight terms originally recurred in a fixed order throughout the psalm. In LXX the psalm is introduced with 'Alleluia', as also are 105–7, 111–18, 135–6, 147A, B, 148–50.

Delitzsch valiantly represents the acrostic scheme in his German translation; for him the psalm is the utterance of a young man in a time of apostasy among the rulers, and has an inner progression of thought as prayer for grace is intensified. Baethgen thinks of a vade-mecum for the young in the early Greek period, the afflictions being those of the people, not an individual. Kirkpatrick says the psalm represents the religious ideas of Deuteronomy as developed in the communion of a devout soul with God. Duhm has scathing remarks about the value of the psalm, which he says only illustrates the perils of book-religion. Gunkel is bemused by the profuse mixture of 'forms' – like a tumble of rocks which scientists have to classify one by one; the psalmist's individual experience is expressed – an old man, teacher of the young in the late Persian period. Mowinckel gives a more appreciative treatment, taking the psalm as a lament, the statements about the Law being motifs for a favourable hearing; it is the supplication of a leader, accused and troubled by the officials of a foreign overlord in the late Persian or early Greek period, and it evinces a piety of devotion to the Law of Moses, the Pentateuch. Kraus follows the view that the psalm is a kind of anthology, a collage of sayings based on scripture and revolving round the theme of wonder at the revelation of the divine will. Allen describes the psalm as a medley of praise, prayer and wisdom features; the 'tora' has a written form and seems to embrace Isaiah, Jeremiah and Proverbs as well as the Pentateuch. The psalm is a literary monument raised in honour of Yahweh's revelation of himself to Israel; Aramaisms support a post-exilic date. But Dahood favours a date around the late seventh century, and he thinks the view that it was composed for a Davidic king or some other leader does not seem improbable; *tora* has its widest sense, including all divine revelation as the guide of life. Soll gives a basic examination of the psalm and its relation to the acrostic traditions of Babylon and Israel; he thinks the *tora* terms refer to a body of covenantal laws with an aspect of promise; he finds coherence and shaping in the content and is inclined to see the psalm as the prayer of the exiled Jehoiachin, grandson of the great *tora* king Josiah. Gerstenberger says it is only formally a prayer; in early Jewish worship, its aim is to instruct especially the young in the correct postures towards the Lord and his will. For Freedman, noting the statistics of the acrostic and word patterns, the symmetries and deviations express the tension of praise and suffering.

[48] The text may have suffered, earlier than LXX, by intrusion of words from the previous line, and one might restore thus; 'And I will lift my hands to you and meditate in your statutes.'

[49a] 'Word' lacks the suffix for 'your' in the Hebrew, though not in LXX and Syriac; perhaps the suffix is understood from the following 'your servant'.

[50b] Most translate 'has given', but a future sense is possible and fits the context well.

[84b] One may wonder if 'judgement' was intended to carry the suffix for 'your', since the required letter is the same as that which follows.

[85b] The literal is perhaps ambiguous: 'that are not according to your law'.

[99] In Jewish tradition the verse was rendered less provocatively 'From all my teachers ...', grammatically possible, but unlikely after v. 98.

[98–100] The choice of future tenses in the translation is quite legitimate, and may suit the psalmist's constant desire to learn better than the perfect tenses usually chosen.

[118] Instead of 'deceiving', LXX reads 'their thought'.

[119a] Another reading, the main tradition, has 'you put an end to'.

[121] A few mss and the Syriac read suitably 'You do what is just and right'.

[122] Some conjecture that 'your servant' is an error for 'your word', thus 'Give your word in surety for my good'.

[126a] The *lamed* before 'Yahweh' may emphasize the vocative (cf. Dahood); others render 'It is time for the Lord to act.'

[128] I have divided the consonants thus: *pqwdyk lysrty*, taking the *lamed* as emphatic.

Psalm 120

A different theory to explain the heading, favoured by Delitzsch, relates the 'steps' to the poetic structure of these psalms; in some of them we notice a stair-like parallelism, a verse making fresh use of words just used (so 121.2, 4, 5, 7, 8). Such a use of the term is not otherwise attested. The ascent up fifteen steps to God was much pondered in later Jewish and Christian tradition (cf. Delitzsch and NL). In addition to expositions of fifteen stages, a threefold division was proposed, corresponding to the three stages of the contemplative way: purgative (120–24), illuminative (125–29), and unitive (130–34).

Gunkel accepts the theory that 'Meshek' is an error for 'Massa' and so another tribe of the Arabian desert (cf. Gen. 25.14); thus the psalmist, an 'individual', laments an enforced sojourn in that region. Mowinckel follows the view that the error is for 'archers' (*moshekey qeshet*), but he leaves open whether the sojourn is literal or metaphorical; he thinks of a king or other military leader. Kraus accepts the view that an individual gives thanks, quoting his earlier lament. Goulder (*Return*) proposes that the fifteen psalms of ascent were for fourteen evening and morning services at Tabernacles under Nehemiah in 445 BCE; he suggests that 'Meshek' and 'Kedar' are allusions to the tribal background of Nehemiah's chief enemies, Sanballat and Geshem. Broyles takes up the observation that almost all these psalms contain a term echoing the blessing of Num. 6.23f.

[5–7] The difficulty did not arise for LXX and Vulgate, which rendered, 'Woe is me, that my sojourning is prolonged' (*m-sh-k* 'to draw out'). The emendation of 'Meshek' to 'Massa' is still accepted by Seybold, the error supposedly arising from an original spelling *ms* (cf. Gen. 10.2 'Mash', paralleled in 1 Chr. 1.17 with 'Meshek').

Psalm 121

Kirkpatrick thinks of pilgrims going up to festivals at Jerusalem, encouraging one another with an antiphonal song as the mountains of Zion come into view; the concluding 'evermore' expresses the national hope. For Gunkel, a priest at the temple answers the lament of an individual, communal interpretation being a sad mistake; the 'hills' are shrines of other gods. Mowinckel thinks the supplicant is a leading or representative figure, or the singular 'you' may mean the community and each individual in it, as in Deuteronomy; a procession in the autumn festival approaches the temple. Kraus (similarly Allen and Davidson) thinks of an individual pilgrim given a blessing on leaving the festival and facing danger in the hills on the way home. Goulder (see above on 120) has the promises addressed to Nehemiah.

[5a] We may compare praise addressed to the Babylonian king Hammurabi (1792–1750): 'Shamash and Adad (gods) are your watchmen' (*TUAT*, p. 727).

[8] In Jewish piety this verse is recited on leaving or entering the house, the hand touching the mezuza (the cylinder fixed to the doorpost and containing a scroll of Deut. 6.4–9 and 11.13–21).

Psalm 122

Gunkel insists on the psalm as an individual's personal outpouring in the wonderful moment of arrival; it could be late monarchy or post-exilic. On similar lines are Kraus, Allen and Davidson; but Kraus sees a reflection of early tribal tradition and allows any time in the monarchy. Kirkpatrick, Dahood and Seybold think the pilgrim has returned home and recalls his experience. Mowinckel thinks of a processional hymn in the autumn festival, taking up the feelings of the pilgrims, and probably post-exilic. Broyles speaks of 'the voice of a representative liturgist'. Goulder (*Return*) again relates to Nehemiah, the rebuilding of the walls, and Tabernacles.

Psalm 123

Even here Gunkel insists the prayer is an individual's; the singer takes thought for fellow-sufferers. Kirkpatrick judges the singer to be the representative of the worshippers and that the affliction matches the time of Nehemiah's first visit. Mowinckel also takes the singer as representative cantor; he thinks a setting in the autumn festival suitable to the thought of liberation and restoration.

Psalm 124

Kirkpatrick thinks of the completion of Nehemiah's walls and the threatened attack which did not materialize. Gunkel classifies as a 'thanks-song of Israel'; he thinks of the Persian period – some event which cannot be identified or a general retrospect. Mowinckel takes the reference as to all the times in history when the Lord saved from the enemy. Allen decides that 'a post-exilic song of thanksgiving composed for a group delivered from a perilous situation has been deemed worthy of wider use by the community at large'.

Psalm 125

Kirkpatrick and Goulder continue to focus on Nehemiah's situation. Allen depicts post-exilic Judah under the control of a foreign power, the situation being aggravated by the collaboration of certain Jews in breach of their ancestral faith. Dahood, however, sees a possible linguistic link with the early sixth century.

Psalm 126

Delitzsch, Kirkpatrick, Kraus, Allen and Broyles join those who think the psalmist recalls the return from the Exile and prays for help in subsequent poor conditions. For Goulder (*Return*) the accomplished salvation is more recent – the completion of Nehemiah's walls. Another approach puts the revival of nature to the fore – good years recalled and a good year sought; Mowinckel and Bentzen incline this way, though Mowinckel allows that the Return could be in mind in vv. 1–3. For Gunkel vv. 1–3 are prophecy of good prospects, followed by lamenting prayer for realization. Dahood takes the entire psalm as thanksgiving, rendering in v. 4 'Yahweh restored our fortunes'; he finds several pointers to a pre-exilic date.

[1–3] The rendering of these verses as a future prospect (Luther, Gunkel) seems forced and not required by the context. Beyerlin (1978) proposed a future prospect with 'we are as dreamers' as a parenthesis alluding to revelation by dream, but this seems even more strained and is criticized by Allen.

Psalm 127

Gunkel treats the sections as two psalms with no inner connection. Kirkpatrick thinks such a view unnecessary, though he allows that the psalmist has wandered somewhat from his opening thought; circumstances of Nehemiah's time can be detected. Kraus sees two wisdom sayings which are united by concern for the family (v. 1 about building a household); Broyles similarly. Allen finds details in the structure that support unity. Mowinckel thinks two sayings have been joined to make a composition for the autumn festival, thanking the Lord for blessings that include the temple, the holy city, harvest provision, and children. Dahood is distinctive, finding the song composed for a king; with God's benediction the king will be able to drive back enemies from the gates.

[2d] The line can also be translated (BCP, RV) 'so he gives sleep to his beloved', implying peace and provision; 'for' is read by two mss and LXX. Instead of 'sleep' Dahood renders 'prosperity' and *LP* 'honour', both looking to Syriac (cf. Allen).

[3–5] The Targum understood the 'children' and 'arrows' to be the disciples in a sage's school, and by Christians also the reference was sometimes understood of the disciples of Christ, born of the will of God, strong in confrontation with the Adversary.

Psalm 128

Kirkpatrick thinks of encouragement addressed to the people in harsh times after the return from exile, and Goulder (*Return*) likewise envisages the need for repopulation in Nehemiah's time. Mowinckel thinks of the priest blessing the people as their procession enters the sanctuary at the autumn festival; Allen similarly, comparing 24.5. Dahood on language grounds inclines to a pre-exilic date.

[3b] The olive is the most important tree in Palestine. The word is not that for 'sucker' (*yoneq*) but for a slip or cutting 'transplanted' (*shatil*). The olive plants are nursed for three years before grafting and do not yield much fruit until about seventeen years old.

Psalm 129

Kirkpatrick continues to set these psalms in Nehemiah's time; history provides ground for hope, and confidence is expressed that foes will be defeated. Kraus takes vv. 5f. as prophetic; Allen similarly. Gunkel, Mowinckel and Dahood take this passage as a wish or curse, as indeed did LXX and Vulgate.

Psalm 130

Gunkel insists on the individuality of the singer – probably someone gravely ill, but widening the concern at the end. Kraus likewise, suggesting that vv. 7–8 were words that had been addressed to the assembly and from which this individual had taken comfort. Allen thinks the original prayer was that of an individual who in vv. 7–8 addresses companions after receiving an (unrecorded) oracle of salvation; later the psalm was used corporately. More simply Kirkpatrick sees the psalmist as a leader such as Nehemiah. Mowinckel also finds a similar leader or a cantor on his behalf; the setting may be atonement ceremonies in the autumn festival, when Israel is under foreign yoke. Broyles speaks of a 'liturgist' leading a congregation, showing the piety to be followed. Johnson (*Prophet*, pp. 312f.) sees a cultic prophet interceding vicariously for a gathering, perhaps at a new moon or sabbath observance; the piece would be introductory to the main liturgy and may be very early in date. Dahood tentatively suggests it is a king's prayer, in view of parallels with 86.

Psalm 131

For Gunkel this was a psalm of trust, using one element common in laments; it expressed an individual's piety, one who had sought great things from God but who now would be content with very little, which he would not even specify; v. 3 would be an addition made when the psalm attained communal use. Seybold further suggests the psalmist is a woman who gives a self-portrait in v. 2, for she has carried her child on the pilgrimage. Broyles sees vv. 1–2 as 'exemplary', a model for the congregation to follow. Dahood says the psalmist may well be the king, in view of parallels in 18.27 and 101.5b.

Psalm 132

Gunkel agrees in the main with Mowinckel and speaks of a 'mystery-play' in the late monarchy, at the feast commemorating the foundation of the temple. For Mowinckel it is part of a dramatic liturgy at the annual reconsecration of the temple within the autumn festival, and the later monarchy is indicated by the prominence of the priests. Johnson (*Prophet*, pp. 67f.) also sees a processional commemoration; the entire psalm is voiced by a cultic prophet in prayer and response, and though the ark is carried, the 'it' in the Hebrew of vv. 6a and 6b is the story of David's vow. Dahood thinks the occasion is David's original procession, 'David' and 'your Anointed' in v. 10 being the same person. Goulder (*Return*) endeavours to explain as from the procession of Neh. 12.27f., a period favoured also by Kirkpatrick.

Psalm 133

Kirkpatrick makes a connection with Nehemiah's efforts to repopulate Jerusalem (Neh. 11), while Goulder (*Return*) relates to the consecration of Nehemiah's wall (Neh. 12.27f.). For Gunkel the psalm is a Wisdom saying praising the practice of brothers living together on an undivided heritage; he conjecturally emends 'Zion' to 'Iyyon' (1 Kings 15.20), a city near Mount Hermon, and so attains a secular song, readily seen to be of northern provenance. Mowinckel allows such an origin, but sees an application to the festal fellowship. Allen's observations on structure tell against deletions and emendations commonly proposed; moreover, he notes, relation to the surrounding psalms indicates how the 'Zion' theme was of central importance for our psalm. Dahood claims philological pointers to a pre-exilic date.

[2–3] Poetic licence has also been heard in more recent times in the cries of Arab carriers of water and sweet drink in the old city of Jerusalem: 'O thirsty one, free water! Drink and pray for the Beautiful (the mosque). It is from Mount Hermon, O thirsty one. God is generous.' The snow-capped Hermon is called by the Arabs 'the Mountain of the Sheikh', as though a venerable and sacred figure with white head and beard. Perhaps such an association was in the psalmist's mind as he passed from bearded Aaron to the thought of Mount Hermon.

Psalm 134

Gunkel takes the first part as a priestly hymn; in the second part the priests turn to bless the laity (a corporate 'you'). Mowinckel has it that first the priests summon the congregation to praise, and then bless them, all at a night ceremony in the autumn festival.

Psalm 135

Gunkel sees this as hardly an independent composition, but an assembly of familiar phrases and lines in the late period to suit the worshippers' love of the familiar. Kraus, noting the absence of the Sinai traditions, suggests a setting in Passover. But Allen thinks of a post-exilic congregation assembled perhaps for Tabernacles. Early commentators relate it to the 'songs of the steps': the praise of God is what awaits the persevering climber (NL).

Psalm 136

Kirkpatrick, following Delitzsch, notes that this psalm was sometimes called the Great Hallel in Jewish tradition, though the phrase was sometimes used to cover 135–6 or even 120–36. The lack of reference to Sinai inclines Kraus to think of a Passover setting in post-exilic times, while Weiser looks to the autumn festival in pre-exilic times.

Psalm 137

The Targum says v. 7 is spoken by 'Michael, Prince of Jerusalem', and v. 8 by 'Gabriel, Prince of Zion'. Gunkel classifies as a form of curse; it is soon after the Exile, the author being still abroad. Mowinckel takes the reference to Babylon in v. 8a as a gloss, so the imprecation was originally all against Edom, easily fitting the 'rock' (so the name of Edom's capital) and the Persian period.

[1a] 'Aloud' represents *gam*, either as an intensive or in the sense 'vocally' (so Dahood from Ugaritic).

[3] 'Those who had despoiled us' represents, in accordance with parallelism and the Targum, a rather puzzling Hebrew word; other suggestions are 'our tormenters' and 'our mockers'.

[8a] 'Great destroyer' follows the understanding of the Targum etc. (*BHS*). The present vowels, however, may be understood as 'you that are doomed to destruction'.

[9] Following Augustine, Littledale (NL) explains of the 'children' of the flesh, 'the first motions of evil thoughts, while they are still new and weak'; they are to be dashed against the rock which is Christ. Jacquet portrays the psalmist not as personally vengeful, but as concerned for Israel's restoration, which he could not imagine without the complete destruction of Babylon.

Psalm 138

Gunkel thinks the form points to a late period, and so the royal character of some parts is due to adaptation of old elements; he thinks v. 2a would not suit a king, who had access to the temple. Kraus likewise thinks of a private individual, probably recovered from sickness, and influenced by conceptions from Second Isaiah. Goulder (*Return*) sees here a thanksgiving of Ezra, who has not yet arrived in Jerusalem. Kirkpatrick takes the psalmist to be speaking for the people, thankful for the return from exile. Delitzsch finds a royal psalmist, and Mowinckel also believes that a king (or later equivalent) gives thanks for some political deliverance. Dahood describes the psalm as 'a royal song of thanksgiving'.

[1b] St Chrysostom comments (LXX 'opposite the angels') that the thought is of angels forming one half of the choir and facing the other half that consists of humans; they provoke each other to emulation in the good work of praise (NL).

[8b] Another reading gives 'works', and the translation could be 'do not slacken from the deeds of your hand' (cf. 28.5; 92.4).

Psalm 139

Gunkel found here a 'higher stage' of religion attained only at a late date; in type it was hymnic, but breaking out of the traditional form. Kraus, adapting a later theory, sees it as the thankful praise of an accused person, cleared in an ordeal trial, and in vv. 19f. citing the earlier petition. Seybold also keeps alive the theory of an ordeal trial, the accusation being one of idolatry. Allen gives detail of numerous proposals, and himself thinks of an accused person seeking a vindicating oracle. Dahood sees the accused person as a religious leader, and suggests, from relation to Job, a date around the seventh century. For Mowinckel the psalmist is the head of the community in the late period; a day of intercession has been called against enemies among the imperial commissars. Goulder finds an evening prayer of Ezra directed against the current high priest. Broyles summarizes evidence against the theory of an 'accused person', and thinks rather of a more general use for the pilgrims' approach to the temple, 'the way everlasting'.

[1] The tenses seem best rendered as general presents, in accordance with the sense of vv. 2f. It is not necessary then to follow Dahood's imperatives, 'Yahweh, examine me . . .', or Kraus who takes 'you have searched me' to show that an ordeal trial has been completed.

[3a] The verb could literally mean 'sift' or 'measure as with a span'; the thought is probably of a detailed knowledge.

[8] (Lit. 'my bed in Sheol'.) It appears that though there was a tradition that Sheol was an 'unclean' region without formal worship (6.5), yet the Lord certainly had power to act there as he wished (cf. Amos 9.2).

[9a] Some assume different vowels with LXX and render 'If I lift my wings to the east or dwell in the farthest west'.

[11a] 'Cover' is perhaps a sense the Hebrew could have (cf. Allen), though many emend for this meaning (*BHS*).

[13a] Lit. 'you that created my kidneys' – the seat especially of conscience.

[14a] The verse has been variously understood; assuming different vowels, some render 'that you are awesomely wonderful'. And some take the verb *plh* here not as 'be wonderful', but 'be set apart'; hence Goulder, 'for I have been set apart for a fearful destiny' (cf. 4.3).

[18b] The present vowels give 'When I awake I am still with you;' though this suits a setting of incubation (cf. 17.15), the immediate context supports an adjustment of spelling to give the sense here (*BHS*).

[20] For 'against you' cf. *BHS*; the main reading can give 'as for those who rise against you'.

Psalm 140

Gunkel classifies this as 'the complaint-song of an individual', taking the references to warfare as poetic exaggeration echoing royal psalms; Kraus similarly. Mowinckel sees a king, or at least an army leader, who suffers the preliminary bombardment of evil words and prays at a special convocation to ward off the danger. Dahood thinks the language points to an early date of composition. Goulder (*Return*) considers it unlikely that an ordinary individual, whether persecuted, accused or sick, would take to himself language attributed to the greatest of Israel's kings; a national leader is indicated, and Goulder's candidate is Ezra.

Psalm 141

Gunkel rejects corporate interpretations and insists on an individual as psalmist in the late period. Kraus takes this path and pictures a social division of those strict and those lax towards the Law, comparing 1 and 119. Mowinckel continues his military-political interpretation from 140 and suggests a threat of war with Edom. Goulder (*Return*) continues with his Ezra story, a struggle with the vested interests of the priesthood. Dahood thinks of a North Israelite after Samaria's fall; living in the dispersion, the man is brought to trial for shunning pagan rites.

[2] This verse gave rise to rich devotion through association with Christ's lifting up of his hands on the cross. Thus NL after Gerhohus: 'And therefore, O Lord, as my trust is in that all-sufficing oblation upon the Cross, let the lifting up of my hands in final penitence, in the evening of my days, when the shadows of the night are coming fast around me, be like that evening sacrifice, and in union with it, be acceptable unto thee, that as I have abided by thy Cross in the sorrows of thy Passion, so I may offer thee the morning sacrifice too, in the bright dawn of the Resurrection.'

[5] 'Oil of the wicked' is from LXX. Our Hebrew has 'oil of the head' or 'oil of venom'.

[7] Some translators supply 'wood' – 'as when wood is chopped . . . on the earth'. A

greater divergence is produced by those who take *sela'*, 'rock', in v. 6 as a title of God, with 'their judges / rulers' as a plural of majesty, giving 'They are thrown down by the hands of the rock, their judge.'

Psalm 142

Kraus sees here an individual, arrested and brought to a sacred trial, the period being unclear. Dahood thinks there may be indications of a pre-exilic date; his 'individual' is on his death-bed, hoping for deliverance from the prison of Sheol. Mowinckel prefers to speak of a leader whose deliverance will be celebrated by the community; the hostility is political, enemies seeking to ensnare him in trouble with an overlord.

Psalm 143

To suit v. 3 especially, Baethgen regarded the prayer as the community's. Gunkel agreed the date was late, but insisted on classifying as 'the complaint-song of an individual'. Kraus sees the psalm as a formulary for someone accused and imprisoned to face a sacred trial; but he questions late dating. Dahood favours royal interpretation, noting some half-dozen verbal indications. Johnson (*Prophet*, pp. 265f.) sees a king preparing for a night of incubation, perhaps even David in his later years. Goulder (*Return*) finds a national leader who sees himself as a latter-day David, namely Ezra.

A vivid glimpse of an application of the psalm to Christ's work is given by an ancient antiphon for Easter Eve (NL): 'I will penetrate into the lower parts of the earth, and I will behold all that sleep, and I will give light to them that hope in the Lord' (Ecclus. 24.45, Vulgate).

Psalm 144

LXX (heading) and Targum (vv. 10–11) relate the psalm to David's combat with Goliath. Kirkpatrick says a leader speaks as representative of the people, and the psalm has a compilatory character. Gunkel splits off vv. 12f. as a separate poem; he classifies vv. 1–11 as a royal psalm. Mowinckel takes vv. 1–11 as a king's prayer in time of war, while vv. 12–15 were added in later use for the community; Allen similarly. Dahood takes the psalm as royal, to be dated tentatively to the tenth century.

Bede (cited in NL) illustrates development of the tradition of a connection with David and Goliath: 'This war of David's was a type to signify the Lord's conflict, that as the one overthrew with the blow of a stone the glory of Goliath, so the Devil's power was conquered by the Rock, which is Christ the Lord.'

Psalm 145

While Mowinckel thinks it a late piece, its theme of kingship fitting the autumn festival, Dahood sees no solid basis for dating, especially as acrostics can be quite ancient; he finds it 'effuses originality and warmth', and is a kind of 'litany of sacred names'. Mays calls it the overture to the final movement of the Psalter.

[5] I have followed a reading from LXX and Qumran; our Hebrew may be rendered: 'Of the splendour of the majesty of your glory, and concerning your marvellous deeds will I sing.'

[12] I have followed the smoother LXX against the Hebrew 'his power ... his reign'.

Psalm 146

Broyles describes the individual voice as that of a liturgist, who represents the exemplary worshipper.

Psalm 147

Mowinckel treats this as three psalms composed for one liturgy in the autumn festival of the late period. Allen speaks of literary references interwoven in an almost midrashic fashion; it is a 'worshipping meditation' based on the return from exile. But Weiser denies that we have here a compilation of quotations; the author in customary fashion draws on the common treasury of worship, and all revolves around two themes: God's power and his grace; the 'outcasts' could be refugees from Samaria after 721.

[1b] The sense is 'how pleasant to give beautiful expression to his praise' (*na'wa* as infinitive, *VT* 1954, pp. 410f.).

[8] The verse does not mention humans, but perhaps LXX preserves a lost phrase at the end, 'and crops for the labour of man', as 104.14. Allen, on structural grounds, argues against this.

[17] (a) depicts the fierce hail as fragments of ice, large as broken bread, and (b) the freezing of 'water' (*may*, but traditionally read *miy*, 'who' – 'who can stand').

[20b] I have followed LXX and the Qumran scroll; the traditional vowels give 'they do not know'.

Psalm 148

From its perspective in the late period, the Benedicite is able to make a significant addition to the list of praisers: 'O ye spirits and souls of the righteous, bless ye the Lord, praise him and magnify him for ever.' The Canticle of St Francis, though not as bold as this psalm in address to each element, well brings out the love that must unite the world at praise: 'Be praised, my Lord ... for Brother Sun ... Sister Moon ... Brother Wind ... Sister Water ... Brother Fire ... our sister, Mother Earth ... Praise and bless my Lord, give thanks to him, and serve him in great humility.' Murray (p. 163) includes 104 and 148 with Job 38–41 as texts weighing against a human-centred world-view which 'has remained a heavy drag-chain on the legs of Christians theologizing about other creatures. The sense of joyful liberation which Francis communicates is doubtless due to his not wearing it.'

[14] Though some look for an allusion here to restoration after the Exile, Gunkel distances himself from this and other specific interpretations. LXX renders: 'And he shall exalt the horn of his people', so also Jerome and BCP, a possible translation, which was sometimes understood as prophecy of the Messiah (cf. 132.17; Luke 1.69; NL). 'Cause for praise' represents *tehilla*, (lit.) 'praise'; some take it in the sense 'renown (for all his people)', so Allen; others apply it to God, 'He is the praise of'. Gunkel suggested that a subscription begins here, a descriptive title of the psalm set at the end; but he still thought that, being metrical, it was meant to be sung.

Psalm 149

Kirkpatrick, from relation to 147, thinks of circumstances in Nehemiah's time. Gunkel compares the return of victorious forces in Judith 15.12f., praising God as they carry weapons, women dance, and prisoners are led in chains; but he thinks the psalmist is imagining the eschatological victory, and may have written for 'a spiritual play' such as 47, 48, 68 presuppose. Kraus and Seybold also envisage some dramatic presentation; the latter suggests a late date, linking with Dan. 7.12 and Wisd. 3.5f., whereas Kraus allows that 'a very old date' is possible. Mowinckel has a setting in the autumn festival with cultic dance and sacred meal (with sitting or lying on 'benches', v. 5b). Johnson (*Prophet*, pp. 91f.) thinks of a prelude to the ritual drama of the pre-exilic autumn festival; it is a night scene, hence the 'bedding' (v. 5b), and the psalm looks to the eschatological conflict. Weiser too favours a setting in the pre-exilic festival cult celebrating the fresh coming of the Lord as king. Brueggemann (pp. 112–132) relates 145–50 to a penetrating meditation on praise.

Psalm 150

Gunkel considered the psalm as late as could be, and (questionably) explained the sequence of instruments as those of priests (v. 3a), Levites (v. 3b), and laity (vv. 4f.). Seybold also looks for subtlety in the sequence, from the introductory signals of the horn to the cymbals that call for quiet listening, and then those that invite the tumultuous cries. Broyles notes how music serves praise by engaging mind, voice, body and heart, capturing 'the emotions and brain, both left and right brain'.

[3–5] The old commentators sometimes found allegorical significance in the various instruments (*NL*). Thus, cymbals, being always used in pairs, could denote those who consider one another, provoking to love, good works and praise of God; they also point to the Old and New Testaments in their complementary harmony, or again, to the double choir of mankind and angels.

Bibliography of Works Cited

Ahlström, G., *Psalm 89: eine Liturgie aus dem Ritual des leidenden Königs*, Lund 1959

Alexander, J. J. G., *The Decorated Letter*, London 1979

Allen, L. C., *Psalms 101–150*, Word Biblical Commentary, Waco 1983

Anderson, A. A., *The Book of Psalms*, New Century Bible, London 1972

Augustine, *Expositions on the Book of Psalms*, ET by A. C. Coxe 1888; reprinted New York 1979

Auwers, J.-M., *La composition du Psautier*, Paris 2000

Baethgen, F., *Die Psalmen*, Göttingen 1892, 1904

Balentine, S. E., *The Tora's Vision of Worship*, Minneapolis 1999

Bentzen, A., *Fortolkning til de Gammeltestamentliger Salmer* (Commentary), Copenhagen 1939

— *Det Sakrale Kongedømme*, Copenhagen 1945

Beyerlin, W., *Die Rettung der Bedrängten in den Feindpsalmen der Einzelnen*, Göttingen 1970.

— 'Der nervus rerum in Ps. 106', *ZAW* 86, 1974, pp. 50–64

— 'Wir sind wie Träumende': *Studien zur 126. Psalm*, Stuttgart 1978

Birkeland, H., *Die Feinde des Individuums in der israelitischen Psalmenliteratur*, Oslo 1933

Botterweck, G. et al. (eds), *Theologisches Wörterbuch zum Alten Testament*, Stuttgart 1970 (ET in progress, Grand Rapids 1977ff.).

Braude, W. G., *Midrash Tehillim*, ET New Haven 1959

Braun, J., *Music in Ancient Israel/Palestine*, Grand Rapids 2002

Briggs, C. and E., *Criticial and Exegetical Commentary on the Book of Psalms*, Edinburgh 1906–7

Brown, F., Driver, S. R. and Briggs, C. A, *A Hebrew English Lexicon of the Old Testament*, Oxford 1907

Broyles, C. C., *Psalms*, New International Biblical Commentary, Peabody 1999

Brueggemann, W., *The Psalms and the Life of Faith*, Minneapolis 1995

Brüning, C., *Mitten im Leben vom Tod umfangen: Ps. 102*, Frankfurt 1992

Buttenweiser, M., *The Psalms Chronologically Treated*, Chicago 1938

Calvin, J., *Commentary on the Book of Psalms*, ET by J. A. Anderson, Edinburgh 1845–9

Cassiodorus, *Explanation of the Psalms*, ET by P. G. Walsh, New York 1990–1

Craigie, P. C., 'The Comparison of Hebrew Poetry: Ps. 104', *Semitics* 4, 1974, pp.10–21

— *Psalms 1–50*, Word Biblical Commentary, Waco 1983

Dahood, M., *Psalms*, Anchor Bible, New York 1966–70

Dalglish, E., *Psalm 51*, Leiden 1962

Danby, H., *The Mishnah*, ET Oxford 1933

Davidson, R., *The Vitality of Worship: Commentary on the Book of Psalms*, Grand Rapids 1998

Davies, J. G. (ed), *A New Dictionary of Liturgy and Worship*, London 1986

Delekat, L., *Asylie und Schutzorakel im Zionheiligtum*, Leiden 1967

Delitzsch, F., *Biblischer Kommentar über die Psalmen*, Leipzig, 5th edn 1894

Devreesse, R., *Le commentaire de Théodore de Mopsueste sur les Psaumes, 1–80*, Vatican 1939

Duhm, B., *Die Psalmen*, Freiburg 1899, 2nd edn 1922

Eaton, J. H., 'Psalms and Israelite Worship', *Tradition & Interpretation* ed G. W. Anderson, Oxford 1979

— *Vision in Worship: The Relation of Prophecy and Worship in the OT*, London 1981

— 'Music's Place in Worship', *Oudtestamentische Studiën 23*, 1984, pp. 85–106

— *The Psalms Come Alive: An Introduction to the Psalms through the Arts*, Oxford 1984

— *Kingship and the Psalms*, Sheffield, 2nd edn 1986

— *The Circle of Creation: Animals in the Light of the Bible*, London 1995

— *Psalms of the Way and the Kingdom*, Sheffield 1995

Flint, P. W., *The Dead Sea Psalms Scroll and the Book of Psalms*, Leiden 1997

Gesenius, *Gesenius' Hebrew Grammar* ed by E. Kautzsch and revd by A. E. Cowley, Oxford, 2nd edn 1910

Gerstenberger, E. S., *Psalms and Lamentations* (Forms of OT Literature 14–15), 2 vols, Grand Rapids 1988, 2001

Gillingham, S. E., *The Poems and Psalms of the Hebrew Bible*, Oxford 1994

Girard, M., *Les Psaumes Redécouverts: 1–50*, Quebec 1996

Goulder, M. D., *The Psalms of the Sons of Korah*, Sheffield 1982

— *The Prayers of David*, Sheffield 1990

— *The Psalms of Asaph and the Pentateuch*, Sheffield 1996

— *The Psalms of the Return (107–150)*, Sheffield 1998

Gruber, M. I., *Rashi's Commentary on Psalms 1–89*, ET Atlanta 1988

Gunkel, H., *Die Psalmen*, Göttingen 1929

— and Begrich, J., *Einleitung in die Psalmen*, Göttingen 1933; ET by J. D. Nogalski, *Introduction to Psalms*, Macon 1998

Haney, K. E., *The Winchester Psalter*, Leicester 1986

Harl, M. (ed), *La Chaîne Palestinienne sur le Ps. 118* (Hebrew 119), Paris 1972

Hengstenberg, E. W., *Commentary on the Psalms*, ET Edinburgh 1845–8

Herder, J. G. von, *On the Spirit of Hebrew Poetry* (1782–3), ET by James Marsh, Burlington, Vermont 1833

Hieke, T., *Psalm 80: Praxis eines Methodenprogramms*, St Ottilien 1997

Holladay, W., *The Psalms through Three Thousand Years*, Minneapolis 1993

Howard, D. M., *The Structure of Psalms 93–100*, Winona Lake 1997

Jacobsen, T., *The Harps that Once: Sumerian Poetry in Translation*, New Haven 1987

Jacquet, L., *Les Psaumes et le coeur de l'homme*, Gembloux 1975–9

Johnson, A. R., *Sacral Kingship in Ancient Israel*, Cardiff, 2nd edn 1967

— *The Cultic Prophet and Israel's Psalmody*, Cardiff 1979

Kaiser, O., *Texte aus der Umwelt des Alten Testaments, II.5–6, Lieder und Gebete*, Gütersloh 1988–91

Keel, O., *Vögel als Boten*, Freiburg 1977

Kennicott, B., *Vetus Testamentum Hebraicum cum variis lectionibus*, Oxford 1776–80

Kirkpatrick, A. F., *The Book of Psalms*, Cambridge 1902

Kraus, H.-J., *Psalmen*, Neukirchen 1961, revd 1978 (ET by H. Oswald, Minneapolis 1988–9)

Lamb, J. A., *The Psalms in Christian Worship*, London 1962

Lipiński, E., *La royauté de Yahwé dans la poésie de l'ancien Israël*, Brussels 1968

Lowth, R., *De sacra poesi Hebraeorum*, Oxford 1753; ET *Lectures on the Sacred Poetry of the Hebrews*, 4th edn London 1839; 1995

Luther, M., *Works*, vols 10–11, *First Lectures on the Psalms*, ET by H. Oswald, St Louis 1974–6; vols 12–14, *Selected Psalms*, ET by J. Pelikan, St Louis 1955–8

Mays, J. L., *The Psalms:* Interpretation, Louisville 1994

McCann, J. C. (ed), *The Shape and Shaping of the Psalter*, Sheffield 1993

— 'Psalms' in *New Interpreters Bible*, vol. 4, Nashville 1996

Mitchell, D. C., *The Message of the Psalter*, Sheffield 1993

McKim, D. (ed), *Historical Handbook of Major Biblical Interpreters*, Leicester 1998

Mowinckel, S., *Det Gamle Testamente IV. 1: Salmeboken* (commentary), Oslo 1955

— *The Psalms in Israel's Worship*, 2 vols, ET Oxford 1962

Murray, R., *The Cosmic Covenant*, London 1992

Neale, J. M. and Littledale, R. F., *A Commentary on the Psalms from Primitive and Mediaeval Writers*, London 1860–74

Noth, M., *The Laws in the Pentateuch and other essays*, ET Edinburgh 1966

— 'Thebes' in *Archaeology and Old Testament Study* ed D. Winton Thomas, Oxford 1967, pp. 21–35

Oesterley, W. O. E., *The Psalms*, London 1955

Popova, O., *Russian Illuminated Manuscripts*, London 1984

Pritchard, J. B., *The Ancient Near East in Pictures*, Princeton 1954

— *Ancient Near Eastern Texts*, Princeton, 2nd edn 1955

— *The Ancient Near East: Supplementary Texts and Pictures*, Princeton 1969

Rad, G. von, *The Problem of the Hexateuch and other Essays*, Edinburgh 1966

Rashi *see* Gruber

Rondeau, M. J., *Les commentaires patristiques du Psautier*, Rome 1982

Rossi, J. B. de, *Variae Lectiones Veteris Testamenti*, Parma 1784–8

Sanders, J. A., *The Psalms Scroll of Qumran Cave II*, Oxford 1965

— *The Dead Sea Psalms Scroll*, New York 1967

Sarna, N., *Songs of the Heart: An Introduction to the Book of Psalms*, New York 1993

Schmidt, H., *Die Psalmen*, Tübingen 1934

Seux, M-J., *Epithètes royales akkadiennes et sumériennes*, Paris 1967

Seybold, K., *Die Psalmen*, Tübingen 1996

Soll, W., *Psalm 119: Matrix, Form, and Setting*, Washington 1991

Spieckerrnann, H., *Heilsgegenwart: eine Theologie der Psalmen*, Göttingen 1989

Spurgeon, C. H., *The Treasury of David*, 1869–83, abridged in 2 vols, Wheaton 1993

Starbuck, S. R. A., *Court Oracles in the Psalms*, Atlanta 1999

Tate, M., *Psalms 51–100*, Word Biblical Commentary, Waco 1990

Terrien, S., *The Psalms*, Eerdmans Critical Commentary, Grand Rapids 2003

Thomas, D. Winton, *The Text of the Revised Psalter*, London 1963

Tillmann, N., *'Das Wasser bis zum Hals': Gestalt . . . des 69. Psalms*, Altenberge 1993

Vantoura, S. H., *La musique de la Bible révélé*, Paris, 2nd edn 1978; ET *The Music of the Bible Revealed*, Berkeley 1991

Vermes, G., *The Dead Sea Scrolls: Qumran in Perspective*, London 1977

— *The Complete Dead Sea Scrolls in English*, Harmondsworth 1997

Weiser, A., *The Psalms*, ET London 1962

Westermann, C., *The Living Psalms* (commentary on selections), ET Edinburgh 1990

Wette, W. M. L. de, *Kommentar über die Psalmen*, Heidelberg 1811

Wilson, G. H., *The Editing of the Hebrew Psalter*, Chico 1995

Index